I0094326

THE DEEDS
OF
AMHERST COUNTY, VIRGINIA
1807-1827
BOOKS L-R

By
THE REVEREND BAILEY FULTON DAVIS

Copyright 1985
By: Southern Historical Press, Inc.

All rights reserved. No part of this publication may be reproduced,
stored in a retrieval system, transmitted in any form, posted on to
the web in any form or by any means without the prior written
permission of the publisher.

Please direct all correspondence and orders to:

www.southernhistoricalpress.com
or
SOUTHERN HISTORICAL PRESS, Inc.
PO BOX 1267
375 West Broad Street
Greenville, SC   29601
southernhistoricalpress@gmail.com

ISBN #0-89308-301-1

Printed in the United States of America

CONTENTS

AMHERST COUNTY, VIRGINIA, COURTHOUSE MINIATURES

DEDICATION

This work is affectionately dedicated to Mary Gayle Pettyjohn of
Green Hills, Monroe, Virginia. She is the only daughter of Thomas
and Mary Hesson Pettyjohn. Mary Gayle and my third son, Thurman
Blanton Davis are to be married in Bethany Methodist Church on the
fifth of March, 1966. They have gone together since the days in
Amherst County High School when she was beauty queen and he was a
captain on the football team. She was graduated from Mary Washington
College and he received his degree from the University of Kentucky.

FOREWORD

This is the second in the triad of works to which I
have referred. It is hoped that researchers will
find it of value.

Bailey F. Davis
Amherst, Virginia

1. 10 April, 1807. GEORGE LOVING, Amherst County, to RICHARD
     POWELL, Town of Warminster, Amherst County...Deed of Trust
5 sh.; debt due WILLIAM BROWN and Company; slave, HARRY, about 16;
slave, GUY, and one negro woman, SELEY. Witnesses: ROBERT MOORE,
SAMUEL JONES, W. H. WILLS. Final proof by MOORE, 21 September, 1807.
To RICHARD POWELL 15 February, 1808.

1. Order to ALBERT, Justice of the Peace: SKILER HARRIS and wife,
     FANNY, 16 October 1801 to J(?) ROBERTS. Two tracts: 1. 200
acres; 2. 29 acres. 17 April 1805. W. S. CRAWFORD, Clerk. Done by
TANDY KEY and GARRET WHITE, 21 October 1805. Recorded Amherst County,
21 September 1807.

2. 21 August 1807. CORNELIUS THOMAS, Amherst County, to REUBEN B.
     PATTERSON and WILLIAM F. CARTER, Amherst County...Deed of Trust;
debt due JAMES MURPHY and Company; 5 sh. 2301 acres south fork
Rockfish. Lines: WILLIAM JOHNSON, EDWARD HARDING, NORBOURN THOMAS,
JOSEPH C. CABELL, WILLIAM BOWMAN and where CORNELIUS THOMAS lives.
Also Buckingham tract of 400 acres. Lines: MILES GIPSON and bought
of LEONARD BALLEAW. Witnesses: WILLIAM H. WILLS, ROBERT FRANKLIN,
ELISHA ESTIS, A. B. SNEAD. To JAMES MURPHY, 9 June 1808.

3. 5 September 1807. THOMAS HAWKINS, Amherst County, to WILLIAM F.
     CARTER and NATHANIEL POWELL, Amherst County...Deed of Trust.
Debt due JAMES MURPHY and Company, 5 sh. 223 acres Cedar Creek and
S. S. BERRY's Mountain. Lines: THOMAS CLASBY, GEO. LOVING, LEROY
ROBERTSON, WILLIAM LAIN, JOSEPH LOVING, JOHN MONROE and where THOMAS
HAWKINS lives. Also five slaves: ESSEX, CHARLES, LUCY, ROSE and
CATE and increase. Deliver to JAMES MURPHY. 9 June 1808. Witnesses:
WILLIAM CLASBY, CHARLES EDMUNDS, THOMAS HARVIE, WILLIAM L. BELL.

4. 3 July 1807. GEORGE MARTIN, Amherst County, to RICHARD POWELL
     and JONATHAN CAMM, Amherst County...Deed of Trust; debt due
WILLIAM BROWN and Company; 5 sh. BROWN is merchant in Warminster.
230 acres Dutch Creek. Lines: JOSHUA WILLOUGHBY; MATTHEW PHILLIPS,
deceased; CHARLES HAMBLET. Bequeathed to GEORGE MARTIN by father,
HENRY MARTIN, deceased, by will and where GEORGE MARTIN lives.
Witnesses: SAMUEL JONES, JAMES VIGUS, JR., ROBERT MOORE, SAMUEL
HANSBROUGH. Delivered to JOHNATHAN CAMM, 4 March 1809.

5. 16 October 1807. CORNELIUS THOMAS and wife, ELIZABETH, Amherst
     County, to EDWARD HARDING, Amherst County. L50 260 acres.
Lines: The glade road; the branch. Witnesses: JAMES MURPHY,
JONATHAN HIGGINBOTHAM, JR., WILLIS H. WILLS, JAMES TURNER. To
EDWARD HARDING, 26 October 1807.

6. 18 March 1807. JAMES HALL, Amherst County, to ANDERSON MOSS,
     Amherst County...many items--fiddle case, walnut table, cow,
one secretary not finished--long and interesting list. Witnesses:
JAMES L. TURNER, JONATHAN SAVAGE, JR. To ANDERSON MOSS, 23 March
1810.

6. 3 September 1807. WILLIAM LONG and wife, ELISABETH (late
     CALLAWAY) to WILLIAM B. GOOCH, Executor of PHILLIP GOOCH,
deceased. L10 5 acres. Tribulation Creek. Lines: JAMES WATSON,
WILLIAM LONG, PHILLIP GOOCH. Witnesses: HUDSON M. GARLAND, SAMUEL
GARLAND, JAMES B. EDWARDS. Note: Tribulation is quite near the
village of Amherst.

7. 22 June 1807. DANIEL THILMAN, Amherst County, to RICHARD
     POWELL, Amherst County...Deed of Trust; debt due NICHOLAS
CABELL--5 sh.--mare and colt. Witnesses: SAMUEL JONES, W. H. WILLS,
JAMES VIGUS, JR.

1

8. 28 April 1807. JAMES GREGORY, Amherst County, to WILLIAM F.
CARTER, Town of New Market, Amherst County...L95-17-2 debt to
JAMES MURPHY and Company. Deed of Talso debt to MURPHY BROWN and
Company; debt to JOSHUA BARTLEY--5 sh., beds etc. Witnesses:
WILLIS H. WILLS, ROBERT FRANKLIN, JONATHAN CREWS.

9. ---180---. WILLIAM S. CRAWFORD, Clerk of Amherst County...order
to JOEL ATKINSON and VAL PEYTON, Lincoln County, Kentucky,
Justice of the Peace; CHARLES, JESSE, PETER, EDWARD, SOLOMON, and
JONATHAN CARTER, 17 November 1806, to NELSON CRAWFORD, Amherst County,
363 acres. Order to quiz their wives. June 13, 1807, the Justice of
the Peace named reported that they quizzed DINAH, FRANCES, ANN, NANCY,
JEMIMA and NANCY--wives of CHARLES, JESSE, PETER, EDWARD, SOLOMON and
JONATHAN CARTER. Also certificate on same date that MARY ANNE CARTER,
widow of PETER CARTER, deceased, relic dower. August 5--THOMAS
MONTGOMERY, County Clerk, as to Justice of the Peace. Recorded in
Amherst County 21 September 1807. To NELSON CRAWFORD 21 August 1809.
Page 10 order to same Justices of the Peace as to deed by various
CARTERS above to HENRY BALLINGER, Amherst County--425 acres. Done
as above.

11. 30 January 1807. ARCHIBALD FREAM, Augusta, to THOMAS JONES,
Amherst County. L48 94 acres south of HATT and RACCOON and
TYE. Lines: THOMAS JONES, JONATHAN JACOBS, JR. Witnesses:
WILLIAM SALE, JESSE JONES, THOMAS R. DRAKE. Note: in summary,
JESSE JONES is called JESSE SALE.

12. 21 September 1807. JOSEPH STRICKLAND and wife, MARY, Amherst
County, to LANDON H. BRENT and JAMES D. BRENT, Amherst County...
L100 head of Hatt Creek--160 acres. Lines: JAMES BRENT, JAMES
WOODS, WILLIAM SMALL. Witnesses: JONATHAN E. FITZPATRICK, GEORGE
SHIELDS.

12. 15 August 1807. WILLIAM LANE, Waggoner, Amherst County, to
SAMUEL PORTER LANE, Amherst County...6 sh. 72½ acres survey
of 25 April 1786. Lines: JONATHAN VIA; North Fork Elk Island Creek.

13. 4 July 1807. BENJAMIN NOEL, Amherst County, to TOLBERT NOEL,
Amherst County...Line 45, 60 acres. Lines: HUGH MC CABE,
along the road; ROBERT KNUCKLES. Witnesses: BENJAMIN SHACKLEFORD,
MOSES RUCKER, RICHARD S. ELLIS, JAMES WAUGH, WILLIAM DAVIS. To
TOLBERT NOEL, per order, 23 January 1809.

14. 4 July 1807. BENJAMIN NOEL, Amherst County, to WILLIAM NOEL,
Amherst County...Line 25, 50 acres. Borders THOMAS MILL
Creek. Lines: SAMUEL NICELEY, BENJAMIN NOEL, ROBERT NUCKELS.
Witnesses: as above.

14. 23 January 1807. Order to Amherst County Justices of the Peace--
WILLIAM WARE and NELSON CRAWFORD--MAURICE HAMNER and wife, MARY;
AMBROSE RUCKER and wife, ELIZABETH; JESSE CARTER and wife, FRANCES;
SAMUEL HAMNER and wife, NANCY; 22 September 1806; to ELIZABETH COLEMAN--
37 acres. Done on 25 January 1807 as to ELIZABETH RUCKER only. On
page 15, 15 September 1807, an order was sent to ALBERT Justice of
the Peace; GARRETT WHITE and CLIFTON GARLAND, as to NANCY HAMNER,
wife of SAMUEL HAMNER. Done on 19 September 1807.

16. 14 October 1807. ARCHELAUS COX and wife, FANNY, Amherst County,
to WILLIAM HUGHES, Amherst County...Line 100, 30 acres Harris
Creek. Witnesses: ELIAS WILLS, REUBEN COX, WILLIAM JONES.

16. 13 October 1807. JONATHAN SHEPHERD and wife, NANCY, Amherst
County, to CONRAD MOWYER, Amherst County...Line 92-10, 85 acres--
pat. 14 June 1788--Rockfish. Lines: JAMES TURNER, BENJAMIN PAYNE,
CORNELIUS MURRELL. Witnesses: HUDSON M. GARLAND, WILLIAM MURRELL,
THOMAS MURRILL.

17.   19 October 1807.   DANIEL MC COY and wife, ANNE, Amherst County,
      to WILLIAM SYME CABELL, Amherst County...$100 60 acre survey
of 14 January 1771, and pat. to WILLIAM CHAMBERLAIN, 30 April 1794.
Borders Naked Creek of RUCKER's Run.   Lines: HENRY KEY. Witnesses:
THOMAS E. FORTUNE, WILLIAM NIMMO, ROBERT COWPER, JAMES POWELL.   To
WILLIAM SYME CABELL, 27 September 1815.

18.   29 September 1807.   DANIEL MEHONE and wife, SARAH, Amherst
      County, to JONATHAN ROBINSON, Lynchburg...$100 22 3/4 acres
north side Lynch road.   Lines: Near fork of Lynch and Tinsley
roads.   Witnessses: REUBEN NORVELL, NICHOLAS HARRISON, PHILIP JOHNSON.
To NICHOLAS HARRISON, 3 December 1807.

18.   29 September 1807.   JONATHAN MERRIT, SR. and wife, MARY, Amherst
      County, to JONATHAN ROBINSON, Lynchburg and Campbell County...
$500 92 acres borders STOVALL and HARRIS.   Lines: Lynch road;
WILLIAM FOWLER, MICAJAH CLARK; ROBERT WARREN, deceased; DANIEL and
JONATHAN BURFORD.   Witnesses: as in previous deed and delivered as
above.

19.   2 July 1807.   HENRY EMMERSON, JR., Amherst County, to JASPER
      and EDMUND ANDERSON of Alb. 2nd part and RICHARD COLE, Alb. 3rd...
Deed of Trust; debt due ANDERSONS; $1.00 160 acres Rockfish.   Lines:
REUBIN T. MITCHELL, DUNMORE DAMRON, WILLIAM DIXON, JAMES TURNER.
Witnesses: DUNMORE DAMRON, JAMES and TERISHA TURNER.

20.   14 October 1807.   REUBEN COX, Amherst County, to WILLIAM HUGHES,
      Amherst County...Line 100, 30 acres Harris Creek.

21.   22 November 1806.   REUBEN NORVELL and wife, POLLY, Amherst
      County, to ELIAS WILLS, Amherst County...$500, 198 acres
Stovall Creek--3 grants--1. 95 acres on 23 April 1805.   2. 52 acres.
3. 51 acres last 2 on 5 August 1806.   Lines: grantee; RUCKER's Road;
JAMES DAVIS; DANIEL DAY; WILLIAM HIGHT.   Witnesses: ARCHIBALD
CREWS, REUBEN CARVER, WILLIAM CLINKSCALES.   Delivered to ELIAS WILLS,
3 December 1815.

21.   17 February 1807.   REUBEN NORVELL and wife, POLLY, Amherst
      County, to ALEXANDER JEWELL, Amherst County...Line 128-10
128½ acres south borders Porridge Creek.   Lines: survey made for
JAMES DILLARD, new road, THOMAS JEWELL, England.   Witnesses: DENNIS
and WILLIAM ENSEY, REUBIN CARVER.   To ALEXANDER JEWELL, 20 August
1810.

22.   19 October 1807.   WILLIAM DAVIS and wife, ELIZABETH, Amherst
      County, to WILLIAM B. HARE, Amherst County...Line 210, 114
acres Piney and where WILLIAM DAVIS lives; part of tract formerly that
of PHILIP DAVIS, deceased.   Graveyard excepted of ¼ to ½ acre.   Lines:
EBENEZER HAYCOCK--at present JAMES THOMPSON.   Witnesses: RANDOLPH
CASH.

23.   17 April 1807.   HENRY EMMERSON, Amherst County, to JONATHAN
      MOSBY, Amherst County...Deed of trust; debt to MORRIS and
MOORE--$1.00--150 acres south south Rockfish.   Lines: JAMES TURNER,
SR.; DR. WILLIAM MARTIN; DUNMORE DAMRON.   Witnesses: BENJAMIN
MOSBY, WILLIAM BAILEY, DANIEL NASH.   To JONATHAN MOORE, 23 September
1808--slaves and stock included in trust.

24.   12 September 1807.   JAMES STEPHENS, JR., Amherst County, to
      JAMES MURPHY, Amherst County--Deed of trust; debt to GEORGE
PURVIS--5 sh. slaves.   Witnesses: WILLIAM LOVING, WILLIAM MC CALEB (?),
JAMES LOVING, JONATHAN BROWN.   To GEORGE PURVIS, 2 August, 1808.

24.   12 May 1807.   Trustees of New Glasgow: SAMUEL MEREDITH,
      WILLIAM S. CRAWFORD, JAMES FRANKLIN, JOSEPH BURRUS, JOEL FRANKLIN,
ROBERT WALKER, WILLIAM MOSS, SPOTSWOOD GARLAND to WILLIAM HALL,
Amherst County, 5 sh and $56.00 to be paid to DAVID S. GARLAND.   One
lot between new and old streets--#18 and joins old garden.

25. 12 May 1807. Same trustees as above to WILLIAM KNIGHT, NEW
    GLASGOW--5sh and L24 to be paid to DAVID S. GARLAND--one lot,
#5, east side of new street.

26. 19 October 1807. HENRY EMMERSON, JR. to WILLIAM H. MOSBY...new
    and old tobacco paid for a mare. Witnesses: WILLIAM ROBERTSON,
JONATHAN MOORE.

26. 26 June 1807. MOSES RUCKER, first part; PETER P. THORNTON,
    second part; JONATHAN and R. L.(S) ELLIS, third...Deed of trust
to secure third parties--$5.00 slaves to be sold at ELLIS' store,
if not redeemed. Witnesses: HENRY BROWN, WILLIAM PRYOR, SR.,
THOMAS N. EUBANK, ARBAM CARTER, NELSON CRAWFORD. To MAJOR JONATHAN
ELLIS, October 5, 1808.

28. 17 October 1807. SARAH BURRUS, widow of CHARLES BURRUS, late
    of Amherst County, to LEONARD HENLEY and JABEZ CAMDEN, Amherst
County...5sh--all interest in 755½ acre conveyed by CHARLES BURRUS, JR.,
my son, and wife, ELIZABETH, to grantees by two deeds of 20 September
1807. Witnesses: J. P. GARLAND, ROBERT COLEMAN, JAMES HALL.

28. 14 October 1807. ROBERT DINWIDDIE, Amherst County, first;
    NATHAN CRAWFORD, second; HUDSON MARTIN and JAMES WOODS, third;
all of Amherst County...Deed of trust; debt to NATHAN CRAWFORD $1.00.
200 acres where ROBERT DINWIDDIE now lives. Lines: ANN DINWIDDIE,
JAMES MORRISON, WILLIAM CRAWFORD, NATHAN CRAWFORD. Tract devised to
ROBERT DINWIDDIE by his deceased father. Witnesses: WILLIAM
CRAWFORD, EDWARD W. JOPLING, NELSON CRAWFORD. To NELSON CRAWFORD, JR.
17 August 1808.

29. 15 October 1807. JAMES SHIELDS and wife, ELIZABETH, Amherst
    County, to DAVID SHIELDS, Amherst County...$10.00 38 acres south
borders Hatt Creek. Witnesses: ROBERT, ALEXANDER and GEORGE SHIELDS
and JONATHAN TOOL.

30. 9 July 1807. Order to Amherst County Justices of the Peace
    JONATHAN CHRISTIAN and DAVID S. GARLAND: WIATT SMITH and wife,
POLLY, June ___, 1807, to JOSEPH HIGGINBOTHAM, JR. 162½ acres. Done,
8 October 1807. To JOSEPH HIGGINBOTHAM, JR. 11 October 1808.

31. 15 August 1807. WILLIAM BALL to JONATHAN BALL...Deed of trust;
    horses and other stock. Witnesses: STERLING CLAIBORNE,
JONATHAN TOOL.

31. 17 November 1807. JAMES BIBB and wife, SARAH, Amherst County,
    to MURPHY BROWN and Company. L218-17 two tracts of 245 acres
south borders RUCKER's Run. 1. Part of tract of WILLIAM ALFORD.
Lines: WILLIAM CRISP, WILLIAM ALFORD. 2. Survey made by WILLIAM
HOLLANDSWORTH for 152 acres on both sides of Berry's Mountain.
Lines: WILLIAM CRISP, CHARLES EDMUNDS, SAMUEL SPENCER's old line;
top of Berry's Mountain; WILLIAM HOLLINSWORTH. To R. RIVES 8 May
1826.

32. 16 April 1807. ANDREW COFFMAN, Rockingham County, to DAVID
    CALDWELL, same county...L140 93 and 1/3 acres Bever Creek;
North border Rockfish. Lines: WARE, JONATHAN COFFMAN, JONATHAN
SMITH, JACOB ARISMAN, FREDERICK WARE. Part of 280 acres sold by
JAMES FLACK to JONATHAN COFFMAN, SR., and by him conveyed to grantor.
To DAVID CALDWELL 18 April 1811.

32. 15 August 1800. Order to Amherst County Justices of the Peace
    WILLIAM and LANDON CABELL, CORNELIUS THOMAS and wife, ELIZABETH...
1800, to Bransford West--554 acres. WILLIAM S. CRAWFORD, Clerk.
Done November 14, 1807.

33. 26 October 1807. Order to same Justices of the Peace: same
    grantors to EDWARD HARDING on 16 October 1807. Done for
260 acres on 21 December 1807.

34. 10 October 1807. Order to Amherst County Justices of the Peace
    JOSEPH BURRUS and PHILIP JOHNSON: CHARLES BURRUS and wife,
ELIZABETH, 20 September 1807, to LEONARD HENLEY. Done 24 October 1807.

35. 10 October 1807. Order to same Justices of the Peace and same
    grantors to JABEZ CAMDEN--232½ acres. Done as above.

35. 9 November 1807. CORNELIUS THOMAS, Amherst County, to REUBEN B.
    PATTESON, Buckingham...P of A A for $1.00 to sell tracts in
Amherst County and Buckingham; to institute suit versus legatees of
LUCY CHILDRESS, deceased. Witnesses: WILLIAM A. HOWARD, DAVID R.
PATTERSON, JONATHAN HIGGINBOTHAM, W. H. WILLS.

36. 27 July 1807. JONATHAN GOODE, Warren County, Ohio, son of
    SAMUEL GOODE, JR., deceased, late of Charlotte County, Virginia...
of lawful age--P of A to his brother, PHILIP GOODE, same Ohio County
to settle with MARTIN PARKS, Amherst County, who is my guardian--to
see that TOM, Slave, from my father's estate is sold. Witnesses:
GAINES GOODE, JONATHAN MC LEAN, SILAS HURIN, Ohio Justice of the
Peace, and DAVID SUTTON, Ohio clerk.

37. 9 November 1807. CORNELIUS THOMAS, Amherst County, to WILLIAM B.
    HARE, Amherst County, and REUBIN B. PATTESON of Buckingham (note:
this is sometimes spelled PATTERSON, too)...Deed of trust; many
slaves named--for benefit of CORNELIUS THOMAS and wife, ELIZABETH,
and after deaths to their children: JONATHAN, SALLY, POLLY, DAVID,
ELIZA, NANCY and CATHERINE THOMAS and any future children. Deduct
for SALLY and POLLY "as may be equal to 1000 acres in Montgomery
County which to each was devised by DAVID PATTESON, SR., Buckingham."
Witnesses: W. H. WILLS, WILLIAM A. HOWARD, D. R. PATTESON, JONATHAN
HIGGINBOTHAM. To REUBIN B. PATTESON 24 October 1825.

37. 17 July 1807. DANIEL NORCUTT and wife, RACHEL, Amherst County,
    to WILLIAM MUSE, SR., Amherst County...L100 53 acres. Lines:
HUGHES' road, MUSE, REYNOLD's Mill Road. Sent to WILLIAM MUSE
8 January 1808.

38. 18 November 1807. CHARLES CHRISTIAN, SR. and wife, SARAY,
    Amherst County, to JONATHAN RICHARDSON, Amherst County...L47
300 acres Michiel Cove; fork of Buffaloe. Lines: WILLIAM LAWLESS
and the cove; MC CLAIN, JACOB PHILLIPS, AMBROSE TOMLINSON, HUGH CAMPBELL.
Witnesses: ROBERT ANDERSON, WILLIAM B. HARE, JOSEPH LOVING, WILLIAM
LEE HARRIS. To JONATHAN RICHARDSON 15 December 1810.

39. 7 August 1807. BENJAMIN CAMDEN, JR., Amherst County, to
    DANIEL HIGGINBOTHAM and Company, Amherst County...Deed of trust;
6 sh, bay mare and saddle. Witnesses: THOMAS ALDRIDGE, STERLING
CLAIBORNE, WILLIAM KNIGHT.

39. 14 August 1807. HANNAH SNEED, Amherst County, to STEPHEN WATTS
    and JAMES SEAY, Amherst County...$50.00 320 acres north side
Buff.--tract sold by REUBEN THORNTON to JONATHAN SNEED, husband of
HANNAH, but deeded by REUBEN THORNTON to WILSON C. NICHOLAS, Alb.
and sold by WILSON C. NICHOLAS to grantees. Lines: HIGGINBOTHAM's
old road, STEPHEN WATTS, SMYTH TANDY. Witnesses: T. S.(?) HOLLOWAY,
W. L. WATTS, HENRY D. BELL, KERR (?) MARTIN.

40. 23 November 1807. GEORGE STONEHAM, late of Amherst County,
    died intestate and children and legal representatives have this
day made distribution. Slaves to HENRY STONEHAM, MARY STONEHAM,
JONATHAN BECKNALL who married ANN STONEHAM, ELIJAH MAYS who married
ELIZABETH STONEHAM. Doubts because of deed of emancipation made by
GEORGE STONEHAM, 22 April 1806, and recorded in Amherst County. If
any are not entitled to freedom, then to be divided as above. Witnesses:
HUDSON M. GARLAND, WILLIAM H. DIGGES, JAMES DILLARD. Note: If a copy
of my will abstract of Book A of NELSON is available, one sees that
JONATHAN LOVING got permission to file old papers found in a prayer
book and they throw light on GEORGE STONEHAM and wife, MARY (N
GOODRIDGE--daughter of WILLIAM GOODRIDGE, Lancaster County, will of

1771). I have never checked on the genealogy of BREVET MAJOR GENERAL
GEORGE STONEHAM who was Federal Officer for first Military District
in Reconstruction days. Was he of this same family? He removed two
county officials here and I have often wondered as to his identity,
but have not pursued my curiosity.

40. December   , 1807. THOMAS PENN and wife, JANE, Amherst County,
     to LEWIS DAVIS, Amherst County...L405 200 acres part of tract.
Lines: Main road, DR. HARE. Witnesses: JAMES GARLAND, WILLIAM
EDMUNDS, MICAJAH CAMDEN. To LEWIS DAVIS 20 August 1810.

41. Please hold your hats tightly as we launch out into the wild
     blue yonder on this one. It is a dilly. 21 December 1807.
JAMES MARTIN, formerly of Amherst County, owned tract conveyed by
CHISWELL out of larger grant on Rockfish--1650 acres in then Alabama.
JAMES died and divided to sons and others the whole tract. Sold or
conveyed to son, JONATHAN MARTIN--310 acres and JONATHAN sold to
SHARAD MARTIN, late of Amherst County, deceased, who devised by will to
his son, GEORGE MARTIN, Amherst County. About same time, JAMES
MARTIN conveyed to his son, OBADIAH MARTIN, tract next to JONATHAN
MARTIN, but mentioned no quantity. However, by lines designated,
OBADIAH MARTIN sold to his cousin, JONATHAN MARTIN, who died intestate,
and tract descended to OBADIAH MARTIN, the younger, son of last
mentioned JONATHAN MARTIN, and OBADIAH, the younger, sold it to
HUDSON MARTIN, Jr., Amherst County. Lines have been discovered to
be different and GEORGE and HUDSON MARTIN, JR. wish to end all disputes
as to lines--$20.00 paid by GEORGE to HUDSON, JR. to hereby establish
the line conveyed by OBADIAH to HUDSON, JR. Lines: COLONEL JONATHAN
COLES, OBADIAH MARTIN. Agreed, too, on his purchase made of OBADIAH,
the younger. Witnesses: GEORGE NORVELL, SR., AARON H. MORRISON,
ALEXANDER REID, JONATHAN GOODWIN.

42. 16 October 1806. GEORGE MARTIN and wife, SALLY, Amherst County,
     to HUDSON MARTIN, Amherst County...L80 42 acres north Rockfish.
Lines: grantee, GIDEON MARTIN. Witnesses: HUDSON, MARTIN, JR.,
JONATHAN GOODWIN, JONATHAN M. MARTIN, NATHANIEL HARLOW, JR.

43. 23 July 1807. ROBERT L.(S) ROSE, New York State and village of
     Geneva, to JAMES FULCHER, Amherst County...L228-12 all interest
in deed of trust executed by ROSE and FULCHER. 114 acres on Big
Piney. Originally conveyed by deed to ROSE for FULCHER. Witnesses:
S. GARLAND, JAMES B. EDWARDS, ARTHUR B. DAVIES.

44. 15 January 1808. WILLIAM HALL, Amherst County, to JONATHAN AYRS,
     Amherst County...$100.00 95 acres north side and joining
Pedlar. Lines: FREDERICK PRICE, JONATHAN D. CRAWFORD, HENRY CAMDEN,
HUGH CAMPBELL. Pat. 16 July 1806 to WILLIAM HALL and ARCHELAUS MAYS.
To JONATHAN AYRS 20 January 1808.

44. 15 February 1806. Ordered to WILLIAM WARE, NELSON CRAWFORD and
     CHARLES TALIAFERRO, Amherst County Justices of the Peace:
JONATHAN WARE and wife, ELIZABETH, 14 December 1805, to NICHOLAS
VANSTAVERN 55 acres. Done by first two named, 19 December 1807.

45. 16 October 1807. WILLIAM FORBUS, Amherst County, to JONATHAN
     EUBANK, JR., Amherst County...Deed of trust; debt to DANIEL
HIGGINBOTHAM; $1.00 stock and furniture etc. Witnesses: HUDSON M.
GARLAND, S. GARLAND, JONATHAN BARNETT.

46. 1 June 1807. JESSE RICHESON and wife, AMELA, Amherst County,
     and LEXINGTON PARISH, to JONATHAN CRAWFORD, Amherst County...
1319-10 213 acres Horsley Creek. Lines: Lomax--old line; THOMAS
GOODRICH; south bank Horsley. To JONATHAN CRAWFORD 20 March 1810.

47. 1 June 1807. Some parties as above--CRAWFORD paid L110 for
     73¼ acres on Horsley. Margin as above.

47. 18 January 1808. JESSE RICHESON and wife as above to EDMOND
     GOODRICH, Amherst County...L156 104 acres Horsley. Lines:

JOSIAH ELLIS, RODERICK MC CULLOCH; grantee. To EDMOND GOODRICH,
22 January 1820.

48. 13 May 1807. JAMES WOOD and wife, NANCY, Amherst County, to
      JONATHAN FARIS, Amherst County...$400 433 acres. Remainder
of tract bought by JAMES WOOD of legatees of CUTHBERT WEBB and whre
JAMES WOOD now lives. Lines: DANIEL MC COY, ELISHA PETERS, GEORGE
VAUGHAN, ELISHA ESTIS, LANDON CABELL. Witnesses: RICHARD POWELL,
JAMES LOVING, JAMES VIGUS, NORBOURN THOMAS, WILLIAM CARTHAN--all
as to JAMES WOODS.

48. 19 October 1807. JONATHAN LOVING, Amherst County, to JONATHAN
      MONROE, Amherst County...L275 275 acres north borders TYE and
south side Berry's Mountain. Part of former survey of JOSEPH MAYS.
Lines: Top of Berry's Mountain, JAMES MAYS, WILLIAM LAINE. To
JOSEPH MAYS, 15 December 1810.

49. 8 August 1807. CORNELIUS POWELL, Amherst County, to WILLIAM
      ARMISTEAD, Amherst County...Deed of Trust; debt to WILLIAM
EDMUNDS, 6 sh, slave, BETTY, and increase. Witnesses: STERLING
CLAIBORNE, ROBERT COLEMAN, WILLIAM FOSTER. Wo WILLIAM ARMISTEAD,
3 June 1808.

50. 16 December 1807. DRURY BELL and wife, CATHERINE T., Amherst
      County, to STEPHEN WATTS, Amherst County...$1240.00 207 acres
both sides Lime Kiln Creek and part of tract of which HENRY BELL
died possessed of and where DRURY BELL lives. Lines: SAMUEL BELL,
Coleman's road, HENRY BELL, deceased, crossing creek. Also one moiety
of a mill seat on Lime Kiln Creek to which DRURY BELL is entitled
under will of HENRY BELL, deceased. Witnesses: HEN HOLLOWAY,
WILLIAM HORSLEY, JOSEPH HORSLEY, HENRY H. WATTS, DAB PHILLIPS. To
JAMES MURPHY, 22 July 1808.

51. 2 November 1807. RICHARD C. POLLARD, Amherst County, to
      WILLIAM F. CARTER and ROBERT FRANKLIN, Amherst County...Deed
of Trust; debt to MURPHY BROWN and Company. 5 sh., slaves. Witnesses:
JOSEPH SHELTON, JAMES TURNER, WILLIS H. WILLS, JEREMIAH YAGER. To
J. M., 9 June 1808.

52. 27 January 1808. WILLIAM BALL and wife, SALLY, Amherst County,
      to his son, WILLIAM BALL, Amherst County...$20.00 325 acres
north side of north fork Rockfish. Lines: JESSE JOPLING on east;
WILLIAM JOHNSON on southeast; EDWARD HARDING on southwest; JONATHAN
SNIDER on west and his lands bought of THOMAS JOPLING on north.
Tract brought of JONATHAN HARDING and deeded to WILLIAM BALL by
EDWARD HARDING. Witnesses: JONATHAN FARRAR, JR., RICHARD BALL,
DAVID ENICKS, SHELTON FARRAR, Memo: father may cultivate any part.

53. 2 April 1805. Order to Amherst County Justices of the Peace:
      JAMES BROOKS and wife, ELIZABETH, Amherst County, to HENRY
MC CLAIN...142½ acres, 13 February 1802. Done by NATHAN CRAWFORD and
HUDSON MARTIN, December 23, 1807.

53. 22 October 1807. CHARLES BURRUS, JR., Amherst County, to
      POLLY H. and ST. GEORGE TUCKER, heirs of DANIEL TUCKER,
Amherst County...to complete a contract as persons interested in said
tract and as heir of CHARLES BURRUS (also his executor) who made bond
13 June 1792 to DANIEL TUCKER, deceased. To tract: 100 acres--part
whereon he then lived--all on east side Mobley's Mountain; survey of
82 acres. Lines: Top of Mobley Mountain; CHARLES BURRUS; WILLIAM
CAMDEN; DANIEL TUCKER, deceased. CHARLES BURRUS, JR. sets forth
that he is executor of father, CHARLES, SR. Witnesses: DAVID S.
GARLAND; ROBERT COLEMAN; JONATHAN EUBANK, JR.; ALLEN BUGG; CHARLES A.
JACOBS.

55. 16 November 1807. SHELTON CROSTHWAIT, Amherst County, to
      JAMES P. COCKE, Alb...6 sh. 250 acres both sides RUCKER's
Run. Lines: HECTOR CABELL, deceased, on northeast tract lately
bought by South Carolina of JONATHAN EDMONDS on south; CHARLES EDMUNDS

on west. Same tract and mills bought by SHELTON CROSTHWAIT of grantee--variety mills; slaves; deed of trust. Witnesses: D. CARR, HENRY HOLLOWAY, NICHOLAS CABELL.

55. 1 October 1801. JAMES CHRISTIAN, son of CHARLES CHRISTIAN, Amherst County, to JONATHAN EUBANK, JR., Amherst County...Deed of Trust; debt to DANIEL HIGGINBOTHAM. $1.00 slaves; furniture, etc. Witnesses: WILLIAM ARMISTEAD, THOMAS ALDRIDGE, BARTLETT THOMPSON, CHARLES A. JACOBS. To JAMES GARLAND, 12 October 1808.

57. 17 December 1807. JAMES CHRISTIAN and wife, CURDILLAH; WILLIAM HORSLEY and wife, SALLY; JAMES MURPHY and wife, BETSY; CHARLES CHRISTIAN and STEPHEN WATTS, trustees of JAMES CHRISTIAN, all of Amherst County, to JAMES DILLARD, Amherst County...$1344.00. 336 acres on JAMES river. Part of tract where GEORGE CHRISTIAN, deceased, formerly lived. Lines: grantee; the old path. Witnesses: REUBEN NORVELL, HEN HOLLOWAY, DRURY BELL, BENJAMIN WATTS. To JAMES MURPHY 19 July 1808.

58. 15 July 1807. HUDSON M. GARLAND, Amherst County, to DAVID S. GARLAND, Amherst County...Deed of Trust; debt to JAMES and DAVID S. GARLAND, late merchants in firm of JAMES and DAVID GARLAND-- $1.00; also debt to DAVID S. GARLAND and DANIEL HIGGINBOTHAM, Amherst County merchants--DANIEL HIGGINBOTHAM and Company--slaves; horse bought from THOMAS ALDRIDGE; long and interesting list of furniture and books in law library. Witnesses: JONATHAN EUBANK, JR.; ROBERT GARLAND; BARTLETT THOMPSON. Sent to HENRY WOODS, 30 June 1810.

60. 28 December 1807. HEZEKIAH HARGROVE and wife, SUSANNA, Amherst County, to JOSEPH HARGROVE, Amherst County...L138-13-5. 100 acres Rucker's Run--south border. Lines: backline of larger tract bought by HEZEKIAH HARGROVE of MARTIN KEYS and where HEZEKIAH HARGROVE lives; road from Loving's Gap to CH; SAMUEL J. CABELL, WILLIAM LOVING. Witnesses: JAMES MURPHY, THOMAS HARGROVE, CHARLES CHRISTIAN, NELSON HARGROVE.

61. 17 November 1807. ELISHA PETERS, Amherst County, to heirs of ALLEN LAVENDER, deceased: AGNES, NANCY, CHARLES, WILLIAM, CLOUGH, ELIZABETH, and JONATHAN LAVENDER...L100 three tracts. 1. 59 acres south side FINLEY's Mountain. 2. 10 acres adjoining number 1. 3. 8½ acres adjoining number 1. Bought by ALLEN LAVENDER from JESSE MARTIN, 21 June, 1794. Witnesses: JESSE PROFFITT, JAMES STEVENS, JR., DUNCAN CAMERON.

62. 6 February 1808. WILLIAM LANE, waggoner, Amherst County, to LEWIS LANE, Amherst County...6 sh.; slave, WESTLEY. Witnesses: THOMAS JOHNS, WOODSON ARRINGTON, MIDDLETON LANE, JAMES PETERS.

62. 15 February 1808. WILLIAM LANE, waggoner, Amherst County, to SAMUEL PORTER LAINE, Amherst County...slaves girl, HALEY. Witnesses: as above, plus WILLIAM HAGER. To SAMUEL LAINE, 9 April 1813.

63. 13 February 1808. HENRY MC CLAIN and wife, ESTHER, Amherst County Parish and Company, to THOMAS WARE, same company and Parish. L5 100 acres. Lines: THOMAS MORRISON, WILLIAM FITZPATRICK, THOMAS FITZPATRICK, JAMES WOODS. Tract conveyed by JAMES WOODS, Amherst County, to RICHARD MC CLAIN, father of grantor, 17 April 1763. Order to quiz ESTHER on same date to NATHAN CRAWFORD and HUDSON MARTIN. Done same day.

64. 23 February 1807. WILLIAM MORTON to JONATHAN EUBANK, JR...Deed of Trust; debt due DAVID S. GARLAND; 5 sh.; furniture and stock. Witnesses: DAB. PHILLIPS, JAMES GARLAND, HENRY LANE, JONATHAN P. COBBS, DANIEL HIGGINBOTHAM.

65. 8 November 1807. RICHARD C. POLLARD and wife, ELIZABETH, Amherst County, to JONATHAN WRIGHT, Amherst County. L100 199 acres Dutch Creek. Lines: the road; top of a mountain.

Witnesses: WILLIS H. WILLS, SYLVANUS BRYANT, RICHARD BRYANT,
CHARLES CHRISTIAN. To J. MURPHY 24 April 1808.

66. 21 October 1807. BENJAMIN RUCKER, SR., Amherst County, to
      JAMES TINSLEY, Bourbon County, Kentucky (spelled Borbon)...
20 sh. 135½ acres border of Hinkston on Somerset border. Lines:
ANTYONY RUCKER's survey; CASSIDAY. Witnesses: GIDEON RUCKER,
CALEB WILTSHIRE, OLIVER TINSLEY, NICHOLAS WEST, ANTHONY RUCKER. To
JAMES TINSLEY 19 October 1809.

67. 6 September 1805. BENJAMIN NOEL, Amherst County, to BENJAMIN
      SHACKLEFORD, Amherst County...$20.00 38 acres. THOMAS MILL
Creek. Lines: RODERICK MC CULLOCH, CHARLES DAVIS. Witnesses:
THOMAS N. EUBANK, THOMAS GOODRICH, LITTLEBERRY BRYANT, CHARLES DAVIS.

68. 1 February 1808. MOSES RUCKER, Amherst County, to PETER P.
      THORNTON, Amherst County...Deed of Trust; debt to JONATHAN
and RICHARD S. (L.) ELLIS and HUGH MC CABE--three slaves. Witnesses:
ABRAM CARTER, THOMAS N. EUBANK, LEONARD HENLEY, WILLIAM WARE. To
MAJOR JONATHAN ELLIS, 5 October 1808.

69. 10 February 1808. ISAAC RUCKER, Executor of AMBROSE RUCKER, to
      RICHARD HARDWICK, Amherst County...L359-6-6 399½ acres HARRIS
Creek. Lines: ELIZABETH COLEMAN, WILLIAM PETERS, TINSLEY RUCKER,
WARE's road, AMBROSE RUCKER.

70. 10 February 1808. ISAAC RUCKER as above to TINSLEY RUCKER,
      Amherst County...L159-19-6 177 3/4 acres head borders HARRIS
Creek. Lines: WARE's road; RICHARD HARDWICK, TINSLEY RUCKER,
tobacco house. To TINSLEY RUCKER, 20 December 1810.

70. 15 February 1808. JONATHAN A. SMITH and wife, MARY, Amherst
      County, to RICHARD HARTLESS, Amherst County...L100 180 acres
pat. at Richmond, 24 July, 1792. Head borders middle fork Pedlar
and south side Little Mount Pleasant. Lines: top of the mountain
that divides Piney and Pedlar; top of the Blue Ridge.

72. 15 February 1808. JONATHAN and JOSEPH LOVING, executors of
      JOSEPH STAPLES, and MARY STAPLES, widow of JOSEPH STAPLES,
to STEPHEN WATTS...Deed of Trust, 783/4 acres debt to STEPHEN WATTS
of L70-17-6. Lines: mouth of small border on Buff; ALLEN BLAIR,
grantee.

73. 4 November 1807. JAMES TINSLEY, Bourbon County, Kentucky,
      power of attorney, to ROBERT and SNTHONY TINSLEY, Amherst
County...to receive legacy of my wife, SUSANNA, from estate of her
father, ISAAC RUCKER, SR., deceased. Witnesses: OLIVER TINSLEY,
EDWARD TINSLEY, JONATHAN SMITH, NICHOLAS WEST.

73. 22 July 1807. CHARLES and BENJAMIN FALIAFERRO, executors
      of WILLIAM TALIAFERRO, late of Amherst County, to REUBEN COLEMAN,
Amherst County...L305 146 acres FRANKLIN and MOLL's Creeks; borders
of Buff. Bought by WILLIAM TALIAFERRO in lifetime from PHILLIP
SMITH, 21 July 1801. Witnesses: HENRY CAMDEN, CHARLES P. TALIAFERRO,
PETER TALIAFERRO.

74. 14 January 1808. WILLIAM TEAS and wife, SARAH, Amherst County,
      to RICHARD PHILLIPS, Amherst County...L82-7 61 acres Naked
Creek. Lines: grantor, SAMUEL J. CABELL, JONATHAN THOMPSON,
grantee. To WILLIAM H. DIGGES, per order--no date.

75. 6 October 1807. ISAAC TUCKER to RICHARD HARRISON...$102.00--
      estate of my father when my mother dies. Witnesses: NICHOLAS
HARRISON, J. P. GARLAND.

75. 14 January 1808. JONATHAN WIATT, Lynchburg, to JAMES FRANKLIN,
      Amherst County...not surveyed as to acres--L600. Lines:
PATRICK ROSE, HUGH ROSE, deceased, LAWRENCE CAMPBELL, SMYTH TANDY,
RUSH and JOSHUA HUDSON. Witnesses: SAMUEL WIATT, STITH MAYNARD,
STERLING CLAIBORNE, ROBERT M. ROSE. To JONATHAN WIATT, 3 October 1811.

9

76. 12 July 1806. Ordered to Amherst County Justices of the Peace:
ISAAC WRIGHT and wife, SUSAN, 17 February 1804, to WILLIAM WARE...
50 acres. Done by JOSIAH ELLIS and NELSON CRAWFORD, 18 April 1808.

77. 4 January 1808. ROBERT DOUTHAT and wife, MARY, Rockbridge, to
ALEXANDER QUARRIER, Richmond...$1.00, 2 tracts. Lime Kiln
Creek and bought by ROBERT DOUTHAT of JACOB KINNEY. ROBERT DOUTHAT
sold to JAMES WELCH and received bond and assigned to QUARRIER and
lost. 1. 80 acres Lines: JAMES CHRISTIAN, DAVID PATTERSON. 2. 180
acres Lines: JAMES CHRISTIAN, HENRY BELL, LARKIN GATEWOOD.

78. 20 March 1806. BENJAMIN SIMMONS, Amherst County, to CALEB TAIT,
Campbell County...L40, Deed of Trust; debt to SAMUEL IRVINE--
$1.00 stock and furniture. Witnesses: JAMES BENAGH, THOMAS R.
CLAYTON, ABRAHAM C. SHELTON, GEORGE CABELL.

79. 12 October 1807. BENNETT JOPLING, Amherst County, to JONATHAN M.
HARRIS, Amherst County...L725 two tracts both sides Rockfish
274 acres. Lines: JONATHAN HARRIS, WILLIAM HARRIS; Also one tract
on south side Rockfish--36 acres. Witnesses: WILLIAM LEE HARRIS,
JONATHAN DIGGS, KILES CHEWNING, THOMAS COCKE.

80. 7 May 1808. BENJAMIN and JAMES MAYS, Iredell County, North
Carolina, power of attorney to JONATHAN B. MAYS, same county...
as to business of estate of our father, ROBERT MAYS, Amherst County,
JOSEPH GUY, J.P. and M. MATHEWS, J.P., JONATHAN NISBET, Clerk.

81. 21 October 1807. ALEXANDER B. ROSE, Amherst County, to
WILLIAM F. CARTER and SHELTON CROSTHWAIT, Amherst County...Deed
of Trust; debt to MURPHY BROWN and Company. 5 (sic) 2530 acres Tye
and Hat Creeks. Lines: THOMAS MASSIE, DAVID S. GARLAND, THOMAS
FITZHUGH, HENRY ROSE, PHILIP RYAN. Part of tract taken from estate
of JONATHAN ROSE, 22 November 1806, and lot of grantor. Witnesses:
RICHARD MURROW, JONATHAN BRYANT, EDWARD H. CARTER.

82. 17 May 1808. CHARLES HUNT, CHRISTIAN, and wife, JANE, Amherst
County, to JACOB PIERCE, Amherst County...L54 36 acres Buff.
Lines: grantee, MIGGINSON's road, BRYDIE, deceased, WILLIAM C.
CHRISTIAN. Witnesses: WALTER CHRISTIAN, RICHARD C. HUCKSTEP,
JONAH PIERCE.

82. 20 June 1808. WILLIAM PENN, JR., Amherst County, to VERNON
METCALFE, Amherst County...no amount. 256 acres of tract
bought by WILLIAM PENN, JR. of COLONEL JOSEPH BURRUSS, 16 January
1804, in first tract. 2. 56 acres surveyed 18 June 1795 on borders
of Rutledge and Huff and granted THOMAS STEWART as assignee of heirs
of JONATHAN DAVIS, deceased, by pat. on 10 July 1799, and by him
conveyed by deed to WILLIAM PENN, JR., 16 April 1807. Lines:
JAMES CALLAWAY, JONATHAN LACKEY, JOSEPH BURRUS, GEORGE MC DANIEL,
JAMES PENDLETON.

83. 4 November 1807. SPENCER NORVELL, Amherst County, to daughter,
SUSANNAH SNEAD, wife of BURWELL SNEAD...two slaves bought from
.sheriff of Amherst County on execution and at death to lawful
heirs--free from control of BURWELL SNEAD. Witnesses: THOMAS MOORE,
PHILLIP JOHNSON.

84. Recorded 21 June 1808. Undersigned commissioners appointed by
Act of General Assembly for fixing permanent seat of Justice
for Amherst County--met at New Glasgow, June 1, 1808--attended by many
of the most respectable citizens from the different parts of the
county; proceeded to consider the pretensions of the different places
recommended as scites (sic) for the public buildings and after a
careful and deliberate view of the subject and consideration of sundry
papers, submitted to us, we are unanimously of opinion that the place
called the Oaks, said to be the property of the devisees of the late
GEORGE COLEMAN, about five miles above New Glasgow, is the most
convenient place. We have designated by setting up stakes a spot on
the said tract, which we think the proper one for the courthouse and

this spot we report to the court of Amherst County as that on which
we have fixed their permanent seat of Justice, June 2, 1808. JACOB
KENNEY, DAVID PATTERSON, PL. (?) CARR, THOMAS PRESTON, ISAAC OTEY,
D. CARR.

84. 2 April 1808. DAVID TINSLEY and wife, NANCY, JONATHAN TINSLEY
     and wife, MARY, ISAAC TINSLEY and wife, JANE, Amherst County,
to JOSHUA TINSLEY, Amherst County...L33 22 acres Harris creek. Lines:
grantee, SPENCER NORVELL, PHILLIP BURFORD, deceased. Witnesses:
RICHARD BURKS, GEORGE M. TINSLEY, GEORGE TINSLEY.

85. 26 December 1807. WILLIAM GUTTRY, JR., and wife, ELIZABETH,
     Amherst County, to BARTLETT EADES, Amherst County...L200 100
acres south borders STOVALL. Witnesses: SAMUEL SCHOOLFIELD,
JONATHAN COX, JONATHAN C. LYNCH, THOMAS HIGGINBOTHAM. To BARTLETT
EADES, 7 September 1809.

86. 26 December 1807. BARTLETT EADES, Amherst County, to WILLIAM
     GUTTRY, JR., Amherst County...600 (sic) 331 acres north and
middle borders STOVALL. Witnesses: JESSE WRIGHT, SAMUEL SCHOOLFIELD
et al. as above. Withdrawn by MR. WILLIAM KENT--no date.

87. 23 April 1807. WILLIAM CAMDEN and wife, SIBELL, Amherst County,
     to MICAJAH CAMDEN, Amherst County...L135 85 acres Huff Creek.
Lines: grantee's spring, JAMES HIGGINBOTHAM, JOSEPH PENN, the road
oldfield, spring branch where it enters Huff, WILLIAM CAMDEN.
Witnesses: CORNELIUS SALE, CHARLES BURRUS, NICHOLAS C. HORSLEY.
To MICAJAH CAMDEN, 31 December 1812.

88. 18 December 1807. JONATHAN LACKEY, Amherst County, to JOSEPH
     DILLARD, Amherst County...L58 58 acres survey of 24 February
1804--both sides north fork Buff. Lines: JACOB PHILLIPS, HENRY
BALLINGER, ZACHARIAL TALIAFERRO. Witnesses: CORNELIUS POWELL,
ALEXANDER WATSON, JAMES OGDON.

89. 13 December 1807. WILLIAM JOHNS, Amherst County, to ISAAC
     TINSLEY, JR., Amherst County...Deed of Trust; debt to RICHARD
BURKS, Amherst County, $1.00 - 57 acres. Lines: MARTIN PARKS, top
of Tobacco Row Mountain, ARTHUR L. DAVIES, HOUCHINS, RICHARD S. ELLIS.
Witnesses: THOMAS L. MC CHENNEY, RODNEY TINSLEY, PETER RUCKER. To
RICHARD BURKS, 6 February 1810.

90. 12 July 1808. JAMES TALIAFERRO to REUBIN COLEMAN...L205 154
     acres Molls and Franklin Creeks; borders of Buff. Bought
from MR. WILLIAM TALIAFERRO, deceased. Lines: WILLIAM SANDIDGE,
ANSELM CLARKSON, DAVID CLARKSON, grantee. Witnesses: BENJAMIN and
CHARLES TALIAFERRO, JESSE BLAND, PETER and RICHARD M. TALIAFERRO.
Carried to court per order, 15 May 1809.

91. 1 June 1808. JESSE BLAND and wife, SALLY, Amherst County, to
     CHARLES P. TALIAFERRO, Amherst County...$300.00 202 acres
Horsley and Puppie Creek. Lines: CHARLES TALIAFERRO, THOMAS WOODROOF,
JONATHAN SMITH, WILLIAM WARE, WILLIAM HOWARD. Witnesses: RICHARD M.
TALIAFERRO, WILLIAM HOWARD, RICHARD BALLINGER.

92. 19 July 1808. WILLIAM BOWMAN, Amherst County, to WILLIAM JORDON...
     Deed of Trust; debt due grantee; slaves. Witnesses: JESSE (?)
ALLEN, S. H. ALLEN, LEROY CAMDEN.

93. 1 January 1808. JONATHAN LACKEY, Amherst County, to WILLIAM
     CAMDEN, Amherst County...slaves and any interest of my mother,
EVE LACKEY. Witnesses: JAMES STINNETT, JONATHAN WHITEHEAD; delivered
to WILLIAM C. CAMDEN 2 December 1809.

93. 9 December 1807. RICHARD JONES and wife, POLLY, to CHARLES
     PALMER, Amherst County...L260 150 acres south borders Porrige.
Lines: grantor JAMES DAVIS, WILLIAM TURNER. Witnesses: WILLIAM
TURNER, JESSE BECK, WILLIAM JONES, WILLIAM GILBERT. Page 94 ordered
to Amherst County Justices of the Peace to quiz POLLY on 28 December
1807. Done, 16 July 1808, by REUBEN NORVELL and PHILLIP JOHNSON.

11

94. 12 December 1807. JAMES DAVIS, Amherst County, to BARTLETT
EADES, Amherst County...L4-12-2 small tracts north borders
Stovall--both contain 3½ acres by survey. 1. EAD's line. 2. At the
creek. Witnesses: WILLIAM GUTTRY, JR., HENRY CALLAWAY, PHILIP
JOHNSON. Final proof at court held at the house occupied by AARON
CAMBELL at the Oaks, 18 July 1808. Note: I have made no attempt to
find property at the Oaks by AARON CAMPBELL; if he owned land. It
is possible that he rented a house here in those long ago days.

95. 19 March 1808. ARCHELAUS MITCHELL, Amherst County, to THOMAS N.
EUBANKS, Amherst County...Deed of trust; debt due JONATHAN
and RICHARD S. (L.) ELLIS; $1.00 400 acres Cashaw Creek; border of
JAMES. Lines: THOMAS JENKINS, ROLAND BYASS. Also stock. Witnesses:
WILLIAM DAVID (C), HENRY BROWN, JAMES WARE, BENJAMIN SALE, THOMAS M.
POPE. To MAJOR JONATHAN ELLIS, 5 October 1808.

97. 18 December 1807. WILLIAM HOWARD, Amherst County, to THOMAS N.
EUBANK, Amherst County...Deed of Trust; debt due JAMES P.
GARLAND; $1.00 117½ acres Puppie Creek. Lines: JONATHAN WARE's
estate, JONATHAN TALIAFERRO, HENRY BALLINGER. Sometimes known as
Frenchburg. Witnesses: WILLIAM MC GAW, WILLIS BROWN, B. STONE.
Sent to JAMES P. GARLAND, 31 August 1808.

98. 21 March 1808. REUBEN NORVELL, Amherst County, to JONATHAN
CAMM and DAVID S. GARLAND, Amherst County...Deed of Trust;
debt due WILLIAM BROWN and Company, Lynchburg--$1.00 400 acres.
Lines: RAWLEY PENN, CHRISTIAN's old line, JONATHAN A. JOHNS, LARKIN
LONDON, JAMES LONDON. Part of 1000 acres formerly owned by JONATHAN
EDLOE and in old survey of 3926 acres made for JONATHAN CHRISTIAN
and WILLIAM BROWN. Also six slaves named and ages. Witnesses:
PHILIP JOHNSON, WILLIAM CAMDEN, ROBERT GARLAND, DANIEL HIGGINBOTHAM,
ARCHIBALD AUSTIN, ARCHAELUS MAYS--he signed for grantee. Sent to
ARCHAELUS MAYS, January 1809.

99. 29 June 1808. MOSES MARTIN and wife, ELIZABETH, Amherst
County, to WILLIAM SANDIDGE, Amherst County...L300 224 acres
Stone House Creek borders. Lines: forks of the road, grantor's
old field, WILLIAM SALES, main road, HENRY CAMDEN, AARON HIGGINBOTHAM,
deceased. Witnesses: WILLIAM SALE, JONATHAN (?) BALLARD, WILLIAM
MAYS, WASH HILL, AMBROSE MC DANIEL.

101. 29 June 1808. MOSES MARTIN and wife, ELIZABETH, Amherst County,
to WILLIAM SANDIDGE, Amherst County...L100 103 acres Stonehouse
borders. Lines: at house, long border. Witnesses: as above plus
EDMOND T. COLEMAN. Margin: as above. February 28, 1822, to WILLIAM
SANDIDGE.

102. 14 May 1808. JONATHAN BOWLING, Amherst County, to REUBEN NORVELL,
Amherst County, and ARCHELUUS MAYS, Lynchburg...Deed of Trust;
debt to WILLIAM BROWN and Company $1.00 230 acres. Lines: DOCTOR
DANIEL BURFORD, JONATHAN COALTER (COULTER), EDWARD WATSON, JONATHAN
MC BRIDE, BENJAMIN RUCKER. Witnesses: SAM WIATT, WILLIAM RADFORD,
THOMAS S. MC CLELLAND. Sent to ARCHELUUS MAYS, January 1809.

103. 1 June 1808. DANIEL BURFORD, JR., Amherst County, to THOMAS
MOORE, ESQ., Amherst County, and ARCHELAUS MAYS, Lynchburg...
Deed of Trust; debt to WILLIAM BROWN and Company, Lynchburg; $1.00--
the one-half of his part of 212 acres in Amherst County. Lines:
NELSON DAWSON, DOCTOR DANIEL BURFORD, AMBROSE BURFORD, LEWIS DAWSON.
Tract was willed to him and AMBROSE BURFORD by their father, JONATHAN
BURFORD, deceased, and divided; 55 gal. still etc. Witnesses:
WILLIAM BRADFORD, HUMPHREY STEWART, JONATHAN LONDON, JONATHAN HORSLEY,
GEORGE CABELL. Margin: as for previous deed.

105. 22 March 1808. WILLIAM MAYS, Amherst County, to ROBERT RIVES,
Amherst County...6 sh; Deed of Trust; colt; debt to ALEXANDER
SALE, executor of BEVERLY WILLIAMSON, deceased. Witnesses: WILLIAM
SALE, MOSES MARTIN, JONATHAN SMITH.

106. 20 June 1808. GEORGE WASHINGTON HIGGINBOTHAM, Amherst County,
       to JOSEPH DILLARD, Amherst County...$600 300 acres surveyed
15 March 1801--Elk Island borders. Lines: JONATHAN and JAMES
HIGGINBOTHAM, JONATHAN THOMPSON, SAMUEL BELL. To JONATHAN LONDON,
21 April 1817.

107. 13 February 1808. JUSTINIAN CARTWRIGHT and wife, FRANCES,
       Livingston County, Kentucky, are legatees of GEORGE GILLESPIE,
Amherst County, deceased, by right of FRANCES as daughter of GEORGE
GILLESPIE. Power of attorney to their son, JAMES CARTWRIGHT, same
county to act for them. ENOCH PRINCE, Clerk; recorded B:5, JAMES
MC NAB, Presiding Justice of the Peace, Recorded, Amherst County,
17 September 1808.

108. 8 April 1808. WILLIAM HOWARD, Amherst County, to WILLIAM WARE,
       Amherst County, and ABRAHAM CARTER, Amherst County...Deed of
Trust; $5.00 paid by CARTER--100 acres whereon CHARLES MAYS lives.
Lines: JAMES TALIAFERRO's estate, RICHARD or HENRY HARTLESS estate,
HENRY BALLINGER, slaves etc. Witnesses: WILLIAM PRYOR, PETER
TALIAFERRO, JESSE BLAND, CHARLES TALIAFERRO.

110. 10 March 1808. JAMES HALL and wife, MARY, Amherst County, to
       DAVID and JAMES GARLAND, Amherst County...L25 lot 17 New
Glasgow. Witnesses: STERLING CLAIBORNE, DANIEL HIGGINBOTHAM, WILLIAM
HALL, H. M. GARLAND, JAMES DILLARD, CHARLES A. JACOBS. To JAMES
GARLAND, 22 September 1808.

110. 14 October 1807. THOMAS JENKINS, Amherst County, to THOMAS N.
       EUBANK, Amherst County, and JONATHAN and RICHARD S. ELLIS,
Amherst County...Deed of Trust; debt to ELLIS men; $5.00 140 acres
Peavine or Chestnut Mountain; Cashaw Creek; border of JAMES and
where THOMAS JENKINS lives. Lines: north by ROWLAND BYAS, west by
ARCHELAUS MITCHELL, east and south by HENRY L. DAVIES. Witnesses:
NATHANIEL J. MANSON, JONATHAN RICHESON, PETER P. THORNTON, WILL
PRYOR. To MAJOR JOHN ELLIS, 5 October 1808.

112. 10 April 1798. Ordered to Amherst County Justices of the Peace
       WILLIAM DAVIS and wife, BENEDICTOR, 16 October 1797, to
WILLIAM WARE...106 acres, WILLIAM S. CRAWFORD, Clerk. To NELSON
CRAWFORD, CHARLES TALIAFERRO, and JOEL FRANKLIN. Done by NELSON
CRAWFORD and CHARLES TALIAFERRO, 19 September 1798, recorded after
court return, 19 September 1808.

113. 2 November 1799. Order to WILLIAM WARWICK and DAVID S. GARLAND,
       Amherst County Justices of the Peace, JAMES SAVAGE and wife,
MARY, 16 September 1799, to ROBERT HOLLOWAY...75 acres. Done by
Justices of the Peace; no date; returned to court, 19 September 1808.

113. 17 November 1807. Agreement between JONATHAN CRAWFORD, agent
       for SALLY BURRUS, to WILLIAM CAMDEN. This item has "error,"
but it is found on the next page.

114. 15 September 1808. ROBERT KNUCKLES and wife, FANNY, Amherst
       County, to BENJAMIN SHACKLEFORD, Amherst County...L75 90 acres--
ROBERT KNUCKLES has lately moved from tract. Lines: grantee,
JONATHAN SLEDD, JAMES BYASS, CHARLES DAVIS. To BENJAMIN SHACKLEFORD,
5 October 1808.

114. 17 November 1807. Agreement between JONATHAN CRAWFORD, agent
       for SALLY BURRUS and WILLIAM CAMDEN...lease of all unsold land
where SALLY lives--"higherd" four negroes for three years; if SALLY
dies, then WILLIAM CAMDEN is to deliver at end of year of her death
within three year period. L15 per year. Witnesses: WILLIAM WARE,
BENJAMIN TALIAFERRO, JONATHAN H. CHILDRESS.

115. 21 June 1799. Order to Alb. Justices of the Peace: JOSEPH
       HORTON and wife, TABITHA, 24 February 1799, to BENJAMIN JORDAN...
1/2 acre lot in Warminster. Done by SAMUEL MURRELL and TANDY KEY;
no date. Returned to Amherst County, 19 September 1808.

116.   22 July 1808.   Ordered to Amherst County Justices of the Peace:
       DRURY BELL and wife, CATHERINE T., 16 December 1807, to
STEPHEN WATTS...207 acres.   Done 12 September 1808 by REUBEN NORGELL
and DAVID S. GARLAND.

117.   22 August 1806.   Order to Amherst County Justices of the Peace:
       HENRY BALLINGER and wife, MARY, 13 July 1805 to PULLIAM SANDIDGE...
two tracts: 213 acres.   Done by NELSON CRAWFORD and CHARLES TALIAFERRO,
28 July 1806 (sic); returned 19 September 1808.

118.   17 September 1808.   DANIEL TRIPLETT, Loudoun County, to
       THOMAS TRIPLETT, Amherst County...$800.00, 150 acres.   Lines:
SMYTH TANDY, Roaling (sic) roads, WILLIAM SPENCER, Raven Creek,
NATHAN HALL, WILLIAM CABELL, JR., SAMUEL ANDERSON.   Witnesses:
SAMUEL BLAIR (?), JAMES B. EDWARDS, CALEB RALLS, S. JONES, PETER
PEARCE.

119.   26 July 1808.   JESSEY BOWEN and wife, POLEY; ELIZABETH GEORGE;
       LODOWICK GEORGE; and NICHOLAS HARRISON, Amherst County, to
EDWARD WATSON, Amherst County...L75-1-6 45½ acres; tract formerly
that of SARAH GEORGE, deceased, and left by her to be equally divided
between ELIZABETH, POLLEY and LODOWICK GEORGE, legatees.   Lines:
REUBEN RUCKER's road.   Witnesses: ALEXANDER WATSON, JONATHAN BLANKS,
WILLIAM KNIGHT.   To EDWARD WATSON, 12 February 1812.

120.   16 February 1808.   THOMAS JENKINS, Amherst County, to ROLLING
       BYAS, Amherst County...L33--no acres--headwaters OTTER and
COCKE's (?).   Lines: grantor.   Witnesses: FLEMING DUNCAN, WILLIAM
SHOEMAKER, LARKIN BIAS, GEORGE MORRIS.

121.   20 October 1806.   JONATHAN CLARKSON, Amherst County, to son,
       DAVID, Amherst County and $100...260 acres both sides FRANKLIN
Creek.   Lines: WILLIAM TALIAFERRO, deceased, ANSELM CLARKSON,
ZACHARIAH TALIAFERRO, JONATHAN SALE.   Witnesses: HUGH CAMPBELL,
ANSELM CLARKSON, ARCHIBALD ROWSEY, HENRY BALLINGER.   To DAVID CLARKSON,
13 April 1816.

123.   8 September 1807.   THOMAS SPRADLING and wife, NANCY, Amherst
       County, to GEORGE SHRADER, Amherst County...L73 72½ acres
both sides north fork Elk Island Creek.   Lines: WILLIAM LAIN.
Witnesses: JAMES FRANKLIN, JR., JAMES P. GARLAND, B. DTONE.

124.   19 September 1808.   JUSTINIAN CARTWRIGHT and wife, FRANCES,
       Livingston County, Kentucky...FRANCES, daughter of GEORGE
GILLESPIE, deceased, to DAVID S. GARLAND, Amherst County, Power of
Attorney, 10 February 1808, to JAMES A. CARTWRIGHT, Livingston
County, Kentucky--to sell her interest in GEORGE GILLESPIE's tract--
L66-13-5--400 acres south side and joining Big Piney.   Lines:
JONATHAN CAMPBELL, MOSES WRIGHT, WILLIAM MOORE, WILLIAM S. CRAWFORD,
JONATHAN FULCHER, JONATHAN CAMDEN, Piney River.   Reference to deed
from CHARLES ROSE to GEORGE GILLESPIE.   FRANCES is entitled to
1/12th.   Note: I have made comments about this land before since my
wife, MILDRED MILLER DAVIS, descends from WILLIAM GILLESPIE who was
a son of GEORGE.   I think that I made an error in stating that
GEORGE GILLESPIE and wife, MARY, were in Alb. in 1776 when they made
a conveyance of record in Alb.   I find that GEORGE and wife, MARY,
were of Amherst.   MARY died sometime between 1776 and 1786 when
GEORGE married widow, MARY FARIS, in Louisa.   All of GEORGE's children
were by first MARY and two of them married daughters of MARY FARIS.
I still contend that the first MARY was a MOORE, but can't prove it.
She and GEORGE had two children with middle name of MOORE: SHEROD
MOORE GILLESPIE, Captain from Amherst County in Revolution, and LILLY
MOORE GILLESPIE who married JAMES BOWLING, SR.   BENJAMIN MOORE and
wife, LETISHA, both left wills in Amherst, but only her name strikes
responsive chord for her will named no GILLESPIES and neither did
his document.   A very early WILLIAM MOORE refers to married children
in will in Amherst County, but I am still in the dark.   GEORGE GILLESPIE
operated a mill on Big Piney and many old-timers refer to the Rose
Mill--now gone, but it stood not far from where GEORGE GILLESPIE was
buried.

126. 10 September 1808. HUGH CAMPBELL and wife, ELIZABETH, CHARLES
      BARRETT and wife, SALLY, JAMES and ANN BARRETT, all of Amherst
County, to PULLIAM SANDIDGE, Amherst County...L845-2 949 acres.
1. JONATHAN BEASLEY's tract of 400 acres pat to him at Williamsburg,
11 November 1761; 2. GEORGE TAYLOR tract of 240 acres pat as above,
25 March 1762. Lines: WILLIAM CABELL, JR. 3. NEILL CAMPBELL
tract of 115 acres pat. 1 March 1773. Lines: his own. 4. NEILL
CAMPBELL's tract--99 acres pat. 20 June 1772. 5. NEILL CAMPBELL's
tract 95 acres pat. 10 September 1767. Witnesses: LINDSEY SANDIDGE,
JAMES and ROLAND SANDIDGE.

130. 19 September 1808. BURCHER WHITEHEAD and wife, NANCY, Amherst
      County, to JONATHAN PENN, JR....L76-2-6 30¼ acres south borders
Buff. and part of where BURCHER WHITEHEAD lives. Lines: MICAJAH
CAMDEN; grantee; a branch; DANIEL TUCER; SCOTT's road. Note: I have
mentioned old WHITEHEAD or COLEMAN, earlier, home just across the
street from my home. The owner is a descendant of both families and
she has invited me to inspect an old WHITEHEAD graveyard which is not
too far away from the house. It is located on land sold off some
years ago, but I have not inspected the graveyard at this date. I
pass within a few yards of it every time that I make a pastoral
call on one of my church families.

131. 26 August 1808. WILLIAM MAYS, Amherst County, to LEROY CAMDEN,
      Amherst County...Deed of Trust; debt to WILLIAM CAMDEN. $1.00--
stock and furniture. Witnesses: WARNER GOODWIN, CHARLES DUNCAN,
JONATHAN WHITEHEAD, NICHOLAS VANSTAVERN. To WILLIAM CAMDEN, 29 October
1808.

133. 20 September 1808. JONATHAN FA. HALL and wife, BETSY, Amherst
      County, to JESSE BLAND, Amherst County...L18 40 acres Pedler.
Lines: JONATHANT HARDW--; at path; ROBERTS; BROWN; RUSSELL.

134. 19 September 1808. HUGH CAMPBELL and wife, ELIZABETH, Amherst
      County, to CHARLES L. BARRET, Amherst County...love and $1.00--
400 acres by pat. on both sides south fork Buff. Lines: JAMES
HIGGINBOTHAM, NEAL CAMPBELL.

135. 19 September 1808. JAMES CLEMENTS and wife, BETSY, Amherst
      County, to ROBERT RIVES, Amherst County...L160 180 acres
border of THRASHER. Lines: AARON HIGGINBOTHAM, SALES.

136. April, 1808. JOHN SMITH, Amherst County, to WILLIAM PRYOR,
      Amherst County...L30 60 north borders Horsley. Lines: WILLIAM
WARE, WILLIAM CARTER (now JESSE BLAND), WILLIAM WARD. Witnesses:
ABRAM CARTER, WILLIAM WARE, NELSON CRAWFORD, THOMAS N. EUBANK.

138. 19 April 1808. CORNELIUS POWELL, Amherst County, to CHARLES A.
      JACOBS, Amherst County...Deed of Trust; debt to DANIEL
HIGGINBOTHAM and Company. 6 sh. three slaves. Witnesses: ANDERSON
MOSS, BARTLETT THOMPSON, THOMPSON NOELL. To CHARLES A. JACOBS,
29 January 1809.

139. 23 January 1808. RICHARD HARDWICK to secure JESSE CLEMENTS on
      three bonds to ISAAC RUCKER, executor of AMBROSE RUCKER,
deceased, to TINSLEY RUCKER...Deed of Trust; 399½ acres on head of
Harris Creek. Tract sold to RICHARD HARDWICK by executor of AMBROSE
RUCKER. Witnesses: SAMUEL COLEMAN, STEPHEN CLEMENTS.

140. 4 July 1807. JONATHAN HOGG, Amherst County, to BENJAMIN NOELL,
      Amherst County...L66 100 acres Otter Creek. Lines: Big branch
of Otter; WILLIAM DAVIES. Witnesses: PETER P. THORNTON, WILLIAM C.
DAVIS, MOSES RUCKER, BENJAMIN SHACKLEFORD. To BENJAMIN NOELL,
6 November 1809.

141. 12 April 1808. WILLIAM HOWARD, Amherst County, to WILLIAM WARE,
      Amherst County...L80 219 acres; Deed of Trust; debt to JONATHAN
SMITH. -- sh. Horsley Creek. Tract. Lines: WILLIAM WARE, WILLIAM
HOWARD, HENRY BALLINGER. All of tracts sold by JONATHAN SMITH to

WILLIAM WARE. Witnesses: JAMES CAMPBELL, SR., PETER TALIAFERRO, JAMES CAMPBELL, JR.

143. 17 April 1808. JONATHAN A. SMITH and wife, POLLY, Amherst
     County, to WILLIAM HOWARD...L160 219 acres Horsley. Lines:
RICHARD LAWLESS, WILLIAM WARE, WILLIAM HOWARD (bought of THOMAS
MITCHELL), HENRY BALLINGER, top of Job's Mountain, WILLIAM LAWLESS.
Witnesses: ABRAM CARTER, PETER TALIAFERRO, JOSEPH MARTIN, WILLIAM
PRYOR, CHARLES TALIAFERRO, JESSE BLAND, WILLIAM WARE. Page 144
order to Amherst County Justices of the Peace to quiz POLLY, 9 (sic)
April 1808; done on same day by CHARLES TALIAFERRO and WILLIAM WARE.

145. 30 April 1804. THOMAS MOORE and wife, SALLY, to DAVID TINSLEY...
     $2560.00 320 acres on James River below Town of Bethel and known
as Rasberry Neck. Lines: The Fluvanna, JESSE WOODROOF, ARTHUR L.
DAVIES, a path. Witnesses: NELSON C. DAWSON, ANTHONY G. TINSLEY,
JAMES WARE, REUBEN PENDLETON. Page 446 order to Amherst County
Justices of the Peace to quiz SALLY, 25 October 1805; done, 30 October
1805 by REUBEN NORVELL and JAMES MONTGOMERY.

147. 23 March 1808. EDWARD WAUGH, Amherst County, to JAMES WAUGH,
     RODERICK WAUGH, and BENJAMIN SHACKLEFORD...Deed of Trust; debt
to THOMAS WAUGH, Bedford--$1.00 six slaves and five horses--names and
ages of slaves.

149. 19 September 1808. HUGH CAMPBELL and wife, ELIZABETH, Amherst
     County, to ANGUS MC CLOUT and JONATHAN H. CLEMENTS, Amherst
County...L50-8 48 acres east side Long Mountain and south fork Buff.
Pat. to NEILL CAMPBELL at Williamsburg, 20 June 1772. Lines:
AARON HIGGINBOTHAM, NEILL CAMPBELL, his own.

150. 10 March 1808. RICHARD LEE, Amherst County, to ARCHIBALD
     ROBERTSON and THOMAS MOORE, both of Campbell County...Deed of
Trust; debt to WILLIAM BROWN and Company, Lynchburg--five slaves
within trust--names and ages. Witnesses: SAMUEL WIATT, ARCHIBALD
MAYS (for County), JONATHAN W. HORSLEY, WILLIAM BLACK, WILLIAM
RADFORD, REUBEN NORVELL, JONATHAN LONDON. To ARCHIBALD ROBERTSON,
January, 1809.

152. 26 August 1808. RICHARD MAYS, Amherst County, to LEROY CAMDEN,
     Amherst County...Deed of Trust; debt to WILLIAM CAMDEN, $1.00;
beds, etc. Witnesses: WARNER GOODWIN, CHARLES DUNCAN, JONATHAN
WHITEHEAD, N. VANSTAVERN. To WILLIAM CAMDEN, 2 December 1809.

153. 21 September 1808. Order to Amherst County Justices of the
     Peace: JAMES HALL and wife, MARY (MAZY?), to DAVID and JAMES
GARLAND, 10 March 1808. One-half a lot in New Glasgow. Done by
JONATHAN WARWICK and REUBEN NORVELL, 22 September 1808.

154. 16 October 1808. SARAH ROSE, executor of CHARLES ROSE, to
     STERLING CLAIBORNE...L1000--over twenty slaves. Witnesses:
WILLIAM ARMISTEAD, JONATHAN P. COBBS, BARTLETT THOMPSON, THOMPSON
NOELL.

155. 19 July 1808. ISAAC TUCKER and wife, ELIZABETH, Amherst County,
     to ABNER SHREVES, Bedford County...L12 for ISAAC's interest
in tract in Nelson County, Kentucky, which is 1/11th under will of
his father, DRURY TUCKER, Amherst County, deceased. Witnesses:
LINDSEY COLEMAN, BURCHER WHITEHEAD, JOSEPH DUNCAN.

156. 10 November 1803. BARTHOLOMEW STAYTON and wife, SARAH,
     Amherst County, to JONATHAN PATTERSON, Rockbridge...L30 50 acres
both sides Middle fork Pedlar. Lines: JOSEPH HIGGINBOTHAM, JR.
Witnesses: WALTER FRASER, JONATHAN FRASER, SAMUEL MC LAIN, WILLIAM
HIGGINBOTHAM. Margin: "This deed ought not to have been recorded
here."

158. 9 September 1806. DANIEL BURFORD and wife, SARY, Amherst
      County, to ELIAS WILLS, Amherst County...L85-15 Deed of Trust;
debt to WILLIAM JONES. $1.00 81 acres Stovall Creek. Lines:
EDWARD WATSON where WILLIAM JONES now lives. Witnesses: JONATHAN
BURFORD, DANIEL MEHONE, THOMAS B. MEHONE.

160. 17 October 1808. JAMES M. MARTIN and wife, NANCY, Amherst
      County, to JONATHAN CAMDEN, SR., Amherst County...L30 270 pat.
to ALEXANDER DUGGENS in Richmond, 24 July 1780. Both sides Pedlar.
Lines: NEILL CAMPBELL's estate, JONATHAN CHILDRESS, MOSES SWEENY.

161. 20 April 1808. JONATHAN OLD and wife, ELIZABETH, heir of
      GEORGE STEELE, deceased, who was legatee of AUGUSTINE STEELE,
deceased, to LINDSEY COLEMAN, Amherst County...Lot No. 2--463/4 acres
for L5-15--"who may be heirs of GEORGE STEELE, deceased." One eighth
of tract survey of 29 June 1799; north borders Buff. Part of 218
acres of AUGUSTINE STEELE and divided by order of Amherst County
court: GEORGE STEELE's part aforesaid. Lines: grantee; lot 1;
HENRY CAMDEN. Witnesses: EDMOND T. COLEMAN, DAVID S. GARLAND,
S. GARLAND, R. H. COLEMAN. Page 161 order to Amherst County Justices
of the Peace to quiz ELIZABETH OLD--one eighth of 46 3/4 acres. Done
by JAMES OLD (signed JONATHAN) and EDWARD GARLAND and recorded
17 October 1808.

163. 15 October 1808. JONATHAN PATTERSON and wife, REBECCA,
      Rockbridge, to WILLIAM CLARK, Amherst County...$150.50--$80.00
in cash; bay mare; one steer; and $50.00--120 acres south and main
fork Pedlar and where a certain JAMES LATIN now lives. Lines:
THOMAS STATON, JOSEPH HIGGINBOTHAM, JR., top of the mountain,
JOSEPH HIGGINBOTHAM, SR. 50 acres. Lines: JOSEPH HIGGINBOTHAM,
middle fork Pedler--in all 120 acres. Witnesses: FIELDING HOLADAY,
SAMUEL MC CLAIN, WILLIAM TONGET, JONATHAN DEPRIEST. To WILLIAM
CLARK, August 1, 1816.

165. 30 November 1808. REUBEN HUDSON and wife, SALLY, Amherst
      County, to RUSH HUDSON, SR., Amherst County...L100 150 acres.
Lines: DAVID S. GARLAND, SAMUEL MEREDITH, LINDSEY COLEMAN, grantee,
old church road. Witnesses: HUDSON M. GARLAND, MICAJAH CAMDEN,
DANIEL HIGGINBOTHAM. To ROBERT RIVES, 13 June 1844.

165. 26 March 1808. Order to Amherst County Justices of the Peace:
      PETER CARTER and wife, BETSY, 14 February 1807, to JONATHAN
TAYLOR--42 acres. Done, 19 December 1808, by WILLIAM WARE and
NELSON CRAWFORD.

166. 5 April 1808. Order to Amherst County Justices of the Peace:
      WILLIAM MITCHELL and wife, JANE, 15 February 1806, to JONATHAN
ROBINSON--two tracts. 1. 66 acres. 2. 200 acres. Done by Justices
of the Peace above, 6 April 1808.

167. 19 July 1808. Order to NELSON and Amherst County Justices of
      the Peace SHELTON CROSTHWAIT, WILLIAM H. DIGGES, REUBEN NORVELL,
and DAVID S. GARLAND--JAMES CHRISTIAN and wife, CURDILLAH, WILLIAM
HORSLEY and wife, SALLY, JAMES MURPHY and wife, BETSY, CHARLES
CHRISTIAN and STEPHEN WATTS and JAMES MURPHY, trustees for JAMES
CHRISTIAN and MARTHA WATTS, 17 December 1807, to JAMES DILLARD--
336 acres--NELSON Justices of the Peace: CROSTHWAIT and DIGGES,
as to SALLY HORSLEY, BETSY MURPHY, and MARTHA WATTS (wife of
STEPHEN WATTS), 16 August 1808. Page 168 Amherst County Justices
of the Peace NORVELL and GARLAND, 12 September 1808, quizzed CURDILLAH
CHRISTIAN.

168. 19 December 1800. WILLIAM WARE, Amherst County, to WILLIAM
      JOPLING...L250 one half of a tract of 400 acres "or something
upwards." Lines: WILLIAM PRYOR, RICHARD S. ELLIS, JOHNSON's estate,
DAVID CRAWFORD's estate--all that I own south and west of first
three mentioned courses. Date seems to be clerical error for it was
recorded 19 December 1808.

169. 5 August 1808. SAMUEL MEREDITH, Amherst County, Power of
      Attorney to DAVID S. GARLAND...and voids previous powers to
JONATHAN HARRIS, Esq. Witnesses: JAMES WOODS, JAMES GARLAND,
BARTLETT THOMPSON, JONATHAN HENDREN.

169. 17 December 1808. CHARLES JOHNSON and wife, MARY, Lynchburg,
      to MERRIT H. WHITE, Amherst County...$100.00--all interest in
estate of half a lot in Town of Bethel. Lot 18 on plot; to us by
trustees under account to establish town by NICHOLAS C. DAVIES and
THOMAS W. COCKE in Amherst County, 31 December 1801. Witnesses:
THOMAS W. COCKE, MAYO DAVIES.

170. 15 December 1808. CHARLES JOHNSON and wife, MARY, Lynchburg,
      to JONATHAN ROBERTSON, Rockbridge...$112.00 one half of lot #6
described as above. Witnesses: THOMAS W. COCKE, WILLIAM PETTYJOHN,
JAMES MOSELEY. To JONATHAN ROBERTSON, 21 April 1809.

171. 1 November 1808. CALEB WATTS and wife, SUSANNAH, Amherst
      County, to MARTIN PARKS, Amherst County...L110-8-4 53 acres
both sides Chach (?) Creek; branch of Pedlar. Witnesses: GEORGE
CABELL, ISAAC TINSLEY, JESSE WOODROOF, THOMAS WOODROOF, BENNETT
TINSLEY.

173. 10 May 1808. REUBEN NORVELL and wife, POLLEY, Amherst County,
      to REUBEN CARVER, Amherst County...L113 113 acres south side
and joining Porridge. Lines: JAMES DILLARD, ALEXANDER JEWELL,
THOMAS JEWELL, JONATHAN LONDON. To REUBEN CARVER--1810.

174. 26 November 1808. DABENY PHILLIPS to DAVID S. GARLAND...L38-4-6
      19 acres south side Buff. Part of tract of WILLIAM PHILLIPS,
deceased, and to DABNEY in division--lot 3. Lines: SEATON M. PENN,
deceased; lots 2 and 3. Witnesses: JAMES FRANKLIN, DANIEL HIGGINBOTHAM,
WIATT SMITH, CHARLES A JACOBS.

175. 1 May 1806. Order to Amherst County Justices of the Peace:
      NICHOLAS HARRISON and wife, NANCY, 6 December 1805, to WILLIAM
EDMUNDS...110 acres. Done by REUBEN NORVELL and PHILLIP JOHNSON,
29 August 1806.

176. 14 November 1808. WILLIAM NOELL and wife, LUCY, Amherst County,
      to CORNELIUS ROACH, Amherst County...L117-10 two tracts.
1. Lines: BENJAMIN NOELL, KNUCKLES, TINSLEY, DAVIS, JAMES FRANKLIN.
2. Lines: CHARLES DAVIS, NICHOLAS DAVIES, deceased, DAVID NOWLING,
JER WHITTEN, JONATHAN STINNETT. Witnesses: BENJAMIN SHACKLEFORD,
ARCHILAUS GILLIAM, JONATHAN DAVIS. To CORNELIUS ROACH, 16 September
1816.

177. 10 January 1809. WILLIAM NOEL and wife, LUCY, Amherst County,
      to HUGH MC CABE, Amherst County...L18 50 acres. Lines:
SAMUEL NUNELY (?NICELY?), BENJAMIN NOEL, ROBERT NUCOLS. To HUGH
MC CABE, 17 September 1810.

178. 6 October 1808. THOMAS N. EUBANK, Amherst County, to JAMES P.
      GARLAND, Amherst County...WILLIAM HOWARD on 18 December 1807,
executor. Deed of Trust to EUBANK--117½ acres Puppie Creek. Lines:
JONATHAN WARE, deceased, JONATHAN TALIAFERRO, MARY BALLINGER--
sometimes known as FRENCHBURG--tract advertised, 16 August 1808, and
GARLAND was highest bidder. Witnesses: WILLIAM G. PENDLETON, JAMES
GARLAND, BARTLETT THOMPSON, MICAJAH CAMDEN. To JAMES GARLAND,
18 December 1809.

180. 5 January 1809. RICHARD LEE, Amherst County, to THOMAS MOORE,
      Amherst County, and RICHARD HARRISON, Patrick County...Deed of
Trust; debt to NICHOLAS HARRISON, Amherst County $1.00 five slaves
and names and ages; stock. Witnesses: RICHARD POWELL, WILLIAM
DOYLE, RICHARD HARRISON.

181.	27 December 1808.	REUBEN GATEWOOD, Amherst County, to CHARLES
	CHRISTIAN, Amherst County...Deed of Trust; 230 acres and slave--
debt evidently due JAMES DILLARD who signed, but is not named in
deed.	Witnesses:	ELIJAH CHRISTIAN, JACOB SMITH, ABNER CHRISTIAN,
ARCHELAUS JOHNS.	DILLARD seems to be JR.

183.	27 December 1808.	JAMES DILLARD to REUBEN GATEWOOD...300 bushels
	of wheat--no sum.	Witnesses:	ELIJAH CHRISTIAN, JACOB SCOTT.

183.	20 October 1808.	DAVID WOODROOF, Amherst County, to WILLIAM
	WOODROOF, Amherst County...$1.00 23+ acres.	Lines:	DAVIS
road, LYNCH road, Church road.	Witnesses:	JONATHAN MC DANIEL,
WILLIAM HARRISON, WIATT MOON.

184.	10 October 1808.	DAVID S. GARLAND, Amherst County, to JACOB
	PEARCE, JR...$1500.00 58 acres south side of Buff and both
sides Rockey Creek.	Tract bought by JACOB WOOD of JAMES FLOYD.
Lines:	east side Rockey Run, JONATHAN CHRISTIAN, Mill pond, CHISEL's
old stumping mill, WILLIAM DILLARD, JACOB G. PEARCE, bank of Buff.
Witnesses:	RICHARD WILSON, JAMES CHRISTIAN, HEN HOLLOWAY.	To
JACOB PEARCE, JR., 30 November 1810.

185.	15 October 1808.	NICHOLAS PRIER, Amherst County, to WILLIAM
	PRIER, Amherst County...$4.00 50 acres Lovelady Creek.	Lines:
grantor, JONATHAN ROBERTS, CHARLES BROWN.	Witnesses:	MARTIN BIBB,
JONATHAN MAYS, FLEMING DUNCAN, DAVID PRIOR, CALEB RALLS.	To WILLIAM
PRIER, January 21, 1857, by JONATHAN PRYOR.

186.	17 February 1809.	RICHARD S. ELLIS and CHARLES TALIAFERRO,
	Amherst County, to LUKE RAY, Bedford...decree of High Court of
Chancery, Richmond District, 4 May, 1807, and subsequent decree by
same court, 9 September 1807, for purpose of carrying out indenture of
20 August 1767, between DAVID DAVENPORT, deceased, to JONATHAN LEWIS
and DAVID ROSS--attorneys in fact for ALEXANDER BAINE in Deed of
Trust--DAVID ROSS has paid, GLOVER, JESSE, and JACK(?) SMITH DAVENPORT,
defendents failed to pay under decree.	ELLIS and TALIAFERRO ordered
to advertise and sell and pay DAVID ROSS and any surplus to defendents.
296 acres of Wilderness Swamp.	L232-6 to buyer, LUKE RAY.

187.	29 March 1805.	Order to Amherst County Justices of the Peace:
	GEORGE GOODWIN and wife, SALLY, 7 September 1799, to AMBROSE
RUCKER, JR...111 acres.	Done by REUBEN NORVELL and THOMAS MOORE,
8 November, 1808.

188.	30 January 1809.	THOMAS N. EUBANK, Amherst County, to BOHN and
	HUBNER, Richmond...Deed of Trust--JACOB PHILIPS to THOMAS N.
EUBANK, to secure DANIEL WARWICK, BOHN and HUBNER were buyers--north
fork Buff.	599 acres six sh.	August 31, 1809, to JAMES COLE, agent
for grantees.

189.	20 February 1809.	NICHOLAS C. DAVIES and wife, ELIZABETH,
	Amherst County, to ASHCRAFT ROACH, Amherst County...L120 113½
acres.	Lines:	JONATHAN GILLIAM, JONATHAN BURKS, old field, ARCHELAU
GILLIAM, grantee.

190.	January --, 1808.	JAMES WOODS and wife, ELIZABETH, Amherst
	County, to JONATHAN THOMPSON, Amherst County...JAMES has sold
to MICAJAH CAMDEN, Amherst County, tract called Dunlora, where he
lives, December 23, 1807.	JONATHAN THOMPSON is appointed trustee
to whom payments are (various dates) to be made for benefit of
ELIZABETH WOODS.	First bond was taken by THOMPSON for MICAJAH CAMDEN
with WILLIAM CAMDEN, bdm., 1 June 1809--others tabulated as due.
If ELIZABETH dies, then to JAMES, if both die, the heirs of ELIZABETH.
Witnesses:	JONATHAN HENDERSON, ANDERSON MOSS, JONATHAN PENN, HENRY
WOODS.

191.	31 October 1808.	JAMES LEE and wife, NANCY, Amherst County, to
	THOMAS CLEMENTS, Amherst County...L299-12-122 acres north side
Hane's Creek (Harris?).	Lines:	LEWIS DAWSON, GEORGE M. TINSLEY.
Witnesses:	ARCH ROBERTSON, GEORGE M. TINSLEY, BANISTER TINSLEY.

192. 10 October 1808. WILSON COLEMAN and wife, LUCY, Orange County, Virginia, to JONATHAN, ROBERT and EDMOND T. COLEMAN, Amherst County...$1.00--all interest is estate of LINDSEY COLEMAN, deceased--save slaves. Witnesses: S. CLAIBORNE, JOSEPH SWANSON, HUDSON M. GARLAND, JAMES M. BROWN, WILLIAM KNIGHT, WILLIAM MOSS. To ROBERT COLEMAN, 9 March 1809.

193. 18 February 1809. CALEB WATTS and wife, SUSANNAH, Amherst County, to AMBROSE RUCKER, JR., Amherst County...L29-8 14 acres Clarke's Creek, part of where CALEB WATTS lives. Lines: Road from Pedlar to Bethel, RODERICK MC CULLOCH, WILLIAM TINSLEY, JR., two small branches, NICHOLAS C. DAVIES. Witnesses: MARTIN PARKS, GEORGE MC DANIEL, SR., ANDERSON CREWS, WILLIAM PETERS, JR., SAMUEL BURKS. To AMBROSE RUCKER, JR., 7 March 1809.

194. 31 October 1808. JAMES LEE and wife, NANCY, Amherst County, to BANISTER TINSLEY...L185-18 103 acres north side Harris Creek. Lines: CHARLES REYNOLDS, LEE's Mill. Witnesses: ARCHIBALD ROBERTSON, GEORGE M. TINSLEY, THOMAS CLEMENTS. To BANISTER TINSLEY, 20 March 1815.

195. 20 September 1808. JESSE CLEMENTS to TINSLEY RUCKER, Amherst County, and ARCHELAUS MAYS, Campbell County...Deed of Trust; debt to WILLIAM BROWN and Company, Lynchburg, $1.00 tract where JESSE CLEMENTS lives: 123 acres Harris Creek. Lines: WILLIAM W. CLEMENTS, TINSLEY RUCKER, LOCAX. Witnesses: A. ROBERTSON, JONATHAN HORSLEY, WILLIAM BLACK, PHILIP JOHNSON, WILLIAM RADFORD, RICHARD HARRISON, JR.

197. 20 February 1808. NICHOLAS C. DAVIES and wife, ELIZABETH, Amherst County, to HENRY ROACH, Amherst County...L30 28½ acres. Lines: ASHCRAFT ROACH, N. MANSON, grantee, J. GILLIAM, JARRET GILLIAM.

197. 29 November 1808. ABNER CHRISTIAN and wife, LUCY F., Amherst County, to WILLIAM B. GOOCH, Amherst County...consideration: one undivided interest which WILLIAM B. GOOCH has in common with LUCY F. CHRISTIAN, late GOOCH, in seven negroes named--which WILLIAM has conveyed to ABNER and LUCY F.--all interest in estate of PHILIP GOOCH, deceased. Witnesses: JAMES DILLARD, HENRY HOLLOWAY, WILLIAM L. SLAUGHTER, JAMES E. HARRIS. Order to Amherst County Justices of the Peace to quiz LUCY F. as to all interest in tracts in Albemarle, Powhatan, and Amherst County. Done by HENRY HOLLOWAY and JAMES DILLARD, 17 March 1809, as to Amherst County tract.

199. 20 September 1808. THOMAS HUNTON, THOMAS M. JOHNSON to NANCY, JONATHAN and MARBLE CAMDEN, infants of MARBLE CAMDEN, deceased... grantors in lifetime of MARBLE CAMDEN bd. to convey to said MARBLE CAMDEN a tract in Green County, Kentucky and MARBLE CAMDEN bd. to convey to JOHNSON a house and lot in Milton. WILLIAM CAMDEN is now guardian of said infants and suit brought--to bring about specific performance, decree of Amherst County Court to grantors to convey--$1.00 1017 acres in Green County, Kentucky. Lines: Camp fork creek. Witnesses: JONATHAN CAMM, HUDSON M. GARLAND, ROBERT GARLAND. To WILLIAM CAMDEN, guardian, 23 September 1809.

201. 3 November 1808. WILLIAM R. COUPLAND and wife, EMILY, Campbell County, to THOMAS ALDRIDGE, Amherst County...$2000.00 180 acres both sides Naked Creek, south border Piney--part of 1872 acres belonging to estate of COLONEL HUGH ROSE, deceased, Amherst County, and divided to legatees by Amherst County order of court. Lot #7 to EMILY COUPLAND (N. ROSE). Lines: WILLIAM CABELL, JR., lot 6, PATRICK ROSE, JAMES FRANKLIN, lot 8 of 200 acres, lot 1, lot 7, tract to PAULINA ROSE, deceased. Grantors own 2/10 of same or 40 acres (lot 7) and interest in lot 8. Witnesses: WILLIAM ARMISTEAD, STERLING CLAIBORNE, WIATT SMITH. Order to Amherst County Justices of the Peace to quiz EMILY, as to interest in PAULINA ROSE's lot and their own--180 acres, 3 November 1808. Done by JAMES FRANKLIN and WILLIAM ARMISTEAD.

204. 5 January 1809. JONATHAN MOORE, Deputy Sheriff, Amherst
      County, January 8th (sic) advertised for sale to satisfy
distress for rent--two beds etc. the property of JONATHAN PUGH,
bought by MICAJAH PENDLETON, but he releases claims because of
distressed condition of JOHN PUGH's children: MARY, JONATHAN, ELIZABETH,
SARAH, WILLIAM and JAMES PUGH. To remain in JOHN's hands for them
until JAMES is 21 and then to divide. Witnesses: WILLIAM LAVENDER,
JAMES COONEY.

205. 8 April 1809. JEREMIAH TAYLOR, Amherst County, first; CALEB
      TAIT, Campbell County, second; and SAMUEL IRVINE, Campbell
County, third...Deed of Trust; debt due IRVINE, $1.00 slaves named
and ages. Witnesses: JONATHAN LONDON, THOMAS W. COCKE, J. D. TOWNS,
ROBERT ADAMS. To SAMUEL IRVINE, 20 March 1811.

207. 15 December 1808. W. S. CRAWFORD and EDMOND PENN, Amherst
      County, to NANCY CALLAWAY, Amherst County...deed executed
3 November 1807, but now wish to revoke it. Witnesses: HUDSON M.
GARLAND, ARTHUR B. DAVIES, JONATHAN N. S. JONES, THOMPSON NOELL,
BARTLETT THOMPSON.

208. 21 April 1809. Order to Amherst County Justices of the Peace:
      CHARLES JOHNSON and wife, MARY, to MERIT M. WHITE, 17 December
1808...½ acre lot in town of Bethel. Justices of the Peace are termed
of Amherst County in order, but clerical error for they reported from
Campbell--1908--JAMES DEERING and ANSELM LYNCH. Recorded in Amherst
County 15 May 1809. On same page--f. is correct order on same date
as to deed by JOHNSON and wife to JONATHAN ROBERTSON for lot in same
town, 15 December 1809. Done as for previous order.

210. 29 May 1809. Order to Amherst County Justices of the Peace:
      REUBEN GATEWOOD and wife, ELIZABETH, 29 August 1807, to WILLIAM B.
GOOCH...68 acres. Done by WILLIAM ARMISTEAD and JAMES M. BROWN,
29 May 1809.

211. 18 May 1809. RICHARD HARRISON and wife, SUCKEY, Patrick County,
      to JAMES WARE, Amherst County...L9 ½ acre in Bethel--#5(?)--on
the hill. Lines: REUBEN PENDLETON. Witnesses: NICHOLAS and WILLIAM
HARRISON, ABSALOM RUCKER.

213. 18 June 1809. THOMAS N. EUBANK, Amherst County, to JOSEPH V.(?)
      HARDWICK, Campbell County...$400.00 200 acres PEGG's branch.
Lines: DAVENPORT, MORRIS, JONATHAN HOGG, ALLERSON MORRIS, JONATHAN
SLEDD (?), BENJAMIN SHACKLEFORD.

214. 30 November 1808. RUSH HUDSON, SR. and wife, LUCY, Amherst
      County, to REUBEN HUDSON, Amherst County...L100 80 acres.
Lines: JAMES FRANKLIN, RUSH HUDSON, old church road, Naked Creek,
grantee, grantor. Witnesses: HUDSON M. GARLAND, MICAJAH CAMDEN,
DANIEL HIGGINBOTHAM. Price paid: L100.

215. 17 April 1809. THOMAS COPPEDGE and wife, ELIZABETH, Amherst
      County, to CHARLES COPPEDGE, Amherst County...L70--no acres--
HARRIS and HUFF. Lines: EDMOND WINSTON (formerly JONATHAN HARVEY).
Witnesses: JONATHAN LACKEY, EDWARD WATSON, JONATHAN LONOGAN. August 9,
1821 to administrator of CHARLES COPPEDGE.

216. 19 June 1809. JONATHAN LONDON, Campbell County, from REUBEN
      CARVER and wife, FANNY, Amherst County...consideration of 200
acres in Amherst County for 100 acres in Amherst County on Porridge.
Lines: JAMES DILLARD, ALEXANDER JEWEL, THOMAS JEWEL, REUBEN NORVELL,
JONATHAN LONDON.

217. 27 March 1809. ROBERT ALLEN, Amherst County, to DENNIS ENSY,
      Amherst County...L140 140 acres south borders of Porridge.
Lines: DAVID S. GARLAND, PLEASANT STORY, JAMES DILLARD, ALEXANDER
JEWELL, SACKVILLE KING. Witnesses: ISAAC RUCKER, wife quizzed,
but no name.

219. 22 November 1809(8?). THOMAS COPPEDGE, Amherst County, to
      GEORGE CORNELIUS, Amherst County...L60 for slave, MARIAH.
Witnesses: RICHARD TANKERSLEY, THOMAS COPPEDGE, JR.

219. 27 March 1809. DENNIS ENSY to ISAAC RUCKER..Deed of trust to
      secure ROBERT ALLEN, tract this day sold see page 217 for lines--
from ALLEN to ENSY.

220. 19 May 1807. Received of COLONEL WILLIAM WARE the amount of
      RICHARD ALCOCK's meeting on Deed of Trust to ALEXANDER SPIERS,
JONATHAN BOWMAN and Company from 26 June 1796. Signed by JONATHAN
TALIAFERRO and THOMAS LUMPKIN. Witness: PETER TALIAFERRO.

221. 15 April 1808. WILLIAM BURFORD, Amherst County, to SPENCER
      NORVELL, STEPHEN HAM, LEWIS DAWSON, PLEASANT DAWSON, SAMUEL
BURK, MICAJAH CLARK, AMBROSE RUCKER, NELSON C. DAWSON, and JAMES
PETIT...$15.00 1 3/4 acres and use of water on my adjoining land--
where meeting house known as Newhope is erected--for Methodist Church.
Lines: near the road. Witnesses: JOSEPH KENNERLY, BENJAMIN WILSON,
HOSON (?) HUGHES, BENJAMIN WATTS, HUGH NORVELL.

222. 26 May 1809. CHARLES REYNOLDS and wife, ANN, Amherst County,
      to JAMES LEE, Amherst County...L559-10 265 acres Harris Creek.
Lines: grantor, PETTIS THACKER, the road. Witnesses: GEORGE POWELL,
JONATHAN TAYLOE, ARCHELAUS REYNOLDS, JONATHAN REYNOLDS, PHIL JOHNSON.

224. 26 May 1809. JAMES LEE and wife, NANCY, Amherst County, to
      GEORGE POWELL, Amherst County...L3/4-8 280 acres Harris Creek.
Lines: mouth of Burrus border, JOSEPH DAWSON. Witnesses: ARCHELAUS
REYNOLDS, JONATHAN TAYLOE, JONATHAN REYNOLDS, RICHARD POWELL.

225. 23 November 1808. THOMAS SLEDD to WILLIAM WARE...L20 85 acres
      Tobacco Row and Horsly. Lines: grantee, top of Tobacco Row,
RICHARD S. ELLIS. Witnesses: MADISON WARE, JOSEPH R. CARTER, BENJAMIN
NORVELL, ABRAM CARTER, WILLIAM PRYOR, CALEB RALLS.

226. 19 June 1809. REUBEN NORVELL and wife, POLLY, Amherst County,
      to JAMES BOLLING, Amherst County...6 sh. 120 acres north borders
STOVALL. Lines: ELIAS WILLS on southeast and west, survey formerly
made for JONATHAN HARDWICK on north and including tract sold by
MITCHEL STONE HAWKER to BOLLING.

227. 28 January 1809. CORNELIUS POWELL, Amherst County, to CHARLES A.
      JACOBS, Amherst County...Deed of Trust; debt to DANIEL HIGGIN-
BOTHAM; 6 sh.; slaves. Witnesses: HENRY WOODS, WILL WOODROOF,
JAMES T. STEVENS. To DANIEL HIGGINBOTHAM, 17 July 1809.

229. 7 March 1809. Order to Amherst County Justices of the Peace:
      CALEB WATTS and wife, SUSANNAH, 14 February 1809, to AMBROSE
RUCKER 14 acres. Done by JOSIAH ELLIS and NELSON C. DAWSON 30 May
1809. To AMBROSE RUCKER, 27, 1817.

230. 13 February 1809. TALBERT NOELL and wife, NANCY, Amherst
      County, to HUGH MC CABE, Amherst County...L28 60 acres. Lines:
grantor, the road, ROBERT KNUCKLES, CAMDEN. To HUGH MC CABE,
17 September 1810.

232. 28 August 1807. ISHAM DAVIS and wife, ELIZABETH, and ELISABETH
      DAVIS, Lexington Parish, Amherst County, to JOSIAH ELLIS, Amherst
County...L1000 418 acres in Lexington Parish on Pedlar, branch of
James River. Lines: JAMES DAVIS, ARCHIBALD GILLIAM, JONATHAN
GILLIAM, CHARLES BURKS, near the road, CHARLES BURKS, SR. Witnesses:
RICHARD S. ELLIS, THOMAS MORRIS, P. THURMAN, JOSEPH DUNCAN, JOSEPH
BIBB, JOSEPH TANKERSLEY, SAMUEL BURKS, MARTIN BIBB. Final proof by
MARTIN BIBB, 19 June 1809.

234. 5 July 1809. DAVID S. GARLAND, Amherst County, to JONATHAN P.
      COBBS, Amherst County...L52-10 5 acres plus. Lines: adjoining
the north and town of New Glasgow. Lines: Lynch Road, JAMES M. BROWN,
east side Main Street, COBBS' yeard--2½ "loots" in New Glasgow.
Reference to plat--Numbers 12 and 13; sold to HENRY CAMDEN and by him
sold to MICAJAH CAMDEN and by him sold to COBBS (sic).

235. 3 July 1809. SAMUEL GOOLSBEY, Amherst County, to JONATHAN BELL,
      Amherst County...Deed of Trust; GOOLSBEY owes MRS. TALIAFERRO
and LOVING on judgment and execution. JONATHAN BALLARD, security;
$1.00; slave and stock. Witnesses: JAMES OGDEN and JAMES GARLAND.
To JONATHAN BALLARD, 15 June 1810.

236. 8 October 1808. Order to Amherst County Justices of the Peace:
      JAMES TURNER and wife, LUCY, 8 February 1807...to HENRRY SMITH
145 acres. Done, 29 April 1809, by JONATHAN MOSBY and JESSE JOPLING.

237. 15 December 1808. WILLIAM WILLIAMS (WILLIAMSON) and wife,
      BARBARY, Amherst County, to HENRY TENISON, Amherst County...
$75.00 18 3/4 acres BOLLING's Creek. Lines: the old path, WARWICK.
Witnesses: CHARLES J. JOHNSON, JONATHAN WILLIAMSON, JAMES JONES.
Written WILLIAMS in deed, but signed WILLIAMSON.

237. This 17, 1809 (sic). JOSEPH HIGGINBOTHAM, Amherst County, to
      JONATHAN COOPER, Amherst County...L150 150 acres south side
middle fork Pedlar. Part of larger survey. Lines: WILLIAM CLARK,
grantor. Witnesses: BENJAMIN HIGGINBOTHAM, JOSEPH MILSTEAD, JOHAN
WAASE, JACOB PHILLIPS. To JONATHAN COOPER, 17 February 1814.

239. 13 February 1809. SALLY, ELIZABETH, SUSANNA, and WILLIAM
      JENKINS, surviving heirs of JONATHAN JENKINS, deceased, Amherst
County, to EZEKIEL and WILLIAM DAYE, Amherst County...$200.00 all
interest in estate of their deceased father, JONATHAN JENKINS, Amherst
County--200 acres. Witnesses: JAMES DAVIS, THOMAS DAY, DANIEL
ROYALTY, NANCY LANDRUM, SALLY PURSLEY, DANIEL DAY.

240. 1 September 1808. JONATHAN HARDEN and wife, PHEBY, Amherst
      County, to JESSE BLAND, Amherst County...$300.00 150 acres
Pedlar. Lines: BURKS, a ridge by path, STEPHEN RUSSELL, JACOB BROWN.
Witnesses: BENJAMIN TALIAFERRO, WILLIAM JOPLING, JESSE RICHESON,
NELSON CRAWFORD.

241. 19 June 1809. JONATHAN LONDON to REUBEN CARVER...consideration
      of 113 acres conveyed this day by REUBEN CARVER to JONATHAN
LONDON--200 acres Juniper Creek and Fall's Creek. Lines: JOSEPH
MAYS, WILLIAM DAMRON, WILLIAM ROBERTSON. To JONATHAN LONDON,
1 November 1813.

242. 12 November 1808. THOMAS COPPEDGE, Amherst County, to ROBERT
      COLEMAN, Amherst County...Deed of Trust; debt to JONATHAN PENN,
JR., who is bondsman to SHEPHERD and LUKE and THOMAS and DANIEL
HIGGINBOTHAM and Company; also execution in hands of Sheriff of
Amherst County in name of LUDLOW and NIMROD BRANHAM versus JONATHAN
PENN, JR., as bondsman $1.00; slaves named. Witnesses: JAMES P.
GARLAND, R. H. COLEMAN, JAMES E. HARRIS.

244. 22 March 1809. HILL CARTER and wife, MARY, Amherst County,
      to JOSEPH PHILLIPS, Amherst County...L296 197 2/3 acres.
Lines: Main Road, New Glasgow Road. To JOSEPH PHILLIPS, 18 January
1813.

245. 19 December 1808. WILLIAM HORSLEY and wife, SALLY, Nelson
      County, to THOMAS SPRADLING, Nelson County...$100.00 57 acres
Pedlar. Lines: JAMES MARTIN, HUGH CAMPBELL. Witnesses: J. C.
CLARKE, JR., MARIAH JORDAN, ROBERT HORSLEY.

246. 15 May 1809. VALENTINE COX, Bedford County, to his grand-
children, JONATHAN FARNSWORTH, SAMUEL, POLLY, JAMES, WILLIAM
and EDWIN FARNSWORTH, children of HENRY FARNSWORTH and his wife,
DAMARIS, and any future increase...love and $1.00 paid me by GEORGE
TINSLEY, Amherst County, and JAMES COX, Bedford, for the children--
trustees for minorities--60 acres Harris Creek. Lines: SHELTON's
road on northwest, MILLER's Creek and HENRY GAUSNEY on northeast,
MARTIN DAWSON and RICHARD SHELTON on south and west, also two
negroes--names and ages, stock, furniture--interesting; to divide
when youngest is 21; for food, clothing, and school. Witnesses:
JONATHAN and JAMES COONEY, DAVID TINSLEY, JR. To HENRY FARNSWORTH,
8 December 1813.

248. 30 May 1809. ELIZABETH PENN, Amherst County, to WILLIAM
EDMUNDS, A.A...L240 120 acres Harris Creek. Lines: JONATHAN
AMBLER, grantee. Witnesses: EDMOND WINSTON, JR., SAMUEL BURKS,
ISAAC TINSLEY, JR. To WILLIAM EDMUNDS, 20 March 1810.

249. 14 February 1809. ROBERT GRANT, Amherst County, to DAVID S.
GARLAND, Amherst County...6sh. 100 acres. Lines: THOMAS
GILLENWATERS, LARKIN LONDON, JAMES DILLARD. Part of upper end of
tract where ROBERT GRANT lives and bought of JONATHAN LONDON. Deed
of Trust; to secure WILLIAM C. CHRISTIAN. Bond to JONATHAN LONDON
and by him assigned to CHARLES CHRISTIAN and by him to WILLIAM C.
CHRISTIAN. Witnesses: HUDSON M. GARLAND, CHARLES A. JACOBS, JONATHAN
PENN, JR., JAMES GARLAND. To WILLIAM C. CHRISTIAN, 14 February 1810.

251. 16 January 1809. VERNON METCALF, Amherst County, to JAMES
PENDLETON, Amherst County...L50 54 3/8 acres. Head borders
Rutledge. Lines: grantee, up the ridge, JONATHAN MC DANIEL.

252. --- 1809. SAMUEL PAXTON and wife, ESTHER, Amherst County, to
JAMES CLARK, Amherst County...L64-17 80 acres. South borders
middle fork Pedlar. Lines: WILLIAM TAYLOR.

253. 17 June 1809. CHARLES REYNOLDS and wife, ANN, Amherst County,
to WILLIAM PETTYJOHN, Amherst County...L300 100 acres south
side Harris. Lines: road crossing of HARRIS, BANISTER TINSLEY,
GEORGE W. TINSLEY, WILLIAM GOODWIN, deceased, WILLIAM PENDLETON,
WILLIAM SCOTT. Witnesses: JAMES LEE, ARCHELAUS REYNOLDS, PHIL JOHNSON.

254. 3 June 1809. JONATHAN AYERS, Amherst County, to SILAS ROGERS,
Amherst County...$5.00 95 acres north side and joining Pedlar.
Lines: FREDERICK PRICE, JONATHAN D. CRAWFORD, HARRY CAMDEN, HUGH
CAMPBELL. Reference to deed: WILLIAM HALL to JONATHAN AYERS,
15 January 1808. Witnesses: ARTHUR B. DAVIES, HUDSON M. GARLAND,
WILLIAM HALL.

255. 17 September 1809. ROBERT KNUCKLES and wife, FANNY, Kentucky,
to JAMES BYAS, Amherst County...$100.00; no acres; north borders
JAMES. Lines: DAVIS, BENJAMIN SHACKLEFORD, grantee, CORNELIUS ROACH.
Witnesses: BENJAMIN SHACKLEFORD, JONATHAN GUE, WILLIAM (?) SHASTED.
To ROBERT KNUCKLES per order of JAMES BYAS, 5 October 1809, J. ALLEN,
D.C.

257. 17 July 1809. ROBERT MAYO, Richmond, lease to JESSE SPINNER,
Amherst County...plantation where JESSE SPINNER lives--8 years
from January 1 last; JESSE SPINNER to pay ½ of costs for all crops,
vegetables; reasonable quantity of cotton flax (for use of own family
excepted); tobacco, corn, wheat, etc. MAYO to pay like amount for
transportation of tobacco and wheat to market. At end of 1810,
JESSE SPINNER to pay himself for new barn and shed, covering old part
of house where he lives and addition of stone chimney. JESSE SPINNER
is not to be responsible for damage by fire, "litening", etc. Witnesses:
GEORGE MAYO, WILLIAM B. GOOCH, DANIEL DAY, JOSIAH TURPIN. To
WILLIAM B. GOOCH, 27 March 1810.

258. 15 July 1809. SAMUEL GOOLSBY, Amherst County, to JONATHAN BALL, Amherst County...Deed of Trust; debt due JAMES and DAVID GARLAND-- bondsmen are JONATHAN BALLARD, JONATHAN and ALEXANDER GOOLSBY, also debt to DANIEL HIGGINBOTHAM and Company. $1.00; slave and stock, furniture, tools. To JONATHAN BALL, 15 June 1810.

259. 16 September 1809. THOMAS N. EUBANK, Amherst County, to JONATHAN TULEY, SR., Amherst County...$1.00 140 acres Peavine or Chestnut Mountain; Cashaw Creek; border of JAMES--some of old survey sold. Lines: ROLAND BYAS on north; ARCHELAUS MITCHELL on west; HENRY L. DAVIES' estate on east and south. Reference to Deed of Trust to EUBANK by THOMAS JEMKINS, 14 October 1807. EUBAND acts at request of JONATHAN and RICHARD S. ELLIS who were highest bidders at public sale; sold to TULEY. To NELSON CRAWFORD, 1 July 1810.

260. 15 September 1809. JESSE BLAND and wife, SALLY, Amherst County, to CHARLES P. TALIAFERRO, Amherst County...$500.00 192 acres south side and joining Pedlar. Lines: JONATHAN ROBERTS, JONATHAN BROWN, STEPHEN RUSSELL, JACOB BROWN. Witnesses: FLETCHER (?) TALIA-FERRO, B. M. TALIAFERRO, LINDSEY COLEMAN.

261. 20 September 1808. JUSTINIAN CARTWRIGHT and wife, FRANCES, Livingston County, Kentucky, gave Power of Attorney to JAMES A. CARTWRIGHT to collect share of FRANCES in estate of GEORGE GILLESPIE-- FRANCES is daughter of GEORGE GILLESPIE--JAMES A. CARTWRIGHT transfers powers to PHILIP THURMOND, Amherst County, to collect slaves and any sums due. Witnesses: DAVID S. GARLAND, FREDERICK FULTZ, JAMES B. EDWARDS, JONATHAN EUBANK, JR.

263. 15 August 1809. MADISON HILL and wife, POLLY, Russell County, to FRANCIS HILL...$60.00 104 acres Buff. ridge. Lines: REUBEN NORVELL, JAMES DILLARD. Witnesses: RICHARD THURMOND, ABNER PADGETT, ARCHIBALD CREWS, WILLIAM LYON.

264. 18 September 1809. JONATHAN LACKEY, Amherst County, to LEROY CAMDEN, Amherst County...Deed of Trust; debt to WILLIAM CAMDEN. $1.00--slave and many items.

265. 21 September 1807. JESSE MAYS, Amherst County, to JONATHAN LOVING, Amherst County...Deed of Trust; debt to WILLIAM WRIGHT, $1.00--slave, BOB. Witnesses: JAMES FULCHER, JAMES WALTERS, ROBERT NIMMO, MICAJAH CAMDEN. To JONATHAN LOVING, 29 November 1809.

267. 15 April 1808. MOSES WRIGHT, Amherst County, to JONATHAN CAMPBELL, Amherst County...L100 50 acres south borders Piney. Lines: grantee.

268. 18 September 1809. JOSEPH MAYS, Amherst County, and wife, JANE, to ELISHA MAYS, Nelson County...$1.00 190 acres Juniper Creek. Lines: WILLIAM DAMRON, deceased, BOLLING, JOSEF MAYS.

269. 15 September 1809. BARTLETT EADES, Amherst County, to CHARLES WINGFIELD, Amherst County...L200 100 acres south borders Stovall. Witnesses: MICAJAH CLARK, JONATHAN BYAN, JONATHAN TANKERSLEY, JOHN MERRITT.

270. 21 August 1809. MOSES HALL, Amherst County, to JONATHAN F. HALL, Amherst County...L14 14 acres near Pedlar. Lines: grantee.

271. 15 April 1809. JONATHAN CAMPBELL, Amherst County, to MOSES WRIGHT, Amherst County...L100 50 acres south borders Piney. Lines: GEORGE GILLESPIE, deceased (now in possession of DAVID S. GARLAND), JONATHAN CAMPBELL.

272. 19 July 1809. RICHARD LAWLESS, Amherst County, to THOMAS N.
EUBANK, Amherst County...Deed of Trust; debt to JONATHAN and
RICHARD S. ELLIS; $1.00 48 acres. Lines: WILLIAM WARE, WILLIAM
PRYOR, WILLIAM HOWARD, stock. Witnesses: ABRAM CARTER, JONATHAN
CRAWFORD, N. VANSTAVERN, BENJAMIN BRYANT, RICHARD BURKS. To JONATHAN
ELLIS, 15 October 1810.

273. 1 May 1809. LEWIS DAWSON and wife, LUCY, Amherst County, to
GEORGE M. TINSLEY, Amherst County...L244 136 acres. Lines:
south bank Harris Creek, R. PENDLETON, grantor, JAMES WILLS, grantee's
Spring Branch. Witnesses: NELSON C. DAWSON, JAMES WARE, THOMAS
CLEMENTS, BANISTER TINSLEY. To NELSON C. DAWSON, 10 June 1811.

275. 19 April 1809. JONATHAN MERRITT, Amherst County, to DANIEL
GRINNAN, Spotslyvania, for PETER MURDOCK, JAMES ROBERSON, and
JOHN HAMBLETON, surviving partners of WILLIAM CUNNINGHAM and Company...
JONATHAN MERRITT owes county on execution issued by Amherst County
clerk from 17 September 1776. 100 acres whereon JONATHAN MERRITT and
RICHARD TANKERSLEY now live. Lines: PHILLIP JOHNSON, BARTLETT EADES,
JONATHAN MERRITT, son of JONATHAN, and JONATHAN MERRITT, son of
THOMAS. Reference to deed from aforesaid JONATHAN to his son, THOMAS,
23 August 1805. Only proved by JONATHAN DEHART and DUDLEY CALLAWAY
and in clerk's office. Witnesses: GEORGE W. TAYLOR, MILLNER COX,
DAVID GEORGE, PHILIP JOHNSON.

277. July --, 1809. CORNELIUS POWELL, Amherst County, to THOMAS
CREWS, Amherst County...Deed of Trust; debt due NICHOLAS HARRISON,
Amherst County and ISAAC CARUTHERS and Company, Rockbridge; $1.00
tract in Buckingham of 188 3/4 acres. Part of tract formerly that of
STEPHEN FORD et al.--south side Slate River. Lines: GEORGE H. ALLEN,
an infant, JOSEPH WATSON, VALENTINE SCRUGGS, deceased, legatees,
ALLEN SCRUGGS. If defaulted, to be advertised at Buckingham CH.
Recorded in Amherst County, September 18, 1809.

278. June --, 1809. WILLIAM COLEMAN, REUBEN COLEMAN and wife,
BELINDA, LINDSEY and ROBERT COLEMAN, heirs and legatees of
GEORGE COLEMAN, deceased, to BENJAMIN RUCKER, JOSIAH ELLIS, WILLIAM
WARE, NELSON CRAWFORD, REUBEN NORVELL, CHARLES TALIAFERRO, DAVID S.
GARLAND, PHILIP JOHNSON, JAMES DILLARD, JAMES M. BROWN, JAMES FRANKLIN,
HENRY HOLLOWAY, JONATHAN N. ROSE, WILL CARTER, EDMOND T. COLEMAN,
BENJAMIN SHACKLEFORD, CHARLES MUNDY, EDMOND WINSTON, BENJAMIN TALIAFERRO,
NELSON C. DAWSON, WILLIAM ARMISTEAD, JONATHAN WARWICK, the acting
magistrates of Amherst County for the time being and for use and benefit
of said county--10 sh. paid BENJAMIN RUCKER, paid amount for all.
Two acres east of main road from New Glasgow to Lynchburg. Part of
tract devised to them by will of GEORGE COLEMAN, 6 July 1787, and
recorded in Amherst County. Lines: stake near the road. Recorded:
August --, 1809. Someone has written in pencil above: "Courthouse
deed"? Such notations are clearly violations of the law. This one
was a violation and also so foolish in light of the record herein
showing that the commissioners met at New Glasgow and decided upon
the GEORGE COLEMAN estate tract as permanent seat of justice for the
county after the division whereby NELSON was formed in 1808. NELSON
abandoned the old site at Colleen and established their courthouse
at Lovingston.

280. 2 September 1809. WIATT SMITH, Amherst County, to DAVID and
JAMES GARLAND...Deed of Trust for L110 due them--has executed
deed of trust for one negro, SQUIRE, and now delivers him to them.
Witnesses: DANIEL HIGGINBOTHAM, JONATHAN HENDREN, CHARLES A. JACOBS,
HENRY WOODS, HENRY HOLLOWAY.

281. 2 September 1809. DAVID and JAMES GARLAND to PHILIP, JAMES, and
MARY SMITH...amount paid by PHILIP SMITH and slave, SQUIRE, in
trust for L110 for use and benefit of WIATT SMITH's children. Slave
was bought from WIATT SMITH. Witnesses: JONATHAN HENDREN, CHARLES A.
JACOBS, JONATHAN MOUNTCASTLE, HENRY HOLLOWAY, HENRY WOODS.

281. 27 November 1806. HENRY ROSE and wife, ANN W., Amherst County,
     to JONATHAN PENN, Amherst County...L378-11-6 136 acres Piney;
pat. to THOMAS WHITE and described in deed from him to GILBERT HAY,
also 301 acres--part of pat. to JONATHAN HARRIS, 10 September 1755,
and reference to same deed as before; also 3 acres adjoining first
two-pat. to JAMES HAY.

284. 27 August 1807. THOMAS ALDRIDGE and wife, POLLY, Amherst County,
     to MICAJAH CAMDEN, Amherst County...$1000.00 162 acres same
tract sold to THOMAS ALDRIDGE by JONATHAN ANDERSON, 18 October 1806,
and reference to deed--JONATHAN ANDERSON from SAMUEL ANDERSON, 20 June
1803. Witnesses: S. GARLAND, JAMES M. BROWN, PEACHY FRANKLIN. To
CORNELIUS POWELL, agent for THOMAS ALDRIDGE, 28 December 1812.

286. 29 August 1808. WILLIAM BURKS, Amherst County, to THOMAS N.
     EUBANK, Amherst County...Deed of Trust; debt to JONATHAN and
RICHARD S. ELLIS; $1.00; two negro girls: AMY and MAHALA. Witnesses:
JONATHAN SLADE, ABRAM CARTER, HENRY BROWN, N. VANSTAVERN.

287. 1 April 1809. JAMES FRANKLIN and wife, NANCY, Amherst County,
     to VERNON METCALFE, Amherst County...L75 190 acres both sides
south fork Huff. Lines: BENJAMIN HIGGINBOTHAM, PATRICK NOWLAND,
JONATHAN COLEMAN. Also 13 acres adjoining. Lines: WILLIAM CAMDEN,
MOSES PENN. Both conveyed to JAMES FRANKLIN by WILLIAM LONG and wife,
ELIZABETH, 26 October 1801. To HOLLOWAY's executor, 25 February, 1812.

289. 15 July 1809. MOSES WRIGHT, Amherst County, to BENJAMIN WRIGHT,
     Amherst County...L100 64 acres headwaters Crawley Creek;
south border Piney. Lines: GEORGE CAMPBELL, deceased.

291. 21 September 1809. HUDSON M. GARLAND, Amherst County, to CASPER
     POTTER, Prebble County, Ohio...30 May 1806, Deed of Trust to
HUDSON M. GARLAND by JONATHAN WILLS, Amherst County; debt due POTTER
on bond of September 10, 1805--then occupied by WILLS in New Glasgow--
Lot No. --; advertised house and lot and sold 21 Setpember 1809,
at 1 P.M. and POTTER bought it for L115. Witnesses: WILLIAM
ARMISTEAD, JAMES GARLAND, WILLIAM HALL, CHARLES A. JACOBS.

293. 16 October 1809. HUGH CAMPBELL and wife, ELIZABETH, Amherst
     County, to JAMES BARRETT, Amherst County...for love and $1.00
200 acres both sides Mitchell Cove Creek, south border of north fork
Buff. Lines: top of fork Mountain; NEILL CAMPBELL, deceased.

294. 16 October 1809. JAMES BARRETT, Amherst County, to JONATHAN
     RICHESON, Amherst County...$800.00 200 acre tract above:
Mitchell's Cove. To JONATHAN RICHESON, 19 May 1817.

295. 17 April 1809. PULLIAM SANDIDGE and wife, LUCY, Amherst County,
     to WILLIAM WILLMORE, Amherst County...L108 228 acres head of
Sbrs. South fork Buff and head borders Horsley. Lines: SOLOMON
CARTER, JONATHAN SANDIDGE, BENJAMIN HIGGINBOTHAM, AARON HIGGINBOTHAM.
To WILLIAM WILLMORE, 16 April 1810.

296. 12 September 1809. RANDAL HOGG, Amherst County, to THOMAS N.
     EUBANK, Amherst County...Deed of Trust; debt to JONATHAN and
RICHARD ELLIS; $1.00 slave, stock, furniture. Witnesses: SAMUEL
HOGG, ROSEMARY GUE, PETER P. THORNTON, ANDREW HAMBLETON, NELSON
CRAWFORD, HENRY BROWN, ARMSTEAD RUCKER. To ELLIS, 3 October 1810.

298. 21 June 1809. HUGH ROSE, a sergeant of the United States Army,
     to SPOTSWOOD GARLAND, Nelson County...10 sh. Lot 3 designated
by Amherst County Court for division to heirs of COLONEL HUGH ROSE,
Amherst County, deceased--230 acres to HUGH ROSE-Piney Woods Commons
in Nelson; also lot N--of PAULINA ROSE--HUGH's interest--one of legatees
and now deceased and descended to her brothers and sisters. GARLAND
is to sell for HUGH ROSE and invest for him. He hopes to receive
$200.00 per year. 28 acres to be sold to WILLIAM SPENCER, now of
Nelson. Witnesses: SAMUEL IRVINE, G. A. ROSE, LANDON CABELL.

300. 15 October 1807. Order to Sumner County, Tennessee, Justices
     of the Peace: EDWARD SANDERSON (SAUNDERSON) and wife, MOLLY,
13 February 1807, to THOMAS MORRIS...210 acres. Done, 5 May 1809,
by ARCHIBALD MARTIN and WILLIAM TRIGG, JR., DAVID SHELBY, clerk of
Pleas and Quarterly Court, EDWARD DOUGLAS, Pres. Magistrate.

301. 15 May 1809. Order to Corporation Court, Lynchburg, JAMES
     TALIAFERRO and wife, MARTHY, 12 July 1808, to REUBEN COLEMAN...
154 acres. Done by MEREDITH LAMBETH and JAMES STEWART, 26 June 1809.

303. 25 October 1809. SPOTSWOOD GARLAND and wife, LUCINDA, Nelson
     County, to JAMES P. GARLAND, Amherst County...L500 289 acres.
Part of tract bought by SPOTSWOOD GARLAND of BENJAMIN RUCKER. Witnesses:
THOMAS MOORE, ELIAS WILLS, DRURY BELL, ISAAC RUCKER.

304. 26 August 1800. JAMES GOODRICH and wife, JANE, Amherst County,
     Lexington Parish, to THOMAS GOODRICH, same county and Parish...
L80 100 acres both sides JACK's Branch, north fork Pedlar. Lines:
WILLIAM WARE, grantor, SAMUEL GIST. Tract bought by LANDON CARTER
from JONATHAN MC CABE. Witnesses: CHARLES FLOOD, JONATHAN FLOOD,
JONATHAN BARKER, WILLIAM BURKS, SAMUEL E. GOODRICH, MOSES RUCKER.
Final proof, 20 November 1809 by JONATHAN FLOOD.

305. 16 October 1807. JESSE CASH and wife, MARGARET, late PARSONS--
     to CHARLES TUCKER...L23-6-8--their dower interests; deed
executed to CHARLES TUCKER by court order, 16 December 1805--by
other legatees of JONATHAN PARSONS, deceased. Recorded November 20,
1809.

306. 18 December 1809. MOSES HALL, Amherst County, to CHARLES and
     RODERICK TALIAFERRO, Amherst County...$20.00 five acres both
sides of river (sic). Lines: Pedlar, grantor, CHARLES P. TALIAFERRO.

307. 13 December 1809. BENJAMIN SHACKLEFORD and wife, FRANCES, Amherst
     County, to CHARLES DAVIS, Amherst County...consideration of
13 acres from DAVIS--13 acres. Lines: old line; ridge.

308. 1 June 1809. MATTHEW WATSON and wife, ELIZA, Rockingham
     County, to NANCY SHIELDS, Amherst County...L1150 235 acres
south side Buff. and where THOMAS POWEL now lives. Witnesses:
WIATT SMITH, J. P. GARLAND, RICHARD HARRISON, JR.

309. 27 October 1809. JAMES P. GARLAND and wife, KITTY, Amherst
     County, to JACOB PIERCE, JR., Amherst County...L360 166 acres
south side PARKS' road and both sides BRAXTON's ridge. Lines:
PARKS' road, grantee, ALEXANDER BRYDIE's estate, CHARLES H. CHRISTIAN,
WALTER CHRISTIAN, JACOB PEARCE. Witnesses: JAMES FRANKLIN, JOSEPH B.
WINGFIELD, JOSIAH PEARCE. To JACOB PIERCE, 30 November 1810.

311. 18 December 1809. JAMES LONDON, JR. to JONATHAN LONDON...$500.00
     140 acres both sides Porridge. Balance of tract formerly that
of JONATHAN LONDON. Lines: JAMES DILLARD, JONATHAN LONDON, REUBEN
NORVELL, JAMES LONDON, SR., ROBERT GRANT. Witnesses: JAMES, MARTIN
and SALLY LONDON, ELIJAH DEHART. To J. LONDON, 1 November 1813.

311. 11 November 1809. BENJAMIN RUCKER, Amherst County, to REUBEN
     RUCKER, Amherst County...5 sh. 34 3/4 acres Harris Creek.
Lines: the road. Witnesses: NELSON C. DAWSON, JR., GIDEON RUCKER,
BENNETT RUCKER.

312. 18 December 1809. JONATHAN LONDON to JAMES LONDON, JR...$500.00
     230 acres Porridge. Had of JONATHAN LONDON from CHARLES CHRISTIAN.
Lines: JAMES LONDON, SR., HENRY TURNER, CHARLES MINDY, CHRISTOPHER
FLETCHER, JONATHAN CREWS, REUBEN NORVELL. Witnesses: JAMES LONDON,
MARTIN and SALLY LONDON. To J. LONDON, 6 March 1818.

313. 13 December 1809. CHARLES DAVIS and wife, SUSANNAH, Amherst
County, to BENJAMIN SHACKLEFORD, Amherst County...consideration
of $5.00 and 13 acres--14 acres THOMAS MILL Creek for free use of land
adjoining and dam not over 15 feet high for public mill, but, if
damaged, can only be rebuilt by permission.

315. 18 December 1809. JAMES LONDON to JONATHAN LONDON...$1.00 and
love of JAMES for his son, JONATHAN. 40 acres Porridge Creek.
Lines: top of Buff. ridge, JAMES LONDON, JR., a brother, JONATHAN
LONDON, and old path on ridge, ROBERT GRANT.

316. 6 December 1809. ALLEN BUGG, Amherst County, to NANCY BUGG,
Amherst County...$1.00 negroes, MARY about seven. Witnesses:
JAMES ALLEN, WILKINS WATSON, RUSH HUDSON, SPOTS A. JONES, LEE W.
HARRIS.

317. 29 September 1809. JONATHAN LONDON to ELIAS WILLS...$40.00
28 acres Stovall Creek. Lines: JAMES BOLLING, grantee, WILLIAM
KNIGHT. Witnesses: R. A. HIGGINBOTHAM, C(?). B. TINDALL, J. WRIGHT.
To ELIAS WILLS, 12 April 1822.

318. 30 November 1809. PAMELIA BURRUS, Amherst County, to JONATHAN
CRAWFORD, Amherst County, power of attorney to transact business...
Witnesses: WILLIAM WARE, NELSON CRAWFORD, ABRAM CARTER. To JONATHAN
CRAWFORD, 24 April 1810.

319. 11 November 1809. REUBEN RUCKER and wife, ELIZABETH, Amherst
County, to BENJAMIN RUCKER, Amherst County...5 sh. 24 3/4 acres
Harris Creek. Lines: BENJAMIN RUCKER, the road. Witnesses: ANTHONY,
GIDEON, and BENNETT RUCKER, NELSON C. DAWSON, SR.

320. 13 January 1800. ARCHER ROWSEY, Amherst County, to WILLIAM
NOELL, Amherst County...L98 420 acres both sides Pedlar. Lines:
JONATHAN CAMDEN, JONATHAN ROBERTSON, GEORGE HOWARD, SAMUEL HOGG,
WILLIAM HARTLESS, HUGH CAMPBELL. Witnesses: JAMES ROWSEY.

321. 16 January 1810. THOMAS N. EUBANK, Amherst County, to ABRAM
CARTER, Amherst County...$9000.00 200 acres Pedlar. Lines:
FIELDING HOLLOWAY. Conveyed by BAILEY to EUBANK.

322. 9 May 1800. JONATHAN LYNCH and wife, MARY, Campbell County,
to WILLIAM SCOTT, same county...L600 tract known as LYNCH's on
both sides Harris Creek and JAMES river bank. Two surveys--300 acres.
Lines: grantee, mouth of Patent Br., Staton, THACKER, WARE. Witnesses:
WILSON DAVENPORT, ANDREW REYNOLDS, WALLER IRVINE, JAMES BENAGH. Final
proof, 19 February 1810, by BENAGH. To JAMES BENAGH, 18 February 1811.

324. 19 February 1810. BALLENGER WADE, Henry County, to EATON
CARPENTER, "of the county"...L90; no acres; Thresher Creek.
Lines: ZACH TALIAFERRO, grantee. Witnesses: SAMUEL IRVINE,
THOMAS ALDRIDGE, THOMAS CREWS. Sent to E. T. TUCKER, administrator of
EATON CARPENTER, 3 October 1848. Note: Plans are under way to build
a series of dams to supply all of Amherst County with an adequate
water system. The plan is to build at least five dams to retain
rainfall in the mountains. The surveys have been made and it is
announced that approval seems certain. Three of the dams will be
on Puppie; Thresher; and Buffalo. One other will be on Mill Creek,
but I forget the location of the fifth one.

325. 19 September 1809. HENRY PEYTON, Amherst County, to ASHCRAFT
ROACH, Amherst County...$60.00 150 acres north bank Fluvanna.
Lines: NICHOLAS VANSTAVERN, side of a mountain, old field, old line
on a branch. Witnesses: BENJAMIN SHACKLEFORD, HENRY ROACH, GEORGE
ROACH.

326. 1 September 1809. HENRY HOLLOWAY, Amherst County, to JEREMIAH
TAYLOR, Amherst County...L400 258 acres and where HENRY HOLLOWAY
lives; surveyed by JAMES HIGGINBOTHAM, late surveyor, 10 October 1804.
Lines: DRURY BELL, DRURY CHRISTIAN, JONATHAN CHRISTIAN's estate,
PHILIP GOOCH, JAMES CHRISTIAN, HENRY BELL, deceased. To JEREMIAH
TAYLOR, 27 September 1811.

327. 5 February 1810. JESSE WOODROOF, Amherst County, to JONATHAN
      CAMM, Amherst County...L500 262½ acres where JESSE WOODROOF
formerly lived. Lines: grantee, ARTHUR DAVIES, the branch, JAMES
WARE, the path. Witnesses: WILLIAM HARRISON, WIATT HAHONE, EDMOND L.
WOODROOF.

328. 26 October 1809. WILLIAM EDMUNDS, Amherst County, and wife,
      POLLY A., Amherst County, to WILLIAM RADFORD, Lynchburg...L997-10
332 acres plus both sides Harris Creek. Lines: SAMUEL BURKS,
JONATHAN AMBLER. To WILLIAM EDMUNDS, 20 March 1810. Page 329 order
to Amherst County Justices of the Peace to quiz POLLY A., 18 November
1809. Done by EDMOND WINSTON and NELSON C. DAWSON--1809. Recorded
February 19, 1810.

330. 27 June 1809. HUDSON M. GARLAND, Amherst County, to STERLING
      CLAIBORNE, Amherst County...Deed of Trust; debt due SPOTSWOOD
and JAMES PARKER GARLAND--$1.00. GARLANDS are bondsmend on tract
bought on execution of Charlottesville District Court--ALLEN BUGG
versus me; also debt to MAJOR JAMES FRANKLIN--1 acre lot in New Glasgow
bought of FRANKLIN; also slaves. Witnesses: RICHARD HARRISON, JR.,
THOMAS N. EUBANK, THOMPSON NOELL, MATTHEW WATSON. To JAMES PARKER
GARLAND, 13 October 1813.

332. 17 February 1810. THOMAS TERRY, Amherst County, to BENJAMIN
      WATTS, Amherst County...Deed of Trust; debt due BENJAMIN WATTS;
no acres; Wills Creek. Lines: PHILIP JOHNSON, LINEAUS BOLLING,
WILLIAM ROBINSON. $1.00 and debt of L52-4.

333. 19 February 1810. ABRAM CARTER, executor of ISAAC WRIGHT,
      will will annexed--not therein--$250.00. 1.1430 acres pat.
27 February 1795, to ISAAC WRIGHT and JONATHAN HUNTER by JAMES WOOD,
Governor of Virginia. Order to be certified to county of Kanawaha
to be recorded. Sold to JONATHAN RICHESON, Amherst County.

333. 17 February 1810. SARAH HUDSON, widow of REUBEN HUDSON, Amherst
      County, to RUSH HUDSON, SR...$1.00 to carry out intent of late
husband--30 November 1808. 150 acres south side Turkey Mountain on
Buffalo. Witnesses: HUDSON M. GARLAND, JAMES GARLAND, DANIEL
HIGGINBOTHAM, THOMPSON NOELL.

334. 15 February 1810. BENJAMIN WILSON and wife, ELIZABETH, Amherst
      County, to THOMAS TERRY, Campbell County...L101 101 acres James
River. Lines: BAILEY's Branch.

335. 19 February 1810. ABRAM CARTER, administrator of ISAAC WRIGHT
      (RIGHT) to WILLIAM PRYOR, Amherst County...L85 100 acres east
side north fork Horsley. Lines: ABRAM CARTER, the road, grantee.

336. 19 February 1810. ABRAM CARTER, as above, to RICHARD S. (L.)
      ELLIS, Amherst County...L134 238 acres Pedlar. Lines:
N. VANSTAVERN. To J. ELLIS, 3 October 1810.

337. 17 February 1810. SAMUEL STAPLES and wife, JUDY P., Amherst
      County, to JAMES SEAY, Nelson County...L26 20 acres Buffaloe.
Lines: grantee, my Spring Branch. Witnesses: J. G. MC CALISTER,
WILLIAM TILLER, JR., ROBERT H. COLEMAN.

338. 19 February 1810. HENRY CAMDEN and wife, LUCY, Amherst County,
      to WILLIAM NOELL, Amherst County...L110 220 acres "in the cain
brakes." Lines: THOMAS VARNER (?), SAMUEL NICELY, ALLISON MORRIS.

339. 12 February 1810. SAMUEL and CHARLES GRISSOM, executors of
      THOMAS GRISSOM, Amherst County, to AMBROSE LUCAS, Amherst County...
L120 123 acres. Lines: DANIEL BURFORD. To AMBROSE LUCAS, 19 October
1812.

341. 17 March 1810. THOMAS N. EUBANK, Amherst County, to CHARLES P.
      TALIAFERRO, Amherst County...L21 17 acres Horsley and Puppie
Creeks. Lines: JONATHAN TALIAFERRO, HENRY HUGS, WILLIAM WARE,
WILLIAM HOWARD.

342. 19 March 1810. SAMUEL COLEMAN, Amherst County, to CHARLES L.
      and WALTER L. CHRISTIAN, Amherst County...L20 98 acres Harris
Creek. Lines: RICHARD HARDWICK, JABEZ CAMDEN, WILLIAM PETERS,
JOSEPH CHILDRESS, former line, AMBROSE RUCKER. To CHARLES L.
CHRISTIAN, 9 January 1811.

343. 20 October 1809. GEORGE STOVALL and wife, NANCY, Elbert County,
      Georgia, to ELIAS WILLS, Amherst County...L505 326 acres Stovall
Creek. Lines: Opossum Island road, PHILLIP JOHNSON, W. WATSON.
Witnesses: HORATIO BENNETT, CHARLES WINGFIELD, JESSE BECK, THOMAS
BADDOW.

344. 17 October 1809. ROBERT NUKLES, Mercer County, Kentucky,
      power of attorney to JAMES BIAS, Amherst County, to sell 136
acres. Witnesses: CHARLES DAVIS, NATHANIEL D. BURKS, MAURICE MORRIS.

345. 16 April 1810. MOSES RUCKER and wife, ELIZABETH, Amherst
      County, to JAMES WARE, Amherst County...$200.00 ½ acre lot in
town of Bethel--Number 11. Witnesses: REUBEN PADGETT, JONATHAN
ELLIS, JAMES S. PENDLETON.

346. 10 January 1810. JOSEPH and BENJAMIN HIGGINBOTHAM, executors
      of JOSEPH HIGGINBOTHAM, deceased, Amherst County, to BENJAMIN
TALIAFERRO, Amherst County...$500.00 404 acres both sides middle fork
Pedlar. Lines: STEWART BALLOW's former line, HUGH MC CABE's former
line. To BENJAMIN TALIAFERRO, 6 September 1834.

348. 19 November 1807. CALEB WILSHER, Amherst County, to WILLIAM
      JOHNS, Amherst County...L18 57 acres. Lines: MARTIN PARKS,
top of Tobacco Row Mountain, ARTHUR L. DAVIES, HOUCHIN, RICHARD S.
ELLIS, MARTIN PARKS. Witnesses: THOMAS L. MC ELHINNEY, RICHARD
BURKS, PETER RUCKER. Final proof, 16 April 1810, by PETER RUCKER.
Sent to WILLIAM JOHNS, 21 August 1810.

349. 15 July 1809. WALTER L. CHRISTIAN, Amherst County, to CHARLES L.
      CHRISTIAN, Amherst County...L30 ½ of tract WALTER CHRISTIAN
bought of BENJAMIN WARREN--71 acres. Lines: WILLIAM DILLARD,
FREDERICK FULTZ, REUBEN PADGETT, PHILIP GOOCH's estate. Witnesses:
WILLIAM B. GOOCH, ABSALOM HOWL, W. D. CHRISTIAN. To CHARLES L.
CHRISTIAN, 9 January 1811.

350. 12 September 1800. JAMES GOODRICH and wife, JANE, JESSE HAYNES
      and wife, MILLY, Amherst County, to THOMAS GOODRICH, Amherst
County...L40 20 plus acres south side Lovelady Mountain and Pedlar.
Lines: JAMES GOODRICH, GIST, HAYNES, road from CAPTAIN WARE's to
WINCANTON, LAIN, WILLIAM WARE. Witnesses: SAMUEL E. GOODRICH, WILLIAM
BURKS, MOSES RUCKER, EDWARD CARTER. Final proof by EDWARD CARTER,
19 March 1810.

351. 21 October 1809. THOMAS MORRIS, Amherst County, to MARTIN
      PARKS, JAMES DAVIS, DAVID J. BURKS, THOMAS MORRIS, NATHANIEL J.
MANSON, Amherst...for good consideration ½ acre Lexington Parish.
Lines: grantor. To be used for meeting house on the republican
plan. Witnesses: NATHANIEL D. BURKS, WILLIAM DUNCAN, NICHOLAS WEST,
EDWARD TINSLEY.

352. 3 September 1808. SPENCER NORVEL, Amherst County, to JAMES
      FRANKLIN, JONATHAN CAMM, THOMAS CREWS, Amherst County...Deed
of Trust; debt to WILLIAM LONG, Richmond--$1.00--tract whereon
SPENCER NORVEL Harris Creek-505 acres. Lines: BENJAMIN RUCKER, DANIEL
BURFORD, ROBERT H. ROSE, PHIL BURFORD, DAVID TINSLEY. Witnesses:
ALEXANDER WATSON, NICK HARRISON, RICHARD HARRISON. To WILLIAM LONG,
16 May 1809.

354. 21 May 1810. NELSON CRAWFORD, Amherst County, and wife, LUCY,
      to GARRET LAIN, Amherst County...$572.00--tract in Green County,
Kentucky on Robinson Creek--1145 acres. Lines: CHARLES ELLIS tract
of 701 acres. To GARRET LAIN, May 27th.

355. 23 May 1810. JAMES POWELL and wife, MILLY, Rockingham, to
     WILLIAM LONG, Richmond...L500 - 5 10 acres at the Oaks. Lines:
LONG, his brick tavern on road from CH to Lynchburg, grantee, first
white oak. Witnesses: JONATHAN LACKEY, WILLIAM COLEMAN, DAVID
WOODROOF, JR., REUBEN COLEMAN. To WILLIAM LONG, 30 May 1810.

356. 4 April 1810. Order to Amherst County Justices of the Peace:
     JAMES FRANKLIN and wife, NANCY, 6 December 1805, to HUDSON M.
GARLAND...tract next to New Glasgow. Done by JONATHAN WARWICK and
JAMES M. BROWN, 18 April 1810.

357. 21 May 1810. JONATHAN BOLLING and wife, SALLY, Amherst County,
     to CHARLES WILLS, Amherst County...L65 61½ acres Lynch road and
part of where JONATHAN BOLLING lives. Lines: grantor, DANIEL
BURFORD. To E. W., 16 January 1815.

358. 9 November 1809. JAMES TINSLEY, Bourbon County, Kentucky
     (spelled Burbin) to ANTHONY G. TINSLEY, Bedford County...all
interest of wife and self in estate of ISAAC RUCKER, deceased--for
value received. Witnesses: ROBERT, LINDSEY and OLIVER TINSLEY.
Recorded in Amherst County 21 May 1810. Proved by LINDSEY and
OLIVER TINSLEY.

359. 24 October 1809. GEORGE STOVALL, Elbert County, Georgia, to
     JONATHAN MERRIT, Amherst County...L100 56 acres south borders
Stovall Creek. Lines: N S of the MARY(?) Branch; FRY's old line.
Witnesses: BARTLETT EADES, GEORGE W. TAYLOR, CHARLES H. CLARK,
WILLIAM M. CLARKE. Final proof, 23 May 1810, by WILLIAM M. CLARKE.

360. 14 February 1810. GABRIEL MOORE, Madison County, Mississippi
     Territory, to JONATHAN WARE, Amherst County...L50 50 acres
south borders north fork Piney River. Witnesses: WILLIAM SLEDD,
N. VANSTAVERN, WILLIAM WARE, JR., SEATON SLEDD, JAMES CLEMENTS. To
JONATHAN WARE, 15 April 1816.

361. 25 October 1809. THOMAS G. GOODRICH, Amherst County, to CHARLES
     TALIAFERRO, Amherst County...Deed of Trust; $1.00; debt to
TALIAFERRO and LOVING and STEWART and TALIAFERRO, County. Lynchburg--
278 plus acres where THOMAS G. GOODRICH lives and bought of JAMES
GOODRICH and wife, 26 June 1800. for 100 acres--21 plus acres bought
from JAMES GOODRICH and wife and ISAAC HANES, 12 September 1800--
157 plus acres. Deeded to THOMAS GOODRICH by ABRAM CARTER and wife,
MARY, 17 June 1805. Derivation of title seems confusing.

363. 23 October 1809. SAMUEL LUCAS, Amherst County, to LEROY CAMDEN,
     Amherst County...Deed of Trust; debt to HENRY CAMDEN, $1.00--
wagon and stock. Witnesses: J. WHITEHEAD, JOSEPH GARNER, WARNER
GOODWIN.

365. 21 May 1810. CHARLES and BENJAMIN TALIAFERRO, Overseers of the
     Poor, Amherst County, in second District to PEYTON KEITH, Amherst
County...order of Court of Appeals, 1810--DAVID HUDSON, 14, bound
out as carpenter's apprentice to KEITH until 21.

367. 15 June 1810. WILLIAM WILLMORE and wife, SUSANNA, Amherst
     County, to WILLIAM DEMPSEY, Amherst County...L7000 inspected
tobacco--120 acres. Lines: JOSEPH HIGGINBOTHAM, BENJAMIN SANDIDGE,
RACHEL ATKINSON. Witnesses: NELSON CARTER. To WILLIAM DEMPSEY,
20 October 1815.

368. 18 June 1810. HENRY WOODS, surviving partner of HENRY and JAMES
     WOODS, Amherst County, to DANIEL HIGGINBOTHAM and Company...
$500.00. 1. 50 acres pat. to CHARLES TYLER, 23 May 1763. 2. 50 acres
pat. to JONATHAN WILSFORD, 29 May 1793. 3. 3 acres pat. to JONATHAN
WILSFORD, 24 May 1794. 4. 20 acres pat. to JAMES WOODS, 28 May 1798.
5. 2½ acres bought of WILLIAM LAWHORN by JAMES WOODS; reference to deed
from JONATHAN WILSFORD to HENRY and JAMES WOODS, 2 March 1803. Also
98 acres bought by WILSFORD of CHARLES TYLER and in aforesaid deed--
all on Indian Creek; south border Piney--except 50 acres on Thresher.

369. 18 June 1810. GODFREY TOLER and wife, CHARITY, Amherst County,
     to WILLIAM SHEPARD, Amherst County...L75 100 acres Horsley.
Lines: THOMAS MORRIS, JOSEPH MILSTEAD, SCOFIELD. To WILLIAM SHEPARD,
7 January 1821, by order of B. A. CRAWFORD.

369. 15 October 1798. RAWLEY PENN and wife, SARAH, Amherst County,
     to WILLIAM BRIANT, Amherst County...L58 92 acres Rutledge Creek.
Bought by RAWLEY PENN of CHARLES CHRISTIAN. Witnesses: R. NORVELL,
PHIL JOHNSON, JONATHAN and HENRY TURNER. Final proof, 18 June 1810,
by HENRY TURNER.

370. 20 February 1810. POLLY CAMPBELL, Amherst County, to BARTHOLOMEW
     WHITEHEAD, Amherst County...L72--no acres. Lines: south border
Piney, JOEL FRANKLIN, deceased, main road. Witnesses: MICAJAH CAMDEN,
JAMES FULCHER, JONATHAN FULCHER.

371. 9 April 1810. AMBROSE RUCKER and wife, ELIZABETH, Bedford
     County, to BRANSFORD HICKS, Amherst County...L140 174 acres north
fork Harris. Lines: RICHARD HARDWICK, BURFORD, ELIZABETH COLEMAN,
the road. Witnesses: JONATHAN PETER, THOMAS GRISSOM, RICHARD TINSLEY,
EDWARD TINSLEY. To BRANSFORD HICKS, 4 October 1810.

372. 28 February 1810. Marriage is shortly to take place between
     NORVELL SPENCER and LUCY SLAUGHTER, my niece--H. HOLLOWAY, her
uncle, gives them four slaves. I am to pay them L480 and--return to
me. Witnesses: JAMES P. PARISH, JONES GILL. To NORVELL SPENCER,
24 September 1811.

372. 16 January 1810. CHRISTOPHER FLETCHER and wife, PHEBE, Amherst
     County, to ROBERT PIERCE, Amherst County...L220 150 acres
Porridge Creek. Lines: THOMAS EDWARDS, JOSEPH HIGGINBOTHAM, RICHARD
JONES, CHARLES MUNDAY, JAMES LONDON, JONATHAN CREWS. Witnesses:
RICHARD WILSON, WILLIAM CLINKSCALES, DENNIS ENSEY.

373. 19 April 1806. THOMAS GUY, agent for heirs of ROBERT JOHNSTON,
     Caroline County, to LITTLEBERRY BRYANT, Amherst County...$50.00
230 acres Rattlesnake branch and James River--reference to pat. and
where BRYANT lives. Witnesses: JONATHAN ELLIS, JONATHAN EUBANK,
THOMAS GOODRICH, N. VANSTAVERN. Final proof, 18 June 1810, by
JONATHAN ELLIS. (or JONATHAN EUBANK?)

374. 18 June 1810. WILLIAM PRYOR and wife, NANCY, Amherst County,
     to WILLIAM S. CRAWFORD, Amherst County...L35 18 acres Horsley.
Lines: CHARLES CRAWFORD opposite mouth of a branch, DAVID CRAWFORD,
a spring near main road. To WILLIAM S. CRAWFORD, 3 October 1810.

374. 2 December 1809. Order to Alb. Justices of the Peace: THOMAS M.
     JOHNSON and THOMAS HUNTON and wife, NANCY, 20 September 1808, to
MARBELL CAMDEN...1117 acres in Green County, Kentucky. Done by
CHARLES B. HUNTON and JONATHAN WATSON, 27 December 1809. Recorded
Amherst County, 18 June 1810.

375. 16 December 1809. HUDSON M. GARLAND, Amherst County, to
     DANIEL HIGGINBOTHAM, second, and DAVID S. GARLAND...Deed of
Trust; to secure GARLAND on bond to Nelson County Sheriff in sale of
mulatto boy, ORANGE, in case of HUDSON M. GARLAND versus RICHARD C.
POLLARD.

376. 16 July 1810. WILLIAM RADFORD and wife, ELIZABETH, Lynchburg,
     to THOMAS CREWS, Amherst County...L773 1/3 332 ½ acres both sides
Harris Creek. Lines: SAMUEL BURKS, JONATHAN AMBLER. Tract bought
by WILLIAM RADFORD from WILLIAM EDMUNDS. Sent to THOMAS CREWS--no date.

377. 16 July 1810. HUGH MC CABE and wife, ELIZABETH, Amherst County,
     to WILLIAM DAVIS, Amherst County...$500.00 261 acres north side
and joining Fluvanna on south side and joining Otter Creek. Part of
404 acres to HUGH MC CABE by WILLIAM VEAL, 25 August 1799. Reference
to pat. lines of 63 acres of 1 August 1772; adjoining tract and granted
to CORNELIUS THOMAS, to line of RICHARD TINSLEY's 206 acres and deed

of same date to HUGH MC CABE and wife. Deed of Trust by ROBERT
JOHNSTON to ALEXANDER SPIERS, JONATHAN BOWMAN, 1772, excepted.

378. 16 July 1810. HUGH MC CABE and wife, ELIZABETH, Amherst County,
to RICHARD TINSLEY, Amherst County...L100 206 acres Otter Creek.
Lines: south bank Otter, Tarrapin Creek, Rattlesnake Branch Fluvanna,
Cedar Brook, CORNELIUS THOMAS, WELSH's Spring. Reference to Deed of
Trust in 1772 as in deed above. To RICHARD TINSLEY, 15 July 1811.
Note: I often wonder about all of these little branches in Otter
Creek area which is now in National Forest. The Sky Line or Blue
Ridge Parkway comes down to Otter Creek and there is a nice restaurant
and camping area called Otter Creek. One drives a short distance to
the James River bridge and soon the beautiful ascent to Peaks of Otter
begins. There is now a museum close to the bridge and one can take
marked trails for nature walks. There is also a ramp walk beneath
the bridge and on other side is a restoration of part of the old
James River canal which is worth walking over to see.

379. 23 March 1810. HUGH MC CABE and wife, ELIZABETH, Amherst
County, to RICHARD TINSLEY...all rights in Otter Creek tract.
Lines: DAVID S. GARLAND, WILLIAM DAVIS, LEWIS BRYANT, deceased.
404 acres. TINSLEY may sell tract; tract has been conveyed to TINSLEY
and WILLIAM DAVIS and not to conflict with 224 acres sold to DAVIS.
Witnesses: RICHARD L. ELLIS, JONATHAN ELLIS, JONATHAN P.(?) BROWN.

380. 17 September 1810. JAMES BISHOP and wife, MARY, Amherst County,
power of attorney to DAVID S. GARLAND, Amherst County...to sell
Georgia land conveyed by THOMAS SHIELDS to WILLIAM SHIELDS, 2 March
1791. --- BISHOP is one of daughters of WILLIAM SHIELDS, deceased,
who died intestate and tract descended to JAMES BISHOP and wife,
MARY, formerly SHIELDS, NANCY SHIELDS and MARTHA WADE.

381. 1 January 1810. DAVID SWANSON, Amherst County, to JAMES
GARLAND, Amherst County...Deed of Trust; debt to DAVID S. GARLAND,
6 sh. wagon and horse. Witnesses: BARTLETT THOMPSON, CHARLES A.
JACOBS, JONATHAN MAYS.

381. 17 September 1810. NATHAN HALL and wife, MARY, Amherst County,
to SAMUEL TURNER, Amherst County...L120 93 acres both sides
north branch Raven Creek of Buffaloe. Part of NICHOLAS CABELL tract.
Lines: JAMES MATHEWS, GILBERT BOWMAN, NICHOLAS CABELL, RICHARD ALCOCK,
WILLIAM CABELL. Witnesses: JAMES FRANKLIN.

382. 17 September 1810. SAMUEL H. ALLEN and wife, POLLY, Amherst
County, to MICAJAH PENDLETON, Nelson County...$500.00 40½ acres--
part of James River tract and Elk Island Creek. Lines: DANIEL
PERROW, WILLIAM JORDAN. Also 16 acres--part of an island in James
and opposite tract above. To M. PAMPLIN, 11 July 1811; returned to
MICAJAH PENDLETON, 25 January 1827, per J. HORSLEY, JR.

383. 4 September 1810. THOMAS TRIPLETT and wife, ELIZABETH, Amherst
County, to PEYTON KEITH, Amherst County...$800.00 150 acres both
sides Raven Creek; north branch Buffaloe. Lines: WILLIAM SPENCER
at Rolling Road, NATHAN HALL, WILLIAM CABELL, SAMUEL ANDERSON.
Witnesses: DAVID S. GARLAND, ISAAC TYREE, DANIEL HIGGINBOTHAM,
HENRY WOODS.

384. 22 November 1809. EZEKIEL GILBERT and wife, ANN ROCKINS,
WILLIAM GIBSON and wife, ELVIRA, PATSY GILBERT, Buckingham,
MATTHEW WATSON and wife, ELIZA, Rockingham, WILMOUTH ANNE GILBERT,
Amherst County, to WILLIAM LONG...L200 80 acres. Lines: JAMES
FRANKLIN, GEORGE COLEMAN, deceased, MARY (?) Br. Part of tract of
JAMES WATSON, deceased. Claimed under deed from JAMES WATSON and wife,
PATSY, 15 October 1796, and recorded 17th. Except MATTHEW WATSON and
wife whose title is derived by deed from WIATT A. GILBERT who claimed
under aforesaid deed from JAMES WATSON. Witnesses: JAMES ALLEN,
SPOTSWOOD JONES, A. B. DAVIES, A. DIBRELL, EZEKIEL B. GILBERT,
WILLIAM B. GILBERT, WILMOUTH A. GILBERT (as to MATTHEW WATSON),
WILLIAM D. MASON, HUMPHREY GILBERT as to P. C. GILBERT. To WILLIAM
LONG, 13 December 1810.

386. 31 August 1810. REUBEN GATEWOOD and wife, ELIZABETH, FRANCIS
      HALL and wife, ELIZABETH, Amherst County, to LEWIS LAINE,
Amherst County...L107-5 71½ acres. Lines: ROBERT COLEMAN, WILLIAM B.
GOOCH, MICAJAH PENDLETON, river below mouth of Green Spring Branch,
GATEWOOD. Witnesses: WILLIAM B. GOOCH, CHARLES L. CHRISTIAN,
SAMUEL P. LAYNE, SHADRICK CARTER.

387. 13 September 1810. WILLIAM TYREE and wife, FRANCES, Amherst
      County, to MATTHEW WATSON, Rockingham County...L66-9 100 acres
north south Buffaloe. Lines: JOSEPH KENNEDY on south, JAMES
HIGGINBOTHAM, JR. on J.; west by Buffaloe. Bought by WILLIAM TYREE
from RICHARD BEAN. Witnesses: HUDSON M. GARLAND, DANIEL HIGGINBOTHAM,
THOMAS ALDRIDGE.

388. 16 July 1810. ABRAM CARTER and wife, POLLY, Amherst County,
      to JONATHAN WARE, Amherst County...$600.00 200 acres north side
and joining north fork Pedlar and on side of Cold Mountain. Pat. to
JAMES SMITH, 10 July 1766, and by him conveyed to PATRICK LOWRY and
by LOWRY to JAMES BAILEY. Lines: JOSEPH HIGGINBOTHAM. To JONATHAN
WARE, 15 April 1816.

388. 20 August 1810. THOMAS TRIPLETT and wife, ELIZABETH, Amherst
      County, to JESSE MILLIKEN, Nelson County...L225 150 acres both
sides Raven Creek, north border Buffaloe. Lines: WILLIAM CABELL
at Rolling Road, NICHOLAS CABELL. Bought by THOMAS TRIPLETT from
SAMUEL ANDERSON 18 March 1799 and recorded 15 April 1799.

389. 20 May 1810. WILLIAM MOON and wife, ELIZABETH, Amherst County,
      to WILLIAM WOODROOF, Amherst County...L83 83 acres. Lines:
top of Paul's Mountain. Witnesses: NICHOLAS HARRISON, DAVID WOODROOF,
JONATHAN T. HILL.

390. 20 August 1810. MOSES HALL and wife, HANNAH, Amherst County,
      to JONATHAN F. HALL, Amherst County...L38 30 acres north side
Pedlar. Lines: grantor, grantee.

391. 18 August 1810. JONATHAN and WALTER FRAZER, Giles County,
      Tennessee, to DAVID BURKS, Amherst County...$462.00 104 acres.
Lines: JAMES COLBERT BLARE's former line, acknowledged in Amherst
County by grantors, 20 August 1810.

391. 18 August 1810. JONATHAN and WALTER FRAZER, Giles County,
      Tennessee to DAVID BURKS, Amherst County...L138-3 153½ acres
borders middle fork Pedlar. Lines: JONATHAN FRAZER, JOSEPH
HIGGINBOTHAM, JONATHAN MARSHALL's former line. Acknowledged as
above.

392. 18 August 1810. Same grantors as above to DAVID BURKS, Amherst
      County...$198.00 99 acres south borders Pedlar. Lines:
WALTER POWERS, deceased.

393. 5 October 1810. JONATHAN DEVEZER and wife, MARY, Amherst
      County, to CHARLES L. BARRET, Amherst County...L100 96 acres.
JONATHAN DEVEZER bought tract from JOSEPH MILSTEAD. Lines: JOSEPH
HIGGINBOTHAM, north side Horsley, CHILDRESS' Gap Road, WILLIAM
SCHOLFIELD, deceased. Witnesses: LYNE S. TALIAFERRO, WILLIAM
COLEMAN, SAMEY (?) G. MARLELBUD (?).

394. 15 October 1810. WILLIAM LAWLESS and wife, ---, Amherst County,
      to ELIJAH BARNES, Amherst County...$100.00 50 acres Horsley.
Lines: WILLIAM WARE, WILLIAM HOWARD, NED (?) CARTER.

395. 8 June 1808. HENRY LANE, SR., Amherst County, to THOMAS N.
      EUBANK, Amherst County...Deed of Trust; debt to JONATHAN and
RICHARD S. ELLIS, $1.00, slaves. Witnesses: JONATHAN LUCAS, WILLIAM
HOWARD, RICHARD H. BURKS, HENRY BROWN, JARRET GILLIAM, THOMAS MOORE,
ARMISTEAD RUCHER, ABRAM CARTER. To JONATHAN ELLIS, 24 March 1813.

396. 18 June 1810. RICHARD RUCKER and wife, PEGGY, Amherst County,
      to NICHOLAS HARRISON, Amherst County...$1000.00 196 acres
Harris Creek and where RICHARD RUCKER lives. Lines: JAMES HILL,
grantee, grantor, BENNETT RUCKER, ANTHONY RUCKER, JAMES TINSLEY.
Witnesses: JAMES WARE, REUBEN NORVELL, JAMES HILL, BENJAMIN RUCKER,
JR.

397. 4 April 1810. CALEB CHENAULT and wife, RACHEL, Amherst County,
      to BENJAMIN WATTS, Amherst County...L90 50 acres Opossum
Island. Lines: MAJOR PHILIP JOHNSON's entry, the road. Witnesses:
PHILLIP JOHNSON, JESSE BECK, one illegible signature. The writing
is terrible in this section of the book.

398. 29 August 1808. BERRY WHITTEN to THOMAS N. EUBANK...Deed of
      Trust; debt to JONATHAN and RICHARD S. ELLIS; $1.00 stock,
furniture, crops. Witnesses: LEWIS and RANSOME WHITTEN, WILLIAM
HOWARD, ARMISTEAD RUCKER, JONATHAN DAVIES, ABRAM CARTER, WILLIAM
PRYOR. To JONATHAN ELLIS, 24 March 1813.

399. 15 October 1810. OBADIAH MARTIN and wife, NANCY, Rockbridge,
      to ARCHY GILLIAM, Amherst County...$396.00. Two tracts
South side Pedlar. 1. Pat. to NATHANIEL HENDERSON, 140 acres.
2. To said MARTIN for 150 acres and other for 106 acres--total of
396 acres. Lines: SAMUEL HOGG, BENJAMIN TALIAFERRO, WILLIAM PAXTON,
JAMES MARTIN, RICHARD L. ELLIS, JONATHAN WARE. Sent to ARCHY GILLIAM,
6 September 1813.

400. 25 September 1788. ANGUS MC DONALD, Amherst County, to
      SAMUEL PAXTON, Rockbridge...L10 18½ acres surveyed by WILLIAM
HAY for JONATHAN TAYLOR, 28 December 1780; part of tract of WILLIAM
TAYLOR -? south of main branch of Pedlar. Lines: WILLIAM TAYLOR.
Witnesses: THOMAS GRAHAM, JAMES FRAZER, WALTER POWER. Final proof
"by three witnesses," 15 October 1810. To SAMUEL PAXTON, 24 August
1812.

401. 15 October 1810. WILLIAM MARTIN and wife, SUSANNAH, Amherst
      County, to LEWIS MARTIN, Amherst County...L60 115 acres north
waters Thresher Creek. Lines: AARON HIGGINBOTHAM, ENOCH CARPENTER,
ZACHARIAH TALIAFERRO. Witnesses: REUBEN and WILLIAM COLEMAN,
JESSE CASH.

402. 15 October 1810. WILLIAM JONES (Mark of WILLIAM JOHNS),
      Amherst County, to RICHARD BURKS, Amherst County...$100.00
57 acres. Lines: MARTIN PARKS, top of Tobacco Row Mountain,
ARTHUR L. DAVIES, HOUCHINS, RICHARD L. ELLIS. To RICHARD BURKS,
19 October 1811.

402. 2 October 1810. THOMAS CURRIE (CURRY) and wife, AILSEY,
      Amherst County, to ROBERT PRICE, Amherst County...L60 121 acres
all CURRY now owns. Lines: WILLIAM SPENCER, KEATH, THOMAS TRIPLETT,
SAMUEL ANDERSON, ALLEN BLAIR. Witnesses: RICHARD WILSON, JAMES
LAYNE, DENNIS ENSEY. Proved by THOMAS CURRIE and wife in open
court, 12 October 1810.

403. 5 October 1810. CHARLES B. PENN, Staunton, Augusta County,
      to SAMUEL BURKS, Amherst County...L160 paid by HENRY HOLLOWAY,
executor of ROBERT HOLLOWAY--80 acres Harris Creek. PENN's part of
400 acres divided to heirs of JOSEPH PENN, deceased, and formerly
that of DANIEL HARVIE and which ROBERT HOLLOWAY, as grandson of
CHARLES PENN, sold to SAMUEL BURKS. Witnesses: NELSON C. DAWSON,
WIATT POWELL, JAMES FRANKLIN, JESSE WOODROOF, REUBIN NORVELL. To
SAMUEL BURKS, 28 September 1815.

404. 11 August 1810. JAMES DILLARD and wife, JANE, to SAMUEL
      SCOTT...100 current Virginia money (sic); 100 acres north
borders Porrage. Witnesses: JOUTH (?) P. HARDWICK, JAMES L. DILLARD,
WILLIAM TABLE (?). To SAMUEL SCOTT, 17 January 1814.

404.   20 August 1810.   Order to Amherst County Justices of the Peace:
       CHARLES NOWELL and wife, POLLY, 17 February 1807, to ALEXANDER
JEWELL...128½ acres.   Done by JAMES DILLARD and CHARLES MUNDY,
first day of ? 1810.   Recorded 15 October 1810.

405.   13 September 1810.   REUBEN NORVELL and wife, POLLY, Amherst
       County, to JAMES LONDON, Amherst County...$850.00; 170 acres
Porrige.   Lines: JAMES LONDON near Glade Road, LARKIN LONDON.
September 20, 1848 to JAMES S. LONDON, present owner of the land.

406.   17 June 1810.   WILLIAM COLEMAN, Amherst County, to ROBERT H.
       COLEMAN, Amherst County...L420--his part of legacy of GEORGE
COLEMAN's estate--Rutledge Creek.   Lines: JAMES FRANKLIN, BENAMMINNI
STONE, GIDEON RUCKER, EDWARD WATSON, WILLIAM GALT, WILLIAM LONG,
EZEKIEL GILBERT.

407.   17 September 1810.   CHARLES B. and SUSANNAH GRISSON, Amherst
       County, to WILLIAM WILLMORE, Amherst County...L60 121 acres
both sides Pedlar.   Bounded as directed by WILLIAM GRISSOM, deceased,
plot.   Lines: PETER MARTIN, HENRY CAMDEN, JAMES MARTIN, CRAWFORD,
GALT.   To WILLIAM WILLMORE, 15 June 1812.

408.   26 July 1810.   JOSEPH MAYO, Powhatan, attorney for DOCTOR
       ROBERT MAYO, Richmond, to WILLIAM SPENCER, Nelson County...
L2500 500 acres James River, that part of estate of late JOSEPH MAYO,
Powhatan, which he divided to his son, ROBERT MAYO, by will.   Lines:
upper point of Buffaloe Island--called DILLARD's Island, Porrage.
NORVELL SPENCER.   To CAPTAIN STEPHEN WATTS, 10 October 1817.

409.   16 July 1810.   WILLIAM CHICK and wife, ELIZABETH, Buckingham
       County, to JAMES and TURNER PENN, Amherst County...$900.00
200 acres Porrage and is tract conveyed by JONATHAN LONDON and
DAVID S. GARLAND to KEZIAH COFLIN.   Lines: Porrage, JAMES DILLARD,
JONATHAN M. WALKER, PLEASANT STORY, DAVID S. GARLAND--all to JAMES
and TURNER PENN, and delivered to both, 25 November 1815.

409.   5 October 1810.   PULLIAM SANDIDGE and wife, LUCY, Amherst
       County, to CHARLES BARRET and ABSALOM HIGGINBOTHAM, Amherst
County...L450 129¼ acres.   Lines: ISAAC MAYFIELD, JONATHAN
HIGGINBOTHAM, south bank of north fork Buffaloe.   Pat., 13 August
1784, at Richmond, also pat. of 5 March 1805.   Lines: his own,
JONATHAN HIGGINBOTHAM, BENJAMIN SANDIDGE, PHILLIPS, LESEER tract,
2 December 1799, north bank south fork Buffaloe, JOSEPH HIGGINBOTHAM,
JR., grantor.   To ABSALOM HIGGINBOTHAM, 3 June 1818--very poor
writing here.

411.   19 November 1810.   WILLIAM GALT, Richmond, to JAMES POWELL...
       $4000.00 360 acres Tribulation.   Lines: Lynch Raod, BALER
WALKER, deceased, EZEKIEL GILBERT.

411.   19 May 1810.   JONATHAN LONDON and wife, TIRZAH, Amherst County,
       to LINAEUS BOLLING, Buckingham County...$100.00 1496 acres;
pat. 10 February 1810 north borders Fluvanna.   Lines: WILLIAM
GALT, POWHATAN BOLLING, deceased, JOSEPH MAYS, WILLIAM ROBINSON,
BENJAMIN WILSON.

413.   26 February 1812 to JONATHAN CAMM--21 September 1810 HENRY
       BALLINGER and wife, POLLY, Amherst County, to JONATHAN CLEMENTS
and JAMES DODD, Amherst County...$1.00 140 acres south borders north
fork Buffaloe and side of Cold Mountain.   Pat. to SAMUEL HIGGINBOTHAM,
3 May 1773.   Witnesses: JONATHAN A. SMITH, JOSEPH DODD, JOSEPH
CHILDRESS.   Final proof, 19 November 1810, by grantor.

414.   23 November 1810.   THOMAS CREWS and wife, SALLY, Amherst
       County, to JONATHAN AMBLER, Richmond...L800 332½ acres both
sides Harris.   Lines: SAMUEL BURKS, grantee.

415. 19 November 1810. JAMES POWELL, Amherst County, to WILLIAM
    GALT, Richmond, second; DAVID S. GARLAND and JONATHAN BULLOCK,
third. Deed of Trust to secure GALT--5 sh paid by third parties.
360 acres Tribulation Creek. Lines: Lynch Road, BALER WALKER,
EZEKIEL GILBERT. To WILLIAM GALT, 12 July 1814.

417. 24 October 1810. Order to Rockingham Justices of the Peace:
    MATTHEW WATSON and wife, ELIZA, 20 November 1809, to WILLIAM
LONG...their interest in 80 acres. Done, 16 November 1810, by
CHARLES LEWIS and GEORGE HUSTON.

418. 6 May 1810. EDMOND PENN, Spotsylvania County, to THOMAS
    CREWS, Amherst County, and WILLIAM LONG, Richmond...Deed of
Trust; debt due LONG: 5 sh. Fourteen named slaves and among these
were "YELLOW and BLACK BILLY." Witnesses: EDMOND RANDOLPH,
RICHARD JEFFRIES. To WILLIAM LONG, 14 December 1810.

419. 8 November 1809. JAMES CHRISTIAN and wife, CURDILLAH, Amherst
    County, JAMES MURPHY and wife, BETSY, CHARLES CHRISTIAN,
WILLIAM HORSLEY and wife, SALLY, orphans of GEORGE CHRISTIAN, to
STEPHEN WATTS, Nelson County...L470 318 acres part of tract next to
grantee. Lines: James River, JAMES DILLARD, SAMUEL BELL. To
STEPHEN WATTS, per his son, 31 December 1810. Witnesses: DABNEY
PHILLIPS, WILLIAM L. BELL, THOMAS S. HOLLOWAY, HENRY H(?) WATTS.
Final proof, 17 December 1810, by all save PHILLIPS.

421. 17 November 1810. JAMES HIGGINBOTHAM, JR., Amherst County,
    to JOSEPH DILLARD, Amherst County...L80 80 acres north
borders Buffaloe. Lines: WILLIAM TYREE, JESSE KENNEDY, deceased,
RICHARD ALCOCK, GEORGE PHILLIPS, JONATHAN PHILLIPS' old line,
JACOB TYREE. Witnesses: HUDSON M. GARLAND, GEORGE W. HIGGINBOTHAM,
PATON KEITH.

422. 26 April 1810. JOSEPH KENNERLY, Amherst County, to DUDLEY
    CALAWAY, Amherst County...no sum, slave named HANNAH. Witnesses:
RICHARD THOMAS, SAMUEL KENNERLY, JAMES MITCHELL. To DUDLEY CALAWAY,
29 September 1812.

423. 29 October 1810. JOSEPH ARBUCKLE and wife, MARY, Amherst
    County, to ANDREW SKINNALL, Amherst County...L45 New Glasgow
lot next to one occupied by JONATHAN SAVAGE, JR., lately occupied by
grantor. Witnesses: JOSEPH DILLARD, JAMES P. PARRISH, MARK LIVELY,
JERE YAGER, THOMPSON NOEL.

423. 6 November 1810. PATRICK ROSE, Nelson County, to heirs of
    JONATHAN FULCHER, deceased, Amherst County...$140.00 two tracts
on Little Piney. 1. About one acre bought of GEORGE GILLESPIE, SR.,
where mill dam was built. 2. Seven acres by survey of 4 November
1801. Lines: north bank Little Piney, Lot #1, old pat. line.
Witnesses: JONATHAN N. ROSE, JAMES FULCHER, MICAJAH CAMDEN. To
CHARLES CHRISTIAN, 22 January 1809.

425. 16 November 1810. JAMES and CHARLES CHRISTIAN, Amherst County,
    to JAMES GARLAND, Amherst County...$1270.00 254 acres Buffaloe
east side Braxton's Ridge. Lines: JACOB PEARCE, top of the ridge,
the road. Witnesses: THOMAS N. EUBANK, JONATHAN LONDON, SAMUEL
FRANKLIN. Page 426 order to quiz SARAH, wife of CHARLES CHRISTIAN,
as to above deed. Done, 24 November 1810, by REUBEN NORVELL and
CHARLES MUNDY.

427. 15 January 1811. Order to Amherst County Justices of the Peace:
    THOMAS MOORE, NELSON C. DAWSON, and JAMES FRANKLIN--THOMAS
CREWS and wife, SALLY, 23 November 1810, to JONATHAN AMBLER...332 acres
Done by last two named Justices of the Peace, 21 January 1811.

428. 5 July 1810. LARKIN SANDIDGE, Lincoln County, Kentucky, to
ABRAM CARTER, Amherst County...power of attorney as my friend--
to recover ten named slaves in hands of estate of JOSIAH ELLIS,
deceased, and claimed by written instrument assigned from JONATHAN
VAUGHAN, MICHAEL STUCKER and wife, NANCY, both of Kentucky and
EDWARD CARTER, Virginia. Bought by LARKIN SANDIDGE of said CARTER and
they are his interest in said slaves by intermarriage with widow of
CORNELIUS VAUGHAN. Reference to Amherst County instrument. Witnesses:
NELSON CRAWFORD, BENNETT A. CRAWFORD.

428. 17 November 1810. Order to Nelson County Justices of the Peace:
JONATHAN BETHEL and wife, POLLY, 21 August 1804, to JONATHAN
BETHEL, JR...346 acres. Done by WILLIAM H. DIGGES and JOSEPH LOVING,
11 December 1810.

429. 2 November 1810. SUDAH WILLIAMSON and wife, LINDSEY, Amherst
County, to EDMOND WILLIAMSON, Amherst County...L200 141 acres
Stone House Creek. Lines: MOSES MARTIN, WILLIAMSON. Witnesses:
WILLIAM SALE, ROBERT RIVES, JONATHAN SMITH. Page 430 order to
Amherst County Justices of the Peace to quiz LINDSAY, 13 November
1810. Done by EDMOND T. COLEMAN and HILL CARTER, 14 November 1810.

432. 21 December 1810. Order to Nelson County Justices of the Peace:
ABRAHAM B. WARWICK and JESSE JOPLING--JAMES CHRISTIAN and wife,
CURDILLAH, JAMES MURPHY and wife, BETSY, CHARLES CHRISTIAN, WILLIAM
HORSLEY and wife, SALLY, orphans of GEORGE CHRISTIAN, 8 November
1809, to STEPHEN WATTS...318 acres. To quiz CURDILLAH, BETSY and
SALLY. Justices of the Peace reported as to last two, 31 December
1810.

433. 15 January 1811. WILLIAM HOWARD and wife, ---, to CHARLES
TALIAFERRO--both of Amherst County...$500.00 no acres--both
sides POWELL's Creek. Lines: grantee. HOWARD's wife is not named
herein.

434. 18 December 1810. DANIEL MAHONE and wife, SARAH, Amherst
County, to EDWARD WATSON, Amherst County...L315 138½ acres.
Lines: DANIEL NORCUTT, Lynch Road, MICAJAH CLARKE, BOWLER CLARKE,
TINSLEY. Witnesses: NELSON C. DAWSON, WILKS WATSON, PHILLIP JOHNSON,
WILLIAM BURFORD. Page 435 order to Amherst County Justices of the
Peace to quiz SARAH, same date. Done, 19 December 1810, by NELSON C.
DAWSON and PHILLIP JOHNSON.

437. 8 October 1810. RICHARD POWELL and JAMES FRANKLIN, Amherst
County, to THOMAS CREWS, Amherst County...L397-9-6--one fourth
of two tracts--late property of JOSEPH CREWS, JR., supposed to be
dead. 587½ acres. Lines: THOMAS CREWS, WILLIAM MOON, JONATHAN
MC DONALD, JAMES PENDLETON, HENRY HOLLOWAY, deceased, EDWARD WATSON,
WIATT POWELL, WILLIAM OLIVER. Note: consult my work on C wills for
data on JOSEPH CREWS, SR., and his mentioning fact that son, JOSEPH,
is supposedly dead. I have never checked CREWS data in Madison County,
Kentucky, but do recall that the family is represented there and
Circuit Court records have material on a CREWS' tract in a suit.

438. 21 January 1811. JONATHAN MONROE and wife, RACHEL, Nelson
County, to DANIEL and SOLOMON DAY, Amherst County...$400.00
100 acres Stovall Creek. Lines: JONATHAN KNIGHT, JOSEPH HIGGINBOTHAM,
JONATHAN TURNER, old field opposite the houses.

439. 24 December 1810. HENRY CAMDEN and wife, LUCY, Amherst County,
to WILLIAM DUNCAN, Amherst County...L123-12-6 86 acres
Stonehouse Creek. Lines: north bank Buffaloe, JAMES HIX, WILLIAM
SANDIDGE, EDMOND T. COLEMAN.

440. 18 February 1811. JAMES TINSLEY and wife, SALLY, Amherst
County, to JAMES WARE, Amherst County...L9-2 6½ acres John's
Creek and part of where JAMES TINSLEY lives. Lines: grantor,
ANTHONY RUCKER, a border.

441. 11 February 1811. JONATHAN RUCKER and wife, NANCY, Amherst
     County, to JAMES WARE, Amherst County...L42 half a lot in town
of Bethel--#8 and whereon JONATHAN RUCKER lately built.

442. 17 February 1811. JAMES POWELL and wife, MILDRED, Amherst
     County, to ROBERT ALLEN, Amherst County...$20.00 lot near
courthouse on main road--one half acre. Lines: WILLIAM LONG. Note:
this lot and adjacent property bought by ALLEN was subject of a bitter
controversy here several years ago. On this property stood an old
house which had not been painted--if ever--for years and no one lived
in it. Fidelity National Bank of Lynchburg secured an option on the
tract and immediately a terrible howl arose. Several folk contended
that this old house was a pre-Revolutionary tavern and dogmatically
stated that they could prove it. I got into the act when it was
stated that deeds could not be found to substantiate anything. I
showed that it was known in deeds as Allen's Tavern and no one ever
brought out data to prove any pre-Revolutionary tavern on the site.
A beautiful bank building is now on the lot.

442. 27 October 1810. GEORGE HUDSON and wife, NANCY, Amherst County,
     to CHARLES BOWLES, Amherst County...$206.00 84 acres Naked
Creek borders. Lines: PATRICK ROSE, REUBEN HUDSON, deceased, where
small branch crosses New Glasgow road. Witnesses: GEORGE RULEY,
BARTLETT THOMPSON, JEREMIAH FRANKLIN. To DAVID S. GARLAND, present
owner, 7 December 1829.

444. 12 July 1810. NICHOLAS VANSTAVERN and wife, CATY, Amherst
     County, to ASHCRAFT ROACH, Amherst County...L66 220 acres
surveyed 21 April 1788--north side and joining Fluvanna and both
sides Cushaw Creek and Rockirow Creek.

445. 18 February 1811. WILLIAM WILLMORE and wife, SUSANNA, to
     JOSEPH BLAND, Amherst County...L108 228 acres borders south
fork Buffaloe and head waters Horsley. Lines: SOLOMON CARTER,
JONATHAN SANDIDGE, BENJAMIN and AARON HIGGINBOTHAM. To JOSEPH BLAND,
11 May 1812.

447. 3 September 1810. JONATHAN and WALTER FRAZIER, Giles County,
     Tennessee...power of attorney to RICHARD HARTLESS, Amherst
County, to act and sell tract next to HENRY HARTLESS--100 acres.
Witnesses: CHARLES L. BARRETT, JOSEPH CREWS, WILLIAM COLEMAN.
Proved by CHARLES L. BARRETT and WILLIAM COLEMAN, 18 February 1811.

448. -- September 1810. PATRICK ROSE, one of the acting executors
     of HENRY ROSE, to THOMAS FITZPATRICK, and wife, LYDE (formerly
CARTWRIGHT) and BENJAMIN NAYLOR and wife, POLLY (formerly NAYLOR--
SIC)..MATTHEW CARTWRIGHT had entered and surveyed by purchase of
JOSEPH LIVELY 148 acres on small borders under Indian Mountain. It
now joins BARTLETT CASH, BENJAMIN ROGERS, CHARLES TUCKER et al. and
returned to Register's Office. MATTHEW CARTWRIGHT employed HENRY
ROSE, attorney-at-law, to enter friendly caveat in name of ROSE.
While pending, ROSE died, intestate, and had named HUGH and PATRICK
ROSE his executors. They recovered caveat in their names and patented
same. HUGH ROSE has since died. LYDE CARTWRIGHT has married THOMAS
FITZPATRICK and POLLY CARTWRIGHT has married BENJAMIN NAYTON (note:
this name is spelled NAYTON; NEYTON; NAYLOR in data) and both are
daughters of MATTHEW CARTWRIGHT, and all expenses of caveat are paid.
They filed bill in Nelson on Chancery side for deed. Order to convey
under pat. of 5 July 1774, $1.00 paid by granteees--148 acres.
Lines: WILLIAM ROSE, HOWARD CASH. Witnesses: C. P. TALIAFERRO,
JONATHAN N. ROSE, HILL CARTER, ANDREW SKINNELL, WILLIAM M. MORGAN.

451. 26 November 1810. MILLY HARRISON to ST. GEORGE TUCKER and
     POLLY WATSON, wife of WILKINS WATSON, and formerly TUCKER, all
of Virginia...L100 for one-eleventh part or interest in undivided
tract of DRURY TUCKER, deceased, which fell to ZACHARIAH TUCKER,
also 1/11th lots of PLEASANT TUCKER, GEORGE DOUGLAS, RICHARD HARRISON,
deceased. Witnesses: ENOCH HAGAN, THOMAS ALEXANDER, AMBROSE RUCKER,
JONATHAN E. HARRISON, deceased (sic), POLLY L. WALDEN. Proved in

Bedford County, 24 December 1810, by HAGAN, AMBROSE RUCKER and by
JONATHAN E. HARRIS (sic). Recorded in Amherst County, 18 March 1811.

452. 1 June 1809. MATTHEW WATSON and wife, ELIZA, Rockingham County,
to NANCY SHIELDS, Amherst County...L750 235 acres south side
Buffaloe and where THOMAS POWELL lives. Witnesses: WIATT SMITH,
J. P. GARLAND, RICHARD HARRISON.

453. 15 December 1810. Order to Amherst County Justices of the Peace:
CHARLES CHRISTIAN and wife, SARAH, 18 November 1807, to
JONATHAN RICHESON...300 acres. Done by CHARLES MONDAY and JAMES
DILLARD, 18 March 1811.

454. 10 February 1811. Order to Campbell County Justices of the
Peace: JONATHAN LYNCH and wife, MARY, 9 May 1800, to WILLIAM S.
SCOTT...300 acres. Done by THOMAS HUMPHREY and THOMAS W. COCKE,
27 February 1811. Delivered to JAMES BENAGH, 15 July 1811.

456. 18 March 1811. THOMAS FITZPATRICK and wife, LYDE, to FERDINAND
LEIGH...$150.00 148 acres small borders Indian Mountain.
Lines: BARTLETT CASH, BENJAMIN ROGERS, CHARLES TUCKER. Sent to
FERDINAND LEIGH, 5 April 1812.

456. 22 November 1809. EZEKIEL GILBERT and wife, ANN ROCKING,
BETSY GILBERT, Amherst County, WILLIAM GIBSON and wife, ELVIRA,
Buckingham County, MATTHEW WATSON and wife, ELIZA, Rockingham County,
and ANN GILBERT, Amherst County, to WILLIAM LONG...L200 80 acres.
Lines: JAMES FRANKLIN, GEORGE COLEMAN, deceased, Mirey Branch.
Part of tract of JAMES WATSON, deceased, and deed by him and wife,
PATSY, 15 October 1796, and recorded on 17th--except MATTHEW WATSON
and wife, ELIZA, whose title is derived by deed from WIATT R. GILBERT
who claimed under aforesaid deed.

458. 15 April 1811. JONATHAN MC DANIEL, Amherst County, to LINDSEY
MC DANIEL, Amherst County...$100 646 acres whereon LINDSEY
MC DANIEL lives. Lines: JAMES PENDLETON, ELIZABETH COLEMAN, EDMOND
WINSTON, THOMAS CREWS. Witnesses: JONATHAN P. WILSON, AMBR. R.
MC DANIEL, JONATHAN WARE, NELSON C. DAWSON. To LINDSEY MC DANIEL,
1813.

459. 3 October 1810. MILLY HARRISON, Bedford County, to MATTHEW
TUCKER, Amherst County...$100 for all slaves, undivided, in
hands of FRANCIS TUCKER under will of DRURY TUCKER, deceased,
Amherst County. Witnesses: COLBY TINSLEY, PATRICK BURTON, WILLIAM
SHELTON, ISAAC TINSLEY.

459. 10 December 1810. RICHARD MILLNOR and wife, MARTHA, Bedford,
to MARY RICHESON, Amherst County...$1.00 120 acres Pedlar.
Part of mansion house tract owned by JONATHAN RICHESON, deceased,
and to MILLNOR on division. Lines: Bethel Road, THOMAS RICHESON,
MARY RICHESON's dower land, JONATHAN EUBANKS, THOMAS GILLIAT (?),
ARMISTEAD RUCKER. Recorded in Amherst County, 15 April 1811.

461. 3 September 1810. JONATHAN FRAZIER and wife, DOLLY, and
WALTER FRAZIER, Giles County, Tennessee, to WILLIAM MACKEY,
Rockbridge...$225.00 90 acres. Lines: WILLIAM TAYLOR, middle fork
Pedlar. Witnesses: CHARLES L. BARRET, JOSEPH GERVIS (?), WILLIAM
COLEMAN, JONATHAN GIBSON, MOSES MARTIN.

463. 16 March 1811. VALENTINE COX, Bedford, and NANCY COX, Bedford
(wife?) to JAMES BENNETT, Amherst County...L200 159 acres
Harris Creek. Lines: DAVID TINSLEY on north, RICHARD SHELTON,
SHELTON's old road, MILLER Creek, HENRY GOSNEY, DANIEL BURFORD,
PHILIP BURFORD. Witnesses: NICHOLAS HARRISON, EDWARD TINSLEY,
DAVID TINSLEY, JR., A. ROBERTSON, HENRY FARNSWORTH.

464. 20 March 1811. WILLIAM MUSE, SR. to WILLIAM MUSE, JR...L100
32 acres. Lines: COX's old line, HUGH's Road, fork in road.
To WILLIAM MUSE, 1818.

465. 20 May 1811. BENJAMIN SANDIDGE and wife, ELIZABETH, Amherst
County, to WILLIAM MC DANIEL, Amherst County...L204 340 acres
both sides middle fork Pedlar. Lines: WILLIAM HIGGINBOTHAM, GEORGE
MC DANIEL, just below a great fall.

466. 23 May 1811. JAMES POWELL and wife, MILDRED, Amherst County,
to WILLIAM HUTCHESON, Amherst County...$20.00 one half acre
lot at Courthouse. Lines: ROBERT ALLEN, the road, COLEMAN. To
ROBERT ALLEN, 10 October 1814. Note: this is part of that contro-
versial land mentioned a few pages back.

467. 31 August 1810. WILLIAM B. GOOCH, Amherst County, to JONATHAN
CARTER, Amherst County...L75 68 acres bought by WILLIAM B.
GOOCH from REUBEN GATEWOOD. Lines: LEWIS LAIN, ROBERT COLEMAN,
EDWARD WILCOX, deceased, STEPHEN WATTS, MICAJAH PENDLETON. Witnesses:
CHARLES L. CHRISTIAN, SAMUEL P. LAINE, REUBEN GATEWOOD.

468. 20 May 1811. SPOTSWOOD GARLAND, trustee for HUGH ROSE, to
STERLING CLAIBORNE, under power of 21 June 1809...L650 200 acres
Tye River. Lines: WILLIAM S. CRAWFORD, WILLIAM SPENCER, JAMES
PLEASANTS. HUGH ROSE's part of father's tract.

469. 6 May 1795. JONATHAN LACKEY and wife, NANCY, EVE LACKEY, and
RACHEL AYRES, Amherst County, to BENJAMIN RUCKER, Amherst
County...L20 16 acres Crooked Run, part of tract sold by JONATHAN
LACKEY to SAMUEL LACKEY, 22 November 1793. Lines: BENJAMIN RUCKER,
JOSEPH HIGGINBOTHAM, SR., JAMES RICHESON, JONATHAN PENDLETON.
Proved by JONATHAN PENDLETON, 22 December 1799, by JAMES RICHESON
PENN (sic), 20 April 1807, final proof, 20 May 1811, by THOMAS
STEWART.

470. 24 January 1811. WILLIAM OLIVER, Amherst County, to JAMES P.
GARLAND and THOMAS CREWS, Amherst County...Deed of Trust; debt
to REUBEN COLEMAN, $1.00 slave and 127 acres where WILLIAM OLIVER
lives. Lines: GEORGE DILLARD, deceased, THOMAS CREWS. Witnesses:
CHARLES L. BARRETT, A. B. DAVIES, THOMAS OLIVER, JONATHAN LACKEY,
JR. (?), THOMAS CREWS, C. POWELL.

472. 15 July 1811. RICHARD TINSLEY, Amherst County, first; WILLIAM
TURNER, second; GEORGE TINSLEY, son of DAVID TINSLEY, third
part...RICHARD to secure right in tract sold by him to GEORGE on
James and Otter Creeks and meeting to ROBERT JOHNSON on debt to
SPEARS BOWMAN and Company and WILLIAM TURNER pays small amount in
Deed of Trust--two negro girls, JUDY and LUCY, valued at $400.00;
to be sold.

473. 4 June 1811. CASPER POTTER, Ohio, to JOSEPH BRADFIELD, New
Glasgow...$200.00 house and lot in New Glasgow; half an acre.
Lines: HENRY CAMDEN's lot on north, Main Street on east, DAVID S.
GARLAND on south and west. Sold by HUDSON M. GARLAND, trustee for
POTTER in Deed of Trust to him by JONATHAN WILLS. Witnesses:
JOHN MYERS, WILLIAM ARMISTEAD, HUDSON M. GARLAND.

474. 17 June 1811. JAMES WARE and wife, NANCY, to JONATHAN COX...
$1000.00 130 acres on John's and Rockey Creeks. Lines:
JONATHAN CAMM, branch known as Tinsley's Spring branch, REUBEN
PENDLETON, MITCHELL's old road, big branch, JAMES WILLS, JOSEPH
HAWKINS, PROSSER POWELL, ANTHONY RUCKER, JAMES TINSLEY, RUCKER.

476. 13 May 1811. SHAROD BUGG and wife, ANN, Amherst County, to
ROBERT COLEMAN, Amherst County...L85 82½ acres north side
Buffaloe and near Turkey Mountain. Lines: LINDSEY COLEMAN at a
branch, line in BESICK's (?), WILLIAM MAYS. Witnesses: DANIEL
HIGGINBOTHAM, JOSEPH DILLARD, JONATHAN LONDON. To ROBERT COLEMAN,
31 March 1813.

478. 20 May 1811. REUBEN NORVELL and wife, POLLY, Amherst County,
to HENRY TURNER, Amherst County...L67 no acres; Porrige Creek.
Lines: grantee, THOMAS JEWELL, JONATHAN LONDON. Witnesses: JONATHAN
LONDON, CHARLES MUNDY, THOMAS T. MAYS.

479. 28 May 1810. WILLIAM MOON and wife, ELIZABETH, Amherst County,
    to WILLIAM WOODROOF, Amherst County...L83 83 acres. Lines:
top of PAUL's Mountain, THOMAS CREWS. Witnesses: NICHOLAS HARRISON,
DAVID WOODROOF, JONATHAN T. HILL.

480. 10 March 1811. NICHOLAS HARRISON and wife, NANCY, to RICHARD
    HARRISON, Amherst County...$1200 196 acres Harris Creek,
bought by NICHOLAS HARRISON of RICHARD RUCKER. Lines: JAMES HILL,
grantor, REUBEN RUCKER, BENNETT RUCKER, ANTHONY RUCKER, old road,
JAMES TINSLEY.

482. 14 June 1811. CALEB WATTS and wife, SUSANNAH, Amherst County,
    to JONATHAN BROWN, Amherst County...L100 50 acres Pedlar.
Lines: MARTIN PARKS, JONATHAN DUNCAN, JONATHAN BURKS, RODERICK
MC CULLOCH. Witnesses: MERIT M. WHITE, ANDREW HAMBLETON, ANDREW A.
BROWN. To JONATHAN BROWN, 16 September 1811.

483. 17 June 1811. WILLIAM HOWARD and wife, BETSY, Amherst County,
    to JONATHAN WARE, Amherst County...L35 28 acres Horsley Creek.
Lines: JAMES GOODRICH, WILLIAM WARE. WILLIAM HOWARD bought tract
from LANDON CARTER.

484. 17 June 1811. JONATHAN MARTIN, Amherst County, to WILLIAM
    MARTIN, Amherst County...L200 250 acres both sides Franklin
Creek. Lines: JACOB SMITH. Witnesses: JONATHAN SMITH, DUDLEY
SANDIDGE, WILLIAM CAMDEN.

485. 18 June 1811. HENRY CAMDEN and wife, LUCY, Amherst County, to
    EDMOND T. COLEMAN, Amherst County...L125 146 acres. Balance
of a tract formerly that of BRAKMAN (?) on Buffaloe. Lines: WILLIAM
DUNCAN, WILLIAM SANDIDGE, main road from SANDIDGE to NELSON old
courthouse, grantee.

486. 17 June 1811. CHARLES L. BARRET and wife, SARAH, Amherst
    County, to WILLIAM DEMPSEY, Amherst County...L100 96 acres.
Bought from JONATHAN DEVASHER and wife. Lines: JOSEPH HIGGINBOTHAM,
north side HORSLEY, Childress' Gap Road, WILLIAM SCHOFIELD, deceased.
Witnesses: BENJAMIN TALIAFERRO, JAMES P. GARLAND, JAMES OGDEN.

487. 1 June 1811. JONATHAN C. DEVASHER and wife, ELIZABETH, Amherst
    County...$400 no acres. Lines: mouth of a branch running
into Long Branch. To WILLIAM DEMPSEY, 20 October 1815.

488. 16 March 1811. WARNER GOODWIN and wife, ESTHER, Amherst County,
    to ALEXANDER PENN, Amherst County...$65 11 acres. Lines:
Indian Creek Ford, JONATHAN PENN, JR., Spring Branch, "grate" road,
forks of road, up Indian Creek road. Witnesses: JONATHAN LACKEY,
JONATHAN PENN, ROBERT COLEMAN, LEWIS W. BANKS,. To ALEXANDER PENN,
16 March 1812.

490. 29 December 1810. Order to Amherst County Justices of the
    Peace: REUBEN PENDLETON and wife, FRANCES, 14 July 1804, to
JAMES WARE...62 acres. Done by NELSON C. DAWSON and THOMAS MOORE,
14 March 1811.

491. 20 November 1810. WILLIAM MEREDITH, Fayette County, Kentucky,
    to DAVID S. GARLAND, Amherst County...$1150.00 for interest
in tract of "about 1150 acres"--both sides Buffaloe, all that tract
of SAMUEL MEREDITH, The Elder. Note: MISS RUTH BLUNT has done some
splendid research on the family which left here and went to Fayette
County, Kentucky. At least one article has appeared in the NSDAR
Magazine.

492. 20 November 1810. WILLIAM MEREDITH, as above, as attorney-in-
    fact for MARY MAY of Fayette County, Kentucky, to DAVID S.
GARLAND...$1500 for all interest in tract as above and now in possession
of MRS. JANE MEREDITH. Witnesses: as above.

493. 18 June 1811. RICHARD TINSLEY, Amherst County, and wife,
        SARY, to BERRY BRYANT, Amherst County...L2-5 paid by BERRY
BRAYANT for one acre. Lines: his own, Rattle snake branch, James
River.

495. 15 October 1810. MARY MAY, Fayette County, Kentucky, to her
        brother, WILLIAM MEREDITH...to sell my interest in tract from
father's will. ROBERT S. TODD, Notary Public of Lexington, Kentucky.
Recorded in Amherst County, 19 June 1811.

495. 6 June 1811. CHARLES P. TALIAFERRO and wife, LOUISA, Amherst
        County, to CHARLES L. BARRET, Amherst County...L350 202 acres
Pedlar. Lines: JONATHAN ROBERTS, JONATHAN BROWN, STEPHEN RUSSELL,
JACOB BROWN. To CHARLES L. BARRET, 29 August 1811.

497. 29 April 1811. RICHARD TINSLEY to HUGH MC CABE..receipt in full
        for payment on Deed of Trust to tract whereon I live to SPIERS
and BOWMAN Company. Witnesses: GEORGE GILLESPIE, FRANCIS TINSLEY,
LINZA BURKS. Note: this is GEORGE GILLESPIE, JR., for his father
was dead by this time.

498. 15 July 1811. CHARLES P. TALIAFERRO and wife, LOUISA, Amherst
        County, to CHARLES TALIAFERRO, Amherst County...$500.00 151½
acres head waters Powell's Creek, south border Puppie Creek. Lines:
JONATHAN WARE.

500. 6 July 1811. CHARLES L. BARRET and wife, SARAH, Amherst County,
        to CHARLES P. TALIAFERRO, Amherst County...L500 412 acres
Puppies Creek. To CHARLES P. TALIAFERRO, 3 January 1822.

501. 9 July 1811. JONATHAN WARD, SR., Campbell County, to BENJAMIN
        SCHOOLFIELD, same county...L500 100 acres James River. Lines:
JOSIAH ELLIS, JONATHAN MILLER. Part of two tracts I bought of
WRIGHT and LYNCH. Witnesses: JONATHAN WEAVER, JONATHAN THURMOND,
AARON SCHOOLFIELD. To BENJAMIN SCHOOLFIELD, 20 September 1819.

503. 15 July 1811. JACOB PEARCE, Amherst County, to FREDERICK FULTZ
        and JONATHAN COLEMAN, Amherst County...L196 28 acres Rockey
Run. Lines: WILLIAM DILLARD, JONATHAN CHRISTIAN, grantor. Part of
a tract bought by JACOB PEARCE from DAVID S. GARLAND. Witnesses:
REUBEN NORVELL, BERNARD (?) OWENS, DAVID S. GARLAND, JACOB SCOTT.
To R.C. (?), 6 February 1812.

504. 1 June 1811. HUGH MC CABE and wife, ELIZABETH, Amherst County,
        to JONATHAN and RICHARD L. ELLIS, Amherst County...$332.00
332 acres on Fluvanna. Lines: JONATHAN BINS (?), WILLIAM NOEL,
THOMAS N. EUBANK, THOMAS HIGGINBOTHAM, ROBERT KNUCKLES, CORNELIUS
ROACH, SAMUEL NICELEY. To JONATHAN ELLIS, 16 September 1811.

505. 15 July 1811. WILLIAM WARE, Amherst County, to CHARLES
        TALIAFERRO, Amherst County...$50.00 12½ acres headwaters Powell's
Creek, south branch of Puppie Creek. Lines: JONATHAN WARE.

507. 10 July 1811. RICHARD TINSLEY and wife, SALLY, Amherst County,
        to GEORGE TINSLEY, Amherst County...$400.00 212 acres James
and Otter Creeks and where said TINSLEY lives. Lines: HENRY L.
DAVIES, mouth of Cedar branch on north bank of James, BERRY BRYANT
and near his house, crossing Tarrapin, Welch Spring Branch. It is
noted that HENRY L. DAVIES is deceased.

509. 18 March 1808. DAVID SAWYERS and wife, ELIZABETH, Augusta
        County, ANDREW ALEXANDER and wife, ISABELLA, WILLIAM PAXTON and
wife, POLLY, JAMES PAXTON, ELISHA PAXTON and wife, PEGGY, Rockbridge
County and JAMES P. PRIOR, Kanawaha, by JAMES PAXTON, his attorney-in-
fact and recorded in Rockbridge...heirs of WILLIAM PAXTON, SR.,
deceased, to JONATHAN PAXTON, Rockbridge $654.33 425 acres near top
of South Mountain. Witnesses: JONATHAN MC NUTT, WILLIAM MC NUTT,
JONATHAN PORTER, JO PAXTON. Acknowledged in Rockbridge, 3 June 1811,
and noted that on 5 June signed by ISABELLA, ALEXANDER, POLLY and

PEGGY PAXTON. Page 512 March 25, 1811 SAWYER's wife relinquished
dower in Augusta. Recorded in Amherst County, 15 July 1811.

513. 1 July 1811. THOMAS T. HOLLOWAY, executor of HENRY HOLLOWAY,
deceased, who was executor of ROBERT HOLLOWAY, deceased, and
grandson for GEORGE T. HOLLOWAY and BETSY CATHERINE SLAUGHTER PENN
HOLLOWAY, infants of ROBERT HOLLOWAY, Amherst County, to DAVID S.
GARLAND, Amherst County. ROBERT HOLLOWAY in will, August 16, 1802,
appointed his brother, HENRY HOLLOWAY, his executor with power to
dispose of tracts and on 21 March 1807 HENRY sold two tracts to
DAVID S. GARLAND--707 acres north side Buffaloe and Higginbotham's
Mill Creek. Lines: FRANK LEE, deceased, EDMOND PENN, WILLIAM
PHILLIPS, deceased, RACHEL BWOEN, WILLIAM ARMISTEAD, WILLIAM CABELL,
BENJAMIN PHILLIPS, and Buffaloe. Reference to agreement between
HENRY HOLLOWAY and DAVID S. GARLAND on same date. 1. 384 acres which
HENRY bought of JAMES PENN, executor of GABL. PENN. Lines: BENJAMIN
PHILLIPS, deceased, north bank Buffaloe, WILLIAM CABELL, HIGGINBOTHAM's
Mill Creek, ISAAC GIBSON, deceased, ROBERT HOLLOWAY, deceased,
mouth of Higginbotham's Mill Creek. 2. 323 acres which ROBERT HOLLOWAY
owned at death. Lines: Mill lot, north bank of Buffaloe, mouth of
Higginbotham's Mill Creek, HENRY HOLLOWAY, ISAAC GIBSON, deceased,
EDMOND PENN, FRANK LEE. HENRY HOLLOWAY failed to execute deed to
DAVID S. GARLAND, but died and by will named THOMAS S. HOLLOWAY,
executor and grandson of ROBERT's children. October Court, 1810,
decree that ROBERT's executor convey--$7000.00. Witnesses: THOMAS
ALDRIDGE, H. M. GARLAND, PEACHY FRANKLIN, JONATHAN MYERS, J. S. (T.)
PENDLETON.

517. 8 September 1810. PETER WATERFIELD, Amherst County, to CHARLES
TALIAFERRO, Amherst County...$1.00; Deed of Trust; debt to
BENJAMIN TALIAFERRO, surviving partner of JONATHAN and BENJAMIN
TALIAFERRO--two tracts of 478 acres on Buffaloe and PETER WATERFIELD
bought them from LARKIN SANDIDGE. Witnesses: RODERICK L. TALIAFERRO,
EDMOND T. COLEMAN, CHARLES TUCKER, WILLIAM SANDIDGE. To CHARLES
TALIAFERRO, 5 September 1811.

520. 16 July 1811. Agreement--JESSE MINTER to CORNELIUS POWELL...
$100.00 for one year, a house left to POWELL for year; at
Buffaloe Springs on the hill side and occupied by DR. JONATHAN CABELL
last summer.

520. 8 December 1810. JOSHUA SHELTON and wife, MARY, Amherst
County, and RACHEL BROWN, Amherst County, to DAVID S. GARLAND,
Amherst County...L65 30½ acres north borders Buffaloe and lot of
MARY GIBSON in division of her late father. Lines: WILLIAM ARMISTEAD,
EDMOND PENN, HARRISON (?) heirs, grantee. Witnesses: WILLIAM
SHELTON, JONATHAN BROWN, ANDREW BROWN, JONATHAN LONDON, ANDERSON
MOSS, JONATHAN MYERS.

522. 16 July 1810. HUGH MC CABE and wife, ELIZABETH, Amherst County,
to WILLIAM DAVIS, Amherst County...$500.00 261 acres north
side and joining Fluvanna and on south side and joining Otter Creek.
Part of 404 acres from WILLIAM VEAL to grantor, 25 August 1799.
Smaller tract of 63 acres, pat. 1 August 1772, adjoining first
tract and granted to CORNELIUS THOMAS--dividing line of RICHARD
TINSLEY's 206 acres included in lines by deed of equal date--executed
by MC CABE and wife, except for Deed of Trust by ROBERT JOHNSON to
ALEXANDER SPIERS, JONATHAN BOWMAN and Company on --- 1772.

524. 20 October 1810. Order to Amherst County Justices of the Peace
REUBEN NORVELL and wife, POLLY, 13 September 1810, to JAMES
LONDON...170 (?) acres. Done by JAMES DILLARD and CHARLES MUNDY,
3 November 1810.

525. 24 December 1810. Order to Amherst County Justices of the
Peace: THOMAS CREWS and wife, SALLY, 16 July 1810, to WILLIAM
RADFORD, Lynchburg...½ acre lot; Campbell County. Done 21 January
1811 by NELSON C. CRAWFORD and JAMES FRANKLIN.

527. 9 November 1810. Order to Amherst County Justices of the Peace:
WILLIAM LAWLESS and wife, SUSANNAH, -- 1810, to ELIJAH BARNES...
50 acres. Done by WILLIAM WARE and NELSON CRAWFORD, 1 November 1810.

528. 17 August 1811. JOSEPH V. HARDWICK and wife, NANCY, Campbell
County, to JONATHAN Y. JOHNSON, Campbell County...$200.00 200
acres both sides Pig's Creek. Lines: THOMAS MORRIS, JONATHAN HOGG,
ALLISON MORRIS, JONATHAN SLEDD, DAVID DAVENPORT. Witnesses: WILLIAM
JOHNSON, THOMAS STEWART, R. H. TAYLOR. This deed is very dim in
spots.

531. 4 June 1811. JOSEPH BRADFIELD, New Glasgow, to WILLIAM ARMISTEAD,
Amherst County...Deed of Trust; debt to CASPER POTTER, Ohio,
for lot in New Glasgow where JONATHAN WILLS, SR., formerly resided;
sold to JOSEPH BRADFIELD by POTTER. $1.00--said lot. Witnesses:
H. M. GARLAND, JONATHAN MYERS, JONATHAN LONDON.

532. 5 August 1811. HANNAH ALLEN, Amherst County, to her sons,
SAMUEL H. and JONATHAN ALLEN...love and $1.00--my lands by will
of husband, SAMUEL ALLEN, deceased--my dower for life. Witnesses:
JONATHAN HORSLEY, JR., WILLIAM L. BELL, MICAJAH PENDLETON, DRURY
BELL. To JONATHAN T. HORSLEY, 25 January 1827.

533. 1 January 1810. WILLIAM SHELTON, guardian and C, Amherst
County, to JONATHAN WARE, SR...part of the plantation as
guardian--Cold Mountain tract on west side of Cold Mountain and north
fork Pedlar. Lease for five years from November 1, last at 6 sh. per
year on December 1--first payment due December 1, 1812. To plant
trees, build log cabins and outhouses, etc. Witnesses: THOMAS N.
EUBANK, WILLIAM JOPLIN, RICHARD EUBANK, NELSON CRAWFORD, JONATHAN
RICHESON. Note: SHELTON never does state names of the wards for
whom he is guardian.

536. 10 June 1808. JAMES KIDD and wife, LUCY, Nelson County, to
NELSON PHILLIPS, Nelson County...no sum; 128 acres on Little
Indian Creek. Witnesses: HENRY T. HARRIS, WILLIAM HARRIS, JR.,
WILLIAM LEE HARRIS. To NELSON PHILLIPS, 29 December 1818. Page 538
order to WILLIAM HARRIS, JONTHAN MOSBY and LANDON CABELL, Nelson
Justices of the Peace as to above deed. Done, 12 July 1808, by
MOSBY and HARRIS. At a court held for Amherst County at the house
occupied by AARON CAMPBELL at the Oaks, Monday, 18 July 1808, it
was proved by HENRY T. HARRIS. Final proof, 19 August 1811, by
acknowledgement. I have not been able to find out location of AARON
CAMPBELL's house at the Oaks, but it was seat of justice for a time.
One story is that the records were kept by WILLIAM S. CRAWFORD at
his home at Tusculum which still stands a few miles north of Amherst.

539. 3 August 1801. Order to Amherst County Justices of the Peace:
JOSEPH C. MIGGINSON and wife, SARAH, 29 August 1800, to WILLIAM
CAMDEN and JAMES FRANKLIN, 91 acres. Done, 22 September 1801, by
WILLIAM WARE and JOSIAH ELLIS. Returned and recorded, 16 September
1811.

540. 18 March 1811. Same grantors as found on page 509. Heirs of
WILLIAM PAXTON, SR., Rockbridge, to JAMES MARTIN, SR., Amherst
County...$131.25 105 acres near top of the South Mountain. Lines:
near a road, top of the mountain. Witnesses: as on page 509.

1. 13 July 1811. ROBERT H. COLEMAN, Amherst County, to REUBEN
    and LINDSEY COLEMAN, Amherst County...L1150 all interest in
551 acres. Lines: north bank Rutledge, Lynch Road, HENRY GILBERT,
PARKS' road, JONATHAN STEWART. Tract given by will of GEORGE COLEMAN
to WILLIAM, ROBERT H., REUBEN and LINDSEY COLEMAN. Witnesses:
WILLIAM LEE, WILLIAM PENN, EDMOND T. COLEMAN, WILLIAM MORAN.

3. September, 1811. JOSEPH BRADFIELD and wife, SARAH, Amherst
    County, to JONATHAN MOUNTCASTLE, Amherst County...$200.00
New Glasgow lot bought of CASPER POTTER, Ohio, and formerly that of
JONATHAN WILLS, SR., and sold by deed of trust to POTTOR--west side
Main Street. One line; north bylot of HENRY CAMDEN, and lands of
DAVID S. GARLAND. One half acre. West: JONATHAN MYERS, JAMES
GARLAND, CHARLES A. JACOBS.

4. 13 September 1811. ISAAC RUCKER, Amherst County, to WILEY
    CAMPBELL, Amherst County...L1100 400 acres where ISAAC RUCKER
lives--small corner sold to JACOB PIERCE. Lines: JOEL CAMPBELL,
ROCKEY RUN, NATHAN WINGFIELD, FREDERICK FULTZ, JACOB PIERCE, STOVALL's
old road, ISAIAH ATKISON. To WILEY CAMPBELL, 1 November 1811.

5. 16 September 1811. DAVID S. GARLAND and wife, JANE, Amherst
    County, to DABNEY HILL, Amherst County...L331-10 110½ acres both
sides Little Piney and part of a tract. Lines: JONATHAN CAMDEN,
JONATHAN FULCHER, deceased, WILLIAM S. CRAWFORD, WILLIAM MOORE,
JONATHAN CAMPBELL. To DABNEY HILL, 11 May 1812.

7. 9 May 1811. LEWIS MARTIN and wife, TABITHA, Amherst County,
    to WILLIAM MARTIN, JR...L200 115 acres north waters Thrasher's
Creek. Lines: AARON HIGGINBOTHAM, ZACHARIAH TALIAFERRO. Witnesses:
JONATHAN BALLARD, JONATHAN WHITHEAD, JONATHAN GOOLSBY.

9. 10 September 1811. JONATHAN DEFREES and wife, POLLY, Rockbridge,
    to WILLIAM CLARK, Amherst County...$165.00; no acres; south
borders Pedlar.

11. 20 February 1811. BARTLETT THOMPSON to WILLIAM G. ARMS...L500
    slaves: ELIJAH, ARMISTEAD, HANNAH, SALLY, and MARY. Witnesses:
JONATHAN P. COBBS, JONATHAN LONDON, STERLING CLAIBORNE. To JAMES
GARLAND, 31 December 1811.

12. 18 November 1811. ISABELLA and WILLIAM CLEMENTS, husband and
    wife--old and infirm...Power of Attorney to THOMAS CLEMENTS,
friend of Amherst County--to transact business in estate of JONATHAN
HILLARD, deceased, New Kent, in right of ISABELLA. Witnesses:
BARTLETT CLEMENTS, JAMES DODD, JONATHAN H. CLEMENTS. Signed
ELIZABETH CLEMENTS. Note: These first pages are very dimmed because
of poor ink and quite difficult to read.

13. 21 October, 1811. CALEB WATTS and wife, SUSANNAH, Amherst County,
    to WILLIAM TINSLEY, Amherst County...L130 52 acres Pedlar.
Lines: AMBROSE RUCKER, N. C. DAVIES, deceased. To WILLIAM TINSLEY
9 March 1812.

15. 21 October 1811. JONATHAN BALL and wife, ELIZABETH, Amherst
    County, to RICHARD SMITH, Amherst County...L200 no acres--
Stonehouse Creek. Lines: EDMOND WILLIAMSON, WILLIAM SALE, WILLIAM
CASH, BEVERLY WILLIAMSON, ENOCH CARPENTER. To RICHARD SMITH,
19 January 1818.

16. 6 August 1811. REUBEN COLEMAN and wife, BELINDA, Amherst
County, to JACOB PIERCE, JR., Amherst County...$1800.00. Two
tracts Franklin and Moll Creeks, borders of Buffaloe. 1. 146 acres
and by WILLIAM TALIAFERRO, deceased, of PHILIP SMITH and conveyed by
deed--no date given. 2. 154 acres. Lines: WILLIAM SANDIDGE,
MOLLY SMITH, first tract, DAVID CLARKSON. First tract conveyd to
REUBEN COLEMAN by JAMES TALIAFERRO and wife and second by CHARLES
and BENJAMIN TALIAFERRO, executors of WILLIAM TALIAFERRO. Witnesses:
HUDSON M. GARLAND, LINDSEY COLEMAN, WILLIAM HARRISON.

18. 11 September 1811. DANIEL CHEATWOOD, Amherst County, to his
children: SALLY W., LEVINIA P., HIRAM, SAMANTHY and ANALISA
CHEATWOOD. Consideration: property received from their deceased
mother--15 negroes named, and to be divided when the youngest child
is 21 or at my death. Will use profits--education. Witnesses:
WILLIAM B. GOOCH, WILL WOODROOF, MARY BISHOP. To WILLIAM B. GOOCH,
14 April 1812.

19. 10 October 1811. JONATHAN MARTIN, Amherst County, to ABRAHAM
MARTIN, Amherst County...L20 21 acres. Lines: Stump near
grantee's house, JAMES CALLAWAY, deceased, grantor. Witnesses:
BENJAMIN TALIAFERRO, JOSEPH and LEWIS MARTIN.

20. 11 September 1811. FRANCES GOOCH, Amherst County, to daughter,
ELIZABETH H. GOOCH...love and $1.00--slave, PETER--COURTNEY's
oldest child, bed and furniture. Witnesses: WILLIAM B. GOOCH, MARY
BISHOP, ELIZABETH WOODROOF. To WILLIAM B. GOOCH, 14 April 1812.

21. 11 September 1811. DANIEL CHEATWOOD, Amherst County, to
FRANCES GOOCH, Amherst County (margin as above as to delivery)...
marriage shortly intended between them, DANIEL relinquishes any claim
versus her property by former husband, PHILIP GOOCH, deceased--three
slaves and list of furniture, stock, and also interest in estate of
GEORGE DILLARD, deceased--reference to suit now pending in high court
of Chancery at Staunton. ELIZABETH may dispose of property without
interference by CHEATWOOD. ELIZABETH makes no claims on fifteen
slaves conveyed by CHEATWOOD to his children by his first wife.
Witnesses: WILL WOODROOF, MARY BISHOP, WILLIAM B. GOOCH.

22. 28 September 1811. JEREMIAH TAYLOR and wife, NANCY, Amherst
County, to JONATHAN M. WALKER, Buckingham...L400 258 acres
where JEREMIAH TAYLOR lives and surveyed 10 October 1804. Lines:
DRURY CHRISTIAN, JONATHAN CHRISTIAN, deceased, PHILIP GOOCH, JAMES
CHRISTIAN, deceased. Witnesses: ABNER CHRISTIAN, DRURY CHRISTIAN,
JAMES CHRISTIAN, SAMUEL GARLAND.

24. 19 August 1811. JONATHAN BALLARD and wife, NANCY, Amherst
County, to JONATHAN BALL, Amherst County...L75-9 125 acres and
3/4 Carter's Mill Creek. Lines: PEGGY GOOLSBY, JAMES FRANKLIN,
BARTLETT CASH. Witnesses: BARTLETT CASH, JESSE JONES, WILLIAM
TUCKER.

26. 16 September 1811. CHARLES P. TALIAFERRO and wife, LOUISA,
Amherst County, to BENJAMIN TALIAFERRO, Amherst County...L206-
10-½ 166½ acres both sides north borders Puppie Creek. Lines:
grantee, top of the hill north of TALIAFERRO's old store. Witnesses:
ANSELM CLARKSON, CHARLES TALIAFERRO, HENRY L. DAVIES, FLETCHER N.
TALIAFERRO, JONATHAN SMITH. To BENJAMIN TALIAFERRO, 22 September
1837.

28. 27 September 1811. WILLIAM HUGHES and wife, JANE, Amherst
County, to JAMES LEE, Amherst County...L126 Harris Creek--two
lots laid off for REUBEN and ARCHELAUS COX, legatees of ARCHELAUS
COX, deceased. Numbers 3 and 4--60 acres. Lines: JONATHAN MAHONE,
PETTIS THACKER, WARD. Witnesses: GEORGE POWELL, JONATHAN REYNOLDS.
Acknowledged by JANE, 15 February 1813.

29. 18 June 1811. Order to Amherst County Justices of the Peace
LEWIS DAWSON and wife, LUCY, 1 May 1809, to GEORGE M. TINSLEY.
Done by PHILIP JOHNSON and NELSON C. DAWSON, 3 July 1811.

31.   31 August 1811. MATTHEW WATSON and wife, ELISA, Rockingham,
      to DAVID S. GARLAND...L50 100 acres north side and joining
Buffaloe. MATTHEW WATSON got it by deed from WILLIAM TYREE. Lines:
JAMES HIGGINBOTHAM, JR., JESSE KENNEDY's heirs. Witnesses: WILKINS
WATSON, THOMAS ALDRIDGE, JONATHAN MYERS, JAMES G. PENDLETON, JAMES
GARLAND.

32.   24 October 1801 (sic). LEWIS H. GILLESPIE, JOSHUA GILLESPIE,
      GEORGE PETTIT, GEORGE GILLESPIE, HENDERSON THURMAN, GABRIEL
GILLESPIE, Kentucky, to DAVID S. GARLAND, Amherst County...$196.20--
interest in 490 acres on south side Piney and joining it. Property
of GEORGE GILLESPIE, The Elder, and grantors are heirs. Madison
County, Kentucky, 24 October 1810, certified by WILLIAM IRVIN, Clerk.
Recorded in Amherst County 21 October 1811. I have referred to this
deed before in writing of my wife, MILDRED MILLER DAVIS, as descendant
of HENDERSON THURMAN. He is one of my enigmas for I can't locate his
parents. These grantors are heirs of WILLIAM GILLESPIE, son of
GEORGE, The Elder, and WILLIAM married ANN HUDSON here on December 23,
1777. WILLIAM and wife went to Madison County, Kentucky, and WILLIAM
was killed in a duel--WINSTON COLEMAN's Kentucky Duels. HENDERSON
THURMAN married in Madison County, Kentucky, MARY GILLESPIE,
November 20, 1809, and she was daughter of WILLIAM and ANN (HUDSON)
GILLESPIE. ANN was daughter of JOSHUA HUDSON--note one son bears
name of JOSHUA. ANN left a will, April 1, 1837, in Madison County
and is styled NANCY GILLESPIE. She named only two children: MARY
THURMAN and LEWIS GILLESPIE. Consult will of later in Madison for
more complete picture on GILLESPIE heirs. Other heirs of GEORGE,
The Elder, remained in Amherst and made separate deed mentioning the
grave site of GEORGE. It is on farm of TAYLOR WRIGHT, deceased.

34.   21 October 1811. JESSE CLEMENTS and wife, ELIZABETH, Amherst
      County, to FRANCIS CLEMENTS, Amherst County...L100 123 acres
head borders Harris. Lines: AMBROSE RUCKER, WILLIAM CLEMENTS.
Witnesses: ABRAM CARTER, JONATHAN CRAWFORD, BERRY COLEMAN, JESSE
BLAND, WILLIAM CLEMENTS.

36.   7 April 1811. ISAAC SCOTT, Amherst County, first; JAMES
      GARLAND, second; DAVID S. GARLAND, third...Deed of Trust;
to DAVID GARLAND, 6 sh. 115 acres Indian Creek. SCOTT bought it of
JONATHAN KIDD and lives thereon. Lines: JONATHAN PENN, WILLIAM
LANGHORN. Witnesses: JONATHAN MYERS, DANIEL HIGGINBOTHAM, JONATHAN
LONDON. To DAVID S. GARLAND, 4 March 1812.

38.   4 November 1811. NICHOLAS HARRISON and wife, NANCY, Amherst
      County, to RICHARD POWELL, Amherst County...$2000.00 201 acres
where NICHOLAS HARRISON lives. Lines: JAMES HILL, RICHARD HARRISON,
REUBEN RUCKER, Lynch Road, JAMES PETIT, SUSANNAH GILLILAND, old field,
JAMES LIVELY. Witnesses: JAMES WARE, REUBEN PENDLETON, DABNEY WARE.
To RICHARD POWELL, 27 January 1812.

40.   21 November 1811. Agreement between SAMUEL P. CHRISTIAN,
      attorney for ELIZABETH BRAXTON, to WILLIAM LEE, Amherst County...
$500.00 in two payments--agreed to compromise suit in High Court of
Chancery, Richmond District: BRAXTON versus LEE's orphans, for
amount due ELIZABETH BRAXTON for said LEE and his sister, SOPHIA
HARRISON, formerly LEE, for ELIZABETH's dower in lands. Each to pay
own costs. Witnesses: JONATHAN WARWICK, JONATHAN PENN, JR., J. P.
GARLAND.

41.   30 August 1811. DAVID S. GARLAND to JONATHAN MAJORS...L43-5
      in trust for ELIZABECH TUCKER, wife of ISAAC TUCKER, and
children--slave bought by GARLAND some time past at Sheriff's sale.

42.   21 June 1811. HENRY BALLINGER to WILLIAM JOPLING...consideration--
      WILLIAM WARE and JONATHAN SMITH are his bondsmen to PETER CARTER's
executors for land bought--Deed of Trust--6 sh. Same tract bought.
425½ acres Horsley and where HENRY BALLINGER lives. Witnesses:
JOHN ROBERTS, JR., JONATHAN WARE, ORMUND WARE, MADISON WARE.

45. 16 December 1811. JAMES HIX, Amherst County, to JONATHAN
     SMITH, Amherst County...Deed of Trust; $1.00; debt to WASHINGTON
HILL--100 acres Buffaloe and Thrasher, except 1 3/4 acres sold by
JAMES HIX for neighborhood school. Lines: SAMUEL CASH, WILLIAM
SANDIDGE, down Buffaloe, JOHANNAH HIGGINBOTHAM, grantor, the road.

48. 16 December 1811. WASHINGTON HILL and wife, SALLY, Amherst
     County, to JAMES HIX, Amherst County...L250 100 acres north
side Buffaloe and lines as above--plus AMBROSE MC DANIEL. To JAMES
HIX, 25 January 1812.

50. 5 April 1803. RICE KEY and wife, SALLY, Amherst County, to
     SAMUEL HOGG, Amherst County...L70 193 acres both sides Pedlar.
Witnesses: JEREMIAH SHOEMAKER, WILLIAM SLEDD, PETER MARTIN, OBADIAH
MARTIN.

51. 25 July 1811. GEORGE POWELL and wife, SOPHIA, Amherst County,
     to WILLIAM HUGHES, Amherst County...L436-16 208 acres Harris.
Lines: Burrus br., tobacco ground. Witnesses: JAMES LEE, WILLIAM R.
COX, HOWSON HUGHES.

52. 6 August 1811. DANIEL BURFORD, Amherst County, to SHADRICK
     TENNISON, Amherst County...$222.00 55½ acres Harris Creek.
Lines: N. DAWSON. Witnesses: WILLIAM BURFORD, CHRISTOPHER GOCC,
AMBROSE BURFORD, LT. ROSE, H. D. MURRELL.

54. 4 October 1805. DANIEL BURFORD, JR. and wife, SALLY, Amherst
     County, to JONATHAN BURFORD, JR...L200 120 acres. Lines:
WILLIAM HUGHES, HIGGINBOTHAM, DAWSON, SHEP, MAHONE, grantor, DANIEL
NORCUTT. Witnesses: WILLIAM DAVENPORT, ROD. TALIAFERRO, JESSE
BECK. Final proof by ROD. TALIAFERRO, 16 December 1811.

56. 16 December 1811. CHARLES BURKS, SR., Amherst County, to
     WILLIAM PARKS, Kanawaha...$200.00 125 acres Cabbin Creek in
Kanawaha; lower end of 500 acres survey for ANDREW DONALLY and includes
FLYNN's Bottom place--end of mountain on west side of creek. Witnesses:
AMBROSE RUCKER, MARTIN PARKS, GEORGE BURKS. To WILLIAM PARKS per
order, 9 February 1814.

57. 11 July 1811. WHITAKER CARTER, Amherst County, to THOMAS
     WILLS, Amherst County...$4000.00 536 acres in Alb. on Moore's
Creek and north side CARTER's Mountain. Lines: WILLIAM DUNMORE,
JAMES MONROE, GILLIAM, BENAGH, GENTRY. Bought by WHITAKER CARTER of
WILLIAM HENING and also conveyed to HILL CARTER, Amherst County, by
WHITAKER CARTER and recorded in Alb. Witnesses: THOMAS ALDRIDGE,
HUDSON M. GARLAND, PEACHY FRANKLIN.

59. -- 1811. DANIEL BURFORD and wife, SARAH, Amherst County, to
     AMBROSE BURFORD, Amherst County...L66-3 53½ acres both sides
Harris Creek and part of tract from DANIEL's father by will. Lines:
NELSON C. DAWSON, DANIEL BURFORD, SR., mouth of Little Mill Creek,
grantee. Witnesses: SHADRICK TENNISON, JOSEPH DUNCAN, DANIEL
BURFORD, WILLIAM BURFORD.

62. 2 November 1811. HUDSON M. GARLAND, Amherst County, to DAVID S.
     GARLAND, Amherst County...Deed of Trust; debt to DAVID S. GARLAND,
JAMES GARLAND, and DANIEL HIGGINBOTHAM, late merchants of DANIEL
HIGGINBOTHAM and Company--$1.00--very interesting and long list of
furniture, law books, etc. Witnesses: JONATHAN HENDERSON, CHARLES A.
JACOBS, ROBERT COLEMAN, THOMAS ALDRIDGE, RICHARD HERNDON. To JONATHAN
LONDON, 1 February 1812.

66. 23 November 1811. SALLY BURFORD, widow of JONATHAN BURFORD, JR.,
     to JAMES STEWART, and RODERICK TALIAFERRO of firm of STEWART
and TALIAFERRO...her dower in two tracts adjoining. 1. 120 acres
conveyed from DANIEL BURFORD, JR. to JONATHAN BURFORD, JR. (sic).
2. 50 acres to JOHN BURFORD, JR., from DANIEL MEHONE--dower by court
order--lots of 175 and 58½ or 1/3 then mentioned--$100.00. Witnesses:
CHARLES TALIAFERRO, RICHARD WHITEHEAD, JONATHAN MERRITT, HUGH NORVELL,
J. WRIGHT.

69. 16 December 1811. ROBERT H. COLEMAN, Amherst County, to FREDERICK
      FULTZ, Amherst County...Power of Attorney to recover or receive
my claim to mill now in occupancy of MAJOR JAMES FRANKLIN. Witnesses:
REUBEN NORVELL, WILLIAM CAMDEN, JONATHAN N. ROSE.

69. 28 August 1800. JAMES WATSON, SR. and wife, PATTEY; JAMES
      WATSON, JR., and wife, ELIZABETH, Amherst County, to DANIEL
BURFORD, SR., Amherst County...L100 210 acres Buffaloe. Part of
tract of JAMES WATSON, SR. Lines: JAMES FRANKLIN, EZEKIEL GILBERT,
ROBERT HOLLOWAY, mouth of a branch. Witnesses: E. GILBERT, WILLIAM
BURFORD, MATTHEW WATSON. Memo by cash paid by order of BROCK and RUCKER
and DAVID GARLAND. Final proof by EZEKIEL GILBERT, 20 June 1812
(January?).

71. 12 February 1811. PETER MARTIN, Amherst County, to WILLIAM
      WILLMORE, Amherst County...L125-5-0 167 acres both sides Pedlar.
Lines: WILLIAM GRISSOM, HENRY CAMDEN, GARLAND, HAULL (sic), WILLIAM
GALT. North side and joining Pedlar. To WILLIAM WILLMORE, 15 June
1812.

73. 2 January 1812. ANN BARRET, Montgomery County, Tennessee, to
      her brother, JAMES BARRET, to sell Louisa County, Virginia,
lands--from father, THOMAS BARRET, and to settle with administrators
of my aunt, NANCY BARRET. JONATHAN H. PORTON (?) and JAMES HAMBLETON,
J.P.'s, WILLIAM C. JAMISON, Clerk, 4 January 1812. Recorded in Amherst
County, 17 February 1812. To C. L. BARRET, 1 August 1812.

74. 2 January 1812. HUGH CAMPBELL and wife, ELIZABETH, Montgomery
      County, Tennessee...power to JAMES BARRET to transact business,
but no family data set forth. Same officials as above. HUGH
CAMPBELL married ELIZABETH BARRET, widow, in Amherst County.

77. 4 February 1812. HUGH CAMPBELL and wife, ELIZABETH, as above,
      to CALEB RALLS, Amherst County...$500.00 390 acres north
borders south fork Buffaloe. Lines: LEONARD BALLOW. By attorney
JAMES BARRET. Witnesses: A. B. DAVIES, HENRY L. DAVIES, CHARLES L.
BARRET, ROBERT COLEMAN. To CALEB RALLS, 12 March 1812.

78. 11 February 1812. JAMES BARRET, to CHARLES L. BARRET, Amherst
      County...to empower him to sell LOUISA lands under power of
attorney from my sister, ANN BARRET. Witnesses: A. B. DAVIES,
HENRY L. DAVIES, JONATHAN M. STEWART.

79. 1 February 1812. CHARLES LANDON CARTER and MARY RANDOLPH CARTER
      in name of heirs of JONATHAN CHISWELL, Spotsylvania, to THOMAS
WINGFIELD, Amherst County...$300.00 for 150 acres north side Buffaloe
Ridge and Rockey Run and Mine(?) Border. Lines: top of Buffaloe
Ridge, DAVID S. GARLAND, NATHAN WINGFIELD, deceased: PADGETT.
Witnesses: J. P. GARLAND, JONATHAN COLEMAN, W. H. WINGFIELD, CHARLES L.
CHRISTIAN. Note: many other heirs show in deed book N which I am now
abstracting in my spare time.

82. 15 February 1812. CHARLES R. ROSE to WILLIAM STERLING CLAIBORNE
      and CHARLES BULLER CLAIBORNE...L480 Piney--part of my father,
CHARLES ROSE, tract and by will to me. Lines: THOMAS and STERLING
CLAIBORNE, Rockey Run, WILLIAM MOSS' legatees, ford on Piney, THOMAS
ALDRIDGE, the road.

83. 16 September 1811. LUCY ROBINSON, Amherst County, to LORENZO
      DOW, Connecticut...$73.00 14 3/r acres Stovall Creek. Lines:
WILLIAM and PHILIP JOHNSON, road opposite old school house. Witnesses:
WILLIAM ROBINSON, J. W. WILLIAMS, AARON SCHOOLFIELD.

85. 4 January 1812. THOMAS STEWART, Lynchburg, to RODERICK TALIAFERRO,
      same town...JONATHAN BURFORD, JR., Amherst County, in life,
4 October 1805, executed Dedd of Trust to THOMAS STEWART--debt to
STEWART and TALIAFERRO, merchants in said town--$1.00 for two adjoining
tracts in Amherst County--120 acres conveydd that day by DANIEL
BURFORD, JR., to JONATHAN BURFORD, JR., other tract of 50 acres to

51

JONATHAN BURFORD, JR., by DANIEL MEHONE--170 acres in all and where
JONATHAN BURFORD, JR., lived. JONATHAN BURFORD, JR., died in default
and advertised, 21 December 1811, to sell at tavern door of CHARLES
HOYLE, Lynchburg. ROD. TALIAFERRO was highest bidder at $700.00.
Witnesses: A. RUCKER, HOWSON HUGHES, AMBROSE BURFORD.

88. 21 November 1811. LEWIS DAWSON and wife, LUCY, Amherst County,
     to JAMES WADE, Lynchburg...$200.00 25 acres on road to Trent's
ferry. Lines: REUBEN PENDLETON, GEORGE M. TINSLEY, the road, grantor.
Witnesses: JAMES LEE, REUBEN PENDLETON, EDWARD TINSLEY. To JAMES
WADE, 15 March 1813.

89. 29 October 1811. JONATHAN COX, Campbell County, to GEORGE
     POWELL, Amherst County...L300 135 acres John's Creek. Lines:
the road, REUBEN PENDLETON, JAMES WILLS, JAMES TINSLEY's spring
branch, JONATHAN CAMM. Witnesses: NICHOLAS HARRISON, FRANCIS HILL,
JOSEPH HAWKINS, T. NOEL.

91. 10 February 1812. JONATHAN LOVING and wife, ELIZABETH, Nelson
     County, to WILLIAM STAPLES, Buckingham County...L1300 289½ acres
on James at mouth of Porrage Creek. Lines: JAMES DILLARD, SAMUEL
TURNER. Witnesses: JOSEPH LOVING, W. H. DIGGS, STEPHEN WATTS,
JONATHAN DILLARD, CHARLES L. CHRISTIAN. P. 92--order to Nelson
County Justices of the Peace to quiz ELIZABETH. 14 February 1812.
Done by JONATHAN DILLARD and W. H. DIGGS, February, 1812; recorded
17 February 1812. To W. S. CREWS, per order, 25 April 1812.

94. 17 February 1812. JOSEPH and BENJAMIN HIGGINBOTHAM, executors
     of JOSEPH HIGGINBOTHAM, Amherst County, to WILLIAM TOMLINSON,
Amherst County...L68-17 102 acres. Lines: ABRAHAM MARTIN, grantee,
the river, PHILIP WALKER, a branch. Witnesses: G. SANDS, ANGUS
MC CLOUD, JAMES HIX.

96. 17 February 1812. BENJAMIN HIGGINBOTHAM, Amherst County, to
     BENJAMIN SANDIDGE, Amherst County...L750 100 acres both sides
Suck (?) branch. Lines: ridge road.

97. 14 February 1812. PETER PIERCE and wife, SARAH, Amherst County,
     to BENJAMIN BURROUGHS, Amherst County...L112 100 acres Rockey
Run. Lines: DAVID S. GARLAND, west side Buffaloe, NATHAN WINGFIELD,
deceased, CHRISTIAN, BROWN. All of tract bought by PETER PIERCE from
JONATHAN A. JOHNS and his late dwelling place at present occupied by
THOMAS WINGFIELD. Witnesses: CHARLES CHRISTIAN, WILLIAM GRANT,
BARNET PAGE. To BENJAMIN BURROUGHS, 8 May, 1813.

99. 10 December 1811. THOMAS T. MAYO, Amherst County, first;
     WILLIAM RADFORD, Lynchburg, second; and JONATHAN BULLOCK,
Lynchburg, third...Deed of Trust; debt due BULLOCK. $1.00 600 acres
James River. Lines: WILLIAM GALT, WILLIAM SPENCER. Witnesses:
GEORGE CABELL, PHILL JOHNSON, NICHOLAS HARRISON, THOMAS S. MC CLELLAND.

101. 12 February 1812. STERLING CLAIBORNE, Amherst County, to sons,
      WILLIAM STERLING and CHARLES BULLER CLAIBORNE...love and $1.00--
1200 acres Geddes tract bought by me of GUSTAVUS ROSE, THOMAS ALDRIDGE,
ANDERSON MOSS, NORVELL SPENCER, JONATHAN MARR, and CHARLES R. ROSE.
Lines: road leading from Bellievett from the ford at present used on
Piney, as road meanders around foot of Geddes Mountain, NORVELL SPENCER's
blacksmith shop on main road where the same crosses Naked Creek,
road to New Glasgow, tract allotted EMILY ROSE on division of HUGH
ROSE's estate, JAMES FRANKLIN, THOMAS LANDRUM, PATRICK ROSE, WILLIAM
MOSS' estate, to Piney River.

103. 12 December 1811. RICHARD HERNDON, first; PEACHY FRANKLIN,
      second; DAVID S. GARLAND, third...Deed of Trust; debt to GARLAND;
$1.00--bay horse nine years old. Witnesses: JONATHAN N. ROSE,
ANDERSON MOSS, JONATHAN P. COBBS.

104. 2 November 1811. Order to Amherst County Justices of the Peace:
      ISAAC RUCKER and wife, MARY ANN, 13 September 1811, to WILEY
CAMPBELL...400 acres. Done by JAMES DILLARD and CHARLES MUNDY, 7 March
1812.

105. 27 January 1812. Order to THOMAS W. COCKE, JONATHAN W. BRADLEY, and SAMUEL SCOTT, Campbell County, Justices of the Peace: NICHOLAS HARRISON and wife, NANCY, 4 November 1811, to RICHARD POWELL... 201 acres. Done by first two named above, 27 February 1812. Recorded in Amherst County 16 March 1812.

107. 25 August 1810. THOMAS ALDRIDGE and wife, CATHERINE, Amherst County, to STERLING CLAIBORNE, Amherst County...L960 320 acres Naked Creek. 180 acres of it formerly that of EMILY ROSE and balance that of PAULINA ROSE. Witnesses: MICAJAH CAMDEN, JONATHAN COLEMAN, JOSEPH SWANSON.

108. 25 August 1810. ANDERSON MOSS and wife, LUCY, to STERLING CLAIBORNE, Amherst County...$800 92 acres Naked Creek whereon ANDERSON MOSS lives. Witnesses: THOMPSON NOEL, REUBEN COLEMAN, JONATHAN SAVAGE, JR.

109. 16 March 1812. JAMES MARTIN and wife, ANNE, Amherst County, to JONATHAN ROBINSON, Rockbridge...7 sh. 105 acres top of South Mountain. Lines: near a road, a branch Del. to Buffaloe, 9 September 1847.

111. 16 March 1812. ALEXANDER PENN and wife, NANCY, Amherst County, to JONATHAN PENN, JR., Amherst County...$65.50 11 acres. Lines: Indian Creek road, JONATHAN PENN, SR. and JR., Spring branch, the great road, fork of the road.

112. 20 December 1811. JONATHAN and RICHARD L. ELLIS, Amherst County, to JAMES WARE, Amherst County...$600 332 acres Fluvanna River. Lines: JONATHAN BYAS, WILLIAM NOEL, near the road, THOMAS N. EUBANK, THOMAS HIGGINBOTHAM, ROBERT KNUCKLES, CORNELIUS ROACH, SAMUEL NIECLEY. To D. WARE, 18 August 1812.

114. 26 February 1812. Order to Amherst County Justices of the Peace: HENRY BALLINGER and wife, POLLY, 21 September 1807, to JONATHAN CLEMENTS and JAMES DODD. Done 29 February 1812, by CHARLES and BENJAMIN TALIAFERRO.

115. 22 December 1810. PHILIP THURMOND, Amherst County, to THOMAS N. EUBANK, Amherst County, second and JONATHAN RICHESON, third. THURMOND qualified as administrator of will of PHILIP THURMOND and RICHESON was bondsman to Amherst County Justices of the Peace: DAVID S. GARLAND, JAMES DILLARD, NELSON C. DAWSON and WILLIAM ARMISTEAD, 23 August 1810. Also THURMOND has bought four hogsheads of tobacco from JESSE and JONATHAN RICHESON. Deed of Trust--$1.00 paid by EUBANK-- eight named slaves; stock; furniture; "farming tools." Witnesses: WILLIS GILLESPIE, DANIEL TAYLOR, THOMAS RICHESON, CHARLES DAVIS, PETER RUCKER. Final proof by EUBANK, 16 March 1812.

120. 17 January 1812. THOMAS REID, Kentucky, attorney-in-fact for WILLSON and SUSANNA GILLESPIE, Kentucky, to DAVID S. GARLAND, Amherst County...L14-16-4 2/9 interest in 400 acres on Piney; tract of GEORGE GILLESPIE, deceased, The Elder, and descended to the children of said GEORGE WILLIAM GILLESPIE, son of GEORGE, died and left nine children prior to death of GOERGE WILSON and SUSANNA are two of WILLIAMS's children. Witnesses: JAMES L. PENDLETON, JAMES GARLAND, THOMAS ALDRIDGE.

122. 14 December 1811. WILLIAM LAVENDER, Nelson County, to THOMAS ALDRIDGE, Amherst County...Deed of Trust; debt due DAVID S. and JAMES GARLAND. 6 sh. stock and furniture and interest in lifetime estate of mother, MILDRED WALTON. Witnesses: ROBERT COLEMAN, JONATHAN CAMM, JAMES S. PENDLETON, JOSEPH KENNEDY.

124.   2 March 1812.   WILLIAM BRYANT, Amherst County, to JACOB SCOTT,
       Amherst County...$910.00 130 acres south side Buffaloe and
northwest side BRAXTON's ridge and bought of MAJOR JAMES FRANKLIN
and LEONARD CLARK.   Lines: CHARLES HIGGINBOTHAM, BARNETT OWEN,
JAMES GARLAND, BRAXTON's old line, WILLIAM C. CHRISTIAN, ALEXANDER
BRIDY, deceased.   Witnesses: CHARLES CHRISTIAN, FLEMING SCOTT,
MEREDITH PARISH.   To JACOB SCOTT, 18 December 1815.

127.   28 July 1810.   JONATHAN MARR and wife, SARAH, Nelson County, to
       STERLING CLAIBORNE, Amherst County...L600 212 acres Naked Creek.
Lines: WILLIAM MOSS.   Bought by JONATHAN MARR of LANDON CABELL.
Witnesses: THOMAS LANDRUM, THOMAS ALDRIDGE, DAVID S. GARLAND.

128.   21 July 1803.   LITTLEBERRY TUCKER, Amherst County, to DAVID
       and JAMES GARLAND, Amherst County...L33-6-8--undivided interest
in estate of DRURY TUCKER, deceased, father of LITTLEBERRY TUCKER.
On Buffaloe.   Witnesses: MATTHEW TUCKER, SHEROD BUGG, THOMAS ALDRIDGE.
Final proof 20 April 1812, but witnesses not named.   However,
SHEROD BUGG and THOMAS ALDRIDGE, proved in on 19 September 1803.

129.   6 February 1812.   THOMAS HUMPHREY and wife, MARY, Campbell
       County, to JONATHAN BOWLING, Amherst County...$1.00 83 acres on
road from Lynchburg by Lynch's ferry to New Glasgow and about 6½ miles
from Madison.   Lines: ROBERT CAMPBELL on east side of Lynch road,
ABEL BLANKENSHIP and WILLIAM DAMERON on north, BENJAMIN RUCKER on
west, DANIEL BURFORD, JR., on south JONATHAN BOWLING did not but it,
but has lived there for years.   THOMAS HUMPHREY does not warrant
title.   Witnesses: G. (?) WRIGHT, JACOB HAAS, WILLIAM I. ISBELL,
W. ROBINSON.

133.   6 February 1812.   THOMAS JOHNSON, late of Lynch's Ferry,
       bought of THOMAS HUMPHREY, Lynchburg, 8 February 1796, same
tract above...83 acres.   Lines: as above.   Sold by me to DANIEL BURFORD,
JR., and by him sold to REUBEN RUCKER, and by him sold to JONATHAN
BOWLING--did not receive conveyance from THOMAS HUMPHREY before last
sale and now authorize THOMAS HUMPHREY to convey to BOWLING.   Final
proof by HAAS, 20 April 1812.

134.   18 April 1812.   JACOB PEARCE, JR., and wife, ELIZABETH, Amherst
       County, to JAMES HUCKSTEP, Amherst County...L320-2 194 acres.
Lines: BENJAMIN RUCKER, deceased, BENJAMIN MILES, GAINES' road.

135.   4 October 1810.   Order to Bedford Justices of the Peace:
       AMBROSE RUCKER and wife, ELIZABETH, to BRANSFORD HICKS,
9 April 1810...174 acres.   Done, 16 March 1812, by WILLIAM HOPKINS
and WILLIAM DICKINSON.   To BRANSFORD HICKS, 6 November 1819.

137.   15 February 1812.   JAMES FRANKLIN and wife, NANCY, Amherst
       County, to WILLIAM BRIANT, Amherst County...L100 64 acres
Rutledge Creek.   Part of BRAXTON's old survey and all that JAMES
FRANKLIN bought of BRAXTON.   Lines: northwest of BRAXTON's ridge,
CHARLES HIGGINBOTHAM, WILLIAM C. CHRISTIAN, ALEXANDER BRYDIE, deceased,
a branch.   Witnesses: CHARLES CHRISTIAN.

139.   27 March 1812.   ISAAC TUCKER, Amherst County, to BURCHER
       WHITEHEAD, Amherst County...Deed of Trust; debt to REUBEN
COLEMAN; $1.00; stock and furniture.   Witnesses: JAMES LAYNE,
FRANCIS PAGE, WILLIAM HUTCHINSON, JAMES FRANKLIN, JR., EDMOND LANIER.

141.   18 May 1812.   JONATHAN WARE and wife, ELIZABETH, Amherst County,
       to JESSE RICHESON, Amherst County...L990 600 acres both sides
Pedlar.   To JONATHAN WARE, no date.

144.   31 March 1812.   THOMAS BADDOW, Amherst County, to JONATHAN
       LONDON...Deed of Trust; debt to WILLIAM TURNER, $1.00, stock
and furniture.   Witnesses: THOMAS T. MAYO, PLEASANT STORY, ROBERT
GRANT.

145.   15 April 1812.   WILLIAM PENN, Amherst County, to JONATHAN
       PENN, JR., Amherst County...Deed of Trust; debt to JONATHAN
PENN, SR., as bondsman to COLONEL JOSEPH BURRUS on judgement; $1.00
476 acres which WILLIAM PENN bought of JOSEPH BURRUS.   Lines: ROBERT
COLEMAN, JONATHAN PENN, SR. and JR.; also slaves and stock, etc.   Also
slaves of ROBERT PENN, son of WILLIAM PENN until ROBERT IS 21--they
were willed to POLLY FURBUSH by her father, WILLIAM FURBUSH, and at
her death to her heirs and ROBERT PENN "is the Air", and son of
WILLIAM.   Witnesses: THOMPSON NOEL, BENNETT CRAWFORD, JONATHAN
LAWHORN.   To JONATHAN PENN, 18 November 1812.

149.   2 June 1812.   REUBEN COLEMAN and wife, BELINDA, Amherst County,
       to JAMES WHITEHEAD, Pittsylvanie...L90 3 acres.   Lines: grantor
and his spring branch.   Witnesses: PETER MARKHAM, RICHARD WHITEHEAD,
JONATHAN LACKEY, HENRY CAMDEN.

151.   26 February 1812.   JONATHAN CLEMENTS and wife, POLLY; JAMES DODD
       and wife, IBY, Amherst County, to LEONARD HENLEY, acting executor
of JOSEPH CHILDRESS, deceased, Amherst County...agreed in lifetime of
JOSEPH CHILDRESS that grantors would convey 140 acres.   JONATHAN
CLEMENTS left will in Amherst County directing that said tract be
sold--$1.00 for 140 acres whereon JONATHAN CLEMENTS lives--bought
from HENRY BALLINGER by CLEMENTS and JAMES DODD.   Witnesses: BENJAMIN
TALIAFERRO, JOSEPH DODD, EDMOND T. COLEMAN.   Page 154 order to
Amherst County Justices of the Peace, 27 February 1812, to quiz
wives above.   Done same date by BENJAMIN TALIAFERRO and EDMOND T.
COLEMAN.

156.   27 October 1811.   JONATHAN TAYLOR and wife, NANCY, Amherst
       County, to RICHARD HARTLESS, Amherst County...L24 42 acres;
patent to LARKIN SANDIDGE, 1794, both sides Piney Mountain between
Buffaloe and Horsley.   Witnesses: JONATHAN WARE, JONATHAN FLOID,
THOMAS TAYLOR, HENRY HARTLESS, RICHARD HATTEN.

158.   10 June 1812.   PHILIP SMITH, Amherst County, to MOLLY SMITH,
       Amherst County...L390 250 acres Franklin Creek.   Lines:
ZACHARIAH TALIAFERRO, main road, WILLIAM SANDIDGE, WILLIAM TALIAFERRO.
Sent to MARY SMITH by PHILIP SMITH, 26 January 1828.

160.   3 January 1811.   JONATHAN CLARKSON, Franklin County, and
       ANSELM CLARKSON, Amherst County to PHILIP SMITH, Amherst
County...L390 250 acres both sides Franklin Creek.   Part of tract of
JONATHAN CLARKSON.   Lines: as above.   Witnesses: DAVID CLARKSON,
RICHARD BALLINGER, HENRY F. SMITH.   It is noted that "wife" consented
in open court, 11 August 1812, but she is not named.

162.   15 June 1812.   JACOB PIERCE, JR., and wife, ---, Amherst County,
       to JONATHAN HENDREN, Nelson County...L400 166 acres south side
PARKS' road and both sides BRAXTON ridge.   Adjoins grantor, ALEXANDER
BRYDIE, deceased, CHARLES H. CHRISTIAN, WALTER C. CHRISTIAN.

164.   22 February 1812.   EDWARD WATSON and wife, ANN, Amherst County,
       to RICHARD RUCKER, Amherst County...L300 99 acres Main Road to
Lynchburg and Harris Creek borders.   Lines: DANIEL NORCUTT.   Witnesses:
JONATHAN LACKEY, WILKINS WATSON, POLLY LACKEY, JAMES MARR (?).   To
RICHARD RUCKER, 27 September 1813.

166.   15 June 1812.   JOSEPH HIGGINBOTHAM, Amherst County, to PHILIP
       SMITH, Amherst County...L500 210 acres.   Lines: BENJAMIN
SANDIDGE, Swapping Creek Road, WILLIAM DENNY, GODFREY TOLER, WALKER
ADKISSON, grantor, a branch.   Witnesses: DUDLEY SANDIDGE, C. P.
TALIAFERRO, WILLIAM SANDIDGE, JESSE JONES, WILLIAM TOMLINSON, BENJAMIN
HIGGINBOTHAM.   To PHILIP SMITH, 17 August 1813.

168. 1 February 1812. CHARLES LANDON CARTER and MARY RANDOLPH CATER,
      heirs of JONATHAN CHISWELL, Spotsylvania, to REUBEN PADGETT,
Amherst County...in name of heirs--$437.50 175 acres north side
Buffaloe ridge, Mine Branch, and Rockey Run. Lines: top of
Buffaloe ridge, PHILIP GOOCH, deceased, grantee, NATHAN WINGFIELD,
deceased. Witnesses: J. P. GARLAND, CHARLES L. CHRISTIAN, WILLIAM H.
WINGFIELD, THOMAS WINGFIELD. I have noted that many more heirs show
in the next deed book. I am of opinion that CHISWELL is called of
Williamsburg and not of Spotsylvania in these deeds. They also sell
land in Pitsylvania in these deeds.

172. 1 May 1812. JONATHAN LOVING and wife, ELIZABETH (late SPENCER
      and child of WILLIAM SPENCER), Nelson County, to WILLIAM STAPLES,
Buckingham County...L1300 289½ acres on James at mouth of Perrage
Creek. Lines: JAMES DILLARD, SAMUEL TURNER, ELIZABETH's share in
division of WILLIAM SPENCER's estate. Witnesses: JONATHAN DILLARD,
STEPHEN WATTS, ALLEN BLAIR, JAMES CHRISTIAN, BENJAMIN WATTS, JAMES
SPENCER. Memo: previously recorded, but by oversight ELIZABETH only
conveyed dower. This is marginal note by clerk.

174. 2 April 1812. JOSEPH HIGGINBOTHAM, Amherst County, to HENRY
      BROWN and JAMES DAVIS, Amherst County...$1.00 1 acre south side
MIGGINSON's Road. Lines: SARAH MONROE, whereon the Baptist Meeting
House now stands and to be open to other groups when not used by
Baptists. Witnesses: GIDEON C. GOODRICH, WILEY CAMPBELL, JOSEPH
BURROUGHS. Note: this one throws me since I am not sure just what
Baptist church is meant. I hope to run down this tract when time
permits. EBENEZER and MT. MORIAH are old sites and latter is now
merged with Central. Ebenezer goes back to about 1771, but records
are lost. I have not had time to pursue this matter in an effort to
identify the church.

175. 2 March 1812. JONATHAN GILLIAM and wife, MARY, Amherst County,
      to JONATHAN ELLIS, Amherst County...$225.00 45 acres. Lines:
grantee, CHARLES BURKS, ARCHY GILLIAM. Witnesses: ABRAM CARTER,
JONATHAN RICHESON, THOMAS LAIN, RICHARD EUBANK.

178. Order to Amherst County Justices of the Peace to quiz MARY
      GILLIAM on 2 March 1812, and done the next day by NATHANIEL J.
MANSON and BENJAMIN SHACKELFORD.

180. 13 June 1812. WILLIAM SCOTT and wife, ANN, Campbell County,
      to WILLIAM PETTYJOHN, Amherst County...L750 303 3/8 acres both
sides Harris at mouth of James River. Bought by SCOTT of JONATHAN
LYNCH and residue of SCOTT's adjoining "the 300 acres." Lines:
mouth of Pole Cat branch, CARRINGTON's former line, THACKER, WARD.
Witnesses: REUBEN NORVELL, RICHARD WHITEHEAD, JAMES LEE.

182. 21 November 1811. LEWIS DAWSON and wife, ---, to RICHARD
      WHITEHEAD, Amherst County...L200 106 acres on road to TRENT's
ferry. Lines: north side Harris Creek. Witnesses: REUBEN PENDLETON,
JAMES LEE, EDWARD TINSLEY. To RICHARD WHITEHEAD, 19 October 1812.

183. 10 February 1812. PETER WATERFIELD and wife, MILLY, Amherst
      County, to CHARLES P. TALIAFERRO, Amherst County...$400.00
502½ acres Buffaloe. Lines: JOSEPH HIGGINBOTHAM, WILLIAM CARTER.
Witnesses: WILLIAM JOPLING, CHARLES TALIAFERRO, HENRY BALLINGER.
Page 185 order to quiz MILLY and done, 10 February 1812, by CHARLES
TALIAFERRO and WILLIAM JOPLING.

187. 6 December 1811. DANIEL SNODDY, Amherst County, to ARMISTEAD
      RUCKER, Amherst County...Deed of Trust; debt to RICHARD BURKS,
Amherst County. Four notes--L7 57 acres. Lines: MARTIN PARKS, top
of Tobacco Row Mountain, ARTHUR L. DAVIES, HOUCHINS, RICHARD L. ELLIS.
Witnesses: THOMAS POWELL, MICAJAH GOODWIN, THOMAS TINSLEY, WILLIAM
WHITE, JONATHAN CRAWFORD.

191. 17 February 1812. JAMES LUCAS and wife, NANCY, Amherst County,
      to THOMAS COPPEDGE, Amherst County...$500 200 acres in Hardin
County, Kentucky, formerly Green, mouth of Panther Creek. Surveyed
by RICHARD BARBOUR for SANNEY (?) HENDERSON, formerly of Orange
County, Virginia. This phase is difficult: "Adjoining a survey made
by the said BARBOUR NANNCY man" (?), for 1000 acres. Witnesses:
JONATHAN LACKEY, RICHARD TANKERSLEY, JONATHAN OGDON, JONATHAN HUDSON,
SR. To THOMAS COPPEDGE, 10 May 1820.

193. 14 February 1800. Received of JOSEPH HIGGINBOTHAM my freedom
      and all other things I was to have. Signed by THORNTON PETERS.
Witnesses: JAMES S. HIGGINBOTHAM and FRANCES HIGGINBOTHAM. Acknowledged in open court, 15 June 1812.

193. 28 February 1812. EDWARD TAYLOR and wife, OZILAR, Amherst
      County, to THOMAS and GEORGE TAYLOR, Amherst County...L40 100
acres Horsley and borders Buffaloe. Witnesses: ABRAM CARTER, NELSON
CRAWFORD, JOSEPH MILSTEAD.

195. 22 October 1811. JOSEPH DILLARD, Amherst County, to EDWARD H.
      CARTER, Nelson County...$30.00 58 acres both sides north fork
Buffaloe; formerly that of JONATHAN LACKEY. Lines: JACOB PHILLIPS,
HENRY BALLINGER, ZACHARIAH TALIAFERRO. Witnesses: JONATHAN J.
DILLARD, HENRY H. WATTS, JOSEPH SWANSON. To EDWARD CARTER, 13 November
1827.

197. 15 June 1812. JESSE MULLICAN and wife, ANN, Nelson to PEYTON
      KEITH, Amherst County...L150 150 acres both sides Raven Creek;
north border Buffaloe. Lines: WILLIAM CABELL at Rolling Road,
NICHOLAS CABELL's old survey. Bought by JESSE MULLICAN of THOMAS
TRIPLETT (Note: MULLICAN is indexed MILLIKEN here). Witnesses:
REUBEN BATES, YOUNG HAWKINS, JAMES GREGORY, A. B. WARWICK, WILLIAM H.
DIGGS. To PEYTON KEITH, 26 June 1812. Note: the old rolling roads
were those upon which tobacco was rolled in hogsheads to the nearest
water outlet for shipment.

200. 4 April 1812. CHARLES CHRISTIAN, SR., Amherst County, to HENRY
      CHRISTIAN, Amherst County...L100 750 acres Porrige Creek.
Lines: EDLOE. Witnesses: WILLIAM CLINKSCALES, WILLIAM HARRISON,
JAMES LONDON, JR. To HENRY CHRISTIAN, 17 November 1814.

201. 27 October 1811. ROBERT COLEMAN, Amherst County, to WILLIAM A.
      HARRIS, Albemarle County...$40.00 1.400 acres partly in counties
of Amherst and Nelson--south borders Buffaloe and north side of
Buffaloe Ridge. Lines: JONATHAN NICHOLAS, deceased. 2. 329 acres
adjoining and in Amherst. Lines: Harris Road, JONATHAN NICHOLAS,
deceased. Bequeathed by will of LINDSEY COLEMAN, father of ROBERT
COLEMAN. Witnesses: JONATHAN MOSS, HENRY HARRIS, JONATHAN CAMM,
ROBERT GARLAND. To WILLIAM A. HARRIS, 20 June 1824.

203. 20 March 1811. HARRISON HUGHES, Amherst County, to WILLIAM
      RADFORD, Lynchburg, and JONATHAN MURRELL, Lynchburg...Deed of
Trust; debt to WILLIAM BROWN and Company, Lynchburg, and BROWN and
ROBERTSON--$1.00 160 acres Harris Creek and hereon is home of HUGHES.
Lines: GEORGE POWELL, WILLIAM HUGHES, PLEASANT DAWSON, AMBROSE
BURFORD. Witnesses: SAMUEL GARLAND, CHARLES A. JACOBS, ALFRED
MC DANIEL, WILLIAM BLACK.

206. 21 December 1811. EDWARD WATSON, Amherst County, and wife,
      ANN, to CHARLES WINGFIELD, Amherst County...L315 135 acres.
Lines: DANIEL NORCUTT at Lynch Road, MICAJAH CLARKE, BOWLER CLARKE,
Spring branch, fork of TINSLEY's Road. Witnesses: A. B. DAVIES,
WILKINS WATSON, WILLIAM JOYNER. To CHARLES WINGFIELD, 15 March 1821.

207. 27 September 1811. CALEB WATTS, Amherst County, to WILLIAM
      RADFORD and JONATHAN MURRELL, Lynchburg...Deed of Trust; debt to
BROWN and ROBERTSON--$1.00; six named slaves and ages. Witnesses:
S. GARLAND, JONATHAN HORSLEY, JR., ALFRED MC DANIEL, D. WOODROOF, JR.,
SAMUEL GARLAND, agent for firm to whom debt is due.

210. 22 April 1812. BENJAMIN WATTS, Amherst County, to WILLIAM
      RADFORD and JONATHAN MURRELL, Lynchburg...Deed of Trust; debt
to late firm of WILLIAM BROWN and Company, Lynchburg; debt to
ARCHIBALD ROBERTSON, surviving partner of firm of BROWN and ROBERTSON--
and ARCHIBALD ROBERTSON and Comapny, Lynchburg. $1.00. Seven slaves
with ages and names. Witnesses: S. GARLAND, JONATHAN HORSLEY, JR.,
LODOWICH MC DANIEL, WILLIAM BLACK.

212. 24 July 1811. SAMUEL COLEMAN, Amherst County, to same grantees
      as above...Deed of Trust for debt to BROWN and ROBERTSON,
Lynchburg; $1.00 slaves--mother, MARIA, about 18 and child, PLEASANT.
Witnesses: S. GARLAND, CHARLES A. JACOBS, WILLIAM BLACK.

214. 20 July 1812. THOMAS N. EUBANK, Amherst County, to JONATHAN P.
      SWINNEY, Amherst County...$50.00 100 acres Tarripin Creek;
border of Fluvanna. Lines: MOSES RUCKER, RICHARD TINSLEY, BERRY
BRYANT. Reference to Deed of Trust to THOMAS N. EUBANK, 22 September
1806, by LEWIS BRYANT on debt to JONATHAN and RICHARD L. ELLIS--
defaulted.

215. 20 July 1812. JABEZ CAMDEN and wife, NANCY, Amherst County,
      to HENRY CAMDEN, Amherst County...L300 232½ acres. Witnesses:
JONATHAN PENN, JR., JONATHAN LACKEY, WILLIAM STINNETT, JONATHAN P.
ASHLEY.

217. 20 July 1812. WILLIAM C. CHRISTIAN, Amherst County, to CHARLES
      TALIAFERRO, DAVID S. GARLAND, JAMES DILLARD, WILLIAM WARE,
PHILIP JOHNSON, PLEASANT DAWSON, WILLIAM JOPLING, BENJAMIN SHACKELFORD,
EDMOND T. COLEMAN, NATHANIEL J. MANSON, CHARLES MUNDY, EDMOND WINSTON,
HILL CARTER, JAMES M. BROWN, JONATHAN WARWICK, EDMOND PENN, JAMES
FRANKLIN, BENJAMIN TALIAFERRO, JONATHAN N. ROSE, JONATHAN ELLIS,
THOMAS N. EUBANK, THOMAS CREWS, JONATHAN COLEMAN, REUBIN NORVELL and
THOMAS MOORE, Acting Justices of the Peace of Amherst County...$670.00
135 acres south border Buffaloe. Lines: JAMES GARLAND, near path
to STOVAL's old road, the raod, JACOB PEARCE, ALEXANDER BRYDIE,
JACOB SCOTT, WEST's old road--except one acre where CHRISTIAN's
Meeting House stands. This is also a puzzle to me. I know of no
such meeting house in present Amherst. I am likewise baffled as to
location of this tract, but have an idea that it may be the WILLIAM
BAILEY tract. This was delivered to WILLIAM DILLARD, 16 August 1847.
No purpose is set forth in this deed, but I am wondering if it was
for a county poor farm. If so, this would be the BAILEY tract.
Here, too, I have made no effort to track down the title.

218. 4 February 1812. HENRY CAMDEN, Amherst County, to THOMAS
      ALDRIDGE, Amherst County...Deed of Trust; debt to DAVID and
JAMES GARLAND--6 sh. 414 acres Beaver Creek; south border Buffaloe
and is part of former tract of GABRIEL PENN, deceased. Lines:
JONATHAN DUNCAN's heirs, WILLIAM CAMDEN, JR., JABEZ CAMDEN, JONATHAN
YOUNG and CHARLES BURRUS. It was conveyed to HENRY by deed of gift
from WILLIAM CAMDEN, 16 July 1804. Witnesses: PEACHY FRANKLIN,
J. P. GARLAND, J. S. PENDLETON. To JAMES GARLAND, 31 December 1812.

220. 28 December 1811. JONATHAN OGDON, Amherst County, to JAMES P.
      GARLAND, second and DAVID S. GARLAND, third...Deed of Trust;
debt due DAVID GARLAND--6 sh. slave, AILEY, and her child, NEOR, at
the breast--bought this day at public auction. Witnesses: WIATT
POWELL, CHARLES JONES, ALEXANDER PENN.

221. 25 January 1812. Order to Amherst County Justices of the
      Peace: EDMOND T. COLEMAN and BENJAMIN TALIAFERRO, WASHINGTON
HILL and wife, SALLY...16 December 1811, to JAMES HIX--100 acres.
Done, 17 June 1812.

223. 11 January 1812. Order to Amherst County Justices of the
      Peace: DAVID S. GARLAND and wife, JANE, 16 September 1811, to
DABNEY HILL...110½ acres. Done by EDMOND PENN and JAMES FRANKLIN,
13 July 1812. to DABNEY HILL, 14 October 1814.

58

224. 4 April 1812. CHARLES CHRISTIAN, The Elder, to JAMES LONDON,
    both of Amherst County...$136.50 19½ acres Porrige and both
sides Jumping Branch. Lines: JAMES LONDON, JR., HENRY CHRISTIAN,
EDLOR, WILLIAM CLINKSCALES, WILLIAM HARRISON, JAMES LONDON.

225. 18 August 1810. NORVELL SPENCER and wife, LUCY, Amherst County,
    to WILLIAM STERLING and CHARLES BULLER CLAIBORNE, infant sons
of STERLING CLAIBORNE, Amherst County...$1000 all of two tracts bought
by NORVELL SPENCER from SPOTSWOOD GARLAND and SAMUEL ROSE--north of
a road from GEDDES House around front of mountain to SPENCER's blacksmith shop of main road to New Glasgow. Also 40 acres--part of
PAULING AORS's lot in division of COLONEL HUGH ROSE estate and
deeded by NORVELL SPENCER to SPOTSWOOD GRALAND.

226. 6 August 1812. JAMES SALE to THOMAS N. EUBANK, Amherst County...
    Deed of Trust; debt to JONATHAN and RICHARD ELLIS--$1.00 my one
third in SALLY and her six children and increases--named. Witnesses:
RICHARD EUBANK, P. THURMOND, TARPLEY MITCHELL. To JONATHAN ELLIS,
24 March 1813.

228. 17 August 1812. JOSEPH WILSHIRE to JACOB PIERCE...Deed of Trust;
    debt to JOSEPH KENNEDY--$1.00--life interest of my wife, SARAH,
in named slaves and my two slaves; stock, furniture, etc.

230. 17 August 1810. STERLING CLAIBORNE and wife, JANE, to NORVELL
    SPENCER...$.00--all of tract formerly that of EMILY ROSE--south
of a road from GEDDES to New Glasgow and including the blacksmith
shop and all above on south side Naked Creek--44 acres--part of HUGH
ROSE tract and laid off to CHARLES L. CHRISTIAN and next to grantee--
survey annexed (not herein).

231. 13 August 1812. WALTER FRAZER, by power from MARTIN TONGATE and
    wife, SUANNAH, and recorded in Giles County, Tennessee, to RICHARD
HARTLESS, Amherst County...L15 50 acres both sides middle fork Pedlar.
Lines: JAMES FRAZIER, deceased.

232. 13 August 1812. JONATHAN and WALTER FRAZIER, Giles County,
    Tennessee, by power from heirs of JAMES FRAZIER, deceased, and
recorded in Giles County, Tennessee, to RICHARD HARTLESS, Amherst
County...$100.00 50 acres both sides Pedlar with residue to WILLIAM
MACKEY, Rockbridge, to out a "currant" for waters of Pedlar through
his own land. Lines: JAMES FRAZIER, deceased, BLAN's Creek, THOMAS
ALLEN.

234. 21 September 1812. ISAAC TINSLEY, Amherst County, and wife,
    JINNEY, to JAMES WARE, Amherst County...L130 interest in tract
on both sides Harris and one-fourth of mill, mill-stones, etc., slave,
stock. To JAMES WARE, 22 April 1816.

235. 21 September 1812. FRANCIS CLEMENTS and wife, FANNY, Amherst
    County, to TINSLEY RUCKER, Amherst County...L45 123 acres
Head borders Harris. Lines: grantee, WILLIAM CLEMENTS.

236. 21 September 1812. Same grantors as above to CHARLES P. TALIAFERRO
    Amherst County...L15 55 acres head borders Harris and Puppie
Creek. Lines: JESSE CLEMENTS, CHARLES TALIAFERRO, JONATHAN SMITH,
THOMAS WOODROOF.

237. 27 February 1807. Order to Lincoln County, Kentucky, Justices
    of the Peace: CHARLES ADAMS and wife, MARY, 17 November 1805,
to JONATHAN S. DAWSON...one-eighth of 512 acres. Done by BENJAMIN
HYATT and JONATHAN MC ROBERTS, 11 November 1811. THOMAS HELM, Clerk.
Recorded in Amherst County 21 September 1812.

239. 27 February 1807. Order to -- Justices of the Peace of --
    County: BENJAMIN DAWSON and wife, MOLLY, 19 November 1805, to
JONATHAN S. DAWSON...one-eighth of 512 acres. Done in Casey County,
Kentucky by WILLIAM SHACKELFORD and WILLIAM GOODE, 9 November 1811.
MOSES RICE, Clerk of Casey County. Recorded in Amherst County
21 September 1812.

242. 21 August 1809. (altered by some clerk and hard to decipher).
      Order to -- Justices of the Peace RICHARD ADAMS and wife,
SUSANNAH, 19 November 1805, to JONATHAN S. DAWSON--interest as above
in 512 acres. Done by same Casey County, Kentucky clerks, 9 November
1811.

244. 14 September 1812. JAMES HIGGINBOTHAM, SR., to son, JAMES
      HIGGINBOTHAM, JR...love and $1.00; part of tract whereon SR.
formerly lived and residue to JOSEPH DILLARD by SR. Lines: JOSEPH
DILLARD, JONATHAN HIGGINBOTHAM, land from house occupied by JR.,
WILLIAM HIGGINBOTHAM, the Glebe, WILLIAM ARMISTEAD, COLONEL WILLIAM
CABELL. Witnesses: S. CLAIBORNE, JONATHAN HIGGINBOTHAM, SAMUEL
STAPLES. To JOSEPH DILLARD, September 28, 1812.

245. 14 September 1812. JAMES HIGGINBOTHAM, SR. to JOSEPH DILLARD,
      son-in-law of JAMES HIGGINBOTHAM, SR. by marriage of DILLARD to
SR.'s daughter, JUDITH...love and $1.00. Where JOSEPH DILLARD lives.
Lines: W. S. CRAWFORD, COLONEL WILLIAM CABELL, JONATHAN HIGGINBOTHAM,
land from house of JAMES HIGGINBOTHAM, WILLIAM HIGGINBOTHAM. Witnesses:
as above and margin as above.

247. 19 September 1812. DAVID SWANSON, Amherst County, to JAMES
      GARLAND, Amherst County...Deed of Trust; debt to DANIEL
HIGGINBOTHAM, Richmond, and assigned to DAVID S. GARLAND...$1.00
interest in four tracts--formerly that of JONATHAN SWANSON, The
Elder, who died some years past and supposed to have escheated to
Commonwealth for want of legal heirs, but relinquished by Commonwealth
to DAVID, JONATHAN, JOSEPH and GABRIEL SWANSON and undivided. DAVID
is entitled to one-fourth. Witnesses: ROBERT L. COLEMAN, CHARLES L.
BARRET, HUDSON M. GARLAND, JONATHAN P. COBBS. To DAVID S. GARLAND,
26 June 1819.

250. 21 March 1812. AMBROSE RUCKER, Bedford, to TINSLEY RUCKER,
      Amherst County...$1.00 540½ acres Harris Creek. Lines:
B. HICKS, R. HARDWICK, WILLIAM WARE, CLEMENTS, WARE Road. Witnesses:
CHARLES L. CHRISTIAN, BLANFORD HICKS, RICHARD HARDWICK, WILLIAM
PETERS, BENJAMIN RUCKER. To R. HARDWICK, 20 January 1814.

252. 15 May 1812. WILLIAM BURFORD, Amherst County, from ELIZABETH
      TENNISON...$5.00 all claim to tract which WILLIAM BURFORD bought
from ARCHIBALD BURFORD, deceased--her dower--Harris Creek. Witnesses:
WILLIAM BURFORD, CHARLES MAYS, JONATHAN R. WHITTEN, RICHARD WHITTEN.

253. 18 September 1812. JONATHAN TINSLEY, Amherst County, to LINDSEY
      TINSLEY, his son...love--where LINDSEY TINSLEY lives. Lines:
J. SHELTON, DAVID TINSLEY, the road. Witnesses: ISAAC TINSLEY,
THOMAS SLEDD, OLIVER TINSLEY, DAVID TINSLEY.

256. 27 March 1812. STERLING CLAIBORNE and wife, JANE, Amherst County,
      to THOMAS ALDRIDGE...$2520.00 95 acres Tye and Piney--part of
a tract formerly that of CHARLES ROSE, deceased. Lines: HUGH ROSE,
grantee, JAMES PLEASANTS, JR., road at ford on Piney--also tract
bought by STERLING CLAIBORNE from HUGH ROSE and part of the tract
which fell to HUGH ROSE, son of HUGH ROSE. Lines: south border Tye,
JAMES PLEASANTS, JR., W. S. CRAWFORD, NORVELL SPENCER. Witnesses:
DAVID S. GARLAND, JAMES S. PENDLETON, WILLIAM COLEMAN, JONATHAN MYERS.

257. 21 September 1812. JAMES WARE and wife, NANCY G., Amherst
      County, to DABNEY WARE, Amherst County...$1105.00 282 acres
headborders Shackelford Mill Creek. Lines: WILLIAM NOEL, ANTHONY
NICELY, JONATHAN BYAS, a road, THOMAS N. EUBANK, THOMAS HIGGINBOTHAM,
ROBERT KNUCKLES. To A. WARE, 20 June 1814.

259. 10 September 1812. EDWARD CARTER and wife, MARY, Amherst County,
      to MARK LIVELY, Amherst County...L200 110 acres. Lines: fork
of the road at Maple Run, main road, New Glasgow road. Witnesses:
WILLIAM G. PENDLETON, JAMES GARLAND, DABNEY HILL.

260. 20 September 1812. JACOB PIERCE to ABSALOM HOWL, both of Amherst
County...L284-9-4 136 acres Rocky Run. Lines: Braxton's old
line, JONATHAN HENDREN, GAINES' road, THOMAS CLASBY, RICHARD WILSON,
ROBERT PIERCE, ISAIAH ATTKINSON, WALTER CHRISTIAN. To ABSALOM HOWL,
21 February 1814.

262. 21 September 1812. WILLIAM NOEL and wife, LUCY, Amherst County,
to WILLIAM WILLMORE, Amherst County...L112 420 acres Pedlar.

264. 15 June 1812. ROBERT WALKER and wife, NANCY, Amherst County,
to VERNON METCALF, Bedford...$75.00 7½ acres adjoining both
parties. Lines: the mountain road, EDWARD WATSON.

265. 3 June 1812. State of South Carolina...LUCAS POWELL, Nelson
County, died owning tracts. 1. Both sides Piney. 2. On Tyre.
3. Plantation where LUCAS died intestate. Title vested in widow,
ELIZABETH, and seven children. SEYMOUR POWELL, Elbert County,
Georgia, son of LUCAS POWELL, for $400 paid by MILDRED TALIAFERRO
(formerly POWELL), Chester District, South Carolina--all my interest
in my father's estate--one-eighth of three tracts save widow's part
and slaves laid off for me, but not conveyed. Witnesses: D. W. CARTER,
WILLIAM TALIAFERRO, J. ROSBOROUGH, Clerk, GEORGE KENNEDY, Notary
Public.

267. 17 July 1812. JAMES SMITH and wife, NANCY, Rockbridge, to
REUBEN COX, Amherst County...$600.00 201 acres Harris Creek
and east side Tobacco Row Mountain. Lines: JAMES BENNETT, ELIZABETH
COLEMAN, BLANDFORD HIX, top of Tobacco Row Mountain, the road. Lot
of NANCY as legatee of late DR. DANIEL BURFORD. Witnesses: REUBIN
NORVELL, JONATHAN R. WHITTEN, HENRY FARNSSORHT. To REUBEN COX,
4 June 1817. Page 268 order to Amherst County Justices of the Peace
to quiz--she is styled of Rockbridge, but done in Amherst County,
30 September 1812, by REUBEN NORVELL and PHILIP JOHNSON.

269. 7 October 1812. THOMAS T. MAYO, Amherst County, to GEORGE
STAPLES, Campbell County...$500 10 acres James River island
between mouths of Porrage and Stovall Creeks. Witnesses: JACOB
WOODSON, WILLIAM TURNER, CHARLES MUNDY. To the grantee, 15 March
1813.

270. 17 October 1812. PULLIAM SANDIDGE and wife, LUCY, Amherst
County, to WILLIAM WILSON, Rockbridge--error written on margin
and lines through deed...L8000 of tobacco and bay cold, Ohio County,
Kentucky, tract.

271. 18 July 1812. MILDRED TALIAFERRO, formerly POWELL, Chester
District, South Carolina--power of attorney to friend, COLONEL
CHARLES TALIAFERRO, Amherst County, to sell Amherst County and Nelson
tracts of SEYMOUR POWELL, Egbert (sic) County, Georgia...by death of
his father, LUCAS POWELL, Nelson County, and conveyed to me by SEYMOUR
POWELL, 3 June 1812. Witnesses: JESSE T. WALLIS, JOSEPH MC COSH,
JONATHAN MC KEE-WALLIS as Justice of the Peace and GEORGE KENNEDY,
Notary Public.

272. 14 October 1812. ISAAC TINSLEY, Amherst County, but about to
remove to Tennessee--power of attorney to AMBROSE RUCKER,
Amherst County, to sell Amherst County tract on Otter. Witnesses:
PETER P. THORNTON, MERRIT M. WHITE, THOMAS CLEMENTS, BANISTER TINSLEY,
WIATT W. BROWN.

273. 19 October 1812. Agreement between GEORGE MAYO and THOMAS T.
MAYO...THOMAS has sold to GEORGE the tract bounded by the river
on south, Porrige on east, north by old line, Bigg Branch on west for
$8000.00. THOMAS is to take a lease on GEORGE's plantation in
Cumberland for at least five years--stipulations as to cultivation,
lease of THOMAS MONTAGUE is to continue, old house to be repaired at
expense of GEORGE, THOMAS has option on it at end of five years at
$12,000 and $8,000 is to be a credit. GEORGE to execute Deed of
Trust to THOMAS and to A. AUSTIN.

275. 19 October 1812. ISAAC RUCKER, Amherst County, to daughter, MARTHA P. RUCKER, Amherst County...$1.00 paid by SAMUEL P. CHRISTIAN, her friend--negro, CREASY.

276. 16 November 1812. THOMAS ALDRIDGE and Company, New Glasgow merchants, to DANIEL HIGGINBOTHAM...power to deliver such bonds as needed by collector of Customs for entries and duties on shipment from MARTIN of Liverpool. to THOMAS ALDRIDGE, 16 November 1812.

277. 31 October 1812. FRANCIS HILL, Amherst County, to JOSEPH HAWKINS, Amherst County...$80.00 104 acres Buffaloe. Lines: REUBEN NORVELL, JAMES DILLARD. Witnesses: JAMES E. HARRIS, NICHOLAS HARRISON, GEORGE POWELL.

278. 3 May 1812. JAMES WARE and wife, NANCY, Amherst County, to JOSEPH HAWKINS, Amherst County...L12 18 acres north bank James River and joins WILLIAM SCOTT, GEORGE GOODWIN. Witnesses: RODNEY TINSLEY, GIDEON P. FLOOD.

279. 12 August 1812. BENJAMIN NOEL, Amherst County, to WILLIAM DAVIS, Amherst County...$100.00 100 acres Otter Creek. Lines: Big Branch, ISAAC TINSLEY, JAMES SHASTEAD, grantee. Witnesses: RICHARD TINSLEY, ROBERT NOEL, BENJAMIN SHACKELFORD, BENNETT TINSLEY, NELSON DAVIS, CHARLES DAVIS, WILLIAM NOEL, RODNEY MC CULLOCH.

280. 23 September 1812. REUBEN NORVELL and wife, POLLY, Amherst County, to THOMAS NORVELL, Richmond...$1.00 853 acres. Lines: JAMES LONDON, LARKIN LONDON, PETER RRINE (?), NATHAN WINGFIELD, deceased, TERISHA TURNER, tract whereon REUBEN NORVELL lately resided, JAMES LONDON, JR., both sides Glade Road. Witnesses: J. HARRISON, THOMAS WIATT, GEORGE D. WINSTON. To REUBEN NORVELL, 2 April --.

281. 17 November 1812. JAMES BENNETT and wife, ELIZABETH, Amherst County, to ELIZABETH COLEMAN, Amherst County...$706 116½ acres south borders Harris. Lines: REUBIN COX, grantee, THOMAS GRISSOM, deceased, AMBROSIA LUCAS, the gulley, the road. Witnesses: REUBEN NORVELL, BLANDFORD HICKS, FLEMING COLEMAN, RICHARD PENDLETON, CHARLES MOORE, EDMOND PADGETT.

282. 19 October 1812. JOSEPH DILLARD and wife, JUDY, Amherst County, to WILLIAM TILLER, Amherst County...L50 80 acres north borders Buffaloe. Lines: DAVID S. GARLAND (formerly WILLIAM TYREE), JESSE KENNEDY, deceased, RICHARD ALLCOCK, MOSES PHILIPS (formerly GEORGE PHILLIPS), JONATHAN PHILLIPS' old line, DAVID S. GARLAND (formerly JACOB TYREE).

283. 22 July 1812. AARON CAMPBELL and NELSON CAMPBELL, Amherst County, to WILLIAM G. PENDLETON, Amherst County...Deed of Trust; debt to JONATHAN ROBINSON--6 sh. furniture and stock. Witnesses: THOMAS ALDRIDGE, JAMES S. PENDLETON, JONATHAN MYERS, CORNELIUS POWELL. I am seeking to get more data on AARON CAMPBELL since data shows that the court met at his home at the Oaks prior to erection of the new courthouse after NELSON was cut from Amherst.

284. 26 June 1812. JONATHAN HALL, Amherst County, to DAVID S. GARLAND, Amherst County...$40.00 100 acres patent to both parties, 19 June 1805 south side and joining north fork Pedlar. Lines: WILLIAM HIGGINBOTHAM, BENJAMIN SANDIDGE, PHILIP BURTON. Witnesses: JAMES S. PENDLETON, JONATHAN MYERS, THOMAS ALDRIDGE, PEACHY FRANKLIN.

286. 17 November 1812. EDWARD WATSON, Amherst County, to JAMES PETTIT, Amherst County...$1100 218½ acres of connected tract bought by EDWARD WATSON of WILLIAM GARROT and JESSE BROWN. Lines: JONATHAN BOLLING, JAMES BOLLING, WILLIAM KNIGHT, RUCKER's road, Lynchburg Road. Witnesses: REUBEN COLEMAN, JOSEPH SWANSON, JONATHAN SCOTT, ZACHARIAH BOWLES. To owner, 30 November 1817.

287.   7 December 1812. RICHARD HATTON, Amherst County, to GEORGE P.
       LUCKE, Amherst County...$108.00 548 acres by survey of 23 October
1799, south borders Horsley. Lines: WILLIAM CABELL's old line,
PHILIP PEYTON's old line, RICHARD ELLIOTT's old line, WILLIAM PATON's
old line. Witnesses: BENNETT CRAWFORD, NELSON CRAWFORD, P. C. BALLINGER.

288.   21 September 1812. PEYTON KEITH, Amherst County, to WILLIAM
       KNIGHT, Amherst County...$40.00 for one lot in New Galsgow--
Number 6, 34 yards in front and 70 yards deep, east side Main and
begins at an alley.

288.   1 January 1813. JONATHAN PENN, JR. and WILLIAM PENN, Amherst
       County, to DAVID S. GARLAND, Amherst County...WILLIAM PENN,
executor, Deed of Trust, 15 April 1812, to JONATHAN PENN, JR.,
tract exposed for sale--476 acres and GARLAND was highest bidder at
$2573.00. On Huff and Buffaloe. Lines: ROBERT COLEMAN, JONATHAN
PENN, JR. and SR. Bought by WILLIAM PENN from JOSEPH BURRUS. It
consists of two tracts: 1. 400 acres south bank Buffaloe. Lines:
TUCKER, deceased, north bank of Huff. 2. 76 acres adjoins on south
bank Buffaloe. Lines: PHILIP BURTON.

290.   10 October 1806. JABEZ CAMDEN and wife, FRANCES, Amherst
       County, to MICAJAH CAMDEN, Amherst County...L215 130 acres
Huff. Lines: AMBROSE PORTER, JONATHAN WHEELER, GEORGE BRAXTON.
Tract was bought by JABEZ CAMDEN of WILLIAM CAMDEN, 1805. Witnesses:
WILLIAM STINNETT, NICHOLAS HORSLEY, JONATHAN WHITEHEAD. Final proof
by WILLIAM STINNETT, 18 January 1813.

292.   18 January 1813. JONATHAN WARE and wife, ELIZABETH, Amherst
       County, to WILLIAM WARE, JR., Amherst County...$1.00 477 acres
Irish Creek, border of Pedlar. Lines: JESSE RICHESON, THOMAS TUCKER,
deceased, RICHARD L. ELLIS, GEORGE HOWARD. To WILLIAM WARE,
18 September 1815.

293.   20 January 1810. Agreement whereby WILLIAM S. CRAWFORD buys,
       as heir, from other heirs and widow of father, DAVID CRAWFORD--
Agreement between WILLIAM S. CRAWFORD, ELIZABETH CRAWFORD, widow of
DAVID CRAWFORD, JOHN, NELSON, CHARLES, NATHAN, REUBEN and DAVID
CRAWFORD, ROWLAND JONES and wife, NANCY, THOMAS W. COCKE and wife,
SALLY, NICHOLAS C. DAVIES and wife, ELIZABETH--all children of DAVID
CRAWFORD (save widow, ELIZABETH)--ELIZABETH is entitled to use and
occupancy of about 780 acres whereon husband lived adjoining Tobacco
Row Mountain for life and then to be divided to children. ELIZABETH
wishes to make certain compensations and to divide in her life and
agrees to relinquish, by sale, includes small entry by purchase of
ELIZABETH from WILLIAM PRYOR, about 18 acres and known as GROOMES'
place. WILLIAM S. CRAWFORD bought for L2000 and bonds made by him.
JONATHAN EUBANK was witness. Page 294 WILLIAM S. CRAWFORD and all
other male CRAWFORD heirs authorized executors of DAVID CRAWFORD to
pay sums to ROWLAND JONES and wife, NANCY, NICHOLAS C. DAVIES and wife,
ELIZABETH--to be charged to all legatees save JONES, DAVIES, and COCKE,
and widow. Witnesses: JONATHAN EUBANK.

295.   16 January 1813. Set forth that DAVID CRAWFORD died on --, 1802
       and will of December 14, 1801, directed that about 765 acres
where he lived on Tobacco Row Mountain should be property of widow,
ELIZABETH, as above recited. This is conveyance by the heirs above
for tract on Horsley and Harris and next to Tobacco Row Mountain.
Lines: CHARLES CRAWFORD, north bank of a branch, WILLIAM THURMOND,
WILLIAM PRYOR's old line. Witnesses: BENNETT A. CRAWFORD, HENRIETTA
ALLEN, MARGARET PRYOR, JONATHAN EUBANK, ROBERT H. CARTER, JAMES B.
RISQUE, CHRISTOPHER ANTHONY, WILLIAM RADFORD.

298.   24 February 1812. LANDON CABELL, Nelson County, to SPOTSWOOD
       GARLAND, same county...SAMUEL ROSE by power of attorney,
8 September 1805, of Kentucky, to CABELL to sell his Amherst County
tracts of 200 acres--his by lot from sister, PAULINA ROSE, deceased.
L50 Geddes tract formerly that of COLONEL HUGH ROSE, deceased, and
divided to legatees by court decree. Recorded in Nelson County
27 Arpil 1812; Amherst County, 18 January 1813.

300. 2 January 1813. MICAJAH CAMDEN and wife, POLLY, Amherst County,
     to ABRAHAM EWERS, Amherst County...$648.00 162 acres--bought by
MICAJAH CAMDEN from THOMAS ALDRIDGE and wife, KITTY, 7 August 1807;
reference to deed by SAMUEL ANDERSON to JONATHAN ANDERSON, 20 June
1803, for lines. Witnesses: THOMAS ALDRIDGE, DAVID S. GARLAND,
JAMES PENDLETON.

301. 16 January 1813. JONATHAN P. COBBS and wife, JANE, Amherst
     County, to NEWELL BAKER, Louisa...$1826 for 100 acres in Louisa
on Cub Creek. Lines: JONATHAN WINSTON, CRENSHAW, THOMAS JACKSON,
AMBLER. Witnesses: WILL G. POINDEXTER, CORNELIUS POWELL, JAMES S.
PENDLETON. Note: See DR. MALCOLM HARRIS' finebook on Louisa for more
on BAKER.

302. 10 November 1812. RICHARD BURKS and wife, POLLY, Amherst County,
     to GEORGE MC DANIEL, Amherst County...$45.00 45 acres east side
Tobacco Row Mountain. Lines: RICHARD S. ELLIS, MARTIN PARKS, ARTHUR L.
DAVIES, HOUCHIN. Witnesses: REUBEN NORVELL, AMBROSE RUCKER, GEORGE H.
BURFORD. Note: GEORGE MC DANIEL is SR.

304. 20 October 1812. GINNEY REDMAN, Amherst County, to parents,
     GEORGE and MARY REEDMOND--note discrepancies in spelling herein--
and my three children: BLANFORD (BLUFORD?), MARY and MINERVY REDMOND--
all of my estate due me from my execution versus JOSEPH MILSTEAD et al.
and one black man, clothes to my sister, NANCY WATKINGS, parents to
be supported and then to my children--also cow and mare. Witnesses:
SAMUEL COLEMAN, BARKSDALE SLEDD, RICHARD TANKERSLEY.

305. 13 January 1813. HUGH CAMPBELL, Tennessee, power of attorney
     to friend, CHARLES L. BARRET, Amherst County...to transact
Virginia business. Witnesses: DAVID S. GARLAND, JONATHAN THOMPSON,
WILLIA BROWN. To CHARLES L. BARRETT, 30 May 1813; recorded Amherst
County, 18 January 1813.

305. 18 January 1813. WILLIAM WILLIAMS and JEREMIAH TAYLOR, Amherst
     County, to ROBERT COLEMAN, grandson of GEORGE L. COLEMAN,
orphan of LINDSEY COLEMAN, deceased...L100 WILLIAM WILLIAMS has sold
ROBERT COLEMAN, grandson. 46 3/4 acres or 1/8th of tract which
GEORGE STEELE, deceased, owned and which descended to CATHERINE WOOD,
formerly STEELE, and sister and heir of GEORGE STEELE. North side
Buffaloe.

306. 18 January 1813. DAVID WOODROOF, Amherst County, to JESSE
     WOODROOF, Amherst County...$1.00 173 acres middle fork Rutledge.
Lines: THOMAS CREWS, DAVID WOODROOF, SR., JR., JONATHAN MC DANIEL.
Witnesses: WILL WOODROOF, DAVID WOODROOF, JR., EDMOND L. WOODROOF.

307. 15 February 1813. MICAJAH CAMDEN and wife, POLLY, Amherst
     County, to BURCHER WHITEHEAD, Amherst County...L150 189 acres
Huff Creek. Lines: WILLIAM CAMDEN's Spring branch, HIGGINBOTHAM,
JOSEPH PENN, JONATHAN PENN, JR., "grate" road.

309. 10 February 1813. CHARLES P. TALIAFERRO and wife, LOUISA,
     Amherst County, to JONATHAN FLOID, Amherst County...$500.00
502½ acres south Buffaloe. Lines: JOSEPH HIGGINBOTHAM, WILLIAM CARTER,
JAMES HENSON, BENJAMIN SANDIDGE. To JONATHAN FLOOD, 26 December 1817.

310. 16 November 1812. JABEZ CAMDEN, Amherst County, to DAVID S.
     and JAMES P. GARLAND, Amherst County...Deed of Trust; debt to
SAMUEL GARLAND, Lynchburg--$1.00; slaves named with ages. Witnesses:
ISAAC TINSLEY, DAVID TINSLEY, J. HAAS. To JAMES P. GARLAND, agent,
26 April 1813.

311. 26 August 1812. ALEXANDER HENDERSON, Amherst County, to
     JOSEPH PENN, Amherst County...Deed of Trust; debt to JONATHAN
PENN, JR. and JONATHAN and WILLIAM PENN--6 sh. furniture, etc.
Witnesses: EDMOND T. COLEMAN, WILLIAM HENDERSON.

313. 9 November 1812. ISHAM JOHNSON, Amherst County, to THOMAS
     ALDRIDGE, Amherst County...Deed of Trust; debt to DAVID S.
GARLAND, assignee of DAVID and JAMES GARLAND--6 sh., furniture and
stock. Witnesses: JAMES L. PENDLETON, CORNELIUS POWELL, JONATHAN
MYERS.

314. 11 February 1813. JOSEPH HIGGINBOTHAM, the elder, Amherst
     County, to DAVID S. GARLAND, Amherst County...L270 270 acres
Huff; south border of Buffaloe. Lines: BENJAMIN HIGGINBOTHAM, CARTER
BRAXTON, JONATHAN HIGGINBOTHAM. Witnesses: JOSEPH DILLARD, WILLIS
BROWN, JESSE KENNEDY, JAMES HIGGINBOTHAM.

316. 18 January 1813. JONATHAN WHITEHEAD, JEREMIAH and PEACHY
     FRANKLIN, commissioners by court to settle estate of REUBEN
HUDSON, deceased, to DAVID S. GARLAND, Amherst County...order of
November court, 1812--public auction--$1000 for several tracts of
342 acres; also 8 acres bought by REUBEN HUDSON of RUSH HUDSON--all
joining on east side Turkey Mountain. Lines: THOMAS ALDRIDGE,
CHARLES BOWLES, JAMES FRANKLIN, RUSH HUDSON--widow's dower of 80 acres
for life, rest to GARLAND.

316. 15 February 1813. RICHARD HARDWICK, Amherst County, to WILLIAM I.
     ISBELL, Amherst County...$1100 399 acres and three-fourths
Harris Creek. Lines: ELIZABETH COLEMAN, WARE's road. Witnesses:
ISAAC RUCKER, BENJAMIN RUCKER, JONATHAN WARE.

318. 2 August 1812. DAVID S. GARLAND, Amherst County, to EDMOND
     PENN, Amherst County...$100 100 acres Otter and both sides.
Lines: DAVID BURKS, HENRY L. DAVIES, deceased. To EDMOND PENN,
19 April 1813.

319. 15 March 1813. THOMAS T. MAYO and wife, ELIZA, to GEORGE
     STAPLES, Amherst County...$500 10 acres Chase Island. To
GEORGE STAPLES, 26 July 1813.

320. 13 March 1813. JONATHAN SMITH, Amherst County, to JACOB SMITH,
     Amherst County...$1000 400 acres on Franklin Creek and bought
from ZACHARIAH TALIAFERRO, 2 October 1780. Lines: JAMES SMITH.

321. 26 August 1812. JONATHAN GOOLSBERRY, Amherst County, to
     JOSEPH PENN, Amherst County...Deed of Trust; debt to JONATHAN
PENN, JR.--cart and stock. Witnesses: RICHARD MAYS, GEORGE LAHARN,
ALLEN BUGG.

322. 15 March 1813. Ejectment pending in County Court of Amherst
     County...ELIZABETH UPSHAW versus ELIZABETH CHRISTIAN, widow of
JONATHAN CHRISTIAN, and administratrix of his estate. A compromise
whereby ELIZABETH UPSHAW relinquishes claim on tracts to ELIZABETH
CHRISTIAN and heirs of JONATHAN CHRISTIAN. ELIZABETH CHRISTIAN to
pay ELIZABETH UPSHAW for two years occupancy of her plantation from
1 January 1811, to 1 January 1813--$800 per year and for rest of life
of ELIZABETH UPSHAW per year. HENRY MOORMAN, attorney-in-fact for
ELIZABETH UPSHAW. All agreements and settlements made by ELIZABETH
UPSHAW and PLEASANT DAWSON versus administratrix of JONATHAN CHRISTIAN
to stand good. Witnesses: PLEASANT DAWSON, JAMES DILLARD. Page 324
ELIZABETH UPSHAW, Amherst County, power of attorney to HENRY MOORMAN,
Campbell County, to recover from ELIZABETH CHRISTIAN as tenant on my
lands on James River. Witnesses: PLEASANT and R. DAWSON. Note: I
have never "understood all that I knew" about ELIZABETH UPSHAW and
do not like to make any dogmatic statements. If one will consult my
C wills, it will be seen that DRURY CHRISTIAN left a will wherein he
speaks of "my beloved companion, ELIZABETH UPSHAW" and all of his
children bear names of UPSHAW rather than CHRISTIAN. JOHN CHRISTIAN
was his brother and DRURY names him in his will, too. One DRURY
CHRISTIAN married here fairly early, but his father, ROBERT, gave
consent.

65

325. 1 August 1812. WILLIAM ARMISTEAD, Amherst County. to DAVID S.
     GARLAND, Amherst County...$100 100 acres both sides Otter.
Lines: DAVID BURKS, HENRY L. DAVIES, deceased. Witnesses: WILLIAM G.
PENDLETON, C. ANTHONY, JAMES BENAGH.

326. 12 March 1813. JONATHAN and RICHARD L. ELLIS, Amherst County,
     to ARCHIBALD GILLIAM, JR., Amherst County...L60 103 acres both
sides Pedlar. Lines: river and a branch.

327. 23 June 1812. Order to THOMAS HUMPHREYS, JONATHAN M. GORDON,
     and THOMAS W. COCKE, Campbell County Justices of the Peace:
WILLIAM SCOTT and wife, ANN, 13 June 1812, to WILLIAM PETTYJOHN...
303 3/8 acres. Done by first two, 22 January 1813.

328. 17 March 1813. ALLEN BUGG, Amherst County, power of attorney
     to CAPTAIN ROBERT COLEMAN, Amherst County...BUGG has considerable
amount versus HUDSON M. GARLAND and pending in court of Appeals and
COLEMAN is to act for him.

329. 23 October 1812. WILLIAM KIDD, Amherst County, to JOSEPH PENN,
     Amherst County...Deed of Trust; debt to JONATHAN PENN, JR.,
6 sh., beds, stock, etc. Witnesses: JONATHAN PENN, SR., WILLIAM
PENN, PATSY LAHORN.

331. 2 October 1812. HENRY CAMDEN, Amherst County, to DAVID S.
     GARLAND, Amherst County...Deed of Trust; debt to JANE REDMAN,
Amherst County--$1.00 230½ acres and bought by HENRY CAMDEN from
JABEZ CAMDEN. Witnesses: PETER P. THORNTON, ABRAM CARTER, B. A.
CRAWFORD.

334. 4 April 1813. GEORGE HOWARD and wife, NANCY, Amherst County,
     to MARKE CAHOON and WILLIAM CAHOON, Amherst County...L36 120
acres south side Pedlar. Lines: HENRY CHILDRESS, top of the blue
ridge. To GEORGE HOWARD, 17 August 1818.

335. 9 April 1813. ROBERT H. ROSE, Orange County; LANDON CABELL;
     SPOTSWOOD (or is it SAMUEL? Very old alteration by some clerk
and signature at end seems to be SA GARLAND), GARLAND, Nelson County;
NANCY IRVINE and GUSTAVUS A. ROSE, Lynchburg--power of attorney to
ROBERT BRACKENRIDGE of town of Lewisville--should be BRECKENRIDGE and
Louisville--to rent or lease for us as co-partners with other brothers
and sisters of SAMUEL ROSE, late of Kentucky, deceased, and to obtain
patents. Witnesses: CHRISTOPHER ANTHONY and S.(?) WIATT.

336. 24 March 1813. LINZA BURKS and wife, POLLY, Amherst County,
     to CURTIS WATTS, Amherst County...L200 270 acres. Lines:
crossing Dancing Creek. Witnesses: PETER P. THORNTON, RICHARD N.
EUBANK, HENRY HAYNES. To CURTIS WATTS, 8 April 1817.

337. 19 April 1813. JAMES BENNETT and wife, ELIZABETH, Amherst
     County, to AMBROSE LUCAS, Amherst County...$47.50 4 3/4 acres
east side Tobacco Row Mountain. Lines: near grantee's house, a
gully, a branch. Part of estate to BENNETT and wife out of division
of estate of DANIEL BURFORD, deceased.

337. 15 February 1813. Order to Amherst County Justices of the
     Peace: GEORGE POWELL and wife, SOPHIA, 25 July 1811, to
WILLIAM HUGHES...208 acres. Done, 11 March 1813, by NELSON C.
DAWSON and THOMAS MOORE.

339. 5 October 1809. Order to Mercer County, Kentucky, Justices of
     the Peace: ARCHIBALD BILBO and LAWSON MOORE...ROBERT KNUCKLES
and wife, FANNY, 17 September 1809, to JAMES BYAS. Done, 6 August
1810, recorded in Amherst County 19 April 1813.

340. 30 March 1813. BENJAMIN BROWN, Amherst County, to THOMAS
     CREWS, Amherst County...consideration of tract from THOMAS
CREWS to BENJAMIN BROWN; Crooked Run and part of tract whereof GEORGE
DILLARD died as owner and BROWN bought from heirs--28 3/4 acres.
Lines: sides, main road, 12 acres thereof exchanged with THOMAS
CREWS by GEORGE DILLARD; BENJAMIN BROWN conveys 31 3/4 acres. Lines:
grantor, MC DANIEL, mouth of a small branch--15 acres of it verbally
exchanged by THOMAS CREWS with GEORGE DILLARD in lifetime--for 12 acres
before mentioned. To THOMAS CREWS, 13 March 1815.

341. 19 April 1813. WALTER CHRISTIAN and ISAAC RUCKER to Amherst
     County Justices of the Peace: CHARLES TALIAFERRO, JONATHAN
WARWICK, JONATHAN N. ROSE, and THOMAS N. EUBANK...WALTER CHRISTIAN
to administrator estate of CHARLES CHRISTIAN. Note: such items
are generally in wills. This one is found--WALTER D. CHRISTIAN as
administrator in C wills.

342. 19 April 1813. BENJAMIN BROWN, Amherst County, to JONATHAN
     MC DANIEL, Amherst County...consideration of tract from JONATHAN
MC DANIEL--Crooked Run--part of GEORGE DILLARD tract and bought by
BENJAMIN BROWN of GEORGE DILLARD's heirs--6 acres. Lines: what was
corner of grantor, HENRY BOURNE (BROWN?), 6 acres then mentioned,
THOMAS CREWS--former line, MC DANIEL. To B(?) BROWN, JR., 18 November
1841.

343. 3 November 1812. BENNETT HUDSON for self and EDWARD HUDSON, two
     of heirs of ROBERT HUDSON, deceased, and LUCY HUDSON, widow of
ROBERT, to RUSH HUDSON, JR. and wife, PAMELIA (one of children of
ROBERT HUDSON). Two slaves, all of their share save lands to be
retained in consideration for slaves. RUSH HUDSON releases one slave,
a boy, to BENNETT HUDSON. Witnesses: GEORGE FARRAR, RUSH HUDSON, SR.

343. 27 September 1810. SAMUEL HOGG and wife, DELANA, to JONATHAN
     and RICHARD ELLIS, Amherst County...L50 193 acres both sides
Pedlar. Witnesses: PETER MILSTEAD, MARTIN PARKS, RODERICK L.
TALIAFERRO, ROSEMARY GUE. Lines: COLEMAN, EDMOND GOODRICH. Final
proof, 17 May, by SAMUEL HOGG. To JONATHAN ELLIS, 27 May 1813.

345. 25 April 1810. SAMUEL H. ALLEN, HANNAH ALLEN, and JONATHAN
     ALLEN, Amherst County, to MICAJAH PENDLETON, Nelson County...
L150 2½ acres Elk Island Creek tract in Amherst County and Nelson for
a mill seat. Witnesses: ROBERT HORSLEY, WILLIAM LAVENDER, JAMES
PETERS. Final proof, 18 May 1813, by ROBERT HORSLEY. To JONATHAN
HORSLEY, 14 October 1814.

346. 16 June 1813. HENRY TURNER and wife, RACHEL, Amherst County,
     to JONATHAN LONDON, Amherst County...L8-10 8½ acres south side
Porrige. Lines: LONDON (JONATHAN scratched), grantee, ALEXANDER
JEWELL, said LONDON. To JONATHAN LONDON, 1 November 1813.

347. 21 June 1813. WILLIAM TURNER and us, SALLY, Amherst County,
     to SAMUEL ANDERSON, Amherst County...L180 180 acres south side
Stovall. Lines: SACKVILLE KING, DAVID S. GARLAND, the road. To
JESSE BECK, administrator of purchaser, 19 August 1833; August 5,
1834, to GRANVILLE LAIN (see rel. of dowers--U:263 on margin).
Acknowledged in court by SALLY TURNER, 16 September 1833.

347. 5 June 1813. JAMES LONDON, JR., to JONATHAN LONDON, Amherst
     County...$500 200 acres north side Porrage and was gift
conveyance from JAMES LONDON, SR., to JAMES, JR. Lines: JAMES
LONDON, SR. on west and north, LARKIN LONDON on east, ROBERT GRANT
on south, and JONATHAN LONDON. Witnesses: HENRY TURNER, CHARLES
MUNDY, WIATT LONDON. To JONATHAN LONDON, 1 November 1813.

348. 25 May 1813. HOWELL DAVIES, Lynchburg, to EDWARD TINSLEY, JR.,
     Amherst County...$700--island in James known as Chestnut Island;
25 acres. Witnesses: PLEASANT DAWSON, JACOB HAAS, JONATHAN
HENDERSON, BENJAMIN RUCKER, RICHARD BURKS, HENRY JACOBS.

349. 10 June 1813. JAMES MARTIN and JONATHAN P. B. CLAYTON, Campbell
County, to NELSON C. DAWSON, Amherst County...twelve negroes
named. L410. Witnesses: ROBERT C. SCOTT and JOSEPH PERKINS. To
NELSON C. DAWSON, 27 September 1819.

349. 2 March 1813. JAMES GATEWOOD, Amherst County, to PHILIP THURMOND,
Amherst County...L50 40 acres by survey of 4 February 1801 on
Lovelady Creek. Lines: ZED. SHOEMAKER, NICHOLAS PRYOR, WILLIAM
PRYOR. Witnesses: LANDON HILEY, JOEL BIAS, THOMAS LAINE, JAMES
ROWSEY, SALLY BIBB.

350. 19 May 1813. RICHARD L. ELLIS, Amherst County, to MARTIN
PARKS, Amherst County...$100 105 acres north side Tobacco Row
Mountain. Lines: grantee, CHARLES ELLIS, PHILIP GOOCH, deceased,
ARTHUR L. DAVIES, GEORGE MC DANIEL (in conveyance made to him by
RICHARD L. ELLIS), RICHARD BURKS tract whereon WILLIAM JOHNS lives--to
extend to first branch of south waters of Harris over Tobacco Row
Mountain. Witnesses: JONATHAN ELLIS, AMBROSE RUCKER, NELSON CRAWFORD,
JAMES WARE, ABRAM (ADAM?) CARET. Plat mentioned.

351. 21 June 1813. WILLIAM HALL, Amherst County, to PULLIAM SANDIDGE,
Amherst County...$20.00 70 acres patent to WILLIAM HALL--Brown
Mountain Creek. Lines: WILLIAM TOMLINSON, WILLIAM NELSON, HUGH
CAMPBELL.

351. 15 May 1802. DANIEL BURFORD and wife, SARAH, Amherst County,
to EDWARD WATSON, Amherst County...L300 300 acres Stovall Creek.
Lines: the road, Opossum Island road, MAYO's path, STOVALL, PHILIP
JOHNSON, MATTHEW RICKETS, WILLIAM DAMERON, JESSE BECK, south fork
STOVALL, a branch. Witnesses: THOMAS MERRITT, WILLIAM OGDON,
DRURY CLEMENTS, WILLIAM BURFORD, WILKINS WATSON. Page 353 order to
quiz SARAH, 15 May 1802, done October 16, 1802 by GEORGE DILLARD
and PHILIP JOHNSON. Final proof, 21 June 1813, by WILLIAM BURFORD.

354. 20 February 1813. DAVID WOODROOF, SR., Amherst County, to
DAVID WOODROOF, JR., Amherst County...$1.00 213 acres Head
borders middle fork Rutledge. Lines: JONATHAN WATTS--formerly,
LYNCH road, JAMES HILL, LIVELY (?). Witnesses: WILLIAM PETTIT,
WILLIAM WOODROOF, JESSE WOODROOF.

355. 19 May 1813. RICHARD L. ELLIS, MARTIN PARKS and wife, NANCY,
Amherst County, to GEORGE MC DANIEL, Amherst County...$205
205 acres. Lines: MARTIN PARKS, CHARLES ELLIS, DAVID BURKS, GEORGE
MC DANIEL. Witnesses: JONATHAN ELLIS, AMBROSE RUCKER, NELSON
CRAWFORD, JAMES WARE, ABRAM CARTER. To AMBROSE RUCKER, 15 September
1817.

355. 20 October 1812. Order to Amherst County Justices of the Peace:
JONATHAN WARE and wife, ELIZABETH, 18 May 1812, to JESSE RICHESON...
Done by THOMAS N. EUBANK and WILLIAM JOPLINS, 18 May 1813. Page 357
order to same Justices of the Peace as to JONATHAN WARE and wife,
ELIZABETH, to WILLIAM WARE, 18 January 1813. Done as above.

358. 14 June 1813. SAMUEL G. W. ANDERSON, SR., Alb., to PEYTON
KEITH, Amherst County...$361 268 acres north Buffaloe. Lines:
the road, MICAJAH CAMDEN, MOSES PHILIPS, MARY PHILIPS, WILLIAM
CABELL, grantee. Witnesses: TERISHA TURNER, WILLIAM F. TURNER,
SAMUEL ANDERSON, JR., HENRY TURNER. To PEYTON KEITH, 29 April 1814.

360. 5 December 1812. Order to Nelson County Justices of the
Peace: ANDREW MORGAN and wife, MARY, 18 May 1807, to GEORGE
WILLIAMS...333 1/3 acres. Done by THOMAS MASSIE and JONATHAN JACOBS,
18 December 1812.

361. 17 April 1812. FREDERICK FULTZ, Amherst County, to ROBERT L.
      COLEMAN, Amherst County...Deed of Trust; debt to WILLIAM CAMDEN,
and for support of his wife and children--6 sh. One third--water
grist mill on Rockey Run with 28 acres; mare and colts by HAMBLETON,
stock, furniture, etc. Witnesses: REUBEN NORVELL, JONATHAN LONDON,
ROBERT WALKER. To L. COLEMAN, 6 May 1817.

362. 19 May 1813. RICHARD L. ELLIS, Amherst County, to AMBROSE
      RUCKER, Amherst County...$60.00 60 acres south Harris. Lines:
ISAAC TINSLEY, grantee, GEORGE MC DANIEL. Witnesses: REUBEN COLEMAN,
MERIT M. WHITE, GARLAND LUCAS, EDMOND GOODRICH, EDWARD TINSLEY,
JAMES WARE, GEORGE ELLIS.

363. 22 May 1813. PHILIP GILLESPIE, Madison County, Kentucky, to
      THOMAS REID, same county...power of attorney to sell to DAVID S.
GARLAND--my part. WILLIAM IRVIN, County Clerk, DAVID IRVINE and
ROBERT CALDWELL, acting Justices of the Peace. Recorded in Amherst
County 22 June 1813; upside down.

364. 22 June 1813. THOMAS REID, Kentucky, attorney for PHILIP
      GILLESPIE, Kentucky, to DAVID S. GARLAND, Amherst County...L7-8-2
for PHILIP's interest in 400 acres on Piney which belonged to GEORGE
GILLESPIE, deceased.

364. 10 March 1813. WILLIAM DUNCAN and wife, SALLY, Amherst County,
      to MARTIN PARKS, Amherst County...L36 140 acres tract formerly
that of JONATHAN DUNCAN, deceased. North Pedlar branches and north
side of Tobacco Row Mountain. Lines: CHARLES ELLIS, CALEB WATTS,
BALLENGER WADE.

365. 19 July 1813. SAMUEL PAXTON and wife, ESTHER, Amherst County,
      to JAMES CLARKE, Amherst County...$100 18½ acres south side main
branch Pedlar and bought from ANGUS MC DANIEL, 5 September 1788.
Lines: WILLIAM TAYLOR--former line. To JAMES CLARKE, 1 August 1814.

366. 15 July 1813. ROBERT RIVES and WILLIAM B. HARE, Commissioners
      of Superior Court of Chancery, Richmond, for District to JAMES
GOVAN, Hanover County...9 October 1800 ZACHARIAH TALIAFERRO, late of
Amherst County, admitted that he and WILLIS WILLS had been merchants and
owed JAMES GOVAN and GEORGE WEIR, London, England, L12, 254-14-5;
ZACHARIAH TALIAFERRO and wife, SALLY, executed Deed of Trust--could
be repaid at Eagle Tavern, Richmond. WILLIS WILLS and wife, ELIZABETH,
executed Deed of Trust on 3 Warminster lots and eight slaves--wholly
unpaid, 7 December 1805, and suit filed and decretal of 17 September
1806, for plaintiffs. CHARLES YANCYE and WILLIAM CABELL also named
as commissioners. Three lots brought only L244. 1. Later decree
in February of current year and defendants forever barred. Six tracts
on 25 June 1812, at the brick house, former reisdence of ZACHARIAH
TALIAFERRO, sold--1510 acres in six tracts. Bought by CHARLES and
BENJAMIN TALIAFERRO as agents for JAMES GOVAN--$1.00 act under act of
13 December 1792, relative to conveyances--all six tracts to GOVAN
and reference to Deed of Trust in General Court. Witnesses: WILLIAM
STAPLES, HILL CARTER, JONATHAN H. ZEVELY, JONATHAN N. ROSE. To
B. TALIAFERRO, 14 July 1814.

371. 16 July 1813. THOMAS T. MAYO and wife, ELIZA B., Amherst
      County, to WILLIAM GALT, Richmond...$1.00--part of tract whereon
THOMAS T. MAYO lives--called upper field of low grounds with high land
adjoining--149½. Lines: old ferry landing, Big Branch, the river.
Witnesses: CHRISTOPHER ANTHONY, RICHARD POWELL, WILLIAM MITCHELL,
JONATHAN BAILEY, JONATHAN BULLOCK.

372. 27 February 1810. HENRY FRANKLIN and wife, JANE, Amherst
      County, to JONATHAN MOSS, Amherst County...$200 their interest
in tract of WILLIAM MOSS, deceased, on Piney. Witnesses: WILLIS
FRANKLIN, NATHANIEL HILL.

373. 19 July 1813. CHARLES L. BARRET and wife, SARAH, Nelson County,
to JONATHAN RICHESON, Amherst County...$800 400 acres Buffaloe.
Lines: JAMES HIGGINBOTHAM, NEIL CAMPBELL, South fork Buffaloe.
Taken out, 19 May 1817, by JONATHAN RICHESON.

374. 16 July 1813. SAMUEL PAXTON and wife, ESTHER, Amherst County,
to HENRY CAMDEN, Amherst County...L110 144 acres south fork
Pedlar. Lines: grantee.

375. 25 October 1807. JAMES MARKHAM and wife, SIBBUNA, Amherst
County, to JONATHAN MC DANIEL, Amherst County...L90 140 acres
Huff. Lines: Coleman on top of the mountain, BENJAMIN NOWEL,
JAMES BYAS, top of the old cove about half-way up the mountain,
CYRUS (?) SLADDEN. Witnesses: WILLIAM MC DANIEL, JAMES and WILLIAM
WOODROOF. At court held at AARON CAMPBELL's place called the Oaks,
20 June 1808, proved by WILLIAM MC DANIEL. Sent to S. STINNETT by
D. J. POWELL, 28 April 1852. Final proof by JAMES WOODROOF 19 July
1813.

376. 5 May 1813. ABRAM CARTER, administrator of ISAAC WRIGHT, to
WILLIAM WARE, Amherst County...$200 46 acres head waters Horsley.
Witnesses: WILLIAM JOPLING, MADISON WARE, ROBERT RIVES.

377. 15 August 1813. WILLIAM CLEMENS and wife, ISABELLA, Amherst
County, old and infirm and are interested in divisions of estate
of WILLIAM HILLARD, deceased, New Kent, in right of ISABELLA--power of
attorney to friend, THOMAS CLEMENS, Amherst County, to act for us.
To THOMAS CLEMENTS, 20 August 1813. Witnesses: JAMES DODD, BARTLETT
CLEMENS, JONATHAN H. CLEMENS.

378. 22 October 1808. SACKVILLE KING, Campbell County, to WILLIAM
TURNER, Amherst County...6 sh. 200 acres north borders Stovall.
Lines: near fork of Stovall road corner, HENRY TURNER, top of
ROBIN WOODS' mountain, grantee. Witnesses: CHARLES MUNDY, HENRY
TURNER, JR., HENRY TURNER. Final proof, 16 August 1813, by HENRY
TURNER.

379. 4 September 1810. DANIEL BURFORD, JR., and wife, SARAH, Amherst
County, to EDWARD WATSON, Amherst County...L198 99 acres south
borders Harris. Lines: DANIEL NORCUTT, JONATHAN BURFORD, JR.,
WILLIAM BURFORD. Witnesses: ALEXANDER WATSON, DANIEL MEHONE,
deceased, WILKINS WATSON.

380. 14 September 1812. JAMES SHARSTEAD (SHASTEAD?), JR. and wife,
PHOEBE, Amherst County, to JONATHAN and RICHARD ELLIS, Amherst
County...L60 100 acres Otter Creek. Lines: ROBERT KNUCKLES, WILLIAM
DAVIS, Big Branch. Witnesses: RICHARD EUBANK, CHARLES BURKS, son
of DAVID, JONATHAN H. ZEVELY, JONATHAN TARDY, PETER MARKHAM.

381. 16 August 1813. SPOTSWOOD GARLAND, Nelson County, to BENAMMI
STONE, Amherst County...6 sh all interest in property from
STONE to GARLAND, 15 July 1801, for benefit of POLLY L. (S) GARLAND,
daughter of said GARLAND--she has since died. Page 382 recital of same
facts, but 1804 instead of 1801--SPOTSWOOD GARLAND to JAMES P. GARLAND
for L250 all right to property conveyed, 19 July 1813. To JAMES P.
GARLAND, 30 December 1813.

382. 20 March 1813. ANGUS MC CLOUT and JONATHAN H. CLEMENTS,
Amherst County, to WILLIAM BOURN, Amherst County...$1.00 Deed
of Trust; debt to JONATHAN BOURN--two tracts. 1. 161 acres both sides
south fork Buffaloe and they bought it from HUGH CAMPBELL, October
1802. Lines: BENJAMIN SANDIDGE on south of south fork Buffaloe.
2. East side Long Mountain and south fork Buffaloe. 48 acres and
they bought it from HUGH CAMPBELL, 19 September 1808. Lines: AARON
HIGGINBOTHAM, NEIL CAMPBELL. Witnesses: ANDERSON SANDIDGE, BENJAMIN
SANDIDGE. To WILLIAM BOURN, 29 October 1818.

384. 20 July 1813. GEORGE W. TRIBLE, Amherst County, to JOSEPH
     DILLARD, Amherst County...Deed of Trust; debt to JESSE JONES--
$1.00 beds, "kitchen furniture", etc. Witnesses: DAVID SWANSON,
J. YAGER, JONATHAN BARNETT, WILLIAM KNIGHT.

385. 20 July 1813. JOSEPH KENNEDY, Nelson County, to JESSE KENNEDY,
     Amherst County...for love and $1.00--slaves and stock--last four
slaves named for duration of life of my mother, SUSANNA ALFRED.
Witnesses: DAVID SWANSON, WILLIAM KNIGHT, JESSE JONES, JONATHAN
BARNETT.

386. 3 July 1813. PHILIP THURMOND, Amherst County, to CHRISTOPHER
     ANTHONY, Amherst County...$1.00 Deed of Trust--named slaves.
JONATHAN KELSO has obtained judgements (five) in Court of Amherst
County versus PHILIP THURMOND.

388. 15 March 1813. EDWARD TINSLEY, Amherst County, and wife,
     LUCY, to SAMUEL BURKS, Amherst County...L778-1 370½ acres.
Lines: fork of Bethel and Pedlar roads, surveyed by REUBEN NORVELL--
a tract. Witnesses: AMBROSE RUCKER, LEWIS WATKINS, WILLIS RUCKER.

389. 11 September 1813. BENNET RUCKER and wife, JOHANNA, to RICHARD
     HARRISON, Amherst County...$1224 102 acres. Lines: road from
RUCKER's to LYNCH Road, REUBEN RUCKER, JONATHAN BOLLING. On Harris
Creek. Witnesses: JAMES P. GARLAND, SAMUEL BURKS, JONATHAN WARE.

390. 30 March 1813. CHARLES R. ROSE, Nelson County, to JONATHAN
     MYERS, Amherst County...Deed of Trust, debt to THOMAS ALDRIDGE,
Amherst County. $1.00 95 acres south fork Piney and Tye--part of
tract called Believett and sold by CHARLES ROSE to STERLING CLAIBORNE
and by STERLING CLAIBORNE sold to THOMAS ALDRIDGE. ROSE has sold
JONATHAN MYERS one third--his interest by will of late father,
CHARLES ROSE. If ALDRIDGE is vested with title or when WILLIAM HENRY
and HARRY ROSE, sons of late CHARLES ROSE, are 21 and shall refuse or
fail to make complete title. Tract to be allotted to them and
JONATHAN MYERS is to sell and pay ALDRIDGE. Witnesses: JONATHAN
COLEMAN, ROBERT L. COLEMAN, DAVID S. GARLAND.

391. 5 November 1813. DAVID WOODROOF, Amherst County, to JAMES
     HILL, Amherst County...L41-10 41½ acres. Lines: Lynch Road,
Church Road. Witnesses: D. WOODROOD, JR., REUBEN NORVELL, GEORGE R.
NORVELL, THOMAS D. HILL.

392. 2 September 1813. GEORGE D. WINSTON and wife, DOLLY S.,
     Campbell County, to ROBERT MORRIS, Lynchburg...$5000.00 497 acres.
Lines: Lynch, JOHNSON, JONATHAN LYNCH, James river bank, small
branch, GEORGE MAY, WARWICK, MRS. ADAMS, THOMAS JOHNSON, PHILIP
JOHNSON. Witnesses: WALTER DUNNINGHTON, NICHOLAS HARRISON,
S. GARLAND, THOMAS W. COCKE.

394. 15 October 1813. STEPHEN WATTS, Nelson County, and wife,
     MARTHA, to WILLIAM L. WATTS, Nelson County...$500.00 195 acres
both sides Buffaloe and next to MICAJAH PENDLETON, also tract on both
sides Freeland's Creek, north border Buffaloe. Lines: JAMES FREELAND,
deceased, JESSE KENNEDY, REUBEN THORNTON, SMITH TANDY, JAMES ROWSEY--
146 acres; also tract starting just below small branch on Buffaloe.
Lines: ALLEN BLAIR, grantor, 73 3/4 acres. To WILLIAM WATTS, 16 July
1821.

396. 3 September 1813. ROBERT MORRIS, Lynchburg, to WALTER DUNNINGTON,
     Lynchburg...$5.00 437 acres on James and conveyed to ROBERT
MORRIS by GEORGE WINSTON and wife, DOROTHA, on even date. Deed of
Trus; debt of ROBERT MORRIS to GEORGE D. WINSTON.

397. 29 September 1813. THOMAS N. EUBANK and wife, JANE, Amherst
     County, to CHARLES ELLIS, Richmond...$1503.00 two tracts to
legatees of JOSIAH ELLIS by commissioners. 1. Top of Tobacco Row
Mountain. Lines: DAVID BURKS, SR. et al. called Duncan and known as
Mt. Murdock--126 acres and patent to JONATHAN DUNCAN, 20 July 1780.
Lines: DAVID BURKS, ROBERT JOHNSON. 2. Pedlar 324 acres. Lines:
RODNEY MC CULLOCH et al. called DAVIS'; patent to NATHANIEL DAVIS,
assignee of ROBERT JOHNSON, 8 November 1782, formerly CHARLES ELLIS'
orphans. Total: 450 acres.

400. 14 October 1813. GEORGE MAY, Petersburg, first; JONATHAN
     WIATT, SAMUEL J. HARRISON, and WILLIAM NORVELL, Lynchburg,
second; BENJAMIN PERKINS, Lynchburg, third...GEORGE MAY, 27 November
last sold to PERKINS for $300.00 half a lot in Madison called the Red
House and to make more complete the title did appoint second patties
as commissioners for conveying for $1.00 paid by them and $1.00 to
MAY from PERKINS. Witnesses: THOMAS S. MC CLELLAND, ROBERT MORRIS,
POWHATAN ELLIS/POWAHATIN B. TINDALE, J. W. DIBRELL, SP. GARLAND,
J. BENAGH. Two blank pages in this section, but not numbered.

401. 16 October 1813. WILLIAM CASH and wife, SALLY, Amherst County,
     to GABRIEL PAGE, Amherst County...$549 122 acres both sides
Stonehouse Creek and Mill Creek. Lines: BEVERLY WILLIAMSON, deceased,
RICHARD SMITH, JONATHAN MARR, deceased. To GABRIEL PAGE, 21 February
1814.

402. 1 July 1811. JONATHAN PAXTON, Rockbridge, to JONATHAN ROBINSON,
     Rockbridge...$654.33 425 acres top of South Mountain and
conveyed to JONATHAN PAXTON from heirs of WILLIAM PAXTON, SR.,
deceased, 18 March 1808. Acknowledged in Rockbridge, 1 July 1811.
Recorded in Amherst County 15 November 1813.

404. 7 August 1813. LITTLEBERRY TUCKER, Lincoln County, Kentucky,
     to brother, ZACHARIAH TUCKER, same county...power to collect
amount due me as child of DRURY TUCKER, deceased, and his wife,
FRANCES, deceased. THOMAS HELM, Clerk; JAMES HICKMAN, Justice of the
Peace.

405. 15 November 1813. WILLIAM OLIVER and wife, WINNEY, Amherst
     County, to THOMAS CREWS, Amherst County...$889.00 127 acres.
Lines: Lynch road, GIDEON RUCKER, grantee, south border north fork
Rutledge, mouth of Big Hill Spring Branch, WIATT POWELL.

406. 15 November 1813. JOSEPH C. HIGGINBOTHAM and wife, LUCY, Bedford
     County; GEORGE W. HIGGINBOTHAM and wife, ELIZABETH; JAMES
HIGGINBOTHAM and wife, ELIZABETH--last two of Amherst County with wives,
to JOSEPH DILLARD, Amherst County...$1500 821 acres south side Buffaloe.
Lines: Loughborough, JONATHAN SCRUGGS, GEORGE HYLTON's heirs, MICAJAH
PENDLETON, GILES DAVIDSON, GOOCH heirs, grantee. Tract allotted to
JAMES HIGGINBOTHAM by Amherst County Chancery decree--JONATHAN and
JAMES HIGGINBOTHAM to divide lands jointly held and conveyed to them
by father, JOSEPH HIGGINBOTHAM, deceased. To JOSEPH DILLARD,
10 February 1814.

407. 18 October 1813. MOSES HALL, SR. and wife, HANNAH, Amherst
     County, to CHARLES L. BARRET and FREDERICK PRICE...L36-10 27 acres
both sides Pedlar. Lines: JONATHAN F. HALL.

408. 18 October 1813. POWHATAN ELLIS, Lynchburg, to RICHARD L.
     ELLIS, Amherst County...L600 197 acres Pedlar. Lines: CHARLES
BURKS, SR. Tract allotted to POWHATAN ELLIS on division of the
estate of his father, JOSIAH ELLIS, and mansion house where he
lived. Witnesses: S. GARLAND, J. BENAGH, J. GREGORY. To RICHARD L.
ELLIS, 19 September 1814.

409. 19 April 1813. HENRY WATTS and wife, ELIZA (who was ELIZA
      DILLARD), to BENJAMIN BROWN, Amherst County...$2962.82 438½
acres both sides Crooked Run. Lines: Main road, tract of GEORGE
DILLARD, deceased, and to his children: JONATHAN J. and ELIZA DILLARD
(now wife of HENRY WATTS). Witnesses: ANDERSON MOSS, ISAAC RUCKER,
F. N. TALIAFERRO.

410. 19 June 1813. MICAJAH PENDLETON and wife, MARY, Amherst
      County, to JONATHAN HORSLEY, JR., Amherst County...L1104-12-3--
one-half of Merchant mill called Elk Mills and lot of 2½ acres in
Amherst County and Nelson. Lines: south border Elk Island Creek.
Also half of two acres formerly known as PAMPLIN's Mill in both
counties and adjoins first tract. Lines: GEORGE HYLTON, SAMUEL ALLEN.

411. 20 December 1813. JONATHAN ROBINSON, Lynchburg, to JONATHAN
      LONDON, Amherst County...200 (sic) 380 acres Main road from
Lynchburg to ACH--it was conveyed by DANIEL BURFORD and wife, SARAH,
to JONATHAN ROBINSON on 18th instant. Lines: a bottom on Lynch
road, near the house, TINSLEY's new road, WILLIAM BURFORD, ROBERT
ROSE, BENNETT RUCKER, JONATHAN BOLLING, BOLLING CLARK, CHARLES
WINGFIELD. To JONATHAN LONDON, 6 March 1818.

412. 20 March 1805. STERLING CLAIBORNE, trustee, in a deed to
      JONATHAN ROBINSON, Lynchburg, January 1, 1805...Deed of Trust by
DANIEL BURFORD, JR., Amherst County, to CLAIBORNE to secure SAMUEL
IRVIN, Lynchburg--500 acres whereon BURFORD, JR., lives on main road
from Lynchburg to New Glasgow and about six miles from the former.
Duly auctioned, 19 March 1805, and JONATHAN ROBINSON paid $1000 for
500 acres. Witnesses: MICAJAH TERRELL, JAMES BENAGH, JACOB ROHR,
THOMAS W. COCKE, JAMES STEWART, R. HORSLEY. Acknowledged in open
court 20 December 1813.

414. 20 December 1813. WILLIAM TURNER and wife, SARAH, Amherst
      County, to WILLIAM JINKINS, Amherst County...$70.00 21 acres
Stovall Creek. Lines: Prize Branch, SAMUEL ANDERSON, DAVID S.
GARLAND, STEPHEN HAM, deceased. To JESSE BECK, 16 September 1833--
margin memo: see rel. Book U: 264--SALLY rel. dower in open court,
16 September 1833.

414. 19 November 1813. WILLIAM TURNER and wife, SARAH, Amherst
      County, to WILLIAM and EZEKIEL DAY, Amherst County...$100
31 acres south borders Stovall. Lines: JONATHAN JINKINS, deceased,
STEPHEN HAM, deceased, grantor, the branch tract bought by WILLIAM
TURNER from JONATHAN JINKINS in his lifetime. Witnesses: WILLIAM
JINKINS, DANIEL RULEY. To WILLIAM and EZEKIEL DAY, 19 August 1833.

415. 4 November 1813. PETER MILSTEAD, Amherst County, to DANIEL
      SHRADER, Amherst County...$100 for many articles. Witnesses:
HENRY CAMDEN, JONATHAN DUNCAN, JABEZ CAMDEN.

416. 18 December 1813. JOSHUA L. ELLIS and wife, PEGGY, Amherst
      County, to RICHARD L. ELLIS, Amherst County...$90 15 acres
south side Pedlar. Lines: both parties; old field. To JOSHUA L.
ELLIS, 27 January 1814.

417. 17 January 1814. JONATHAN SCRUGGS and wife, ELIZABETH, Nelson,
      to LEWIS JEFFERSON, Nelson County...L80 110 acres Pack (?)
branch; Elk Island Creek. Lines: JONATHAN HIGGINBOTHAM, Lufborough.
To LEWIS JEFFERSON, 21 October 1833.

418. 8 January 1814. SHADRICK TENNISON and wife, ELIZABETH, Amherst
      County, to PLEASANT DAWSON, Amherst County...L80 55½ acres
Harris Creek. Lines: WILLIAM BURFORD, JOSEPH MC RAY, Little Mill
Creek (a branch). Witnesses: WILLIAM J. BURFORD, SAMUEL TENISON,
RICHARD WHITTEN, WILLIAM B. DAMERON. To PLEASANT DAWSON, 14 March
1815.

418. 17 January 1814. JONATHAN LONDON and wife, TIRZAH, Amherst
     County, to WILLIAM BURFORD, Amherst County...L100 paid by
BURFORD for 23½ acres Harris Creek. Lines: grantee, ROBERT ROSE,
TINSLEY's road.

419. 17 January 1814. WILLIAM BURFORD and wife, SUSANNAH, Amherst
     County, to JONATHAN LONDON, Amherst County...L100 23½ acres on
road from Lynchburg to ACH--both sides of road. Lines: grantor,
grantee, ELIAS WILLS (on south side).

420. 4 November 1813. CHARLES P. TALIAFERRO and wife, LOUISA,
     Amherst County, to BENJAMIN SHACKELFORD, Amherst County...$1000
260 acres Puppies Creek. Lines: Main road, top of themt. To
BENJAMIN SHACKELFORD, 19 July 1814. Witnesses: LYNE S. TALIAFERRO,
FLETCHER N. TALIAFERRO.

421. 16 July 1813. JOSEPH HIGGINBOTHAM, Amherst County, to CHARLES P.
     TALIAFERRO, Amherst County...$1600 267 acres Buffaloe. Lines:
ford of the road above one to Buffaloe Springs; mouth of Willmere's
branch, BALLOW's old line, JOSEPH DODD. To CHARLES P. TALIAFERRO,
16 February 1815. Witnesses: BENJAMIN HIGGINBOTHAM, FLETCHER N.
TALIAFERRO, BENJAMIN TALIAFERRO, JAMES F. TALIAFERRO.

422. 30 September 1813. REUBEN GATEWOOD, Kentucky, to LEWIS LAYNE,
     Amherst County...L42-5 84 acres south side Buffaloe. Lines:
his own, HARRIS, CHARLES L. CHRISTIAN, WATERMILION Br. (Note: this
br. is always so spelled). To LEWIS LAYNE, 17 January 1817. Witnesses:
CHARLES L. CHRISTIAN, EDWARD LEWIS, MARY LEWIS, ELIJAH L. CHRISTIAN,
JONATHAN PHILIPS.

423. 24 December 1813. JAMES POWELL and wife, MILDRED, Amherst
     County, to ROBERT ALLEN, Amherst County...$100 one acre adjoining
lot on which ALLEN now lives. Lines: Lynch road, grantor, grantee,
WILLIAM LONG, WILLIAM HUTCHINSON. Witnesses: REUBEN COLEMAN,
JONATHAN P. BLOUNT, RICHARD BALLINGER. To ROBERT ALLEN, 10 October
1814.

423. 4 January 1814. JACOB PIERCE, Amherst County, to GEORGE SHRADER,
     Amherst County...L220 35 acres south side Buffaloe and both
sides Rockey Creek. Island tract sold by JAMES FLOID to JACOB WOOD--
except part taken off for COLEMAN's and FULTZ's mill. Lines: East
side Rockey Run, JONATHAN CHRISTIAN, mill pond, Buffaloe Bank, mouth
of Rockey Run. Witnesses: JONAS PIERCE, JAMES KNIGHT, GEROGE L.
SHRADER.

424. 27 May 1812. ELIZABETH LUCAS, Amherst County, to JAMES and
     SAMUEL GARLAND, one of Campbell and one of Amherst County...Deed
of Trust; debt to JAMES P. GARLAND Company by ELIZABETH GARLAND and
her bondsman, JONATHAN LUCAS. $1.00 mare bought of JAMES P. GARLAND,
other stock and furniture. Witnesses: HUDSON M. GARLAND, A. B. DAVIES,
H. L. DAVIES.

436. -- The pages are so numbered and no comment is inserted by any
     clerk to indicate missing pages. The book does not give any
sign of pages having been torn out in the past. It is impossible to
come to any conclusion as to missing pages since deeds do not follow
a chronological pattern for some deeds. 21 December 1813, order to
Amherst County Justices of the Peace: HENRY WATTS and wife, ELIZA,
19 April 1813, to BENJAMIN BROWN--438½ acres done by JAMES DILLARD
and JONATHAN COLEMAN, 13 January 1814. To BENJAMIN BROWN, 13 April
1815.

437. 26 July 1813. Order to Amherst County Justices of the Peace:
     THOMAS T. MAYO and wife, ELIZA, 15 March 1813, to GEORGE
STAPLES...10 acres. Done by JAMES DILLARD and CHARLES MUNDY, 9 October
1813.

438. 1 October 1813. JAMES WARE and wife, NANCY, Amherst County, to
     JONATHAN CAMM, JONATHAN BULLOCK, and POWHATAN ELLIS...Deed of
Trust; debt to CHARLES ELLIS, Richmond--45¼ acres--tract from ELLIS
to WARE on Horsley--nine bonds due; $1.00 tract with mills-Pedlar
Mills and Horsley. Lines: EDMOND GOODRICH, the canal, JONATHAN EUBANK.
Witnesses: NATHANIEL D. BURKS, THOMAS GOODRICH, RICHARD EUBANK,
JONATHAN ELLIS, DAVID BURKS, JR. To CHARLES ELLIS, 8 September 1815.

440. 16 February 1811. PROSSER POWELL, Amherst County, to RICHARD
     POWELL, Amherst County...L100 66 acres. Witnesses: MADISON
WARE, WILLIAM WARE, RICHARD POWELL.

441. 7 January 1814. THOMAS GREGORY, Pitsylvania County, to JONATHAN
     LONDON...$500.00 slaves and furniture for benefit of POLLY
GREGORY, wife of THOMAS, and their children: WILLIAM, JONATHAN,
LEWIS, and REUBIN GREGORY and any future children. Witnesses:
STARK WHITTINGTON, JONATHAN L. GLENN, FRANCIS CHUMBLEY, HENRY TURNER
(LINNER?), WILLIAM TURNER.

442. 15 September 1813. JONATHAN HYLTON, Redford, to REUBEN L. TYREE,
     Nelson County...L50 50 acres both sides Elk Island Creek.
Lines: road in Lufborough's line, JOHN SCRUGGS. Witnesses: WILLIAM
CUNNINGHAM, VALENTINE HYLTON, JAMES CUNNINGHAM, JR.

443. 27 January 1814. Order to Amherst County Justices of the Peace:
     JOSHUA L. ELLIS and wife, PEGGY, 18 December 1813, to RICHARD L.
ELLIS...15 acres. Done, 18 February 1814, by JONATHAN ELLIS and
THOMAS N. EUBANK.

444. 2 October 1813. DAVID WOODROOF, Amherst County, to JONATHAN
     MORTON, Amherst County...$100 27 acres Harris. Witnesses:
WILL WOODROOF, WILLIAM MC DANIEL, JAMES PETTIT.

444. 16 January 1814. WILLIAM B. GOOCH, acting executor of PHILIP
     GOOCH, Amherst County, to THOMPSON NOEL, Amherst County...$1000
and 3000 bushels of wheat, no acres given, south side Buffaloe.
Lines: JONATHAN PENN, SR., WILLIAM LONG, NANCY SHIELDS. Whole of
tract bought by PHILIP GOOCH of JAMES WATSON, WILLIAM LONG, and
JOHN PENN, SR. Witnesses: POWELL, J. EUBANK, HORACE WILSON.

445. 17 January 1814. THOMPSON NOEL and wife, NANCY, Amherst County,
     to WILLIAM B. GOOCH, as above...$1.00 Deed of Trust to secure
DANIEL CHEATWOOD, bondsman for NOEL to GOOCH--3000 bushels of wheat
to be delivered at Gates, Pendleton, or Stephen mills on the James.
Buffaloe tract. Lines: JONATHAN PENN, SR., WILLIAM LONG, NANCY SHIELDS
and which THOMPSON NOEL bought of WILLIAM B. GOOCH as described in above
deed. Witnesses: J. POWELL, JONATHAN EUBANK, H. WILSON.

447. 21 February 1814. THOMAS JEWELL and wife, SALLY, Amherst County,
     to HENRY TURNER, Amherst County...$1.00 46 3/4 acres Porrige;
part of 100 acres conveyed by REUBEN NORVELL to THOMAS JEWELL. Lines:
grantee, Staples road.

448. 21 February 1813. PHILIP THURMOND, Amherst County, to WILLIAM
     GATEWOOD, Amherst County...$90 40 acres Lovelady Creek. Lines:
ZED. SHOEMAKER, NICHOLAS PRYOR, WILLIAM PRYOR.

448. 21 February 1814. ANDERSON WARE and wife, CYNTHIA, late
     BURFORD and the daughter of PHILIP BURFORD, Amherst County,
to JAMES BENNETT, Amherst County...$352.00 44 acres Harris--CYNTHIA's
share of father's land at west end of tract where father lived.
Lines: grantee, DAVID TINSLEY, PHILIP BURFORD, JR., MARY BURFORD's
dower tract.

449. 21 February 1814. WILLIAM JINKINS and wife, PEGGY, Amherst
     County, to SAMUEL ANDERSON, Amherst County...$55 21 acres north
borders Stovall and bought by WILLIAM JINKINS of WILLIAM TURNER.
Lines: Prize Branch, grantee, DAVID S. GARLAND, STEPHEN HAM, deceased.
To GRANVILLE LAIN, 5 August 1834.

450. 3 January 1814. GUERRANT PERROW, Amherst County, to DANIEL
PERROW, Amherst County...Power of attorney to recieve my interest
in tract surveyed 25 January 1803--421 acres and devised by DANIEL
PERRO to three sons by will: GUERRANT, CHARLES, and DANIEL and my
interest is one-third. To sell and amount is for benefit of my wife
and children. Witnesses: S. GARLAND, JAMES WATSON, HENRY H. WATTS,
DAVID G. DAVIDSON, WILLIAM HORSLEY.

451. 21 March 1814. SAMUEL STAPLES and wife, JUDITH, Nelson County,
to GEORGE WASHINGTON HIGGINBOTHAM, Amherst County...$200.00
all interest as heirs of JOSEPH STAPLES, deceased, Amherst County,
in tracts on Buffaloe. To GEORGE WASHINGTON HIGGINBOTHAM, --.

453. 21 February 1814. THOMAS JEWELL and wife, SALLY, Amherst
County, to HENRY TURNER, Amherst County...$1.00 46 3/4 acres
Porrige. Part of 100 acres to THOMAS JEWELL by deed from REUBEN
NORVELL. Lines: grantee, Staples road.

453. 25 December 1813. JONATHAN TULEY, SR., and wife, MARY, Amherst
County, to RICHARD L. ELLIS, Amherst County...$400.00 two tracts.
1. 112 acres north side and joining Pedlar. Lines: JONATHAN MAYS, SR.,
RICHARD HATTEN, HALL. 2. 140 acres Pea Vine or Chestnut Mountain on
Cashaw Creek, branch of James. Lines: north by ROLAND BYAS, west by
ARCHELAUS MITCHELL, east and south be estate of HENRY L. DAVIES,
deceased. Witnesses: THOMAS LAIN, HENRY BROWN, WILLIAM JOPLING,
ABRAM CARTER. To RICHARD L. ELLIS, 26 July 1814.

455. 18 December 1813. JONATHAN ROBINSON, Lynchburg, to DANIEL
BURFORD, Amherst County...$1.00 40 acres Harris. Balance of
tract which BURFORD this day conveyed to ROBINSON and where the house
stands. Lines: Lynch road, TINSLEY's road. Witnesses: JONATHAN
LONDON, THOMAS BEDDOW, WILLIAM BURFORD.

456. 18 December 1813. DANIEL BURFORD and wife, SARAH, Amherst
County, to JONATHAN ROBINSON, Lynchburg...$2000.00 380 acres
Harris and Stovall Creeks and both sides of road from Lynchburg to
ACH. Part of tract to DANIEL BURFORD from STERLING CLAIBORNE on
trust for benefit of SAMUEL IRVINE, deceased. Tract sold and ROBINSON
bought under Deed of Trust and has this day conveyed to DANIEL
BURFORD the balance of tract--say 40 acres where the house stands.
Lines: Bottom on Lynch road, near the house, Tinsley's new road,
WILLIAM BURFORD, ROBERS ROSE, BENNETT RUCKER, JONATHAN BOLLING,
ELIAS WILLS, BOLLING CLARK, CHARLES WINGFIELD. Witnesses: JONATHAN
LONDON, THOMAS P. BEDDOW, WILLIAM BURFORD. Page 458 order to quiz
SARAH, 19 March 1814. Done by NELSON C. DAWSON and CHARLES MUNDY on
same date.

460. 15 March 1814. JAMES HIGGINBOTHAM and wife, ELIZA, Amherst
County, to JOSEPH DILLARD, Amherst County...L270 Higginbotham
Mill Creek. Part of tract by deed to JAMES from his father, JAMES
HIGGINBOTHAM. Lines: grantee, WILLIAM HIGGINBOTHAM, EDMOND PENN,
JAMES HIGGINBOTHAM's Spring Branch, grantor. To JOSEPH DILLARD,
16 January 1814--sic.

461. 21 March 1814. JAMES BARRETT, attorney for HUGH CAMPBELL and
wife, ELIZABETH, Montgomery County, Tennessee, CHARLES L.
BARRETT, JAMES BARRETT and JAMES BARRETT as attorney for ANN BARRETT,
Montgomery County, Tennessee, to JONATHAN WARE, Amherst County...$350
154 acres both sides Pedlar, also 99 acres adjoining on bank of
Pedlar. To JONATHAN WARE, 15 April 1816.

463. 14 September 1813. NELSON CRAWFORD and wife, LUCY, Amherst
County, to ABRAM CARTER, Amherst County...$456 57 acres both
sides Horsley. Part of tract. Lines: both parties, RICHARD HATTEN,
P. CARTER. To ABRAM CARTER, 22 May 1814.

465. 21 March 1814. ABRAM CARTER and wife, MOLLY, Amherst County,
to NELSON CRAWFORD, Amherst County...$1.00; no acres. Lines:
grantee, EDWARD CARTER, grantor, the road, Horsley.

466. 21 February 1814. REUBEN NORVELL and wife, POLLY, Amherst
County, to HENRY TURNER, Amherst County...$220 65½ acres Porrige
and west side Staples Ferry road. Lines: Staples road, tract bought
by TURNER from THOMAS JEWELL.

467. 16 April 1814. JOSEPH MILSTEAD and BENJAMIN HIGGINBOTHAM,
Amherst County, to JONATHAN and RICHARD L. ELLIS, Amherst
County...$1600 three negro girls: FRANCES, NANCY, POLLY, also 350
acres both sides Horsley. Lines: WILLIAM DEMPSEY, WILLIAM SCHOLFIELD's
estate, WILLIAM SHEPHERD, WILLIAM CRAWFORD, DANIEL SHRADER, Spring
road, Long Branch. Witnesses: THOMAS N. EUBANK, WILLIAM COLEMAN,
PETER CARTER, JESSE CLEMENS. To R. EUBANK, 26 July 1814.

469. 1 April 1814. JAMES SALE to THOMAS N. EUBANK, Amherst County...
Deed of Trust; debt to JONATHAN and RICHARD L. ELLIS, $1.00,
my one-third of SALLY and her children: REUBEN, MOURNING, JINCY,
CIDA, JACK, and COLEMAN and increase. Witnesses: PETER P. THORNTON,
RICHARD N. EUBANK, JAMES WARE. To JONATHAN and RICHARD L. ELLIS,
19 September 1814.

471. 18 October 1813. MARTHA MAYO, widow of JOSEPH MAYO, late of
Powhatan, deceased, to WILLIAM GALT, Richmond...GALT bought of
THOMAS T. MAYO, Amherst County, 149½ acres on James and next to GALT,
16 July 1813--Stovall Creek as well. Part of tract left to THOMAS T.
MAYO by his father, JOSEPH MAYO, aforesaid. MARTHA considers that she
is entitled to dower and for $1.00 released it. Witnesses: ELLIS
PURYEAR, THOMAS PEERS, BENJAMIN HUGHES, GEORGE MAYO. Acknowledged
in Goochland by MARTHA and witnesses: PURYEAR, PEERS and HUGHES,
15 November 1813.

472. 27 July 1813. Order to Amherst County Justices of the Peace:
THOMAS T. MAYO and wife, ELIZA, 16 July 1813, to WILLIAM GALT...
149½ acres. Done by JAMES DILLARD and CHARLES MUNDY, 9 October 1813.

474. 22 October 1813. DANIEL NORCUTT and wife, RACHEL, Amherst County,
to WILLIAM MUSE, JR., Amherst County...$110 2 acres west side
Lynch road. Lines: GEORGE W. TAYLOR, the road. Witnesses: REUBEN
NORVELL, ELIAS WILLS, WILLIAM MUSE, SR., GEORGE W. TAYLOR. To WILLIAM
MUSE, JR., 1818.

475. 15 May 1814. FERDINAND LEIGH and wife, ELIZABETH, Amherst
County, to WILLIAM CASH, Amherst County...$400 148 acres--small
branch under Indian Will's (sic) Mountain. Lines: BARTLETT CASH,
BENJAMIN ROGERS, CHARLES TUCKER. Witnesses: LINDSEY SANDIDGE, B.
BROWN, AMBROSE R. MC DANIEL. To WILLIAM CASH, 27 October 1828.

476. 4 October 1813. ANDERSON MOSS, Amherst County, to WILLIAM G.
PENDLETON, Amherst County, and THOMAS ALDRIDGE, Amherst County...
Deed of Trust; debt to THOMAS ALDRIDGE and Company--judgement in
County Court of Amherst County by DAVID and JAMES GARLAND versus
MOSS, confirmed by Superior court of Amherst County; also a judgement
by DAVID GARLAND, assignee of DANIEL HIGGINBOTHAM and Company versus
AMDERSON MOSS, one bond executed to STERLING CLAIBORNE in 1811--$1.00
paid by PENDLETON--two slaves, ADAM and CALEB, woman, CHARLOTTE,
woman, PHEBE, and three children: LUCY, ELLICK and AFFREY, girl,
MILLY, woman, PEREAN and her nine children (named), stock. Witnesses:
JAMES S. PENDLETON, JONATHAN L. BLAIR, ROBERT ALDRIDGE, JONATHAN
MYERS. To THOMAS ALDRIDGE, 27 August 1814.

480. 10 December 1813. BENJAMIN WATTS, Amherst County, to WILLIAM
ROBINSON and JAMES LEE, Amherst County...Deed of Trust; debt
to SAMUEL BRANSFORD, Buckingham County. $1.00--named slaves, stock,
furniture. Witnesses: JESSE BECK, JONATHAN D. BURFORD, WILLIAM
ISBELL.

482. 4 December 1813. LEROY CAMDEN, Amherst County, to WILLIAM G.
PENDLETON, Amherst County...Deed of Trust; debt to THOMAS
ALDRIDGE, Amherst County--$1.00 slaves named with children. Witnesses:
JOSEPH DILLARD, EDMOND PENN, ROBERT ALDRIDGE, JONATHAN S. BLAIR.

484. 29 May 1810. Order to Amherst County Justices of the Peace:
JAMES POWELL and wife, MILDRED, 23 May 1810, to WILLIAM LONG...
ten acres. Done by EDMOND PENN and THOMAS CREWS, 24 March 1814.

485. 23 May 1810. JAMES POWELL and wife, MILLY, Buckingham, to
WILLIAM LONG, Richmond...L500 10 acres at the Oaks. Lines:
grantee, near brick tavern on road by courthouse to Lynchburg--oblong
square. Witnesses: JONATHAN LACKEY, WILLIAM COLEMAN, D. WOODROOF,
REUBEN COLEMAN.

485. 7 October 1813. WILLIAM CAMDEN, Amherst County, died testate
and the will makes ample provision for widow, SYBLEE CAMDEN,
as to personal estate, but no provision for real estate. WILLIAM
gave son, LEROY CAMDEN, tract whereon WILLIAM lived with mansion
house. LEROY wishes to provide for his mother--two rooms on first
floor and one in cellar in east end of house and a lumber room above
stairs with room in north end of kitchen, joining use of smoke house
and Dairywell house and yard; part of garden, use of a small stable,
privilege to take fire wood and timber for repairs. LEROY will not
use rest of house save for his own family during her lifetime.
Witnesses: MICAJAH CAMDEN, JORDAN P. CAMDEN, WARNER GOODWIN.

487. 27 January 1814. Order to Amherst County Justices of the Peace:
JOSHUA ELLIS and wife, PEGGY, 18 December 1813, to RICHARD L.
ELLIS...15 acres. Done by JONATHAN ELLIS and THOMAS N. EUBANK,
18 February 1814. Someone has written on margin: "Twice recorded."

488. 2 April 1814. JAMES BIAS, attorney for ROBERT KNUCKLES, Amherst
County, to BOLLING MITCHELL, Amherst County...$150.00 136 acres
north side Otter. Lines: JEREMIAH WHITTEN, JONATHAN HOGG.

489. 23 November 1813. THOMAS RICHESON, Amherst County, to THOMAS N.
EUBANK, Amherst County...Deed of Trust; debt to JONATHAN and
RICHARD L. ELLIS, bond executed by RICHARD MILNER, Bedford, to
THOMAS RICHESON. $1.00--slaves named. Witnesses: RICHARD EUBANK,
NATHANIEL DAVIS, RICHARD H. BURKS, TARLTON GILLESPIE, JAMES WARE,
PETER P. THORNTON, HENRY BROWN. To JONATHAN and RICHARD ELLIS,
19 September 1814.

490. 15 June 1814. REEUBEN COLEMAN and wife, BELINDA, Amherst County,
to LINDSEY COLEMAN, Amherst County, and wife, NANCY...GEORGE
COLEMAN died owning Amherst County land and descended to his sons:
WILLIAM, ROBERT H., REUBEN, and LINDSEY COLEMAN. WILLIAM conveyed to
ROBERT H. his rights, ROBERT H. conveyed to REUBEN and LINDSEY his
rights. REUBEN and LINDSEY hereby make partition. REUBEN and wife
to own. Lines: the road, a spring, Migginson's road, Rutledge
Creek, GIDEON RUCKER, Lynch road--217½ acres. The part to LINDSEY
and wife. Lines: north bank Rutledge, Lynch Road, REUBEN COLEMAN,
a spring, Migginson's road--378 acres.

492. 18 May 1814. JONATHAN N. ROSE and wife, MARY, Amherst County,
to HILL CARTER, Amherst County...L78 52 acres. Lines: Carter's
old line.

493. 1 December 1813. BERRY BRYANT, Amherst County, to FINNEY
BRYANT, Amherst County...L21 140 acres. Lines: his own.

494. 21 April 1814. GEORGE PENN and wife, PAMELIA, Amherst County,
to ROBERT LEWIS JEFFERSON, Nelson County...L425 195 acres
borders Elk Island Creek. Lines: JONATHAN THOMPSON, JONATHAN
CHRISTIAN's old line. Also 38 acres adjoining. Lines: PHILIP GOOCH,
grantor. To ROBERT LEWIS JEFFERSON, 1 June 1814. Witnesses:
JONATHAN HORSLY, JR., JOSEPH HORSLEY, JONATHAN ALLEN, WILLIAM L. BELL.

495. 22 November 1813. JABEZ CAMDEN, Amherst County, to JONATHAN
      MYERS, Amherst County...Deed of Trust; debt to THOMAS ALDRIDGE,
$1.00; slaves and tract conveyed to JABEZ CAMDEN by father, WILLIAM
CAMDEN--700 acres head waters Huff. Lines: TINSLEY RUCKER, CHRISTOPHER
ISBELL, CHARLES TALIAFERRO. It is whole of tract where JABEZ CAMDEN
lives. Also one tract bought by JABEZ CAMDEN of JONATHAN WHITEHEAD,
HENRY CAMDEN, et al. on Huff. Lines: WILLIAM STINNETT, LEROY CAMDEN,
MICAJAH CAMDEN--500 acres; also five negroes, men, four women, two
girls. Witnesses: JAMES L. PENDLETON, JONATHAN L. BLAIR, ROBERT
ALDRIDGE. To THOMAS ALDRIDGE, 11 October 1816.

498. 25 November 1813. MOZA PETER, Amherst County, to JAMES P.
      GARLAND, Amherst County...Deed of Trust--incomplete and ends--
clerk has scratched through it. Complete on 509.

498. 29 May 1814. DANIEL BURFORD, JR., and wife, SUSANNA, Amherst
      County, to JAMES MARR, Amherst County...$268.70 53 3/4 acres
headborders Porrige. Lines: grantee, THOMAS WILLCOX, deceased,
ELIZABETH THURMOND, JAMES PETTIT. Witnesses: REUBEN NORVELL, RICHARD
JONES, JONATHAN HUTCHINSON. Page 499 order to quiz SUSANNA, 18 April
1814; done by CHARLES MUNDY and PHILIP JOHNSON, 10 June 1810 (sic).
Recorded June 11, 1814.

500. 27 January 1814. JESSE RICHESON and wife, AMELIA, JONATHAN
      RICHESON and wife, NANCY, ARMISTEAD RUCKER and wife, ELIZABETH,
and THOMAS RICHESON--heirs of JONATHAN RICHESON, deceased, to RICHARD
MILLNER, Amherst County...$1.00 432 acres Pedlar. Part of MH tract
of JONATHAN RICHESON. Witnesses: REUBEN NORVELL, BENJAMIN RUCKER,
JAMES L. DILLARD. To THOMAS RICHESON, 14 May 1814.

502. 28 May 1806. BENJAMIN RUCKER, Amherst County, to BENAMMI STONE,
      Amherst County...$1.00 16 acres--part of tract on Rutledge.
Lines: JOSEPH HIGGINBOTHAM, JR., south bank of Rutledge, mouth of a
small branch, grantee. Witnesses: J. P. GARLAND, BENNETT RUCKER,
NELSON C. DAWSON, JR. Final proof by NELSON C. DAWSON, JR. 13 July
1814.

503. 18 July 1814. DAVID S. GARLAND and wife, JANE, Amherst County,
      to JONATHAN LONDON, Amherst County...$2500 five tracts on
Porrige, north branch James. 1. 360 acres. Lines: WILLIAM GALT,
JOSEPH MAYO, deceased. Bought by DAVID S. GARLAND of SACKVILLE
KING's executors. 2. Located by both and next to Number one--378
acres. Lines: STEPHEN HAM, SACKVILLE KING, WILLIAM GALT, JONATHAN
LONDON. 3. Located by LONDON and next to 70 acres in Number two.
Lines: JAMES DILLARD, JOSEPH MAYO, SACKVILLE KING, LONDON, GARLAND.
4. 76½ acres located by LONDON. Lines: GARLAND, KING, STEPHEN HAM,
POWHATAN BOWLING, deceased, WILLIAM GALT. 5 200 acres part reserved
by GARLAND and LONDON out of 400 acres, 27 March 1802, conveyance to
KEZIAH COFLAN (alias SMITH, alias KNIGHT). To JONATHAN LONDON,
15 August 1814.

505. 18 July 1814. WILLIAM LEE and wife, BETSY, Amherst County, to
      DAVID S. GARLAND, Amherst County...$2664 296 acres north side
Buffaloe. Lines: GARLAND on north bank Buffaloe, EDMOND PENN, THOMAS
ALDRIDGE. To DAVID S. GARLAND, 2 December 1827.

506. 18 July 1814. JONATHAN LONDON and wife, TIRZA, Amherst County,
      to BENJAMIN RUCKER, Amherst County...$3800 380 acres both sides
Lynch road. Part of tract formerly that of DANIEL BURFORD. Lines:
Lynch road, TINSLEY road. Except 40 acres reserved for DANIEL BURFORD
and wife at survey at intersection of Lynch and Tinsley's roads.
To BENJAMIN RUCKER, 15 August 1815.

508. 14 July 1814. THOMAS T. MAYO and wife, ELIZABETH, GEORGE MAYO,
      Cumberland, to WILLIAM GALT, Richmond...$2560 154½ acres.
Lines: bank of James, DAVID S. GARLAND, WILLIAM GALT.

509. 25 November 1813. MOZA PETERS, Amherst County, to JAMES P.
GARLAND, Amherst County...Deed of Trust; debt to WILLIAM C.
CHRISTIAN, Amherst County--$1.00 slaves. Witnesses: JONATHAN
ROBINSON, REUBEN COLEMAN.

510. 16 February 1814. JONATHAN MOSS and wife, POLLY H., Amherst
County, to WILLIS FRANKLIN, Amherst County. L120--interest
in tract of WILLIAM MOSS, deceased. Piney River. Witnesses:
CHARLOTTE POWELL. Page 511 order to quiz MARY H., 28 June 1814.
Done, 14 July 1814, by HILL CARTER and JONATHAN N. ROSE.

513. 15 August 1814. JONATHAN LONDON and wife, TIRZA, Amherst County,
to THOMAS JEWELL, Amherst County...$416.60 151½ acres both
sides Porrage Creek. Lines: THOMAS BURLEY, TURNER PENN, PLEASANT
STORY, DENNIS ENSEY.

514. 22 July 1814. WILLIAM TOMLINSON and wife, BETSY, Amherst County,
to JONATHAN WARE, Amherst County...L15 70 acres Pedlar. Lines:
JONATHAN HALL, BEASLEY, BROWN. Witnesses: JONATHAN TOMLINSON, JESSE
CLEMENTS, DAVID TOMLINSON. To JONATHAN WARE, 15 July 1816.

515. 30 July 1803. JONATHAN DAKIN, Campbell County, to DAVID MOORE,
same county...L30 15 acres. Lines: Lynch road, JONATHAN WARE,
JONATHAN HANSFORD. Witnesses: JACOB RHOR, WILL B. BANKS, WILSON
DAVENPORT, HENRY D. TENISON. Proved Amherst County, 15 January 1814,
by WILSON DAVENPORT and JACOB RHOR. Final proof 15 August 1814 by
HENRY D. TENISON. To DAVID MOORE, 26 August 1815.

516. 26 May 1814. DANIEL PERROW, attorney-in-fact for GUERRANT
PERROW, Amherst County, to CHARLES PERROW, Nelson County...
$1200 all of GUERRANT's interest in tract willed by DANIEL PERROW,
deceased, to his three sons--survey of 1803--undivided part of
421 acres. Witnesses: WILLIAM MEGGINSON, MEREDITH FORTUNE, ELEANOR
PERROW.

517. 9 August 1814. GEORGE CAMPBELL and wife, EADY, Amherst County,
to HILL CARTER, Amherst County...$2352 143 acres Piney--100 acres
of it conveyed by deed to GEORGE by heirs of GEORGE CAMPBELL, 1 December
1806, and 46 acres devised to GEORGE and 30 acres of the 40 acres as
one of heirs of his father, GEORGE CAMPBELL. 16 acres of it bought
from JONATHAN CAMPBELL, JR., another of heirs of GEORGE. Lines:
Piney, main road from Rose Mill to Buffaloe Springs, heirs of GEORGE
CAMPBELL. Also 30 acres--part of tract of GEORGE CAMPBELL, deceased,
and allotted to SAMUEL CAMPBELL, heir of GEORGE, and by SAMUEL sold
to GEORGE. Also 30 acres--share of CORNELIUS CAMPBELL--heir of GEORGE,
and sold by him to GEORGE--206 acres--$12.00 per acre for first 146
acres and $10 per acre for two tracts of 30 acres each. Witnesses:
JONATHAN THOWETT (?), S. CLAIBORNE, JONATHAN N. ROSE.

520. 18 February 1814. REUBEN NORVELL, Amherst County, to CHRISTOPHER
ANTHONY and JONATHAN BULLOCK, Lynchburg...Deed of Trust; debt
to WILLIAM NORVELL and JONATHAN WIATT, merchants--$1.00 twelve slaves--
ages and names. If not paid, to be sold at tavern or house now
occupied by RICHARD POWELL in Amherst or at NORVELL's home. Witnesses:
W. HARRISON, E. B. NORVELL, WILL NORVELL.

522. 1 February 1814. DAVID CRAWFORD, Amherst County, to HENRY L.
DAVIES, Amherst County...Deed of Trust; debt to ARTHUR B. DAVIES
as bondsman on three suits; THOMAS W. COCKE for benefit of P. DUDLEY
and NATHAN CRAWFORD versus DAVID CRAWFORD--$1.00; one negroe, MOLLY.
Witnesses: JAMES FRANKLIN, JAMES LUCAS, DAVID CLARKSON. To HENRY L.
DAVIES, 2 September 1814.

524. 15 August 1814. THOMAS JEWELL and wife, SALLY, Amherst County,
to ALEXANDER JEWELL, Amherst County...L53-5 53¾ acres south
side Porrage and is balance of 100 acres bought by THOMAS JEWELL from
REUBEN NORVELL. Lines: grantee, JONATHAN LONDON, HENRY TURNER. To
ALEXANDER JEWELL, August, 1820.

525. 15 August 1814. WILLIAM A. HARRIS, Nelson, to ROBERT COLEMAN,
      Amherst County...$3600 for two tracts. 1. 400 acres in Amherst
County and Nelson--south borders Buffaloe and north side Buffaloe
Ridge. Lines: JONATHAN NICHOLAS, deceased. 2. 329 acres adjoining
and in Amherst County. Lines: Harris old road, JONATHAN NICHOLAS,
deceased, a branch. Bought by HARRIS from COLEMAN. Witnesses:
CORNELIUS POWELL. To H. T. HARRIS, 15 July 1816.

526. 8 November 1802. JONATHAN CAMM, Amherst County, to JONATHAN
      WARWICK, Amherst County...$188 16 acres north borders Buffaloe.
Part of tract bought by JONATHAN CAMM from WILLIAM WARWICK. Lines:
main road from Lynchburg to New Glasgow, his own. Witnesses:
EDMOND T. COLEMAN, EDMOND PENN, DAVID S. GARLAND, HUDSON M. GARLAND.
Acknowledged in court, 16 August 1814.

528. 7 August 1814. DABNEY WARE and wife, ELIZABETH, Amherst County,
      to ANDERSON WARE, Amherst County...$705 282 acres Headborders
of SHACKELFORD's Mill Creek. Lines: WILLIAM NOEL, ANTHONY NICELY,
JONATHAN BYAS, a road, THOMAS N. EUBANK, THOMAS HIGGINBOTHAM, ROBERT
KNUCKLES.

529. 22 March 1814. THOMPSON NOEL, Amherst County, to STERLING
      CLAIBORNE, Amherst County...Deed of Trust; debt to DANIEL
CHEATWOOD--$10.00 DANIEL CHEATWOOD on bond to WILLIAM B. GOOCH,
executor of PHILIP GOOCH to secure payment of L3000 wheat--nine
named slaves, stock, and furniture. Witnesses: PETER CHRISTIAN,
SAMUEL CHRISTIAN, ELIZABETH H. GOODE.

530. 1 August 1814. ISAAC RUCKER, executor of AMBROSE RUCKER,
      deceased, to JONATHAN HANSARD, Amherst County...L1270 473 acres.
Lines: BENJAMIN RUCKER on south, WILLIAM TINSLEY et al. on west,
JONATHAN AMBLER on north, WILLIAM MC DANILE on east.

531. 19 July 1814. Order to Amherst County Justices of the Peace:
      CHARLES P. TALIAFERRO and wife, LOUISA, 4 November 1813, to
BENJAMIN SHACKELFORD...260 acres. Done, 10 August 1814, by CHARLES
and BENJAMIN TALIAFERRO. Page 533 order of same date as to CHARLES P.
TALIAFERRO and wife, LOUISA, to BENJAMIN TALIAFERRO--66½ acres. Done,
10 August 1814, by CHARLES TALIAFERRO and BENJAMIN SHACKELFORD.
Margin: To B. SHACKELFORD, 19 June 1815, and to B. TALIAFERRO,
22 September 1837.

534. 19 July 1814. ROBERT H. COLEMAN, Amherst County, to WILLIAM
      COLEMAN, Amherst County...$1.00 and other considerations--
tract in Madison County, Kentucky, on Silver and Muddy Creeks--part
of tract--250 acres and on north side of larger tract. Witnesses:
A. B. DAVIES, WILL G. PENDLETON, SAMUEL P. CHRISTIAN. To WILLIAM
COLEMAN, 4 December 1814.

534. 31 August 1814. WILLIS FRANKLIN, Amherst County, to THOMAS
      ALDRIDGE, Amherst County...$850 two tracts out of larger tract
to legatees of WILLIAM MOSS, deceased. Numbers two and six--50 acres
each and all to FRANKLIN. Reference to commissioners report. L10
for two lots in New Glasgow and houses--also property of legatees of
WILLIAM MOSS. Numbers 23 and 24--1/9th of them. To THOMAS ALDRIDGE,
13 October 1822.

537. 7 February 1814. WILLIAM LONG and wife, BETSY, Richmond, to
      MICAJAH CAMDEN, Amherst County...$3000 25 acres--a brick tavern.
Lines: a white oak near the road, JAMES POWELL, grantor, a branch,
Lynch road. Witnesses: HENRY L. DAVIES, A. B. DAVIES, HUDSON M.
GARLAND, HENRY BALLINGER. To MICAJAH CAMDEN, 31 October 1814.

538. 1 September 1814. WARNER GOODWIN and wife, ESTHER, Amherst
      County, to MICAJAH CAMDEN, Amherst County...$500 150 acres all
that WARNER GOODWIN now owns of tract bought of ROBERT HOLLOWAY
except that between the two roads where his dwelling house is located.
Lines: near main road, JONATHAN PENN, ROBERT WALKER, JOSEPH PENN.

539. 1 September 1814. MICAJAH CAMDEN and wife, POLLY, Amherst
      County, to DAVID S. GARLAND, Amherst County...L2000 298 acres
south side and joining Piney. Lines: WILLIAM GALT, JOEL FRANKLIN's
estate, JAMES FULCHER, WILLIAM S. CRAWFORD.

541. 14 June 1814. JONATHAN WARWICK, Amherst County, to THOMAS
      ALDRIDGE, Amherst County...$5000.00 two tracts. 1. 16 acres
north borders Buffaloe--tract bought by JONATHAN WARWICK of JONATHAN
CAMM. Lines: main road from Lynchburg to New Glasgow, grantor,
branch. 2. 357 acres which he bought of GABRIEL PENN's executors.
North side and joining Buffaloe, part of PENN tract. Lines: WILLIAM
LEE, THOMAS ALDRIDGE. Witnesses: ROBERT ALDRIDGE, JONATHAN P. COBB,
JONATHAN WHITE. To JONATHAN WHITE, 15 December 1817.

543. 1 September 1814. JOSEPH SWANSON and wife, SUSANNA, Amherst
      County, to WILLIAM HIGGINBOTHAM, Amherst County...$200--bought
by both of THOMAS ALDRIDGE--half of three quarters of an acre--lot 1
in New Glasgow, east side Main Street. Lines: north by Church lot,
DAVID S. GARLAND, THOMAS ALDRIDGE, Main Street.

544. 21 July 1814. CHARLES P. TALIAFERRO, Amherst County, to
      ZACHARIAH DRUMMOND, Amherst County...$50 17 acres headwaters
Puppie Creek. Lines: grantee. To ZACHARIAH DRUMMOND, 2 August
1817. Witmesses: LYNE TALIAFERRO.

545. 9 September 1814. LEONARD TENNISON, Amherst County, to JOSEPH
      NEEDHAM, Campbell County...$400 40 acres both sides Steel Creek
and both sides of Opossum Island Road. Lines: JONATHAN LYNCH, JR. (?),
MAJOR WILLIAM WARWICK, HENRY TENNISON, MRS. LUCY ROBINSON, LINEAS
BOLLING. Witmesses: THOMAS W. COCKE, JONATHAN HARDWICK, JONATHAN Y.
JOHNSON.

546. 19 September 1814. GEORGE W. HIGGINBOTHAM and wife, ELIZABETH,
      Amherst County, to ANGUISH MC CLOUD, Amherst County...L50
98 acres south fork Buffaloe. Lines: BENJAMIN SANDIDGE, NEAL CAMPBELL,
deceased, JAMES HIGGINBOTHAM. Witmesses: LINDSEYY SANDIDGE, JONATHAN
SMITH, LEONARD HENLEY.

548. 9 September 1814. JOSEPH and BENJAMIN HIGGINBOTHAM, Amherst
      County, to JONATHAN HUTCHESON, Amherst County...they act as
executors of JOSEPH HIGGINBOTHAM--L500 248 acres Porrage Creek.
Lines: EDWARD EIDSON, JAMES CHRISTIAN. Witnesses: LINDSEY MC DANIEL,
JAMES HIX, DABNEY SANDIDGE, AMBROSE N. MC DANIEL. To JOSEPH
HIGGINBOTHAM, 20 January 1817.

549. 18 August 1814. ROBERT HUNTER and wife, NANCY, Campbell
      County, to JOSHUA L. ELLIS, Amherst County...L300 three tracts
in Amherst County and descended to HUNTER and wife on division of the
estate of late JOSIAH ELLIS by marriage of HUNTER to NANCY, daughter
of JOSIAH ELLIS. 1. 287 acres known as Combs tract on south side and
joining Pedlar and both sides Cedar Creek. Lines: DAVID BURKS, SR.,
LARKIN BYAS. 2. 366 acres on Dancing Creek--Harper's tract. Lines:
JOSIAH JOPLING, ZED. SHOEMAKER, north side Dancing Creek, LARKIN
BYAS, DRURY BOWMAN. 3. 91 acres Dancing Creek borders. Lines:
ZED. SHOEMAKER, JOSIAH JOPLING, WILLIAM SHOEMAKER. Witnesses:
R. L. ELLIS, JAMES WARE, RICHARD N. EUBANK, JONATHAN ELLIS.

551. 15 September 1814. ISAAC RUCKER, executor of AMBROSE RUCKER,
      Amherst County, to RICHARD HARRISON, Amherst County...L37
35 acres part of ISAAC RUCKER, deceased, tract and joining RICHARD
HARRISON where he lives, JAMES HILL, ANTHONY RUCKER. Note: I think
copyist made a mistake and meant AMBROSE RUCKER, deceased, and not
ISAAC RUCKER, deceased.

552. 19 September 1814. JONATHAN EUBANK, JR., Amherst County, to
      WILLIAM MITCHELL, Amherst County...$800 112½ acres Horsley.
Lines: RICHARD L. ELLIS, RICHARD MILLNER, CHRISTIE ELLIS. Witnesses:
THOMAS M. EUBANK, JOSHUA L. ELLIS, JAMES WARE, R. N. EUBANK.

553. 6 September 1814. THOMAS MONTGOMERY, Lincoln County, Kentucky,
    to infant daughter, MARY WRIGHT ELLIS MONTGOMERY, by my late
wife, MARY WRIGHT MONTGOMERY...three slaves--two boys and one girl--
to maintain and educate her. Witnesses: R. S. ELLIS, JONATHAN
ELLIS, RICHARD N. EUBANK.

554. 15 September 1814. JONATHAN WARE, SR. and WILLIAM JOPLING,
    executor of WILLIAM WARE, to THOMAS LANE, Amherst County...
L58-13 46 acres headwaters Horsley. Lines: WILLIAM PRYOR. To
THOMAS LANE, 3 January 1820.

555. 11 July 1811. Order to Nelson County Justices of the Peace:
    SAMUEL H. ALLEN and wife, POLLY, 17 September 1810, to MICAJAH
PENDLETON...40½ acres. Done, 5 October 1811, by WILLIAM HORSLEY and
GEORGE VARNUM.

556. 27 August 1814. Order to Amherst County Justices of the Peace:
    JONATHAN LONDON and wife, TIRZA, 15 August 1814, to THOMAS
JEWELL...Done by JONATHAN COLEMAN and CHARLES MUNDY, 14 September
1814. To THOMAS JEWELL, 15 November 1824.

557. 14 December 1813. THOMAS ALDRIDGE, Amherst County, to JAMES
    GARLAND, Amherst County--4 February 1812, HENRY CAMDEN, Amherst
County, to THOMAS ALDRIDGE...Deed of Trust, Beaver Creek, south fork
Buffaloe tract and part of former tract of GABRIEL PENN, deceased--
414 acres. Lines: JONATHAN DUNCAN's heirs, WILLIAM CAMDEN, JR.,
JABEZ CAMDEN, JONATHAN YOUNG (?), CHARLES BURRUS--it was conveyed
to WILLIAM CAMDEN by HENRY CAMDEN, deed of gift, 16 July 1804. HENRY
CAMDEN defaulted on debt due DAVID and JAMES GARLAND. December 14,
1811, HENRY CAMDEN made Deed ofTrust to JAMES S. PENDLETON and JONATHAN
MYERS on debt to THOMAS ALDRIDGE, transferred to JAMES GARLAND and
ALDRIDGE as trustees. At sale JAMES GARLAND bought at $700. To JAMES
PENDLETON, 31 January 1816.

560. 9 September 1814. JOSEPH NEEDHAM, Campbell County, to ISAIAH
    ALLEY, Amherst County...Deed of Trust; debt to LEONARD TENNISON,
Amherst County...$1.00 40 acres both sides Steel's Creek and both sides
Opossum Island road. Lines: JONATHAN LYNCH, JR., MAJOR WILLIAM
WARWICK, HENRY TENNISON, MRS. LUCY ROBINSON, LINEAUS BOLLING.
Witnesses: THOMAS W. COCKE, JONATHAN Y. JOHNSON, JOSEPH V. HARDWICK.

562. 15 August 1814. Order to Amherst County Justices of the Peace:
    DAVID S. GARLAND and wife, JANE, Amherst County, 18 July 1814,
to JONATHAN LONDON...five tracts. 1. 360 acres, 2. 378 acres, 3. 70
acres. 4. 70½ acres, 5. 200 acres. Done by EDMOND PENN and EDMOND
COLEMAN, 31 August 1814. To JONATHAN LONDON, 4 November 1814.

563. 15 August 1814. Order to Amherst County Justices of the Peace:
    JONATHAN LONDON and wife, TIRZA, 18 July 1814, to BENJAMIN
RUCKER...380 acres. Done by JONATHAN COLEMAN and CHARLES MUNDY,
14 September 1814.

564. 19 October 1814. JAMES BENNETT and wife, ELIZABETH, Amherst
    County, to RICHARD SHELTON, Amherst County...$290 58 acres
Miller's Creek. Lines: Shelton's road, grantee. Part of tract
bought by JAMES BENNETT of VALENTINE COX. Witnesses: WILL F. LEE,
WILLIAM PENDLETON, JAMES MC DANIEL, JONATHAN ELLIS, WILLIAM SHELTON.

566. 11 March 1814. LORENZO DOW, Connecticut, and wife, PEGGY, to
    STITH MEAD, Lynchburg...$75.00 14½ acres. Lines: WILLIAM and
PHILIP JOHNSON, road opposite old school house. Witnesses: JONATHAN
WEST, JR., EDMOND WRIGHT, JONATHAN WRIGHT. PEGGY DOW rel. dower in
Richmond, Virginia, 11 March 1814--CHARLES WHITLOCK and L. JONES,
Justices of the Peace. Recorded in Amherst County 17 October 1814.

567. 17 October 1814. SAMUEL CAMPBELL, Amherst County, to GEORGE
    CAMPBELL, Amherst County...L72 30 acres Piney. Lines: main
road, Piney, BARTLETT WHITEHEAD.

568. 19 September 1814. NICHOLAS HARRISON and wife, NANCY, Campbell
      County, to GEORGE MC DANIEL, SR., Amherst County...$200.00
100 acres Harris Creek, survey of 20 November 1806. Lines: GEORGE
MC DANIEL, -- ELLIS, PARKS, CALEB WILCHER, HENRY L. DAVIES.

569. 25 September 1814. DAVID S. GARLAND, Amherst County, to WILLIAM
      KNIGHT, Amherst County...$100.00 for three lots in New Glasgow:
No. 22 north side Main Street--35 yards by 49 yards and opposite
KNIGHT's improved lot No. 5; also No. 4 on south side Main Street
and joining No. 5 on south--35 yards on Main and 70 yards deep, on
south by Market Street; also No. 7 on south side Main Street--35
yards by 70 yards--alley on north. Witnesses: JONATHAN WHITEHEAD,
JERE YAGER, JONATHAN MOUNTCASTLE, FREDERICK ALDRIDGE. Taken out by
WILLIAM KNIGHT, 13 April 1817. Note: there was a time when New
Glasgow was the center of activity in Amherst County, but the establish-
ment of the seat of justice at the Oaks seems to have begun its gradual
decline. It is now just a small village and goes by the name of
Clifford. There was once a race track there and a thriving academy,
but today it is usually known as the village near the cemetery where
SARAH HENRY is buried at nearby Winton. GARLAND was disappointed in
his dreams for New Glasgow just as NICHOLAS CABELL was doomed to
defeat in his efforts to make a prosperous town out of Warminster.
GARLAND would at least have the satisfaction of seeing a friendly
little village on the site of his dream and his beautiful home is
still occupied, but CABELL would find only a country store at the
location of Warminster in present Nelson. The village of Amherst is
actually not the hub of activities in Amherst County. This distinction
belongs rather to Madison Heights which is really a suburb of Lynchburg.
It is here that one finds the large Lynchburg Training School which is
a state institution employing many people. A large shopping center and
much traffic on the recently improved U.S. 29 give Madison Heights an
air of activity which is not belied. On the other hand, the area is
still not incorporated and is a Sanitary District for Amherst County.
There is a steady growth in population and the day should come when
the former Scuffletown will have its own mayor and local government.

570. 17 October 1814. CORNELIUS CAMPBELL, Amherst County, to GEORGE
      CAMPBELL, Amherst County...$300 30 acres on Piney. Lines:
main road, CATHERINE CAMPBELL, ELIZABETH CAMPBELL's share.

571. 12 October 1814. BENJAMIN WATTS and wife, FRANCES, Amherst
      County, to JONATHAN WADE, Lynchburg...$300.00 68 acres on road
to Opossum Island. Lines: PHILIP JOHNSON. Witnesses: NELSON C.
DAWSON, J. ROBINSON, SPENCER NORVELL, PLEASANT DAWSON. To JONATHAN
WADE, 25 April 1815.

572. 27 June 1814. DANIEL L. BURFORD and wife, RUTH, Amherst County,
      to JOSEPH MC CRAE, Amherst County...$600 two tracts on Harris,
parts of tract whereon late DR. DANIEL BURFORD lived, and where
DANIEL L. BURFORD now lives--110 acres. Lines: MARY BURFORD's dower,
WILLIAM BURFORD, SHADRICK TENNISON, NELSON C. DAWSON on Harris--7 acres
also part of tract where grantor lives. To JOSEPH MC CRAE, 29 December
1814.

573. 14 November 1814. WILLIAM CLINKSCALES and wife, ANN G.,
      Amherst County, to JONATHAN WARWICK, Amherst County...L662
331 acres Rocky Run. Lines: ROBERT PEARCE on Rockey Run, JOEL
CAMPBELL, STOVALL's old road, REUBEN NORVELL. To JONATHAN WARWICK,
1 November 1814.

575. 16 October 1813. WILLIAM PETTYJOHN and wife, ELIZABETH, Amherst
      County, to WILLIAM MITCHELL, Lynchburg...L800 33 acres mill
seat, mouth of Harris. Lines: JONATHAN WARD, formerly that of JONATHAN
LYNCH, Lynchburg and LYNCH bought it of PETTIS THACKER, LYNCH sold to
WILLIAM SCOTT and PETTYJOHN bought tract from SCOTT. Also 600 yards
from mouth of Harris to this line and dividing fence. Witnesses:
NICHOLAS HARRISON, GEORGE CABELL, ROBERT RIDGWAY. To W. P.,
22 November 1814, to JAMES BRUCE, present owner, 9 May 1829.

576. 21 November 1814. JONATHAN LONDON and WILLIAM L. CHRISTIAN
      to PHILIP JOHNSON...no amount--14 acres Stovall and Bolling
Creeks. Lines: grantee. Witnesses: R. NORVELL, HENRY TURNER,
ELIAS WILLS, WILLIAM BREEDLOVE, attorney-in-fact for WILLIAM L.
CHRISTIAN.

577. 21 November 1814. HENRY TURNER and wife, RACHEL, Amherst
      County, to CHARLES MUNDY, Amherst County...$276 three tracts
on Porrage. 1. 16 acres. Lines: glade road, grantee MUNDY's road
from his mill to ACH. 2. 11½ acres. Lines: grantee, WILLIAM TURNER.
3. 7 acres LN side Porrage in road to Lynchburg. Total: 34½ acres.
To JESSE MUNDY, 16 October 1826.

578. 15 November 1814. JONATHAN and RICHARD L. ELLIS, Amherst
      County, to THOMAS RICHESON, Amherst County...$1750 350 acres
Horsley. Lines: WILLIAM DEMPSEY, WILLIAM SCHOFIELD, WILLIAM SHEPHERD,
DANIEL SHRADER, Spring road, fork of Long Branch. Witnesses: PETER P.
THORNTON, TARLTON GILLESPIE, JOSHUA L. ELLIS, R. N. EUBANK, JONATHAN
GOODWIN.

579. 17 May 1813. Order to Amherst County Justices of the Peace:
      SAMUEL HOGG and wife, DELANY, 27 September 1810, to JONATHAN
and RICHARD L. ELLIS...Done 8 October 1814, by BENJAMIN SHACKELFORD
and JAMES WARE.

581. 10 October 1814. Order to Amherst County Justices of the Peace:
      JAMES POWELL and wife, MILLY, 24 December 1813, to ROBERT
ALLEN...half an acre. Done by JONATHAN WARWICK and J. M. BROWN,
5 November 1814. To ROBERT ALLEN, 10 January 1814, sic.

582. 10 October 1814. Order to same Justices of the Peace: POWELL
      and wife, MILLY, 17 February 1811, to ROBERT ALLEN...half a
lot. Done by same men on same date. To ROBERT ALLEN, 10 January
1814, sic.

583. 10 October 1814. Order to same Justices of the Peace: JAMES
      POWELL and wife, MILLY, 23 May 1811, to WILLIAM HUTCHESON...
half acre lot. Done as above and margin as above.

585. 28 September 1814. Description of negro woman--property of
      WILLIAM ROACH, and removed from Kentucky and arrived 18 of this
present month--SUCKY, about 17, mulatto, of middle size. Sworn to
before THOMAS N. EUBANK by ROACH. Intent to keep in Virginia and no
intent of avoiding laws--inherited from father of his wife. Recorded
21 November 1814.

585. 3 October 1814. WILLIAM L. CHRISTIAN, Warren County, Kentucky,
      power of attorney to WILLIAM BREEDLOVE to sell Amherst County
tract...Lines: PHILIP JOHNSON and survey entry in my name and JOHN
LONDON's jointly. JONATHAN HINES and D. MAXWELL, Warren County
Justices of the Peace, JONATHAN HOBSON, Clerk, JONATHAN ROWNTREE,
Presiding Justice County Court.

587. 8 December 1814. JONATHAN LONDON and wife, TIRZA, Amherst
      County, to WILLIAM GALT, Richmond...$1307.50 515 acres James
River. Lines: grantee, JONATHAN LONDON, SACKVILLE KING, SAMUEL
ANDERSON, STEPHEN HAM, deceased, LINEAS BOLLING. Witnesses: WILL
NORVELL, CHRIS WINFREE, LINDSEY MC DANIEL, JONATHAN BULLOCK. To
JONATHAN LONDON, 16 January 1815.

589. 15 November 1814. Order to Amherst County Justices of the
      Peace: WILLIAM CLINKSCALES and wife, ANN, 14 November 1814,
to JONATHAN WARWICK--331 acres. Done by JONATHAN COLEMAN and CHARLES
MUNDY, 12 December 1814.

590. 29 December 1814. JOSEPH PENN, Amherst County, to CHARLES B.
      PENN, Staunton...$1200, no acres. Lines: CAMDEN, GOODWIN.
Tract from division of father, JOSEPH PENN, also one slave, DILSY,
and her two children. To CHARLES B. PENN, 9 June 1841.

591. 16 January 1815. JOSEPH DILLARD and wife, JUDAH, JONATHAN
      LONDON and wife, TIRZA, Amherst County, to JONATHAN COLEMAN,
Amherst County...$3476.00 1638 acres south side Buffaloe ridge and
Elk Island Creek--both sides and known as Higginbotham's Surveys.
Lines: SWANSON's heirs, GOOCH's heirs, GILES DAVIDSON, MICAJAH
PENDLETON, GEORGE HYLTON's heirs, LEWIS JEFFERSON, NATHANIEL LOFBOROUGH,
JONATHAN COLEMAN. To JOSEPH DILLARD, 10 February 1814.

593. 16 January 1813. JOSEPH DILLARD and wife, JUDAH, Amherst
      County, to JONATHAN COLEMAN, Amherst County...$674.00 337 acres
south side Buffaloe Ridge and Elk Island Creek. Lines: grantor,
JONATHAN LONDON, P. GOOCH's heirs. To JOSEPH DILLARD, 10 February
1814.

594. 29 August 1814. JONATHAN STAPLES, Amherst County, to GEORGE
      WASHINGTON HIGGINBOTHAM, Amherst County...L53-15 one full
fourth--except part in original tract sold by JONATHAN LOVING to
CAPTAIN STEPHEN WATTS--Buffaloe. Lines: CAPTAIN STEPHEN WATTS.
Devised by JOSEPH STAPLES to his sons, SAMUEL, JOSEPH, WILLIAM and
JONATHAN STAPLES and last of whom is "bagainor" in this deed. Tract--
exclusive of that sold to STEPHEN WATTS--380 acres and not intended
to convey remaining 3/4 which belongs to SAMUEL, JOSEPH and WILLIAM
STAPLES. HIGGINBOTHAM is intended to be considered a tenant in
common and not joint tenant. Witnesses: SAMUEL P. LAYNE, HENRY
CASHWELL, JAMES SEAY.

597. 16 January 1815. ELIAS WILLS, Amherst County, to THOMAS MURRELL,
      Amherst County...$500 62½ acres headwaters Stovall and joining
Lynch Road. Lines: JAMES BOLLING, WILLIAM BURFORD. To ELIAS WILLS,
20 October 1817.

598. 3 March 1815. WARNER GOODWIN and wife, HESSE, Amherst County,
      to MICAJAH CAMDEN, Amherst County...$100.00, no acres. Lines:
JONATHAN PENN, JR., CHARLES B. PENN. Part of tract of WARNER GOODWIN
bought of JOSEPH PENN's executors. Witnesses: RICHARD HARRISON,
BENJAMIN HARRISON, WILLIAM LEE.

599. 18 February 1815. CHARLES P. TALIAFERRO and wife, LOUISA,
      Amherst County, to BENJAMIN SANDIDGE, Amherst County...$2100
267 acres Buffaloe. Lines: ford of the river above one leading to
Buffaloe Springs, mouth of Willmore's Branch, BALLOW's old line,
JOSEPH DODD.

600. 7 March 1815. WARNER GOODWIN and wife, HESSE, Amherst County,
      to MICAJAH CAMDEN, Amherst County...L100 9 acres--part of tract
bought by WARNER GOODWIN of ROBERT HOLLOWAY and wife. Memo: deed
is made for same tract as in deed of 3 March 1815. To MICAJAH
CAMDEN, 29 January 1816.

601. 13 July 1814. ARMISTEAD RUCKER, Amherst County, to WILLIAM
      RADFORD, Lynchburg, and JONATHAN MURRELL, Lynchburg...Deed of
Trust; debt to READ and ROBERTSON, Lynchburg--to ARCHIBALD ROBERTSON,
surviving partner of BROWN and ROBERTSON, late of Lynchburg--$1.00,
slaves--ages and names. Witnesses: SAMUEL GARLAND, HENRY JACOBS,
ALFRED MC DANIEL. To ARMISTEAD RUCKER, 22 December 1818.

604. 10 March 1815. JONATHAN and RICHARD L. ELLIS, Amherst County,
      to ROWLAND GILLESPIE, Amherst County...$280.00 112 acres north
side and joining Pedlar. Lines: JONATHAN F. HALL, MAYS. Sent to
ROWLAND GILLESPIE, 29 April 1817.

605. 18 February 1815. WILLIAM WOODROOF and wife, ELIZABETH, Amherst
      County, to ROBERT ALLEN, Amherst County...L173 83 acres.
Lines: top of Paul's Mountain, THOMAS CREWS.

606. 17 March 1815. ROBERT ALLEN and wife, ELIZABETH, Amherst County,
      to WILLIAM WOODROOF, Amherst County...$1000.00 lot or lots on
west side of road to Lynchburg. ROBERT ALLEN bought from JAMES
POWELL in two deeds. 1. half acre. 2. one acre and they adjoin.
REUBEN COLEMAN was also joint buyer with WOODROOF.

607. 14 March 1815. Order to Amherst County Justices of the Peace:
      SHADRICK TENNISON and wife, ELIZABETH, to PLEASANT DAWSON,
8 January 1814...55½ acres. Done, 14 March 1815, by REUBEN NORVELL
and PHILIP JOHNSON.

608. 16 January 1815. Order to Amherst County Justices of the Peace:
      JONATHAN LONDON and wife, TIRZA, 8 December 1814, to WILLIAM
GALT...515 acres. Done by JONATHAN COLEMAN and CHARLES MUNDY,
31 January 1815.

609. 9 February 1815. Order to Amherst County Justices of the Peace:
      JOSEPH DILLARD and wife, JUDAH, 16 January 1815, to JONATHAN
COLEMAN...337 acres. Done by EDMOND PENN and THOMAS ALDRIDGE,
10 February 1815. To J. L., no date.

610. 9 February 1815. Order to Amherst County Justices of the Peace:
      JOSEPH DILLARD and wife, JUDAH, JONATHAN LONDON and wife,
TIRZA, 16 January 1815, to JONATHAN COLEMAN--1638 acres. Done by
same Justices of the Peace as above and date. Margin as above.

610. 18 August 1814. GEORGE MAYO, to his brother, JOSEPH MAYO,
      Richmond...$2000 245½ acres on James. Lines: corner of tract
lately sold by GEORGE MAYO to WILLIAM GALT on north, Porrage Creek.
Witnesses: ROBERT and PHILIP MAYO, THOMAS T. MAYO. Acknowledged
by GEORGE MAYO in Richmond before JONATHAN ALLEN and CHARLES WHITLOCK,
Justices of the Peace, 19 August 1814. Recorded in Amherst County
7 April 1815.

613. 6 March 1815. Order to Amherst County Justices of the Peace:
      RICHARD RUCKER and wife, PEGGY, 18 June 1810, to NICHOLAS
HARRISON...196 acres. Done by PHILIP JOHNSON and NELSON C. DAWSON,
7 March 1815.

614. 20 March 1815. ELISHA EVANS and wife, JUDAH, Buckingham County,
      to CALEB RALLS, Amherst County...$200.00 300 acres both sides
Lovelady Creek. To RICHARD CRAWFORD for NELSON CRAWFORD, 14 January
1824.

615. 20 March 1815. RUSH HUDSON, SR. and wife, LUCY, Amherst County,
      to JONATHAN P. COBBS, Amherst County...$750 150 acres north
borders Buffaloe. Lines: DAVID S. GARLAND, SAMUEL MEREDITH, deceased,
LINDSEY COLEMAN, deceased, old church road. To JONATHAN P. COBBS,
25 October 1815.

616. 20 March 1815. JONATHAN LONDON and wife, TIRZA, Amherst County,
      to JONATHAN BROWN and WILLIAM BROWN...HENRY BROWN, late of Amherst
County, by will directed sale of tract where he lived. JONATHAN and
WILLIAM BROWN, executors of HENRY BROWN, bought at public sale at
L2013 and resold to executors for same amount by this deed--Rutledge
whereon HENRY BROWN lived at death--554½ acres. HENRY BROWN bought
of MICHAEL COLTER and residue of 152½ acres bought from COLONEL
JONATHAN WIATT. To WILLIAM BROWN, 22 June 1815.

618. 20 March 1815. JONATHAN and WILLIAM BROWN, executors of HENRY
      BROWN, Amherst County, to JOHN LONDON, Amherst County...will
recited as above and two tracts as above. Lines: JONATHAN MC DANIEL,
BENJAMIN BROWN, JAMES SMITH, PETER CASHWELL, JAMES LIVELY, deceased.
L2013.

619. 24 November 1814. PATRICK ROSE and wife, MARY, Nelson County,
     to THOMAS ALDRIDGE...L1902 951 acres both sides main road from
ROSE's mill on Piney to New Glasgow. Lines: THOMAS LANDRUM, JAMES
FRANKLIN, CHARLES BURKS, DAVID S. GARLAND, NATHANIEL MANTIPLY, HILL
CARTER, JONATHAN N. ROSE. Witnesses: THOMAS CREWS, HUDSON M. GARLAND,
S. CLAIBORNE. To THOMAS ALDRIDGE, -- 1823.

620. 4 February 185. PULLIAM SANDIDGE and wife, LUCY, to JACKEY
     CARTER...L60 99 acres north borders Brown Mountain Creek.

622. 20 March 1815. WILLIAM JOHNS (B) to THOMAS N. EUBANK, Amherst
     County...Deed of Trust; debt to JONATHAN and RICHARD L. ELLIS,
$1000 stock, furniture. Witnesses: EDMOND PENN, BENJAMIN SHACKELFORD,
RICHARD HARRISON. To JONATHAN ELLIS, 15 October 1815.

623. 1 December 1814. JONATHAN HIGGINBOTHAM, Nelson County, and
     THOMAS HIGGINBOTHAM, Campbell County, executors of JOSEPH
HIGGINBOTHAM, to JONATHAN LONDON...will of 22 June 1813, in Amherst
County empowered executors to sell and LONDON was highest bidder at
$606--721 acres east side Buffaloe ridge. Lines: JONATHAN COLEMAN,
CHISWELL's heirs, SWANSON heirs, JOSEPH GOOCH, GOOCH heirs. Part of
three tracts patent to JONATHAN and JAMES HIGGINBOTHAM, deceased, and
to JONATHAN in Chancery decree of County Court in suit between JONATHAN
and JAMES. To JONATHAN LONDON, 21 April 1817.

625. 16 December 1814. Same executors as above to RICHARD HARRISON...
     200 acres Rutledge branches at $4061. Lines: WILLIAM MORRISON.

627. 17 September 1814. RICHARD HARRISON and wife, SOPHIA, Amherst
     County, to THOMAS HIGGINBOTHAM, Campbell County...$4061 200 acres
above. To THOMAS HIGGINBOTHAM, 25 April 1822, by JESSE HIGGINBOTHAM.

628. 17 May 1814. JESSE CARTER and wife, FRANCES (formerly LUCAS
     and child of THOMAS LUCAS) to MORRIS HAMNER, Charlotte County...
LUCAS died intestate and tract was patent to him, 13 May 1794, for
150 acres. CARTER and wife sell one fourth: L25 for LUCAS left four
children. Lines: SAMUEL GUEST, JONATHAN BRYANT, WILLIAM SHOEMAKER,
Pounding Mill Creek, NICHOLAS PRYOR. Page 630 certified in Lincoln
County, Kentucky that CARTER and wife appeared and she rel. dower,
17 May 1814. THOMAS HELM, Clerk, JAMES LOGAN, Presiding Justice.

631. 18 July 1814. Order to Cumberland Justices of the Peace:
     THOMAS T. MAYO and wife, ELIZA, B. and GEORGE MAYO, 14 July
1814, to WILLIAM GALT...154½ acres. Done by CONRINGTON CARRINGTON
and DAVID SHIELDS, 2 August 1814. Recorded in Amherst County 17 April
1815. To WILLIAM GALT, 2 June 1815.

632. 26 February 1814. Order to Amherst County Justices of the Peace:
     JAMES SMITH and wife, SUSANNAH, 29 January 1815, to CHARLES P.
TALIAFERRO...200 acres. Done by EDMOND T. COLEMAN and BENJAMIN
SHACKELFORD, 28 February 1815.

633. 29 January 1815. JAMES SMITH and wife, SUSANNAH, formerly
     HIGGINBOTHAM, Amherst County, to CHARLES P. TALIAFERRO, Amherst
County...$1800 200 acres both sides Rutledge. Witnesses: JONATHAN
EUBANK, JR., GEORGE EUBANK, JR., LUCINDA SMITH. To CHARLES P.
TALIAFERRO, 11 December 1815.

634. 15 November 1814. THOMAS RICHESON, Amherst County, to THOMAS N.
     EUBANK, Amherst County...Deed of Trust to EUBANK, debt to JONATHAN
and RICHARD L. ELLIS--$1.00 350 acres Horsley. Lines: DANIEL SHRADER.
Sold by JONATHAN and RICHARD ELLIS to JONATHAN RICHESON (sic).
Witnesses: PETER P. THORNTON, TARLTON GILLESPIE, JOSHUA L. ELLIS,
R. N. EUBANK, JONATHAN GOODWIN.

635. 10 August 1814. JOSEPH MAYO, Richmond and JONATHAN GRANTLAND,
      Richmond, to WILLIAM GALT, Richmond...GEORGE MAYO, 19 October
1813, conveyed to JONATHAN GRANTLAND and JOSEPH MAYO and recorded in
General Court for benefit of THOMAS T. MAYO--GEORGE and THOMAS T.,
14 July 1814, and ELIZA B., to WILLIAM GALT--154½ acres. James River.
THOMAS T. requested release from Deed of Trust. Memo: 10 August
1814, Cumberland County--THOMAS T. MAYO consented to sale. Witnesses:
C. J. SHELTON, acknowledged in Richmond 10 October 1814 by JOSEPH
MAYO and JONATHAN GRANTLAND. To WILLIAM GALT, executor of WILLIAM
GALT, 26 July 1827.

637. 8 April 1815. WILLIAM H. MARKHAM, Amherst County, to ARTHUR B.
      DAVIES, second; ELIJAH FLETCHER, third...Deed of Trust; debt to
FLETCHER--$1.00 three acres whereon WILLIAM H. MARKHAM lives. Lines:
MICAJAH CAMDEN, a ten yard and house. Note: ELIJAH FLETCHER came
here from north as school teacher at New Glasgow Academy. He married
daughter of WILLIAM S. CRAWFORD and he became a money lender and
published a paper in Lynchburg. His will of 1850's is in my F will
work. He wrote it at Sweet Briar plantation and shows that the tract
was acquired by various foreclosures. His daughter, INDIANA FLETCHER,
inherited Sweet Briar and her will set up what is today the famed
Sweet Briar College.

638. 18 March 1815. THOMAS WAUGH and wife, FRANCES, Bedford, to
      EDWARD WAUGH, Amherst County...L500 100 acres north side and
joining Fluvanna River. Part of tract bought by THOMAS WAUGH and
RODERICK MC CULLOCH from JONATHAN THOMAS, Alb. Lines: JAMES WAUGH.
Witnesses: WILLIAM H. MC CULLOCH, ROBERT H. MC CULLOCH, ROSEMARY GUE.

639. 25 September 1814. DAVID S. GARLAND to SARAH HUDSON, Amherst
      County...$1.00 lot #20 New Glasgow on north side Mane (sic)
Street--75 yards in front and 50 yards deep on which is framed dwelling
house where SARAH lives--life interest and reverts to GARLAND.
Witnesses: JONATHAN WHITEHEAD, WILLIAM KNIGHT, J. YAGER. To DAVID S.
GARLAND, 6 April 1828.

639. 25 September 1814. SARAH HUDSON, Amherst County, to DAVID S.
      GARLAND, Amherst County...$1.00 80 acres dower in estate of
late husband, REUBEN HUDSON. Lines: JAMES FRANKLIN, old church road,
mouth of a lane, top of Turkey Mountain. Witnesses: as above.
Margin: as above.

640. 31 March 1815. DAVID S. GARLAND, Amherst County, to JAMES L.
      PENDLETON, Amherst County...L268 134 acres Little Piney--surveyed
5 November 1803. Lines: WILLIAM WIDDERBOURN.

641. 17 April 1815. JONATHAN MC DANIEL and wife, LUCY, Amherst
      County, to JAMES WILMORE, Amherst County...L50 140 acres Huff.
Lines: JONATHAN COLEMAN, top of the mountain, BENJAMIN NORVELL,
JAMES BYAS, top of old cove about half-way up the mountain, TYREE
SLADING. To JAMES WILMORE, 16 October 1820.

642. 1 April 1815. GEORGE P. LUCK, Amherst County, to JONATHAN F.
      HALL, Amherst County...L85 54 acres south borders Horsley and
north borders Pedlar. Lines: PHILIP PAYTON, RICHARD ELLIOTT, WILLIAM
PRYOR, WILLIAM CABELL. Witnesses: PETER P. THORNTON, THOMAS N.
EUBANK, NELSON CRAWFORD, JONATHAN EUBANK, JR.

643. 26 March 1814. GEORGE W. TRIBLE, Amherst County, to JAMES L.
      PENDLETON...Deed of Trust; debt to THOMAS ALDRIDGE--$1.00
slaves. Witnesses: ROBERT ALDRIDGE, JONATHAN L. BLAIN, STERLING
CLAIBORNE. To JAMES L. PENDLETON, 9 July 1814.

645. 17 April 1815. JONATHAN JAMES DILLARD, Amherst County, to
      BENJAMIN BROWN, Amherst County...$3129.50 438½ acres both sides
Crooked Run; reference to deed by HENRY WATTS and wife to BROWN for
lines: Tract whereon GEORGE DILLARD died as owner and descended to
JONATHAN JAMES and ELIZA (now WATTS, wife of HENRY WATTS) DILLARD.
Witnesses: HENRY T. HARRIS, CHARLES TALIAFERRO, WILLIAM ARMISTEAD,
PETER P. THORNTON.

646. 1 April 1815. JONATHAN F. HALL, Amherst County, to PETER P.
      THORNTON and NELSON CRAWFORD...Deed of Trust; debt to GEORGE P.
LUCK, $1.00--54 acres surveyed 23 October 1799. Lines: WILLIAM
CABELL's old line, PHILIP PEYTON, RICHARD ELLIOTT, WILLIAM PEYTON.
Witnesses: THOMAS N. EUBANK, JONATHAN EUBANK, JR., JONATHAN ELLIS.

648. 24 April 1815. THOMAS ALDRIDGE and wife, CATHERINE, Amherst
      County, to JONATHAN WHITE, Louisa County...L1808 452 acres Tye.
Lines: NORVELL SPENCER, STERLING CLAIBORNE, WILLIAM S. CRAWFORD,
HUGH and CHARLES ROSE, deceased, road from Belevit to Geddes.
Witnesses: DAVID S. GARLAND, EDMOND PENN, JONATHAN S. BLAIN.
CATHERINE rel. dower, same date: DAVID S. GARLAND and EDMOND PENN,
Justices of the Peace.

650. 24 January 1810. ALEXANDER SALE, executor of BEVERLY WILLIAMSON,
      to ENOCH CARPENTER, Amherst County...L181-10 121 acres Stone
House Creek borders. Witnesses: MICAJAH CAMDEN, BENJAMIN TALIAFERRO,
ROBERT RIVES, EDMOND LANIER. Final proof, 15 May 1815, by ROBERT
RIVES.

651. 15 April 1815. HENRY BALLINGER, Amherst County, to WIATT SMITH,
      Amherst County...Deed of Trust; $1.00 debt to ANSELM CLARKSON,
bondsman to JONATHAN and RICHARD ELLIS--long and interesting list of
articles and one negroe. Witnesses: RICHARD BALLINGER, JONATHAN
TAYLOR, JONATHAN BALLINGER. To ANSELM CLARKSON, 25 November 1814.

653. 10 November 1814. NELLY MORTON, widow of JONATHAN MORTON,
      WILLIAM RUCKER and wife, SALLY, JOSHUA RUCKER and wife, LUCY,
and NANCY MORTON--SALLY, LUCY and NANCY are children of JONATHAN
MORTON--to RICHARD HARRISON...JONATHAN MORTON died owning one-third of
water mill and 20 acres adjoining on Harris and cattle in common with
JOSHUA and DAVID TINSLEY--TINSLEY's Mill, MORTON died intestate.
L200 for their interest. Witnesses: THOMAS L. HILL, WILLIAM BOURNE,
JAMES WOODROOF.

655. 3 October 1814. MICAJAH CAMDEN and wife, MARY, Amherst County,
      to ANDERSON L. CREWS, Amherst County...$60 half acre. Lines:
WILLIAM HUTCHINSON, JAMES POWELL, the road. Witnesses: BAYLOR
WALKER, RICHARD BALLINGER, WILLIAM LEE. Acknowledged by MARY CAMDEN,
18 January 1819. It is noted that several relinquishments of dower
are recorded without the usual orders to Justices of the Peace.

655. 24 September 1814. RUSH HUDSON, the elder, to DAVID S. GARLAND,
      Amherst County...10 shi. 8 acres Turkey Mountain. Lines:
RUSH HUDSON, LINDSEY COLEMAN, grantee. Witnesses: ROBERT GARLAND,
DAVID SWANSON, MICAJAH PENDLETON, WILLIS BROWN, CORNELIUS POWELL.
To DAVID GARLAND, 6 April 1818.

657. 10 November 1814. WILLIAM MC DANIEL and JOSHUA RUCKER are
      bound to RICHARD HARRISON for L400...HARRISON has bought interest
of JONATHAN MORTON's heirs to mill, 20 acres, and stock--TINSLEY's
Mill. Bond to protect him during non-age of NANCY MORTON. Witnesses:
WILLIAM BOURNE, JAMES WOODROOF, THOMAS D. HILL. This simply means
that NANCY is still a minor.

658. 10 November 1841. NELLY MORTON, widow of JONATHAN MORTON and
      other heirs--see page 653--to WILLIAM MC DANIEL...L126 123 acres
Harris. Lines: grantee, CAPTAIN DAVID WOODROOF. Witnesses:
LINDSEY MC DANIEL, JONATHAN HANSARD, JAMES PENDLETON, RICHARD
HARRISON, JAMES WOODROOF.

659. 18 April 1815. THOMAS S. HOLLOWAY and JAMES POWELL, Amherst
      County Justices of the Peace, certify that NANCY COLEMAN, wife
of LINDSEY COLEMAN, relinquish dower to REUBEN COLEMAN, 15 June
1814, deed.

660. 26 May 1815. ROBERT ALLEN, Amherst County, to WILLIAM WOODROOF,
      Amherst County...$300 83 acres. Lines: top of Paul's Mountain,
THOMAS CREWS. To WILLIAM WOODROOF, 30 December 1815.

661. 10 June 1815. Order to Amherst County Justices of the Peace:
HENRY CAMDEN and wife, LUCY, 18 June 1811, to EDMOND T. COLEMAN...
146 acres. Done by BENJAMIN TALIAFERRO and BENJAMIN SHACKELFORD,
19 June 1815.

662. 15 June 1815. SAMUEL SCOTT and wife, JUDAH, Amherst County,
to REUBEN CARVER, Amherst County...$400 100 acres north borders
Porrage, south side bought of JAMES DILLARD and 4½ acre not conveyed
herein--agreement with JONATHAN LONDON and CARVER. Lines: JAMES
DILLARD, JAMES PENN. To REUBEN CARVER, 17 March 1817.

663. -- June 1815. STEPHEN WATTS, Nelson, to HENRY WATTS, Amherst
County...love for STEPHEN for his son, HENRY, and $1.00 two
tracts. 1. 318 acres adjoining the James River and bought by STEPHEN
WATTS from representatives of GEORGE CHRISTIAN, deceased. 2. 207
acres on Lime Kiln Creek and joining Number 1 and bought by STEPHEN
WATTS from DRURY BELL. To HENRY H. WATTS, 5 January 1831.

664. 28 January 1815. THOMPSON NOELL and wife NANCY, Amherst County,
to ROBERT RIVERS, Amherst County...L1200 404 acres Buffaloe--
belonged to estate of PHILIP GOOCH and conveyed by his executor,
WILLIAM B. GOOCH, to THOMPSON NOELL--called Watson tract. Lines:
JONATHAN PENN, SR., WILLIAM LONG, NANCY SHIELDS. Witnesses:
STERLING CLAIBORNE, SARAH NOEL, FRANCES NOEL.

665. 9 June 1815. JAMES WADE and wife, ANNE, Lynchburg, to JONATHAN
DAWSON, Lynchburg...$300 25 acres on road to Trent's ferry in
Amherst County. Lines: REUBEN PENDLETON, GEORGE M. TINSLEY, LEWIS
DAWSON, south side of road to Trent's ferry. Witnesses: SOLOMON
and WILLIAM DAY, STITH MEAD.

666. 20 June 1815. CHARLES HUNT CHRISTIAN and wife, JINCEY, Amherst
County, to JOSEPH HIGGINBOTHAM, Amherst County...$632 79 acres--
tract is share of JINCEY in division of estate of SAMUEL HUCKSTEP.
Lines: Migginson road, BENJAMIN MILES, grantee, dower line. Witnesses:
STERLING CLAIBORNE, WILLIAM ARMISTEAD, HUDSON M. GARLAND. To JOSEPH
HIGGINBOTHAM, June, 1816.

667. 17 June 1815. ROBERT WRIGHT and wife, KEZIAH, late GILLENWATERS,
and JAMES GILLENWATERS, Campbell County, to ELISHA GILLENWATERS,
Amherst County...$1.00 our interest in estate of our brother, THOMAS
GILLENWATERS, deceased, in Amherst County tract. Lines: JAMES DILLARD,
ROBERT GRANT, LARKIN LONDON--120 acres. Witnesses: ROBERT GRANT,
LEWIS JOHNS, WILLIAM ENSEY.

669. 15 June 1815. DAVID S. GRALAND and wife, JANE, to -- incomplete
report by EDMOND PENN and JAMES POWELL.

669. 20 June 1815. ELIZABETH PIERCE, wife of JACOB PIERCE, to
FREDERICK FULTZ, 15 July 1811...Done by REUBEN NORVELL and JAMES
POWELL.

670. 8 June 1815. Report as to JAMES FLOYD and wife, ELEANOR, to
JACOB WOOD, 17 October 1804, by Bedford Justices of the Peace:
NICHOLAS ROBERTSON and SAMUEL HANCOCK.

670. 10 December 1814. JAMES HIX and wife, NANCY, Amherst County,
to AARON HIGGINBOTHAM, Amherst County...NANCY was formerly
HIGGINBOTHAM and widow of AARON HIGGINBOTHAM, the elder--L75 for her
one-seventh interest. To AARON HIGGINBOTHAM, 19 July 1815. Note
that is of record in T(?):500.

671. 17 July 1815. RICHARD HUCKSTEP and ELIZABETH FULCHER to JINCEY
CHRISTIAN...SAMUEL HUCKSTEP's estate divided by commissioners of
County Court in Chancery in case of RICHARD HUCKSTEP et al.--all are
heirs of SAMUEL HUCKSTEP--JINCEY and husband, CHARLES H. CHRISTIAN
relinquish one-seventh part of RICHARD HUCKSTEP and ELIZABETH FULCHER--
$1.00 paid by JINCEY--part of tract with mansion house--residue to
ANNE, widow, and to RICHARD--79 acres. Lines: Migginson road,
JOSEPH HIGGINBOTHAM.

672. 17 July 1815. CHARLES H. CHRISTIAN and wife, JINCEY, to RICHARD
HUCKSTEP and ELIZABETH FULCHER--SAMUEL HUCKSTEP estate as above...
$1.00 142 acres--part of tract. Lines: JAMES P. GARLAND, ANNE,
widow of SAMULEL HUCKSTEP.

674. 17 July 1815. CHARLES H. CHRISTIAN and wife, JINCEY, formerly
HUCKSTEP and ELIZABETH FULCHER, formerly HUCKSTEP, to RICHARD
HUCKSTEP...as above. $1.00. Lines: MRS. MONROE, dower line,
RICHARD WILSON, the road, near dwelling house.

675. 17 July 1815. EDMOND PENN to THOMAS CREWS and DAVID S. GARLAND...
Deed of Trust; various debts--interest by marriage with present
wife in Fredericksburg and interest in western by said marriage;
estate of WILLIAM DRUMMOND, deceased, and interest in estate of deceased
father at mother's death--long list--library etc. Debts to Farmers
bank, Lynchburg; THOMAS ALDRIDGE, THOMAS CREWS, JONATHAN MC DANIEL,
MRS. JANE MEREDITH, MICAJAH CAMDEN, bondsman, DAVID S. GARLAND,
NICHOLAS HARRISON, assignee of JAMES PENN, JONATHAN PENN, JR.,
GEORGE MYERS and Company, WILLIAM KNIGHT, JAMES FULCHER, JONATHAN P.
COBBS, JAMES M. BROWN, JONATHAN ROBERTSON, ROCKBRIDGE, WHITEHEAD
and HIGGINBOTHAM. To THOMAS CREWS, 18 March 1823.

677. 15 July 1815. THOMAS CREWS, Amherst County, to DAVID S. GARLAND,
Amherst County, and WILLIAM LONG...Deed of Trust; $1800 slaves
named for benefit of MRS. JANE PENN, wife of EDMOND PENN and children
or future ones. Witnesses: B. BROWN, RICHARD HARRISON.

678. 15 July 1815. EDMOND PENN to DAVID S. GARLAND...$100 100 acres
Otter Creek. Lines: DAVID BURKS, HENRY L. DAVIES, deceased.

679. 10 July 1813 (15?). Recorded 17 July 1815. HENRY BALLINGER
and wife, POLLY, to WILLIAM LONG...$912 228 acres. Lines:
Horsley borders. Lines: MATTHEW TUCKER, HARTLESS, HOWARD, NELSON
CRAWFORD. To WILLIAM LONG, 20 September 1815.

680. 17 July 1815. WILLIAM JOPLING to WILLIAM LONG for consideration...
LONG has paid a debt due from HENRY BALLINGER, WILLIAM WARE,
and JONATHAN SMITH to executor of PETER CARTER; Deed of Trust to
WILLIAM JOPLING from BALLINGER on Amherst County tract and "deed is
on other part of this page." Witnesses: BENJAMIN BROWN.

680. 21 November 1814. WILLIAM HARRISON to ELIAS WILLS, Amherst
County, and JONATHAN CAMM...Deed of Trust; debt to NICHOLAS
HARRISON, RICHARD HARRISON as bondsman on County Court judgement by
DAVIS and MAYNARD and as bondsman to WILLIAM COLEMAN, administrator
of DRURY TUCKER and Superior Court judgement; also bondsman to
HARRISON HUGHES--$1.00 named slaves etc. Witnesses: MERIT M. WHITE,
BAYLOR WALKER, H. T. HARRIS. To RICHARD HARRISON, 19 June 1816,
per order by R. H. BLANKS, April 4, 1822, to WILLS.

684. 28 December 1814. JAMES WARREN, Lincoln County, Kentucky,
to JAMES GARLAND, Amherst County...Deed of Trust; debt to DAVID
and JAMES GARLAND--$1.00 all interest in estate of WILLIAM BRYANT at
his death--WARREN married VICEY BRYANT, daughter of WILLIAM, and she
may become one of her father's heirs. Witnesses: HUDSON M. GARLAND
and JACOB SCOTT.

685. 13 March 1815. JOSEPH HAWKINS, Amherst County, to WILLIAM
RADFORD, Bedford, and JONATHAN MURRELL, Campbell County...Deed
of Trust; debt to ARCHIBALD ROBERTSON and Company, Lynchburg--$1.00
90 acres. Lines: GEORGE POWELL, JONATHAN GILES, also named slaves.
Witnesses: JAMES S. PENDLETON, ALFRED MC DANILE, S. GARLAND. To
JONATHAN WILSON, 31 January 1815.

688.   5 July 1815.   ARTHUR L. DAVIES and wife, LUCY C., Gloucester
        County, to JONATHAN CAMM, Amherst County...L450 500 acres Salt
Creek--part of tract surveyed by CAPTAIN JAMES WARE, 14 April 1814.
Lines: grantor, grantee, Bethel road, Bethel tract, SAMUEL BURKS,
Pedlar road at junction with Bethel road. Witnesses: THOMAS C.
AMORY and WILLIAM ROBINS, Justices of the Peace of Gloucester. Page
689 10 June 1815 (sic) order to them to quiz LUCY. Deed to JONATHAN
CAMM, Clerk of Amherst County and signed by him. Done 5 July 1815.
Dates are so recorded.

690.   4 February 1815.   Agreement between SUSANNAH DAVIS, widow of
        CHARLES DAVIS, Amherst County, and his legatees: CHARLES L.
and ELIZABETH E. DAVIS, WILLIAM DOUGLAS and SALLY DAVIS--all relinquish
interest in any lots drawn by them--CHARLES L. is to have his land
taken off at that part where he now lives. Witnesses: PETER P.
THORNTON, NATHANIEL STEWART, JONATHAN P. BURKS, SUSANNAH GILLESPIE,
WILLIAM DAVIS. To H. W. QUARLES, 28 November 1852. Returned
30 November 1852. All of these heirs seem to be relinquishing
interest in lots drawn by others and are not surrendering theirs.

691.   24 May 1815.   JONATHAN HUTCHESON, THOMAS EDWARDS and wife,
        NANCY, REUBEN PADGET and wife, CATHERINE, and THOMAS HUTCHESON,
Amherst County, to ROBERT ALLEN, Amherst County...$70.00 half acre
lot near Amherst County Court House. Lines: ALLEN, the road,
COLEMAN.

692.   18 May 1815.   Same grantors above plus ROBERT ALLEN and wife,
        ELIZABETH, Amherst County, to MICAJAH CAMDEN, Amherst County...
$636.25 half acre lot at Amherst County Court House--thereon is brick
tenement and is tract sold to ROBERT ALLEN by DR. JAMES POWELL.
Lines: former line of WILLIAM LONG, the road. Witnesses: STERLING
CLAIBORNE, WIATT SMITH, JESSE KENNERLY. To MICAJAH CAMDEN, 19 February
1817.

693.   22 June 1815.   Order to Amherst County Justices of the Peace:
        JONATHAN LONDON and wife, TIRZA, 20 March 1815, to JONATHAN
and WILLIAM BOURN...554½ acres. Done by CHARLES MUNDY and JONATHAN
WARWCIK, 11 August 1815.

694.   21 August 1815.   JOSEPH KENNERLY, Amherst County, to FRANCES
        EVINS, Amherst County...$30.00 nine acres where FRANCES EVINS
lives. Lines: COLONEL PHILIP JOHNSON, MATTHEW RICKETS, on Opossum
Island road.

695.   1 August 1815.   CALEB WATTS and wife, SUSANNAH, Amherst County,
        to ANDREW MORELAND, Amherst County...$180.00 15 acres north
side Pedlar. Lines: CAPTAIN MARTIN PARKS, grantee, CAPTAIN RODERICK
MC CULLOCH. Witnesses: WILLIAM SHELTON, JONATHAN GOODWIN, JAMES
MC DANIEL. To ANDREW MORELAND, 24 September 1816.

696.   19 June 1815.   LINESEY TINSLEY and wife, LUCY, Amherst County,
        to DAVID TINSLEY, Amherst County, Sr...$408 48 acres. Lines:
grantee, Harris Creek, JOSHAU SHELTON, deceased, road to Bethel,
JONATHAN TINSLEY. Witnesses: ALEXANDER TINSLEY, HUGH NORVELL, ANSON
TINSLEY, ALLEN NIMMO.

697.   25 December 1814.   LEROY CAMDEN, Amherst County, to GEORGE
        MYERS, Amherst County...Deed of Trust; debt to THOMAS ALDRIDGE...
$1.00 1313 acres Hough (Huff) and Beaver--all of tract willed to
LEROY CAMDEN by WILLIAM CAMDEN, deceased, also slaves. Witnesses:
MICAJAH PENDLETON, PEACHY FRANKLIN, JAMES N. EDMUNDS, JONATHAN S.
BLAINE.

700.   21 August 1815.   JOSEPH KENNERLEY and WILLIAM WILLIAMS, Amherst
        County, to NATHAN WILLIAMS, Amherst County...$60.00 two lots
near town of Madison, Amherst County. 1. half acre lot. Lines:
COLONEL PHILIP JOHNSON, CHRISTOPHER ISBELL and on road from Lynchburg
to Amherst County Court House. 2. One-sixth acre adjoining No. 1.
Lines: JONATHAN LYNCH and opposite tan yard lot. Witnesses: WILLIAM
RADFORD, JONATHAN N. URQUHART, JAMES BENAGH.

701. 10 July 1815. PULLIAM SANDIDGE and wife, LUCY, Amherst County,
to LINDSEY TINSLEY, Amherst County...$1350 150 acres Swamping
Camp Creek and Buffaloe. Lines: BENJAMIN SANDIDGE, AMBROSE TOMLINSON,
JESSE RICHESON, JESSE RICHESON's tract bought of CAPTAIN WARE.
Witnesses: JOSHUA, JAMES and WALLER SANDIDGE.

703. 10 July 1815. PULLIAM SANDIDGE and wife, LUCY, Amherst County,
to JESSE RICHESON, Amherst County...$650 65 acres Swamping Camp
Creek, branch of Pedlar. Witnesses: as above. To JESSE RICHESON,
29 March 1832, by WILLIAM A. RICHESON.

704. 17 August 1815. SPENCER NORVELL to CHRISTOPHER ANTHONY and
WILLIAM RADFORD, second, and EDMOND WINSTON and JOSEPH KENNERLEY,
third...Deed of Trust; $5.00, nine named slaves.

705. 1 August 1815. JONATHAN BROWN and wife, ANNE, to ANDREW
MORELAND...$600.00 50 acres. Lines: CAPTAIN MARTIN PARKS,
JONATHAN DUNCAN, JONATHAN BURKS. Witnesses: JAMES WARE, ANDERSON
WARE, JAMES MC DANIEL, JONATHAN GOODWIN, WILLIAM SHELTON. To ANDREW
MORELAND, 25 September 1816.

707. 12 July 1815. NATHANIEL J. MANSON and wife, SARAH, Amherst
County, to THOMAS N. EUBANK, Amherst County...$5968.00 746
acres. Lines: NICHOLAS C. DAVIES, north side Fluvanna, ALLISON
MORRIS, HENRY L. DAVIES, HENRY ROACH, ASHCRAFT ROACH, RODERICK
MC CULLOCH. Witnesses: R. L. ELLIS, JAMES WARE, AMBROSE RUCKER,
RICHARD HARRISON. To ROBERT COLEMAN, 23 March 1817.

708. 5 July 1815. ERASMUS STRIBLING and wife, MATILDA, Augusta,
to JAMES ROSS, Fredericksburg...$4038.75 900 acres north side
Buffaloe. Lines: DAVID S. GARLAND, SAMUEL MEREDITH, JONATHAN CAMM,
WILLIAM ARMISTEAD, WILLIAM CABELL, JAMES HIGGINBOTHAM. Same tract
conveyed by EDMOND PENN to JONATHAN CRUMP in Deed of Trust to indemnify
JAMES ROSS, 22 April 1809, and recorded in General Court. EDMOND PENN
afterwards conveyed to THOMAS H. DREW and JONATHAN FOX in Deed of
Trust, 9 August 1809, and STRIBLING bought it and conveyed from DREW
and FOX and recorded in General Court. Witnesses: ANTHONY BURTT (?),
ADAM COOPER, HORACE MARSHALL, JONATHAN W. GREEN. Acknowledged before
JONATHAN WAYT and ALEXANDER ST. CLAIR, Augusta Justices of the Peace,
5 August 1815, and wife relinquished dower. To RICHARD ROBEY, agent,
12 December 1815.

711. 7 July 1815. JONATHAN CRUMP, Fredericksburg Corporation, to
JAMES ROSS, same Corporation...reference to EDMOND PENN as
above, 22 April 1809--known as the Glebe--Deed of Trust to indemnify
JAMES STEVENSON and JAMES ROSS paid GARRAT MINOR, administrator of
STEVENSON $1923.10. Advertised in Virginia Herald, Fredericksburg;
sold at Buck's (?) auction room in Fredericksburg. Superior Court of
Chancery, Staunton District: ERASMUS STRIBLING versus EDMOND PENN,
JAMES ROSS, and JONATHAN CRUMP. CRUMP enjoined to sell enough to
raise $1295.71 and costs. JAMES ROSS bought at this price and costs
of $67.28. 900 acres. The Glebe. Lines: DAVID S. GARLAND, COLONEL
WILLIAM CABELL, JAMES HIGGINBOTHAM, WILLIAM ARMISTEAD. Margin: as
above. WILLIAM S. STONE and JONATHAN S. WILLFORD, Fredericksburg
Justices of the Peace.

713. 1 May 1815. HENRY F. CARTER, Nelson County, to STERLING
CLAIBORNE, Amherst County, and ROBERT H. ANDERSON...Deed of
Trust; debt to MURPHY BROWN and Company--$1.00 four slaves named.
Witnesses: CHARLES C. CARTER, JAMES THOMPSON, THOMAS L. CARTER,
JONATHAN THOMPSON, JR., GEORGE T. WILLIAMS.

715. 17 July 1815. Order to Amherst County Justices of the Peace:
JAMES MARTIN and wife, ANNE, 16 March 1812, to JONATHAN
ROBERSON...105 acres. Done 19 August 1815, by JONATHAN ELLIS and
EDMOND T. COLEMAN, JONATHAN CAMM, Clerk.

717.   26 April 1815.   BENNETT RUCKER and wife, JOHANNAH, Amherst
        County, to RICHARD HARRISON, Amherst County...$6870.50 490 3/4
acres. Lines: SPENCER NORVELL, the road. Witnesses: ARMISTEAD
and RUBEN RUCKER, HENRY BURKS. To RICHARD HARRISON, 19 September
1815.

718.   17 April 1815.   GIDEON RUCKER and wife, JOYCE, Amherst County,
        to REUBEN COLEMAN, Amherst County...$8598.75 573¾ acres Rutledge
and where GIDEON RUCKER lives. Lines: Lynch road, THOMAS CREWS,
a branch, north fork Rutledge, WIATT POWELL, EDWARD WATSON, MICAJAH
CAMDEN, FRANKLIN's mill pond. To REUBEN COLEMAN, 9 October 1815.
Also joins JOSEPH HIGGINBOTHAM, THOMAS HIGGINBOTHAM, CHARLES P.
TALIAFERRO, BENJAMIN BROWN. Witnesses: HUDSON M. GARLAND, THOMAS
ALDRIDGE, DAVID S. GARLAND.

719.   18 September 1815.   GEORGE M. BROWN and wife, SALLY, Amherst
        County, to CHARLES L. BARRET, Amherst County...L62 50 acres
Pedlar. Lines: JONATHAN BROWN, MURRY HENSON, JONATHAN ROBERTS,
JONATHAN ROBERTS, NELSON CRAWFORD--crops now growing.

721.   12 September 1815.   JESSE BLAN and wife, SARAH, Amherst County,
        to SAMUEL TURNER, Amherst County...$100 228 acres head of south
borders of south fork Buffaloe and head borders Horsley. Lines:
SOLOMON CARTER, JONATHAN SANDIDGE, AARON HIGGINBOTHAM.

722.   16 September 1815.   JOSEPH HIGGINBOTHAM, Amherst County, to
        JONATHAN RICHESON, Amherst County...$3000 500 acres. Lines:
ford of the river opposite LINDSEY SANDIDGE, road to BENJAMIN SANDIDGE
near the old meeting house, THOMAS N. EUBANK, ARCHY ROWSEY, WILLIAM
DEMPSEY, BENJAMIN SANDIDGE--known as PHILLIPS' old place, ABSALOM
HIGGINBOTHAM, JONATHAN TOMLINSON, AMBROSE TOMLINSON, JOSEPH DODD,
BENJAMIN SANDIDGE line to tract he bought of CHARLES P. TALIAFERRO.
Witnesses: THOMAS RICHESON, RICHARD BALLINGER, WIATT P. SMITH,
WIATT SMITH.

723.   16 September 1815.   JAMES WARE and wife, NANCY, Amherst County,
        to JONATHAN CAMM, Amherst County, JONATHAN BULLOCK and POWHATAN
ELLIS...Deed of Trust; debt to CHARLES ELLIS, Richmond--tract and mills
bought on Horsley. Ten bonds made for payments from January, 1814--
$1.00 tract and mill--Pedlar Mills on Pedlar and Horsley 45¾ acres.
Lines: EDMOND GOODRICH, the canal, WILLIAM MITCHELL, RICHARD L. ELLIS.
To CHARLES ELLIS, 17 September 1823. Witnesses: JONATHAN ELLIS,
JAMES DAVIS, R. N. EUBANK, JAMES R. LIVELY, WILLIAM BATES.

726.   19 November 1814.   DANIEL NORCUTT and wife, RACHEL, Amherst
        County, to RODERICK TALIAFERRO, Lynchburg...$800 50½ acres
north borders Harris. Witnesses: WILLIAM M. CLARK, BENJAMIN HENSLEY,
MICAJAH CLARK.

727.   29 April 1815.   JOSEPH KENNERLEY and wife, SARAH, Amherst County,
        to DANIEL HOFFMAN and County, Lynchburg...$4000.00 two acres.
Lines: Main road leading to town of Madison and where JOSEPH
KENNERLEY lives. Witnesses: RICHARD W. CHANDLER, WILLIAM B. GOOCH,
and ellegible signature--E. A. (?).

728.   15 August 1815.   REUBEN COLEMAN, Amherst County, to MICAJAH
        CAMDEN, Amherst County...$10,000 218 acres. Lines: LINDSEY
COLEMAN, GIDEON RUCKER, JAMES POWELL, BENAMMI STONE--commonly called
The Oaks and includes the tavern. Witnesses: THOMAS ALDRIDGE,
HUDSON M. GARLAND, DAVID S. GARLAND. To MICAJAH CAMDEN, 29 January
1815.

729.   25 September 1815.   Order to Amherst County Justices of the
        Peace: CHRISTOPHER FLETCHER and wife, PHEBE, 16 January 1815,
to ROBERT PIERCE...150 acres. JONATHAN CAMM, Clerk. Done by CHARLES
MUNDY and JONATHAN WARWICK, 26 September 1815.

730.   29 August 1815. WILLIAM HARTLESS and wife, NANCY, HENRY HARTLESS
      and wife, JANE, RICHARD HARTLESS and wife, MARY, JONATHAN COOPER
and wife, TABITHA, WILLIAM WILSON and wife, NANCY, JAMES GRAHAM and
wife, ISABELLA, MARYANT, ANNIS and JAMES HARTLESS, representatives of
JOSEPH JARVIS and wife, NANCY, ROBIN PETERS and us, SUSANNAH, NATHAN
COOPER and wife, PATSY, JONATHAN CLARK and wife, POLLY, RICHARD
HARTLESS by his grandson, WILLIAM HARTLESS, Rockbridge, and Amherst
County to JAMES SANDIDGE, Amherst County...$100 Buffaloe on Long
Mountain. Lines: JONATHAN BEVERLY, near Little Swamping Creek,
top of Long Mountain, AARON HIGGINBOTHAM--no acres; also 35 acres.
Witnesses: JONATHAN S. CARTER, FREDERICK PAINTER, JONATHAN PAINTER.
To JAMES SANDIDGE, 8 September 1816.

732.   18 August 1815. EDMOND HUDSON and wife, SUSANNAH, BENNETT
      HUDSON and wife, SALLY, RUSH HUDSON, JR., and wife, PAMELA, and
LUCY HUDSON, Amherst County, to HUGH TAGGATT, Amherst County...$515.00
103 1/3 acres--part of tract allotted to EDMOND HUDSON--B borders
Buffaloe. Lines: LINDSEY COLEMAN, formerly STULZ (?), EDWARD CARTER,
BENNETT HUDSON. Witnesses: EDMOND T. COLEMAN to all but SALLY HUDSON,
HILL CARTER--same, JONATHAN PENN, JR., --same, SUSANNAH, PAMELA, and
LUCY relinquished dowers before HILL CARTER and EDMOND T. COLEMAN,
18 August 1815. To R. TINSLEY, 26 August 1820.

733.   29 September 1814. MRS. MARY MAY, Nelson County, Kentucky...
      power of attorney, to WILL L. MAY to go for her to Virginia to
sell my part or share from slaves in estate of my late father,
SAMUEL MEREDITH. AUSTIN HUBBARD and JOSEPH LEWIS, Nelson Justices
of the Peace. BENJAMIN GRAYSON, Clerk, TRAVIS DAVIS, Presiding
Justices of the Peace.

734.   8 May 1815. WILLIAM L. MAY, under powers above, to DAVID S.
      GARLAND, Amherst County...$1500 slaves held by JANE MEREDITH
for life under will of SAMUEL MEREDITH to his four children: WILLIAM,
SAMUEL (both MEREDITHS), SARAH ARMISTEAD, JANE H. GARLAND, and MARY
MAY--note five instead of four children. Witnesses: CORNELIUS
POWELL, PEYTON KEITH. To DAVID S. GARLAND, no date.

735.   26 September 1815. WILLIAM WILLIAMS, Amherst County, to STITH
      MEAD, Lynchburg...$1286 128 5/8 acres Boling Creek. Lines:
PHILIP JOHNSON, widow LUCY ROBINSON, old road, white oak with a swell
on it, DENNIS, a path, WILLIAM WARWICK, THOMAS JOHNSON, HOYLE, grantor.
Witnesses: JONATHAN H. WILLIAMS. To STITH MEAD, 24 May 1822.

736.   23 September 1815. THOMAS WIATT and wife, SARAH, Amherst
      County, to STITH MEAD, Lynchburg...$2000.00 100 acres northwest
side main road to Lynchburg from Amherst County House. To STITH MEAD,
21 April 1817.

7373. 9 October 1815. Order to Amherst County Justices of the Peace:
      GIDEON RUCKER and wife, JOYCE, 17 April 1815, to REUBEN COLEMAN...
573¼ acres. Done by THOMAS S. HOLLOWAY and JAMES POWELL, 9 October
1815.

738.   26 September 1815. ROBERT PIERCE and wife, JANE, to JAMES
      LONDON, JR., Amherst County...$800 150 acres Porrige. ROBERT
PIERCE bought of CHRISTOPHER FLETCHER. Lines: THOMAS EDWARDS,
JONATHAN HUTCHINSON, RICHARD JONES, CHARLES MUNDY, grantee, JONATHAN
CREWS. Witnesses: JONATHAN WARWICK, CHARLES MUNDY. Page 739 order
to quiz JANE, same date, done by CHARLES MUNDY and JONATHAN WARWICK,
same date.

740.   26 September 1815. ROBERT PIERCE and wife, JANE, Amherst County,
      to JAMES POWELL, Amherst County...L807 403¼ acres where ROBERT
PIERCE lives--headwaters Rockey Run. Lines: JONATHAN WARWICK,
JONATHAN CASHWELL, widow MONROE, RICHARD WILSON, ABSALOM OWL (sic),
JACOB PIERCE, ISAIAH ATTKINSON, JOEL CAMPBELL. Witnesses: as above
and ordered as above.

742.   18 January 1815. REUBEN COLEMAN and wife, MELINDA, LINDSEY
       COLEMAN and wife, NANCY, and ROBERT COLEMAN, Amherst County,
to NANCY COPER FRANKLIN and ELIZABETH HENRY FRANKLIN, devisees of
JAMES FRANKLIN, deceased, Amherst County...L45 paid by their grandson,
THOMAS CREWS--3 3/4 acres north side Rutledge. Lines: mouth of oak
springs branch, north border Rutledge. Part of tract of GEORGE
COLEMAN, deceased. One acre of it was formerly that of BENAMMI STONE.
Witnesses: MICAJAH CAMDEN, JOSEPH LEE, P. G. CAMDEN.

743.   26 September 1815. BENJAMIN SHACKELFORD and wife, FRANCES,
       Amherst County, to JAMES PENDLETON, Amherst County...$2000.00
260 acres Puppie Creek. Lines: main road, top of the mountain.
Page 744 order to quiz FRANCES, 9 October 1815, done by BENJAMIN
TALIAFERRO and WILLIAM JOPLING, -- 1815; recorded in Amherst County,
16 October 1815.

746.   3 -- 1815. EDMOND WILLIAMSON and wife, NANCY, Amherst County,
       to WILLIAM TUCKER, Amherst County...$1060 237 acres. Lines:
ridge at corner of grantor's frnce, Ball's Spring branch, Stone
House Creek, LUDAH WILLIAMSON, MOSES MARTIN. Page 747 ordered to
quiz NANCY, 9 October 1815, done by HILL CARTER and EDMOND T. COLEMAN,
10 October 1815. Witnesses: are then named: JONATHAN EUBANK,
ALEXANDER and JAMES HIX.

ABSTRACT OF DEED BOOK N OF AMHERST COUNTY, VIRGINIA

by

BAILEY FULTON DAVIS

1. 18 March 1816. JOSEPH HIGGINBOTHAM to BENJAMIN SANDIDGE, both
of Amherst County...$150 25 acres south fork Buffaloe. Lines:
HUGH CAMPBELL, both parties. Part of a tract. Witnesses: JONATHAN
ELLIS, CHARLES P. TALIAFERRO, LINDSEY SANDIDGE, ABRAM CARTER, ZACH
DRUMMOND. To BENJAMIN SANDIDGE, 5 April 1816.

2. 20 March 1815. JABEZ CAMDEN, Amherst County, to JONATHAN
MYERS, Amherst County...Deed of Trust; debt due THOMAS ALDRIDGE;
$1.00, four male slaves named; six boys named; four women named;
two girls named. Witnesses: STERLING CLAIBORNE, JONATHAN S. BLAIR,
JONATHAN WHITEHEAD. To THOMAS ALDRIDGE, 11 October 1816.

4. 13 May 1815. JOSEPH MC CRAY to DANIEL S. BURFORD and ISAAC
RUCKER...$1,000.00 two slaves. Witness: R. POWELL, JR.

4. 28 July 1815. WILLIAM MARTIN and wife, MARY ANN, Amherst
County, to ABRAHAM MARTIN, JR...L100 115 acres north Thrasher
Creek. Lines: AARON HIGGINBOTHAM, ENOCH CARPENTER, ZACHARIAH
TALIAFERRO.

5. 16 October 1815. PIERCE W. MAYES and wife, POLLY, Amherst
County, to JESSE MAYES, Amherst County...$525 104 acres.
Lines: grantee, JOEL MAYES, BEVERLY WILLIAMSON, deceased, PETER
CASH.

6. 21 September 1815. JOSEPH MAYO and wife, JANE, Richmond, to
WILLIAM GALT, Richmond...$3500.00 243½ acres. Lines: the river,
tract lately sold by GEORGE MAYO to GALT, DAVID S. GARLAND, Porrage
Creek. Witnesses: DAVID JOHNSON, WILL P. STROTHER, CHARLES H. HYDE.
S. JACOBS and WILLIAM H. FITZSIMMONS (?)--clerk has bad time with this
name in this book--Richmond Justices of the Peace, 30 October 1815;
also JONATHAN PARKHILL, Justice of the Peace.

8. 14 August 1814. BENJAMIN RUCKER and wife, SALLY, Amherst County,
to WILLIAM LEE, Amherst County...$4560.00 309 acres Harris
Creek. Lines: DAVID WOODROOF, WILLIAM MC DANIEL, the road, JONATHAN
HANSARD, ANTHONY RUCKER. Witnesses: TINSLEY RUCKER, PHILIP JOHNSON,
JAMES S. DILLARD. Page 9 order to quiz SALLY; done by NELSON C.
DAWSON and PHILIP JOHNSON, 18 September 1815.

10. 6 November 1815. JONATHAN BURCH and wife, ELIZABETH, Amherst
County, to JONATHAN LONDON, Amherst County...$200.00 104 acres
Christian Creek. Lines: JONATHAN and CHARLES CHRISTIAN, JAMES
DILLARD. Witnesses: FRANCIS R. HIGGINBOTHAM, JAMES S. DILLARD,
WILLIAM GRANT. To JONATHAN LONDON, 1 May 1817.

11. 18 November 1815. NICHOLAS WEST and wife, ELIZABETH, Amherst
County, to SAMUEL BURKS, Amherst County...280 (sic) 169 acres.
Patent to ROBERT DAVIS, JR., 3 March 1760. Lines: THOMAS MORRIS,
SAMUEL BURKS, JR., ARTHUR TULEY, MICAJAH CLARK. Also 20 acres
adjoining. Lines: JOSHUA ELLIS, DAVID BURKS. Also 100 acres adjoin-
ing. Lines: STEPHEN GOOLSBY--bought from MATTHEW WILSON, 3 July
1773. Witnesses: JAMES WARE, R. R. BURKS, DAVID BURKS, JR., JOSHUA
ELLIS, RICHARD EUBANKS, THOMAS MORRIS, R. L. ELLIS.

13. 26 October 1815. JOSEPH ALLCOCK and wife, STILLY, Amherst
County, to JONATHAN ALLEN, Amherst County...L300 200 acres north
borders Buffaloe. Lines: RICHARD ALLCOCK, WILLIAM GATEWOOD, JAMES
FREELAND, deceased, GUERLAND PENN (?), deceased, JAMES ROWSEY.
Witnesses: JAC TYREE, WILLIAM L. WATTS, JOSEPH KENNEDY. Page 14
order to quiz STILLY; done, 28 October 1815, by THOMAS ALDRIDGE and
JAMES POWELL.

15. 17 February 1806. JAMES LASHWELL, Campbell County, to CHRISTOPHER
    ISBELL, Amherst County...to CHRISTOPHER ISBELL, 16 September
1816--L150 nine acres both sides Lynch road near town of Madison.
Lines: stable at road, near the spring, WARD, LYNCH, steep hill
side. Witnesses: CORNELIUS POWELL, JOSEPH KENNERLEY, JOSIAH LEAKE,
THOMAS S. MC CLELLAND. Proved by MC CLELLAND, 20 November 1815, and
by KENNERLEY and POWELL, 18 December 1816.

16. 20 November 1815. JONATHAN SMITH, acting executor of PHILIP
    SMITH, deceased, to PHILIP WELCH, Wilkes County, North Carolina...
PHILIP SMITH by will gave daughter, RODA WELCH, $200.00 and rest of
property to be divided between her and his son, THOMAS SMITH--her
part to be in negroes for her life and then to her children--free
from control of her husband, ANDREW WELCH. Executors has L126-1-2
besides her $200.00 and has bought DICE, a woman, for RODA and to her
son, PHILIP WELCH, as trustee. Witnesses: ROBERT RIVERS, JONATHAN
SMITH, JR., ROBERTSON.

17. 4 September 1815. WALTER and JAMES FRAZIER, late of Giles
    County, Tennessee...power of attorney to trusty friend,
WILLIAM FRAZIER, Giles County, Tennessee--to act in Virginia.
JONATHAN DICKEY, Presiding Justice, as to GERMAN LESTER, Clerk,
8 September 1815. Recorded in Amherst County, 20 November 1815.

19. 7 November 1815. POLLY PADGETT and WILLIAM CROUCHER to JAMES
    FULCHER...$500 82½ acres. Lines: LINDSEY COLEMAN, deceased,
NATHANIEL MANTIPLY, the estate of LINDSEY COLEMAN to BEVERLY PADGETT
and formerly that of SHERAD BUGG. Witnesses: ROBERT RIVERS,
STERLING CLAIBORNE, JONATHAN SMITH.

19. 21 March 1815. WILLIAM COLEMAN, Amherst County, to ROBERT H.
    COLEMAN, Amherst County...L200 under deed of 19 July 1814--
tract in Madison County, Kentucky, on Silver and Muddy Creeks. Part
of ROBERT H. COLEMAN tract. 250 acres on north side larger tract.

20. 6 June 1815. TALBERT NOEL to THOMAS N. EUBANK...Deed of Trust;
    debt to JONATHAN and R. L. ELLIS; $1.00 boy about seven; stock
etc. Witnesses: RICHARD N. EUBANK, PETER P. THORNTON, NELSON
CRAWFORD, CHARLES L. BARRET, JAMES WARE, JOSHUA L. ELLIS.

21. 21 November 1815. WILLIAM EVANS and wife, JOYCE, Amherst County,
    to GEORGE CAMPBELL, Amherst County...$1480 391½ acres both
sides Little Piney. Lines: WILLIAM MOORE, CLARKSON, CAMPBELL.

22. 21 November 1815. JOSEPH and NANCY HAWKINS, Amherst County, to
    CHARLES Y. JOHNSON, Lynchburg...no amount--18 acres surveyed
1 April 1806, on Fluvanna River. Lines: WILLIAM SCOTT, GEORGE
GOODWIN.

23. 1 November 1815. PLEASANT DAWSON and wife, JEMIMA, Amherst
    County, to NELSON C. DAWSON, Amherst County...$1260 127½ acres
north side Harris. Lines: LEWIS DAWSON.

24. 15 December 1815. WILLIAM I. ISBELL to ZACH ISBELL...$3200
    400 acres Headwaters Harris and bought from RICHARD HARDWICK
and THOMAS NORVELL lives there as overseer. Lines: ELIZABETH
COLEMAN, WILLIAM PETERS, RICHARD HARRISON. To WILLIAM PENDLETON,
15 April 1822.

25. 7 December 1815. PATRICK P. BURTON and wife, EMILY W., Bedford,
    to ISAAC RUCKER, Amherst County...$1000 433 acres not by acres,
but by boundaries; reference to deed of 19 August 1802, from GEORGE
MC DANIEL to PHILIP BURTON. JOSEPH SLAUGHTER and BALDA MC DANIEL,
Bedford Justices of the Peace, 15 December 1815, as to acknowledgement.
To ISAAC RUCKER's son, 16 August 1816.

26. 7 December 1815. WILLIAM, CHARLES, WIATT TUCKER, DABNEY HILL
     and wife, ELIZABETH, JAMES ANGUS and wife, MARY, BARNETT CASH
and wife, SARAH, to JONATHAN TUCKER, Amherst County...4 June 1817
(27?) to D. HILL. Grantors are heirs of CHARLES TUCKER, the elder--
interest for $1000 100 acres Indian Creek. Part of 400 acres patent
to JONATHAN HARRIS, 10 September 1755, and the 100 acres was conveyed
by deed from DAVID HARRIS, 6 March 1769, to JONATHAN PARSONS, the
younger, et al. (JONATHAN PARSONS) to CHARLES TUCKER, deceased.
14 December 1805. Lines: HENRY ROSE, the creek. Witnesses:
WILLIAM CASH, ENOCH CARPENTER, JAMES CASH, JONATHAN SMITH, EDMOND T.
COLEMAN.

28. 7 December 1815. PATRICK P. BURTON and wife, EMILY W.,
     Bedford, to NELSON C. DAWSON, Amherst County...$3000 353 acres
and refrence to deed: GEORGE MC DANIEL, JR., to PHILIP BURTON,
2 March 1799. To NELSON C. DAWSON, 3 July 1827. Acknowledged as
on page 25f.

29. 12 December 1815. ELISHA GILLENWATERS and wife, BETSY, Amherst
     County, to JONATHAN LONDON, Amherst County...$250 110 acres
Porrage Creek. Same tract JONATHAN LONDON sold to THOMAS GILLENWATERS.
Lines: Buffaloe Ridge, JOSEPH HAWKINS, JAMES DILLARD, ROBERT GRANT,
DAVID S. GARLAND.

30. 28 December 1815. BARKSDALE SLEDD, 1; BENJAMIN HARRISON, 2;
     WILLIAM WOODROOF, 3...Deed of Trust; debt to WILLIAM WOODROOF
as bondsman in WILLIAM HENDERSON for benefit of THOMAS L. HOLLOWAY
versus SLEDD and NATHANIEL TATE--slaves; stock, etc.

32. ROBINETTE NELSON, ROBINSON NELSON, CHARLES CHISWELL NELSON,
     children of SUSAN NELSON, by their father, ROBERT NELSON,
SUSAN WHITING, PEYTON R. NELSON and wife, SARAH B., MARY G(IVENS?)
NELSON, NATHANIEL NELSON, ANN FITZHUGH NELSON, LUCY CHISWELL NELSON,
ETHELINDE NELSON to CHARLES LANDON CARTER, Town of Fredericksburg...
grantors are heirs of JONATHAN CHISWELL, deceased, Williamsburg;
$1.00 paid by CARTER as devisee of his mother, ELIZABETH CARTER, who
was also heir of JONATHAN CHISWELL--three tracts, two in Amherst
County and one in Pitsylvanie County--all received lately by law
under right of said CHISWELL from SHELTON, WINGFIELD et al. ROBERT
NELSON for self and--grandson of ROBINETTE, ROBINSON, and CHARLES C.
NELSON--Charles City County, December 1815, parties appeared before
WILLIAM E. HILL and BENJAMIN HARRISON, Justices of the Peace.

33. 14 November 1815. WILLIAM BOYD and wife, MARY H., who was
     MARY H. ROBINSON, to CHARLES LONDON CARTER, as above...BOYD
and wife are legatees of JONATHAN CHISWELL--$1.00 three tracts
above. Certified in King and Queen, 14 November 1815, by grantors
before JAMES G. RORR and WILLIAM ROBERTSON, Justices of the Peace.

34. 19 October 1815. WILLIAM N. WILLFORD, JANE C. WILLFORD, MARY C.
     WILLFORD by JONATHAN S. WILLFORD, father and grandson and
children of FRS N. WILLFORD, deceased, WILLIAM WILLFORD, SUSAN R.
WILLFORD, ELIZABETH NELSON, HUGH NELSON, ARMISTEAD NELSON, son of
COLONEL WILLIAM NELSON, deceased, by CHARLES C. PAGE, grandson,
ROBERT PAGE, CHARLES L. PAGE, JONATHAN F. PAGE, sons of MANN(?) PAGE
and MARY C. PAGE, by CHARLES C. PAGE, grandson, CHARLES C. PAGE,
SARAH C. PAGE, WILLIAM R. NELSON, WILLIAM MEUX, LUCY MEUX to CHARLES
LANDON CARTER as above...grantors as heirs of JONATHAN CHISWELL.
Fredericksburg Corporation as to WILLFORDS: BENJAMIN DAY and JONATHAN
CRUMP, Justices of the Peace. Page 36 King William County: ARMISTEAD
NELSON, son of COLONEL WILLIAM NELSON, by CHARLES C. PAGE, grandson.
ROBERT PAGE, CHARLES LANDON PAGE, JONATHAN FRANCIS PAGE--sons of MANN
PAGE and MARY CHISWELL PAGE, by CHARLES C. PAGE, grandson, CHARLES C.
PAGE, SARAH C. PAGE, WILLIAM R. NELSON, WILLIAM MEUX, LUCY MEUX--
GEORGE and BENJAMIN DABNEY, Justices of the Peace: 10 November 1815.

37. 28 November 1815. MATTHEW WHITING BROOK and wife, ELIZABETH,
     late ELIZABETH LEWIS, JONATHAN LEWIS and wife, ANN CHISWELL,
MARGARET P. OLIVER, MARY A. OLIVER, WARREN L. OLIVER, infant children
under 21 by AUGUSTINE OLIVER, their father and grandson, JONATHAN W.
FOX by grandson, JONATHAN LEWIS, THOMAS NELSON and wife, MARY
CHISWELL, late MARY C. PEYTON, who was MARY C. LEWIS to CHARLES
LANDON CARTER as above..heirs of JONATHAN CHISWELL, formerly of
Williamsburg, PEYTON, 1 December 1815: THOMAS ARCHER and ROBERT
GIBBONS, Justices of the Peace.   Gloucester County: acknowledged
by M. W. BROOKS and wife, ELIZABETH, 29 November 1815, JONATHAN LEWIS
and WILLIAM ROBBINS, Justices of the Peace. Also Gloucester ack-
nowledged by JONATHAN LEWIS for self and as grandson of JONATHAN W.
FOX and ANN C. LEWIS: WILLIAM ROBINS and ROBERT THURSTON, Justices
of the Peace. Also same county for acknowledgement by AUGUSTINE
OLIVER as grandson of MARGARET P., MARY A., and WARNER L. OLIVER, his
children, 29 November 1815. JONATHAN LEWIS and WILLIAM ROBINS,
Justices of the Peace.

39. 2 February 1816. NICHOLAS HARRISON and wife, NANCY, Lynchburg,
     to THOMAS MORRIS, Amherst County...$186 93 acres both sides
Peg's Creek--part of 200 acres of grantor. Lines: grantee, the
road. Witnesses: JAMES WARE, RICHARD HARRISON, THOMAS CREWS.

40. 13 December 1815. JEREMIAH TAYLOR to JAMES and JONATHAN BROWN,
     WILLIAM COLEMAN, CHARLES L. BARRET, bondsman on delinquent bond
to Amherst County Sheriff for benefit of THOMAS L. HOLLOWAY, executor
of HENRY HOLLOWAY, deceased, for parcel of tobacco...Deed of Trust;
$1.00, two negroes: CHARLES and KEZIAH. Witnesses: WILLIAM SHELTON,
RICHARD H. BURKS, MITCHELL WATTS, FRANCIS A. K. DAVIES.

42. 8 January 1816. JONATHAN MERRITT, SR., Amherst County, to
     JONATHAN MERRITT, JR., Amherst County...$1500 103 acres Stovall.
Lines: CHARLES WINGFIELD, PHILIP JOHNSON. Witnesses: J. L. WINGFIELD,
CORNELIUS MERRITT, CHARLES WINGFIELD, JONATHAN L. BURFORD, GEORGE W.
TAYLOR.

42. 8 December 1815. JAMES POWELL and wife, MILDRED, Amherst
     County, to CATLETT CAMPBELL, Amherst County...$1372.50 152½
acres north borders Rocky Run. Lines: JOSIAH ATKINSON, ABSALOM
HOWL, RICHARD WILSON, a road, JONATHAN WARWICK, JOEL CAMPBELL.
Witnesses: HENRY H. WATTS, J. M. BROWN, R. POWELL, JR.

43. 15 February 1816. LINDSEY MC DANIEL, Amherst County, to
     SAMUEL WATTS, Amherst County...$900 195 acres and where SAMUEL
lives. Lines: grantor, EDMOND WINSTON, CHARLES COPPEDGE, Huff
Creek, JAMES PENDLETON. To SAMUEL WATTS, July, 1819.

44. 19 February 1816. JAMES LONDON, Amherst County, to JONATHAN
     and THOMAS HUTCHESON--JR. for LONDON...$1.00 39 3/4 acres
called Griffith's Place which JAMES LONDON bought from ROBERT PIERCE.
Lines: CHARLES MUNDY, FLETCHER's Far field, THOMAS EDWARDS, grantee,
RICHARD JONES.

45. -- January 1816. JONATHAN DAWSON and wife, SALLY, to JAMES WADE,
     Lynchburg...$200 25 acres on road to Trent's ferry. Lines:
REUBEN PENDLETON, GEORGE TINSLEY, south side road, LEWIS DAWSON.
Witnesses: RICHARD H. BURKS, CHARLES WINGFIELD, GEORGE W. TAYLOR.
To JONATHAN DAWSON, 8 July 1816.

46. 28 December 1815. JONATHAN HYLTON to ROWLAND VIAH...L50 50
     acres balance of tract willed to grantor by GEORGE HYLTON after
deducting 50 acres sold to REUBEN TERY. Witnesses: JAMES L. DILLARD,
CHARLES L. BARRET, WILLIAM L. WATTS, WILLIAM HORSLEY, JAMES CUNNINGHAM.

47. 15 January 1815. DAVID S. GARLAND to WILLIS DUNCAN, Amherst
     County...$200 197 acres south borders Buffaloe. Lines:
JONATHAN DUNCAN, JACOB SMITH, deceased, JONATHAN YOUNG. To WILLIS
DUNCAN, 23 October 1816.

48. 15 January 1816. RUSH HUDSON, SR., Amherst County, to daughter,
     MILDRED HUDSON...$10.00; she is infirm and decrepit and now
resides with me--a mullatto (sic) boy, JOURDAN WINSTON.

49. 1 January 1816. WILLIAM BURFORD and wife, SUSANNAH, Amherst
     County, to JONATHAN L. WINGFIELD, Amherst County...$2500 232
acres Stovall Creek. Lines: BENJAMIN RUCKER, ROLLING CLARK, ELIAS
WILLS. Witnesses: CHARLES WINGFIELD, JONATHAN L. BURFORD, JONATHAN
MERRITT, JR. To JONATHAN L. WINGFIELD, 18 November 1817, by T. RUCKER
per order.

49. 18 March 1816. JOSEPH HIGGINBOTHAM, Amherst County, to ABRAM
     CARTER, Amherst County...$123 41 acres north borders Buffaloe
on both sides Fork Mountain; reference to patent survey of 12 March
1802; Book Number 48:505. Witnesses: JONATHAN ELLIS, CHARLES P.
TALIAFERRO, LINDSEY and DUDLEY SANDIDGE, ZACHARIAH DRUMMOND.

50. 4 December 1815. JOSEPH and BENJAMIN HIGGINBOTHAM, executors
     of JOSEPH HIGGINBOTHAM, to ABRAM CARTER, Amherst County...no
amount; 140 acres Fork Mountain between heads of north and south fork
Buffaloe. Patent of 13 December 1791. Lines: JOSEPH HIGGINBOTHAM,
JAMES HIGGINBOTHAM. Witnesses: NELSON CRAWFORD, THOMAS N. EUBANK,
BENJAMIN TALIAFERRO, ANSELM CLARKSON, PHILIP SMITH, ZACH DRUMMOND,
LINDSEY SANDIDGE, JONATHAN ELLIS. To ANSELM CLARKSON, 20 May 1823.

52. 24 February 1816. JAMES WAUGH, Amherst County, to GARRET LANE,
     Amherst County...$1.00 150 acres in Green County, Kentucky--
on Robinson Creek. Part of 1145 acres surveyed for NELSON CRAWFORD
and sold by GARRET LANE to JAMES WAUGH, 8 October 1810--sic. Lines:
CHARLES ELLIS, ROBERT TODD, NELSON CRAWFORD. Witnesses: THOMAS N.
EUBANK, JONATHAN and JOSHUA ELLIS.

52. 11 August 1815. WILLIAM NOEL and wife, LUCY, Amherst County,
     to ANDERSON WARE, Amherst County...500 (sic) 115 acres. Lines:
WALTER WILLIAMS, ANTHONY NICELY, JONATHAN BYAS, WILLIAM PRYOR,
JONATHAN ELLIS, JONATHAN WARE, MOSES RUCKER.

53. 21 August 1815. WILLIAM NOEL and wife, LUCY, Amherst County,
     to WALTER WILLIAMS, Amherst County...L30 40 acres. Lines:
ALLISON MORRIS, ANTHONY NICELY, SAMUEL NICELY, ANDERSON WARE.

54. 15 September 1815. CHARLES ELLIS and wife, MARGARET R.,
     Richmond, to JAMES WARE, Amherst County...$8000 45½ acres
Pedlar Mills tract on Horsley and Pedlar--mills thereon. Divided
by commissioners to CHARLES ELLIS on division of MAJOR JOSIAH ELLIS,
deceased. Lines: EDMOND GOODRICH, by the canal, WILLIAM MITCHELL,
RICHARD L. ELLIS. Witnesses: JONATHAN ELLIS, JAMES DAVIS, R. N.
EUBANK, JAMES R. LIVELY, WILLIAM BATES.

56. 8 September 1815. HARRISON HUGHES and wife, NANCY, Amherst
     County, to PLEASANT DAWSON, Amherst County...$336 38 acres
Harris Creek. Lines: grantee, grantor, WILLIAM HUGHES, deceased,
DANIEL NORCUTT, RODNEY TALIAFERRO. Witnesses: LEE (?), WILLIAM B.
DAWSON, RUSSELL DAMERON, BRAXTON DAMERON. To PLEASANT DAWSON,
11 June 1816.

57. 2 February 1816. NICHOLAS HARRISON and wife, NANCY, Lynchburg,
     to JOHN ELLIS, Amherst County...$208 104 acres. Lines: THOMAS
MORRIS, ALLISON MORRIS, LUKE RAY, BENJAMIN SHACKELFORD. Witnesses:
BENJAMIN HARRISON, JAMES WARE, JAMES L. LAMKIN. To JOHN ELLIS,
30 April 1817.

58. 18 March 1816. WILLIAM WOODROOF, Amherst County to LINDSEY
     MC DANIEL, Amherst County...$316.68 83 acres. Lines: top of
PALL's Mountain (probably PAUL's).

59. 22 March 1816. HENRY CAMDEN and wife, LUCY, Amherst County, to AMBROSE WILMORE, Amherst County...$400 155 acres Huff Creek. Lines: HENRY HOLLOWAY, deceased, ELIZABETH COLEMAN, JAMES WILMORE, JORDAN P. CAMDEN. Witnesses: WILLIAM ARMISTEAD, R. H. BURKS, WIATT LONDON.

60. 20 December 1813. Order to Amherst County Justices of the Peace: BENNETT RUCKER and wife, JOHANNAH, 11 September 1813, to RICHARD HARRISON...102 acres. Done by AMBROSE RUCKER and NELSON C. DAWSON, 22 September 1815. Page 62; order as to same grantors to RICHARD HARRISON, 26 April 1815; 493 3/4 acres. Done as above.

62. 15 March 1815. LIEUTENANT COLONEL ANDREW J. MECONICE, Commander of 35th Regiment of the United States Infantry at Norfolk: GARLAND LUCAS is private in CAPTAIN BENJAMIN HARDAWAY's Company of regiment cited. Has served proper term and is honorably discharged. To prevent its falling into other hands, he is 25 years old, light hair, light eyes and complexion--5 feet 7 inches, waggoner by occupation. R. W. SCOTT, Lieutenant, and acting Adjutant Inf. Signed at Norfolk by LUCAS and he states that he had received from United States full amount of bounty, clothing, and rations up to time of discharge. Recorded Amherst County, 22 March 1816.

62. 22 February 1816. JOSEPH HAWKINS and wife, NANCY, Amherst County, to JONATHAN LONDON, Amherst County...L49-15 104 acres south side Buffaloe Ridge and Porrige Creek. JOSEPH HAWKINS bought it of FRANCIS HILL. Lines: grantee, REUBEN NORVELL, JAMES DILLARD, tract LONDON bought of JONATHAN BENIT (?), top of Buffaloe Ridge. Witnesses: JONATHAN and F. K. HIGGINBOTHAM, HENRY and RICHARD TURNER.

63. 15 April 1816. CALEB RALLS, Amherst County, to ANDREW M. STATON and CHARLES STINNETT, Amherst County...L104 104 acres Pedlar. Lines: MARTIN BIBB, Lovelady Creek, THOMAS LUCAS, SAMUEL GIST, JONATHAN MAYS, PRYOR. To ANDREW M. STATON, 6 December 1817.

64. 10 April 1816. NELSON C. DAWSON and wife, NANCY, Amherst County, to DABNEY WARE, Amherst County...$1.00; 302 acres Grahams Creek. Lines: ARTHUR L. DAVIES, GEORGE MC DANIEL, SR., grantor, RICHARD SHELTON, SAMUEL BURKS.

65. 20 February 1816. JONATHAN COALTER, Henrico, to PHILIP JOHNSON, Amherst County, and JAMES BOWLING, third...MICHAEL COALTER in life bought jointly with JOHNSON two tracts. 1. Scuffle Town. 2. Tract joining JONATHAN WINGIFLED, THOMAS MURRELL, JONATHAN and JAMES BOWLING-- 120 acres. Agreed to divide, but MICHAEL died intestate and descended to his children: DAVID COALTER, JAMES COALTER, ELIZABETH MC PHEETERS, JONATHAN COALTER, JANE NAILEN (?), MARGARET COALTER, MICAJAH COALTER, PATSY COALTER. Memo: JAMES died shortly and interest descended to brothers and sisters--all united in conveyance--POLLY is still minor, to JONATHAN COALTER, 15 January 1802, and recorded in General Court 11 October 1808. JONATHAN COALTER agreed with JAMES BOWLING-- JONATHAN then of Augusta--MICHAEL was to take tract of above joining BOWLING and JOHNSON--Scuffle Town. JONATHAN sold BOWLING 196 acres, but no warranty. BOWLING to execute title. BOWLING to give reasonable notice for $800. In hands of JOHNSON for safe-keeping. $1.00 now paid to JOHNSON by BOWLING. POLLY is now wife of NATHANIEL BEVERLEY TUCKER. JOHNSON to hold Scuffle Town tract. JONATHAN G. GAMBLE and JONATHAN PARKILL, Henrico Justices of the Peace. Witnesses: WILLIAM PETTYJOHN, NATHANIEL DODSON, JONATHAN H. SMITH.

68. 14 April 1816. WILLIAM GATEWOOD and wife, CATHERINE, Amherst County, to BARBARA NOEL, Amherst County...L31-10 40 acres Lovelady Creek; border of Pedlar. Lines: ZED. SHOEMAKER, NICHOLAS PRYOR.

69.   8 April 1816.   JONATHAN LONDON and wife, TIRZA, Amherst County,
        to IRVING L. LONDON, Amherst County...$850 tract JONATHAN LONDON
bought of JAMES LONDON, JR.--by deed of gift from JAMES LONDON, SR.
to JAMES LONDON, JR.--171 3/4 acres--200 acres mentioned first and
then this acreage. Lines: south side Buffaloe Ridge: JONATHAN LONDON,
ROBERT GRANT, LARKIN LONDON, JAMES LONDON, Glade Branch, JAMES LONDON,
SR. and JR. Witness: WIATT LONDON.

70.   4 December 1815.   THOMAS N. EUBANK and wife, JANE, Amherst
        County, to JONATHAN EUBANK, JR., Amherst County...$1300 210
acres. Lines: WILLIAM DEMPSEY, ARCHELAUS ROWZEY, BENJAMIN SANDIDGE,
Buffaloe Springs tract, GODFREY TOLER, JOSEPH HIGGINBOTHAM. Witnesses:
WILLIAM BOURNE, JAMES F. TALIAFERRO, BENJAMIN TALIAFERRO. To
JONATHAN EUBANK, JR., 13 September 1818.

72.   29 March 1816.   SACKVILLE KING and wife, ANNE, Campbell County,
        to WILLIAM TURNER, Amherst County...$700 208 acres Porrage
and Stovall Creeks. Lines: grantee, road to Staples Mill near where
road crosses Stovall road, WILLIAM GALT, JONATHAN LONDON, THOMAS
JEWELL, ALEXANDER JEWELL on 100 acres survey; bought by ALEXANDER
JEWELL, from REUBEN NORVELL and NORVELL bought of JONATHAN HIGGINBOTHAM,
SAMUEL ANDERSON. Witnesses: JONATHAN LONDON, WILLIAM GREGORY,
WILLIAM T. and JONATHAN L. TURNER.

73.   7 September 1802.   JAMES COLEMAN and wife, NANCY, JESSE COLEMAN
        and wife, SUSANNAH, LITTLEBERRY COLEMAN and wife, MILLY, DANIEL
COLEMAN and wife, MARY, WILLIAM COLEMAN, SPILSBY COLEMAN and wife,
ELIZABETH, of Counties of Amherst and Campbell (sic) to NELSON CRAWFORD,
Amherst County...L55 98 acres north fork Piney. Also 50 acres south
fork Piney. Lines: JONATHAN WARNOR (?). Witnesses: WILSON
DAVENPORT, WILLIAM B. BANKS, THOMAS W. COCKE, ARCH. ROBERTSON,
SAMUEL ROSE. Final proof, 20 May 1816, by ROSE.

75.   18 December 1815.   DENNIS ENSEY and wife, JUDAH, Amherst
        County, to THOMAS JEWELL, Amherst County...$250 140 acres
south Porrage and bought from ROBERT ALLEN. Lines: JONATHAN LONDON,
PLEASANT STORY, JAMES DILLARD, ALEXANDER JEWELL, SACKVILLE KING.

75.   18 December 1815.   DENNIS ENSEY as above and seems to be same
        deed.

75.   18 March 1816.   JESSE CAMPBELL and wife, NANCY, Amherst County,
        to DABNEY HILL, Amherst County...NANCY is child and heir of
JONATHAN FULCHER who departed this life intestate--$330--their
interest in FULCHER's tract on Piney. Lines: JAMES FULCHER,
grantee--213 acres. To DABNEY HILL, 21 July 1817.

77.   15 September 1815.   DAVID S. GARLAND to EDMOND PENN, Amherst
        County...$100 100 acres both sides Otter Creek. Lines:
DAVID BURKS, HENRY L. DAVIES, deceased. Witnesses: PEACHY FRANKLIN,
JEREMIAH WILSON, JONATHAN SAVAGE. To EDMOND PENN, 1819.

78.   16 April 1816.   CHARLES MOORE and wife, POLLY, Amherst County,
        to JONATHAN LONDON, Amherst County...$2000 228 acres both sides
Porrage. Tract was sold by JONATHAN CREWS to RICHARD HARRISON
and HARRISON sold to CHARLES MOORE. Lines: JONATHAN WARWICK,
JONATHAN PADGETT, THOMAS EDWARDS, JAMES LONDON, JR., CHRISTIAN
heirs. To J. J. LONDON, 14 July 1845.

78.   5 March 1816.   LEROY CAMDEN and wife, BETHEMIA, Amherst County,
        to STERLING CLAIBORNE, Amherst County...$10,000 135 acres
where WILLIAM CAMDEN, deceased, formerly lived and devised by him
to grantor. Lines: JABEZ CAMDEN, CHARLES BURRUS, BURCHER WHITEHEAD,
MICAJAH CAMDEN. Witnesses: JONATHAN THOMPSON, JOSEPH DILLARD,
JONATHAN L. BLAIR.

79. 23 April 1816. JAMES P. GARLAND and wife, KETURAH, Amherst
     County, to ZACHARIAH T. DRUMMOND, Amherst County...$300 117
acres Puppie Creek. Lines: JONATHAN WARE, JONATHAN TALIAFERRO,
deceased, HENRY BALLINGER. Known as Frenchburg, formerly that of
WILLIAM HOWARD and bought by GARLAND under Deed of Trust. To
ZACHARIAH DRUMMOND, 2 August 1817.

80. 18 April 1816. DANIEL BURFORD, JR., 1; BENJAMIN RUCKER, 2;
     RICHARD BURKS, 3...Deed of Trust; debt to RUCKER. $1.00 paid
by BURKS 33 acres--junction of Lynch and Tinsley roads. Lines:
BENJAMIN RUCKER, DANIEL M. BURFORD, ROBERT H. ROSE. Witnesses:
RICHARD H. BURKS, JOSEPH DUNCAN, BERRY COLEMAN.

82. 25 April 1816. SAMUEL BURKS, SR., Amherst County, and wife,
     PEGGY, to RICHARD BURKS, Amherst County...L500 161½ acres
both sides Harris. Lines: JONATHAN AMBLER, JONATHAN SHELTON, RICHARD
BURKS. To RICHARD BURKS, 21 April 1817.

82. 23 April 1816. RICHARD HARRISON and wife, SOPJIA, Amherst
     County, to AMBROSE RUCKER, Amherst County...L200 20 all interest
in tract both sides Harris. Lines: JONATHAN TINSLEY, DAVID TINSLEY,
JOSHUA TINSLEY--including mill--TINSLEY's mill, stones, slave; stock--
one third of it.

83. 23 August 1815. EDWARD WAUGH, Amherst County, to LUKE RAY,
     Amherst County...$818.00 200 acres. Lines: CAPTAIN BENJAMIN
SHACKELFORD, JAMES BIAS, SAMUEL NICLEY, ALLISON MORRIS, NICHOLAS
HARRISON--bond to make title. Witnesses: WILLIAM RAY, FANNY J. RAY,
SIMEON RAY.

84. 24 April 1816. WILLIAM GALT, Richmond, to WILLIAM M. WALLER,
     Amherst County...$10,800 900 acres. Lines: JOEL FRANKLIN,
BARTLETT CASH, WILLIAM S. CRAWFORD, deceased. Witnesses: CHARLES L.
CHRISTIAN, GABRIEL PAGE, DILLARD H. PAGE, JOSEPH PHILLIPS. To
WILLIAM M. WALLER, 16 May 1820.

85. 24 April 1816. WILLIAM M. WALLER, Amherst County, to WILLIAM
     GALT, Richmond, 2, and DAVID S. GARLAND and BENJAMIN BROWN, 3...
Deed of Trust; debt to GALT and $1.00 paid by DAVID S. GARLAND and
BENJAMIN BROWN's 800 acres. Lines and witnesses as above.

87. 22 January 1816. DANIEL BURFORD, SR., to JONATHAN BURFORD...
     $133 81 acres both sides south fork Stovall and whre grantor
lives; includes water grist mill. Lines: EDWARD WATSON, south bank
of creek, STOVALL's line at MAYO's path, ELIAS WILLS, JESSE BECK.
Witnesses: MERIT M. WHITE, JAMES HAMBLETON, WILLIAM WHITE.

88. 14 May 1816. AARON HIGGINBOTHAM, ABSALOM HIGGINBOTHAM and
     wife, POLLY, to WILLIAM DUNCAN, Amherst County...$2500 160 acres
south side Buffaloe. Lines: on Buffaloe just above mouth of Thrasher
Creek, JAMES HICKS, WILLIAM DUNCAN, WILLIAM SANDIDGE, old field.

89. 17 May 1816. EDMOND PENN and wife, JANE, 1; THOMAS CREWS and
     DAVID S. GARLAND, 2; WILLIAM LONG, 3...Deed of Trust; $1.00
paid by second parties to secure WILLIAM LONG on bond to BOYD MILLER,
surviving partner of WILLIAM BROWN and Company, late Lynchburg
merchants. Fredericksburg tract in Spotsylvania--a lot and house
occupied by JONATHAN M. SHEPHERD as a tavern: The Golden Ball,
JANE is owner as heir of ANN FOX DRUMMOND, late widow and only heir
of WILLIAM DRUMMOND, deceased. Also interest in tract of between
nine and ten hundred acres in Amherst County--the Glebe and where
PENN lives. Final certification 19 August 1818. To WILLIAM LONG,
17 October 1816.

92. 10 May 1816. EDMOND PENN, 1; H. M. GARLAND and PEACHY FRANKLIN,
     2; WILLIAM LONG, 3...Deed of Trust; debt to WILLIAM LONG; $1.00
paid by two parties to secure LONG on bond to BOYD MILLER; slaves
named. Witnesses: WILLIAM ARMISTEAD, JONATHAN S. BLAIR, R.
HIGGINBOTHAM. To WILLIAM LONG, 7 October 1816.

93. 20 May 1816. JONATHAN LONDON and wife, TIRZA, Amherst County,
to WILLIAM GALT, Richmond...$878.75 351½ acres west side
Porrage. Lines: GALT, JEWELL, the creek. Witnesses: JAMES LONDON,
JR., JONATHAN GARTH, JONATHAN R. HIGGINBOTHAM. To ROBERT TINSLEY,
9 November 1827.

94. 6 May 1816. JONATHAN LONDON and wife, TIRZA, Amherst County,
to JAMES LONDON, JR., Amherst County...$800 128 acres Porrage.
Part of tract JONATHAN bought of CHARLES MOORE. Lines: JONATHAN
WARWICK, JONATHAN PADGETT, tract JAMES bought of ROBERT PIERCE and
where JAMES lives; tract JONATHAN WARWICK bought of CHARLES CHRISTIAN's
heirs.

95. 20 May 1816. JAMES LONDON, JR., to JONATHAN LONDON, Amherst
County...$400 65 acres part of tract JAMES LONDON, JR. bought
of ROBERT PIERCE--both sides Porrage. Lines: CHARLES MUNDY, JONATHAN
and THOMAS HUTCHESON, THOMAS EDWARDS, JONATHAN LONDON, between house
and creek.

95. 20 May 1816. WILLIAM TURNER and wife, SALLY, Amherst County,
to SAMUEL ANDERSON, Amherst County...$250 53 acres Stovall
Creek. Lines: road, STEPHEN HAM, deceased, grantee. SALLY relinquished dower in court, 6 September 1833. To JEESE BECK, administrator of purchaser, 19 August 1833. To GRANVILLE LAIN, 5 August 1834.

96. 20 May 1816. JONATHAN PADGETT and wife, PEGGY, REUBEN PADGETT
and wife, CATY, Amherst County, to EPHRAIM PADGETT, Amherst
County...L138 69 acres Porrage. Lines: THOMAS EDWARDS, JONATHAN
WARWICK, JONATHAN CASHWELL, his own.

97. 4 March 1816. CHARLES PERROW and wife, ELEANOR, ANNA PERROW,
to DRURY CHRISTIAN, SALLY and MARY CHRISTIAN, infants of
JONATHAN CHRISTIAN, deceased...$3500 paid by JONATHAN DILLARD,
grandson. 221 acres James River, upper end of tract devised by will
of DANIEL PERROW--low grounds to tract of JONATHAN HORSLEY (bought
from DANIEL PERROW), tenants in common and not joint tenants.
Witnesses: JONATHAN P. COBBS, JAMES DILLARD, WILLIAM M. RYAN. To
ALEXANDER MUNDY, 16 October 1837.

98. 18 April 1816. JEREMIAH TAYLOR, Amherst County, to JAMES
BROWN, COLEMAN and BARRET, and JAMES TAYLOR...Deed of Trust;
debt to COLEMAN and BARRET and to JAMES TAYLOR. $1.00 paid by
JAMES BROWN--three negroes named; furniture; stock, etc. Witnesses:
WILLIAM WHITE, JAMES HAMBLETON, DAVID CRAWFORD, JONATHAN HAMBLETON,
JONATHAN GILES.

99. 25 February 1816. WILLIAM EVANS and DAVID S. GARLAND to
GEORGE CAMPBELL, Amherst County...$180 90 acres Little Piney.
Lines: EVANS. Witnesses: JAMES FULCHER, JONATHAN CAMPBELL,
WILLIAM CAMPBELL.

100. 13 December 1815. JONATHAN CREWS and wife, CHRISTIAN, to
CHARLES MOORE, Amherst County...$1068 228 acres Porrage.
Lines: JONATHAN WARWICK, JONATHAN PADGETT, THOMAS EDWARDS, JAMES
LONDON, CHRISTIAN. Witnesses: JONATHAN WARWICK, CHARLES MUNDY,
JAMES LONDON, JR.

100. 16 June 1816. LUCY ROBINSON, Amherst County, to STITH MEAD,
Amherst County...$626.25 41 3/4 acres both sides Opossum Island
Road. Lines: COLONEL PHILIP JOHNSON, junction of road with Lynchburg
road, TERRY's path, WILLIAM ROBINSON. Witnesses: WILLIAM ROBINSON,
STITH MEAD, JR., JONATHAN M. WILLIAMS. To STITH MEAD, 21 April 1816.

101. 18 December 1815. Order to Amherst County Justices of the
Peace: DENNIS ENSEY and wife, JUDAH, 18 December 1815, to
THOMAS JEWELL, 140 acres. Done by CHARLES MUNDY and JONATHAN WARWICK,
25 January 1816.

102. 29 January 1816. Order to Amherst County Justices of the Peace:
JACOB PIERCE and wife, ELIZABETH, 15 June 1812, to JONATHAN
HENDREN...166 acres. Done by JONATHAN WARWICK and JONATHAN COLEMAN,
15 April 1816. To JONATHAN HENDREN, 16 April 1817.

103. 15 February 1804. ROBERT DE GRAFFENREID, Lunenberg, to CHARLES
BRYDIE, same county...L210 270 acres which ROBERT bought of
HUGH PAUL, Augusta, and part of 577 acres granted to JONATHAN PRICE,
Amherst County. Witnesses: MEREWETHER HUNT, THOMAS FARMER, PATON
SMITH, ZACH DE GRAFFENREID. Acknowledged in Lunenberg by ROBERT
DE GRAFFENREID, 12 April 1804, WILLIAM TAYLOR, Clerk. Certified in
Amherst County, 17 June 1816. To SAMUEL LEAK, agent for CHARLES
BRYDIE, 10 March 1829.

104. 16 August 1814. Order to Amherst County Justices of the Peace:
THOMAS N. EUBANK and wife, JANE, 29 September 1814, to CHARLES
ELLIS...450 acres. Done by JONATHAN ELLIS and BENJAMIN SHACKELFORD,
24 December 1814.

105. 10 May 1816. HENRY CAMDEN and wife, LUCY, Amherst County, to
HUGHEY TYGET...$300 80 acres north side Buffaloe and part of
estate of DANIEL TUCKER, deceased. Lines: EDWARD CARTER's, Mill
Creek, COLONEL BRAXTON, LINDSEY COLEMAN, deceased, CHARLES PARKS and
now in possession of said COLEMAN's heirs, grantee, formerly HUDSON
heirs. Witnesses: WILLIAM H. CAMDEN, WESLEY L. DUNCAN, JABEZ CAMDEN.
To R. TINSLEY to get relinquishment of dower, 26 August 1820.

106. 15 December 1815. AMBROSE RUCKER and wife, ELIZABETH, Bedford,
MORRIS HAMNER and wife, LUCY F., SAMUEL HAMNER and wife,
NANCY, Charlotte County to JOSHUA MAYS, Amherst County...THOMAS LUCAS,
late of Amherst County, died intestate and left 150 acres on Pedlar
and descended equally to his children. MORRIS HAMNER some time ago
bought of JESSE CARTER and wife, FRANCES, one of children of LUCAS,
and all grantors married daughters of LUCAS. $500. Lines: SAMUEL
GUEST, JONATHAN BRYANT, WILLIAM SHOEMAKER, Mill Creek, NICHOLAS PRYOR.
Witnesses: ROBERT MORTON, JONATHAN DENNIS who also certified as
Justice of the Peace of Charlotte, SAMUEL HAMBER, 15 December 1815,
and relinquished of dower. WILLIAM DICKINSON and RICHARD HOBSON,
Bedford Justices of the Peace, 10 February 1816, as to RUCKER and
wife.

108. 22 November 1815. Order to Amherst County Justices of the
Peace: JAMES DILLARD and wife, JANE, 11 August 1810, to
SAMUEL SCOTT...100 acres. Done by CHARLES MUNDY and JONATHAN HORSLEY,
15 March 1816.

109. 31 October 1814. Order to Amherst County Justices of the
Peace: WILLIAM LONG and wife, ELIZABETH, 7 February 1814, to
MICAJAH CAMDEN...25 acres. Done by THOMAS CREWS and THOMAS L.
HOLLOWAY, 17 March 1815.

110. 20 May 1816. JAMES POWELL and wife, MILDRED, to CHARLES MOORE...
$2102 262 3/4 acres headwaters Rocky Run. Lines: JONATHAN
CASHWELL, JAMES GRISSOM's old line, the road, ANDREW MONROE, deceased.
To CHARLES MOORE, 21 June 1819.

110. 8 February 1816. ANN M. KNOX, Mecklenberg, only heir of
ALEXANDER GORDON, deceased, to GEORGE and JONATHAN M. EUBANK,
Bedford...$2590.50 863½ acres south borders Buffaloe and head borders
Horsley. Lines: WILLIAM HARTLESS, ZACH DRUMMOND, JAMES PENDLETON,
GOVAN, HIGGINBOTHAM, TAYLOR. Witnesses: F. WHITTLE, THOMAS (?)
GOODE, S. (L) GOODE. Certified by SAMUEL GOODE and JONES GEE, Justices
of the Peace of Mecklenberg, 8 February 1816. To JONATHAN M. EUBANK,
16 May 1820.

112.   28 September 1815.   RICHARD BURKS and wife, POLLY, Amherst
        County, to CLOTWORTHY BARBER, Petersburg...$1490 53 acres both
sides Harris and both sides road from BURKS to ACH. Lines: JONATHAN
AMBLER. Witnesses: REUBEN NORVELL, BENJAMIN SHACKELFORD, PHILIP
JOHNSON, CHARLES TALIAFERRO. Order to quiz POLLY and done by
Amherst County Justices of the Peace: REUBEN NORVELL and AMBROSE
RUCKER, 29 September 1815. To CLOTWORTHY BARBER, 22 September 1817.

113.   25 October 1815.   JOSEPH BURROUGHS and wife, MARY, Amherst
        County, to WILLIAM DOWNS, Amherst County...L120 100 acres
Rocky Run. Lines: DAVID S. GARLAND on northwest side Buffaloe
Ridge, NATHAN WINGFIELD, deceased, CHRISTIAN and BROWN's order line.
All that tract that JOSEPH BURROUGHS bought of PETER PIERCE--his
late dwelling place. Witnesses: JONATHAN SCOTT, JONATHAN BURROUGHS,
JAMES BURROUGHS. Page 114 order to quiz MARY, 19 December 1815, and
done on that date by THOMAS S. HOLLOWAY and JAMES POWELL.

115.   8 June 1816.   DAVID S. GARLAND and wife, JANE, Amherst County,
        to JOSEPH KENNEDY, Amherst County...$1000 200 acres north side
Buffaloe. Lines: DILLARD's road, JESSE KENNEDY, JONATHAN CHRISTIAN,
EVANS' spring branch. Witnesses: CORNELIUS POWELL, JONATHAN N.
ROSE, WILLIAM HALL.

116.   10 June 1816.   JONATHAN LUCK, Augusta, to JONATHAN WARE, Amherst
        County...$750 218 acres middle fork Pedlar. Lines: ADAM REID,
now HENRY CAMDEN--sic; Copied from patent, but 18 acres to be excepted--
sold by ANGUS MC DONALD and has been in possession of SAMUEL PAXTON
and now JAMES CLARK's. To JONATHAN WARE, 19 April 1819. Page 117
acknowledged by JONATHAN LUCK in Rockbridge: WILLIAM CARUTHERS and
J. ALEXANDER, Justices of the Peace, 11 June 1816.

117.   10 June 1816.   WILLIAM LYLE, attorney-in-fact for ANGUS
        MC DONALD, to JONATHAN LUSK--LUCK above--19 August 1788...
MC DONALD executor to JONATHAN LUSK a title bond as to 218 acres on
Pedlar; part of 236 acre patent to ANGUS MC DONALD, 1 May 1784.
ANGUS MC DONALD to comply did on 27 September 1788, executor to
WILLIAM LYLE a power of attorney to convey as soon as JONATHAN LUSK
paid L35 and ANGUS MC DONALD assigned to LYLE--power of attorney in
Rockbridge. JONATHAN LUSK has paid with interest. Tract on middle
fork Pedlar. Lines: ASEN (?) REED, now HENRY CAMPBELL, 18 acres
excluded as in above deed. Same Rockbridge Justices of the Peace
on 10 June 1816, as to acknowledgement.

118.   28 November 1815.   JONATHAN WILLIAMSON and wife, POLLY,
        Bedford County, Tennessee to ALEXANDER SALE, Amherst County...
$250 all interest in estate of BEVERLY WILLIAMSON, deceased, on
Stonehouse Creek in two or three tracts. One sixth as legatees;
left by will for division to six legatees and recorded in Amherst
County. Witnesses: EDMOND T. COLEMAN, ROBERT RIVERS, WILLIAM SALE,
REUBEN NORVELL, WILLIAM TUCKER. To ALEXANDER SALE, 7 October 1818.

119.   9 February 1816.   PHILIP JOHNOSN, Amherst County, to REUBEN
        NORVELL, Amherst County...$5.00 35 acres east side and joining
Opossum Island road. Lines: STITH MEAD, WILLIAM ROBINSON. Witnesses:
JONATHAN PADGETT, GEORGE W. TAYLOR, RICHARD HARRISON, T. S. HOLLOWAY.
To REUBEN NORVELL, 16 September 1816.

120.   21 August 1815.   ROBERT MC CULPIN and wife, POLLY, Rockbridge,
        to RICHARD BURKS, Amherst County...L190 196 acres east side
Tobacco Row Mountain. POLLY's share of estate of her late grandfather,
DR. DANIEL BURFORD. Lines: the road leading through CRAWFORD's Gap,
AMBROSE LUCAS' house. Witnesses: REUBEN NORVELL, JOSEPH MC CRAY,
REUBEN BURFORD. To REUBEN BURFORD, per MATTHEW BURKS, 5 March 1823.
Order on same day to quiz POLLY and done by DAVID EDMUNDSON and
DAVID TEMPLETON, 4 June 1816. County is not named in order or by
Justices of the Peace, but Rockbridge in deed.

122. 24 June 1816. ROBERT PIERCE and wife, JEAN, Pitsylvania, to
      PEYTON KEITH, Amherst County...$350 121 acres Raven Creek.
North border Buffaloe. Lines: ALLEN BLAIR, STEPHEN WATTS, SAMUEL
SPENCER, grantee. Witnesses: ALLEN BLAIR, ROBERT G. KIDD, WILLIAM H.
ANDERSON. To PEYTON KEITH, 8 March 1817.

122. 13 July 1816. NATHANIEL WILSON and wife, RACHEL, Amherst
      County, to ARCHELAUS ROWSEY, Amherst County...L55 136 acres--part
of 254 acres. Lines: south end Suck Mountain, GODFRY TOLER,
JONATHAN HUGHBANKS (sic--EUBANKS), top of the mountain down to
JOSEPH HIGGINBOTHAM. Memo: at death of RACHEL WILSON, said land to
be returned to MOLLY ADKERSON--all save one third. Witnesses:
PULLIAM SANDIDGE. To NATHANIEL WILSON, 1 August 1816.

123. 15 July 1816. WILLIAM STAPLES, Amherst County, to GEORGE W.
      HIGGINBOTHAM, Amherst County...$200 one full fourth of tract
devised by JOSEPH STAPLES, deceased, to his sons: SAMUEL, JOSEPH,
JOHN and WILLIAM, who is grantor, will in Amherst County, on Buffaloe.
Lines: STEPHEN WATTS, ALLEN BLAIR. GEORGE W. HIGGINBOTHAM tenant in
common and not joint tenant. To GEORGE W. HIGGINBOTHAM, 5 March 1817.

124. 29 April 1816. JONATHAN MERRIT, SR., Amherst County, to
      MILLNER COX, Amherst County...$997.50 66½ acres on both sides
south fork Stovall near its head. Lines: PHILIP JOHNSON, ELIAS
WILLS, JONATHAN MERRIT, JR. Witnesses: REUBEN NORVELL, JONATHAN
MERRIT, JR., ARCHIBALD AUSTIN, WILLIAM HARRISON, THOMAS D. HILL,
ABSALOM RUCKER, REUBEN HENDERSON.

125. 16 July 1815. JONATHAN CAMM and wife, ELIZABETH, Amherst
      County, to THOMAS ALDRIDGE, Amherst County...L760 384 acres
north side and joining Buffaloe. Bought by JONATHAN CAMM from
WILLIAM WARWICK, 17 June 1802--except 16 acres sold by JONATHAN
CAMM to JONATHAN WARWICK.

125. 17 July 1816. REUBEN COLEMAN, Amherst County, to JOSEPH
      POWELL, Amherst County...$1327.00 118 acres part of tract.
Lines: Lynch road, THOMAS CREWS, Rutledge Creek, WIATT POWELL.

126. 1 November 1804. LEONARD ROWSEY and wife, ELIZABETH, Amherst
      County, to HENRY CAMDEN, Amherst County...L150 170 acres.
Lines: top of Blue Ridge. Witnesses: MICAJAH CAMDEN, WILLIAM
CAMDEN, LEROY CAMDEN. Final proof by MICAJAH CAMDEN, 26 June 1816.
To WILLIAM H. CAMDEN, 24 July 1816.

127. 19 August 1816. JONATHAN LONDON and wife, TIRZA, Amherst
      County, to JONATHAN SCOTT, Amherst County...$260 104 acres
Christian Mill Creek and bought by JONATHAN LONDON from JONATHAN
BURCH. Lines: JAMES DILLARD, JONATHAN LONDON, CHRISTIAN heirs.

128. 8 August 1816. JORDAN P. CAMDEN, Amherst County, to WILLIAM H.
      CAMDEN, Amherst County...$138 60 acres "The Cove"; devised by
WILLIAM CAMDEN in will in Amherst County to grantor.

128. 29 July 1816. DAVID CLARKSON, Amherst County, to WASHINGTON
      HILL, Rockbridge...$2800 no acres; both sides Franklin Creek.
Lines: WILLIAM TALIAFERRO, ANSELM CLARKSON, ZACHARIAH TALIAFERRO,
WILLIAM S. CRAWFORD, JONATHAN SALE. Witnesses: WIATT SMITH,
JOEL F. SMITH, JAMES DODD. To WASHINGTON HILL, 27 April 1819.

129. 5 October 1814. CHARLES REYNOLDS and wife, ANN, JAMES LEE and
      wife, NANCY, to ELIAS WILLS...L200 14 acres both sides Harris
and including the mill. Lines: BANISTER TINSLEY, the road.
Witnesses: SOLOMON DAY, CHARLES DAMERON, JONATHAN D. WILLS. To
WILLS, 16 September 1816.

130.   15 July 1816. SAMUEL SALE and wife, CLARISA, THOMAS V. GOODRICH
       and wife, NANCY, WILEY CAMPBELL and wife, ELIZABETH, ALEXANDER
SALE and wife, SARAH, all of Amherst County, to JONATHAN JONES and
wife, MARTHA, Nelson County, and THOMAS SALE, Bedford County, and
CORNELIUS SALE, Amherst County...$2100 all interest in 600 acres as
well as interest in conformity of will of JONATHAN SALE, deceased--
Buffaloe. Lines: HIGGINBOTHAM, JONATHAN SMITH. To THOMAS C. SALES,
29 July 1817. CHARLES P. TALIAFERRO and EDMOND T. COLEMAN, Amherst
County Justices of the Peace as to CLARISA, NANCY, SARAH C., and
MARTHA, 17 August 1816.

132.   13 March 1816. JOSEPH and BENJAMIN HIGGINBOTHA, executors of
       JOSEPH HIGGINBOTHAM, Amherst County, to BENJAMIN TALIAFERRO,
Amherst County...$18.00 18 acres south borders middle fork Pedlar
and north borders south ford Pedlar. Lines: tract surveyed for
JOSEPH HIGGINBOTHAM. Witnesses: ANSELM CLARKSON, GEORGE EUBANK,
DAVID CLARKSON.

133.   18 May 1816. ANSELM CLARKSON, Amherst County, to THOMAS N.
       EUBANK, Amherst County...Deed of Trust; debt to JONATHAN and
RICHARD L. ELLIS; $1.00 four named slaves. Witnesses: GEORGE L.
SHRADER, LANDON TULEY, JONATHAN EUBANK, SR. To JONATHAN and RICHARD L.
ELLIS, 4 November 1816.

133.   16 May 1816. Order to Amherst County Justices of the Peace:
       JESSE RICHESON and wife, AMELIA, JONATHAN RICHESON and wife,
NANCY, ARMISTEAD RUCKER and wife, ELIZABETH and THOMAS RICHESON,
children of JONATHAN RICHESON, deceased, 27 January 1814, to RICHARD
MILLNER...432 acres. Done by BENJAMIN TALIAFERRO and THOMAS N. EUBANK,
17 August 1816, as to NANCY. To RICHARD MILLNER, 2 May 1817.

134.   1 August 1816. JOSEPH HAWKINS, Amherst County, to WILLIAM
       RADFORD...Deed of Trust; debt to ARCHIBALD ROBERTSON; $1.00
90 acres tract adjoins GEORGE POWELL, JONATHAN GILES, slaves and
children named. Witnesses: JACOB HAAS, S. GARLAND, T. HOLCOMB,
JONATHAN P. WILSON. To JONATHAN P. WILSON, 18 November 1816.

136.   16 March 1816. DANIEL NORCUTT, Amherst County, to WILLIAM
       RADFORD, Bedford...Deed of Trust; debt to BOYD MILLER; $1.00
400 acres. Lines: MICAJAH CLARK, WILLIAM MUSE, HARRISON HUGHES,
ELIAS WILLS. Witnesses: JONATHAN P. WILSON, BENJAMIN HARRISON,
RICHARD H. BURKS.

137.   10 July 1816. RICHARD WILSON and wife, ANNE, Amherst County,
       to JONATHAN P. WILSON, Campbell County...$1000 101 acres.
Lines: ABSALOM HOWL, CAMPBELL, MONROE, HUCKSTEP, CLASBY. Witnesses:
JAMES S. HIGGINBOTHAM, WILLIAM TURNER, THOMAS NEIGHBOURS. To
JONATHAN P. WILSON, 30 October 1816. Page 138 17 June 1816 (sic)
order to quiz ANNE; done, 7 August 1816, by JONATHAN COLEMAN and
JONATHAN WARWICK.

139.   18 May 1816. CHRISTOPHER ISBELL and wife, ELIZABETH, to
       ELIZABETH CREASY...$500 one half acre on Lynch road where
ELIZABETH CREASY lives; also half acre opposite first lot and where
THOMAS B. MEHONE lives. Witnesses: WILLIAM I. ISBELL, JONATHAN
WOODSON, LUCY FREELAND. To WILLIAM I. ISBELL, 24 September 1816.

140.   10 September 1816. CORNELIUS ROACH and wife, ELIZABETH,
       Amherst County, to JONATHAN WARE, SR., Amherst County...$600
two tracts where CORNELIUS ROACH lives north borders Otter and
joining. 1. Lines: GEORGE MORRIS, NICHOLAS C. DAVIES, deceased,
DAVID NOLAND, JEREMIAH WHITTEN, JONATHAN STINNETT. 74 acres.
2. 117 acres. Lines: BEN NOEL, TINSLEY, DAVIS, KNUCKLES, JAMES
FRANKLIN. To JONATHAN WARE, JR., 9 October 1815 sic.

141. 14 September 1816. CORNELIUS ROACH and wife, ELIZABETH,
      Amherst County, to GEORGE ROACH, Amherst County...$404.00
52 acre tract was lot of CORNELIUS ROACH from father's estate.
Lines: HENRY and GEORGE ROACH, ARCHER DAVIES, THOMAS N. EUBANK,
RICHARD BURKS. To GEORGE ROACH, 9 October 1816.

142. 2 September 1816. JOSEPH PHILIPS to HILL CARTER...L540 197 2/3
      acres. Lines: main road, Maple Run, New Glasgow road, Mine
Hill road.

142. 20 August 1816. CHARLES P. TALIAFERRO, Amherst County, to
      RICHARD HARRISON, Amherst County...$100 55 acres on Tobacco
Row Mountain. Lines: CHARLES TALIAFERRO.

143. 1 November 1815. BANISTER TINSLEY and wife, MILLY, Amherst
      County, to ELIAS WILLS, Amherst County...$1200 103 acres north
side Harris. Lines: WILLIAM PETTYJOHN, near WILLS' mill and dam.
Witnesses: JONATHAN BULLOCK, GEORGE M. TINSLEY, JONATHAN BAILEY.
To ELIAS WILLS, 29 January 1820.

144. 16 September 1816. WILLIAM FRAZER for self and by power of
      attorney from JAMES FRAZER, both of Giles County, Tennessee,
to CHARLES P. TALIAFERRO, Amherst County...$1000.00--ancient survey
of 380 acres--south borders of middle fork Pedlar. Lines: DAVID
BURKS, their share of late father's estate and patent to WALTER
POWERS, 1782.

145. 16 September 1816. WILLIAM FRAZER for self and by power of
      attorney from WALTER and JAMES FRAZER, both of Giles County,
Tennessee to ADDISON TALIAFERRO, Amherst County...$50 100 acres by
ancient survey--south side Blue Ridge. Lines: HENRY HARTLESS.
Residue of larger tract patent to JAMES FRAZZER.

145. 1 March 1816. PHILIP JOHNSON, Amherst County, to DAVID
      HOFFMAN and Company, Lynchburg...$5.00 half acre near Lynchburg
on east side Lynch road and next to tan yard of grantee. Witnesses:
REUBEN NORVELL, ROB MORRIS, HUGH NORVELL, JESSE BECK, JESSE KENNERLY.

146. 21 August 1816. NOTLEY SMOOT to STERLING CLAIBORNE...Deed of
      Trust; debt to JESSE KENNERLEY; $1.00; wagon, team, stock.
Witnesses: JONATHAN PENN, JR., THOMAS CREWS, B. (?) WALKER. To
JESSE KENNERLEY, 22 January 1817.

147. 16 August 1816. REUBEN CARVER and wife, FANNY, to CHRISTOPHER
      ISBELL...$2000 200 acres Juniper and Falls Creeks. Lines:
JOSEPH MAYS, WILLIAM DAMERON, deceased, WILLIAM ROBERTSON. Witnesses:
JONATHAN GARTH, A. L. HARRISON, JONATHAN L. BURFORD. To CHRISTOPHER
ISBELL, 2 November 1816.

147. 29 August 1816. JOSEPH and BENJAMIN HIGGINBOTHAM, executors
      of JOSEPH HIGGINBOTHAM, to PETER MARTIN, Amherst County...L68-17
102 acres Buffaloe. Lines: WILLIAM TOMLINSON, ABRAHAM MARTIN.
Witnesses: CHARLES P. TALIAFERRO, WIATT SMITH, ROBERT M. EUBANK,
WILLIAM HENLEY. To PETER MARTIN, 5 October 1818.

148. 26 June 1816. PULLIAM SANDIDGE, Amherst County, to JOSEPH
      HIGGINBOTHAM, Amherst County...L213 north side Buffaloe.
1. 185 acres and where LINDSEY SANDIDGE lives. Lines: JAMES GOVAN,
JOSEPH DODD, old patent. 2. 28 acres an entry by STEWART BELLOW
and assigned to ZACHARIAH TALIAFERRO and by him to THOMAS DICKINSON.
Witnesses: CHARLES P. TALIAFERRO, WIATT SMITH, ADDISON TALIAFERRO,
ROBERT M. EUBANK, WILLIAM HENLEY.

149. 6 August 1816. ANN CHENAULT, Tennessee, power of attorney
     to WILLIAM I. ISBELL, Amherst County...as to my estate in
Amherst County due me from administrator of THOMAS RICKETTS and wife,
or in hands of my grandson, CHRISTOPHER ISBELL. Witnesses: ELISHA
UNZELL, ROBERT MC CRATHEN (?), JEREMIAH CHENY, REDDISH ROBINSON,
August 1816, Maury County, Tennessee, JOSEPH B. PORTER, Clerk of
Court of Pleas and grants by deputy, P. BELSON, JAMES T. LANDFORD,
Presiding Justice of the Peace. Recorded Amherst County, 16 September
1816. To WILLIAM I. ISBELL, 2 November 1816.

151. 16 October 1816. NICHOLAS VANSTAVERN and wife, CATHERINE,
     Amherst County, to WALTER CHRISTIAN, SR., Amherst County...
$1000 55 acres both sides Irish Creek. Lines: JESSE RICHESON.
Bought in 1805 by NICHOLAS VANSTAVERN from JONATHAN WARE and wife,
ELIZABETH. Witnesses: JOSEPH DILLARD, DANIEL F. CHRISTIAN, THOMAS C.
CHRISTIAN. To WALTER CHRISTIAN, 25 October 1816.

152. 28 June 1816. MICAJAH TERRELL and wife, MARTHA ELIZA, Natchez,
     Mississippi, Territory--power of attorney to JONATHAN LYNCH, JR.,
Lynchburg...to convey 196 acres on Seneca Creek in Campbell. Lines:
CHARLES L. TERRELL, GERRARD JOHNSON. Also Amherst County tract on
Bowling Creek about three miles from Lynchburg--60 acres--sold by
MICAJAH TERRELL, SR., to his agent, JONATHAN CALLAWAY, and by him
to some others, but SR. never made title and we empower attorney to
do so. Also to sue MORRIS of Goochland or from PAUL DISMUKES,
grandson of MARTHA ELIZA--then SAMPSON. Witnesses: JONATHAN
RICHARDS, E. TURNER, RICHARD TERRELL, President of Selectman of city
in Mississippi, and Justice of the Peace of Adams County, E. TURNER.

154. 6 August 1816. ANN CHENAULT to WILLIAM I. ISBELL, Amherst
     County...$200 100 acres whereon MARTHA RICKETTS lives. Lines:
near the road. Witnesses: ROBERT MC CRACKEN, JEREMIAH CHERRY,
ELISHA UZZELL--Maury County, Tennessee, acknowledged by ANN; JOSEPH P.
PORTER, Clerk. JAMES T. SANDFORD (LANDFORD), Presiding Justice of
the Peace. To WILLIAM I. ISBELL, 2 November 1816.

155. 20 September 1816. DANIEL NORCUTT and wife, RACHEL, Amherst
     County, to RODERICK TALIAFERRO, Lynchburg...$1500 125 acres.
Lines: RICHARD RUCKER, WILLIAM HUGHES, deceased, grantee, grantor.
Part of where DANIEL NORCUTT lives. Witnesses: REUBEN NORVELL,
PHILIP JOHNSON, WILLIAM M. CLARKE, CHARLES W. CARY (?).

156. 24 September 1816. CHARLES TALIAFERRO, Amherst County, to
     EDMOND and THOMAS MASSIE, Amherst County...MILDRED TALIAFERRO,
Chester District, South Carolina, 18 July 1812, empowered CHARLES to
convey Amherst County tract and part in Nelson--both sides Piney;
LUCAS POWELL's quarter, drawn by SEYMOUR POWELL and sold by him to
MILDRED--723 acres surveyed by JAMES CAMDEN lately--$353.00.

158. 31 July 1816. WILLIAM MITCHELL and wife, SALLY, Amherst County,
     to THOMAS HIGGINBOTHAM, and CHISWELL DABNEY...Deed of Trust;
debt to JONATHAN WARD, JR.; $1.00; 798 3/4 acres; one acre excepted
at mouth of Harris given by JONATHAN WARD, SR., to JONATHAN LYNCH, SR.
and sold by EDWARD LYNCH, son of JONATHAN, to WILLIAM MITCHELL.
Tract conveyed to WILLIAM MITCHELL by JONATHAN WARD, SR., 3 July
1816. Acknowledged in Lynchburg: JONATHAN SCHOOLFIELD and DANIEL
BROWN, Justices of the Peace. To JONATHAN WARD, JR., 16 December
1816.

161. 30 July 1816. BENJAMIN PERKINS to CHISWELL DABNEY...Deed of
     Trust; debt to JONATHAN WARD, JR.--margin as above. $1.00
98 acres. Conveyed to BENJAMIN PERKINS by JONATHAN WARD, SR., 3 July
1816. Acknowledged in Lynchburg as above.

163. 1 October 1816. JONATHAN CLARKE and wife, POLLY, and RICHARD
      WARDROPE (?) HARTLESS, Amherst County, power of attorney to
HENRY CLARKE, Rockbridge...to sell tract of JAMES HARTLESS, deceased,
also to convey title to estate of HENRY HARTLESS, deceased--JAMES was
a legatee. Witnesses: ISAAC RUCKER, FIELDING HOLIDAY, WILLIAM
TUNGETT, SAMUEL SWANSON, NATHANIEL WILSON.

164. 18 October 1816. JONATHAN CASWELL (sic), Amherst County, to
      PETER CASHWELL, Amherst County...$2000 200 acres Rocky Run.
Lines: RUBEN PADGETT, EPHRAIM PADGETT, grantee, SARAH MONROE,
Mixon on road, CHARLES MOORE. To PETER CASHWELL, 1 January 1818.
Mixon seems to be the name of a road: Mixon road. This book is
terrible as to script in some parts.

166. 8 October 1816. ARCHIBALD GILLIAM, Amherst County, to children
      of my daughter, ELIZABETH SLAUGHTER, Kanawha...slave to them.
Witnesses: NATHANIEL BURKS, JAMES GILLIAM, JOHN GILLIAM, ARCHELAUS
GILLIAM, JR.

166. 24 August 1816. JONATHAN LONDON, Amherst County, and wife,
      TIRZA, to JONATHAN HAYTHE, Lynchburg...$3044.25 338½ acres
both sides Porrage and where JONATHAN LONDON lives. Lines: JAMES
DILLARD, THOMAS JEWELL, ALEXANDER JEWELL, HENRY TURNER, JAMES LONDON,
ROBERT GRANT. Witnesses: WILL W. NORVELL, JAMES PENAGH, JONATHAN
MC DANIEL. To JONATHAN HAYTHE, March, 1817.

167. 12 April 1816. JONATHAN GILLIAM and wife, MARY, Amherst County,
      to WILLIAM ROACH, Amherst County...$1072.50 143 acres. Lines:
grantor, MC CULLOCH, RICHARD BURKS, old field, grantee. Witnesses:
ROWLAND P. BURKS, WILLIAM A. GILLIAM.

169. 10 October 1816. JONATHAN BURKS and wife, ELIZABETH, Rockbridge,
      to RICHARD L. ELLIS, Amherst County...$4225 422½ acres Swaters
Pedlar. Lines: grantee, CHARLES BURKS, SR., SAMUEL BURKS, JONATHAN
ELLIS, JAMES DAVID, DAVID BURKS, SR. Witnesses: NATHANIEL D. BURKS,
THOMAS N. EUBANK, JOSHUA L. ELLIS, MARTIN PARKS, GEORGE BURKS, son
of DAVID, WILLIAM SHELTON, JONATHAN GILLIAM.

170. 9 October 1816. Order to Amherst County Justices of the Peace:
      CORNELIUS ROACH and wife, ELIZABETH, 10 September 1816, to
JONATHAN WARE, JR...74 acres and 117 acres. Done by BENJAMIN
SHACKLEFORD and THOMAS N. EUBANK, 10 October 1816. Page 171 order
to same justices of the peace: CORNELIUS ROACH and wife, ELIZABETH,
14 September 1816, to GEORGE ROACH 52 acres. Done as above.

172. 18 October 1816. ARCHILLUS GILLIAM, Amherst County, to JAMES
      ROWLEY, Amherst County...L84 193 acres both sides Pedlar. To
JAMES ROWLEY, 21 July 1817.

173. 3 July 1816. JONATHAN WARD, SR., Campbell County, to BENJAMIN
      PERKINS, Amherst County...L882 98 acres. Lines: BENJAMIN
SHACKLEFORD, James River. BENJAMIN HADEN and ANSELM LYNCH, Campbell
Justices of the Peace as to JONATHAN WARD's acknowledgement.

177. 18 November 1816. JONATHAN H. PARISH and wife, MARY, to WALTER
      CHRISTIAN, Amherst County...$1200 140 acres. Lines: JAMES P.
GARLAND. Allotment of ELIZABETH FULCHER on division of SAMUEL
HUCKSTEP and deeded by her to grantor. Witnesses: JABEZ CAMDEN,
JOSEPH HORSLEY, ROBERT ALDRIDGE. To WALTER CHRISTIAN, 22 June 1818.

177. 23 September 1816. JOSEPH HIGGINBOTHAM and wife, RACHEL,
      Amherst County, to ELLIS T. OMOHUNDRO, Amherst County...$100
122½ acres Rutledge. Lines: Megginson road, PETER CASHWELL, SAMUEL
HUCKSTEP's estate, grantor's old tract. To ELLIS T. OMOHUNDRO,
2 August 1817.

178. 18 November 1816. WILLIAM DUNCAN and wife, SALLY, Amherst
     County, to JAMES HIX, Amherst County...L250 86 acres north
side Buffaloe and both sides Stonehouse Creek. Lines: grantee,
WILLIAM SANDIDGE, the road, EDMOND T. COLEMAN.

180. 11 November 1816. JOSEPH HIGGINBOTHAM to BENJAMIN SANDIDGE,
     Amherst County for both...$210 14½ acres Buffaloe. Lines:
his own, the road, mouth of a branch. Witnesses: CHARLES P.
TALIAFERRO, JAMES SMITH, CORNELIUS SALE, DUDLEY SANDIDGE, LINDSEY
SANDIDGE.

181. 30 September 1816. MARK LIVELY and wife, MARY, to EDWARD
     CARTER, Amherst County...$1000 no acres. Lines: HILL CARTER,
JAMES FRANKLIN, deceased. Witnesses: JONATHAN SMITH, DABNEY HILL,
JAMES W. SMITH. HILL CARTER and THOMAS ALDRIDGE, Amherst County
Justices of the Peace, as to MARY, 14 October 1816.

182. 25 October 1816. Order to Amherst County Justices of the
     Peace: NICHOLAS VANSTAVERN and wife, CATHERINE, 16 October
1816, to WALTER CHRISTIAN, SR...55 acres. Done by WILLIAM JOPLING
and BENJAMIN SHACKELFORD, 26 October 1816. To WALTER CHRISTIAN,
22 June 1818.

183. 7 September 1816. RICHARD JANNEY, Nelson County, to WILLIAM
     KNIGHT, Amherst County...Deed of Trust; debt to WILLIAM HALL;
$1000 one lot in New Glasgow between old and new sts. No. 18.
Lines: an alley, the old garden, new street, alley between it and
No. 17. Witnesses: JOSEPH DILLARD, PEACHY FRANKLIN, JONATHAN
LONDON, STERLING CLAIBORNE, H. M. GARLAND. To WILLIAM HALL,
16 December 1816.

185. 19 November 1816. WILLIAM RADFORD, Bedford, to PROSSER
     POWELL, Amherst County...JOSEPH HAWKINS by Deed of Trust,
13 March 1815, to RADFORD and JONATHAN MURREL; debt to ARCHIBALD
ROBERTSON and Comapny; and 1 August 1816, for same purposes. Lines:
GEORGE POWELL, JONATHAN GILES--90 acres; also sundry slaves. POWELL
has bought of HAWKINS the 90 acres and paid ROBERTSON $400.00.

186. 29 October 1816. JACK CARTER and wife, KEZIAH, Amherst County,
     to ANDERSON TINSLEY, Amherst County...$650 90 acres Brown
Mountain Creek. Witnesses: NATHANIEL WILSON, ISAAC RUCKER, JONATHAN H.
CLEMENT. BENJAMIN and CHARLES P. TALIAFERRO, Amherst County Justices
of the Peace, as to KEZIAH, 16 November 1816. To ANDERSON TINSLEY,
20 August 1817.

187. 20 August 1816. WILLIAM DOWNS and wife, MARY, Amherst County,
     to THOMAS WINGFIELD, Amherst County...$400 100 acres north
side Buffaloe. Lines: NATHAN WINGFIELD, deceased, tract called
Edloe, DAVID S. GARLAND. Witnesses: WILLIAM A. WINGFIELD, CHARLES
MUNDY, ISAAC RUCKER. CHARLES MUNDY and JONATHAN COLEMAN, Amherst
County Justices of the Peace, as to MARY, 18 November 1816.

189. 18 October 1815. JONATHAN DILLARD, Nelson County, to NANCY
     SHIELDS, Amherst County...L500 slaves conveyed by NANCY SHIELDS
to him and money; note from WILLIAM KNIGHT, Z. (?) MARTIN, JOSEPH
ENDAY, SAMUEL FRANKLIN, NICHOLAS HARRISON. NANCY, late LEE, conveyed
these and beds etc. to DILLARD, April 1802, in Deed of Trust for her
and heirs.

190. 11 November 1816. JOANTHAN PANCOAT, Loudoun County, to DANIEL
     SHRADER, Amherst County...L50 91 acres north fork Horsley. Also
tract conveyed by NELSON CRAWFORD to JOSEPH MC KEE and from thence to
PANCOAT--six acres Horsley. Lines: CRAFFORD (sic), THOMAS W. MOTT,
DC of Loudoun. Recorded: Amherst County, 13 December 1816.

191. 12 December 1816. DANIEL SHRADER and wife, PATSEY, Amherst
County, to PHILIP THURMOND, Amherst County...$1400 107 acres
Horsley. Lines: JONATHAN DEVAZEAR, a branch, JOSEPH MILSTEAD, the
road. Also tract on north side Horsley, 91 acres. Lines: down the
branch. Also tract from NELSON CRAWFORD to JOSEPH MC KEE and then
to JONATHAN PANCOAT and then to SHRADER on Horsley. Lines: CRAWFORD--
six acres. Witnesses: NELSON CRAWFORD, ROBERT W. EUBANK, RICHARD
MILLNER, JAMES WARE, R. L. ELLIS.

193. 11 December 1816. THOMAS CREWS and wife, SALLY, Amherst
County, to JAMES POWELL, Amherst County...$400 50 3/4 acres
north fork Rutledge. Lines: grantee on Lynch road, mouth of a
branch.

193. 27 November 1816. THOMAS CREWS to SALLY CREWS, Amherst County...
$2448 136½ acres north borders Rutledge. Lines: WIATT POWELL,
grantor. To THOMAS CREWS, 22 December 1818.

194. 23 November 1816. BENJAMIN D. PETTIT, Fayette County,
Kentucky...power of attorney to NATHANIEL PETTIT, same county,
to act for him in Amherst County as to interest in estate of JACOB G.
PIERCE, also as to business as grandson of SARAH ANNIS, infant of
JONATHAN N. ANNIS, who is legatee of PIERCE. JONATHAN D. YOUNG,
NATHANIEL PETTIT of Lexington, Kentucky. Recorded: Amherst County,
16 December 1816.

195. 12 December 1816. JACOB G. PIERCE died owning considerable
estate of real and personal property--intestate, and BENJAMIN D.
PETTIT, Fayette County, Kentucky, is a legatee...NATHANIEL PETTIT
under power of attorney has received from JONAS PIERCE, agent of
JACOB PIERCE, acting executor of JACOB G. PIERCE, $450. Witnesses:
JONATHAN D. URQUHART, JONAS PIERCE, WILLIAM M. RIVES. To JACOB G.
PIERCE, 24 October 1818.

196. 4 November 1816. REUBEN RUCKER and wife, ELIZABETH, Amherst
County, to RICHARD HARRISON, Amherst County...$6000 300 acres
north borders Harris and west side Lynch road. Lines: old field,
JOSHUA RUCKER, RICHARD POWELL, JAMES PETTIT, the road, REUBEN NORVELL,
grantee, HARMON GENTRY, a road.

197. 9 December 1816. RICHARD JONES and wife, POLLY, Amherst County,
to JONATHAN LONDON, Amherst County...$3357 373 acres Porrage.
Lines: CHARLES MUNDY, JONATHAN HUTCHERSON, CHARLES PALMER, JAMES
DAVIES, DANIEL DAY. To JONATHAN LONDON, 8 June 1818.

198. 27 July 1816. DAVID CRAWFORD, Amherst County, to RICHARD
PERKINS, Campbell County...all his interest in 216 acres on
Buffaloe Ridge--one fourth by father's will--$100. DAVID CRAWFORD
was his father. Witnesses: WILLIAM B. GOOCH, I. H. MOORMAN,
WILLIAM PETTYJOHN. Certified in Lynchburg before Justices of the
Peace: FORTUNATUS SYDNOR and ROBERT MORRIS, 14 December 1816.

199. 31 July 1816. DANIEL BURFORD, SR., Amherst County, to JONATHAN
BURFORD, Amherst County...L59-1 50 acres north side and joining
Lynch road and on east side and joining TINSLEY's road. Lines:
junction of the roads, BENJAMIN RUCKER. Witnesses: CHARLES Y. JOHNSON,
THOMAS ALLEY, DAVID ACRIE, DABNEY T. PHILLIPS, MERRIT M. WHITE, WILLIAM
WHITE.

200. 9 December 1816. FREDERICK FULTZ and wife, HANNAH, to BOYD
MILLER, survey partner of WILLIAM BROWN and Company...FREDERICK
FULTZ executed by Deed of Trust to ROBERT WALKER and THOMAS CREWS
201 (?) acres on Rocky River. Lines: WILEY CAMPBELL, WILLIAM
DILLARD--to secure WILLIAM BROWN and Company--$1.00. Witnesses:
A. ROBERTSON, ROBERT L. COLEMAN, JONATHAN COLEMAN, THOMAS CREWS--later
two Amherst County Justices of the Peace as to HANNAH on same day--
order on page 201.

202.   16 December 1816. Agreement: JONATHAN WHITEHEAD, executor of
       BURCHER WHITEHEAD and JABEZ CAMDEN...lease from 1 January 1816
for five years--tract on both sides of road from ACH to WILLIAM
SANDIDGE; to fence two fields. Lines: JONATHAN PENN, JR., field
cleared by WILLIAM COLENAN, top of a hill. $50 per year for last
three years; may use timber save in two fields.

204.   18 December 1816. THOMAS RICHESON, Amherst County, to PHILIP
       THURMOND, Amherst County...$1800 345 acres Horsley. Bought by
THOMAS RICHESON from JONATHAN and RICHARD L. ELLIS--4 6/10 acres
excepted and sold to HENRY BALLINGER.

204.   2 January 1817. CHARLES B. PENN, Augusta, to JABEZ CAMDEN,
       Amherst County...$1650 166 acres Huff. Lines: BAYLOR WALKER,
old patent line, PARK's road.

205.   2 January 1817. JABEZ CAMDEN, Amherst County, to ARTHUR B.
       DAVIES...Deed of Trust; debt to CHARLES B. PENN--166 acres
above. To CHARLES B. PENN, 19 November 1823.

207.   14 January 1817. DANIEL and SOLOMON DAY, Amherst County, to
       JONATHAN LONDON, Amherst County...$3450 314 acres Stovall and
Porrage. Bought of SUSANNAH MARTAIN and JONATHAN MONROE. Lines:
JAMES MARR, WILLIAM KNIGHT, JONATHAN HUTCHERSON, grantee, JAMES
DAVIE, ELIAS WILLS. Witnesses: JONATHAN KNIGHT, EUGENE HIGGINBOTHAM,
WILLIAM DAY. Very poor scribe here. To JONATHAN J. LONDON, 2 July
1833.

208.   21 June 1816. WESTLEY L. DUNCAN, Amherst County, to CHARLES
       PERROW, Amherst County...Deed of Trust; debt to DAVID S.
GARLAND; $1.00; 66 acres. Lines: JAMES WOOD, island tract cut off
for WESTLEY L. DUNCAN in division of estate of JONATHAN DUNCAN,
deceased's stock, about 50 hogs at the Sill (sic) house of WESTLEY L.
DUNCAN and "rendered" of JONATHAN PENN, JR. Witnesses: JEREMIAH
WILSON, PEACHY FRANKLIN, DAVID G. DUNCAN.

209.   15 December 1816. JOSEPH HIGGINBOTHAM and wife, RACHEL,
       Amherst County, to THOMAS HIGGINBOTHAM, Campbell County...$440
44 acres both sides Rutledge. Lines: grantee, dividing line between
them, CHARLES P. TALIAFERRO, PETER CASHWELL, ELLIS P. OMONHUNDRO.

210.   1 January 1817. PHILIP THURMOND, Amherst County, to RICHARD
       MILLNER, Amherst County...$6000 734 acres north side Tobacco
Row and north borders Horsley and whereon PHILIP THURMOND lives and
all that PHILIP THURMOND, SR., died owning. Lines: JONATHAN EUBANK,
SR., EDMOND GOODRICH, CHARLES ELLIS, RICHARD L. ELLIS, WILLIAM
THURMOND, CHARLES CRAWFORD, THOMAS N. EUBANK. Witnesses: JAMES
WARE, WILLIAM WARE, ANDERSON WARE, MANSFIELD WARE, WILLIAM T. THURMOND,
JONATHAN WARE, THOMAS RICHESON. To RICHARD MILLNER, 25 September
1817.

211.   20 January 1817. JONATHAN HOLCOMBE, JR., Marshall of Superior
       Court of Amherst County and Lynchburg District, to DANIEL
CHEATWOOD, under decree of Chancery, 14 October 1816...at public
auction--$2010 201 acres; conveyed 3 January 1806 by FREDERICK FULTZ
to ROBERT WALKER, GEORGE DILLARD, and THOMAS CREWS in Deed of Trust
to secure WILLIAM BROWN and Company. Lines: AMBROSE RUCKER, REUBEN
PADGETT, WILLIAM DILLARD, JONATHAN TYLOR. Also to secure JAMES
FRANKLIN.

212.   21 January 1817. THOMAS CREWS, executor of JAMES FRANKLIN,
       and grandson of his children, to SAMUEL SIMMONS, Amherst
County...$3000 2 3/4 acres Rutledge. Lines: BENAMMI STONE, with
grist mill known as Montpelier and part of FRANKLIN's estate. To
SAMUEL SIMMONS, 17 April 1820.

212.   21 January 1817. SAMUEL SIMMONS and wife, CYNTHIA, Amherst
       County, to BENJAMIN BROWN, Amherst County...Deed of Trust to
secure THOMAS CREWS; $1.00; tract above. To THOMAS CREWS, 5 November
'829.

214. 7 March 1809. Order to Amherst County Justices of the Peace:
     CALEB WATTS and wife, SUSANNAH, 1 November 1808, to MARTIN
PARKS...53 acres. Done 30 May 1809 by JOSIAH ELLIS and NELSON DAWSON
and recorded 20 January 1817. This seems to be another of those
rainy days affairs when clerk caught up on back work.

214. 29 November 1816. ANDREW MORELAND and wife, ELIZABETH, Amherst
     County, to MARTIN PARKS, Amherst County...$1600 65 acres Pedlar
and where grantors live. Lines: grantee, JONATHAN DUNCAN, JONATHAN
BURKS, RODNEY MC CULLOCH. Order to quiz ELIZABETH; done by JONATHAN
ELLIS and JAMES WARE, 29 November 1816; recorded 20 January 1817.

216. 29 November 1816. Order to same Justices of the Peace: CALEB
     WATTS and wife, SUSANNAH, 14 June 1811, to JONATHAN BROWN...
50 acres; done on order date and recorded as above.

217. 18 November 1816. WALTER CHRISTIAN, Amherst County, to
     STERLING CLAIBORNE, Amherst County...Deed of Trust; debt to
ELIZABETH FULCHER; $1.00 140 acres. Lines: JAMES P. GARLAND.
Tract conveyed by ELIZABETH to JONATHAN H. PARRISH and by him to
WALTER CHRISTIAN; her share of SAMUEL HUCKSTEP's estate Witnesses:
JAMES L. PENDLETON, JABEZ CAMDEN, JOSEPH HORSLEY. To STERLING
CLAIBORNE, 29 May 1819.

219. 24 September 1816. Order to Amherst County Justices of the
     Peace: CALEB WATTS and wife, SUSANNAH, 1 August 1815, to
ANDREW MORELAND...Done by JONATHAN ELLIS and JAMES WARE, 29 November
1816; recorded 20 January 1817.

220. 5 November 1816. JONATHAN TAYLOR and wife, SALLY, to THOMAS A.
     (?) HOLCOMBE and JONATHAN MOORE...Deed of Trust; debt to
BENJAMIN PERKINS; $1.00; 98 acres bought by PERKINS from JONATHAN
WARD. Lines: BENJAMIN SCHOOLFIELD, JONATHAN LYNCH, James River.
Witnesses: D. SAUNDERS, SAMUEL MILLER, THOMAS MOORE, JR. Acknowledged
in Lynchburg by SALLY, 18 January 1817, before Justices of the Peace:
ROBERT MORRIS and THOMAS SCHOOLFIELD.

223. 13 January 1817. THOMAS NEIGHBOURS, Amherst County, to
     ARTHUR B. DAVIES...Deed of Trust; debt to SAMUEL SIMMONS;
$1.00; horse.

223. 2 February 1816. JAMES WHITEHEAD and wife, ELIZABETH,
     Pitsylvania, to JOSEPH KENNERLEY, Amherst County...$800 three
acres whereon WILLIAM H. MARKHAM lives. Lines: MICAJAH CAMDEN.
Tract was bought by JAMES WHITEHEAD from REUBEN COLEMAN.

224. 21 October 1816. REUBEN RUCKER and wife, ELIZABETH, RICHARD
     HARRISON and wife, SOPHIA, Amherst County to HARRISON GENTRY,
Amherst County...$800 52 3/4 acres north borders Harris. Lines:
RICHARD HARRISON, JOSHUA RUCKER, ANTHONY RUCKER. Witnesses:
RICHARD H. BURKS, JOSEPH C. LEE, BENJAMIN HARRISON.

225. 27 January 1817. JAMES SMITH to heirs of my brother, WIATT
     SMITH...for $1.00 and love; two slaves named. Witnesses:
WILLIAM DEMSEY, WILLIAM COLEMAN, BENJAMIN HIGGINBOTHAM, ROWLAND
GILLESPIE.

225. 10 February 1817. STERLING CLAIBORNE and wife, JANE, to
     MICAJAH CAMDEN...$7162.66 at special request of LEROY CAMDEN
who assents to deed--1350 acres and where WILLIAM CAMDEN, JR.
formerly lived and by him devised to LEROY CAMDEN. Lines: JABEZ
CAMDEN, CHARLES BURRUS, BURCHER WHITEHEAD, MICAJAH CAMDEN. Conveyed
to STERLING CLAIBORNE by LEROY in Deed of Trust; 5 March 1816. To
MICAJAH CAMDEN, 7 November 1828.

226.   6 February 1817.   LEROY CAMDEN and wife, PETHEMIAH, Amherst
       County, to MICAJAH CAMDEN...Deed of Trust above set forth--
from deceased father, WILLIAM, to LEROY--some difficulties have
arisen, between CLAIBORNE and LEROY and LEROY sued in Superior Court
of Chancery, Lynchburg Districe versus THOMAS ALDRIDGE and CLAIBORNE
to void Deed of Trust. Compromised and dismissed. MICAJAH agrees
to give LEROY $9,213 and $7,162.66 to be paid to CLAIBORNE. Residue
to LEROY. Witnesses: WILLIAM BAILEY, W. L. DUNCAN, WILLIAM DUNCAN.
To MICAJAH CAMDEN, 18 September 1817.

228.   18 February 1817.   REUBEN COLEMAN, WILLIAM WOODROOF and wife,
       ELIZABETH, to JONATHAN L. (S) MOORE...$1000 1 5/2 acres near
ACH--ALLEN's Tavern.   To JONATHAN L. (S) MOORE, 27 February 1819.

228.   9 October 1816.   HANNAH ALLEN, Amherst County, to PETER
       RUTHERFORD, Amherst County...L75-10 her dower in estate of
SAMUEL ALLEN--Elk Island tract on west side--also her interest in
fishery on ALLEN's Island--38 acres apart from fishery. Witnesses:
CHARLES PERROW, DANIEL PERROW, JONATHAN ALLEN, STEPHEN DAWSON,
illegible signature.

229.   22 July 1816.   WILKINS WATSON and wife, POLLY, formerly TUCKER,
       to GEORGE TUCKER, Amherst County...$800 interest in Buffaloe
tract of DANIEL TUCKER and interest at death of his widow, JUDITH
TUCKER.   Several tracts and references to plat--not herein. Witnesses:
EDMOND T. COLEMAN, AUSTIN DAVIS, WILLIAM DUNCAN, JAMES W. SMITH.
To GEORGE TUCKER, 24 January 1823.

230.   9 October 1816.   PETER RUTHERFORD, Amherst County, to LEWIS
       TINDALL, Amherst County...L72-10 all interest in dower tract
of HANNAH ALLEN, widow of SAMUEL ALLEN--Elk Island and fishery.   In
possession of grantor.

231.   19 August 1816.   Recital of law--Act. of Assembly--for sheriff
       to sell delinquent tracts--could find no lands to cover tax of
ROBERT DOUTHAT who owes for 1796, 1799. Advertised, August court,
1816, and first day of court sold by RICHARD HARRISON, deputy for
CHARLES TALIAFERRO, Sheriff. ROBERT GRALAND bought for $2.54, amount
due, three tracts of 260, 180 and 80. There are many of these items
in this book and no descriptions of land.

232.   19 August 1816.   WILLIAM CARTER owns no property to pay tax...
       700 acres sold under act by HARRISON, Deputy Sheriff. ROBERT
GRALAND bought for amount due of $3.47. GARLAND of Nelson County.
No description, as stated.

233.   12 December 1816.   JONATHAN H. GOODWIN, administrator of PHILIP
       JOHNSON...power of attorney to REUBEN NORVELL, Amherst County.

234.   21 November 1816.   JAMES HIX and wife, NANCY, Amherst County,
       to EDMOND T. COLEMAN, Amherst County...$860 86 acres both
sides Stonehouse Creek and north side Buffaloe. Lines: grantor,
WILLIAM SANDIDGE, the road, grantee. Witnesses: WILLIAM DUNCAN,
JONATHAN SMITH, LEWIS W. BANKS.

235.   15 February 1817.   JONATHAN CREWS, Henry County, to HARRISON
       HUGHES, Amherst County...L1200 tobacco--no acres--Pond (?)
Creek. Lines: grantee, LEWIS DAWSON, WILLIAM HUGHES, JR., deceased.
Witnesses: BENJAMIN HARRISON, ALLISON OGDON, DAVID A. GILBERT.

236.   24 February 1817.   SAMUEL ANDERSON, Alb., to PEYTON KEITH,
       Amherst County...$1020 127½ acres Raven Creek. Lines: ABRAHAM
EWERS, ALLEN BLAIR, grantee, the road. Witnesses: WINSTON BLAIR,
JOSEPH BROWN, ROBERT G. KIDD, WILLIAM H. ADNERSON. To PEYTON KEITH,
8 March 1817.

237.   24 February 1817.   SAMUEL ANDERSON, Alb., to ALLEN BLAIR, Amherst
       County...$25 2½ acres Raven Creek. Lines: his own, grantee.
Witnesses: as above.

238. 2 May 1817. JOSEPH KENNERLEY and wife, SARAH, Patrick County,
     to SAMUEL HEISKELL, Amherst County...$2000 three acre tract
was sold by REUBEN COLEMAN to JAMES WHITEHEAD. Lines: MICAJAH
CAMDEN (formerly REUBEN COLEMAN), Spring Branch, old field.

239. 15 January 1817. JONATHAN LONDON and wife, TIRZA, Amherst
     County to CHARLES PALMER, Amherst County...$1250 113 3/4 acres
Porrage. Lines: CHARLES MUNDY, grantee. Witnesses: EUGENE
HIGGINBOTHAM, JONATHAN HUTCHESON, THOMAS HUTCHESON. To CHARLES
PALMER, 22 May 1818.

239. 22 November 1816. HENRY CHRISTIAN, Amherst County, to JONATHAN
     WARWICK, Amherst County...$827.50 75 acres Porrage and where
HENRY CHRISTIAN lives. Reference to deed from CHARLES CHRISTIAN, SR.
to HENRY CHRISTIAN, 4 April 1812. Witnesses: WALTER L. CHRISTIAN,
DANIEL F. CHRISTIAN, LEWIS PADGETT.

241. 26 October 1816. WILLIAM HENRY ROSE to GEORGE CAMPBELL...$400
     215 acres headwaters Piney. Lines: WILLIAM EVANS (now
CAMPBELL's). Witnesses: GEORGE MYERS, JAMES S. PENDLETON, JONATHAN S.
BLAIR.

242. 21 April 1817. GEORGE CAMPBELL to WILLIAM CAMPBELL...$135.00
     54 acres both sides and joining Little Piney--part of former
tract of WILLIAM EVANS and now GEORGE CAMPBELL's.

243. 10 April 1817. GEORGE CAMPBELL to JONATHAN CAMPBELL...$663
     119 acres both sides Little Piney. Part of two tracts formerly
of JAMES TURNER and WILLIAM EVANS and now GEORGE CAMPBELL's.

244. 21 April 1817. JONATHAN HENDREN and wife, ELIZABETH ELDRIDGE,
     Amherst County, to CHARLES HUNT CHRISTIAN and WALTER D.
CHRISTIAN, Amherst County...$2000 160 acres south side PARKS' road
and both sides BRAXTON's Ridge. Lines: JACOB PIERCE, ALEXANDER
BRYDIE, deceased, WALTER CHRISTIAN, CHARLES H. CHRISTIAN. To
CHARLES HUNT CHRISTIAN, 27 July 1824.

245. 11 February 1817. JAMES DAVIS and wife, MILDRED, Amherst
     County, to WILLIAM GUTTRY, Amherst County...$358.87 32 5/8 acres
Stovall. Lines: RUCKER's Road, grantee, ELIAS WILLS, north fork
Stovall. Witnesses: JONATHAN LONDON, JAMES HEIGHT, F. R. HIGGINBOTHAM.
To WILLIAM KENT, commissioner, to sell lands of WILLIAM GUTTRY,
17 July 1848.

246. 21 April 1817. CHARLES H. CHRISTIAN, Amherst County, to
     JONATHAN WARWICK, Amherst County, and JONATHAN COLEMAN,
Amherst County...Deed of Trust; debt to JONATHAN HENDREN. $1.00
160 acres lately sold to them by JONATHAN HENDREN.

247. 24 April 1817. JONATHAN ALLEN, Amherst County, to JONATHAN
     MYERS and Company...Deed of Trust; debt to ARTHUR B. DAVIES;
$1.00 slaves. To LEWIS TINDALL, per order ot E. FLETCHER to
P. RUTHERFORD, 17 May 1817.

249. 10 February 1817. JONATHAN LONDON and wife, TIRZA, Amherst
     County, to JAMES DAVIS, Amherst County...$500 34½ acres
Stovall. Lines: both. Witnesses: JAMES KNIGHT, F. R. HIGGINBOTHAM,
WILLIAM GUTTRY. To JAMES DAVIS, 31 August 1831.

250. 19 December 1816. WILLIAM H. CAMDEN, Amherst County, to MICAJAH
     CAMDEN, Amherst County...$238 60 acres The Cove. Tract sold to
WILLIAM by JORDAN R. (P) CAMDEN, 12 August 1816. Witnesses:
JONATHAN PENN, JR., HENRY CAMDEN.

251. 21 April 1817. PEGGY GOOLSBY, Amherst County, to LYNE S.
     TALIAFERRO, Amherst County...$475 124 acres. Lines: JONATHAN
BALL, JONATHAN SMITH, grantor. Witnesses: CHARLES P. TALIAFERRO,
JAMES F. TALIAFERRO, ADDISON TALIAFERRO.

251. 27 September 1816. Deed of release--PHILIP SLAUGHTER, Culpepper,
     to ROBERT RIVERS, Amherst County...Deed of Trust executed by
RIVERS to SLAUGHTER, 19 August 1805; recorded Amherst County,
16 December; 862 acres. Witnesses: THOMAS S. HOLLOWAY, EDWARD
CARTER, HILL CARTER, JONATHAN SMITH.

252. 13 March 1817. DANIEL MEHONE, Amherst County, to DANIEL
     BURFORD, Amherst County...consideration--one batteaux for
19½ acres. Lynch road--part of tract in possession of BENJAMIN
RUCKER et al. Lines: TINSLEY road. Witnesses: REUBEN COX, JONATHAN R.
WHITTEN, WILLIAM MUSE, SR., WILLIAM MEHONE.

253. 13 March 1817. DANIEL MEHONE to his son, JONATHAN MEHONE,
     Amherst County...L10--part of tract deeded to DANIEL BURFORD
on same estate--Lynch and Tinsley roads. 1½ acres. To JONATHAN
MEHONE, 26 February 1830. Witnesses: as above.

254. 5 May 1815. BENAMMI STONE, Amherst County, to ROBERT WALKER,
     Amherst County...$1.00; slaves for benefit of my daughter,
NANCY GARLAND and child, if any. Witnesses: A. B. DAVIES, B. WALKER.
To J. P. GARLAND, agent, 16 August 1826. Note: I am not sure just
who is buried in the old graveyard at Hunting Tower which is old
Gilbert home near Central High School. I have mentioned home before
and it is now property of MR. and MRS. MADISON SETTLE. MADISON
tells me that some GARLANDS are buried in lot which is quite near the
house.

255. 7 January 1817. HENRY CAMDEN and wife, LUCY, Amherst County,
     to MICAJAH CAMDEN, Amherst County...$830 150 acres head borders
Huff. Lines: JABEZ CAMDEN. Tract patent to BENJAMIN NOEL, 16 February
1771. Witnesses: LEORY CAMDEN, W. L. DUNCAN, LITTLEBERRY CARTER.
To MICAJAH CAMDEN, 17 January 1826.

256. 21 April 1817. ROBERT L. COLEMAN and wife, MARY F., Amherst
     County, to DAVID S. GARLAND, Amherst County...$5000 377½ acres
south side Buffaloe. Lines: grantee, Huff Creek, JONATHAN PENN,
SAMUEL MEREDITH, deceased. BURTON--includes Mill house and dam. To
H. M. GARLAND, 6 April 1828.

258. 21 April 1817. ROBERT L. COLEMAN and wife, MARY F., Amherst
     County, to DAVID S. GARLAND...L202-10 141 acres south side
Buffaloe. Lines: grantee, which he bought of WILLIAM PENN, deceased,
JONATHAN PENN, deceased, DANIEL TUCKER's heirs. Margin as above,
but DAVID S. and not H. M. GARLAND recorded deed.

259. 21 April 1817. ROBERT L. COLEMAN and wife, MARY F., Amherst
     County, to WILLIAM CARTER, Nelson County...$1065 106½ acres
south Buffaloe and Green Spring Branch. Part of a tract. Lines:
LAYNE, CHARLES L. CHRISTIAN, W. S. CRAWFORD, deceased. To WILLIAM
CARTER, 15 April 1822.

260. 23 September 1816. BENJAMIN RUCKER and wife, SALLY, Amherst
     County, to THOMAS MURRELL, Amherst County...$118 nine acres
east side and joining Lynch road. Lines: JONATHAN WINGFIELD,
grantee. To THOMAS MURRELL, 20 October 1817.

261. 10 February 1817. JAMES DAVIS, Amherst County, and wife,
     MILDRED, to JONATHAN LONDON, Amherst County...$400. 1. 37½
acres. Lines: CHARLES PALMER, grantee and grantor, Stovall road.
2. 1½ acres. Lines: grantor, RUCKER. Witnesses: JAMES KNIGHT,
F. R. HIGGINBOTHAM, WILLIAM GUTTRY.

262. 5 November 1816. BENJAMIN PERKINS to JONATHAN TAYLOR...$5880
     98 acres bought by BENJAMIN PERKINS from JONATHAN WARD. Lines:
BENJAMIN SCHOOLFIELD, STITH MEAD, JONATHAN LYNCH, James River.
Witnesses: THOMAS A. HOLCOMBE, SAMUEL MILLER, D. SAUNDERS, JR. Certi-
fied in Lynchburg, 18 January 1817, before ROBERT MORRIS and JONATHAN
SCHOOLFIELD. To JONATHAN TAYLOR, 9 July 1819.

263.   11 March 1817.   MICAJAH CAMDEN and wife, POLLY, Amherst
       County, to ARTHUR B. DAVIES, Amherst County...$2791.25 79 3/4
acres north side Rutledge. Lines: POWELL, WATSON, REUBEN COLEMAN,
mill dam. Acknowledged by MARY CAMDEN in court, 19 January 1819.
To JONATHAN THOMPSON, JR., 30 July 1842. Note: JONATHAN THOMPSON,
JR. appears in data as much as does DAVID S. GARLAND. He gave the
Amherst Baptist Church an acre of ground many years later and I am
wondering if it was in this particular tract. Rutledge Creek is
quite close to church.

264.   27 November 1816.   SALLY CREWS, Amherst County, to THOMAS
       CREWS, Amherst County...$1716; all interest in tracts of
JOSEPH CREWS, JR., deceased. To THOMAS CREWS, 23 December 1828.

265.   13 March 1816.   JOSEPH and BENJAMIN HIGGINBOTHAM, executors
       of JOSEPH HIGGINBOTHAM, to NELSON CRAWFORD and BENJAMIN
TALIAFERRO...$141 275 acres borders middle fork Pedlar. Witnesses:
ANSELM CLARKSON, GEORGE EUBANK, DAVID CLARKSON.

267.   20 April 1817.   MATTHEW RICKETTS, Amherst County and wife,
       WINIFRED, to WILLIAM I. ISBELL, Amherst County...$1.00 100 acres
south borders Stovall. Lines: Opossum Island road, WILLIAM DUNCAN,
deceased, the Spring. To WILLIAM I. ISBELL, 2 August 1818.

268.   27 March 1817.   RANDALL HOGG and wife, MARY, Rockbridge, to
       RICHARD L. ELLIS, Amherst County...$100 43 acres Maple Creek
borders. Lines: THOMAS MORRIS, JONATHAN HOGG, ZED SHOEMAKER,
NANCY HOGG. Tract descended to me by my deceased father, JONATHAN
HOGG; lot three in survey. Witnesses: SAMUEL HOGG, ROSEMARY GUE,
JONATHAN BURKS, JR., JONATHAN MC CLELAND, ROBERT WHITE--last two
Rockbridge Justices of the Peace as to MARY, 1 April 1817. To
RICHARD L. ELLIS, 17 May 1819.

269.   20 March 1817.   GEORGE GILLESPIE, Amherst County, to JONATHAN
       TAYLOE, Amherst County...$600 387 acres Cedar; border of Pedlar--
one-eighth excepted for cemetery where my companion is buried.
Lines: THOMAS MORRIS, JOSIAH JOBBLING, JOSEPH CABELL, JONATHAN
GOODRICH. Witnesses: SAMUEL MILLER, THOMAS MOORE, JR., GEORGE M.
PERKINS. Acknowledged in Lynchburg by GEORGE GILLESPIE, 24 March
1817. JONATHAN M. GORDON, Mayor, and JONATHAN SCHOOLFIELD, Justice
of the Peace.

271.   3 July 1816.   JONATHAN WARD, SR., Campbell County, to WILLIAM
       MITCHELL, Amherst County...L7658 798 3/4 north side and joining
Fluvanna and little above town of Lynchburg. One acre excepted at
mouth of Harris given by me to JONATHAN LYNCH, SR. and sold by his
son, EDWARD LYNCH, to MITCHELL. Lines: BENJAMIN SCHOOLFIELD, REUBEN
COX, MILLNER COX. Acknowledged in Campbell County, 13 July 1816.
BENJAMIN HADEN and ANSELM LYNCH, Justices of the Peace. To WILLIAM
MITCHELL, 20 October 1817.

273.   27 February 1817.   JONATHAN LONDON and wife, TIRZA, Amherst
       County, to JONATHAN HUTCHESON, Amherst County...$250 Porrage
Creek. 1. 17½ acres. Lines: THOMAS EDWARDS, dividing line between
grantor and grantee, CHARLES MUNDY. 2. 5 acres adjacent both of
them. Witnesses: JONATHAN KNIGHT, EUGENE HIGGINBOTHAM. To JONATHAN
MEHONE, 4 September 1835.

274.   20 August 1816.   JAMES DILLARD and wife, JANE, Amherst County,
       to JAMES S. and JONATHAN DILLARD, Amherst County...$1.00 200
acres north borders Indian Creek. Lines: WILLIAM PARKS, branch,
WILLIAM BIBB.

275.   4 November 1816.   RICHARD HARRISON and wife, SOPHIA, Amherst
       County, to JOSHUA RUCKER, Amherst County...$1200 110½ acres
B borders Harris. Lines: grantor, RICHARD POWELL, JAMES HILL,
ANTHONY RUCKER, HARRISON (?) GENTRY.

276. 21 April 1817. ARTHUR B. DAVIES, grandson for RODERICK DAVIES, to GEORGE BURKS...$200 no acres--north side Pedlar and ward's share of estate of NICHOLAS DAVIES, deceased, as descendant. To GEORGE BURKS, 1822.

277. 15 May 1817. ELIZABETH CREASY, Amherst County, to JORDAN CREASY, Amherst County...half acre Lynch road and where THOMAS B. MARKHAM lives. $700. Witnesses: ANDERSON JOHNSON, WINSTON LAIN, SIMEON ROBERSON.

278. 1 April 1817. JOSEPH NEEDHAM and wife, MARY, Campbell County, to THOMAS WIATT, Amherst County...$1000 40 acres Bolling Creek. Lines: MRS. LUCY ROBINSON, HENRY TENNISON, WILLIAM WARWICK, LINEAS BOLLING, THOMAS TERRY. Acknowledged in Lynchburg before MATTHEW BROWN and JONATHAN SCHOOLFIELD, Justices of the Peace. To THOMAS WIATT, 1827.

281. 4 February 1817. JAMES SMITH and SUSANNAH SMITH, Amherst County, to LYNE S. TALIAFERRO, Amherst County...Deed of Trust; debt to GARLAND and CHARLES P. TALIAFERRO, headwaters Horsley--258 acres. One of tracts devised to SUSANNAH by JOSEPH HIGGINBOTHAM. Witnesses: ANGUS MC CLOUD, JONATHAN W. YOUNG, ABRAM VENABLE, JAMES F. TALIAFERRO, RICHARD HATTEN. Order to quiz SUSANNAH, wife of JAMES SMITH; done by CHARLES TALIAFERRO and BENJAMIN TALIAFERRO, 13 March 1817. To LYNE S. TALIAFERRO, August, 1817.

284. 19 May 1817. RUBEN NORVELL and wife, POLLY, Amherst County, to JAMES PETTIT, Amherst County...$100 19 acres west side Lynch road. Lines: RICHARD HARRISON, grantee, JONATHAN MC BRIDE, deceased.

285. 29 April 1817. RICHARD L. ELLIS, Amherst County, to CHARLES ELLIS, Richmond...$180 180 acres north borders Pedlar. Lines: PHILIP GOOCH, deceased, JOSHUA ELLIS, deceased, GEORGE MC DANIEL, RUCKER, CARTER, THURMOND, JOSIAH ELLIS.

287. 19 April 1817. NANCY HOGG, Amherst County, to RICHARD L. ELLIS, Amherst County...$202 50½ acres Maple Creek, border of Pedlar. Lines: THOMAS MORRIS. Devised to me by deceased father, JONATHAN HOGG, as a legatee. Witnesses: SAMUEL HOGG, ROSEMARY GUE, JONATHAN TANKERSLEY, JAMES EUBANK, ROBERT EUBANK, JAMES WARE, BENJAMIN SHACKELFORD, AMBROSE RUCKER, PETER THORNTON. To RICHARD L. ELLIS, 18 May 1819.

288. 19 April 1817. ROSEMARY GUE and wife, MARY ANN, to RICHARD L. ELLIS...$200 50½ acres Maple Creek--from estate of JONATHAN HOGG, as legatees on division. Page 289 order to quiz MARY ANN; done by THOMAS N. EUBANK and JAMES WARE, 5 May 1817. To RICHARD L. ELLIS, 18 May 1819.

290. 31 January 1817. JONATHA P. COBBS and wife, JANE, Amherst County, to JANE SOWELL, Amherst County...$1000 150 acres. In JANE G's possession. Lines: north borders Buffaloe, DAVID S. GARLAND, SAMUEL MEREDITH, deceased, LINDSEY COLEMAN, deceased, old Church Road. Witnesses: HENRY G. PADGETT, DRURY D. CHRISTIAN, THOMAS PARROCK. To JANE SOWELL, 6 November 1819, by DAVID S. GARLAND.

291. 7 November 1816. JOSEPH HAWKINS and wife, NANCY, Bedford, to PROSSER POWELL, Amherst County...L150 90 acres John's Creek. Lines: JAMES HILL (?), GEORGE POWELL, grantee. Bought by JAMES HILL of JAMES WARE. Witnesses: JONATHAN P. WILSON, R. POWELL, GEORGE POWELL, A. ROBERTSON. To PROSSER POWELL, 12 August 1817.

292. 28 February 1817. BENJAMIN HIGGINBOTHAM to JOSEPH HIGGINBOTHAM... $7000 536 acres. Lines: ELIJAH FLETCHER, JAMES GOVAN, GEORGE EUBANK, WILLIAM DEMPSEY, JONATHAN EUBANK, BENJAMIN SANDIDGE. Witnesses: NELSON CRAWFORD, CHARLES P. TALIAFERRO, LYNE S. TALIAFERRO.

293. 30 April 1816. SAMUEL HEISKELL, Amherst County, to ARTHUR B.
DAVIES, Amherst County...Deed of Trust; debt to JOSEPH KENNERLEY;
$1.00; three acres bought from REUBEN COLEMAN by JAMES WHITEHEAD,
and 1 November 1816 by JOSEPH KENNERLEY and wife to HEISKELL. Lines:
CAMDEN's spring branch, old field.

296. 1 May 1817. NICHOLAS VANSTAVERN and wife, CATHERINE, Botetourt,
to WILLIAM MITCHELL, Amherst County...$60 150 acres Rockyrow
and Cashaw Creeks. Lines: ARCHIBALD MITCHELL, HENRY L. DAVIES,
HENRY PEYTON, Z. TALIAFERRO. Witnesses: R. L. ELLIS, JAMES WARE,
ROBERT EUBANK. To WILLIAM MITCHELL, 20 June 1825.

297. 6 December 1816. JONATHAN LONDON and wife, TIRZA, Amherst
County, to SAMUEL SCOTT, Amherst County...$300 110 acres north
borders Porrage. Bought by JONATHAN LONDON of ELISHA GILLENWATERS.
Lines: ROBERT GRANT, JAMES DILLARD, DAVID S. GARLAND, tract JONATHAN
LONDON bought of JOSEPH HAWKINS. Witnesses: JONATHAN GARTH. To
SAMUEL SCOTT, 27 October 1820.

298. 16 October 1795. JONATHAN MERRITT and DANIEL MEHONE to DANIEL
BURFORD, JR., Amherst County...L50 116 acres both sides Lynch
road. Lines: P. BURFORD, CLARKE, TINSLEY's road. Witnesses:
HENRY ROBINSON, AMBROSE BURFORD, JAMES LASHWELL, WILLIAM DICKS.
Final proof by AMBROSE BURFORD, 6 May 1817.

300. 20 April 1817. WILLIAM I. ISBELL, attorney for ANN CHENAULT,
Tennessee, to MATTHEW RICKETTS, Amherst County...$1.00; no
acres; south borders Stovall. Lines: EDWARD WATSON, WILLIAM I.
ISBELL. To ISBELL, 21 July 1817.

301. 5 February 1817. BARLTETT EADES, Logan County, Kentucky, to
ANTHONY RUCKER, AMBROSE RUCKER, and NELSON C. DAWSON, Amherst
County...power of attorney to divide my lands and slaves in Amherst
County in three lots to my children: NANCY R. LONDON, WILLIAM EADES,
and REBECCA B. EADES--last two are still minors--and to appoint
guardians. Witnesses: FRANCIS A. WHITTLE and SAMUEL G. WHITE.
SPENCER CURD, Logan County Clerk; ROBERT EWINIG (EWING?), Presiding
Justice of the Peace.

303. 2 May 1817. ARMISTEAD RUCKER and wife, ELIZABETH, THOMAS
RICHESON, heirs of JONATHAN RICHESON, deceased, Amherst County,
to RICHARD MILLNER, Amherst County...$1.00 432 acres Pedlar. Part
of Mansion house tract JONATHAN RICHESON. ELISABETH relinquished
dower, 2 May 1817, before Amherst County Justices of the Peace:
WILLIAM JOPLING and NELSON CRAWFORD.

305. 4 June 1817. ABNER CHRISTIAN and wife, LUCY F., formerly
GOOCH, Bedford, to CLAIBORNE W. GOOCH, Richmond...WILLIAM B.
GOOCH, late of Amherst County, was brother of LUCY F. of the whole
blood and has died without heirs--intestate and LUCY F. is legatee.
$1500.00 all interest in real and personal property of WILLIAM B.
GOOCH. To CLAIBORNE W. GOOCH, 14 June 1817. Memo: They do not sell
that part of estate of COLONEL CHARLES FLEMING to which WILLIAM B.
has claim; do sell all interest in undivided estate of PHILIP GOOCH,
deceased. Witnesses: THOMAS LOGWOOD, THOMAS SALE, also as Justices
of the Peace of Bedford, 5 June 1817. To be recorded in Bedford,
Amherst and Albemarle.

307. 16 June 1817. GEORGE H. BURFORD, Amherst County, to DAVID
TINSLEY, SR., Amherst County...$440 44 acres Harris Creek.
Lines: grantee, JOSHUA TINSLEY. Witnesses: AMBROSE RUCKER, RICHARD H.
BURKS, BENJAMIN HARRISON.

308. 12 June 1817. WILLIAM GALT, Richmond, to JONATHAN WARE,
Amherst County...$1.00 82 acres Brown Mountain. To JESSE
RICHESON, 28 December 1840, by WILLIAM A. RICHESON.

309. 12 June 1817. WILLIAM GALT, Richmond, to JONATHAN D. CRAWFORD,
       Amherst County...$1.00 320 acres. Conveyed to GALT by WILLIAM
WARWICK, 1 September 1815.

311. 16 June 1816. RICHARD BURKS and wife, POLLY, Amherst County,
       to AMBROSE LUCAS, Amherst County...$5.00 two tracts on Harris.
1. Seven acres. Lines: grantee, WILLIAM PRYOR. 2. Small tract
on south side of road from THOMAS COLEMAN's to CRAWFORD's Gap.
Lines: grantee. To AMBROSE LUCAS, 11 May 1819.

311. 16 June 1817. AMBROSE LUCAS and wife, ELIZABETH, Amherst
       County, to RICHARD BURKS, Amherst County...$5.00 50 acres
Harris Creek and Tobacco Row Mountain. Lines: RICHARD BURKS,
ISBELL, old patent line, WILLIAM TERRY. Surveyed by CHARLES L.
CHRISTIAN. To RICHARD BURKS per M. BURKS, 5 March 1823.

313. 13 March 1817. AMBROSE RUCKER and wife, ELIZABETH, Bedford,
       to AMBROSE LUCAS, Amherst County...$180 180 acres H borders
Harris. Lines: BURKS, HARRISON, WARE, CRAWFORD, DANIEL BURFORD,
grantee. SAMUEL HANCOCK and LAWRENCE W. GEORGE, Bedford Justices of
the Peace, same date, as to ELIZABETH.

315. 31 May 1817. ARTHUR B. DAVIES, Amherst County, to SAMUEL
       SIMMONS, Amherst County...$175 3½ acres north side Rutledge.
Lines: mill dam.

316. 5 June 1816. ADDISON TALIAFERRO, Amherst County, to JAMES F.
       TALIAFERRO, Amherst County...$50 100 acres south side Blue
Ridge. Lines: HENRY HEARTLESS. Bought of WILLIAM FRAZER S. (sic).
Witnesses: CHARLES P. TALIAFERRO, JONATHAN W. YOUNG, RICHARD H.
BURKS.

316. 2 September 1815. GEORGE MC DANIEL and wife, DOLLY, Campbell
       County, to WILLIAM GALT, Richmond...$1.00 82 acres. Lines:
Brown Mountain. Patent to GEORGE MC DANIEL, 20 June 1780, and by
him sold to JOHN HALL, Amherst County. Certified in Lynchburg on
same date as to DOLLY: JONATHAN M. GORDON, Magistrate and Recorder
and HENRY DAVIS (D?), Justice of the Peace.

319. 16 June 1817. CHARLES L. BARRET and wife, SARAH, to FREDERICK
       PRICE...consieration; PRICE having built a saw and grist mill--
one half of tract ot PRICE, BARRET bought tract from CHARLES P.
TALIAFERRO, 6 July 1811--202 acres. Lines: DAVID PRYOR, JONATHAN
BURKS, JONATHAN BROWN, Pedlar River. Witnesses: JONATHAN ROBINSON,
WILLIS WHITE, WILLIAM COLEMAN. To CHARLES L. BARRET, 18 August 1818.

319. 2 August 1816. CHARLES BOWLES and wife, ELIZABETH, Amherst
       County, to DAVID S. GARLAND, Amherst County...$300 84 acres
Naked Creek and Turkey Mountain. Lines: THOMAS ALDRIDGE, JAMES
FRANKLIN, grantee. Where CHARLES BOWLES lives and he bought it from
GEORGE HUDSON. Witnesses: CORNELIUS POWELL, HENRY G. PADGETT,
GEORGE W. TRIBBLE. To DAVID S. GARLAND, April, 1828.

320. No date. Order to Amherst County Justices of the Peace:
       JAMES BENNETT and wife, ELIZABETH, 7 November 1812, to ELIZABETH
COLEMAN...116¾. This order stops at bottom of page 320 and is to
NELSON C. DAWSON and AMBROSE RUCKER and last words are "and being
in." It is evidently as to the next deed below.

321. 7 November 1812. JAMES BENNETT and wife, ELIZABETH, Amherst
       County, to ELIZABETH COLEMAN, Amherst County...$706 116¾ acres
south borders Harris. Lines: REUBEN COX, grantee, THOMIS GRISSOM,
deceased, AMBROSE LUCAS, the road. Witnesses: REUBEN NORVELL,
BLANFORD HICKS, FLEMING COLEMAN, RICHARD PENDLETON, CHARLES MOORE,
EDMOND PADGETT. To THOMAS COLEMAN, 20 October 1819. Page 322
order to NELSON C. DAWSON and AMBROSE RUCKER to quiz ELIZABETH:
done 24 May 1817.

323. 17 October 1816. JONATHAN PATTEN and wife, SARAH, WILLIAM
     VANNERSON and wife, HENRIETTA, ALDEN B. SPOONER and wife,
ELIZABETH H., to JONATHAN MC DANIEL and RICHARD JONES. SARAH PATTEN,
Richmond, HENRIETTA VANNERSON and ELIZABETH H. SPOONER, Petersburg,
daughters of WILLIAM S. CRAWFORD, deceased...$11,775 785 acres
Tobacco Row Plantation. Harris and Horsley Creeks. Lines: CHARLES
CRAWFORD, WILLIAM THURMOND, WILLIAM PRYOR--this is 765 acres; other
part of 20 acres. Lines: CHARLES CRAWFORD, DAVID CRAWFORD, a spring
near main road. To R. JONES, 19 March 1821. Petersburg Justices
of the Peace: SAMUEL CRAWFORD and JOEL HARRISON (HAMMON?) as to
HENRIETTA and ELIZABETH H., 17 October 1816. Richmond Justices
of the Peace, CARTER B. PAGE and JAMES BIVINOM (?) as to SARAH
PATTEN, 22 November 1816. Recorded, Amherst County: 3 July 1817.

327. 11 July 1817. Receipt by A. B. DAVIES, Deputy Clerk of
     Amherst County, from CLAIBORNE W. GOOCH's administrator with
will annexed...$32.29 for taxes, damages and fees on 400 acres in
Amherst County--returned delinquent by Sheriff and sold to DANIEL
CHEATWOOD. Returned in name of estate of JONATHAN HARVEY, CHEATWOOD
also signed receipt for above amount.

327. 20 January 1817. A. B. DAVIES as above--from THOMAS TERRY...
     $2.00 on 106 acres returned in name of THOMAS TERRY; delinquent
in 1810. I have noted that the descriptions are not with these
delinquent tax items.

327. 8 April 1817. A. B. DAVIES, Deputy Clerk, to CAPTAIN JAMES
     DILLARD...L1-1-3 for BENJAMIN COFFAND--COFLAND or COFFLIN--
delinquent on 170 acres in 1791.

327. 20 May 1817. A. B. DAVIES received of ROBERT WHITE by
     JONATHAN ROBERSON...$3.25 for 252 acres sold by Sheriff, August
Court, 1816, for delinquent taxes--1801, 1804, 1806, 1807, 1810 and
1811 in name of DAVID WILSON.

327. 8 April 1817. A. B. DAVIES received $7.58 from LEWIS JEFFERSON...
     two tracts delinquent in name of JOEL WALKER's estate--155
acres for 1796, 1807, 1808, 1810, 1811. Sold by sheriff to JAMES P.
GARLAND at August Court, 1816.

328. 12 July 1817. FREDERICK FULTZ and wife, HANNAH, JONATHAN
     COLEMAN and wife, SARAH W., Amherst County, to ROBERT COLEMAN,
Amherst County...$1.00 one third of a tract and water grist mill on
Rocky Creek--28 acres. Bought by FULTZ and COLEMAN of JACOB PIERCE.
Lines: JONATHA CHRISTIAN, B, WILLIAM DILLARD.

329. 29 March 1817. DANIEL PERROW, CHARLES PERROW and wife,
     ELEANOR, and ANNA PERROW, widow of DANIEL PERROW, deceased, to
JONATHAN HORSLEY, JR...$4000 209 acres James River. Lines: MRS.
ALLEN. Part of tract devised to GUERRANT, CHARLES, and DANIEL PERROW
by their father, DANIEL PERROW, deceased. Acknowledged in Nelson by
grantors, 28 March 1817--sic, ROBERT F. (?) KINCAID and F (?) MATTHEWS,
Justices of the Peace. To JONATHAN HORSLEY, 21 July 1817.

340. 27 June 1817. (pages so numbered) SUSAN ARRINGTON, Nelson
     County, to PETER F. CHRISTIAN...power of attorney to act for
her. Witnesses: LEWIS LAYNE, DANIEL F. CHRISTIAN, BEVERLY DAVIES.

341. 25 December 1816. WILLIAM VANNERSON, Petersburg, to SOPHIA
     CRAWFORD, A. B. SPOONER--VANNERSON has lately married HENRIETTA
ALLEN, formerly CRAWFORD, Amherst County, and she is heir of WILLIAM S.
CRAWFORD, deceased, Amherst County and estate has been devised to widow
and heirs by Amherst County decree--a slave, ALFRED, given to HENRIETTA
and portion of real estate; contracted to sell to JONATHAN MC DANIEL
and RICHARD JONES and they are to make bond and they have joined in
deed. WILLIAM agrees to secure his wife and child or future ones.
WILLIAM is a merchant, but has no capital of his own--$1265.80 and
$20.00--slave and bonds due from JONES and MC DANIEL--in trust for
WILLIAM's wife and child. ALFRED is to be retained by WILLIAM and,

if sold, is to be replaced. JONATHAN WINN (WYNN) and JONATHAN H. BROWN, Petersburg Justices of the Peace, 5 July 1817. Acknowledged by SOPHIA CRAWFORD in Amherst County before EDMOND PENN and JAMES M. BROWN, 9 July 1817. In Petersburg as to SPOONER, and recorded in Amherst County, 19 July 1817. To ELIJAH FLETCHER, 17 September 1817.

345. 19 August 1816. SAMUEL DEAN, delinquent on 290 acres for 1790...
     decree to sell, 19 August 1816, RICHARD HARRISON, deputy
sheriff for CHARLES TALIAFERRO, bought by RICHARD ELLIS for $2.12
due. Redeemed by CHARLES P. TALIAFERRO, 17 February 1817, and
signed by ELLIS. To RICHARD ELLIS, 17 May 1819.

347. 19 August 1816. JOSPEH LYLE, delinquent for 1803, 1804, and
     1805...140 acres. RICHARD HARRISON as above and bought for
$4.83 due by CHARLES P. TALIAFERRO--100 acres. Later 140 acres and
100 acres is a part. Redeemed by JOSEPH HIGGINBOTHA; recorded
21 July 1817.

349. 21 July 1817. JAMES PENN and wife JINNEY, Amherst County, to
     TURNER PENN, Amherst County...$1.00 108 acres where TURNER PENN
lives. They bought together from WILLIAM CHICK. Lines: JONATHAN W.
WALKER, both above; JAMES and TURNER, THOMAS BAILEY, THOMAS JEWELL,
WILLIAM GALT, JAMES DILLARD.

350. 21 July 1817. JONATHAN SCOTT and wife, JANE, Amherst County,
     to WIATT LONDON, Amherst County...$260 104 acres Christian Mill
Creek and bought from JONATHAN LONDON by JONATHAN SCOTT. Lines:
JONATHAN LONDON on Buffaloe ridge, JAMES DILLARD, CHRISTIAN heirs,
REUBEN NORVELL.

351. 21 July 1817. JAMES PENN and wife, JINSEY, TURNER PENN and wife,
     JOYCE, Amherst County, to REUBEN CARVER, Amherst County...$100
112 acres Porrage Creek and whereon JAMES PENN lives. Lines:
JONATHAN M. WALKER, grantors , THOMAS BURLEY, PLEASANT STORY, JAMES
DILLARD, grantee. To REUBEN CARVER, 20 July 1818.

352. 21 July 1817. THOMAS COLEMAN and wife, NANCY, Amherst County,
     to GEORGE CABELL, Campbell County...to THOMAS COLEMAN, 23 September
1817--$1000 390 acres. Lines: JONATHAN AMBLER, formerly JONATHAN
HARVEY, deceased, JONATHAN COLEMAN, deceased, JOSEPH CHILDRESS. Bought
by THOMAS COLEMAN, 15 March 1806, from SAMUEL COLEMAN and wife,
JUDITH. Patent to SAMUEL COLEMAN and JOSEPH CHILDRESS--40 acres patent
to SAMUEL COLEMAN, 4 April 1805, and to JOSEPH CHILDRESS, 29 June
1796 for 350 acres.

354. 21 July 1816. JONATHAN LONDON and wife, TIRZA, Amherst County,
     to JAMES PENN, Amherst County...$1000 130 acres both sides
Porrage. Lines: JAMES LONDON, JR., JONATHAN PADGETT, THOMAS EDWARDS,
JOHN HUTCHERSON, CHARLES MUNDY.

355. 19 August 1817. JAMES PARKER GARLAND and wife, KETURAH,
     Nelson County, BENAMMI STONE and wife, ELIZABETH, Amherst
County, to JONATHAN H. SMITH, Lynchburg...$5730 382 acres where
GARLAND lived formerly. Lines: PARKS' road, GARLAND, JONATHAN
HENDREN, WALTER CHRISTIAN, SR. BENJAMIN MILES, B. STONE. Late
survey by CHARLES L. CHRISTIAN. To JAMES PARKER GARLAND, 20 January
1818.

356. 11 August 1817. FLETCHER N. TALIAFERRO and wife, NANCY, Amherst
     County, to CHARLES P. TALIAFERRO, Amherst County...$500 one
fifth of estate of JONATHAN TALIAFERRO, deceased--46 acres in hands
of widow, ELIZABETH, for life. Witnesses: H. GEORGE TUCKER,
WILLIAM DUNCAN, JONATHAN EUBANK, JR., JAMES F. TALIAFERRO. To
CHARLES P. TALIAFERRO, 3 January 1823.

357. 1 September 1815. WILLIAM WARWICK, trustee for JONATHAN HALL,
      Amherst County, for benefit of DANIEL WARWICK, then of Amherst
County and now of Richmond, to WILLIAM GALT, Richmond...$100 320 acres
and part of 432 acres in three tracts in trust to WARWICK, 30 October
1800. Borders of Pedlar. Lines: CHARLES BLAN. Patent to JOSEPH
EDWARDS, July, 1780. Witnesses: NICHOLAS HARRISON, JAMES BULLOCK,
WILLIAM R. ROANE. Acknowledged in Lynchburg, 9 July 1817, by
WILLIAM WARWICK: ROBERT MORRIS and JONATHAN M. SETTLES, Justices of
the Peace.

357. 6 August 1817. WIATT P. SMITH, Amherst County, to JAMES F.
      TALIAFERRO, Amherst County...$202.50--interest in estate of late
WILLIAM SMITH--33 1/3 acres and in hands of PHILADELPHIT SMITH,
widow of WILLIAM on Puppies Creek. Witnesses: CHARLES P. TALIAFERRO,
BENJAMIN and F. W. TALIAFERRO. To JAMES F. TALIAFERRO, 15 January
1818.

360. 16 April 1817. JOSEPH HIGGINBOTHAM to BENJAMIN SANDIDGE...
      $2412 201 acres Buffaloe on south side. Lines: Road from
Buffaloe Springs to the house on Buffaloe lately occupied by CHARLES P.
TALIAFERRO, mouth of Wilmore Bt., path or road. Witnesses: LINDSEY
SANDIDGE, BENJAMIN HIGGINBOTHAM, RICHARD H. BURKS.

361. 5 August 1817. RICHARD MILLNER and wife, PATSY (MARTHA),
      Amherst County, to RICHARD L. ELLIS, Amherst County...$4776.75
434½ acres Pedlar. Lines: grantee, WILLIAM MITCHELL, THOMAS
GILLIAM, WINCANTON, SAMUEL GUEST, deceased. Witnesses: JOSHUA ELLIS,
JAMES EUBANK, JONATHAN ELLIS, TARPLEY MITCHELL, RODNEY M. THORNTON,
JOSIAH ELLIS. To RICHARD L. ELLIS, 1819. Page 363 order to Amherst
County Justices of the Peace to quiz MARTHA MILLNER. Done by JONATHAN
ELLIS and JAMES WARE on same day.

364. 18 July 1817. REUBEN COX, Amherst County, to TINSLEY RUCKER,
      Bedford...$925 37 acres forks of Lynch and Dawson roads. Lines:
RODNEY TALIAFERRO, RICHARD RUCKER, ELIAS WILLS. Witnesses: THOMAS R.
BADDOW, REUBEN NORVELL, JONATHAN R. (B) WHITTEN.

365. 13 August 1817. JAMES SMITH to CHARLES P. TALIAFERRO and
      JAMES HIGGINBOTHAM, Amherst County...$1500 Deed of Trust;
debt to GARLAND and TALIAFERRO, merchants of Amherst County--$1.00
for support of SMITH's wife--crops and stock on plantation where he
lives; seven slaves named. Witnesses: ADDISON TALIAFERRO, BENJAMIN
HIGGINBOTHAM, PHILIP SMITH, JR., STERLING CLAIBORNE. To CHARLES P.
TALIAFERRO, 15 September 1817.

366. 25 April 1816. SAMUEL BURKS, SR., and wife, PEGGY, Amherst
      County, to RICHARD BURKS, Amherst County...L500 161 acres both
sides Harris. Lines: JONATHAN AMBLER, JONATHAN SHELTON, RICHARD
BURKS. Page 367 order to quiz PEGGY, 21 April 1817; done by AMBROSE
RUCKER and NELSON C. DAWSON, 14 August 1817.

368. 11 August 1817. CHALRES L. BARRET and wife, SARAH, Amherst
      County, to CHARLES P. TALIAFERRO, Amherst County...$200 one
fifth of dower tract of estate of JONATHAN TALIAFERRO, deceased--
46 acres in possession of ELIZABETH, widow of JONATHAN on Puppies
Creek. To CHARLES P. TALIAFERRO, 3 January 1822.

369. 7 December 1817. HENRY L. DAVIES, Lynchburg, to FRANCIS K.
      DAVIES, Amherst County...$2500 210 acres north side and joining
James River. Tract allotted to HENRY L. DAVIES as heir and descendant
of NICHOLAS DAVIES. Lines: FRANCIS A. K. DAVIES, JONATHAN DAVIES,
BEVERLY DAVIES.

370. 22 September 1817. ISAAC RUCKER, executor of AMBROSE RUCKER,
     Amherst County, to TINSLEY and GARLAND RUCKER, Bedford County...
$1604.30 under will 610 acres in two tracts Harris and southeast
side of Tobacco Row Mountain. Lines: top of Tobacco Row, ROBERT
JOHNSON, WILLIAM PENDLETON, HENRY MC DANIEL. 2. DANIEL BURFORD,
AMBROSE RUCKER, JR., AMBROSE RUCKER, deceased, THOMAS GRISSOM. To
TINSLEY RUCKER, 15 July 1819.

372. 2 May 1817. JOSEPH KENNERLEY and wife, SARAH, Patrick County,
     to SAMUEL HEISKELL, Amherst County...$200 three acre tract sold
by REUBEN COLEMAN to JAMES WHITEHEAD. Lines: MICAJAH CAMDEN, formerly
REUBEN COLEMAN, Spring Branch. To SAMUEL HEISKELL, 20 January 1819.
GRANSVILLE and THOMAS PENN, Patrick Justices of the Peace as to
SARAH, 11 September 1817.

375. 18 August 1817 (so numbered). NANCY SHIELDS to STEPHEN WATTS,
     JONATHAN PENN, JR. and WILLIAM LEE...$1.00 tract whereon she
lives and bought by her from MATTHEW WATSON; also named slaves. She
has life interest only for her benefit.

377. 11 September 1817. BENJAMIN BROWN, Amherst County, to CHARLES P.
     TALIAFERRO, Amherst County...$195 6½ acres Crooked Run. Lines:
grantor, HENRY BROWN, MOVITON's (?) Spring, grantee.

377. 1 August 1815. JONATHAN BROWN and wife, ANNA, Amherst County,
     to ANDREW MORELAND, Amherst County...$600 50 acres north borders
Pedlar. Lines: MARTIN PARKS, JONATHAN DUNCAN, JONATHAN BURKS.
Witnesses: JAMES WARE, ANDERSON WARE, JAMES MC DANIEL, JONATHAN
GOODWIN, WILLIAM SHELTON. Order to quiz ANNA, 21 September 1816;
done by JONATHAN ELLIS and JAMES WARE, Amherst County Justices of the
Peace, 8 February 1817.

379. 12 July 1817. FREDERICK FULTZ and wife, HANNAH, Amherst County,
     JONATHAN COLEMAN and wife, SARAH, Amherst County, to ROBERT L.
COLEMAN, Amherst County...$1.00 one third of tract and mill on Rocky
Creek; 28 acres. Bought by grantors from JACOB PIERCE. Lines:
JONATHAN CHRISTIAN, B, WILLIAM DILLARD. Order to quiz wives, 17 July
1817; done, same day, by JONATHAN WARWICK and CHARLES MUNDY.

381. 18 September 1817. Order to Amherst County Justices of the
     Peace: LEROY CAMDEN and wife, BETHEMIAH, 6 February 1817,
to MICAJAH CAMDEN--767 3/4 acres. Done by THOMAS CREWS and EDMOND
PENN, 18 September 1817.

382. 9 February 1817. Order to Amherst County Justices of the
     Peace: JOSEPH C. HIGGINBOTHAM and wife, LUCY, GEORGE W.
HIGGINBOTHAM and wife ELIZABETH, JAMES HIGGINBOTHAM and wife,
ELIZABETH, 15 November 1813, to JOSEPH DILLARD...821 acres. Done
by JAMES M. BROWN and THOMAS ALDRIDGE, 9 May 1817, but only as to
both ELIZABETHS.

383. 9 September 1817. BOWLING MITCHELL and wife, NANCY, Amherst
     County, to GEORGE M. TINSLEY, Amherst County...$275 136 acres
north side Otter. Lines: JEREMIAH WHITTEN, JONATHAN HOGG. Witnesses:
NELSON C. DAWSON. Order to quiz NANCY, page 384, 10 September 1817;
done by NELSON C. DAWSON and AMBROSE RUCKER, same day. To GEORGE M.
TINSLEY, 18 November 1818.

385. 14 October 1817. HENRY BALLINGER and wife, MARY, Amherst County,
     to MATTHEW TUCKER, Amherst County...$794 198 acres Horsley
Creek. Lines: JOSEPH MILSTED, NELSON CRAWFORD, WILLIAM LONG,
WILLIAM HARTLESS, EDWARD TAYLOR. To WILLIAM ROAD, by JONATHAN
PRYOR, 2 September 1834.

385. 6 September 1817. PHILADELPHIA SMITH, MILLY P. SMITH, JOEL F.
     SMITH, WIATT P. SMITH, HENRY F. SMITH, WILLIS GILLESPIE and
wife, HARRIET, late SMITH, and RICHARD SMITH, JR., heirs of WILLIAM
SMITH, deceased, Amherst County, to BENJAMIN TALIAFERRO, Amherst
County...L235-10 two tracts 118½ acres 56 3/4 acres conveyed to
BENJAMIN TALIAFERRO, 11 December 1809, by PHILADELPHIA, MILLY and
JOEL. Part of tract devised by JACOB SMITH and joining dower tract
of said WILLIAM and now in hands of PHILADELPHI, widow of WILLIAM.
Lines: grantee, old road, fork leading to TALIAFERRO's house, road
of late JONATHAN YOUNG, main road. Witnesses: CHARLES P. TALIAFERRO,
LYNE S. TALIAFERRO, JAMES HIX, JONATHAN W. YOUNG as to GILLESPIE.

387. 23 September 1817. NELSON CRAWFORD, JOSEPH HIGGINBOTHAM,
     WILLIAM JOPLING, JONATHAN WARE, surviving executors of JACOB
SMITH. to BENJAMIN TALIAFERRO...under will--tracts to be sold and sums
divided to MILLY, JOEL, WIATT P., HENRY F., and RICHARD SMITH, JR.,
and HARRIET GILLESPIE, late SMITH, and husband, WILLIS GILLESPIE--all
of age and have conveyed to BENJAMIN TALIAFERRO, as above, for $1.00
paid by TALIAFERRO--relinquished all claims total tracts. Witnesses:
CHARLES L. BARRET, J. P. GARLAND, MICAJAH CAMDEN, ROBERT GARLAND,
LYNE S. TALIAFERRO, CHARLES P. TALIAFERRO, JAMES HIX, JAMES TALIAFERRO,
RICHARD H. BURKS, JONATHAN W. YOUNG. HARRIET GILLESPIE relinquished
dower, 6 September 1817, deed, on 18 October 1817. CHARLES P. and
CHARLES TALIAFERRO, Amherst County Justices of the Peace.

388. 7 August 1817. JOSEPH HAWKINS and wife, NANCY, Bedford County,
     to PROSSER POWELL, Amherst County...$125 102½ acres on James.
Lines: grantee--lately sold to him by JOSEPH ENTIRE tract where late
JONATHAN GILES lived and HAWKINS and wife own by descent "as only
heir." Witnesses: JONATHAN R. COOK, P. H. BURTON, S. GARLAND,
T. WIATT. Certified Lynchburg, 20 August 1817, by JOSEPH HAWKINS,
before JONATHAN M. SETTLE and ROBERT MORRIS, Justices of the Peace.
Order to quiz NANCY, 12 August 1817, and done by same Justices of the
Peace on 20 August 1817.

390. 20 May 1817. LYNE S. TALIAFERRO, Amherst County, to CHARLES P.
     TALIAFERRO, Amherst County...Deed of Trust; 4 February 1817
from JAMES SMITH and wife, SUSANNAH, to LYNE S. TALIAFERRO, to secure
GARLAND, TALIAFERRO and CHARLES P. TALIAFERRO--258 acres devised by
JOSEPH HIGGINBOTHAM, deceased, to SUSANNAH. Lines: JONATHAN HARDING.
Witnesses: ABRAHAM VENABLE, JAMES F. TALIAFERRO, RICHARD HATTEN,
ANGUS MC CLOUD. LYNE S. TALIAFERRO under Deed of Trust, 15 May 1817,
sold at auction and CHARLES P. TALIAFERRO was highest bidder at
$112. Witnesses: WILLIAM DUNCAN, BEVERLY DAVIES, JESSE KENNEDY.
To CHARLES P. TALIAFERRO, 3 January 1822.

391. 20 August 1817. LYNE S. TALIAFERRO and wife, MILDRED T. (?),
     Amherst County, to CHARLES P. TALIAFERRO, Amherst County...$400
one fifth of dowry tract of JONATHAN TALIAFERRO, deceased, 46 acres
and in hands of ELIZABETH TALIAFERRO, widow of JONATHAN for her life.
Witnesses: WILLIAM DUNCAN, BEVERLY DAVIES, JESSE KENNEDY. To
CHARLES P. TALIAFERRO, 3 January 1822.

392. 17 November 1816. JOSEPH HAWKINS and wife, NANCY, Bedford,
     to PROSSER POWELL, Amherst County...L150 90 acres John's Creek.
Lines: JAMES WILLS, GEORGE POWELL. Witnesses: JONATHAN P. WILSON,
R. and GEORGE POWELL, A. ROBERTSON. Order to JONATHAN M. SETTLE and
ROBERT MORRIS, 12 August 1817, by JONATHAN CAMM, Amherst County Clerk
to quiz NANCY and done by them in Lynchburg, 20 August 1817. To
PROSSER POWELL, 4 June 1818.

394. 1 September 1817. ANDERSON TINSLEY and wife, SYNTHIA, Amherst
     County, to ISAAC RUCKER and JONATHAN H. CLEMENTS, Amherst
County...$550 99 acres Brown Mountain Creek with tobacco, corn,
"whath", vegetables, rye. Witnesses: BARTLETT CLEMENTS, YOUNGER
HOLLIDAY, FIELDING HOLLIDAY. Certified as to SYNTHAI by BENJAMIN and
CHARLES P. TALIAFERRO, Amherst County Justices of the Peace,
10 September 1817.

129

395. 20 October 1817. THOMAS CLASBY and wife, CATHERINE, Nelson
      County, to THOMAS MILES, Amherst County...$900 101½ acres;
part of former tract of RICHARD WILSON. Lines: PRICE (?), on road,
RICHARD WILSON, SAMUEL HUCKSTEP, BENJAMIN MILES.

396. 3 October 1817. BENJAMIN SANDIDGE and wife, ELIZABETH, Amherst
      County, to AARON HIGGINBOTHAM, Amherst County...$2000 300 acres
north borders of south fork Buffaloe. Lines: JONATHAN RICHESON,
ABRAM CARTER (former), JOSEPH HIGGINBOTHAM, grantor, LINDSEY SANDIDGE
(formerly JAMES HIGGINBOTHAM, JR.), ANGUISH MC CLOUD (formerly
GEORGE W. HIGGINBOTHAM), JONATHAN RICHARDSON--sic. Witnesses:
WILLIAM COLEMAN, THOMAS SANDS, MANSFIELD WARE. To AARON HIGGINBOTHAM,
21 July 1818.

398. 7 October 1817. ROWLAND PROFFITT and wife, KEZIAH, FLEMING
      EDWARDS and wife, RACHEL, Nelson County, to JAMES BALL, Sumner
County, Tennessee...$1200; all interest in estate of JONATHAN BALL,
late of Amherst County--dower of ELIZABETH BALL, widow of JONATHAN,
for life by will--125 acres and five named slaves. Witnesses:
CORNELIUS POWELL, HUDSON M. GARLAND, JONATHAN DILLARD.

399. 10 October 1817. JAMES F. TALIAFERRO from WILLIS GILLESPIE and
      wife, HARRIET, Amherst County...$200 one sixth of dower tract
of WILLIAM SMITH, deceased--23 1/3 acres Puppies Creek. Lines:
WILLIAM SANDIDGE. Witnesses: CHALRES P. TALIAFERRO, JAMES HIX,
ADDISON TALIAFERRO. To JAMES F. TALIAFERRO, 15 January 1819.

400. 27 May 1817. LEROY CAMDEN, Amherst County, to DAVID SHEPHERD,
      Amherst County...Deed of Trust; debt to DAVID S. GARLAND.
$1.00; named slaves. Witnesses: E. FLETCHER, JAMES WARE, CORNELIUS
POWELL. To DAVID S. GARLAND, 3 June 1818.

401. 21 November 1815. JONATHAN H. GOODWIN, Pitsylvania, to ROBERT
      GOODWIN, Amherst County...$200 half acre lot. Lines: JAMES
LASHWELL's former lot; COLONEL PHILIP JOHNOSN. Witnesses: WILLIAM
LEFWICH, GEORGE H. ENGLISH, PHIL GOODWIN, MOORE CONKIN (?), JONATHAN
RICHESON, BUNCH VIRMILLION MOORE. Acknowledged in Pitsylvania,
15 April 1816; WILL TANSTALL (?), Clerk.

402. 12 September 1817. ISAIAH ALLEY and wife, BETSY, Amherst County,
      to WILLIAM BURD, Campbell County...$3815 190 3/4 acres Frost's
branch. Lines: JONATHAN HANSARD, WILLIAM MITCHELL, CHISWELL DABNEY.
To CHISWELL DABNEY, 16 July 1832. BETSY relinquished dower, 11 October
1817, before REUBEN NORVELL and AMBROSE RUCKER, Amherst County Justices
of the Peace.

404. 13 October 1800. EDWARD HARDEN and wife, POLLY, to JAMES
      HARDEN, Amherst County...GROVES HARDEN, Amherst County, deceased,
by will devised to son, EDWARD 300 acres and to son, JONATHAN, 300 acres
and 410 acres. Agreed to exchange and EDWARD hereby conveys 300 acres.
This is a bit confusing, but appears that only two tracts were
exchanged of 300 of EDWARD and 410 of JONATHAN. Witnesses: ROBERT
RIVES, WILLIAM H. CABELL, JESSE HIGGINBOTHAM, W. B. HARE, WILLIS
WILLS.

405. 22 August 1817. REUBEN L. TYREE and wife, JEMIMA, Amherst
      County, to JONATHAN HORSLEY, JR...L69 50 acres both sides Elk
Island Creek. Lines: LUFBOROUGH, ROBERT L. JEFFERSON. To JONATHAN
HORSLEY, 16 March 1818. Witnesses: ROBERT HORSLEY, JOSEPH HORSLEY,
JONATHAN TORCY (?).

406. 5 September 1817. HENRY F. SMITH, Amherst County, to JAMES F.
      TALIAFERRO, Amherst County...$150--one sixth of dower estate
of WILLIAM SMITH--33 2/3 acres and in hands of PHILADELPHIA SMITH,
widow of WILLIAM SMITH, for life. Puppies Creek. Witnesses: JACOB
SMITH, JONATHAN W. YOUNG, RICHARD SMITH, PHILIP SMITH. To JAMES F.
TALIAFERRO, 15 January 1819.

407.	28 August 1817.	CHARLES CRAWFORD and wife, SALLY, Amherst
	County, to CHARLES C. (?) CARTER, Nelson County...L1840 460 acres
Horsley Creek. Lines: RALLS, south border Horsley, THURMOND, the
road. Witnesses: JONATHAN MC DANIEL, NELSON CRAWFORD, CHARLES
TALIAFERRO, JONATHAN PRYOR. SALLY relinquished dower, 30 August
1817, before CHARLES TALIAFERRO and NELSON CRAWFORD.

409.	4 October 1817.	JONATHAN BROWN and wife, MARY, Amherst County,
	to TARPLEY MITCHELL, Amherst County...L100 120 acres south
side Pedlar. Lines: Brown's Creek. MARY relinquished dower,
18 October 1817, before NELSON CRAWFORD and WILLIAM JOPLING.

411.	1 August 1816.	Order to Amherst County Justices of the Peace:
	NATHANIEL WILSON and wife, RACHEL, 13 July 1816, to ARCHIBALD
ROWSEY...136 acres. Done by NELSON CRAWFORD and BENJAMIN TALIAFERRO,
14 August 1816. Recorded 15 February 1817. To ARCHIBALD ROWSEY,
13 December 1817.

413.	29 September 1817.	(there is no 412 page) JAMES LONDON and
	wife, MARY, Amherst County, to REUBEN NORVELL, Amherst County...
$1200 170 acres east side Glade road and joining it. Lines: grantor,
LARKIN LONDON. Bought by grantor from grantee. Witnesses: JONATHAN
LONDON, MARTIN LONDON, JOSEPH DILLARD.

414.	16 December 1817.	Order to Amherst County Justices of the
	Peace: JAMES POWELL and wife, MILDRED, 18 December 1815, to
CATLETT CAMPBELL...152½ acres. Done by JONATHAN COLEMAN and T. S.
HOLLOWAY, 18 November 1817.

414.	17 October 1817.	BENJAMIN SHACKELFORD and wife, FRANCES, Amherst
	County, to JAMES WAUGH, Amherst County...$2632 four tracts by
patent. 1. 200 acres patent to HUGH MORRIS--Thomas Mill Creek.
Lines: HUGH MORRIS, former line, DAVENPORT, former line, crossing
road. 2. 38 acres same creek. Lines: RODNEY MC CULLOCH, CHARLES
DAVIES. 3. Adjoins first two tracts on south side creek. 4. Tract
bought by BENJAMIN SHACKELFORD from ROBERT NUCKLES; 90 acres; part
conveyed to CHARLES DAVIS, deceased, and remainder of about 77 acres.
FRANCES relinquished dower, 25 October 1817. JONATHAN ELLIS and
JAMES WARE, Amherst County Justices of the Peace.

417.	6 October 1817.	JOSEPH HIGGINBOTHAM, Amherst County, to
	STERLING CLAIBORNE, Amherst County...$5000 534 acres on Buffaloe
near Springs by that name. Bought by JOSEPH from BENJAMIN HIGGINBOTHAM.
Lines: BENJAMIN SANDIDGE, JAMES GOVAN. Witnesses: BENJAMIN
HIGGINBOTHAM, JAMES SMITH, HILL CARTER, HENRY J. ROSE. To STERLING
CLAIBORNE, 27 October 1820.

418.	Received from ARTHUR B. DAVIES, Deputy Clerk, $26.30 to redeem
	lands bought by MR. DAVIES at sales by Sheriff, August Court,
1816. Signed by WILLIAM DAVIES. Witnesses: BEVERLY DAVIES.

418.	Received from DAVIES, $2.91 damages on tract bought by me under
	Sheriff's sale, August 1816; delinquent taxes in name of
JONATHAN MARKLIAM (MARKHAM?). Signed by THOMAS CREWS.

419.	REUBEN COLEMAN's receipt to DAVIES, $10.68 four tracts bought
	by REUBEN COLEMAN as above--tracts of JAMES SMILEY, JONATHAN
MC HAMM or HANN, JONATHAN HUTCHESON's estate and JONATHAN MORRISON.

419.	ROBERT GARLAND, same: $6.75 for 260 acres; 180 acres; 80 acres--
	tracts of ROBERT DOUTHAT or DOWTHAT.

419.	BENJAMIN TALIAFERRO as above: $3.00 as to LEONARD ROWSEY's
	tract of 170 acres. Also as to GEORGE CLARKE's tract of
166 acres for $5.36. Also DR. PARKER's tract of 200 acres for
$20.44.

419.	CHARLES P. TALIAFERRO as above: $2.00 no acres or owners.

420.   THOMAS N. EUBANK as above: $35.67; no tracts or owners.

420.   ROBERT GARLAND as above: $8.17 800 acres WILLIAM CARTER's
       tract and 700 acres of it sold by Sheriff, August Court, 1816.

420.   R. POWELL: $8.85; no owner or tract.

420.   JAMES T. (S) PENDLETON: $22.03; no owner named or tract.

420.   CHARLES P. TALIAFERRO bought various tracts: $201.73--40 acres
       of JAMES GATEWOOD; 105 acres of CHARLES OVERSTREET; 100 acres
of WILLIAM SCHOFIELD; 70 acres of ROBERT EDMUNDSON; 100 acres of
WILSON C. NICHOLAS; 140 acres of JOSEPH LYLE.

420.   12 November 1817. REUBEN COX and wife, PATSY, Amherst County,
       to WILLIAM MITCHELL, Amherst County...$825 33 acres headborders
Buck Branch and Pole Cat Branch. Lines: grantee, JONATHAN MEHONE,
JAMES LEE. To REUBEN COX, 23 December 1817; 19 June 1829, to JAMES
BRUCE, present owner. Deed Book O: 165 for relinquishment of
dower.

421.   16 August 1817. REUBEN COX and wife, PATSY, Amherst County,
       to ALEXANDER TINSLEY, Amherst County...$1000 201 acres Harris
and east side Tobacco Row Mountain. Lines: ELIZABETH COLEMAN,
top of mountain, RICHARD BURKS, CRAWFORD Gap road. To REUBEN COX,
5 December 1817. Witnesses: J. S. WINGFIELD, JONATHAN R. WHITTEN,
GEORGE W. TAYLOR.

423.   13 December 1817. JAMES HILL, SR., Amherst County, to JAMES
       HILL, JR., Amherst County...$350 41½ acres. Lines: Lynch
road, Church road. Witnesses: JAMES WOODROOF, HUGH NORVELL, PHILIP
LIVELY. To JAMES HILL, JR., 12 February 1829 (?).

423.   12 November 1817. ARTHUR L. DAVIES and wife, LUCY C., Gloucester
       County, to AMBROSE RUCKER, Amherst County...$3400 1600 acres
near Bethel, surveyed by JAMES WARE. Lines: JONATHAN CAMM, BETHEL,
JONATHAN DAVIES, around Indian grave on the mountain, WILLIAM ROBINS
and JONATHAN R. CAREY (?), Gloucester Justices of the Peace as to
LUCY C., 14 November 1817. To AMBROSE RUCKER, 16 February 1818.

426.   21 October 1817. JONATHAN SALE and wife, NANCY, Green County,
       Ohio, ROBERT SALE and wife, MAGDALEN, Warren County, Ohio, to
THOMAS SALE, Bedford, and CORNELIUS SALE, Amherst County...$820 600
acres Buffaloe. Lines: Higginbotham, JONATHAN SMITH. Witnesses:
P. GOODE, P. G. GOODE, JOSEPH HAMILL, Justices of the Peace, Green
County, Ohio, as to wives, 21 October 1817. JOSIAH GROVER, Green
County Clerk. ORRIE (?) PARRISH, Presiding Judge.

428.   17 November 1817. JONATHAN CLEMONS and RICHARD HARRISON,
       Amherst County, to ZACH ISBELL, Amherst County...$4998.75
879 acres headwaters Harris Creek. Lines: grantee, JABEZ CAMDEN,
CHARLES TALIAFERRO, THOMAS WOODROOF, deceased, JONATHAN COLEMAN,
WILLIAM WARE, RICHARD BURKS, BRANSFORD HICKS. Also 120 3/4 acres
adjoining. Lines: grantee, WILLIAM WARE, THOMAS WOODROOF, JR.,
deceased. To ZACH ISBELL, 28 September 1820.

430.   21 June 1817. ROBERT MORRIS and wife, SARAH, Lynchburg County,
       to GEORGE WHITLOCKE, same plave...blank sum; 20 3/4 acres
bought by ROBERT MORRIS from GEORGE D. WINSTON and joining JONATHAN
LYNCH, SR. Lines: LYNCH, BENJAMIN PERKINS. To GEORGE WHITLOCKE,
26 June 1826. Witnesses: WILL MITCHELL, GEORGE CABELL, A. ROBERTSON.
JONATHAN M. SETTLE and JONATHAN SCHOOLFIELD, Lynchburg Justices of
the Peace, as to SARAH, 25 June 1817.

432. 1 November 1816. JACOB TYREE, Amherst County, from WIATT
     DUNCAN and wife, POLLY, WILLIS DUNCAN and wife, JANE, POLLY
DUNCAN, JONATHAN DUNCAN, WASH CAMDEN and wife, NANCY formerly DUNCAN,
Rockbridge...$1100 246 acres south borders Buffaloe--as heirs of
JONATHAN DUNCAN, our father. Lines: JAMES GARLAND, deceased,
CHARLES DUNCAN, CHARLES BURRUS, PATSY DUNCAN. Witnesses: ELIJAH
STATON, JAMES WOOD, NANCY WOOD, SAMUEL WOOD.

433. 5 April 1817. BENJAMIN NOEL and wife, JUDY, Amherst County,
     to WILLIAM MITCHELL, Amherst County...L2-10 30 acres Cashaw
Creek. Lines: ARCHELAUS MITCHELL, HENRY L. CUNDAN. Witnesses:
JAMES ROWSEY, WILLIAM NOEL, BOWLING MITCHELL.

434. 5 April 1817. BENJAMIN NOEL and wife, JUDY, Amherst County,
     to WILLIAM MITCHELL, Amherst County...L2-10 16 acres James
River. Lines: ARCHIBALD MITCHELL, NICHOLAS VANSTAVERN, ZACHARIAH
TALIAFERRO. Witnesses: as above.

435. 24 June 1817. WILLIAM CLARKE, SR., Amherst County, to BENJAMIN
     TALIAFERRO, Amherst County...$400 three tracts for total of
220 acres on south and middle forks Pedlar. 1. 70 acres. Lines:
THOMAS STATON, formerly, JOSEPH HIGGINBOTHA, JR., top of the mountain,
JOSEPH HIGGINBOTHAM, SR., formerly. 2. 50 acre patent to HUGH MC CABE,
6 April 1769. Lines: JOSEPH HIGGINBOTHAM, JR., middle fork Pedlar.
3. 100 acres bought from JOSEPH HIGGINBOTHAM, 6 December 1796.
Lines: HIGGINBOTHAM. Witnesses: CHARLES BURKS, son of DAVID,
JONATHAN D. CRAWFORD, SR., JONATHAN CRAWFORD.

437. 11 November 1817. CHARLES and MOLLY HOUCHIN, Hardin County,
     Kentucky, to THOMAS SALE, Bedford...$420 100 acres. Lines:
HIGGINBOTHAM. Witnesses: JONATHAN D. HOUCHIN, ASEL ---?, CORNELIUS
SALE. To J. THOMPSON, attorney for parties, 17 September 1857.

438. 19 August 1817. JONATHAN H. SMITH, Lynchburg, to DAVID S.
     GARLAND, Amherst County...Deed of Trust; debt to JAMES P.
GARLAND; $1.00; 382 acres conveyed this day by JAMES P. GARLAND and
BENAMMI STONE. Witnesses: MICAJAH CAMDEN, JAMES POWELL, REUBEN
COLEMAN. To JAMES P. GARLAND, 20 January 1818.

439. 7 April 1817. JONATHAN LYNCH and wife, MARY, Lynchburg, to
     JONATHAN M. GORDON, same plave...$3150 four lots or two acres
southwest end of town of Madison--plan attached (not in book).
Lines: Main Street, alley, third street, seventh alley. Witnesses:
WILLIAM SNEAD, EDWARD LYNCH, RICHARD TYREE, CHRISTOPHER ANTHONY,
WILLIAM M. RIVES, JONATHAN D. URQUHART. JONATHAN SCHOOLFIELD and
ROBERT MORRIS, Lynchburg Justices of the Peace. To JONATHAN M.
GORDON, 17 April 1820; to W. R. RIVES, 18 July 1821.

441. 7 April 1817. JONATHAN LYNCH and wife, MARY, Lynchburg, to
     DANIEL and DAVID HOFFMAN, same place...$2000 5 3/4 acres. Lines:
southwest corner of grantees on east side Main Street in town of
Madison; JONATHAN MILLER. Witnesses: JONATHAN N. ROSE, JAMES BENAGH,
JONATHAN H. SMITH, JONATHAN D. URQUHART. To PITT WOODROOF, present
owner, 8 November 1842. Same Justices of the Peace as above.

442. 7 April 1817. JONATHAN LYNCH and wife, MARY, Lynchburg, to
     JONATHAN ROBINSON, same place...$2880 four lots--southwest
end of town of Madison. Lines: junction of first or Main, second
street, seventh alley. To JONATHAN ROBINSON, 17 April 1820; to
WILLIAM M. RIVES, 18 July 1821. Witnesses: WILLIAM SNEAD, EDWARD
LYNCH, RICHARD TYREE, C. ANTHONY, WILLIAM M. RIVES, JONATHAN D.
URQUHART. Justices of the Peace as above.

443. -- 1817; recorded 19 January 1818. WILLIAM WOODROOF and wife,
     ELIZABETH, Amherst County, to THOMAS CREWS, Amherst County...$140
1. six acres north fork Haw Branch. 2. Six acres in fork of Lynch
road and Mc Daniels road.

444. 19 January 1818. ELIAS WILLS, Amherst County, to JONATHAN
LONDON, Amherst County...$560 70 acres Stovall. Lines:
WILLIAM KNIGHT tract JONATHAN LONDON bought from DANIEL DAY, JAMES
BOLLING, RUCKER's road, JAMES DAVIS. Received by JONATHAN J. LONDON,
16 July 1845.

445. 14 January 1818. DAVID S. GARLAND and wife, JANE, Amherst
County, to JONATHAN MOUNTCASTLE, town of New Glasgow, Amherst
County...$1.00; lot in said town. Lines: east by Main, north by
WILLIAM JUSE, No. 24, west by grantor, south by 25 and 26. Witnesses:
WILLIAM ARMISTEAD, JONATHAN COLEMAN, JONATHAN J. DILLARD, JONATHAN
DILLARD.

447. 13 December 1817. JONATHAN N. ROSE and wife, MARY, to
JONATHAN THOMPSON, JR., Amherst County...mill on Piney. Lines:
Spring used by WILLIAM STAPLES, HILL CARTER, COLONEL PATRICK ROSE,
small island--36 acres plus--known as ROSE's Mill; $4000. Witnesses:
JONATHAN L. BLAIR, JONATHAN MYERS, G. W. DILLARD. To JONATHAN
THOMPSON, JR., 18 January 1821.

449. 17 January 1818. NELSON C. DAWSON and wife, NANCY, Amherst
County, to JONATHAN M. EDWARDS, Amherst County...$1300 84 acres.
Lines: JONATHAN SHELTON, JONATHAN RUCKER, deceased. To JONATHAN M.
EDWARDS, 29 December 1818.

450. 11 December 1817. GEORGE W. HIGGINBOTHAM and wife, ELIZABETH,
Amherst County, to JABEZ CAMDEN, Amherst County...$50 42 acres
Huff. Lines: JONATHAN COLEMAN, deceased--his survey, BENJAMIN NOEL's
old line, HENRY CAMDEN, WILLIAM STINNETT.

451. 17 January 1818. DABNEY WARE and wife, ELIZABETH, Amherst
County, to JONATHAN M. EDWARDS, Amherst County...$400 20 acres
Graham Creek. Lines: WILLIAM SHELTON, AMBROSE RUCKER. To JONATHAN M.
EDWARDS, 29 December 1818.

452. 29 September 1817. JONATHAN MC DANIEL, Amherst County, to
BENJAMIN BROWN, Amherst County...exchange of land on Crooked
Run and joins both and THOMAS CREWS, the path--5 1/4 acres. Second
tract BROWN to MC DANIEL. Lines: the road, WILLIAM BOURN, BROWN--
5¼ acres.

452. 26 December 1817. JACOB HASS and wife, SUSANNAH, Lynchburg,
to JONATHAN L. WINGFIELD, Amherst County...$4125 165 acres.
Lines: NICHOLAS C. DAVIES, deceased, CALEB WATTS, RODNEY MC CULLOCH,
ELLIS. Tract devised to SUSANNAH by WILLIAM TINSLEY. Witnesses:
JAMES SHURLEY. JONATHAN SCHOOLFIELD and JONATHAN M. SETTLE, Lynchburg
Justices of the Peace as to SUSANNAH, 28 December 1818.

454. 11 December 1817. EDWARD CARTER and wife, MARY, Amherst County,
to WILLIAM, NELSON and SAMUEL MANTIPLY, Amherst County...$7186.67
539 acres. Part of tract. Lines: CARTER's Mill branch, NATHANIEL
MANTIPLY, deceased, ROBERT RIVERS. Witnesses: CORNELIUS POWELL,
HENRY FRANKLIN, DAVID S. GARLAND. To SAMUEL MANTIPLY, 16 February
1818.

456. 31 October 1817. LARKIN BIAS and wife, MARY, Amherst County,
to GEORGE P. LUCK, Amherst County...$3400 340 acres. Lines:
SAMUEL GIST, deceased, south bank Pedlar, EDWARD HARPER, FLEMING H.
DUNCAN, GEORGE MORRIS, SR., DAVID BURKS, JOSHUA S. ELLIS, Cedar
Creek. Witnesses: PETER P. THORNTON, FLEMING H. DUNCAN, ARCHER
GILLIAM, ROBERT MILLNER. To T. N. EUBANK, 19 November 1818.

457. 15 December 1817. Order to Amherst County Justices of the
Peace: JONATHAN WARWICK and wife, MARY, 14 June 1814, to
THOMAS ALDRIDGE...373 acres. Done by CHARLES MUNDY and THOMAS S.
HOLLOWAY, 19 December 1817.

457.   22 December 1817.   (two such pages numbered)   Order to Amherst
        County Justices of the Peace: JONATHAN CAMM and wife, ELIZABETH,
to JONATHAN WARWICK...16 acres. Signed by JONATHAN CAMM, Clerk.
Done by NELSON C. DAWSON and AMBROSE RUCKER, 22 December 1817.

458.   22 March 1810. SARAH PHILLIPS, Garrard County, Kentucky...power
        of attorney to her son, JACOB PHILLIPS, to sell dower in tract
of land of late husband, JACOB PHILLIPS, in Amherst County. BENJAMIN
LETCHER, Clerk; CHARLES SPILMAN, Presiding Justice of the Peace.
Recorded in Amherst County, 19 January 1818.

459.   4 November 1817. BETSY BALL, Amherst County, to JAMES BALL,
        Sumner County, Tennessee...heirs of JONATHAN BALL, deceased.
JAMES BALL conveyed from heirs of JONATHAN, October Term, 1817, to
JAMES SMITH, Amherst County. $725 for 125 3/4 acres CARTER's Mill
Creek. Lines: JAMES FRANKLIN, BARTLETT CASH, ELIZABETH GOOLSBY.
Witnesses: JONATHAN W. YOUNG, JONATHAN B. DUNCAN, CORNELIUS POWELL,
ZACH DRUMMOND, WILLIAM SALE. Page 461 order to Amherst County
Justices of the Peace to quiz BETSY; done, 8 January 1818, by JAMES M.
BROWN and THOMAS ALDRIDGE.

462.   22 January 1818. JAMES WADE and wife, ANNE, Campbell County,
        to WILLIAM ROBERTSON, Amherst County...$100.00--ten--47½ acres
west side and joining Opossum Island Road. Lines: PHILIP JOHNSON,
deceased, ROBERT MORRIS and JONATHAN SCHOOLFIELD, Lynchburg Justices
of the Peace on same date as to ANNE.

463.   19 January 1818. JAMES LONDON, JR., Amherst County, to
        JAMES PENN, Amherst County...$360 19 acres Porrage Creek.
Lines: Spring Branch, CHARLES MUNDY, house where PENN lives, grantor,
grantee.

464.   23 October 1815. WILLIAM DAVIS and JOSEPH HAYNES, heirs of
        JONATHAN ROACH, deceased, by marriage...power of attorney to
WILLIAM ROACH, Amherst County, to collect from estate of ASHCRAFT
ROACH, deceased, Amherst County. Mercer County, Kentucky: THOMAS
ALLEN, Clerk as to both of them. JAMES WESTERFIELD, Presiding Justice
of the Peace. Recorded Amherst County: 15 September 1817.

465.   9 December 1817. HENRY CAMDEN, Amherst County, to ARTHUR B.
        DAVIES, Amherst County...Deed of Trust; debt to LEROY CAMDEN
who is on bond to DAVID S. and JAMES P. GARLAND, executors of JAMES
GARLAND, deceased. MICAJAH CAMDEN is also on bond. $1.00. 750 acres
bought by HENRY CAMDEN from THOMAS GRYMES. Witnesses: JONATHAN ALLEN,
THOMAS P. ESKRIDGE, G. W. DILLARD.

467.   17 November 1817. WILLIAM DOUGLAS and wife, SUSANNAH, to
        JAMES WAUGH...$652 163 acres Thomas Mill Creek. SUSANNAH's
share as daughter of CHARLES DAVIS. Witnesses: JAMES DAVIS,
R. N. EUBANK, THOMAS N. EUBANK, JAMES WARE, RICHARD H. BURKS. To
JAMES WAUGH, 21 April 1818.

467.   23 September 1817. NOTLEY SMOOT, SR., Amherst County, to
        ROBERT TINSLEY...Deed of Trust; debt to DAVID S. GARLAND.
$1.00 furniture and stock. Witnesses: HES. S. FULCHER, B. SHEPHARD,
CORNELIUS POWELL, PEACHY FRANKLIN. To DAVID S. GARLAND, 10 November
1818.

469.   26 September 1817. JONATHAN ALLEN, Amherst County, to DAVID
        SHEPHARD and ROBERT TINSLEY...Deed of Trust; debt as above.
$1.00 four named slaves. Witnesses: as above, minus DAVID SHEPHARD.
To DAVID S. GARLAND, 3 June 1818.

470. 20 October 1817. SAMUEL CASH and wife, JOANNA H., Amherst
County, to BARNETT CASH, Amherst County...they are in joint
possession of 400 acres on Thrasher Creek and received from their
father patent to RICHARD POWELL, 1 June 1750. Lines: JAMES SMITH,
PIERCE WADE--$1800 for 400 acres. Order to NELSON CRAWFORD and
THOMAS S. HOLLOWAY to quiz JOANNA H.; done on same date.

472. 23 October 1817. THOMAS APPLING, JR., and wife, POLLY, Amherst
County, to ALEXANDER SALE, Amherst County...whereas BEVERLY
WILLIAMSON, SR. (?) owned two tracts on Stonehouse; branch of Buffaloe.
Lines: WILLIAM TUCKER, RICHARD SMITH, GABRIEL PAGE. Devised to his
six children and POLLY is one of them--reference to will of WILLIAMSON.
L95 for one sixth--no division has been made. Witnesses: WILEY
CAMPBELL, CATLETT CAMPBELL, JONATHAN WARWICK, JONATHAN COLEMAN.
Order to quiz POLLY and done by JONATHAN WARWICK and JONATHAN COLEMAN,
27 October 1817. To ALEXANDER SALE, 7 October 1818.

474. 29 October 1817. SUCKEY ROBERTS, Amherst County, to CHARLES P.
TALIAFERRO, Amherst County...$150 45 acres Pedlar. Lines:
HUDSON, grantee. Tract devised to her by JONATHAN ROBERTS, deceased.
Witnesses: CHARLES L. BARRET, JAMES F. TALIAFERRO, ADDISON TALIAFERRO.

475. -- 1817. Recorded 15 February 1818. THOMAS APPLING, JR.,
Amherst County...power of attorney to his father, THOMAS
APPLING, Amherst County, to settle accounts with ALEXANDER SALE,
executor of BEVERLY WILLIAMSON. Witnesses: T. S. HOLLOWAY, LEWIS
LAYNE, DAVID APPLING, ALEXANDER SALE.

476. 20 January 1818. AMBROSE RUCKER, AMherst County, to GEORGE
MC DANIEL, SR., Amherst County...$1400 280 acres south side
Tobacco Row Mountain and headwaters Graham Creek--late survey by
CAPTAIN JAMES WARE. Tract bought from ARTHUR L. DAVIES. Lines:
DABNEY WARE, SAMUEL BURKS, top of the ridge from JOHNS' to Indiangrave
Gap by WATTS, MARTIN PARKS, grantee. Witnesses: DABNEY WARE,
JONATHAN EDWARDS, SAMUEL P. (?) MITCHELL, THOMAS EUBANK.

477. 1 October 1817. WILLIAM PRYOR, Amherst County, to his son,
JONATHAN PRYOR, Amherst County...love and for support--60 acres
HOrsley. Lines: WILLIAM WARE, WILLIAM CARTER. Witnesses: PETER P.
THORNTON, P. THURMOND, CHARLES P. TALIAFERRO, WILLIAM JOPLING.

477. 16 February 1818. JONATHAN LONDON and wife, TIRZA, Amherst
County, to JONATHAN HUTCHESON, Amherst County...$150 15 acres
Porrage Creek. Lines: grantee, path to MUNDY's Mill. To JONATHAN
MEHONE, 4 September 1835.

478. 16 February 1818. JONATHAN HUTCHESON and wife, LUCINDA, Amherst
County, to JONATHAN LONDON, Amherst County...$70 two tracts.
1. Six acres. Lines: west side Stovall road, grantee, JAMES MARRS,
deceased. 2. One acre. Lines: grantee, where he lives, grantor,
the path to LONDON's house. To JONATHAN J. LONDON, agent for
JONATHAN LONDON's administrator, 24 October 1833.

479. 17 November 1817. THOMAS MURRELL and wife, ELIZABETH, Amherst
County, to NELSON C. DAWSON, Amherst County...$1430 71½ acres
Lynch road. Lines: JONATHAN BOLLING, JAMES BOLLING, JONATHAN WINGFIELD.
To THOMAS MURRELL, 7 May 1819.

480. 16 February 1818. JAMES POWELL and wife, MILDRED, Amherst
County, to ARTHUR B. DAVIES, Amherst County...$2531 168 3/4
acres. JAMES POWELL bought it from REUBEN COLEMAN and JAMES L. (S)
WALKER. Witnesses: FRANCIS HILL, WILKINS WATSON, EZEKIEL B. GILBERT.
To ARTHUR B. DAVIES, 26 December 1818.

480. 17 February 1818. MICAJAH CAMDEN to CHARLES P. TALIAFERRO...
$1800 half acre tract bought by MICAJAH CAMDEN from heirs of
WILLIAM HUTCHISON. Lines: WILLIAM LONG, the road, WILLIAM LONG's
former tract.

481. 23 September 1817. Order to Amherst County Justices of the
    Peace: THOMAS COLEMAN and wife, NANCY, 21 July 1817, to
GEORGE CABELL...390 acres. Done by AMBROSE RUCKER and WILLIAM
JOPLING, 16 February 1818.

482. 18 October 1817. SAMUEL SALE...power of attorney to ALEXANDER
    SALE. Witnesses: ZA DRUMMOND, ROBERT RIVERS.

482. 22 March 1817. Order to Bedford Justices of the Peace:
    NATHANIEL J. MANSON and wife, SALLY, 12 July 1815, to THOMAS N.
EUBANK...746 acres. Done by BALDA MC DANIEL and TAMERLAND W. DAVIES,
25 April 1817.

483. 12 February 1818. MICAJAH TERRELL and wife, MARTHA ELIZABETH,
    Natchez, Mississippi, to JONATHAN LYNCH, Lynchburg...$2000
340 acres both sides Bolling Creek. Lines: ROBERT MORRIS, LINEAS
BOLLING, Opossum Island road, ROBINSON, WARWICK. Witnesses:
JONATHAN TAYLOR, Presiding Judge of Superior Court of Mississippi as
to relinquish of dower. DAVID HOLMES, Governor of Mississippi as to
TAYLOR. Recorded Amherst County, 16 March 1818.

485. 15 December 1817. CALEB RALLS, Amherst County, to RICHARD EUBANK,
    Amherst County...CALEB seals for $3870 322½ acres both sides
Horsley. Lines: GILBERT, CARTER, top Gum Mountain, JONATHAN
CRAWFORD, the road, HARRIS. Part of tract bought by CALEB RALLS
from PHILIP THURMOND. Description given to P. P. THORNTON, Commissioner
of Revenue, this December. Witnesses: WILLIAM JOPLING, NELSON
CRAWFORD, PETER P. THORNTON, THOMAS LAINE.

486. 7 March 1818. BENJAMIN HIGGINBOTHAM, Amherst County, to
    STERLING CLAIBORNE, Amherst County...$500 for between 280 and
300 acres and adjacent tracts. Lines: BENJAMIN TALIAFERRO, CHARLES
BURKS, JONATHAN COOPER, HENRY HARTLESS, Pedlar.

486. 13 February 1818. GEORGE MC DANIEL, SR., Amherst County, to
    AMBROSE RUCKER, Amherst County...$15,001 1350 acres southeast
Tobacco Row and headwaters Miller and Graham Creeks; includes where
I live. Lines: Top of them Mountain leading to Indian Grave Gap,
MARTIN PARKS, grantee's tract bought from ARTHUR L. DAVIES, SAMUEL
BURKS, DABNEY WARE, the road, two springs, RICHARD SHELTON, PHILIP
BURTON, deceased--former tract, the field, AMBROSE RUCKER, deceased--
former tract, CHARLES ELLIS, DAVID BURKS. Witnesses: DABNEY WARE,
JONATHAN M..EDWARDS, THOMAS EUBANK, SAMUEL MITCHELL, SAMUEL BURKS.
This deed is very dim, hard to decipher some of it.

488. 10 August 1817. JONATHAN BURKS and wife, ELIZABETH, Rockbridge,
    to JAMES WARE, Amherst County...$570 95 acres. Lines: ELIZABETH
HENLEY. Witnesses: JONATHAN P. BURKS, WILLIAM H. MC CULLOCH, JAMES
DAVIES.

489. 1 March 1818. JAMES F. TALIAFERRO, Amherst County, to CLIFTON
    HARRIS, Amherst County ..$200 100 acres south side Blue Ridge.
Lines: HENRY HARTLESS. To CLIFTON HARRIS, 27 February 1819.

490. 1 September 1817. WILLIAM CABELL and wife, ANNE, Nelson
    County, to their son, WILLIAM J. CABELL, Nelson County...love--
674 acres Higginbotham Mill Creek. Part of a tract. Lines:
JONATHAN HIGGINBOTHAM, WILLIAM ARMISTEAD, JAMES HIGGINBOTHAM, DAVID S.
GARLAND, PEYTON KEITH, grantor. Witnesses: JAMES S. (L) PENDLETON,
JAMES MURPHY, DAVID S. GARLAND, THOMAS S. MC CLELLAND. To WILLIAM J.
CABELL, 20 July 1818.

491. 16 March 1818. WILLIAM WOODROOF and wife, BETSY, Amherst
    County, to BENJAMIN R. DAWSON, Amherst County...$1185 79 acres
Rutledge on east and joining Lynch road. Lines: JESSE WOODROOF,
THOMAS CREWS. To BENJAMIN R. DAWSON, 19 April 1819.

491. 6 March 1818. LUCY SLEDD, Amherst County, to RICHARD L. ELLIS,
     Amherst County...$200 53 acres Maple Creek, a border of
James. Tract devised to me by late father, JONATHAN HOGG. Witnesses:
THOMAS N. EUBANK, JOSHUA S. ELLIS, SEATON SLEDD, JAMES WARE, ROBERT N.
EUBANK, ROBERT MILLNER, W. P. SANDERSON. To RICHARD L. ELLIS, 17 March
1819.

492. 9 January 1818. ELIJAH MAYS and wife, ELIZABETH, Nelson County,
     to LANDON C. RIVES, Lynchburg...$2985 199 acres Juniper Creek.
Lines: JOSEPH MAYS, DAMERON, BOWLING. Witnesses: JONATHAN M.
HOLLANDSWORTH, JOSEPH MAYS, DANDRIDGE CLASBY. Page 493 order to
Nelson Justices of the Peace as to ELIZABETH; done by ROBERT J.
KINCAID and S. MATHEWS, 16 January 1818.

494. 8 May 1817. RICE and SALY KEY, North Carolina, to RICHARD L.
     ELLIS, Amherst County...L50 50 acres south borders Cedar.
Lines: GEORGE GILLESPIE, THOMAS MORRIS. Descendant to me from late
JONATHAN HOGG as one of legatees. To RICHARD L. ELLIS, 17 May 1819.
Witnesses: JAMES WARE, JONATHAN ELLIS, MANSFIELD WARE, PETER RUCKER,
JOSHUA L. ELLIS, ROBERT E. EUBANK, ROSEMARY GUE. Page 495 order to
quiz SALLY KEY; done by JONATHAN ELLIS and JAMES WARE, Amherst County
Justices of the Peace, 28 November 1817.

496. 6 March 1818. ZED. SHOEMAKER, Amherst County, to RICHARD L.
     ELLIS, Amherst County...$200 44 acres Maple Creek, branch of
James. Descended to me from JONATHAN HOGG, deceased. Witnesses:
PETER P. THORNTON, THOMAS N. EUBANK, W. P. SANDERSON, ROBERT N.
EUBANK, ROBERT MILLNER, JOSHUA L. ELLIS, JAMES WARE. To RICHARD L.
ELLIS, 17 May 1819.

497. 13 September 1817. THOMAS WIATT, acting executor of JONATHAN
     MILLER, to ROBERT MORRIS...under will--$8085 108 acres east
side Main road from Lynchburg to ACH; part of a tract. Lines:
CHARLES HOYLE--near his gate, JOHNSON, PHILIP JOHNSON, old field, main
road, HOYLE's road. Witnesses: W. ROBINSON, HENRY CLARK, WILLIAM
BURD. To C. DABNEY, 22 March 1820. WILLIAM BURD and JONATHAN
SCHOOLFIELD, Lynchburg Justices of the Peace as to THOMAS WIATT,
14 March 1818. Recorded Amherst County: 16 March 1818.

498. 14 February 1818. THOMAS WIATT as above to CHISWELL DABNEY...
     $2220 37 acres. Lines: Main road from Lynchburg to New Glasgow--
short distance below WIATT's dwelling house; alley. To CHISWELL
DABNEY, 24 April 1823. Lynchburg Justices of the Peace as above.

499. 22 December 1817. Order to Amherst County Justices of the
     Peace: REUBEN COX and wife, PATSY, 16 August 1817, to ALEXANDER
TINSLEY...201 acres. Done by REUBEN NORVELL and CHARLES P. TALIAFERRO;
no date. Recorded 20 April 1818. To ALEXANDER TINSLEY, 18 March 1819.

500. 21 January 1818. RICHARD SMITH, Amherst County, to GABRIEL
     PAGE, Amherst County...$204 34 acres Stonehouse Creek--part of
tract. Lines: the road, WILLIAM TUCKER, WILLIAMSON, deceased,
grantee. To GABRIEL H. PAGE, 7 April 1857.

501. 2 March 1818. EDWARD GOODRICH and wife, SALLY, Amherst County,
     to JONATHAN HAAS, Campbell County...$150 3½ acres Horsley Creek.
Part of tract bought by EDMOND GOODRICH. Lines: JOSIAH ELLIS,
JAMES WARE. Witnesses: R. N. EUBANK, JAMES WARE, NATHANIEL D. BURKS.
To JONATHAN HAAS, 20 September 1820.

502. 11 November 1817. PLEASANT DAWSON and wife, JEMIMA, Amherst
     County, to AMBROSE BURFORD, Amherst County...$600 55 acres
Harris Creek. Lines: grantee, JOSEPH MC CRAY, REUBEN COX. Witnesses:
LEWIS BURFORD, NELSON C. DAWSON, SPENCER NORVELL, SAMUEL BURKS.
19 March 1818, JEMIMA relinquished dower. NELSON C. DAWSON and
AMBROSE RUCKER, Amherst County Justices of the Peace.

503.   2 September 1817. ANTHONY NICELY, Amherst County, to ANDERSON
       WARE, Amherst County...$300 100 acres Peg's Creek. Lines:
JONATHAN BYAS, JONATHAN HOGG's heirs, ALLISON MORRIS, ANDERSON WARE.
Witnesses: JAMES WARE, PETER RUCKER, SAMUEL TULEY, R. N. EUBANK.

504.   23 August 1817. ANSELM CLARKSON, Franklin County, to JONATHAN
       EUBANK, Amherst County...Deed of Trust; debt to PHILIP THURMOND
and he is bondsman to GARLAND and TALIAFERRO. $1.00 slave; also
interest in my father's estate by will--JONATHAN CLARKSON, father.
Witnesses: WILLIAM H. CAMDEN, DAVID CLARKSON, WILLIAM COLEMAN,
JOSEPH MILSTRED--he is scratched.

505.   21 October 1817. JABEZ CAMDEN to JAMES S. PENDLETON and PEACHY
       FRANKLIN...Deed of Trust; debt to S. CLAIBORNE--$1.00 500 acres.
Lines: MICAJAH CAMDEN, CORNELIUS STINNETT. Tract was bought from
THOMAS LUMKIN, HENRY CAMDEN et al., also three named slaves--boys,
five women. Witnesses: WILLIAM ARMISTEAD, JONATHAN S. BLAIR,
ROBERT HIGGINBOTHAM. To S. CLAIBORNE, 23 March 1820.

507.   15 April 1818. DABNEY WARE and wife, ELIZABETH, Amherst
       County, to JONATHAN L. WINGFIELD, Amherst County...$1250 where
DABNEY WARE lives--Grayham Creek. 282 acres. Lines: RICHARD SHELTON,
SAMUEL BURKS, AMBROSE RUCKER, EDWARDS. Witnesses: R. L. ELLIS,
AMBROSE RUCKER, JAMES DAVIS.

507.   30 March 1818. JAMES S. WALKER, Amherst County, to BENJAMIN
       BROWN, Amherst County...$1.00; Deed of Trust; debt to THOMAS
CREWS. No acres. Lines: Lynch road, JAMES POWELL, north fork
Rutledge, CREWS' old line, WILLIAM OLIVER, grantee, THOMAS CREWS.
To THOMAS CREWS, 25 May 1819.

508.   29 January 1818. WIATT SMITH, Amherst County, to JONATHAN
       EUBANK, Amherst County...Deed of Trust; debt to PHILIP THURMOND
and JOSEPH MILSTRED as bondsman to CHARLES L. BARRET; $1.00; beds,
stock, crops on tract where I live. Witnesses: HENRY H. EVANS,
HARDEN HAYNES. To PHILIP THURMOND, 19 March 1819.

509.   27 October 1817. WILLIAM P. MUSE and wife, NANCY, Amherst
       County, to CHARLES WINGFIELD, Amherst County...Deed of Trust;
debt to MILLNER COX, $1.00, 40 acres whereon MUSE lives. Lines:
GEORGE W. TAILOR, DANIEL NORCUTT, WILLIAM MUSE, SR., JONATHAN MEHONE,
MILLNER COX. Three acres occupied by JEREMIAH COATS on Lynch road.
Lines: GEORGE W. TAILOR, MICAJAH CLARK, DANIEL NORCUTT. Witnesses:
REUBEN NORVELL, ABSALOM RUCKER, THOMAS NEIGHBORS, ARCHIBALD COX.
To CHARLES WINGFIELD, 15 June 1818.

511.   19 November 1817. JONATHAN MONROE, Amherst County, to DAVID S.
       GARLAND, Amherst County...ANDREW MONROE, late of Amherst County,
by will of 10 April 1808, devised to his brother, JONATHAN MONROE
of this instrument--one woman slave and to remain in possession of
SARAH MONROE, widow of testator for life--slave, MINNE, has issue,
MARIAH, since then--about eight or nine and in possession of SARAH.
$150 paid by GARLAND for MARIAH and to be delivered at death of
SARAH MONROE. Witnesses: THOMAS PENN, CORNELIUS POWELL, ROBERT
TINSLEY.

512.   24 March 1818. JONATHAN HAYTHE and wife, SUSAN, Campbell
       County, to JONATHAN LONDON, Amherst County...$4000 338½ acres
Porrage. Tract bought by JONATHAN HAYTHE from LONDON. MATTHEW
BROWN and WILLIAM BURD, Lynchburg Justices of the Peace as to SUSAN,
25 March 1818.

513. 10 April 1818. HENRY CAMDEN, Amherst County, to WILLIAM H.
      CAMDEN, SALLY W. DUNCAN, wife of WESTLEY DUNCAN, MARY C. CAMDEN,
and HENRY L. W. CAMDEN...love of HENRY for them as his children--and
$1.00 260 acres where HENRY lives and bought from JABEZ CAMDEN. Also
170 acres known as Rowsey tract; 580 acres in Greensville County;
327 acres adjacent 170 acres; also 307 acres; also 55½ acres in Green
County, Kentucky on Parish Creek; branch of Green; also slaves and
other property. Witnesses: BENJAMIN NORVELL, REUBEN T. NEVIL,
JOSEPH C. LEE. To WILLIAM H. CAMDEN, 15 May 1819.

515. 23 May 1818. SAMUEL BYERS to SAMUEL SIMMONS...Deed of Trust;
      debt to JONATHAN MYRERS and Company; all of Amherst County
$1.00 slave girl, LURANCE.

515. 15 April 1818. JONATHAN HAYTH and wife, SUSAN, Lynchburg, to
      CORNELIUS D. PIERCE, Amherst County...$1200 two tracts.
1. Adjacent town of Madison and southwest of JONATHAN HAY--lot 43
on first alley to lot occupied by GEDIAN SHAW, JONATHAN HAYTH--1 acre.
2. Two lots in town of Madison--43 and 44--one acre. Lines:
junction of second street andfirst alley; Clark Street. JONATHAN
SCHOOLFIELD and WILLIAM MORGAN, Lynchburg Justices of the Peace as
to SUSAN, 5 May 1818.

517. 12 March 1818. ARCHIBALD ROWSEY, Amherst County, to ROBERT
      WHITE, Rockbridge...$200 269 acres Brown Mountain Creek.
Lines: HUGH CAMPBELL, HENRY CAMDEN, WILLIAM GALT, WILLIAM TOMLINSON.

518. 20 October 1817. JOSEPH HIGGINBOTHAM, Amherst County, to
      BENJAMIN SANDIDGE, Amherst County...no amount; 14½ acres south
side Buffaloe. Lines: the road. Witnesses: CHARLES L. BARRET,
WILLIAM COLENA, WILLIAM DEMPSEY, DAVID CLARKSON, WILLIAM COLEMAN.

519. 15 June 1818. RICHARD HARRISON and wife, SOPHIA, Amherst
      County, to DAVID S. GARLAND, Amherst County...$1700 152 acres
south side Buffaloe and north side Rutledge. It was tract of
SEATON M. PENN, late of Amherst County, and descends to heirs who
are wards of RICHARD HARRISON and wife, late PENN. SEATON bought it
from BENJAMIN PHILLIPS, deceased. Lines: grantee, JAMES FRANKLIN,
deceased, CHARLES HIGGINBOTHA, deceased, PHILLIPS, BENJAMIN PHILLIPS'
tract bought from ROBERT HOLLOWAY, deceased, mouth of a branch.

521. 15 June 1818. DAVID S. GARLAND and wife, JANE, Amherst County,
      to RICHARD HARRISON, Amherst County...$500 500 acres Rocky Run
and Lime Kiln and Christian Mill Creek. Tract patent to ELIZABETH
LONG, late CALLAWAY, and administratrix and devisee of JAMES CALLAWAY,
deceased, and by JAMES CALLAWAY conveyed to WILLIAM LONG and by LONG
to BARTLETT STEEL and by STEEL to GARLAND. Lines: ROBERT MARRS,
JONATHAN SWANSON, JONATHAN CHRISTIAN, JONATHAN A. JOHNS. To WILLIAM
GILBERT for RICHARD HARRISON, 5 May 1821.

522. 22 December 1817. JONATHAN LOVING, son of CHRISTOPHER LOVING,
      to STERLING CLAIBORNE and HILL CARTER...Deed of Trust; debt to
ROSE and THOMPSON--wagon, horse bought from JONATHAN WRIGHT. LOVING
uses wagon and team in their services. Witnesses: SEYMOUR POELL
(sic), GEORGE B. NICHOLSON, JONATHAN CHRISTIAN. To JONATHAN THOMPSON,
23 May 1818.

523. 6 April 1818. SAMUEL COLEMAN, Amherst County, to BLANFORD
      HICKS and DAVID S. GARLAND...Deed of Trust; debt to JAMES P.
GARLAND, Nelson County, WINSTON COLEMAN also owes JAMES P. GARLAND--
$1.00 98 acres Harris Creek. Lines: WILLIAM PETERS, deceased,
ZACH ISBELL. Also slaves and furniture and interest in estate of
JONATHAN COLEMAN; also interest in estate of his mother, ELIZABETH
COLEMAN, at her death. To JAMES P. GARLAND, 19 June 1820.

524. 19 March 1817. REUBEN NORVELL and wife, POLLY, Amherst County,
      to ROBERT MORRIS, Lynchburg...$100 three acres north side and
joining Fluvanna. Lines: grantee, BOLLING. POLLY relinquished dower,
1817. NELSON C. DAWSON and AMBROSE RUCKER, Amherst County Justices of
the Peace.

140

526. 28 May 1818. Order to Amherst County Justices of the Peace:
SAMUEL SALE and wife, CLARISA, JONATHAN V. GOODRICH and wife,
NANCY, WILEY CAMPBELL and wife, ELIZABETH, ALEXANDER SALE and wife,
--, JONATHAN JONES and wife, --, 15 July 1816, to THOMAS and CORNELIUS
SALE...600 acres. ELIZABETH CAMPBELL relinquished dower, 1 June 1818;
REUBEN NORVELL and WILLIAM JOPLING.

527. 13 September 1817. ROBERT MORRIS, executor of JONATHAN MILLER,
to WILLIAM ROBINSON and CHISWELL DABNEY...debt to THOMAS WIATT,
executor of JONATHAN MILLER; $1.00 108 acres east side of road from
Lynchburg to Amherst County and bought this day from WIATT. I feel
that the statement as to MORRIS as executor of MILLER is error.
WIATT was executor. Witnesses: WILLIAM BURD, JONATHAN SCHOOLFIELD,
HENRY CLARK.

528. 20 October 1817. ELIZABETH DOUGLAS, formerly TERRELL, EDWARD
LYNCH and wife, MARY, formerly TERRELL, Lynchburg, CHARLES L.
TERRELL, Campbell County...heirs of MICAJAH TERRELL, deceased, to
JONATHAN LYNCH, JR., Lynchburg. MICAJAH, SR., sold to MICAJAH TERRELL,
JR. in life Amherst County tract on Bolling, but no deed was made.
JR. brought Chancery suit in Amherst County versus SR.'s heirs as he
has sold tract to JONATHAN LYNCH, JR. $1.00--both sides Bolling
Creek. 340 acres and formerly tract of MICAJAH, SR. Lines: Bolling,
MORRIS, a road, ROBINSON, WARWICK. Witnesses: WILLIAM C. DOBSON,
MARGARET FOX, ANSELM LYNCH. Acknowledged by CHARLES TERRELL in
Campbell County. BENJAMIN HADEN and SANSELM LYNCH, Justices of the
Peace, 20 December 1817. Acknowledged in Lynchburg by EDWARD LYNCH
and wife, MARY, and ELIZABETH DOUGLAS, 2 June 1818. DAVID HOFFMAN
and L. J. HARRISON, Justices of the Peace.

531. 16 June 1818. JONATHAN GOODWIN, Amherst County, administrator
of MICAJAH B. GOOWIN, late soldier in United States Army and
Fifth Regiment of Infantry...power of attorney to HONORABLE HUGH
NELSON, Esq., to collect from United States for all heirs. Witnesses:
DAVID S. GARLAND.

531. 1 June 1818. LYNE S. TALIAFERRO and wife, MILDRED, Amherst
County, to CLIFTON HARRIS, Albemarle...$1300 226½ acres
Franklin Creek on both sides Gill Creek. Lines: FLETCHER N.
TALIAFERRO. To LYNE S. TALIAFERRO, 28 July 1818.

532. 19 March 1818. ELIZABETH and EPHY GOOLSBY, Amherst County, to
JACOB SMITH and JAMES F. TALIAFERRO, Amherst County...Deed of
Trust; debt to JAMES W. SMITH and LYNE S. TALIAFERRO; $1.00 73 acres.
Lines: BARTLETT CASH, POLLY GOOLSBY. Witnesses: JAMES CAMDEN,
FLEMING EDMUNDS, JONATHAN GOOLSBY, JONATHAN SMITH. To LYNE S.
TALIAFERRO, 28 July 1818.

533. 6 May 1818. JONATHAN LONDON and wife, TIRZA, Amherst County,
to DAVID STAPLES, Amherst County...$402 201 acres south borders
Porrage. Lines: WILLIAM GALT, THOMAS JEWELL, WILLIAM TURNER.

534. 28 June 1818. FREDERICK PRICE and wife, MARY ANN, Amherst
County, to WILLIAM COLEMAN, Amherst County...$3000 Pedlar.
1. Tract to FREDERICK PRICE from CHARLES L. BARRET. 2. Tract
bought by FREDERICK PRICE and BARRET from JOSEPH MAGANN. 3. Tract
of MOSES HALL whereon mills and Tilt hammer shop stand. Reference
to deed from MOSES HALL to BARRET and PRICE and tract bought by them
from his heirs. Witnesses: WILLIAM SHOEMAKER, NATHANIEL MORRIS,
ORMUND WARE.

535. 22 November 1817. JOSHUA RUCKER and wife, EMELA, Bedford, to
RICHARD HARRISON, Amherst County...$2225 111¼ acres north
borders Harris Creek. Lines: RICHARD POWELL, grantee, HARRISON
GENTRY, ANTHONY RUCKER, JAMES HIL. Signed EMILY. Witnesses:
BENJAMIN RUCKER, JAMES PETIT, JONATHAN H. SMITH.

536. 25 June 1818. WILLIAM WOODROOF and wife, ELIZABETH, Amherst
County, to WILLIAM LEE, Amherst County...$2940 127½ acres
patent of tract formerly that of DAVID WOODROOF, SR. Lines: the
road, Lynch road. Witnesses: RICHARD HARRISON, WILLIAM KNIGHT, JR.,
JAMES WOODROOF, DAVID GLASS, RICHARD WILTSHIRE. To WILLIAM LEE,
14 May 1821.

537. -- 1817. ABRAHAM MARTIN, JR., Amherst County, to ABRAHAM MARTIN,
SR., Amherst County...$500 115 acres north Thresher Creek.
Lines: AARON HIGGINBOTHAM, ENOCH CARPENTER, ZACHARIAH TALIAFERRO.

538. 20 July 1818. JACOB PIERCE, Amherst County, to PHINEAS PIERCE,
Amherst County...$1.00 200 acres. Part of tract of REUBEN COLEMAN
and bought from him in two tracts 6 August 1811--to include dwelling
house. Witnesses: WILLIAM ARMISTEAD, DABNEY HILL, THOMAS L. (?)
HILL.

539. 19 March 1818. ELIZABETH and EPHY GOOLSBY, Amherst County, to
JAMES W. SMITH and LYNE S. TALIAFERRO, Amherst County...$100
20 acres. Lines: BARTLETT CASH, JAMES W. SMITH. Witnesses: JAMES
CAMDEN, FLEMING EDMUNDS, JONATHAN GOOLSBY, JONATHAN SMITH, JR.

540. 17 January 1818. EPHEY and ELIZABETH GOOLSBY, Amherst County,
to JAMES W. SMITH...sometime ago ELIZABETH conveyed by Deed
of Trust to her mother, EPHY, a tract for life. JAMES W. SMITH has
bought portion of it and has paid both a valid consideration: $125
25 acres by recent survey by JAMES CAMDEN. Lines: grantee.

541. 4 August 1818. WESTLEY L. DUNCAN, Amherst County, to JAMES
WOOD, Amherst County...$150 66 acres south border Buffaloe.
Lines: SPICEY DUNCAN, SARAH DUNCAN, widow of JONATHAN DUNCAN,
JAMES WOOD, PATSY DUNCAN.

542. 20 July 1818. JAMES SHIELDS and wife, ELIZABETH, late
HIGGINBOTHAM, Nelson County, WASHINGTON HILL and wife, SALLY,
late HIGGINBOTHAM, Rockbridge County, AARON HIGGINBOTHAM and wife,
ELIZABETH, Amherst County, and LINDSEY SANDIDGE and wife, CLARY G.,
late HIGGINBOTHAM, Amherst County, to ABSALOM HIGGINBOTHAM, Amherst
County...grantors are heirs of AARON HIGGINBOTHAM, The Elder, -- his
widow, NANCY bought lands after his death. AARON HIGGINBOTHAM, JR.,
and wife, ELIZABETH, are entitled to one seventh by purchase from
JAMES HICKS and wife, NANCY, late HIGGINBOTHAM, and heir of AARON
HIGGINBOTHAM, SR. Tract in possession of NANCY, widow, for life--
$2500 for our interests. Witnesses: CORNELIUS SALE, ENOCH CARPENTER,
EATON CARPENTER. To AARON HIGGINBOTHAM, 18 August 1818.

544. 23 April 1818. TINSLEY RUCKER and wife, NANCY, Bedford, to
REUBEN NORVELL, Amherst County...$5800 327 3/4 acres Harris
Creek, where PLEASANT DAWSON lives. Lines: AMBROSE BURFORD,
HARRISON HUGHES, REUBEN COX, RODNEY TALIAFERRO, WILLIAM HUGHES,
deceased. Witnesses: ROBERT P. RICHARDSON, GEORGE WHITLOCKE, THOMAS A.
OLIVER. Certified in Bedford by SAMUEL HANCOCK and LAWRENCE MC GEORGE,
30 April 1818.

546. 20 July 1818. CHARLES L. BARRET and wife, SARAH, ABSALOM
HIGGINBOTHAM and wife, POLLY, to JACK CARTER...L450 Buffaloe.
1. 129½ acres. Lines: ISAAC MAYFIELD, JONATHAN HIGGINBOTHAM.
2. Lines: PULLIAM SANDIDGE, JONATHAN HIGGINBOTHAM, BENJAMIN
SANDIDGE, PHILLIPS. 3. Lines: north bank of southfork Buffaloe.
Lines: JOSEPH HIGGINBOTHAM, JR., PULLIAM SANDIDGE--all join. No
acres on some. To CHARLES L. BARRET, August, 1818.

547. 26 June 1818. SAMUEL HOGG and wife, DELPHIA, to RICHARD L.
ELLIS, Amherst County...$150 46 acres Maple Creek. Descended to
SAMUEL from father, JONATHAN HOGG, deceased, lot seven. Witnesses:
JONATHAN ELLIS, SEATON SLEDD, FLEMING H. DUNCAN, JAMES WARE, R. N.
EUBANK, ANDERSON WARE. Order to quiz DELANEY, 27 June 1818; done by
JONATHAN ELLIS and JAMES WARE, same date. To RICHARD L. ELLIS,
17 May 1819.

550. 1 May 1818. JESSE JOPLING and JAMES MURPHY, Nelson County
     Justices of the Peace as to POLLY HARDING, wife of EDWARD
HARDING...deed of 30 October 1800 to JONATHAN HARDING.

550. 12 December 1817. JONATHAN HUDSON and wife, MARY, Amherst
     County, to JONATHAN TUCKER, Amherst County...$196 499 acres.
Lines: grantor, GEORGE HUDSON. Witnesses: PHILIP THURMOND, JR.,
T. COPPEDGE, JR. and SR. THOMAS GEORGE W. HUDSON. To D. HILL,
4 June 1820.

551. 17 April 1817. JONATHAN LYNCH and wife, MARY, Lynchburg, to
     WILLIAM I. ISBELL, Amherst County...$131.25 3 3/4 acres.
Lines: JONATHAN TAYLOR (OE?), JOHNSON, Main Street in town of
Madison, a branch. Witnesses: JONATHAN D. URQUHART, JONATHAN N.
ROSE, JAMES BENAGH, JONATHAN H. SMITH. To WILLIAM I. ISBELL,
22 August 1856.

553. 20 July 1818. JACOB PIERCE, Amherst County, to JONA PIERCE,
     Amherst County...$1.00 158 acres south side Buffaloe. To
JONA PIERCE, 22 August 1835.

553. 17 January 1818. CHARLES H. CHRISTIAN and wife, JANE, Amherst
     County, and WALTER D. CHRISTIAN, Amherst County, to WILLIAM
SIMMONS, Amherst County...$1000 55 acres. Lines: Bridie on road,
JONATHAN H. SMITH.

554. 26 December 1816. WILLIAM HALL to JOSEPH SEAY...$45.50 50 acres
     north borders Pedlar. Lines: JAMES FRAZER, deceased, WALTER
FRAZER, JOSEPH HIGGINBOTHAM, MARTIN and ZACH TUNKETT (?). Witnesses:
STERLING CLAIBORNE, WILLIAM H. ROSE, JONATHAN EUBANK, JR.

555. 16 April 1817. JONATHAN RICHESON and wife, NANCY, to JOSEPH
     HIGGINBOTHAM...$1.00 201 acres Buffaloe and south side. Lines:
road from Buffaloe Springs to house on Buffaloe lately occupied by
CHARLES P. TALIAFERRO, WILMER's branch, path or road. JONATHAN
RICHESON is not responsible--if deficient in quantity. Witnesses:
LINDSAY SANDIDGE, STERLING CLAIBORNE, DAVID CLARKSON, BENJAMIN
HIGGINBOTHAM.

557. 17 August 1818. JONATHAN LONDON and wife, TIRZA, Amherst
     County, to GEORGE STAPLES, Amherst County...$3700 338½ acres
both sides Porrage. Lines: JAMES DILLARD, THOMAS JEWELL, HENRY
TURNER, JAMES LONDON, ROBERT GRANT, top of a ridge.

558. 17 June 1818. JOSEPH MAYS and wife, JANE, Amherst County, to
     JONATHAN MERRITT, JR., Amherst County...$1340.00 134 acres
headborders Juniper Creek. Lines: JONATHAN BONDS, deceased,
ELIJAH MAYS, JAMES BOLING, REUBEN NORVELL and THOMAS CREWS, Amherst
County Justices of the Peace, as to JANE, 20 June 1818.

560. 12 September 1818. MICAJAH CAMDEN and wife, POLLY, Amherst
     County, to SAMUEL HEISKELL, Amherst County...$380 3 1/5 acres
near courthouse. Lines: the branch. To MICAJAH CAMDEN, 19 January
1819. To SAMUEL HEISKELL, 1 April 1819.

561. 21 September 1818. MARK CAHOON and wife, SARAH, WILLIAM CAHOON
     and wife, DEBORAH, Amherst County, to LINDSEY TINSLEY, Amherst
County...$400 120 acres south side Pedlar. Lines: HENRY CHILDRESS,
top of Blue Ridge. Witnesses: WILLIAM TOMLINSON.

561. 4 September 1818. MITCHELL FLOYD and wife, POLLY, late GOOLSBY,
     Amherst County, to LYNE S. TALIAFERRO, Amherst County...$200
60 acres. Lines: the orchard, joint property of grantors, the road,
GABRIEL PAGE, BEVERLY WILLIAMSON, deceased, grantee. Witnesses:
JONATHAN SMITH, SR., JONATHAN SMITH, JR., EZEKIEL GILBERT, JAMES W.
SMITH. To LYNE S. TALIAFERRO, 26 January 1819.

562. 21 September 1818. HENSLEY CARPENTER and wife, RHODA, Amherst
County, to THOMAS WILLIAMSON, Amherst County...$400 70 3/4
acres north borders Buffaloe. Lines: JAMES HIGGINBOTHAM, BALLINGER
MAYS, JOSEPH MAYS, ABSALOM HIGGINBOTHAM.

563. 12 August 1818. THOMAS N. EUBANK, Amherst County, to WALTER
WILLIAMS, Amherst County...$1.00 330 acres Johnson Branch.
Lines: JONATHAN TOOLY, TANDY TOOLY, THOMAS CUMPTON, WILLIAM HANNAH,
DAVID heirs, PHILIP THURMOND, ROWLAND BYAS. Balance of 400 acres
sold by THOMAS N. EUBANK as trustee of ARCHELAUS MITCHELL for benefit
of JONATHAN and RICHARD L. ELLIS. MITCHELL is to have lifetime on
old plantation where he lives and sufficient timber. Witnesses:
R. N. EUBANK, JAMES EUBANK, JONATHAN DAVIES, JONATHAN MITCHELL.

564. 17 August 1818. NELSON CRAWFORD and wife, LUCY, Amherst County,
to THOMAS ALDRIDGE, Amherst County...$740 Piney. 1. 98 acres
on north fork Piney. 2. 50 acres south fork Piney. Lines: JONATHAN
MONROE (?). To THOMAS ALDRIDGE, 5 June 1820.

565. 29 April 1818. THOMAS ALDRIDGE and wife, CATHERINE, Amherst
County, to JAMES S. PENDLETON, Amherst County...$8000 750 acres
Buffaloe. Lines: DAVID S. GARLAND, EDMOND PENN, JAMES MEREDITH.
Tract bought by THOMAS ALDRIDGE from JONATHAN CAMM and JONATHAN
WARWICK. 1 May 1818 JONATHAN COLEMAN and EDMOND PENN, Amherst County
Justices of the Peace, as to CATHERINE.

566. 26 May 1818. PROSSER POWELL, JAMES LEE, RICHARD POWELL, executors
of RICHARD POWELL, deceased, Amherst County, to RICHARD SHELTON,
SR., Amherst County...under will to SHELTON--L1963-10 385 acres
Graham Creek--except graveyard of one acre. Lines: grantee, DABNEY
WARE, SAMUEL BURKS, JONATHAN CAMM. Witnesses: NELSON C. DAWSON,
JAMES BENNETT, GABRIEL GOSNEY, HENRY GOSNEY. I do not take it that
SHELTON is legatee, but they sell under authority from will.

568. 12 August 1818. THOMAS N. EUBANK, Amherst County, to JONATHAN
TOOLY, Amherst County...$1.00 58 acres on Johnson Branch.
Lines: TANDY TOOLY. Part of tract sold by THOMAS N. EUBANK as
trustee of ARCHELAUS MITCHELL to WILLIAM ROACH and deed is made at
request of WILLIAM ROACH. Witnesses: R. N. EUBANK, JAMES EUBANK,
JONATHAN DAVIES, JONATHAN MITCHELL.

569. 12 August 1818. THOMAS N. EUBANK, Amherst County, to TANDY
TOOLY, Amherst County...$100 50 acres--data as in previous
deed and joins WALTER WILLIAMS. Witnesses: as above.

570. 24 November 1817. THOMAS N. EUBANK, Amherst County, to LARKIN
BYAS. EUBANK is joined by wife, JANE...$1600 on Rocky Row
Mountain on Creek of same name. No acres. Patent 1 September 1782.
Witnesses: R. N. EUBANK, JONATHAN ELLIS, R. H. BURKS, RICHARD L.
ELLIS, FLEMING H. DUNCAN, WILLIAM DAVIES. To THOMAS N. EUBANK,
19 November 1818.

571. 21 September 1818. MITCHELL FLOYD and wife, POLLY, late
GOOLSBY, Amherst County, to LYNE S. TALIAFERRO, Amherst County...
$400 60 acres. Lines: GABRIEL PAGE, grantee. Witnesses: JAMES F.
TALIAFERRO, JONATHAN DAVIES, ORMUND WARE.

572. 21 September 1818. ALEXANDER SALE and wife, SARAH C., Amherst
County, to GABRIEL PAGE, Amherst County...$800 one third
undivided interest in late BEVERLY WILLIAMSON's tract on Stonehouse--
reference to Amherst County will--to six children. This third belonged
to JONATHAN WILLIAMSON and THOMAS APPLING and wife, POLLY, and conveyed
by them two deeds to sale in 1815 and 1817.

573. 6 April 1818. PLEASANT DAWSON and wife, JEMIMA, Amherst County,
    to TINSLEY RUCKER, Bedford County...$5713 327 3/4 acres Harris
Creek. Lines: AMBROSE BURFORD, grantor, REUBEN COX, RODNEY TALIAFERRO,
WILLIAM HUGHES, the road. Witnesses: REUBEN NORVELL, SAMUEL BURKS,
GEORGE H. BURFORD, AMBROSE RUCKER. Amherst County Justices of the
Peace: JAMES WARE and AMBROSE RUCKER, 21 April 1818, as to JEMIMA.

575. 6 April 1818. TINSLEY RUCKER and wife, NANCY, Bedford County,
    to PLEASANT DAWSON, Amherst County...$4450 222½ acres east
side and joining Lynch Road. Lines: BENJAMIN RUCKER, BOLLING
CLARKE, ELIAS WILLS, JAMES BOLLING, THOMAS MURRELL. Witnesses: as
above.

576. 18 March 1818. WILLIAM LONG and wife, BETSY, to JONATHAN M.
    and JONATHAN EUBANK, JR...$1040 228 acres. Lines: Henley
Creek, HARTLESS, HOWARD, NELSON CRAWFORD. Witnesses: J. MYERS,
PETER P. THORNTON THOMAS ALDRIDGE. To B. A. CRAWFORD, 1819.

577. 27 January 1818. HENRY CAMDEN and wife, LUCY, Amherst County,
    to DAVID S. GARLAND, Amherst County...$4400 899 acres south
fork Pedlar and Nicholson Run. 899 acres granted to DAVID MOORE;
also 102 acres granted to ANGUS MC DANIEL; 240 acres to same; 250
acres granted to ARTHUR TOOLY; 46 acres granted to WILLIAM TAYLOR;
144 acres granted to JACOB PHILLIPS. Lines: HENRY LAINE, grantor,
CARTWRIGHT, JOSEPH HIGGINBOTHAM, LUCK, WILLIAM HALL, HUGH CAMPBELL,
WILLIAM WILSON, JONATHAN D. CRAWFORD, GARLAND, HALL. To DAVID S.
GARLAND, 1 July 1819. Witnesses: ROBERT TINSLEY, W. L. DUNCAN,
WILLIAM H. CAMDEN.

579. 19 September 1818. JONATHAN F. HALL and wife, ELIZABETH,
    Amherst County, to CHARLES L. BARRET, Amherst County...$105
seven acres. Lines: NELSON CRAWFORD near road leading up to Pedlar,
HALL's old line, THOMAS MORRIS. To CHARLES L. BARRET, 17 November 1818.

580. 6 December 1817. JONATHAN H. GOODWIN and wife, MARY,
    Pitsylvania County, to MARY BUSTER, CLAUDIUS BUSTER and wife,
NANCY, Kanawha County...$10.00 two tracts and part of land of late
COLONEL PHILIP JOHNSON and allot. to MARY, CLAUDIUS, and NANCY as
JOHNSON's heirs. 1. 1062 3/4 acres. Lines: ELIAS WILLS, MATTHEW
RICKETTS, FRANKEY EVANS, WILLIAM ROBINSON, STITH MEAD, CHARLES
HOYLE, JONATHAN MUNDY, and new line laid off for GOODWIN and wife,
MARY. 2. 137½ acres on Fall Creek and known as BAILEY tract.
Lines: WILLIAM TERRY, CHRISTOPHER ISBELL, SAMUEL HARRISON, STITH
MEAD. Acknowledged in Amherst County by GOODWIN before RUBEN NORVELL
and NELSON C. DAWSON, 6 December 1817, and MARY relinquished dower,
too.

581. 26 June 1818. BENJAMIN GOSNEY and wife, ELIZABETH, Pitsylvania,
    to ELIAS WILLS, Amherst County...two tracts for $2840.
1. 105½ acres--a gap is in deed--"said creek." Second tract must
have been described in missing part. WILLIAM BEAM and JOSEPH CARTER,
Pitsylvania Justices of the Peace on same date as to ELIZABETH.

582. At this point we begin a series of delinquent tax land sales
    and they continue to end of this book. They were sold under
Act of Assembly, 9 February 1814, and it was duty of sheriff to sell
when he could find no property. All were sold without descriptions as
to locations by RICHARD HARRISON, deputy for C. TALIAFERRO, Sheriff,
in 1816. JOEL STINNETT--100 acres; taxes for 1792, 1794, 1801.
WILLIAM DAVIS bought for $5.47 and on 19 December 1816, HARRISON made
deed to DAVIS. This form prevails in data and there is no need to
repeat it each time. Amounts refer to taxes due.

583. WILLIAM SMITH--delinquent on 213 acres for 1790. EDMOND T.
    COLEMAN paid $2.06.

584. WILLIAM MEHONE--delinquent on 240 acres for 1790. EDMOND T.
    COLEMAN paid $3.41.

585. JOHN PARSONA and later JONATHAN PAXTON--no acres; $3.73 for 1813. EDMOND T. COLEMAN was the buyer.

586. RICHARD OGLESBY--90 acres for 1797; 182-(sic); 1803. EDMOND T. COLEMAN bought for $2.59.

587. MARY ALFRED--372 acres for 1793, 1794, 1795, 1799; also 174 acres. WILLIAM HILL--also HALL in one place--$6.48 paid.

588. CHALRES PATTERSON--4 acres for 1790; 171 (sic); 1796, 1807, 1809, 1810, 1811. DAVID S. GARLAND was buyer at $5.17.

589. CHARLES TYLER--355; 353; and 80 acres for 1790, 1791, 1792, 1794. DAVID S. GARLAND paid $11.39.

589. JONATHAN WILSFORD--150 and 45 acres for 1791, 1792. DAVID S. GARLAND was the buyer at $2.61.

590. JAMES ROBERTS--81 acres for 1796. DAVID S. GARLAND paid $1.61.

591. JAMES FOREST--93 acres for 1796, 1797. DAVID S. GARLAND paid $2.08.

592. JONATHAN HENDERSON's estate--660, 420, 410, 1008 acres for 1790, 1796, 1797, 1798, 1799 and 1806. DAVID S. GARLAND paid $31.24.

593. JONATHAN CARTWRIGHT--71 acres for 1789, 1790, 1795. DAVID S. GARLAND paid $2.28.

594. JESSE MULLICAN--$1.80 paid by DAVID S. GARLAND for 1811 taxes. No acres set forth.

595. JONATHAN OLD--1793, 1794, 1803, 1805, 1806, 1808. DAVID S. GARLAND was buyer, but "quantity not known."

596. THOMAS JOHNS--1811. No acres; DAVID S. GARLAND paid $2.34.

597. MATTHEW WATSON--1811. DAVID S. GARLAND paid $2.70; no acres set forth.

598. ELISHA CHRISTIAN--$1.37; no tax year and no acres. DAVID S. GARLAND was the buyer.

598. THOMAS CLASBY--101 acres; two years taxes, but no dates. JAMES P. GARLAND was buyer at $2.36.

599. HENRY and JAMES WOODS--305 acres; no years. DAVID S. GARLAND paid $2.91.

600. JAMES LACEY--1810; 20 acres. DAVID S. GARLAND paid $1.54.

601. ALEXANDER QUARRIES--1810, 1811, 1812; 180 acres. DAVID S. GARLAND paid $3.54.

602. WILLIAM WIDDEBORNE--164 acres; 1799, 1804, 1806, 1807, 1812, 1811, and 1813. DAVID S. GARLAND paid $5.87.

603. WILLIAM MARTIN (B)--sic--65 acres for 1804. DAVID S. GARLAND paid $1.88.

603. RANDOLPH HOGG--161 acres for 1813. RICHARD L. ELLIS paid $2.25.

604. HENDERSON MC CALL and Company for 1804; 300 acres. JAMES S. PENDLETON paid $2.87.

605. JAMES RICE--1819 (sic) 128 acres. JOSEPH DILLARD paid $1.60.

606. HUGH MC CABE--200 and 143 acres; 1812 and 1813. GEORGE TINSLEY paid $4.33

607. JAMES MARR (also MAIN)--400 acres for 1794. JAMES S. PENDLETON paid $2.05.

608. NICHOLAS JONES--1810, 1811, 1812; 40 acres. Two amounts are set forth for buyer, BENNET A. CRAWFORD--$1.38 and $4.83.

608. JAMES GOODRICH--1801; no acres set forth. THOMAS N. EUBANK paid $1.88.

609. JONATHAN BALLOW--1804, 1807, 1808, 1810, 1811; 284 acres. BENNET A. CRAWFORD paid $6.03.

610. WILLIAM COY--100 acres for 1794. RICHARD N. EUBANK paid $1.59.

These prices seem ridiculous in light of present day tax rates. Did someof these owners just go off into Kentucky and other points and desert these tracts? The answer lies in pursuing each one in data here in wills, but this is not being done by the compiler.

1. 6 October 1818. PETER MARTIN, Amherst County, to WILLIAM
    TOMLINSON, Amherst County...$550 102 acres Buffaloe. Lines:
grantee, ABRAM MARTIN. To WILLIAM TOMLINSON, 2 February 1820.

1. 7 October 1818. WILLIAM SIMMONS, Amherst County, to ROBERT
    WALTON, Amherst County...$1100 55 acres. Lines: Brydie, the
road.

2. 1 November 1817. ELIJAH FLETCHER and wife, MARIA ANTOINETTA,
    and ALDEN B. SPOONER and wife, ELIZABETH H., Petersburg, to
PULLIAM SANDIDGE-FLETCHER of Amherst County...grantors and wives are
daughers and heirs of W. S. CRAWFORD, late of Amherst County--Chancery
decree of Amherst County to sell tract of W. S. CRAWFORD--L2000 in
three adjacent tracts. 1. 300 acres. 2. 390 acres. 3. 236 acres--
survey of 24 April 1795--both sides Buffaloe and borders of Franklin
Creek and Davis Mountain. Lines: JAMES GOVAN, formerly ZACHARIAH
TALIAFERRO, JACOB SMITH's former line, Petersburg, 1 November 1817,
EDWARD PENNEL and ROBERT RITCHIE, Justices of the Peace or aldermen,
as to SPOONER and wife.

5. 27 August 1818. MOORMAN JOHNSON, Campbell County, to MERRIT M.
    WHITE, Amherst County...$30 four lots of half acre each in
town of Bethel--numbers 20, 21, 22, 23. Witnesses: HUGH NORVELL,
WILLIS WHITE, P. HARDWICK, JONATHAN BURFORD, AMBROSE RUCKER.

6. 4 March 1817. REUBEN NORVELL and wife, POLLY, Amherst County,
    to SAMUEL J. HARRISON, Lynchburg...$5144.25 180½ acres Falls
Creek and east side Opossum Island road and joining. Lines: STITE
MEAD, PHILIP JOHNSON, deceased, CHRISTOPHER ISBELL. Witnesses:
WILLIAM BAILEY, JAMES BULLOCK, GEORGE P. RICHARDSON, NELSON C.
DAWSON and AMBROSE RUCKER, Amherst County Justices of the Peace as
to POLLY, 14 March 1817.

7. 30 September 1818. JONATHAN RICHESON and wife, NANCY, Amherst
    County, to RICHARD MILLNER, Amherst County...$2920 365 acres
forks of Buffaloe and both sides. Part of several tracts which
JONATHAN RICHESON bought of JOSEPH HIGGINBOTHAM. Lines: BENJAMIN
SANDIDGE, JONATHAN DODD, WILLIAM LONG, AMBROSE TOMBOLING, WILLIAM
TOMBOLING, CARTER. To RICHARD MILLNER, 16 November 1818.

8. 7 April 1817. Trustees of town of Madison, Amherst County, to
    ROBERT C. WILLIAMS, Lynchburg and JONATHAN TAYLOR, Amherst
County...$1.00 two lots--24 and 25. Lines: junction of second
street and Clark, third alley. Trustees: JONATHAN WIATT, W. WARWICK,
WILLIAM PETTYJOHN, NELSON C. DAWSON, PLEASANT DAWSON, DAVID TINSLEY,
SR. Witnesses: JONATHAN H. SMITH, RICHARD TYREE, WILLIAM SNEAD,
JAMES WARWICK, EDWARD LYNCH.

9. 7 April 1817. Trustees as above to BENJAMIN PHILLIPS, Lynchburg...
    $1.00 lot 27. Lines: fourth alley, half acre. Witnesses:
as above.

10. 7 April 1817. Trustees as above to BENJAMIN PERKINS, Lynchburg...
     $1.00 two lots: 21 and 42. Lines: junction of first and Main
and first alley, PLEASANT THURMOND on third. Witnesses: as above.

11. 8 January 1818. ABRAM CARTER and ROWLAND GILLESPIE...agreement--
     ABRAM CARTER has sold to ROWLAND GILLESPIE for $450 tract on
Horsley known as Schofield place. Deed of Trust and conveyed as such
to PETER P. THORNTON. Witnesses: WILLIAM COLEMAN, HENRY BALLINGER,
BENJAMIN SALE, MADISON WARE, MOSES (?) TAYLOR, EZEKIEL GILBERT.

12. 23 September 1818. WILLIAM MARTIN and wife, SUSANNAH, Amherst
     County, to TINSLEY RUCKER, Bedford...L157 157 acres George
and Indian Creeks. Lines: JAMES DILLARD, ZACHARIAH TALIAFERRO,
WILLIAM EVINS. Witnesses: JAMES H. MARTIN, ISAAC RUCKER, ROBERT
LAWHORN. To JOSEPH DILLARD, present owner, 27 March 1845.

13. 29 November 1817. JONATHAN RICHESON is bound to PHILIP THURMOND
     for $2920 to make title to 365 acres on both sides Buffaloe.
Lines: BENJAMIN SANDIDGE, AMBROSE TOMLINSON. Witnesses: DANIEL B.
TURNER.

14. 25 April 1818. ROBERT TINSLEY, Bedford, from EDWARD TINSLEY
     and wife, LUCY, Bedford County; NICHOLAS WEST and wife,
ELIZABETH, Henry County; ANTHONY G. TINSLEY and wife, JUDITH TINSLEY;
OLIVER TINSLEY and wife, SOPHIA; RICHARD FOWLER and wife, LUCY,
Bedford County...$3900 356 acres Harris Creek. Lines: DAVID TINSLEY,
RICHARD BURKS, former tract of JONATHAN TINSLEY, deceased, is sold.
Henry County: ROBERT ALLEN and GEORGE HAIRSTON, Justices of the
Peace as to WEST and wife, ELIZABETH. Bedford Justices of the Peace:
RICHARD HOBSON and PLEASANT M. GOGGIN, Justices of the Peace as to
EDWARD TINSLEY and wife, LUCY. Bedford Justices of the Peace:
BALDA MC DANIEL and NATHANIEL J. MANSON as to SOPHIA TINSLEY, wife
of OLIVER, and LUCY FOWLER, wife of RICHARD FOWLER, 28 April 1818.

17. 26 January 1818. DANIEL NORCUTT and wife, RACHEL, Amherst
     County, to REUBEN NORVELL, Amherst County...$525 21 acres north
side of Mitchell Mill Road. Lines: HUGHES' road, WILLIAM MUSE,
the branch. Witnesses: HUGH NORVELL, WILLIAM NORCUTT, WILLIAM MUSE,
SR., WILLIAM S. MUSE.

18. 29 September 1818. THOMAS WILLIAMSON and wife, POLLY B., to
     GABRIEL PAGE, Amherst County...$414 one sixth of undivided
tract of BEVERLY WILLIAMSON, deceased, and by will to his six children
and THOMAS is one of them. Witnesses: ROBERT TINSLEY, filed in
Lynchburg in case of WILLIAMSON versus WILLIAMSON--margin. JONATHAN
WARWICK and HILL CARTER, Amherst County Justices of the Peace,
30 September 1818, as to POLLY.

20. 1 October 1818. ARTHUS B. and JONATHAN DAVIES, Amherst County,
     to RICHARD L. ELLIS, Amherst County...$4000 310 acres James
River. Lines: Bethel tract near a spring, AMBROSE RUCKER, the road,
E. DAVIES, POTATO HILL, F. A. K. DAVIES. Tract descended to JONATHAN
DAVIES from father, NICHOLAS C. DAVIES, deceased. To RICHARD L.
ELLIS, 17 May 1819.

21. 7 April 1817. Madison Trustees to FLEMING MERRITT, Lynchburg...
     $1.00 Lot 58. Lines: THOMAS B. MEHONE, JOHN MILLER, fourth
alley, half acre. Witnesses and trustees as on page 8ff.

22. 7 April 1817. Madison trustees to THOMAS ANTRIM, Lynchburg...
     $1.00 two lots 49 and 50. Lines: junction of second street,
fourth alley, BENJAMIN PERKINS. Witnesses and trustees as on page 8ff.

23. 7 April 1817. Madison trustees to THOMAS B. MEHONE, Amherst
     County...$1.00 lot 7 at junction of first or Main, JOHNSON,
fourth alley--half acre; also lot 59 with lines on third street,
southwest corner of JONATHAN MERRITT, third alley, JONATHAN MILLER--
half acre. Witnesses and trustees as on page 8ff.

25. 7 April 1817. Trustees of Madison to JORDAN CREASY, Amherst
     County...$1.00 lot 29. Junction of second street and fifth
alley, CHARLES Y. JOHNSON--half acre. Witnesses and trustees as on
page 8ff.

26.   7 April 1817.   JONATHAN LYNCH and wife, MARY, Lynchburg, to
      JONATHAN MILLER and ROBERT C. WILLIAMS, Lynchburg...$4136 48 acres
partly joining town of Madison.   Lines: DAVID and DANIEL HOFFMAN at
northeast corner of lot 55; northeast corner of 60; the branch near
Madison Warehouse "Manners".   To ELIJAH FLETCHER, 5 April 1819.
Witnesses: RICHARD TYREE, WILLIAM SNEAD, EDWARD LYNCH.

27.   7 April 1817.   Madoson trustees to PLEASANT DAWSON, Amherst
      County...$1.00 lot 17 at junction of first or main and third
alley--half acre.   Witnesses and trustees as on page 8f.

28.   1 January 1818.   SAMUEL BURKS, JR., and wife, MARY, Amherst
      County, to CHARLES M. CHRISTIAN, Amherst County...$1700 70 3/4
acres; part of tract of DRURY CHRISTIAN, deceased, of 842½ acres.
Lot No. 1.   Lines: JONATHAN CHRISTIAN, NELSON C. DAWSON and AMBROSE
RUCKER on same date as to relinquishment of dower by wife, but crossed
out in book.   SAMUEL's acknowledgement is recorded 19 January 1818.

29.   5 December 1817.   MARY BUSTER, CLAUDIUS BUSTER and wife,
      NANCY, Kanawaha County, to JONATHAN H. GOODWIN and wife, MARY,
Pitsylvania County...$10.00 654 acres head borders of Bolling Creek.
Lines: WILLIAM COX, GEORGE W. TAYLOR, CHARLES WINGFIELD, JONATHAN
MERRITT, ELIAS WILLS--includes mansion house of late COLONEL PHILIP
JOHNSON, deceased, Amherst County...REUBEN NORVELL and NELSON C.
DAWSON as to MARY and CLAUDIUS in Amherst County on 6 December 1817;
Kanawaha Justices of the Peace: JONATHAN HANSFORD and DAVID MILBURN
as to NANCY, 28 March 1818.

31.   22 September 1818.   PLEASANT PARTIN, Lynchburg, to WILLIAM I.
      ISBELL, Amherst County...$1.00 lot in Madison at junction of
second street and Clarke, BENJAMIN PERKINS, PLEASANT THURMOND--half
acre.   Acknowledged in Lynchburg by PARTIN before JAMES NEWHALL and
DAVID HOFFMAN.   To WILLIAM I. ISBELL, 16 November 1818.

32.   19 October 1818.   BENJAMIN RUCKER and wife, SALLY, Amherst
      County, to JOSHUA RUCKER, Bedford...$287.50 115½ acres west
and joining Lynch road.   Lines: WILLIAM PETTYJOHN, JONATHAN BOLLING,
WILLIAM MC DANIEL, Amherst County Justices of the Peace: REUBEN NORVELL
and NELSON C. DAWSON as to SALLY on same date.

34.   6 October 1818.   JONATHAN MERRITT and wife, RHOAD, Amherst
      County, to CHARLES WINGFIELD, Amherst County...$1742 135 acres.
Lines: ELIJAH MAYS, LINEAS BOLLING, JONATHAN BONDS, deceased.
Same Justices of the Peace as above as to RHODA, 19 October 1818.

35.   2 September 1818.   THOMAS MOORE, REUBEN PENDLETON, JONATHAN
      ELLIS, NELSON CRAWFORD, LEWIS DAWSON, JAMES WARE, Bethel
Trustees to MOORMAN JOHNSON, Campbell County...$1.00 four lots of
half acre each: 20, 21, 22, 23--under Act of 31 December 1801, for
NICHOLAS C. DAVIES and THOMAS W. COCKE to establish town. Witnesses:
JOHN HARDWICK and JAMES BULLOCK.   Note: the activities of Madison
trustees to sell lots must have spurred these Bethel trustees. I
have commented on fact that Bethel never got off of the launching
pad, but Madison is now known as Madison Heights and is "busting out"
all over and is actually only a suburb of Lynchburg.

37.   30 March 1818.   THOMAS CREWS and wife, SALLY, Amherst County,
      to JAMES S. WALKER...$1000.   Lines: Lynch, JAMES POWELL,
north fork Rutledge, grantor, WILLIAM OLIVER, BENJAMIN BROWN.   Residue
of deed of 22 March 1816 and WALKER sold to JAMES POWELL and CREWS
has made deed to POWELL.   Witnesses: B. BROWN.   To JAMES S. WALKER,
16 November 1818.

38.   28 August 1818.   NELSON C. DAWSON and AMBROSE RUCKER as to
      RUTH BURFORD, wife of DANIEL BURFORD...27 June 1814, deed to
JOSEPH MC CRAY.

38. 9 October 1818. CHARLES ROACH and wife, ELIZABETH, Rockbridge
County, to HENRY ROACH, Amherst County...$651 108½ acres--lot
of CHARLES ROACH from father, ASHCRAFT ROACH, in division of estate.
Lines: ARCHIUS GILLIAM, WILLIAM ROACH, BENJAMIN KELLY (now GEORGE
ROACH), HENRY ROACH, DANIEL PEYTON, all of CHARLES' share. Rockbridge
Justices of the Peace: JOSEPH GILMORE and JOSEPH CLOYD, same day,
as to ELIZABETH.

39. -- October 1818. DAVID TINSLEY, SR. and wife, NANCY, Amherst
County, to EDWARD TINSLEY, JR., Amherst County...$3000 320 acres
James River below Bethel--Bowling Neck. Lines: JONATHAN CAMM,
deceased. Witnesses: AMBROSE RUCKER, CHARLES MUNDY, WILLIAM COLEMAN.
To EDWARD TINSLEY, 16 September 1822.

40. 22 July 1818. JAMES WARE and wife, NANCY, Amherst County, and
ANDREW MORELAND, Amherst County, to MARTIN PARKS, Amherst
County...$1170 95 acres. Tract sold by JONATHAN BURKS, SR., to
JAMES WARE on Pedlar. Lines: ELIZABETH HORSLEY.

42. 14 October 1818. WILLIAM KNIGHT and wife, TEMPERANCE, Amherst
County, to JONATHAN LONDON, Amherst County...$5244.75 364 acres
both sides north fork Stovall and both sides Stovall Road. Lines:
JONATHAN LONDON, JAMES BOLLING, JAMES PETTIT. REUBEN NORVELL and
CHARLES MUNDY, same day, as to wife.

43. 28 August 1818. JOSEPH MC CRAE and wife, SOPHIA, Amherst
County, to WILLIAM F. LEE, Amherst County...$1035 110 acres
both sides Harris; part of tract whereon late DR. DANIEL BURFORD
lived. Lines: Dower tract of MRS. MARY BURFORD, WILLIAM BURFORD,
SHADRICK TENNISON, NELSON C. DAWSON. Same day, NELSON C. DAWSON
and AMBROSE RUCKER as to wife.

45. 2 October 1818. MOORMAN JOHNSON, Campbell County, to MERRIT M.
WHITE, Amherst County...$30 half acre lot in Bethel--his
interest--#17.

45. 31 September 1818. GARLAND LUCAS to CHARLES L. BARRETT...power
of attorney to receive amount due me as soldier in late war
under CAPTAIN BENJAMIN HARDAWAY. Witnesses: A. B. DAVIES, WILLIAM S.
CRAWFORD. To CHARLES L. BARRETT, 19 November 1818.

46. 16 November 1818. JONATHAN CAMDEN, Nelson County, to his son,
JAMES CAMDEN, Amherst County...love and $1841.25 which JONATHAN
intends to pay son--122 3/4 acres on Piney. If JONATHAN dies
intestate. Lines: JONATHAN F. CAMDEN, mouth of Little Piney. To
JAMES CAMDEN, 18 September 1820.

47. 25 July 1818. DAVID S. GARLAND and wife, JANE, Amherst County,
to JONATHAN WARE, Amherst County...patent of 10 May 1805 under
hand of JONATHAN PAGE, Governor, to DAVID S. GARLAND and WILLIAM
HALL on Pedlar...200 acres. Lines: WILLIAM TOMLINSON, JONATHAN HALL,
JONATHAN CRAWFORD, HUGH CAMPBELL, WILLIAM HARTLESS, JONATHAN BEASLEY.
$100.00 for half of this Pedlar tract. Witnesses: ROBERT TINSLEY,
C. POWEL, J. PENN. To JONATHAN WARE, 19 August 1830.

49. 18 June 1818. DAVID S. GARLAND to JONATHAN HALL, Amherst
County...$1.00 half of tract. Lines: WILLIAM GALT, REUBEN
TINSLEY, HUGH CAMPBELL, mouth of border on river, JAMES BALLINGER.

49. 19 October 1818. RICHARD RUBANK and wife, MARGARET, Amherst
County, to WILLIAM GIBSON, Amherst County...$4000 322½ acres
Horsley. Lines: road, GILBRAID (?), KIRBY, CARTER, top of Gun
Mountain, JONATHAN CRAWFORD, HAYNES. Witnesses: JONATHAN GARTH,
EZEKIEL B. GILBERT, JONATHAN PRYOR, PETER P. THORNTON. NELSON
CRAWFORD and JONATHAN WARE, 14 November 1818, as to MARGARET L.

51.   15 March 1818. WILLIAM MUSE, SR., Amherst County, to REUBEN
       NORVELL, Amherst County...$500 56 acres both sides Mitchell's
Mill road and joining DANIEL NORCUTT, deceased, HUGHES' road,
JONATHAN MEHONE, WILLIAM MUSE, JR. Witnesses: JOSEPH PETTYJOHN,
WILLIAM SILLINGE (?), WIATT PETTYJOHN.

51.   23 October 1818. WILLIAM JOPLING and JAMES WARE, Amherst
       County Justices of the Peace, as to POLLY JONES, wife of
RICHARD JONES, as to deed to JONATHAN LONDON, 9 December 1816.

52.   20 November 1817. MARGARET RUCKER, Amherst County, to TINSLEY
       RUCKER, Bedford County...$1.00 all her interest in Amherst
County tract. Lines: RODNEY TALIAFERRO, REUBEN COX--100 acres--
sold by RICHARD RUCKER to TINSLEY RUCKER, second day last. Witnesses:
CHARLES WINGFIELD, MARTIN MORGAN, THOMAS MURRELL. To TINSLEY RUCKER,
15 July 1819.

53.   25 September 1818. THOMAS LANE, Amherst County, to MERRIT M.
       WHITE, Amherst County...Deed of Trust; debt to MAYO DAVIES,
Amherst County...$1.00 slaves. To MERRIT M. WHITE, 21 December 1818.

53.   17 November 1818. JAMES PETTIT and wife, FRANCES, Amherst
       County, to RICHARD HARRISON, Amherst County...$325 16½ acres
north borders Harris. Lines: grantee, a road. Witnesses: NICHOLAS
HARRISON, BENJAMIN RUCKER, JOSHUA D. RUCKER. JONATHAN H. SMITH.

54.   16 November 1818. RICHARD MILLNER and wife, MARTHA, to
       LINDSEY SANDIDGE and JACK CARTER...$3376.25 365 acres both
sides Buffaloe. Part of several tracts which RICHARD MILLNER bought
of JONATHAN RICHESON. Lines: BENJAMIN SANDIDGE, JOSEPH DODD,
WILLIAM LONG, AMBROSE TOMLING, WILLIAM TOMBLING, CARTER, crossing
both prongs of river. To JONATHAN RICHESON, 27 March 1820.

55.   16 November 1818. JONATHAN CAMDEN, Amherst County, to his son,
       JONATHAN F. CAMDEN, Amherst County...love and $2066.25 which
JONATHAN intends to pay so--if JONATHAN dies intestate. Piney
River tract. Lines: JAMES CAMDEN, DAVID S. GARLAND, Big Piney--
137 3/4 acres. To JONATHAN F. CAMDEN, 20 December 1819.

57.   9 December 1818. ARTHUR B. DAVIES, Amherst County, to CHARLES B.
       PENN, Amherst County...tract sold under Deed of Trust--JABEZ
CAMDEN to DAVIES for 166 acres and PENN bought at $500.00.

57.   15 October 1818. JAMES and JONATHAN KNIGHT, Amherst County...
       power of attorney to DANIEL and WILLIAM DAY. Witnesses:
MATTHEW LIVELY, HENRY ROBERTS.

58.   15 October 1818. CHARLES LANDON CARTER and wife, MARY R.,
       Fredericksburg, to RICHARD HARRISON, Amherst County...$1.00.
Lines: JONATHAN COLEMAN, REUBEN PADGETT, MRS. WINGFIELD. Remainder
of tract of 848 acres sold to PADGETT and WINGFIELD--531 acres.
Patent to WALLER (?) R. CATTER et al., 28 April 1806, and conveyed
to CHARLES LANDON CARTER. Witnesses: GEORGE W. DILLARD, T. S.
HOLLOWAY, GEORGE L. SHRADER. Justices of the Peace of Fredericksburg:
GARRET MINOR and JONATHAN HUNT, same date, as to MARY R.

59.   15 October 1818. WILLIAM KNIGHT, Amherst County, power of
       attorney to DANIEL and WILLIAM DAY, Amherst County...Witnesses:
MATTHEW LIVELY, HENRY ROBERTS.

60.   18 December 1818. PAMELIA BURRUS, Amherst County, to sister,
       LUCY CAMDEN, wife of HENRY CAMDEN, and her children: W. H.
CAMDEN, SALLY W. DUNCAN, POLLY C. CAMDEN, and HENRY L. W. CAMDEN...love
and $1.00--slaves in which she has life estate for her support.
Witnesses: WILLIAM SALE, HENLEY DRUMMONG, JONATHAN B. DUNCAN.

60. 29 November 1818. DAVID S. GARLAND to GEORGE W. HIGGINBOTHAM,
     Amherst County...$205.96 all interest of JOSEPH STABLES, Shelby
County, Kentucky. Lines: JAMES SEAY, ALLEN BLAIR. Devised by
JOSEPH STAPLES, SR., to wife for life and then to his four sons:
SAMUEL, JOSEPH, JONATHAN and WILLIAM STAPLES. Conveyed in Amherst
County to GARLAND. Witnesses: CORNELIUS POWELL, JOSEPH PENN,
HENRY HAGER, CHARLES L. CHRISTIAN. Note: I was reared in Shelby
County, Kentucky, and was in same high school class with EMMA STAPLES.
She had an older brother, BEN STAPLES, and there was also a younger
sister.

61. 12 November 1818. MARY STAPLES, Amherst County, to son,
     JOSEPH STAPLES, Shelby County, Kentucky...love and $1.00 88 acres
Buffaloe. Lines: as above. Tract of his father, JOSEPH, and my
life dower. Witnesses: PHILIP THURMOND, WIATT SMITH, WILLIAM WAUGH,
THOMAS SMOOT.

62. 17 November 1818. JOSEPH STAPLES, JR., Shelby County, Kentucky,
     to DAVID S. GARLAND, Amherst County...facts as above. JOSEPH
died some years ago testate--to four sons as above. South side
Buffaloe--one fourth interest for $200.96. Witnesses: CORNELIUS
POWELL, HEZEKIAH FULCHER, JONATHAN PENN, HENRY HAGER, JONATHAN P.
COBBS.

63. 14 September 1816. HENRY TENNSION and wife, PEGGY, Amherst
     County, to STITH MEAD, Amherst County...$750 50 acres Bolling
Creek. Witnesses: THOMAS WIATT, JONATHAN Y. JOHNSON, JONATHAN M.
WILLIAMS, WILLIAM PICKETT, JR. NELSON C. DAWSON and AMBROSE RUCKER
as to PEGGY, 19 September 1816. Final proof by WIATT and JOHNSON,
21 April 1817.

65. 27 May 1818. PAMELIA BURRUS, Amherst County, to HENRY CAMDEN...
     power of attorney. Witnesses: SAMUEL BYERS, JAC TYREE, CHARLES
DUNCAN, MICAJAH CAMDEN.

65. 4 January 1819. ROBERT RIVERS and wife, ANNA, Amherst County,
     to WILEY DICKERSON, Albemarle...L6465 862 acres. Lines: south
side Main road, LINDSEY COLEMAN, JONATHAN SMITH above CARTER's old
mill, Mill Creek, JAMES FRANKLIN, Main county road, EDWARD CARTER.
To WILEY DICKERSON, 30 September 1819.

66. 4 January 1819. WILEY DICKERSON, Albemarle, to ROBERT RIVERS...
     $1.00 862 acres; Deed of Trust; conveyed as above.

67. 24 December 1818. JABEZ CAMDEN, Amherst County, to THOMAS S.
     HOLLOWAY, Amherst County...Deed of Trust; debt to G. S.
HOLLOWAY--two slaves brought over by sale from G. S. HOLLOWAY to
JABEZ CAMDEN. Witnesses: J. POWELL. To G. S. HOLLOWAY, 7 February
1818.

68. 16 January 1819. JONATHAN MAJOR, Bedford, power of attorney
     to HENRY CAMDEN...Witnesses: WILLIAM H.; P. G.; CAMDEN and
THOMAS LAIN.

69. 18 January 1819. DAVID R. CLARKSON and wife, REBECCA, to
     JONATHAN CAMDEN, JR., and BENJAMIN CAMDEN...$270 81 acres south
fork Piney. Lines: GILBERT HAYS, GEORGE MONROE, the mill. Tract
conveyed by GEORGE GILLESPIE and wife, MARY, to JAMES ROBERTS, then
of Goochland, 5 October 1792.

70. 30 October 1818. HENRY HARTLESS and wife, JANE, Amherst County,
     to ROBERT TINSLEY, Bedford County...$608 304 acres. Lines:
ARCHILUS ROWSEY. Witnesses: ISAAC RUCKER, WILLIAM DUNCAN, JAMES M.
SMITH, CHARLES L. BARRET. To JONATHAN B. ROBERTSON, present owner,
15 August 1885.

71. 3 February 1819. JOSIAH ELLIS, Richmond, to RICHARD L. ELLIS,
Amherst County...$13,000 325 acres Pedlar. Lines: JAMES WARE
on Pedlar, EDMOND GOODRICH, RODNEY MC CULLOCH. Descended to me from
my father, JOSIAH ELLIS on division. Sold, 18 December 1818, to
RICHARD L. ELLIS. Also slaves, stock. Witnesses: R. N. EUBANK,
JOSHUA S. ELLIS, THOMAS N. RUBANK, JONATHAN ELLIS.

72. 15 January 1819. JONATHAN MERRITT and wife, RHODA, Amherst
County, to CHARLES WINGFIELD, Amherst County...$100 two tracts
head of Northfork Stovall. 1. 100 3/4 acres. Lines: grantor, a
lane, MILLNER COX, JONATHAN H. GOODWIN. 2. 46 3/4 acres. Lines:
BOLLING CLARK, grantee. 18 January 1819, NELSON C. DAWSON and
REUBEN NORVELL, Amherst County Justices of the Peace, as to RHODA.
To CHARLES WINGFIELD, 19 July 1824.

73. 25 June 1818. EPHY and PEGGY GOOLSBY, Amherst County, to
JAMES W. SMITH and JONATHAN GOOLSBY, Amherst County...Deed of
Trust; debt to LYNE S. TALIAFERRO. One bay horse and two cows, etc.
Witnesses: CHARLES P. TALIAFERRO, BENJAMIN TALIAFERRO, JONATHAN
SMITH.

74. 15 December 1818. JONATHAN M. EDWARDS and wife, POLLY, Amherst
County, to WILLIS RUCKER, Amherst County...$2000 where JONATHAN M.
EDWARDS lives. Lines: AMBROSE RUCKER, RICHARD SHELTON, DABNEY WARE.
104 acres. Signed by MARY L. EDWARDS. NELSON C. DAWSON and AMBROSE
RUCKER as to wife, 13 February 1819.

75. 7 April 1817. Trusttes of Madison to PLEASANT PARTIN, Lynchburg...
$1.00 lot 20 at junction of second street and Clarke, BENJAMIN
PERKINS, PLEASANT THURMOND--half acre. Witnesses and trustees as on
page 8f.

76. 28 July 1818. WILLIAM WARE and wife, ROSANNAH, Amherst County,
to PETER MARTIN, Amherst County...L233-5 477 acres. Lines:
JESSE RICHESON, THOMAS TUCKER's estate, RICHARD L. ELLIS, GEORGE
HOWARD. Witnesses: AMBROSE RUCKER, NELSON C. DAWSON, DABNEY WARE,
WILLIS RUCKER. NELSON C. DAWSON and AMBROSE RUCKER, 13 February 1819,
as to wife.

77. 2 November 1818. JONATHAN LYNCH, JR., Lynchburg, attorney-in-fact
for MICAJAH TERRELL and wife, MARTHA ELIZA, Natchez, Mississippi,
to ROBERT MORRIS, Lynchburg...MICAJAH TERRELL, the Elder, owned
tract of about 400 acres on both sides Bolling Creek and sold 61 acres
to JONATHAN CALLAWAY, who sold to GEORGE MAY, who sold to ROBERT MORRIS.
He sold the rest to his son, MICAJAH TERRELL, JR., but died without
making a deed. Upon advice of JONATHAN CALLAWAY, who sued as to
61 acres in Amherst County versus heirs and was given deed for
whole tract--$1.00. 61 acres to ROBERT MORRIS. Lines: WARWICK on
south fork Bolling Creek, James River, grantee. Acknowledged by
JONATHAN LYNCH in Lynchburg before SAMUEL J. HARRISON and JAMES
NEWHALL, Aldermen, 30 November 1818.

79. 26 January 1819. JEREMIAH FRANKLIN, Amherst County, receipt...
from father, BARNARD FRANKLIN, North Carolina--JEREMIAH FRANKLIN
has received slave boy, WESLEY, about ten and nothing remarkable in
description. Acknowledged before DAVID S. GARLAND, Justice of the
Peace, on same date.

79. February Term, 1819. Bertie County, North Caroline, SOLOMON DAY
swore that he came into possession of several named slaves--also
ages. 8 February 1819, THOMAS TAYLOE, Clerk. December 21, 1818 DAY
certified that he brought them to Virginia--not to sell. JONATHAN
COLEMAN, Amherst County Justice of the Peace.

80. 29 June 1818. ROBERT MORRIS and wife, SARAH, Lynchburg, to
     President and Directors of Farmers' Bank of Virginia...Deed of
Trust; debts to bank, etc. $1.00 one house and lot where ROBERT
MORRIS lives in Lynchburg; 430 acres in Amherst County on James--
conveyed by GEORGE WINSTON and wife, DOROTHA, to ROBERT MORRIS;
also adjacent tract of 62 acres and bought by ROBERT MORRIS from
GEORGE MAY, also Campbell County tract. Lines: CAMPBELL CHILTON--
930 acres and bought by ROBERT MORRIS from MICAJAH C. MOORMAN.
ROBERT MORRIS is partner of WILLIAM MITCHELL. 9 July 1819, Lynchburg
Justices of the Peace, WILLIAM MORGAN and SAMUEL J. HARRISON, as to
SARAH.

82. 15 January 1819. ANTHONY Rucker and wife, REBECCA, Amherst
     County, to RICHARD HARRISON, Amherst County...$100 161½ acres
Harris Creek. Lines: ISAAC TINSLEY, SHELTON, the road, WARE's road.
Witnesses: REUBEN NORVELL, TINSLEY RUCKER, HUGH NORVELL, THOMAS
GRISSOM.

84. 6 September 1813. DANIEL NORCUTT and wife, RACHEL, Amherst
     County, to ELIAS WILLS, Amherst County...L68-15 12½ acres
surveyed lately by REUBEN NORVELL, head of one of borders of Harris.
Lines: Lynch road, old smith's shop, CHARLES WINGFIELD, MICAJAH
CLARK, WILLIAM BURFORD, RICHARD RUCKER. Witnesses: THOMAS WILLS,
DABNEY PHILLIPS, WILLIAM SNEAD. Margin: Recorded in this book
through mistake.

85. 15 March 1815. JOSEPH NICHOLS and wife, ANNA, Lynchburg, to
     LEWIS NICHOLS, their son...tract on north side James. Lines:
HENRY TRENT, WILLIAM LEE, deceased. To D. R. EDLEY, per order of
LEWIS NICHOLS, 17 February 1824.

85. 15 October 1819. BENJAMIN BROWN and THOMAS CREWS...an exchange--
     part of tract where BENJAMIN BROWN lives and joins CREWS.
Lines: Lynch road, grantor--3 1/4 acres at $25.00. CREWS deeds to
BENJAMIN BROWN whereon he lives. Lines: west side Crooked Run,
JONATHAN MC DANIEL, both. 1 3/4 acres at $30.00. CREWS to put
$40 to credit of BENJAMIN BROWN.

87. 12 March 1819. ROBERT MORRIS and wife, SARAH, Lynchburg, to
     SAMUEL GARLAND, Lynchburg, and JONATHAN H. SMITH, Lynchburg...
Deed of Trust; debt to ROBERT L. COLEMAN, NICHOLAS HARRISON, JONATHAN M.
SETTLE, JAMES PENN, and NICHOLAS HARRISON of HARRISON and PENN,
Lynchburg merchants. ROBERT COLEMAN has endorsed notes for MORRIS
and MITCHELL, who are partners, also debt to JAMES DUNNINGTO. $1.00
house and lot where ROBERT MORRIS lives in Lynchburg, lots at opposite
corner of West and Main streets in Lynchburg on which are school
house and baker shop and fronting on Main; except 20 feet on back
which is property of DR. JONATHAN CABELL. Also tract in Campbell--
600 acres. Lines: CAMPBELL, DINWIDDIE, also tract ROBERT MORRIS
bought from MICAJAH C. MOORMAN--930 acres and joins first tract.
Also Amherst County tract on James. Lines: WILLIAM WARWICK,
GEORGE WHITLOCK--500 acres and bought by ROBERT MORRIS from GEORGE D.
WINSTON. To ROBERT L. COLEMAN, 15 March 1819. Witnesses: WILL
MITCHELL, JR., D. SAUNDERS, JO. B. COVINGTON, JONATHAN WATSON.
JAMES BENAGE, Deputy Clerk, Lynchburg, 20 March 1818.

91. 4 February 1819. CARTER B. PAGE and WILLIAM F. WIKHAM,
     trustees of estate of SAMUEL GIST, deceased, both of Richmond,
to JONATHAN ELLIS, Amherst County...$15840 1056 acres on both sides
Pedlar. Lines: GEORGE P. LUCKE, ABRAM CARTER, A. RUCKER, RICHARD L.
ELLIS. Surveyed by REUBEN NORVELL, 19 December 1818, and plat annexed
(not in book). WILLIAM H. FITZHYLSOM (?) and WILLIAM P. SMITH,
Richmond Aldermen, as to both trustees. To JONATHAN ELLIS, 19 May
1819.

92. 3 April 1819. WILLIAM SIMMONS, Amherst County, to CHARLES H.
     CHRISTIAN...all interest in Deed of Trust by ROBERT WALTON to
JESSE KENNERLEY for benefit of WILLIAM SIMMONS--55 acres. CHARLES H.
CHRISTIAN releases Deed of Trust versus WILLIAM SIMMONS.

93.   8 February 1819. RICHARD HARRISON and wife, SOPHIA, Amherst
      County, to JOSHUA TINSLEY, Amherst County...$100 164½ acres
Harris Creek. Lines: ISAAC TINSLEY, SHELTON's road, WARE's road.
Witnesses: ALEXANDER TINSLEY, CHARLES L. CHRISTIAN, BENJAMIN HARRISON,
NICHOLAS HARRISON. To ALEXANDER TINSLEY, 17 June 1822.

94.   8 February 1819. CHARLES BURRUS and wife, ELIZABETH, Alabama
      Territory, to MICAJAH CAMDEN, Amherst County...$4000 600 acres
devised to CHARLES BURRUS by deceased father. Lines: LEONARD
HENLEY, HENRY CAMDEN, CHARLES DUNCAN, MICAJAH CAMDEN. Witnesses:
ROBERT COLEMAN, CORNELIUS POWELL, WILLIAM CASH.

95.   9 March 1819. JOSEPH SEAY and wife, NANCY, Amherst County,
      to STERLING CLAIBORNE, Amherst County...$230 (blurred could be
$290) 1. 180 acres. 2. 50 acres. Lines of 1: PRICE, CRAWFORD,
WILLIAM and JOSEPH HIGGINBOTHAM, BENJAMIN SANDIDGE, TUCKER (?),
JAMES FRAZER, deceased, LUCK. 180 acres and to JOSEPH SEAY from
WILLIAM HALL and JAMES MAYS by deed. 2. 50 acres. Lines: north
bank Pedlar, JAMES FRAZER, deceased, WALTER FRAZER, JOSEPH HIGGINBOTHAM,
MARTIN and ZACH TUNKEL (?). Bought by JOSEPH SEAY from WILLIAM HALL.
Witnesses: HUDSON M. GARLAND, HENRY T. HARRIS, B. BROWN.

97.   15 March 1819. SAMUEL D. CHRISTIAN and wife, JANE, Amherst
      County, to DABNEY HILL...$400 all interest in Piney tract and
formerly that of JONATHAN FULCHER and bought by him from ROBERT L.
ROSE. JANE is heir of JONATHAN FULCHER. Witnesses: JONATHAN SMITH,
JABEZ CAMDEN, THOMAS CREWS. To SAMUDL D. CHRISTIAN, 4 September 1821.

97.   27 February 1819. JAMES WADE and wife, ANNE, Lynchburg, to
      ELIAS WILLS, Amherst County...$400 25 acres on road to TRENT's
ferry. Lines: REUBEN PENDLETON, GEORGE M. TINSLEY, LEWIS DAWSON.
Witnesses: C. DABNEY, RICHARD HARRISON, NICHOLAS HARRISON, ABNER
PADGETT, LEWIS PADGETT. Lynchburg Justices of the Peace: WILLIAM
BURD and JAMES NEWHALL as to ANNE on same date. To ELIAS WILLS,
12 April 1822.

99.   1 August 1818. GEORGE H. BELL, Amherst County, and ALEXANDER
      TOLLE and wife, SOPHIA, Campbell County, to JONATHAN M. WALKER,
Buckingham...SAMUEL BELL, late of Amherst County, by will directed
that tract where he lived, and present home of his widow, SARAH
BELL, be sold at her death or marriage and divided to his five children.
GEORGE H. is a son and SOPHIA is a daughter and wife of ALEXANDER
TOLLEY. They sell their undivided interest. Certified in Buckingham
as to BELL and TOLLE, 24 November 1818. PHILIP DUVALL and GEORGE
CHRISTIAN, Justices of the Pease as to SOPHIA in Buckingham; same
date. To JONATHAN M. WALKER, 25 August 1820.

101. 23 April 1818. REUBEN NORVELL to GEORGE WHITLOCKE and GEORGE P.
      RICHARDSON...Deed of Trust; debt to RINSLEY RUCKER. 327 3/4
acres on Harris where PLEASANT DAWSON lives. Lines: HARRISON HUGHES,
REUBEN COX, RODNEY TALIAFERRO, WILLIAM HUGHES, deceased. Certified
in Lynchburg, 4 November 1818, by all. JAMES BENAGH, Deputy Clerk.
To RUCKER, 26 April 1819.

103. 13 April 1818. EDWARD DDNINGTON, Staunton in Augusta, power
      of attorney to BENNETT A. CRAWFORD, Amherst County...to sell
126 acres in Amherst County. ERASMUS STRIBLING, clerk of court,
23 March 1819.

104. 25 November 1818. FIELDING HOLLIDAY and wife, MARY, Amherst
      County, to ISAAC RUCKER, Amherst County...$5000 300 acres
north and middle fork Pedlar. Also 154 acres on both sides north
fork Pedlar. Lines: his own; also 57 acres north fork Pedlar.
Lines: his own, DENNIS BAGBY. Witnesses: JONATHAN MEYERS, ALEXANDER
GOSNEY, LINDSEY MC DANIEL, BENJAMIN TALIAFERRO and NELSON V. DAWSON
as to wife on same date.

105. 7 October 1818. ROBERT WALTON, Amherst County, to JESSE
     KENNERLY, Amherst County...Deed of Trust; debt to WILLIAM
SIMMONS. $1.00; tract sold by ROBERT WALTON to WILLIAM SIMMONS--
55 acres. To JESSE KENNERLY, 14 April 1819.

106. 20 August 1818. LEROY CAMDEN, Amherst County, to JABEZ CAMDEN,
     Amherst County...Deed of Trust; debt to JESSE KENNERLEY. $1.00;
also to secure MICAJAH CAMDEN on note to RICHARDSON TAYLOR, STEPHEN
WATTS as trustee for NANCY SHIELDS, ELIJAH FLETCHER, DANIEL CHEATWOOD--
slave, furniture, stock. Witnesses: WILLIAM P. CASHWELL, JONATHAN L.
MOORE, SAMUEL BYAS. To JESSE KENNERLEY, 1819.

108. 29 June 1818. ROBERT MORRIS and wife, SARAH, Lynchburg, to
     President and Directors of Farmers' Bank of Virginia. $1.00--
this seems to be same as Deed of Trust previously recorded--page 80.
To WILLIAM RADFORD, 28 April 1819. It bears same date and seems to
contain same data.

110. 9 December 1818. WILLIAM PETTYJOHN and wife, ELIZABETH, Amherst
     County, to ROBERT RIDGWAY, Amherst County...$2132.06 274 acres
both sides Lynch road. Lines: PLEASANT DAWSON, BOWLING CLARK,
CHARLES WINGFIELD, JONATHAN BURFORD, TINSLEY's road, ROBERT H. ROSE,
WILLIAM MC DANIEL, ridge road. Witnesses: GEORGE W. TINSLEY,
WESLEY PADGETT, GEORGE W. PETTYJOHN. To ROBERT RIDGWAY, 18 August
1840.

112. 27 September 1788. ANGUS MC DONALD, Amherst County, power of
     attorney to WILLIAM LYLE, Rockbridge...to convey to JONATHAN
LUCK--218½ acres. Witnesses: J. GOULD, SAMUEL HOUSTON, N. HOUSTON,
JR., WILLIAM CARRUTHERS, JONATHAN HOPKINS. Proved in Rockbridge by
WILLIAM CARRUTHERS, 6 May 1816; Calohill Deputy Clerk. Proved there
by GOULD, 4 June 1816. Recorded Amherst County: 19 April 1819.

113. 10 April 1819. NELSON C. DAWSON, Amherst County, to SAMUEL
     BURKS, Amherst County...$200 20 acres headwaters Graham Creek.
Lines: both, ARTHUR L. DAVIES.

113. 20 March 1819. ROBERT L. COLEMAN and wife, MARY, Campbell
     County, to NELSON MANTIPLY, Amherst County...$400 82½ acres
north fork Buffaloe near Turkey Mountain. Lines: LINDSEY COLEMAN,
deceased, LINN BANKS, WILLIAM MAYS. Witnesses: THOMAS S. CARTER,
WILLIAM H. ROSE, JONATHAN C. CARTER, JR. To NELSON MANTIPLY,
4 February 1821.

114. 19 October 1818. OLIVER TINSLEY, Bedford, from JOSEPH NORCUTT
     and wife, SALLY, VERMILIA MILES, WILLIAM NORCUTT and JAMES
NORCUTT, Amherst County...$2075 121½ acres--one fifth equal part
belongs to SOPHIA TINSLEY, wife of OLIVER, and is not conveyed.
Lines: REUBEN NORVELL, Lynch road. NELSON C. DAWSON and REUBEN
NORVELL, Amherst County Justices of the Peace, as to JOSEPH, PERMELIA
MIL S, WILLIAM and JAMES NORCUTT, same date, and to SALLY, wife of
JOSEPH NORCUTT, 15 March 1819.

116. 21 September 1818. NANCY MC CREDIE, formerly BRYDIE, and widow
     of ALEXANDER BRYDIE, Richmond, WILLIAM H. DYER and wife,
MARGARET, Albemarle, and WILLIAM and BETSY BRYDIE, Richmond...MARGARET
and WILLIAM and BETSY are ALEX's children, to CHARLES MUNDY, Amherst
County. BRYDIE, by will, devised Amherst County tract--651 acres, to
wife for life and then to children--$976 5. Lines: PARKS' road,
JACOB PIERCE, Poor house tract, JACOB SCOTT, the branch, CHARLES
HIGGINBOTHAM, deceased, RUTLEDGE, JAMES FRANKLIN, deceased, PARKS'
old road--WILLIAM and BETSY are minors. Richmond: S. JACOBS and
WILLIAM H. FITZHYPSOM (Clerk had a hard time with this name in all
Richmond deeds), as to NANCY, 13 November 1818; Albemarle: MARTIN
DAWSON and JOSEPH COFFMAN, 11 December 1818, as to DYER and wife,
Recorded Amherst County: 23 March 1819.

119. 1 October 1818. CHRISTOPHER SMITH, Lord Mayor of London,
England, certified that MARTIN PEACHES, Howley Street, Parish
of St. Mary de Bone, Middlesex County, and wife, MARY, appeared before
him at Windale...under this order any two judges or mayor of chief
cities in Kingdom of Great Britain--as to deed of 3 August 1818, by
them to CARTER B. PAGE and WILLIAM F. WICKHAM--tract in Amherst
County, MARY is resident of Great Britain. ARTHUR B. DAVIES, Amherst
County, 5 August 1818. This is indexed PEACKES, but appears to be
PARKS in places.

120. 3 August 1818. MARTIN PEACHKES, upper Howley Street, Middlesex,
and wife, MARY, eldest of two daughters of SAMUEL GEST, late
of Gower Street in parish of St. Giles in the Field, Middlesex,
deceased, to CARTER BRAXTON PAGE and WILLIAM FANNING WICKHAM,
Richmond, Virginia...under Act of Assembly, May 1782, to invest
estate of SAMUEL GIST (GEST) in MARY, then wife of WILLIAM ANDERSON
(now PEACHKES), and all vested in her. SAMUEL GIST made will of
22 June 1806 and codicil as to exception of plantations and freed
slaves. February 26, 1816, Act, to give effect to will of SAMUEL
GIST, late of London. PAGE and WICKHAM were made trustees as to
Virginia slaves--10 sh paid to PEACKES and wife--all interest in the
estate. Witnesses: EDWARD LODGEGLE and EDWARD JOHN CARLOS, 1 October
1818. CHRISTOPHER SMITH, Lord Mayor of London, certified that MARY
relinquished dower rights.

123. No date. PHILIP THURMOND to ANSELM CLARKSON...deed acknowledged
in court and certified of Court of Franklin. Sent by PHILIP
THURMOND to County, 29 May 1819.

123. No date. ANSELM CLARKSON to JONATHAN EUBANK...Deed of Trust;
debt to P. THURMOND. Margin as above. Also acknowledged in
court by EUBANK and THURMOND. Three witnesses not named. Margin
as above.

123. 22 November 1818. ANDERSON L. CREWS and wife, DEBORAH, Amherst
County, to JEREMIAH COATS, Amherst County...$250 half acre lot.
Lines: WILLIAM HUTCHISON, JAMES POWELL, MICHAJAH CAMDEN, CHARLES
MUNDY, JONATHAN WARWICK--last two Justices of the Peace as to wife,
2 February 1819.

124. 24 December 1816. BARBARA NOEL, Amherst County, to JAMES TAYLOR,
Amherst County...L45 40 acres Lovelady Creek--border of Pedlar.
Lines: FREDERICK SHOEMAKER, NICHOLAS PRYOR. Witnesses: THOMAS N.
EUBANK, JAMES WARE, WILLIAM HAYNES, WILLIAM L. THURMOND, WALTER
WILLIAMS.

125. 31 December 1818. ROBERT MORRIS and wife, SARAH, Lynchburg,
to JONATHAN PATTEN, same town...$4937.50 39½ acres. Lines:
G. WHITLOCKE, STITH MEAD, JONATHAN MILLER. JONATHAN THURMOND and
PL. LABBY, Lynchburg Justices of the Peace, 10 May 1819, as to
ROBERT MORRIS. Margin: to JONATHAN PATTEN, 11 December 1821; also
to him on 9 August 1819.

127. 18 May 1819. WILLIAM F. GOOCH, Amherst County, to CLAIBORNE W.
GOOCH, Richmond...WILLIAM is entitled to share under will of
father, PHILIP GOOCH, and late brother, of the half-blood, WILLIAM B.
GOOCH, who died without issue-- $3000 for all interest in both estates.
to CLAIBORNE W. GOOCH, June, 1819.

128. 15 December 1818. ROBERT MORRIS and wife, SARAH, Lynchburg,
to JONATHAN PATTEN, same town...$880 11 acres; bought by
ROBERT MORRIS from GEORGE D. WINSTON. Lines: ADAMS, PHILIP JOHNSON,
deceased, PERKINS, a road. Certified as on page 125 as to SARAH,
10 May 1819.

129. 17 May 1819. JONATHAN B. CHRISTIAN, Amherst County, to JONAS
PIERCE, Amherst County...$36 six acres south side Buffaloe.
Lines: grantee. Signed: JONATHAN CHRISTIAN, B.

130. 20 May 1819. JONATHAN COLEMAN and wife, SALLY, ROBERT L. COLEMAN
and wife, MARY, Amherst County, to RICHARD HARRISON, Amherst
County...$7000 28 acres 2/3 of tract and mill on Rocky Creek. Lines:
JOHN CHRISTIAN, B, WILLIAM DILLARD.

131. 17 May 1819. HENRY CAMDEN, WILLIAM H. CAMDEN, WESTLEY L.
DUNCAN and wife, SALLY W. to A. B. DAVIES, STERLING CLAIBORNE,
and JAMES POWELL...Deed of Trust; $1.00; debt to RICHARD H. BURKS,
former sheriff (deputy) for DAVID S. GARLAND, Sheriff--judgement in
Superior Court for Amherst County--appeal pending--327 acres. Lines:
ROWSEY tract. Also 307 acres and reference to deed of HENRY CAMDEN
to WILLIAM H. CAMDEN, 19 May 1818. Witnesses: B. A. CRAWFORD,
W. S. CRAWFORD, RICHARD BURKS, DAVID S. GARLAND, LINDSEY COLEMAN.
To RICHARD H. BURKS, 15 December 1819.

133. 17 May 1819. WILLIAM LONG and wife, BETSY, to THOMAS COLEMAN,
Amherst County...$15 30 acres Huff. Lines: HENRY CAMDEN,
ELISABETH LONG (late CALLAWAY), JONATHAN COLEMAN, deceased.

133. 4 June 1819. EDMOND PENN, Amherst County, to DAVID S. GARLAND,
Amherst County...$500 slave girl about eleven; riding horse.
To DAVID S. GARLAND, 13 August 1821.

134. 15 November 1818. JONATHAN EUBANK, Amherst County, from WILLIAM
NOEL, Amherst County...$1.00 120 acres north borders Maple
Creek and bought by JONATHAN EUBANK from ZACHARIAH TAYLOR and sold
by JONATHAN EUBANK to JONATHAN GOODRICH; by will of JONATHAN GOODRICH
to RANDOLPH HOGG who married JONATHAN GOODRICH's daughter, POLLY.
Sold by RANDOLPH HOGG to THOMAS N. EUBANK and by him to LINDSAY BURKS
and by him to WILLIAM NOEL. Lines: JONATHAN HOGG's tract, ANDERSON
WARE, JONATHAN TAYLOR, and whereon WILLIAM NOEL lives. Witnesses:
JONATHAN ELLIS, CHARLES HAYNES, ANDREW MORELAND, R. L. ELLIS, R. N.
EUBANK.

135. 22 October 1818. JONATHAN BURKS, JR., and wife, ELIZABETH,
Rockbridge, to JONATHAN ELLIS, Amherst County...$3075 205
acres Pedlar. Lines: grantee, ARCHIBALD GILLIAM, DANIEL PEYTON,
old field, JARRETT GILLIAM, tract sold by JONATHAN P. BURKS to
CAPTAIN JAMES DAVIS. Witnesses: CHARLES L. CHRISTIAN, ANDREW
MORELAND, THOMAS LAIN, SAMUEL BURKS (SC-sic*; JOSIAH ELLIS.)

136. 2 January 1819. PHILIP THURMOND, Amherst County, to RICHARD
MILLNER, Amherst County...$6000 750 acres both sides Horsley.
Lines: the road, the path, NELSON CRAWFORD, WILLIAM DEMPSEY.
Witnesses: R. L. ELLIS, JAMES WARE, THOMAS N. EUBANK, PETER RUCKER,
A. EUBANK. To WILLIAM MILLNER, 24 November 1834.

137. 27 November 1818. THOMAS POINDEXTER, Spotsylvania, to DAVID S.
GARLAND, Amherst County...$800 400 acres Buffaloe. Patent
to AARON TRUEHART, 20 September 1759, and by deed to JONATHAN SERJEANT
to JONATHAN POINDEXTER and by JONATHAN to THOMAS. Witnesses:
GEORGE W. VAUGHAN, J. PENN, CORNELIUS POWELL.

138. 17 May 1819. THOMAS COLEMAN, Amherst County, to WILLIAM
RADFORD, Bedford, and SAMUEL GARLAND, Lynchburg...Deed of
Trust; debt to ARCHIBALD ROBERTSON of BROWN and ROBERTSON and
surviving partner; debt to READ and ROBERTSON on LITTLEBERRY COLEMAN's
account. $1.00 slaves and children. Witnesses: W. S. CRAWFORD,
JAMES P. GARLAND, HILL CARTER. To SAMUEL GARLAND, 18 January 1820.

139. 30 April 1819. ROWLAND KYLE and wife, SOPHIA, Amherst County,
to JONATHAN M. WALKER, Buckingham...DRURY CHRISTIAN, Amherst
County, died intestate, and had tract whereon he died--840½ acres--
left five children and tract divided by commissioners. KYLE married a
daughter of DRURY, SOPHIA. Sells one fifth interest and one fifth of
dower at death of widow. $1830 lot four of 143 acres. Lines: CHARLES
CHRISTIAN, JONATHAN M. WALKER (formerly JONATHAN CHRISTIAN; H seems to
be initial), deceased, CHARLES MUNDY and JONATHAN HORSLEY, JR. Amherst
County Justices of the Peace as to SOPHIA, same date. To JONATHAN M.
WALKER, 19 March 1822.

141.   17 May 1819.   JOSEPH B. MAY and wife, SALLY, Amherst County,
      to GABRIEL PAGE, Amherst County...$400 one sixth 1/6th of
undivided tract bequeathed by BEVERLY WILLIAMSON to six children and
MAYS' first wife was one; after her death her interest sold by
commissioners and he bought it and now sells. Witnesses: JOSEPH W.
SMITH, RICHARD SMITH, JOEL F. SMITH.

141.   22 December 1818.   JONATHAN CHRISTIAN, B, and wife, JUDITH,
      Amherst County, to RICHARD HARRIS, Amherst County...$1507.50
101½ acres Rocky Creek and part of where JONATHAN CHRISTIAN lives.
Lines: grantor, FOLLY tract, WILLIAM DILLARD, MILL tract, the road.
Witnesses: ELIJAH L. CHRISTIAN, CHARLES L. CHRISTIAN, LAWSON WILSHER,
JAMES HILL, ROBERT PAGE, T. S. HOLLOWAY. 22 August 1820, to take
dower.

143.   2 April 1819.   WILLIAM A. PATTESON and wife, MARTHA in own
      right and as grandsons for JAMES H., DAVID N., SAMUEL A.,
JONATHAN J. and SARAH ANN PATTESON, infant heirs of JAMES A. PATTESON,
deceased, Chesterfield County, to JONATHAN M. WALKER, Buckingham...
Note: this appears to be PATTERSON in some places, but is signed as
PATTESON--JAMES A. in life, 1 April 1816, contracted with WALKER to
sell tract--November term of Chesterfield County Court Chancery, to
make title: JONATHAN M. WALKER versus MARTHA and WILLIAM A. PATTESON
and infants named and as sec. or JAMES A.--$5.00 400 acres in Amherst
County. Lines: the river, CHRISTIAN, Lime Kiln Creek. Also 2/3
undivided interest in Buckingham tract called Goings' Hill--392
acres. Lines: river, JAMES CHRISTIAN. Chesterfield Justices of
the Peace: DANIEL WESINGER and NICHOLAS MILLS, as to WILLIAM and
wife, 20 May 1819. To JONATHAN M. WALKER, 25 August 1820.

146.   5 April 1819.   SOPHIA R. MORGAN, formerly MARR, and husband,
      BENJAMIN H. MORGAN, ALEXANDER D. MARR and wife, ELIZA, SARAH S.
MARR, AMBROSE R. MARR, MATILDA W. MARR, heirs of JAMES MARR, deceased,
to JONATHAN LONDON, Amherst County...$5124--ALEXANDER MARR as executor
of JAMES--Porage Creek. Lines: JONATHAN HUTVHINSON, THOMAS WILCOX,
deceased, ELIZABETH THURMAN, RICHARD POWELL, JAMES PETTIT, tract
JAMES bought of WILLIAM KNIGHT. MARR sold to LONDON in life and
whereon he lived. 336¾ acres. Certified in Pitsylvania as to
ALEXANDER D. MARR and wife, 5 April 1819. THOMAS SHELTON and JAMES
HOPKINS, Justices of the Peace. Certified in Bedford as to ELIZABETH,
widow of JAMES MARR, SOPHIA R. MORGAN, 14 April 1819. JONATHAN
HEADEN and NICHOLAS ROBERTSON, Justices of the Peace. Also as to
SARAH L., AMBROSE R. and MATILDA W. MARR. To JONATHAN LONDON, 15 July
1819.

148.   15 March 1819.   Suit pending in Amherst County Court: JONATHAN
      LONDON versus heirs of JAMES MARR and heirs ordered to convey...
328 3/4 acres. AMBROSE RUCKER appointed to execute deed for infants:
JONATHAN, JAMES, ISAAC, MARY, ELIZABETH, CAWLIN (CAROLINE?), MARTHA
and FRANCES MARR, infant heirs of JAMES MARR: eight undivided
parts. Lines: JAMES PETTIT, WILLIAM KNIGHT (now JONATHAN LONDON).
Witnesses: REUBEN COLEMAN, RICHARD BURKS, WILLIAM BOURNE, H. GEORGE
TUCKER, THOMAS D. HILL, R. POWELL, THOMAS KNIGHT, TINSLEY RUCKER.
To JONATHAN LONDON, 15 July 1819.

149.   25 June 1818.   NICHOLAS HARRISON and wife, Campbell County, to
      -- NANCY, wife of NICHOLAS HARRISON...JONATHAN MORRIS and
JAMES BULLOCK, Justices of the Peace. They are called Buckingham
Justices of the Peace at end, but order is to Bedford at start. It
will be noted that there are many of these incomplete dower items
in this book. In many cases they do not name grantees.

150.   26 January 1819.   Order to Amherst County Justices of the Peace:
      MITCHELL FLOYD and wife, POLLY, 21 September 1818, to LYNE S.
TALIAFERRO...60 acres. Done, 23 April 1819, by BENJAMIN TALIAFERRO
and WILLIAM JOPLING.

151.   8 May 1819.   JABEZ CAMDEN to JOSEPH PENN...Deed of Trust; debt
       to DAVID S. GARLAND $1.00 100 acres Huff and where I live;
bought from MICAJAH CAMDEN and he bought it from WARNER GOODWIN.
Witnesses: HUDSON M. GARLAND, EDMOND PENN, WIATT SMITH. To JOSEPH
PENN, 5 July 1820.

152.   19 June 1819.   JAMES WARE and wife, NANCY, Amherst County, to
       GEORGE H. BURFORD, Amherst County...$300 half acre lot in
Bethel--#8 and whereon GEORGE H. BURFORD lives. To GEORGE H. BURFORD,
15 May 1820.

152.   8 June 1819.   JONATHAN TAYLOE, Amherst County, to CHISWELL
       DABNEY and JONATHAN LONDON, Amherst County...Deed of Trust;
debt to WILLIAM TURNER as bondsman to Branch Bank and Deposit at
Lynchburg. $1.00 slaves; two acres in Lynchburg and next to WILLIAM B.
LYNCH and JONATHAN TAYLOE bought it from LEWIS BROWN, Lynchburg.
Also furniture. Witnesses: JONATHAN WRIGHT, THOMAS MURRELL. To
WILLIAM TURNER, 1819.

154.   26 November 1818.   WILLIAM MITCHELL, Lynchburg, to STITH MEAD,
       Amherst County...$500 two lots in town of Madison: 11 and 32.
Junction of first or Main and sixth alley--two half acres. Witnesses:
JONATHAN F. WIATT, ABRAM R. NORTH, ANSELM LYNCH, JR.

155.   19 September 1818.   JONATHAN L. WINGFIELD and wife, POLLY,
       Amherst County, to DABNEY WARE, Amherst County...$11,280 where
WARE lives: Graham Creek. 282 acres. Lines: RICHARD SHELTON,
SAMUEL BURKS, AMBROSE RUCKER, JONATHAN M. EDWARDS. Witnesses:
SAMUEL DAWSON, SAMUEL BURKS, PLEASANT DAWSON.

155.   7 April 1817.   JONATHAN LYNCH and wife, MARY, Lynchburg, to
       ROBERT C. and FIELDING L. WILLIAMS, Lynchburg...$1245 four
lots at southwest end of town of Madison: 80, 81, 82, 83. Lines:
junction of third street and seventh alley, JONATHAN TAYLOR--two
acres. Witnesses: EDWARD LYNCH, HENRY CLARK, JONATHAN LYNCH, JR.,
ROBERT ADAMS, Lynchburg Justices of the Peace: JAMES STEWART and
MICAJAH DAVIS, JR., as to JONATHAN LYNCH.

157.   12 September 1816.   Order to Amherst County Justices of the
       Peace: WALTER CHRISTIAN and wife, PATSY, 20 December 1794,
to ISAIAH ATKINS...71 acres. Done by JONATHAN WARWICK and JONATHAN
COLEMAN, 18 December 1816.

158.   12 November 1818.   JONATHAN HAYTHE and wife, SUSANNA, Lynchburg,
       to WILLIAM MITCHELL, JR., same town...$500 two lots in Madison:
11 and 32. Junction of first or Main and sixth alley; second street--
half acre each. Witnesses: C. DABNEY, JONATHAN D. URQUHART, WILLIAM M.
RIVES. Campbell County Justices of the Peace: ADAM CLEMENT and
THOMAS COCKE, as to wife, 29 May 1819.

159.   12 September 1816.   Order to Amherst County Justices of the
       Peace: WALTER CHRISTIAN and wife, PATSY, 3 October 1798, to
ISAIAH ATKINSON...23 3/4 acres. Done by JONATHAN WARWICK and
JONATHAN COLEMAN, 18 December 1816. Recorded: 21 June 1819.

160.   21 June 1819.   Order to Amherst County Justices of the Peace:
       JAMES POWELL and wife, MILDRED, 20 May 1816, to CHARLES MOORE...
262 3/4 acres. Done by EDMOND WINSTON and T. S. HOLLOWAY, same day.

161.   22 November 1814.   Order to Amherst County Justices of the
       Peace: WILLIAM PETTYJOHN and wife, ELIZABETH, 16 October
1813, to WILLIAM MITCHELL...mill seat at mouth of Harris--33 acres
and tract between JAMES and creek--square cress 10. Done by PHILIP
JOHNSON and NELSON C. DAWSON, 25 November 1814; recorded 21 June 1819.

162.   18 August 1818.   Order to Amherst County Justices of the Peace:
       CHARLES L. BARRET and wife, SARAH, 16 June 1817, to FREDERICK
PRICE...202 acres. Done by BENJAMIN TALIAFERRO and NELSON CRAWFORD,
22 May 1819.

163. 20 September 1815. Order to Amherst County Justices of the
     Peace: HENRY BALLINGER and wife, POLLY, 13 July 1815, to
WILLIAM LONG...228 acres. Done by NELSON CRAWFORD and WILLIAM
JOPLING, 14 October 1815; recorded 21 June 1819.

164. Order to Amherst County Justices of the Peace: FREDERICK PRICE
     and wife, MARY ANN, 28 June 1817, to WILLIAM COLEMAN...three
tracts on Pedlar. Done, 22 May 1819, by NELSON CRAWFORD and BENJAMIN
TALIAFERRO.

165. 22 December 1817. Order to Amherst County Justices of the
     Peace: REUBEN COX and wife, PATSY, 12 November 1817, to
WILLIAM MITCHELL...33 acres. Done by CHARLES P. TALIAFERRO and
REUBEN NORVELL, 28 December 1817. Margin: see Deed Book N:420 for
--; 19 June 1829, to JAMES BRUCE, present owner.

166. 18 November 1818. Order to Amherst County Justices of the
     Peace: JONATHAN F. HALL and wife, ELIZABETH, 19 September
1818, to CHARLES L. BARRET...seven acres. Done, 22 May 1819, by
NELSON CRAWFORD and BENJAMIN TALIAFERRO.

167: 20 April 1818. Order to Amherst County Justices of the
     Peace: WILLIAM DOUGLAS and wife, SUSANNA, 17 November 1817, to
JAMES WARE...163 acres. Done by THOMAS N. EUBANK and JAMES WARE,
25 August 1818.

168. 12 November 1818. ROBERT MORRIS and wife, SARAH, Lynchburg, to
     DANIEL, WILLIAM and CORBAN WARWICK, merchants of Richmond...firm
of DANIEL, WILLIAM, etc. WARWICK. Deed of Trust; executed to
CHRISTOPHER WINFREE, Lynchburg, by MORRIS for self and WILLIAM
MITCHELL, Lynchburg merchants. $1.00 four tracts in Campbell; two
lots in Lynchburg; twenty slaves. One tract in Campbell known as
BENNETT and HILL tracts below Oxford Iron Works--350 acres. Lines:
WOODSON LASHELL and tenanted (?; illegible) to GIBSON and RICE. Tract
in Campbell--750 acres and bought of TAYLOR and MARTIN and cultivated
by ROBERT MORRIS; one tract in Campbell--800 acres and bought from
ARMISTEAD and formerly JONES tract and tenanted to IRVINE; one tract
in CAmpbell--headwaters of Linden (? 0-300 acres; formerly LAMB's
tract; one house and lot in Lynchburg--formerly that of HENRY MEREDITH
on -- Street--1/4 acre and occupied by MEREDITH), one lot at junction
of fifth and Market and bought by ROBERT MORRIS from CHRISTOPHER
ANTHONY, twenty slaves named. Witnesses: E. N. LANE, I. H. MITCHELL,
JONATHAN M. MITVHELL. To CORBAN WARWICK, 27 October 1819. Certified
by JAMES BENAGH, Deputy Clerk of Lynchburg, 4 March 1819.

172. 19 July 1819. DANIEL PEYTON and wife, MARY, Kentucky, to
     WILLIAM MITCHELL, Amherst County...$1.00 100 acres James River.
Lines: HENRY ROACH, JARRET GILLIAM--known as LEWIS PLACE. Acknowledged
in Amherst County by wife, same day. To WIATT DUNCAN per WILLIAM
MITCHELL's order, 29 September 1829.

173. 17 July 1819. ROWLAND GILLESPIE and wife, LUCY, Amherst County,
     to COLEMAN and BARRET, Amherst County...$450 112 acres north
side Pedlar. Lines: JONATHAN F. HALL, MAYS. Witnesses: WALLER
SANDIDGE, JONATHAN COLEMAN, GEORGE LOLLAM (?).

173. 19 June 1819. ROWLAND GILLESPIE and wife to same grantees as
     above...Deed of Trust; debt to CHARLES L. BARRET and Company--
JAMES BROWN, trustee and conveyed to him. Half acre tract whereon
ROWLAND GILLESPIE lives--70 acres out of 140 acres. Lines: ROWLAND
BYAS, WALTER WILLIAMS. Witnesses: JONATHAN R. SHELTON, JOSEPH M.
VENABLE, WILLIAM PRICE, JONATHAN COLEMAN, WALLER SANDIDGE, GEORGE
LOLLAM.

162

175. 12 July 1819. JONATHAN WHITE and wife, MARTHA, Spotsylvania,
     to JONATHAN THOMPSON, JR., Amherst County...$12,000 452 acres
Tye. Lines: the road, NORVELL SPENCER, deceased, STERLING CLAIBORNE,
WILLIAM S. CRAWFORD, deceased, HUGH and CHARLES ROSE, deceased,
road from Belevet to Geddes. JOSEPH HERNDON and WILLIAM WALLER,
Spotsylvania Justices of the Peace, as to wife, 10 July 1819--sic.

176. 16 (10?) June 1819. BALLINGER MAYS and wife, MARY, Salina in
     Botetourt, to THOMAS WILLIAMSON, Amherst County...$350 117 acres
Stonehouse Creek. Devised by his father, ROBERT MAYS, by will.
Lines: grantee, NANCY HIGGINBOTHAM, JESSE MAYS, JOSEPH B. MAYS.
HENRY SNIDER and NATHANIEL BURWELL, Botetourt Justices of the Peace,
as to wife, 17 June 1819.

178. 28 June 1819. CHARLES H. CHRISTIAN and wife, JANE, Amherst
     County, to JONATHAN H. SMITH, Lynchburg...$432 36 acres.
Lines: WALTER CHRISTIAN, grantee, SIMMONS, Rocky Run and Rutledge.
Surveyed by CHARLES L. CHRISTIAN, 18 July 1818.

179. 12 July 1819. JONATHAN THOMPSON, JR., Amherst County, to
     JONATHAN P. COBBS, Nelson County, and ARTHUR CLAYTON, Louisa
County...Deed of Trust; debt to JONATHAN WHITE, Spotsylvania. $1.00
tract which JONATHAN THOMPSON, JR. bought from JONATHAN WHITE and
JONATHAN WHITE bought it from THOMAS ALDRIDGE on Tye. 452 acres.
Lines: STERLING CLAIBORNE, NORVELL SPENCER, deceased, WILLIAM
CRAWFORD, deceased, THOMAS ALDRIDGE. Witnesses: ARTHUR CLAYTON,
WILLIAM F. WHITE. To JONATHAN WHITE, 20 September 1819. WILLIAM
HARWOOD and ALEXANDER M. CLAYTON were also witnesses.

181. 12 July 1819. JOSEPH GILMORE and JOSEPH CLOYD, Rockbridge
     Justices of the Peace as to NANCY CAMDEN, wife of WASHINGTON
CAMDEN, 1 November 1816, to JACOB TYREE...same page: JONATHAN
CARUTHERS and ROBERT WHITE, Justices of the Peace in same county as
to JANE DUNCAN, wife of WILLIS DUNCAN, as to same deed.

181. 19 July 1819. CHARLES TALIAFERRO and BENJAMIN TALIAFERRO,
     Amherst County Justices of the Peace, as to POLLY CAMDEN,
formerly DUNCAN, as to deed above.

182. 11 August 1819. JONATHAN L. MOORE, Amherst County, to BENNETT A.
     CRAWFORD...Deed of Trust; debt to JONATHAN MYERS--bondsman in
suit JESSE KENNEDY and JAMES W. HILL, merchants, versus JONATHAN L.
MOORE. $1.00 house and lot near CCH on west side Lynch road. Occupied
by JAMES MOORE. To BENNETT A. CRAWFORD, 25 November 1820.

183. 22 December 1818. WILLIAM MITCHELL and wife, SALLY, Amherst
     County, to CHARLES JOHNSTON and SAMUEL PANNELL, Campbell
County...Deed of Trust; debt to JAMES BRUCE, Halifax. $1.00 Amherst
County mills called Farmer (?). Lines: above Buck br., James River,
PETTIS THACKER, deceased, WILLIAM PETTYJOHN, JAMES LEE. 384 acres.
Acknowledged in Richmond by WILLIAM MITCHELL, 24 December 1818, and
in Lynchburg by SALLY, 11 August 1819. JONATHAN THURMOND and PLEASANT
LABBY. L. JACOBS and WILLIAM H. FITZUHYLOM in Richmond as Justices
of the Peace. To C. DABNEY, 17 January 1820.

185. 13 February 1819. NELSON C. DAWSON and AMBROSE RUCKER,
     Amherst County Justices of the Peace, as to ELIZABETH WARE,
wife of DABNEY WARE...to JONATHAN M. EDWARD, 17 January 1818.

185. 2 May 1817. WILLIAM HALL, Amherst County, to ANDERSON MOSS,
     Amherst County...$10.00 200 acres. Patent to JONATHAN CHRISTIAN
and WILLIAM HALL and HALL conveys his half. Head branches Pedlar.
Lines: WILLIAM CLARKE, Blue Ridge, JAMES HARTLESS, FREDERICK PRICE,
FRAZER. Witnesses: JONATHAN MYERS, JONATHAN L. BLAIR, GEORGE MYERS.
To ANDERSON MOSS, 16 May 1826.

187.   22 July 1818. THOMAS CUMPTON, Philadelphia, Pennsylvania,
        to DAVID HOFFMAN, Baltimore, Maryland, and coulsellor-at-law...
THOMAS CUMPTON bought tract from WILLIAM FENWICK and wife, CATHERINE,
25 September 1802. $6919 35,512½ acres by survey of 4 November 1794,
in Botetourt on Craig Creek, branch of James and Potter's Creek,
branch of Jackson River and joins survey for JONATHAN MILLER, WILLIAM
ROYALL, BOSTON SHAVER, SAMUEL DEW, WOLF, JACOB JOHNSON. This tract
patent under hand of ROBERT BROOKE, Governor, 20 August 1795--reference
to Book 33:115 granted under WILLIAM FENWICK. Also 10,400 acres
surveyed 3 February 1795, in Botetourt and Montgomery on Casey and
east side. Patent to FENWICK, 1 October 1795: Book 33:207--it also
included 300 acres reserved; also 2000 acres surveyed 30 October 1794,
in Botetourt on Pounding Mill, branch of Jackson. Lines: MITVHELL,
HELMONTELLEM (?), PETER WRIGHT, deceased. Patent 28 August 1795,
to FENWICK. Book 33:119. Also 3000 acres surveyed 3 November 1794,
in Botetourt on north side James. Lines: JONATHAN ALLEN. Patent
28 August 1795, to FENWICK. Book 33:124. Also 4442 acres in Amherst
County, surveyed 20 March 1795, on north side and joining Fluvanna
on Blue Ridge. Patent to FENWICK, 30 September 1795. Book 33:202.
Witnesses: EDWARD PARRY, SAMUEL WILLIAMS, JAMES M. BROWN. Philadelphia,
22 July 1818, ROBERT WHARTON, Mayor, as to THOMAS CUMPTON. Acknowledged
in Botetourt, March Court, 1819, as above. JONATHAN M. POWYER,
Deputy Clerk. Recorded Amherst County: 16 August 1819.

191.   25 November 1818. ISAAC RUCKER to BENJAMIN TALIAFERRO,
        JONATHAN WARE, SR., and JAMES WARE, Amherst County...Deed of
Trust; debt to FIELDING HOLLOWAY. $1.00; three tracts bought by
ISAAC RUCKER from FIELDING HOLLOWAY; reference to deed. Witnesses:
ALEXANDER TINSLEY, LINDSEY MC DANIEL, WILLIAM WARE, JONATHAN MYERS,
ADDISON TALIAFERRO, WILLIAM H. CAMDEN, JAMES F. TALIAFERRO. To
BENJAMIN TALIAFERRO, 6 April 1820.

193.   2 January 1819. WILLIAM JOPLING and JAMES WARE, Amherst County
        Justices of the Peace, as to MARTHA MILLNER, wife of RICHARD,
24 December 1818, to JESSE RICHESON.

194.   22 May 1819. CHARLES DUNCAN to CORNELIUS POWELL...Deed of
        Trust; debt to DAVID S. GARLAND. $1.00 slaves, stock, furniture.
Witnesses: JONATHAN S. BLAIR, JONATHAN SHEPHARD, SAMUEL M. GARLAND.
To THOMAS PENN, agent, 20 December 1819.

195.   31 July 1819. THOMAS WILLIAMSON and wife, POLLY, Amherst County,
        to JOSEPH B. MAYS, Amherst County...$350 117 acres headwaters
Stonehouse Creek. CHARLES TALIAFERRO and BENJAMIN TALIAFERRO as
to wife, same date.

196.   6 January 1819. WILLIAM ROBERTSON and wife, LUCY, Amherst
        County, to SAMUEL TAYLOR, Amherst County...$10.00 10 3/4 acres
both sides Falls' Creek. Lines: WILLIAM TERRY, a branch, LINEAS
BOLLING, grantee. Witnesses: NELSON C. DAWSON, REUBEN NORVELL,
WILLIAM DAY.

197.   8 July 1819. SAMUEL J. HARRISON and wife, SALLY, to THOMAS
        WIATT and RICHARD TYREE...Deed of Trust; debt to WILLIAM
ROBINSON and JESSE BECK. 181½ acres. Lines: L. BOLLING, CHRISTOPHER
ISBELL, PHILIP JOHNSON. Tract bought by SAMUEL J. HARRISON from
REUBEN NORVELL. Witnesses: STITH MEAD, PRUDENCE W. MEAD, LUCY
ROBINSON. Acknowledged in Lynchburg by SAMUEL J. HARRISON, July
term, 1819; JAMES BENAGH, Deputy Clerk. To WILLIAM ROBINSON,
29 October 1822.

199.   3 August 1819. JOSEPH HIGGINBOTHAM, SR., Amherst County,
        to JOSEPH MILSTRED, Amherst County...$100 both sides Long
Branch. Lines: the road, WILLIAM DEMPSEY, GORDAN's old line,
JONATHAN EUBANK. Witnesses: CHARLES L. BARRETT, JONATHAN RICHESON,
PHILIP SMITH, DAVID CLARKSON.

200. 22 July 1819. JONATHAN H. GOODWIN, Amherst County, administrator
        of PHILIP JOHNSON, Amherst County...revokes power of attorney,
12 December 1816, to REUBEN NORVELL. Witnesses: WILLIAM MUSE, SR.,
JONATHAN H. GOODWIN, JR., RICHARD BALLINGER, JONATHAN VEST.

201. 28 June 1818. WALLER SANDIDGE, SR., to PETER P. THORNTON,
        Amherst County...Deed of Trust; debt to COLEMAN and BARRETT,
JONATHAN FLOOD as bondsman to WILLIAM TUCKER. CHARLES L. BARRETT.
$1.00 16 acres bought from BENJAMIN CARTER, slave, stock, furniture,
etc. Witnesses: ZA. DRUMMOND, GEORGE L. SHRADER, A. EUBANK.

202. 18 August 1818. Order to Amherst County Justices of the Peace:
        JAMES SHIELDS and wife, ELIZABETH, WASHINGTON HILL and wife,
SALLY, AARON HIGGINBOTHAM and wife, ELIZABETH, LINDSEY SANDIDGE and
wife, CLARY, 20 July 1818, to ABSALOM HIGGINBOTHAM...one seventh of
land left by AARON HIGGINBOTHAM. CHARLES TALIAFERRO and BENJAMIN
TALIAFERRO, 16 July 1819, as to all wives.

204. 28 July 1819. JONATHAN HUDSON, son of RUSH HUDSON, Amherst
        County, to JOSEPH PENN, Amherst County...Deed of Trust; debt
to DAVID S. GARLAND. $1.00 stock. Witnesses: HUDSON M. GARLAND,
D. SHEPHARD, JONATHAN J. DILLARD.

205. 31 July 1819. JOSEPH B. MAYS and wife, SARAH, late HATTEN,
        Amherst County, to THOMAS WILLIAMSON...$100 12½ acres Stonehouse
Creek. Lines: ARAON HIGGINBOTHAM, deceased, grantee. CHARLES and
BENJAMIN TALIAFERRO as to SARAH, same date.

207. 15 June 1819. CORNELIUS PIERCE to RODERICK TALIAFERRO and
        JONATHAN D. URQUHART...Deed of Trust; debt to JOSEPH and
JONATHAN BOYCE, HENRY MOTLEY, WILLIAM BARNETT for benefit of BOYD and
MILLER and Company; judgement obtained in Campbell County--two acres
of unenclosed and unimproved tract in Madison and bought by CORNELIUS
PIERCE from JONATHAN HAYTHE; also 32 feet in Lynchburg--near POE's
Tanyard and bought by CORNELIUS PIERCE from JACOB HAAS. Also interest
in small tract in Amherst County. Lines: JONATHAN TAYLOR--four or
five acres and bought by CORNELIUS PIERCE to AMMON HANCOCK and
JONATHAN BULLOCK for benefit of WILLIAM DAVIS, SR., in Bedford;
also tract in trust in Lynchburg to THOMAS A. HOLCOMB for benefit
of DAVID ROSSER. Lynchburg Hustinss, July 1819; acknowledged by
CORNELIUS PIERCE; JAMES BENAGH, Deputy Clerk.

209. 10 August 1819. JONATHAN TARDY and wife, COURTNEY, Amherst
        County, to WILLIS FRANKLIN, Amherst County...$400 65 acres
formerly that of WILLIAM MOSS, deceased, and that part divided to
COURTNEY, daughter of MOSS. To WILLIS FRANKLIN, 8 August 1820.

210. 14 September 1819. Order to Amherst County Justices of the
        Peace: THOMAS N. EUBANK and wife, JANE, 4 December 1815, to
JONATHAN EUBANK, JR...210 acres. Done 7 August 1819, by HILL CARTER
and JONATHAN ELLIS.

211. 16 August 1819. WILLIAM KNIGHT, Amherst County, to WILLIAM
        HALL, Amherst County...Deed of Trust; September 7, 1816, and
recorded in Amherst County 18 November 1816 by RICHARD JANNEY, late
of Amherst County, to KNIGHT...One lot in New Glasgow between new
and old streets--#18. Lines: an alley, the old garden. HALL bought
at public sale for $180. Witnesses: WILLIAM M. RIVERS, HUDSON M.
GARLAND, G. L. HOLLOWAY.

214. -- August 1819. WILSON CARY NICHOLAS and wife, MARGARET,
Albemarle, 1; JONATHAN BROCKENBOROUGH, Richmond; JONATHAN
HARTWELL COCKE, Fluvanna; RANDOLPH HARRISON, Cumberland, 2; President
and Masters of Professors of William and Mary College; JONATHAN
PRESTON, Richmond; PHILIP NORBORN NICHOLAS, Richmond; DURO (?) BLAIR
and CARROLL, merchants, Richmond; JONATHAN GRAHAM, Richmond; WILLIAM
GALT, Richmond; JONATHAN PATTISON, Baltimore; JAMES MORRISON,
Lexington, Kentucky; WILLIAM H. CABELL, Buckingham; THOMAS JEFFERSON,
Albemarle; LEWIS NICHOLAS, Albemarle; LEWIS NICHOLAS, Albemarle;
THOMAS J. RANDOLPH, Albemarle; WILLIAM B. GILES, Amelia; HERON
LINTON and Company, Richmond merchants; JONATHAN MARSHALL, Richmond;
RICHARD ANDERSON, Richmond; JAMES BROWN, Richmond. BROWN is SR...
This is about as complicated a document setting forth various debts
as can be imagined: Deed of Trust; WILLIAM H. CABELL, bondsman for
WILSON CARY NICHOLAS to bank of US at Richmond; RICHARD ANDERSON
also bondsman; THOMAS JEFFERSON also bondsman to bank; also JONATHAN
PRESTON, PHILIP NORBORN NICHOLAS; LEWIS NICHOLAS, HERON SINTON
(LINTON?), WILLIAM B. GILES, JONATHAN MARSHALL, JONATHAN PATTESON,
THOMAS J. RANDOLPH, JAMES BROWN, SR. Some of others have paid part
of debt due WILLIAM and MARY: JONATHAN BROCKENBROUGH, JONATHAN H.
COCKE, RANDOLPH HARRISON. He executes Deed of Trust for $10.00 paid
by these three just named. His holdings enormous, but I wonder if he
ever got out of the strait. His holdings are as follows: Albemarle
tract. Lines: James River, JONATHAN HARRIS, PRICE PERKINS, ZACHARIAH
LEWIS, ROBERT RIVERS, THOMAS GOOLSBY, JESSE JOPLING, WILLIAM--2500
acres; already under Deed of Trust to WILLIAM and MARY; Albemarle
tract bought by him from ABRAHAM EADES--200 acres; tract in Albemarle
bought by him from REZON PORTER--175 acres. Also Albemarle tract
called CARROLL's--185 acres. All are encumbered. Six lots in
Warren in Albemarle; Buckingham tract bought by him from executors
of THOMAS ANDERSON--200 acres. Lines: P. PERKINS, HOWARD's road on
James. Also August a tract on Back Creek and bought by him from
GEORGE PETTS STEVENSON and held in common--600 acres. Tract in
Cabell County on Ohio River--Green Bottoms and patent to FRY and sold
by JOSHUA FRY and PEYTON SHORT to him--4444 acres and Deed of Trust
on it to ROBERT GAMBLE and WILLIAM WEST to secure WILLIAM H. CABELL;
also tract on Little Bird in Goochland--formerly of WILLIAM ANDERSON,
deceased. 1718 acres--Deed of Trust to JOSEPH SMITH, Augusta, and
ANDERSON's executors. Also 40,000 acres in Nelson, Amherst County,
and Bedford and patent to him. Also undivided tract in Greenbrier--one
fourth of 50,000 acres in common with JAMES BROWN, ROBERT BURTON,
HUDSON MARTIN and patent to him. Also all stock, books, etc. in
Albemarle and Richmond. Also claim upon estate of JONATHAN HATLEY
NORTON (?), deceased--about $6000; claim upon estate of EDWARD AMBLER
and pending in Court of Appeals; also all claims upon COLONEL
JONATHAN AMBLER; also all debts due him on certain Buckingham tracts
by and from DAVID, SAMUEL and NELSON PATTESON and BENJAMIN CLOPTON--
about $15,000. Also bonds in hands of DAVID BULLOCK and JAMES M.
MORRIS; many slaves named--some worked at Green Bottoms in Cabell.
Due, January 1, 1822. Henrico: T. H. ROSSER and WILLIAM PRICE,
Mayor, 6 August 1819, and ordered to certify to Goochland, Albemarle,
Buckingham, Augusta, Nelson, Amherst, Bedford, Cabell and Greenbrier
Counties.

229. 1 October 1818. JAMES GRAHAM and wife, ISABELLA, late HARTLESS,
Rockbridge...power of attorney to son, WILSON GRAHAM, Rockbridge,
to sell interest in estate of HENRY HARTLESS, deceased, late of
Amherst County. ISABELLA is daughter of HENRY. Two tracts of about
150 acres and bought by ISABELLA at a sale. JAMES CARUTHERS and
ALEXANDER SHIELDS, Rockbridge Justices of the Peace, 1 April 1818, as
to both grantors. Recorded Amherst County: 20 September 1819.

231. 18 September 1819. WILLIAM LONG and wife, BETSY, Amherst
      County, to THOMAS CREWS, Amherst County...WILLIAM BRYDIE, now
of Great Britain--BETSY BRYDIE and NANCY MC CREDIE, formerly BRYDIE--
of Richmond. L10 81½ acres. Lines: LINDSEY COLEMAN, JAMES FRANKLIN,
deceased, NANCY SHIELDS. Also 860 acres in Amherst County called
Lanivelle (?). Lines: JAMES POWELL, -- RIVERS, NANCY SHIELDS,
LINDSEY COLEMAN. Also many named slaves; mahogony custard bed, etc,;
long and interesting list. Deed of Trust; debt to CREWS. BRYDIES are
legatees of ALEXANDER BRYDIE, deceased, and reference to HENNICO
will. LONG is his executor. Reference to Superior Court of Richmond
and amount paid WILLIAM H. DYER as legatee by marriage of BRYDIE.
Married MARGARET, daughter of ALEXANDER BRYDIE.

235. 15 June 1817. JESSE KENNEDY, Amherst County, to WILLIAM
      POLLARD, Amherst County...$355.25 50 3/4 acres. Lines:
JONATHAN H. SMITH, on the road. Tract was part of one sold by
JESSE KENNEDY in Deed of Trust from ROBERT WALTON; debt due CHARLES H.
CHRISTIAN.

236. 2 April 1804. WOOSON P. CLARKE, Amherst County, to DAVID HUNTER,
      Martinsburg, Berkley County...Deed of Trust; debt to JONATHAN
ROBERSON, Martinsburg 5 sh. Tract bought by his father, NATHANIEL
CLARKE, in life from THOMAS GOODWIN and within three miles of MOORE's
Iron Works in Amherst County--my part is 183 acres. Margin: blanks
because deed was blotted. Witnesses: JAMES PENDLETON, WILLIAM BELL,
SAMUEL REID, ELISHA BOYD, HENRY S. G. TUCKER, W. R. LOWRY. Certified
from Jefferson County, 11 September 1804. Recorded Amherst County
21 June 1819.

237. 11 December 1809. PHILADELPHIA SMITH, MILLY and JOEL SMITH,
      Amherst County, to BENJAMIN TALIAFERRO, Amherst County...L113-10
56 3/4 acres south fork Puppie Creek. Lines: grantee. Witnesses:
JONATHAN SMITH, JEREMIAH FRANKLIN, STEPHEN CASH. Proved, 16 April
1810, by SMITH and CASH, and by FRANKLIN, 20 September 1819.

238. 22 May 1819. BENJAMIN SALE, Amherst County, to THOMAS N.
      EUBANK, Amherst County...Deed of Trust; debt to JONATHAN and
RICHARD L. ELLIS. $1.00 slaves and stock, furniture. Witnesses:
R. N. EUBANK, M. PENDLETON, JAMES EUBANK, CHARLES STINNETT. To
RICHARD ELLIS, 10 March 1822.

240. 19 July 1819. JAMES F. TALIAFERRO and JACOB SMITH to JAMES W.
      SMITH--the grantors are trustees in Deed of Trust by ELIZABETH
and EPHY GOOLSBY, 19 March 1818, to secure JAMES W. SMITH and LYNE S.
TALIAFERRO. Public sale--73 acres. Lines: BARTLETT CASH, POLLY
GOOLSBY. For amount of debt. Witnesses: JAMES HIX, JOEL F. SMITH.

241. 18 January 1819. SUSANNAH HOGG, Washington County, Kentucky,
      to MILBOURN HOGG, same county...$110 34 acres Maple Creek and
whereon JONATHAN HOGG died--mandion house tract. Witnesses: STEPHEN
BROWN, Deputy Clerk, JONATHAN HUGHES, Clerk, DAVID CLEVER, Presiding
Justice. August 12, 1819. I lived in Washington County for over
eight years. I do not recall doing any work on HOGG family, but
MILBOURN name is well known. It is usually MILBURN and I suspect
one of my lines stems from there to western Kentucky: MILBURN-
GLASSCOCK line.

242. 11 June 1819. ROBERT MORRIS, Lynchburg, to ARCHIBALD ROBERTSON,
      Lynchburg...Deed of Trust; debt to ROBERT TINSLEY, Bedford.
MORRIS and MITCHELL are partners and owe debts. $1.00 furniture in
ROBERT MORRIS's Lynchburg home--except china press and sideboard, and
four horses and wagon used by ROBERT MORRIS to haul wood and other
things about Lynchburg. Four horses are at Amherst County plantation.
Place in Campbell County called Long Mountain and interest in store-
house occupied by JAMES DUNNINGTON and WILLIAM M. WALLACE on Second (?)
Street in Lynchburg and Main--encumbered. Witnesses: ROBERT
ROBERTSON, JONATHAN M. MITCHELL, JAMES FITZPATRICK.

245. 16 February 1819. JABEZ CAMDEN to LEROY CAMDEN...Deed of
     Trust; debt to WILLIAM STINNETT--$1.00 slave and smith's tools.
Witnesses: ELIJAH STATON, SAMUEL BYERS, RICHARD STINNETT.

246. 27 May 1817. Clerk was wool-gathering on this one: Order
     to Amherst County Justices of the Peace as to GEORGE STOVALL
and wife, NANCY, 20 October 1809, to ELIAS WILLS...326 acres. Done
in Franklin County, Georgia, by JAMES H. LITTLE and NEELY DOBSON.
MASEFIELD PAYNE, Clerk. Done, 12 December 1818. Recorded Amherst
County: 21 June 1819. To ELIAS WILLS, 12 April 1822.

248. 29 September 1819. LINDSEY TINSLEY and wife, LUCY, Amherst
     County, to JONATHAN ROBINSON, Lynchburg...$120 120 acres south
side Pedlar. Lines: HENRY CHILDRESS, top of Blue Ridge.

249. 13 August 1819. ANN C. FRANKLIN, Amherst County, to SAMUEL
     SIMMONS...THOMAS CREWS as executor of JAMES FRANKLIN and as
grandson of children, 21 January 1817, conveyed to SAMUEL 5 3/4 acres
and mill as part of estate of JAMES FRANKLIN. ANN C. FRANKLIN is
now of age--$1.00. Witnesses: JONATHAN MORE, THOMAS CREWS, JOSEPH C.
LEE, B. STONE.

250. 20 August 1819. JAMES WOODROOF, Amherst County, to ARCHIBALD
     ROBERTSON and Company...$1.00 all interest in estate of DAVID
WOODROOF, SR.; two slaves; personal property; debts and money.
Witnesses: WILLIAM MITCHELL, GEORGE W. TURNER. To ARCHIBALD ROBERTSON,
23 March 1825.

251. 18 October 1819. CHALRES H. CHRISTIAN and wife, JANE, Amherst
     County, to LEWIS B. SIMPSON, Amherst County...L90 50 acres
Rutledge and Rocky Run. Lines: JOSEPH HIGGINBOTHAM, RICHARD
HUCKSTEP, road, MONROE.

252. 30 September 1813. JOSEPH HIGGINBOTHAM and PHILIP SMITH,
     Amherst County, to THOMAS N. EUBANK, Amherst County...L369-5
210 acres. Lines: Buffaloe Springs, BENJAMIN SANDIDGE at Swaping
Camp Road, WILLIAM DEMPSEY, GODFREY TOLER, WALKER ATTKINSON, JOSEPH
HIGGINBOTHAM, a branch. Witnesses: BENJAMIN HIGGINBOTHAM, WIATT
SMITH, DABNEY SANDIDGE, DUDLEY SANDIDGE. Final proof by DABNEY SANDIDGE,
18 October 1819. DUDLEY SANDIDGE.

252. 21 September 1819. JAMES L. WALKER and wife, ELIZABETH, Amherst
     County, to JAMES POWELL, Amherst County...$499 80 acres. Lines:
north side Lynch road, grantee, north fork Rutledge, THOMAS CREWS old
line--formerly between CREWS and WILLIAM OLIVER, BENJAMIN BROWN.
Witnesses: JONATHAN COLEMAN, JESSE KENNEDY, HUGH NORVELL. To
JAMES POWELL, 18 January 1821.

254. 30 September 1819. RICHARD HUCKSTEP, ELIZABETH FULCHER,
     CHARLES HUNT CHRISTIAN and wife, JANE, Amherst County...in
division of estate of SAMUEL HUCKSTEP, his widow received 52 acres
next to ELIZABETH FULCHER and 88 acres given to CHRISTIAN and
RICHARD HUCKSTEP. ANN, the widow, has died and grantors agree to
divide and have named friends, JACOB PIERCE, WILLIAM TURNER, CHARLES
MUNDY and JONATHAN LONDON to do so. ELIZABETH gets 52 acres and to
account to JANE for nine acres at $8.00 per acre. RICHARD gets
43 acres--part of 88--and rest to JANE and joins CHARLES H. CHRISTIAN.
All agree and convey. Witnesses: HENRY G. FULCHER, DELILAH FULCHER,
SAMUEL D. CHRISTIAN.

255. 17 April 1818. JOSEPH ANTRIM and wife, SUSAN, Lynchburg, to
     BEVERLY STAPLES, Lynchburg...$160 two tracts northwest of
Second Street in Madison--#'s 49 and 50. Junction of Second Street
to fifth alley. Two lots of half acre each. JONATHAN THURMON and
CHARLES WINFREE, Lynchburg Justices of the Peace, 9 April 1819, as
to wife. To DAVID STAPLES, 18 March 1822.

257. 28 August 1817. CHALRES C. CARTER, Nelson County, to JONATHAN
        BULLOCK...Deed of Trust; debt to CHARLES CRAWFORD, Lynchburg
L5 460 acres Horsley and whereon CRAWFORD lived for many years.
Lines: RICHARD MILLNER, WILLIAM THURMOND, RICHARD JONES, WILLIAM
JOPLING, JONATHAN CRAWFORD, CALEB RALLS, THOM S GILLIAM. Witnesses:
NELSON CRAWFORD, JONATHAN PRYOR, JONATHAN MC DANIEL, CHARLES TALIAFERRO.
(To JONATHAN BULLOCK, 1819--blotted)

259. 19 July 1819. JAMES W. SMITH to LYNE S. TALIAFERRO...SMITH
        bought tract sold by trustees of ELIZABETH and EPHY GOOLSBY--
73 acres. Debt due SMITH and TALIAFERRO on Deed of Trust and they
have divided tract--17 acres to TALIAFERRO. Lines: SMITH, JAMES
CASH, grantee. Witnesses: JACOB SMITH, JAMES SANDS, JONATHAN SMITH,
JR.

260. 23 August 1819. EDMOND EDNINGTON, Augusta, to ZACH DRUMMOND,
        Amherst County...$250 Tract conveyed by CARTER BEVERLY to
JACOB KINNEY and ERASMUS STRIBLING as trustees for WILLIAM MC MAKIN
and JAMES P. HEATH, Baltimore, 12 June 1802--General Court at Richmond.
Sold by CHARLES OVERSTREET to WILLIAM JOHNSTON and described in
BEVERLY's deed as 126 acres and by OVERSTREET for 105 acres.
Augusta Justices of the Peace: JAMES A MC CUE and JONATHAN C. SOWERS,
as to EDMOND EDNINGTON, 23 August 1819.

261. 26 January 1819. Order to Amherst County Justices of the
        Peace: MITCHELL FLOYD and wife, POLLY, 4 September 1818, to
LYNE S. TALIAFERRO...60 acres. Done by BENJAMIN TALIAFERRO and
WILLIAM JOPLING, 23 April 1819.

262. 10 April 1819. SAMUEL BURKS, Amherst County, to NELSON C.
        DAWSON, Amherst County...$200 30 acres headwaters Graham
Creek. Lines: grantor, ARTHUR L. DAVIES.

263. 16 October 1819. WILLIAM B. BANKS, Halifax, to LANDON CABELL,
        Nelson County, and ROBERT H. ROSE, Orange County...Deed of
Trust; debt to CABELL. $1.00 paid by LANDON CABELL. Harris Creek--
former tract of SPENCER NORVELL--505 acres and slaves. Conveyed by
Deed of Trust from ROSE to BANKS and JONATHAN CAMM, deceased, 21 May
1801, to secure CABELL as bondsman in suit of JAMES SHORT, deceased,
and CHARLES CREIGHTON, assignee of ROBERT KING, at Richmond. MARTIN
DAWSON, then of Millton in Albemarle, the other bondsman for ROSE.
Witnesses: H. M. GARLAND, REUBEN NORVELL, JONATHAN H. SMITH,
WILLIAM ARMISTEAD.

265. 3 August 1819. JOSEPH MILSTRED, Amherst County, to PHILIP
        THURMOND, SR., trustee, 2; CHALRES L. BARRET and Company, 3;
JONATHAN RICHESON, 4...Deed of Trust; debt to CHARLES L. BARRET and
Company and JONATHAN RICHESON; and JONATHAN and RICHARD ELLIS. $1.00
paid by THURMOND. Tract on both sides Long Branch. Lines: the
road, WILLIAM DEMPSEY, GORDON's old line, JONATHAN EUBANK. Bought by
JOSEPH MILSTRED from JOSEPH HIGGINBOTHAM, also crops on RICHARD
MILLNER's lands, slave, stock. Witnesses: DAVID CLARKSON, SAMUEL
HANSBROUGH, HENRY F. SMITH, WILLIAM COLEMAN. To BARRETT, 4 January
1820.

268. 23 September 1819. DAVID GLASS, 1; BENNETT A. CRAWFORD, 2;
        JONATHAN MYERS, 3...all of Amherst County. MYERS on bond for
GLASS: JONATHAN M. SETTLE versus GLASS suit. Deed of Trust; $1.00
house and lot near MC DANIEL's blacksmith shop and occupied by GLASS.
Witnesses: EZEKIEL HILL, THOMAS P. DILLARD, SAMUEL SWANSON.

269. 23 October 1819. ENOCH CARPENTER and wife, SALLY, Amherst County,
        to EATON CARPENTER, Amherst County...$968. Lines: RICHARD
SMITH, BARNETT CASH. Bought by grantor from WILLIAMS's executors.
Witnesses: CHARLES P. TALIAFERRO and LINDSEY COLEMAN who also acted
as Justices of the Peace as to wife, 27 October 1819. To E. P. TUCKER,
executor of grantee, 3 October 1848.

271. 15 August 1819. ROBERT TINSLEY and wife, JUDITH C., Bedford,
     to DAVID TINSLEY, Amherst County...$3632.00 363½ acres south
side Harris. Lines: SHELTON's road, grantee, RICHARD BURKS, mouth
of a branch. Tract whereon JONATHAN TINSLEY, deceased, lived.
BALDA MC DANIEL and NATHANIEL J. MANSON, Bedford Justices of the
Peace, 27 August 1819, as to wife.

273. 23 October 1819. ENOCH CARPENTER and wife, SALLY, Amherst
     County, to EATON CARPENTER, Amherst County...$1104 138 acres
Thrasher Creek. Lines: DAVID S. GARLAND. Justices of the Peace
and margin as on page 269.

274. 24 June 1816. SELY HOGG, JAMES CLARKE and wife, LUCY, MICHAEL
     ENSEY and wife, CHESY, JONATHAN STEWART and wife, SALLY, SUSANNAH,
CATY HOGG, DELILA LUCAS and JONATHAN HOGG, all of Pendleton County,
Kentucky, to SUSANNAH HOGG, same county...L27 34 acres--JONATHAN
HOGG's tract in Amherst County. JEDIAH ASHCRAFT and WILLIAM ANIDE (?),
Justices of the Peace. WILLIAM C. KENNETT, Clerk.

277. 9 August 1819. WIATT P. SMITH, Amherst County, to JOSEPH PENN,
     and DAVID S. GARLAND, Amherst County...Deed of Trust; debt to
GARLAND. $1.00 paid by PENN--slaves. Witnesses: JAMES L. PENDLETON,
HUDSON M. GARLAND, WILLIAM C. CHRISTIAN. To JOSEPH PENN, agent,
10 August 1819.

278. 10 November 1819. JAMES SEAY and wife, JANE, late SOWELL,
     Amherst County, to DAVID S. GARLAND...$500 150 acres north
borders Buffaloe and JANE bought it from JONATHAN P. COBBS, 31 January
1817. Lines: grantee, SAMUEL MEREDITH, deceased, GEORGE COLEMAN,
old church road. Witnesses: C. POWELL, THOMAS ALDRIDGE, JONATHAN
COLEMAN. Last two as Justices of the Peace as to wife, same day.

280. 16 November 1819. JAMES SANDS, 1; CORNELIUS POWELL, 2; DAVID
     and DANIEL HIGGINBOTHAM and Company, 3...Deed of Trust; debt
to DAVID and DANIEL HIGGINBOTHAM and Company; $1.00 paid by CORNELIUS
POWELL--beds, etc.

281. 13 November 1818. LEORY CAMDEN and wife, BETHEMIAH, Amherst
     County, to THOMAS ALDRIDGE, Amherst County...$300 two lots in
town of Duiguidsville on Bent Creek. LEROY CAMDEN bought of WILLIAM J.
FREELAND in Buckingham County. Witnesses: JESSE KENNEDY, W. D.
CHRISTIAN, WILLIAM P. CASHWELL.

282. 12 July 1819. WILLIAM MITCHELL, Amherst County, 1; EDWARD
     WATTS, Campbell County, 2, and HENRY L. LANGHORNE, 2; CHARLES
JOHNSTON, Campbell County, 3...Deed of Trust; debt to CHARLES
JOHNSTON. $1.00 paid by EDWARD WATTS and HENRY L. LANGHORNE; 60 acres
bought by WILLIAM MITCHELL from WILLIAM PETTYJOHN and whereon stands
Farm Mills and about 40 acres adjoining which WILLIAM MITCHELL bought
from PETTIS THACKER; also 31 acres bought by WILLIAM MITCHELL from
REUBEN COX. Lines: MILNER COX, JONATHAN MEHONE, JAMES Lee; lands
bought by WILLIAM MITCHELL from JONATHAN WARD. (To HENRY L. LANGHORNE,
30 December 1819). Also stone lumber yard and groves on Black Water
Creek and near Lynchburg limits; also twenty slaves in Prostonville
County; also 85 named slaves. Various debts: notes to Farmers
Bank; to CHARLES JOHNSTON, GEORGE GORDON CLOYD, Montgomery County,
JONATHAN WATTS, Bedford, CHRISTOPHER CLARK and in hands of DR. GEORGE
CABELL, Lynchburg, CHARLES M. MITCHELL, JOSEPH MARRS (?), Richmond,
JMAES W. SWAN, CHARLES P. JOHNSON, MICAJAH DAVIS, JR., and JAMES
STEWART, Lynchburg Justices of the Peace as to WILLIAM MITCHELL,
24 December 1819.

286. 15 November 1819. RUSSEL DAWSON, 1; AMBROSE RUCKER, 2;
     SAMUEL BURKS, SR., 3...Deed of Trust; debt to SAMUEL BURKS, SR.
$..00 paid by AMBROSE RUCKER--beds, etc. Witnesses: JAMES LEE,
ROBERT RIDGWAY, BENJAMIN OGDEN.

287. 13 November 1819. RICHARD HARRISON and wife, SOPHIA, to
STERLING CLAIBORNE...$1600 100½ acres. Lines: Rocky Mills.
Bought by RICHARD HARRISON from JONATHAN CHRISTIAN, B. Witnesses:
D. P. GOOCH, JAMES R. LIVELY, DRURY CHRISTIAN.

288. 10 December 1819. --27 October 1817. WILLIAM P. MUSE and wife,
NANCY, executor Deed of Trust to CHARLES WINGFIELD for benefit
of MILLNER COX...Lines: GEORGE W. TAYLOR, DANIEL NORCUTT, WILLIAM
MUSE, SR., MILLNER COX. At request of COX, public sale, and WILLIAM
PETTYJOHN has bought at $270.00.

289. 14 September 1819. JONATHAN THOMPSON, JR., Amherst County, to
THOMAS ALDRIDGE, Amherst County...$12,000 452 acres Tye and
JONATHAN THOMPSON, JR. bought it from JONATHAN WHITE. To THOMAS
ALDRIDGE, 12 November 1823.

289. 1 October 1819. WILLIAM H. CAMDEN, Amherst County, CORNELIUS
POWELL, 2; DAVID and DANIEL HIGGINBOTHAM and Company, 3...Deed
of Trust; debt to DAVID and DANIEL HIGGINBOTHAM. $1.00 furniture,
stock--interest in tract from HENRY CAMDEN to me and others, stock
three slaves left to me by CHARLES BURRUS, SR. To CORNELIUS POWELL,
12 February 1820.

290. 16 December 1819. JAMES POWELL and wife, MILDRED, Amherst
County, to JONATHAN LONDON, Amherst County...$500 80 acres.
Lines: north side Lynch road, grantee, north fork Rutledge, THOMAS
CREWS' old line--formerly between CREWS and WILLIAM OLIVER, BENJAMIN
BROWN. Tract bought by JAMES POWELL from JAMES S. WALKER. To
JONATHAN LONDON, 4 November 1820.

291. 16 November 1819. THOMAS NEVIL, 1; ALDRIDGE, MYERS and
PENDLETON, 2; STERLING CLAIBORNE, 3...Deed of Trust; $1.00
paid by STERLING CLAIBORNE. Debts to ALDRIDGE, MYERS and PENDLETON;
JABEZ CAMDEN, JONATHAN MYERS and Company--200 acres in Montgomery
County on Burks fork. Deeded to THOMAS NEVIL by JAMES NEVIL. To
THOMAS ALDRIDGE, to be certified by Montgomery Clerk. 30 August 1820.

293. 8 August 1818. HENRY HARTLESS and wife, JANE, RICHARD HARTLESS
and wife, MARY, WILLIAM WILSON and wife, NANCY, JAMES GRAHAM
and wife, ISBELL, MARIAH HARTLESS, ANNIS HARTLESS, JONATHAN CLARK
and wife, MARY, JONATHAN COOPER and wife, TABITHA, HENRY CLARK as
attorney for JONATHAN CLARK, JOSEPH GARVIS and wife, NANCY, REUBEN
PETERS and wife, SUSANNAH, NATHANIEL COOPER and wife, PATSY, Amherst
County, to WILLIAM HARTLESS...6 sh. 58½ acres. Lines: JONATHAN
COOPER on top of a mountain, north fork Pedlar, JOSEPH HIGGINBOTHAM,
JR., LYLE.

294. 13 December 1816. Order to Amherst County Justices of the
Peace: DANIEL SHRADER and wife, PATSY, 12 December 1816, to
PHILIP THURMOND...107 acres, 91 acres, 6 acres. Done by JAMES M.
BROWN and JAMES POWELL--181--recorded: December --, 1816.

295. 8 August 1818. Same grantors as on page 293. HARTLESS et al.
to WILLIAM HARTLESS...L295 330 acres Howl Creek. Lines:
SOLOMON CARTER, WILLIAM CABELL, JONATHAN TALIAFERRO.

297. 7 April 1817. JONATHAN LYNCH and wife, MARY, Lynchburg, to
JONATHAN TAYLOE, Amherst County...$6986.25 paid by TAYLOE--
1. Beginning at southwest corner of lot occupied by GIDEON SHAW and
joining road from the bridge, grantee, WILLIAM ISBELL, BENJAMIN
PERKINS--28 3/4 acres. 2. Lines: BENJAMIN PERKINS, the horse ford
road--5 3/4 acres. Witnesses: JONATHAN D. URQUHART, JONATHAN N.
ROSE, JAMES BENAGH, JONATHAN H. SMITH, JAMES BULLOCK and RICHARD
PERKINS, Campbell County Justices of the Peace, 4 November 1819, as
to MARY. To SETH WOODROOF, 5 June 1829, per order of JONATHAN
TAYLOE.

298. 7 May 1819. Order to Amherst County Justices of the Peace:
THOMAS MURRELL and wife, ELIZABETH, 17 November 1817, to
NELSON C. DAWSON...71½ acres. Done by DAVID S. GARLAND and CHARLES P.
TALIAFERRO, 12 November 1819.

299. 2 April 1819. JONATHAN TAYLOE, Amherst County, 1; CHRISTOPHER
ANTHONY and JORDAN ANTHONY, Lynchburg, 2; JAMES C. MOORMAN,
Campbell County, 3...Deed of Trust; $5.00 paid by CHRISTOPHER ANTHONY
and JORDAN ANTHONY. 28 3/4 acres--tract conveyed from JONATHAN LYNCH
and wife, 7 April 1817; also slaves. If not paid, to sell at Market
House in Lynchburg. Witnesses: GEORGE WHITLOCKE, T. W. ASHELLL (?),
JR., WILLIAM RADFORD. JAMES BULLOCK and RICHARD PERKINS, Campbell
County Justices of the Peace as to JONATHAN TAYLOE, 2 April 1819.
To MOORMAN, 29 March 1820.

301. 18 November 1819. STERLING CLAIBORNE and wife, JANE, Amherst
County, to RICHARD HARRISON, Amherst County...$2500 530 acres
headwaters Pedlar. 1. 300 acres bought from BENJAMIN HIGGINBOTHAM.
Lines: BENJAMIN TALIAFERRO, JONATHAN COOPER. 2. 230 acres--part of
it bought by STERLING CLAIBORNE from JOSEPH SEAY. Witnesses:
C. DABNEY, HENRY T. HARRIS, C. ANTHONY. To RICHARD HARRISON, 1821.

302. 18 November 1819. RICHARD HARRISON and wife, SOPHIA, to
STERLING CLAIBORNE, Amherst County...$4700 2/3 of Rocky Mills
and tract with it--between 28 and 29 2/3 acres and bought from
JONATHAN and ROBERT COLEMAN. Witnesses: as above.

303. 16 September 1819. HENRY BALLINGER, 1; JOSEPH PENN, 2; DAVID S.
GARLAND, 3...GARLAND is bondsman in suit of JONATHAN and RICHARD
ELLIS versus HENRY BALLINGER; also debt to GEORGE W. TAYLOR. Deed
of Trust; $1.00 paid by JOSEPH PENN--named horses; slave, furniture.
Witnesses: ROBERT TINSLEY, CORNELIUS POWELL, JOSEPH DILLARD.

304. 2 August 1819. JONATHAN LYNCH and wife, MARY...SR., ELIZABETH
DOUGLAS, widow of ARCHILLES DOUGLAS, deceased, NEWBY JOHNSON
and wife, SARAH (formerly DOUGLAS), JONATHAN JOHNSON and wife,
JUDITH, formerly DOUGLAS, RICHARD TYREE and wife, MILDRED, formerly
DOUGLAS, WILLIAM BUTLER and wife, DEBORAH, formerly DOUGLAS, MAHLON
CADWALLADER and wife, ELIZABETH, formerly DOUGLAS, MARY, JONATHAN L.
and ARCHILLES DOUGLAS, heirs of ARCHILLES DOUGLAS, deceased, to
JONATHAN LYNCH, JR. May 14, 1792, MICAJAH TERRELL sold to JONATHAN
LYNCH, SR., and ARCHILLES DOUGLAS 376 acres on both sides Bolling
Creek. Conveyed absolute title, but meant to be Deed of Trust to
secure PARSONS ANTHONY and Company and now paid. JONATHAN LYNCH, SR.
and JR. have bought part of tract and title appears to be vested in
SR. and DOUGLAS heirs--$1.00--to JR. for 340 acres--part of tract.
Lines: ROBERT MORRIS, Bolling, near Opossum Island road, WARWICK,
ROBINSON. Acknowledged by all in Lynchburg; Justices of the Peace:
JONATHAN THURMOND, ARCHIBALD ROBERSTSON, HENRY DAVIS, MICAJAH DAVIS, JR.

308. 6 December 1819. CHARLES M. BURKS, Amherst County, to RICHARD H.
BURKS, son of CD (sic), Amherst County, and WILLIAM GRANT,
Kanawaha County...love for my sister, ELIZABETH GATEWOOD, wife of
RANSOM GATEWOOD and concessions by her to me in division of our
father's estate and $1.00--slaves named--for her and her children.
Witnesses: STERLING CLAIBORNE, JAMES WARE, JAMES DAVIS. To CHARLES M.
BURKS, 18 December 1820.

310. 22 December 1819. JAMES W. HILL, 1; JOSEPH PENN, 2; GEORGE S.
HOLLOWAY, 3...Deed of Trust; debt to GEORGE S. HOLLOWAY. $1.00
paid by JOSEPH PENN--tract adjoining JAMES POWELL and HILL has
recently erected building with three chimneys, a slave, all claims
versus KENNEDY and HILL firm; claim on THOMAS CREWS. To GEORGE S.
HOLLOWAY, 26 February 1820.

312. 23 December 1818. SAMUEL J. HARRISON and wife, SARAH, Lynchburg,
      to EDMOND LYNCH, Lynchburg...$1.00 part of an island in James
just below Lynchburg and formerly that of GEORGE D. WINSTON and
konwn as WINSTON's Island. Lines: north side Lynch, south side--
24½ acres at low water mark. MICAJAH DAVIS, JR. and HENRY DAVIES,
Lynchburg Justices of the Peace as to wife, 16 October 1819.

313. 10 August 1819. WILLIAM STINNETT, Amherst County 1; DAVID and
      DANIEL HIGGINBOTHAM and Company, 2; JOHN S. BLAIR, 3...Deed of
Trust; $1.00 paid by JOHN S. BLAIR. Slave, stock, furniture. To
C. POWELL, agent for DAVID and DANIEL HIGGINBOTHAM, 1824.

314. 20 December 1819. POLLY COLEMAN, Amherst County, to JAMES
      COLEMAN, Amherst County...$4800 142 acres head borders Huff.
Part of tract of JONATHAN COLEMAN, deceased, and her share from his
estate as his daughter. Lines: PETERS, WILLMORE. Witnesses:
SAMUEL COLEMAN, BARRET O. MOON, FLEMING COLEMAN, JONATHAN COLEMAN.

315. 6 January 1820. JAMES COLEMAN, Amherst County, to POLLY COLEMAN,
      Amherst County...$1000 45 acres north border and south side
Tobacco Row Mountain and Harris. Part of tract of DANIEL BURFORD,
deceased, as to JAMES COLEMAN at division of his mother's estate.
Lines: BURKS, SAMUEL COLEMAN, BURFORD's old line. Witnesses: as
above. To DANIEL F. CHRISTIAN, 25 April 1822.

316. 4 January 1820. POLLY CAMDEN, Amherst County, to her nephew,
      CHRISTIAN COLEMAN, Amherst County...love and $1.00--girl about
twelve or thirteen and from estate of POLLY's mother. To CHRISTIAN
COLEMAN, 6 September 1831.

317. 20 December 1819. JAMES COLEMAN to POLLY COLEMAN...$4800 300
      acres both sides Harris. Part of tract of JONATHAN COLEMAN,
deceased, and to his son, JAMES. Lines: DR. CABELL, LINGUS (?), the
road. Witnesses: as above. To DANIEL F. CHRISTIAN as above, page
315.

318. 2 August 1819. JONATHAN LYNCH, SR., and wife, MARY and
      DOUGLAS heirs as on page 304...same facts set forth and this
deed is to ROBERT MORRIS 376 acres on both sides Bolling Creek.
$1.00 for 60 acres bought by MORRIS. Lines: Bolling, James River,
grantee, WARWICK, JONATHAN LYNCH, JR., JONATHAN THURMOND et al. as
to wives as on page 304.

322. 9 June 1819. JONATHAN LONDON and wife, TIRZA, Amherst County,
      to RICHARD WYATT, Louisa County...$5000 330 acres Porrage Creek
and where JONATHAN LONDON lives on east side Stovall road. Lines:
JAMES DAVIS, CHARLES PALMORE, CHARLES MUNDY, JOHN HUTCHISON. Witnesses:
DANIEL DAY, SOLOMON DAY, EZEKIEL DAY. CHARLES MUNDY and TINSLEY
RUCKER, Amherst County Justices of the Peace, as to TIRZA, 11 November
1819. To WILLIAM DAY, 1 May 1820.

323. 13 March 1818. JAMES HIGGINBOTHAM and wife, ELIZA, Amherst
      County, to LINDSEY SANDIDGE, Amherst County...L6 ten acres
Buffaloe. Lines: BENJAMIN SANDIDGE. To LINDSEY SANDIDGE, 17 April
1820.

324. 14 June 1819. BENJAMIN PERKINS and wife, MARY, Lynchburg, to
      RICHARD PERKINS, Campbell County...$1500--all land bought by
BENJAMIN PERKINS at sale conducted by WHITLOCK and RICHARDSON, 4 April
1817--eight lots in Madison: 21, 42, 70, 77, 78, 79, 84, 85 and
three small tracts of 4½, 3/4, and 1 3/4 adjoining Madison. SACKVILLE
KING and MEREDITH LAMBETH, Campbell Justices of the Peace as to
BENJAMIN PERKINS, 20 December 1819.

325. 19 July 1819. LYNE S. TALIAFERRO and wife, MILDRED, Amherst
     County, to JAMES W. SMITH, Amherst County...joint owners of
tract on headwaters of CARTER's Creek, branch of Buffaloe. Lines:
BARTLETT CASH. Bought from ELIZA and EPHY GOOLSBY--27 acres.
$40.00 for half interest. Witnesses: JONATHAN SMITH, JR., JAMES
SANDS, JACOB SMITH.

326. 31 December 1819. CATHERINE METCALFE, widow of VERNON METCALFE,
     ROBERT MORRIS, executor of VERNON METCALFE, ARTHUR B. DAVIES,
commissioner by Amherst County Court decree, November, 1818, on behalf
of JAMES METCALFE, infant son of VERNON, to GEORGE LETTON HOLLOWAY
and E. C. L. P. KINNEY L1760. Tract bought by THOMAS L. HOLLOWAY,
executor of HENRY HOLLOWAY, deceased, from VERNON METCALFE--916 3/4
acres. Lines: the road, R. WALKER, CAMDEN, COLEMAN, the creek,
MC DANIEL, PENDLETON, POWELL. Witnesses: S. GARLAND, REUBEN NORVELL,
JONATHAN D. URQUHART. Bedford County Justices of the Peace: NATHANIEL J.
MANSON and BALDA MC DANIEL, as to CATHERINE, same date.

328. 21 December 1819. NICHOLAS HARRISON and JONATHAN M. SETTLE and
     Company to JONATHAN H. SMITH...Deed of Trust by JONATHAN H.
SMITH to NICHOLAS HARRISON to secure SETTLE. Tracts near Amherst
County Court House and JONATHAN H. SMITH is ready to release.
Witnesses: JAMES L. PENDLETON, HILL CARTER, RICHARD HARRISON.

328. 12 July 1819. WILLIAM MITCHELL, Amherst County, to THOMAS
     HIGGINBOTHAM, Lynchburg...Deed of Trust; debt to MATTHEW
HARVEY. $1.00 670 acres. 21 acres excepted and sold to GEORGE
TUCKER, but not deeded. Tract bought by WILLIAM MITCHELL from
JONATHAN WARD. On south side James River. Lines: MILLNER COX,
BENJAMIN SCHOOLFIELD, WILLIAM BYRD, JONATHAN HANSFORD, tract bought
by WILLIAM MITCHELL from REUBEN COX, PETTIS THACKER's heirs--it is
where WILLIAM MITCHELL lives. Witnesses: EDWARD P. JOHNSON,
WILLIAM LINTHICUM, JONATHAN WHITE. Acknowledged in Lynchburg:
MICAJAH DAVIS, JR. and A. ROBERSTSON, Justices of the Peace.

330. 8 November 1819. RICHARD HARRISON, Amherst County, to SAMUEL
     SIMMONS, Amherst County...$1000 530 acres Buffaloe ridge and
bought by RICHARD HARRISON from ROBERT R. CARTER. Witnesses:
ARTHUR B. DAVIES, GEORGE HOLLOWAY, BEVERLY DAVIES.

331. 12 August 1818. WILLIAM HARTLESS and wife, NANCY, join other
     HARTLESS et al. who are named on pages 293 and 295 to sell to
some of those named...grantors--in other deeds: JONATHAN CLARK,
JOSEPH GARVIS, REUBEN PETERS, and NATHANIEL COOPER paid $2.00.
1. 82 acres headwaters Pedlar. Lines: top of Blue Ridge, HENRY
HARTLESS. 2. 53 acres and next to 1. WILLIAM WILSON, attorney for
JAMES GRAHAM.

333. 23 May 1819. DAVID HOFFMAN and wife, MARY, DANIEL HOFFMAN and
     wife, ELIZABETH, 1; PLEASANT LABBY, 2; CHISWELL DABNEY and
WILLIAM ROBINSON, 3...first are partners and LABBY is bondsman at
Lynchburg Bank. Deed of Trust; $1.00 paid by CHISWELL DABNEY and
WILLIAM ROBINSON--5 3/4 acres in town of Madison--two acres of it
includes tanyard and bought from JOSEPH KENNEDY; rest bought from
JONATHAN LYNCH, SR. Witnesses: JAMES WEAKS, JONATHAN J. CHAMBERS,
THOMAS WELSH, REID BROWN, WILLIAM STEEN, JOHN BOYD, ARCHIBALD ROBERTSON
and JONATHAN THURMON as Justices of the Peace in Lynchburg, 17 July
1819, as to DABNEY and ROBINSON, DAVID HOFFMAN, LABBY and MARY S. W.
HOFFMAN. Rockbridge Justices of the Peace: ALEXANDER SHIELDS and
JONATHAN ALEXANDER, 2 May 1819, as to ELIZA N. HOFFMAN, wife of
DANIEL.

337. 2 December 1819. WILLIAM H. CAMDEN and wife, POLLY, Amherst
     County, to JAMES W. SMITH, Amherst County...Deed of Trust;
debt to TANDY RUTHERFORD--interest in estate of SALLY DUNCAN's dower--
POLLY is due child's part at SALLY's death. Witnesses: JAC TYREE,
JAMES WOOD, CHARLES DUNCAN. To TANDY RUTHERFORD, November, 1827.

338. 20 December 1819. JESSE RICHESON and wife, KITTY, Amherst
County, to WILLIAM GATEWOOD, Amherst County...$1.00 13½ acres.
Lines: Brown's Creek. To WILLIAM GATEWOOD, 13 June 1821.

338. 20 December 1819. JESSE RICHESON and wife, KITTY, Amherst
County, to MOSES MARTIN, Amherst County...$500 487½ acres.
1. Surveyed for JOSIAH ELLIS. 2. Surveyed for JACOB BROWN. Lines:
JOSIAH ELLIS. 3. Surveyed for JONATHAN RICHESON on Brown's Creek.

340. 11 December 1819. JONATHAN H. SMITH and wife, MARY C., Lynchburg,
to STERLING CLAIBORNE, Amherst County...$6000--tract within
two miles of Amherst County Court House. Lines: BEN STONE, MILES,
grantee, CHARLES W. CHRISTIAN, separated from late JAMES FRANKLIN
by public road. Bought from JAMES P. GARLAND, BEN STONE and wife,
and CHARLES, HUNT CHRISTIAN by deeds. All that SMITH owns in
Amherst County. Witnesses: WILL CARTER, RICHARD HARRISON, JAMES L.
PENDLETON.

341. 27 December 1819. OLIVER TINSLEY and wife, SOPHIA, Bedford
County, to TINSLEY RUCKER, Amherst County...$2100.75 121½ acres
by survey of REUBEN NORVELL--Lynch road. NATHANIEL J. MANSON and
BALDA MC DANIEL, Bedford Justices of the Peace, as to wife, same date.

342. 18 January 1820. WILLIAM H. CAMDEN, Amherst County, 1;
BENNET A. CRAWFORD, Amherst County, 2; JONATHAN MYERS, 3...
Deed of Trust; $1.00 paid by BENNET A. CRAWFORD 214 acres bought by
HENRY CAMDEN from JABEZ CAMDEN. Lines: MICAJAH CAMDEN, CHARLES
DUNCAN.

343. 27 May 1819. TINSLEY RUCKER to WILLIAM R. PORTER, ANTHONY
RUCKER, and WILLIAM J. WALKER, Bedford...Deed of Trust; to
secure AMBROSE and GARLAND RUCKER (10 May 1821 to AMBROSE RUCKER)
on bond to ISHAM CLARK by TINSLEY RUCKER, JAMES JOPLING, GARLAND
RUCKER and JONATHAN MOORE. $1.00--slaves named. Witnesses: CAWHILL
MENEES, FREDERICK ANNSPAUGH, JESSE HACKWORTH. Certified by J.
STEPTOE, Bedford Clerk, 27 December 1819.

343. 27 December 1819. TINSLEY RUCKER and wife, NANCY, Amherst
County, to ROBERT TINSLEY, Bedford...Deed of Trust; to secure
OLIVER TINSLEY, Bedford. $1.00 121½ acres conveyed by OLIVER TINSLEY
to TINSLEY RUCKER on even date. To OLIVER TINSLEY, 11 February 1822.

346. 1 August 1819. JONATHAN PATTEN, 1; A. B. DAVIES, 2; SOPHIA
CRAWFORD, 3...Deed of Trust $1.00 paid by A. B. DAVIES--slave,
furniture, stock. Tract bought from BENJAMIN PERKINS and deeded by
ROBERT MORRIS--25 acres. Part of 39½ acres bought. Witnesses:
E. FLETCHER, JOSEPH DILLARD, W. S. CRAWFORD.

348. 19 May 1819. STITH MEAD and wife, PRUDENCE W., Amherst County,
to PEYTON ANDERSON, Chesterfield County...$3200. Lines:
WILLIAM BURD, B. SCHOLFIELD, TAYLOR, grantor, WYATT, DABNEY.
Witnesses: WILLIAM P. MARTIN, GEORGE M. ANDREWS, BENJAMIN HOPKINS,
TINSLEY RUCKER, JAMES L. LAMKIN--last two as Justices of the Peace,
1 February 1820, as to wife.

349. 29 January 1820. THOMAS WIATT and wife, SALLY, Amherst County,
to DANIEL BROWN and CHISWELL DABNEY...Deed of Trust; to secure
Bank of Virginia--$1.00 40 acres. Lines: WILLIAM WARWICK, STITH
MEAD, WILLIAM ROBINSON--formerly part of where he lives and bought
from JOSEPH NEEDHAM and wife, slaves named. A. ROBERTSON and HENRY
DAVIS, Lynchburg Justice of thePeace, 1 February 1820, as to grantors.

351. 17 January 1820. LINDSEY TINSLEY, Amherst County, 1; ISAAC
     RUCKER, 2; NATHANIEL J. MANSON, 2; ROBERT TINSLEY, Bedford, 3...
Deed of Trust; debts to ROBERT TINSLEY, executor of JONATHAN TINSLEY,
ISAIA ATKISON, JESSE RICHESON, administrator of WILLIAM SLEDD, THOMAS
PENN, Nelson County, CALE B. RALLS, CHARLES TOOLEY, CHARLES L. BARRET,
JONATHAN CLEMENTS. $1.00 paid by ISAAC RUCKER and NATHANIEL J. MANSON.
Slaves named, stock, furniture. Witnesses: MERIT M. WHITE, J. S.
DILLARD, RICHARD BURKS, WILLIAM WHITE. To ROBERT TINSLEY, 30 March
1820.

353. 16 December 1816. CALEB RALLS, Amherst County, to JAMES
     SANDIDGE, Amherst County...$1000 390 acres north borders south
fork Buffaloe. Lines: LEONARD BALLOW, his own. Witnesses:
NELSON CRAWFORD, JAMES RALLS, EZEKIEL GILBERT, ROBERT SEBREE, WILLIAM
CARPENTER. 1819 final proof by CRAWFORD.

354. 7 June 1819. STITH MEAD, Amherst County, 1; THOMAS MURRELL, 2;
     NELSON DAWSON, 3...Deed of Trust; debt to 4 (?). $1.00 paid
by THOMAS MURRELL and NELSON DAWSON. Horses named. Debt to 4:
REVEREND CHRISTOPHER S. MOORINGS (?). Witnesses: PLEASANT THURMOND,
JORDAN CREASY, LEWIS ROBINSON. To THOMAS MURRELL, 16 December 1822.

356. 10 September 1819. ROWLAND SANDIDGE, Amherst County, to
     JONATHAN IRVINE, Rockbridge, and WILLIAM CARTER, Amherst
County...Deed of Trust; debt to JAMES LAIRD, Rockbridge. Slaves
named and stock. To remain in ROWLAND SANDIDGE's hands, if not
removed from Virginia. Witnesses: W. JOPLING, JONATHAN CARUTHERS
and ROBERT WHITE, Rockbridge Justices of the Peace as to IRVINE and
LAIRD, CHARLES and BENJAMIN TALIAFERRO, Amherst County Justices of
the Peace, as to SANDIDGE and CARTER. Recorded 9 February 1820.
To JAMES LAIRD, 7 August 1822.

357. 10 June 1819. ALEXANDER HENDERSON, Amherst County, to JONATHAN
     COLEMAN, Amherst County...Deed of Trust; debt to ROBERT L.
COLEMAN, Lynchburg. $1.00, furniture, stock.

358. 3 May 1819. STITH MEAD, Amherst County, to JONATHAN ALCOCK
     and AMBROSE RUCKER...Deed of Trust; debt to MRS. MARY BLAKEY
and ELIZA BLAKEY, Henrico. Witnesses: B. STONE, THOMAS LANDRUM,
JONATHAN EWERS. To JONATHAN ALCOCK, 27 December 1822--slaves named
in Deed of Trust.

360. 14 July 1819. STITH MEAD and wife, PRUDENCE, Amherst County,
     to WILLIAM ROBINSON and CHISWELL DABNEY...Deed of Trust; debt
to JAMES GILLIAM, Lynchburg, on bond to Bank of Virginia. $1.00
tract where STITH MEAD lives--233 acres; four small tracts. 1. 48 3/4
acres bought from HENRY TENISON. 2. 128 acres bought from WILLIAM
WILLIAMS. 3. 41 3/4 acres bought from LUCY ROBINSON. 4. 14½ acres
bought from LORENZO DOW and wife, PEGGY, 11 March 1814. Witnesses:
ABRAM R. NORTH, JONATHAN T. MASON, WILLIAM H. CLARK. Lynchburg
Justices of the Peace: HENRY DAVIS and CHRIS WINFREE, as to PRUDENCE,
24 August 1819. To W. NORVELL, 13 June 1822.

364. 31 August 1819. LUCY ROBINSON, Amherst County, to STITH MEAD,
     Amherst County...$105 three acres. Lines: both, road. Witnesses:
WILLIAM MARTIN, WILLIAM and LEWIS RONBINSON. TINSLEY RUCKER and
JAMES L. LAMKIN, Amherst County Justices of the Peace, as to LUCY,
1 February 1820. To STITH MEAD, 24 May 1824.

364. 2 February 1820. MICAJAH CAMDEN and wife, POLLY, Amherst
     County, to A. B. DAVIES, Amherst County...$1040. Lines:
Spring branch, grantor, main road. Witnesses: REUBEN NORVELL,
BENNET A. CRAWFORD, WARNER GOODWIN. To A. B. DAVIES, 31 July 1823.

365. 7 February 1820. JEREMIAH N. COATS, Amherst County, to BENNET A.
     CRAWFORD...Deed of Trust; debt to HANNAH HALL. $1.00 house and
lot near Amherst County Court House and where JEREMIAH N. COATS lives.
To BENNET A. CRAWFORD, 27 September 1821.

366. 29 January 1820. THOMAS WIATT and wife, SALLY, Amherst County,
      to CHISWELL DABNEY and DANIEL BROWN...Deed of Trust; debt to
Bank of Virginia; $1.00 40 acres in Amherst County. Lines: WILLIAM
WARWICK, STITH MEAD, MRS. ROBINSON (formerly part of where she lives).
Bought by THOMAS WIATT from JOSEPH NEEDHAM and wife, slaves named.
ARCHIBALD ROBERTSON and HENRY DAVIS, Lynchburg Justices of the
Peace, 1 February 1820, as to grantors.

369. 14 September 1819. JONATHAN BARNETT, Nelson County, to
      CORNELIUS POWELL...Deed of Trust; debt to EDMOND F. COFFEY,
Nelson County. $1.00 slaves in hands of THOMAS JANNER, Augusta,
crops on Amherst County plantation where JONATHAN BARNETT lives and
rented from DAVID S. GARLAND on Buffaloe. JAMES BRIDGE, overseer,
to be secured as to his part. Witnesses: HUDSON M. GARLAND, J. PENN,
W. C. JORDAN. To EDMOND F. COFFEY, 18 April 1820.

372. 30 March 1820. RICHARD HARRISON and wife, SOPHIA, Amherst
      County, to SAMUEL GARLAND, Lynchburg, and TIPTON B. HARRISON,
same town...Deed of Trust; debt to WILLIAM and G. H. MITCHELL,
Richmond. 300 acres next to where RICHARD HARRISON lives and bought
from REUBEN RUCKER. Lines: JOSHUA RUCKER, RICHARD POWELL, JAMES
PETTIT. Witnesses: JONATHAN B. CARRINGTON, GEORGE HOLLOWAY, JR.,
JAMES PENN.

374. 15 May 1820. DAVID S. GARLAND, Amherst County, power of
      attorney to friend, JONATHAN P. COBBS, Nelson County...to act
in Ohio to divide land. Witnesses: JOSEPH PENN, SAMUEL M. GARLAND.

374. 4 February 1820. JONATHAN S. MOORE, Amherst County, to
      REUBEN COLEMAN, Amherst County...$800 1 5/8 acres near ACH--
ALLEN's Tavern.

375. 20 November 1819. STITH MEAD, 1; THOMAS MURRELL, 2; CHISWELL
      DABNEY, 3...Deed of Trust; debt to THOMAS MURRELL. $1.00 paid
by CHISWELL DABNEY; smith's tools bought from WILLIAM I. ISBELL and
itemized; tools in wheelwright shop and smith's shop and wood shop
used by JONATHAN WRIGHT--itemized; furniture in MEAD's home--itemized--
long and interesting; horse bought from ARMISTEAD TRUSLOW; more tools
itemized. Witnesses: ALEXANDER DANDRIDGE, JORDAN CREASY, HENRY
WILLIAMSON. Lynchburg Justices of the Peace, ARCHIBALD ROBERTSON and
JONATHAN THURMOND, as to STITH MEAD, same day.

379. 1 December 1819. WILLIAM WRIGHT and wife, CHYTHIA, JOSEPH
      KENNEDY and wife, BETSY, NION WHITTLE and wife, ONEY, WILLIAM
KELLY and wife, NANCY, JONATHAN FARRAR and wife, MARY, WIATT SMOOT
and wife, SUSANNA, JESSE KENNEDY, JANE KENNEDY, JONATHAN POINDEXTER
and wife, DRUSILLA, heirs and children of JESSE KENNEDY, late of
Amherst County, to JOSEPH DILLARD and JONATHAN LONDON, Amherst County...
$663.50. Lines: CHARLES L. CHRISTIAN, THOMAS APPLING, JONATHAN
ALLCOCK, RICHARD ALLCOCK, WILLIAM TILLER, deceased, DAVID S. GARLAND--
380½ acres. SUSANNA, is widow and her part is undivided. Rutherford
County, Tennessee, December Term, 1819, BLACKMORE COLEMAN, Clerk of
Pleas, as to NINION WHITTLE and wife, ONEY, WIATT SMOOT and wife,
SUSANNA, December 16, 1819, FREDERICK BARFIELD, Chariman of Court of
Pleas.

382. 19 January 1820. JAMES HIX, Amherst County, to JAMES W. SMITH,
      Amherst County...Deed of Trust; debt to DUDLEY SANDIDGE...$1.00
100 acres Buffaloe and Thrasher. Lines: WILLIAM SANDIDGE, BARNET
CASH. Part of where JAMES HIX lives and bought from WASH HILL.
Witnesses: JONATHAN SMITH, SR., RANDOLPH CASH, JONATHAN SMITH, JR.
to DUDLEY SANDIDGE, 25 September 1820.

384. 19 February 1820. SAMUEL COLEMAN, Amherst County, to WILLIAM
      PENDLETON, Amherst County...L165 95 acres and his part drawn
from mother's land out of BENNETT's tract, Harris Creek. Lines:
TINSLEY, DANIEL CHRISTIAN, RUCKER, BURKS. Witnesses: WIATT LONDON,
DANIEL F. CHRISTIAN, FLEMING COLEMAN. To WILLIAM PENDLETON, JR.,
15 April 1822.

385. 14 February 1820. SAMUEL COLEMAN, Amherst County, to FLEMING
      COLEMAN, Amherst County...$275 55 acres Harris Creek. Lines:
RICHARD BURKS, PETERS, sink hole, ISBELL, COLEMAN. Witnesses:
CHARLES L. CHRISTIAN, DANIEL F. CHRISTINA, WILLIAM PETER, THOMAS
COLEMAN.

386. 18 January 1820. WILLIS RUCKER, Amherst County, and wife,
      TABITHA, to JONATHAN SHELTON, Amherst County...$1200 104 acres
whereon JONATHAN M. EDWARDS formerly lived, Graham creek. Sold by
DABNEY WARE to EDWARDS. Lines: RICHARD SHELTON, SR., AMBROSE RUCKER,
DABNEY WARE. Witnesses: AMBROSE RUCKER, NELSON C. DAWSON, RICHARD
SHELTON, JR. NELSON C. DAWSON and AMBROSE RUCKER, Amherst County
Justices of the Peace, as to TABITHA, 18 February 1820.

388. 5 January 1820. JAMES PENN and wife, JINSEY, Amherst County,
      to THOMAS HUTCHESON, Amherst County...$2250 150 acres Porrage.
Lines: JAMES LONDON, JR., JONATHAN PADGETT, THOMAS EDWARDS, JONATHAN
HUTCHESON, CHARLES MUNDY. Witnesses: WILLIAM and EZEKIEL DAY,
JONATHAN HUTCHESON.

389. 25 January 1820. WILLIAM GATEWOOD to JONATHAN RICHESON...Deed
      of Trust; debt to JESSE RICHESON--$1.00 stock, furniture--long
and interesting list. Witnesses: JONATHAN A. CUMMINGS, SAMUEL MC CRAY.

391. 6 February 1820. GEORGE PENN, Amherst County, to JAMES PENN
      and JOSEPH KYLE, Amherst County...Deed of Trust for benefit
of GEORGE's wife and children (until of age)--slaves named, stock,
furniture, interest in estate of MACE FREELAND, deceased, by marriage
to his daughter, PAMILA FREELAND. At age of maturity, then division
to be made and JAMES PENN is heir of GEORGE and so is KYLE--son-in-law
of GEORGE PENN.

393. 18 March 1820. BENJAMIN BITTLE, Amherst County, to ROBERT
      RIVERS, Amherst County...$200 half acre lot in Madison #38 and
bought from WILLIAM PICKET and for title holds bond of THOMAS JOHNSON,
28 September 1816. Witnesses: ABRAM NORTH, JONATHAN THURMOND and
A. ROBERTSON, Lynchburg Justices of the Peace as to BENJAMIN BITTLE,
same day. To JOSEPH KYLE, 1 August 1826.

394. 20 January 1820. JAMES BROWN, Amherst County, to JONATHAN F.
      HALL...Deed of Trust; debt to CHARLES L. BARRET and Company.
$1.00 horse, furniture, tailor's goose and shears. Witnesses:
JONATHAN T. HILL, JONATHAN R. SHELTON, N. A. GILBERST.

395. 3 March 1819. WILLIAM WOODROOF and wife, ELIZABETH, Amherst
      County, to JESSE WOODROOF, Amherst County...$1700 south borders
Rutledge and joins Lynch Road. Part of MH tract of DAVID WOODROOF, SR.,
deceased. Lines: BENJAMIN DAWSON, DAVID WOODROOF, JR., deceased,
grantee. To JESSE WOODROOF, 22 July 1822.

396. 30 October 1819. WILLIAM BARBER and wife, MARY, to RICHARD
      BURKS, Amherst County...$1490 53 acres both sides Harris, both
sides road from Burks to ACH. Lines: JONATHAN AMBLER. Witnesses:
WILLIAM HORSLEY, THOMAS H. BASS, HENRY FARNSWORTH. Final proof,
24 April 1820, by "a third witness."

397. 18 October 1819. WILLIAM WRIGHT et al. as heirs of JESSE
      KENNEDY--see page 379 for long list of heirs, to same grantees
as on 379...$2663.50 for 380½ acres. Lines: CHARLES L. CHRISTIAN,
THOMAS APPLING, JONATHAN and RICHARD ALCOCK, WILLIAM TILLER, deceased,
DAVID S. GARLAND. One third of SUSANNA, widow of JESSE and not
divided.

400. 12 March 1820. THOMAS RICHESON, Amherst County, to JESSE
      RICHESON, Amherst County...Deed of Trust; debt to JESSEE--all
my interest in firm of CHARLES L. BARRETT and Company. Witnesses:
SEATON SLEDD, BENJAMIN CARTER, WESLEY E. CHRISTIAN.

404. 11 March 1820. JONATHAN MERRIT, Amherst County, to CHISWELL
DABNEY...Deed of Trust; debt to ALEXANDER CLEMENT, Campbell
County...$1.00 slaves, stock, furniture. Witnesses: ACHILLES D.
JOHNSON, DAVID CRAWFORD, JONATHAN T. HILL. PLEASANT LABBY and
ARCHIBALD ROBERTSON, Lynchburg Justices of the Peace, as to acknowl-
edgement, same day. To CHISWELL DABNEY, 16 August 1825.

407. 18 March 1820. RICHARD EUBANK to JOSEPH R. CARTER...Deed of
Trust, WILLIAM JOPLING is bondsman to THOMAS LAIN; three slaves.
Witnesses: JONATHAN PRYOR, JONATHAN EUBANK, JR.

409. 18 June 1819. WILLIAM DUNCAN, executor of JONATHAN CAMDEN,
to WILLIAM WILLMORE, Amherst County...$120 117 acres Pedlar.
Former tract of JONATHAN CAMDEN, SR.--Pointer Falls tract. Lines:
JONATHAN ROBERTSON, HENRY CAMDEN, WILLIAM WILLMORE.

410. 27 October 1819. ANDERSON WARE and wife, CYNTHAI, to GEORGE
MORRIS, JR....$1.25 50 acres. Lines: GEORGE M. TINSLEY, JAMES
BYAS, SAMUEL NICLEY. Witnesses: THOMAS RICHESON, MARTIN N. DAWSON,
JONATHAN WARE.

411. 17 June 1819. GEORGE CRAWFORD, Dinwiddie County, to DRURY
BURGE, Petersburg...Deed of Trust; debt due GREEN M. BURGE,
Petersburg, on judgement of Superior Court, Pr. GEORGE, in GREEN M.
BURGE's name. 104 acres. Lines: ROBERT ALLEN, JONATHAN DILLARD
Bought from JONATHAN LONDON and wife, TIRZA. WILLIAM GILMOUR and
R. F. HAMMON, Justices of the Peace, same day. To DRURY BURGE,
20 October 1821.

413. 11 March 1820. JAMES POWELL, Amherst County and A. B. DAVIES,
Amherst County, to RICHARD HARRISON and RICHARD H. BURKS,
Amherst County...Deed of Trust; to first two and STERLING CLAIBORNE
by HENRY CAMDEN on 327 acres--reference to Deed of Trust. HARRISON
and BURKS became buyers at $168.50. Page 414 same date and parties
as to 307 acres for $75.75. To RICHARD HARRISON, 27 April 1821.

415. 20 October 1819. THOMAS GRISSOM, JR. and wife, NANCY, Bedford
County, JONATHAN GRISSOM and wife, LUCY, Adair County, Kentucky,
EDWARD GOODRICH and wife, SALLY, Amherst County, WILLIAM WILLMORE and
wife, SUSANNA, Amherst County, to RICHARD BURKS, Amherst County...$3650
400 acres south borders Harris. Devised to grantors by deceased
father, THOMAS GRISSOM, SR. Lines: MILLICENT COLEMAN, J. AMBLER,
DANIEL BURFORD, ELIZABETH COLEMAN, WILLIAM PETERS, THOMAS COLEMAN.
Witnesses: R. L. ELLIS as to SALLY GOODRICH, JAMES WARE, RICHARD
EUBANK, R. N. EUBANK, B. G. PETERS or BATES. Bedford Justices of
the Peace: PLEASANT M. GOGGINS and STEPHEN PRESTON as to THOMAS
GRISSOM, JR., and wife, 30 December 1819. CHARLES TALIAFERRO and
BENJAMIN TALIAFERRO, Amherst County Justices of the Peace, as to
SUDANNAH WILLMORE, 15 January 1820. Adair County, Kentucky, WILLIAM
CALDWELL, Clerk of Court as to JONATHAN GRISSOM and wife, LUCY,
20 October 1819; WILLIAM PATTERSON, Justice of the Peace.

420. 19 July 1819. CHARLES DAIRY, 1; ALDRIDGE, MYERS and PENDLETON,
2; STERLING CLAIBORNE, 3...Deed of Trust; $1.00 paid by
STERLING CLAIBORNE. Tract bought of ROBERT RIVERS and received of
him on Superior Court Chancery, Lynchburg District. Witnesses:
PEACHY FRANKLIN, HENRY G. PADGETT, JAMES FULCHER. EDMOND PENN and
ROBERT TINSLEY, Amherst County Justices of the Peace, as to CHARLES
DAIRY and ALDRIDGE--acting partner of ALDRIDGE, MYERS and PENDLETON,
7 February 1820. To THOMAS ALDRIDGE, 30 August 1820.

422. 22 July 1819. AUSTIN DAVIES, Amherst County, to JAMES W. SMITH...
Deed of Trust; debt to SANDIDGE and TINSLEY, JAMES BOLLING--
stock, furniture, etc. Witnesses: JACOB SMITH, RICHARD SMITH,
JONATHAN SMITH. To DABNEY SANDIDGE, 25 August 1821.

424. 29 March 1820. ZACHARIAL ISBELL to CORNELIUS POWELL...Deed of
      Trust; debt to DAVID and DANIEL HIGGINBOTHAM; $1.00 slaves
named. Witnesses: WILLIAM DILLARD, RICHARDSON HENLEY. To CORNELIUS
POWELL, 17 October 1820.

426. 27 October 1819. JONATHAN M. WARE and wife, POLLY, Amherst
      County, to GEORGE MORRIS, JR., Amherst County...$900 191 acres
north borders Otter. Lines: grantee, WILLIAM DAVIS, ISAAC TINSELY,
GEORGE M. TINSLEY, JAMES BIAS. Witnesses: THOMAS RICHESON, MARTIN N.
DAWSON, ANDERSON WARE, THOMAS MORRIS. To JONATHAN M. PARKS, 8 March
1838.

427. 17 May 1819. WASH HILL and wife, SALLY, Rockbridge County,
      to THOMAS GOODRICH, Amherst County...$4520 260 acres both sides
Franklin Creek. Lines: JACOB PIERCE, POLLY SMITH, JAMES GOVENS,
PULLIAM SANDIDGE, THOMAS V. GOODRICH, JACOB PIEREC. To THOMAS
GOODRICH, 23 April 1822.

429. 8 April 1820. ELIAS WILLS and wife, MARY G., Amherst County,
      to JAMES S. PENDLETON and RICHARD H. BURKS, Amherst County...
Deed of Trust; debt to RICHARD HARRISON and JONATHAN M. SETTLE. $1.00
103 acres bought by ELIAS WILLS from BANISTER TINSLEY; 106 acres
bought from BENJAMIN GOSNEY, slaves. To RICHARD HARRISON, 21 May 1821.

430. 8 April 1820. ROBERT MORRIS and wife, SARAH, Lynchburg, to
      THOMAS WIATT, acting executor of JONATHAN MILLER...$5400 108
acres east side Main road from Lynchburg to ACH. Lines: CHARLES
HOYLE, PHILIP JOHNSON. Tract conveyed by WIATT as executor to ROBERT
MORRIS, 13 September 1817. JONATHAN THURMON and A. ROBERTSON, Lynchburg
Justices of the Peace, same day as to wife.

433. 7 April 1820. JONATHAN MAYS, Amherst County, to COLEMAN and
      BARRET, Amherst County...$12.00 1½ acres Pedlar. Lines:
grantee. Witnesses: ABRAM CARTER, JOSEPH R. CARTER, THOMAS NEVIL.

434. 8 April 1820. RICHARD HARRISON and wife, SOPHIA, Amherst
      County, to JAMES L. PENDLETON and RICHARD H. BURKS...Deed of
Trust; debt to ELIAS WILLS and JONATHAN M. SETTLE and RICHARD BURKS.
$1.00 530 acres Pedlar. Tract bought from grantees--and STERLING
CLAIBORNE. Also slaves.

436. 27 November 1819. MARY PHILLIPS, Amherst County, to DAVID S.
      GARLAND, Amherst County...$1.00 in trust for love of daughter,
POLLY SMITH--furniture. Witnesses: GEORGE P. FARRAR, FRANCIS L.
FARRAR, JAMES L. PENDLETON, DRURY BELL, STEPHEN WATTS. To WIATT
SMITH, 17 October 1828.

437. 17 April 1820. ZACH TYREE, Amherst County, to JONATHAN W.
      YOUNG...Deed of Trust; debt to COLEMAN and BARRET. $1.00;
stock, etc.

438. 7 October 1819. HARRISON HUGHES and wife, NANCY, Amherst
      County, to WILLIAM PETTYJOHN, Amherst County...$1000 184½ acres
Fawn Creek. Lines: the road. Witnesses: JONATHAN R. WHITTON,
G. A. ROSE, JONATHAN HAMBDEN PLEASANTS, TINSLEY RUCKER, JAMES L.
LAMKIN, WIATT LONDON. TINSLEY RUCKER and LAMKIN as to wife, 10 October
1819.

440. 11 March 1820. ANTHONY RUCKER and wife, REBECCA, Amherst
      County, to BENJAMIN OGDEN, Amherst County...$130 213 acres
both sides John's Creek and bought from AMBROSE RUCKER some years
past and where BENJAMIN OGDEN lives. Lines: JAMES TINSLEY, EDWARD
TINSLEY, PROSSER POWELL, GEORGE POWELL, deceased. Witnesses:
AMBROSE RUCKER, ABSALOM RUCKER, ANTHONY RUCKER, JR.

442.   24 April 1820.   CHARLES P. TALIAFERRO and BENJAMIN BROWN...
      agreement--new road lately opened from Main road and between
their plantations--cuts off small portions: one or two acres.
BROWN eschanges south of branch called Crooked--TALIAFERRO to BROWN:
one or one and a half acres. Witnesses: BENJAMIN HARRISON.

443.   20 April 1820.   MILLNER COX and wife, SALLY, Amherst County,
      to WILLIAM MUSE, Amherst County...$100 three acres west side
and joining Lynch road. Lines: TINSLEY RUCKER, GEROGE W. TAYLOR,
NELSON C. DAWSON and JAMES L. LAMKIN as to wife, 22 April 1820.

445.   24 April 1820.   WILLIAM P. MUSE and wife, PEMELIA, to REUBEN
      NORVELL...MUSE has executor bonds to MILLNER COX. Deed of
Trust; MUSE has bought new batteaux for $80.00. 1. 40 acres bought
from--both sides MITCHELL's Mill road. Lines: REUBEN NORVELL,
GEORGE W. TAYLOR, MILLNER COX. 2. Three acres west side and joining
Lynch road. Lines: TINALSEY RUCKER, GEORGE W. TAYLOR. Witnesses:
JONATHAN H. GOODWIN, ROBERT GOODWIN, JONATHAN R. WHITTINTON.

447.   20 April 1820.   WILLIAM PETTYJOHN and wife, ELIZABETH, Amherst
      County, to WILLIAM P. MUSE, Amherst County...$260 40 acres
Mitchell Mill Road. Lines: as above. Tract conveyed by MUSE in
Deed of Trust to CHARLES WINGFIELD and by CHARLES WINGFIELD to PETTYJOHN.
NELSON C. DAWSON and JAMES L. LAMKIN as to wife, 22 April 1820.

449.   Not dated.   RICHARD HARRISON to BENNETT A. CRAWFORD and
      RICHARD HENRY BURKS, Amherst County...Deed of Trust; three
named slaves; WILKINS WATSON has bought mill which was late property
of JAMES FRANKLIN, but Deed of Trust thereon from SAMUEL SIMMONS and
THOMAS CREWS. To secure WATSON and CREWS. Witnesses: ROBERT L.
COLEMAN, BENJAMIN HARRISON, BENJAMIN BROWN. To BENNETT A. CRAWFORD,
7 November 1820.

451.   22 April 1820.   GARLAND LUCAS, Amherst County, to BENJAMIN
      HARRISON, Amherst County...Deed of Trust; debt to JONATHAN
ALLEN. $1.00 all bounty lands due as soldier in late ware between
United States and Great Britain. HARRISON is to secure patents.
Witnesses: GEORGE W. DILLARD, REUBEN J. NEVIL, THOMAS D. BALIRE of
Blaine. To JONATHAN ALLEN, 7 August 1820.

452.   2 April 1820.   LAINE JONES, Amherst County, to CHARLES P.
      DORMAN, Rockbridge...Deed of Trust; debt to JONATHAN ROBINSON,
Rockbridge; $1.00 beds, etc. Witnesses: R. H. LEWIS.

454.   27 April 1820.   ANDERSON EVANS, Amherst County to WILLIAM
      ARMISTEAD, Amherst County...Deed of Trust; debt to JONATHAN
TARDY, Amherst County--one mare. Debt to SOPHIA CRAWFORD and TARDY
is bondsman.

455.   28 April 1820.   SAMUEL SIMMONS and wife, CYNTHIA, Amherst
      County, to JAMES POWELL and WILKINS WATSON, Amherst County...
$4827.50 2 3/4 acres Rutledge Creek. Lines: BEN STONE, MONTPELIER
MILLS and formerly that of JAMES FRANKLIN and to SAMUEL SIMMONS from
THOMAS CREWS. Memo: THOMAS CREWS has Deed of Trust on it. SAMUEL
SIMMONS sold mill to RICHARD HARRISON who bought subject to Deed of
Trust, but SAMUEL SIMMONS is in no way bound--only HARRISON. To
C. P. TALIAFERRO, 1821, for relinquishment of dower.

457.   12 February 1820.   PETER F. CHRISTIAN, Amherst County, to
      WILLIAM HASLIP, Amherst County...$80 46 acres Brown Mountain
Creek and Buffaloe. Lines: WILSON C. NICHOLAS.

458.   1 October 1819.   ANDERSON EVANS, Amherst County, to JONATHAN
      EUBANK, JR., Amherst County...Deed of Trust; debt to PHILIP
THURMOND as bondsman to JOSEPH MILSTEAD and assigned to WILLIAM
CLARKSON who sued and traded to THURMOND. $1.00 mare, carpenter's
tools, furniture. Witnesses: ROBERT MILLNER, WILLIAM THURMOND. To
PHILIP THURMOND, 7 October 1820.

459. 15 May 1820. JACOB SMITH, Amherst County, to CHARLES TUCKER,
      Amherst County...$1885 400 acres Franklin Creek. JACOB bought
it from JONATHAN SMITH who bought from ZACHARIAH TALIAFERRO. To
CHARLES TUCKER, 20 November 1820.

460. 11 March 1820. PULLIAM SANDIDGE and wife, LUCY, Amherst
      County, to CALEB RALLS, Amherst County and Lexington Parish...
$2400 400 acres. Lines: the road, JONATHAN RICHESON, JONATHAN H.
CLEMENTS, Horsley, CHRISTIAN. CHARLES and BENJAMIN TALIAFERRO as
to wife, 11 March 1820. To RICHARD CRAWFORD, agent of NELSON
CRAWFORD, executor of CALEB RALLS, 12 January 1824.

461. 17 April 1820. WILLIAM WOODROOF and wife, ELIZABETH, Amherst
      County, to WILLIAM MC DANIEL, Amherst County...$450 1100 acres
west side and joining Lynch road. Part of MH tract of DAVID WOODROOF,
deceased. Reference to plat, but not herein. TINSLEY RUCKER and
DABNEY WARE as to wife, 24 April 1820.

463. 20 November 1819. JOSEPH BRYANT, Amherst County, to JONATHAN L.
      BETT...Deed of Trust; debt to HORSELY and FARRIS of Bent Creek--
stock. To JONATHAN HORSLEY, 22 August 1820.

464. 1 March 1820. EDWARD LYNCH and wife, MARY, Lynchburg, to
      JONATHAN PERCIVALL, same town...$1.00 lower part of Island
below town toll bridge. Lines: JAMES C. MOORMAN's fish trap.
JONATHAN THURMOND and CHRIS WINFREE, Lynchburg Justices of the
Peace as to wife, 15 March 1820. To JONATHAN PERCIVALL, 27 August
1832.

467. 7 March 1820. WILLIAM F. HOGG and wife, POLLY, Rockbridge,
      to TOLBERT NOEL, Amherst County...$200 47 acres. Lines:
Maple Creek, RICHARD L. ELLIS. Part of tract of JONATHAN HOGG,
deceased. Witnesses: JAMES WARE, R. N. EUBANK, R. L. ELLIS, SAMUEL
HOGG. JAMES WARE and RICHARD N. EUBANK, same day, as to wife.

468. 16 May 1820. HUMPHREY GILBERT, Amherst County, to TINSLEY
      RUCKER.,.Deed of Trust; JOSEPH R. CARTER is bondsman to
JONATHAN RICHARDSON. Horses, etc. To JONATHAN RICHARDSON, 21 November
1820. "Supplement Record: R:134."

469. 18 May 1820. WILLIAM POLLARD and wife, ELIZABETH, Amherst
      County, to SAMUEL D. CHRISTIAN, Amherst County...$382.50 51 acres
WILLIAM POLLARD bought it from CHARLES H. CHRISTIAN.

470. 18 May 1820. JESSE KENNEDY, Amherst County, to SAMUEL D.
      CHRISTIAN, Amherst County...$69.06½ 4½ acres. Part of tract
bought from ROBERT WALTON in trust and bought at sale.

471. 26 February 1820. WILLIAM MITCHELL and wife, SALLY, Amherst
      County, to EDMOND WINSTON and WILLIAM LANGHORNE, Amherst
County...$5.00 tract on James--Farm Mills--350 or 400 acres. Lines:
MRS. JENKINS, TEMPEY THACKER's heirs, WILLIAM PETTYJOHN, Deed of
Trust; debts to MATTHEW HARVEY and bondsmen are CHRISTOPHER CLARK,
JAMES C. STEPTOE, and ROBERT MITCHELL. HARVEY is then called
ROBERT HARVEY; debts to HENRY BOWYER, WILLIAM C. BOWYER, ELIJAH
MC CLANAHAN, NATHANIEL BURWELL, JAMES C. STEPTOE, PLEASANT LABBY,
MRS. ELIZABETH MOSELY, EDWARD WATTS, CHARLES JOHNSON. Some have
sued. Witnesses: WILLIAM MITCHELL, JR., CORNELIUS CROW, FRED KUHN.
Certified in Amherst County as to WILLIAM MITCHELL by TINSLEY
RUCKER and JAMES L. LAMKIN, 3 May 1820.

476.   7 December 1819. WILLIAM MITCHELL and wife, SALLY, to EDMOND
       WINSTON and WILLIAM LANGHORNE...Deed of Trust; debts to JAMES C.
STEPTOE, CHARLES M. MITCHELL, ROBERT MITCHELL. $5.00 Stone Lumber
house, Lynchburg; 31 acres in Amherst County and adjoining tract
whereon WILLIAM MITCHELL lives and bought from REUBEN COX; slaves
named--long list; already in Deed of Trust to EDWARD WATTS and HENRY
LANGHORNE; 18 horses, 100 hogs, other stock and furniture, tools at
Farm Mills, houses on Turnpike, Bank debts, too. Witnesses: JAMES
BULLOCK, WILLIAM D. THOMPSON, JAMES GARNETT, JONITHAN B. DABNEY.   To
ROBERT MITCHELL, 22 October 1824.

480.   27 May 1820. WIATT P. SMITH, Amherst County, to JAMES W.
       SMITH...Deed of Trust; debt to DABNEY SANDIDGE as bondsman to
JONATHAN RICHESON. $1.00 slaves. Witnesses: ROBERT TINSLEY.   To
DABNEY SANDIDGE, 20 November 1820.

483.   1820. JAMES DILLARD and wife, JANE, JAMES S. DILLARD and wife,
       NARCISSA, JONATHAN DILLARD and wife, NANCY F., to TINSLEY RUCKER...
$1080 216 acres. North borders Indian Creek. To COLONEL DILLARD,
20 November 1820, for relinquishment of dower.

484.   19 June 1820. TINSLEY RUCKER and wife, NANCY, to A. B. DAVIES
       and WILLIAM DILLARD...Deed of Trust; debt to JAMES DILLARD.
216 acres above on Indian Creek; also adjoining tract. Lines:
JONATHAN PENN. Bought by TINSLEY RUCKER of -- 150 acres. To
TINSLEY RUCKER, to take dower as above.

487.   2 June 1820. JONATHAN TAYLOR and wife, SALLY, Amherst County,
       to THOMAS MORRIS, Amherst County...$1000 387 acres. Cedar
Creek, branch of Pedlar. Lines: grantee, JOSIAH JOPLING, JOSEPH
CABELL, JONATHAN GOODRICH. JONATHAN THURMON and PLEASANT LABBY,
Lynchburg Justices of the Peace, 5 June 1820, as to wife.

490.   22 November 1819. THOMAS FITZPATRICK and wife, LYDIA, late
       CARTWRIGHT, Nelson County, to DAVID S. GARLAND, Amherst County...
$740 296 acres Nicholston Run, border of Pedlar. Lines: JAMES
FRAZER, top of Blue Ridge, JONATHAN MOSBY and JAMES MURPHY, Nelson
Justices of the Peace, same date, as to wife.

492.   12 June 1820. AMBROSE TOMLINSON, SR., Amherst County, to
       JONATHAN TOMLINSON, Amherst County...L100 100 acres both sides
north fork Buffaloe. Lines: JONATHAN HIGGINBOTHAM, JR., deceased.

493.   30 May 1820. ROBERT MILLNER and wife, PATSY, Bedford County,
       to LANDON TOOLEY, Amherst County...$220 220 acres north side
Fluvanna and both sides Cashaw, Otter and Rocky Row. Lynchburg
Justices of the Peace: JONATHAN THURMON and JACOB N. CARDOZA, same
date, as to wife.

495.   2 May 1820. WILLIAM CAMPBELL and wife, FRANCES, Amherst County,
       to WILLIAM I. MAY, Amherst County...L3000 tob. at Tye WH 100
acres George Creek, border of Little Piney. Lines: GEORGE CAMPBELL.
Located by WILLIAM CAMPBELL and patent signed by GOVERNOR JAMES P.
PRESTON. Witnesses: WILLIAM ARMISTEAD, SAMUEL CAMPBELL, JONATHAN S.
BLAIR. To WILLIAM CAMPBELL to get dower, 21 May 1821.

497.   27 May 1819. TINSLEY RUCKER, Bedford County, CHRISTOPHER ANTHONY
       and WILLIAM COOK...Deed of Trust; debt to SAMUEL PHILLIPS.
$1.00 147 acres Harris Creek and where TINSLEY RUCKER lives. Lines:
RODNEY TALIAFERRO, CHARLES WINGFIELD. Witnesses: ROBERT MITCHELL,
CAHOHILL MENNIS, WILLIAM P. PORTER. Bedford Clerk, J. STEPTOE,
25 August 1819. To CHRISTOPHER ANTHONY, 17 April 1821.

499.   18 August 1818. Order to Amherst County Justices of the Peace:
       CHARLES L. BARRET and wife, SARAH, ABSALOM HIGGINBOTHAM and
wife, POLLY, 20 July 1818, to JACK CARTER...129½ acres. Done by
NELSON CRAWFORD and CHARLES TALIAFERRO, 12 February 1820.

500. 21 July 1818. Order to BENJAMIN and CHARLES P. TALIAFERRO and
WILLIAM JOPLING, Amherst County Justices of the Peace:
LYNE S. TALIAFERRO and wife, MILDRED, 1 June 1818, to CLIFTON HARRIS...
226½ acres in Franklin County. Done by first two, 28 July 1818. To
CLIFTON HARRIS, 2 January 1822.

502. 22 December 1818. Order to REUBEN NORVELL and TINSLEY RUCKER,
Amherst County Justices of the Peace: THOMAS CREWS and wife,
SALLY, 27 November 1816, to SALLY CREWS...136½ acres. Done, 17 April
1820.

503. 25 June 1818. Order to Amherst County Justices of the Peace:
JAMES HIGGINBOTHAM and wife, ELIZA, 15 March 1814, to JOSEPH
DILLARD...90. Done, 26 January 1820, by EDMOND PENN and ROBERT
TINSLEY. To JOSEPH DILLARD, 13 December 1820.

504. 11 November 1819. MILDRED COLEMAN, widow of EDMOND T. COLEMAN,
Amherst County...love for her children: DANIEL L. and MARY
COLEMAN, infants--$1.00--slaves named; mine under will, void, if she
remarries. To children as grantees. Witnesses: JONATHAN COLEMAN,
LINDSEY COGHILL, CAROLINE FRANKLIN. To HILL, 31 October 1826.

506. 20 June 1820. FERGUS FERGUSON and wife, ELIZABETH H. (formerly
GOOCH), Prince Edward County, to CLAIBORNE W. GOOCH, Richmond...
ELISABETH is heir of late father, PHILIP GOOCH, and brother of half-
blood, WILLIAM B. GOOCH, deceased--will of former and laws of land--
$3500 all interest in both estates. Certified in Amherst County as
to ELIZABETH H. by NELSON C. DAWSON and DABNEY WARE, same date. To
DABNEY P. GOOCH, 22 July 1820.

507. 1 June 1820. CHARLES P. TALIAFERRO and wife, LOUISA, Amherst
County, to JONATHAN WARE, Amherst County...L45 45 acres. Lines:
CHARLES TALIAFERRO, WILLIAM PRYOR, grantee.

508. 1 July 1819. Order to Amherst County Justices of the Peace:
HENRY CAMDEN and wife, LUCY, 22 January 1818, to DAVID S.
GARLAND...899 acres. Done by ROBERT TINSLEY and EDWARD PENN,
12 November 1819.

509. 30 June 1820. ROBERT MITCHELL, Amherst County, to DAVIDSON
BRADFUTE, Lynchburg...Deed of Trust; debt to bank. $1.00
sixteen slaves named. HENRY DAVIS and JONATHAN VICTOR, Lynchburg
Aldermen, 12 July 1820.

511. 1 July 1820. WILLIAM MITCHELL and wife, SALLY, Amherst County,
to GEORGE TUCKER, Amherst County...$1600 21¼ acres. Part of
tract bought by WILLIAM MITCHELL from JONATHAN WARD, Pitsylvania
County. Lines: road to free bridge, HANSFORD, new road. To
GEORGE TUCKER, 22 August 1820.

512. 28 June 1820. SAMUEL PANNILL to JAMES BRUCE...WILLIAM MITCHELL
by deed, 22 December 1818, sold to SAMUEL PANNILL and CHARLES
JOHNSON, mills in Amherst County--Farm Mills. Lines: tract above
Back Creek, James River, PETTIS THACKER's heirs, WILLIAM PETTYJOHN,
JAMES LEE--384 acres--Deed of Trust; sold, 27 June 1820, to BRUCE
at $13,799.00. Certified as to SAMUEL PANNILL in Lynchburg: JAMES
STEWART and MICAJAH DAVIS, JR., same day.

513. 1 September 1819. DAVID GLASS, Amherst County, to JONATHAN D.
WILLS, Amherst County...GLASS woes ELIAS WILLS; Deed of Trust;
$1.00--long list of items, slave, etc. Witnesses: THOMAS RICKETTS,
GEORGE H. DAMERON, JONATHAN L. RICKETTS.

515. 17 July 1820. BAZIL SLEDD, Amherst County, to CHRISTOPHER
ISBELL, Amherst County...Deed of Trust; debt to MICAJAH DAVIS
and Company--JR. for DAVIS, $1.00, oxen, other stock. Witnesses:
ROBERT TINSLEY, MANSFIELD WARE. To CHRISTOPHER ISBELL, 15 January 1821.

516. 17 July 1820. GEORGE CAMPBELL, Amherst County, and wife, LUCY,
      to JONATHAN STINNETT, Amherst County...$3.00 152 acres Little
Piney. Lines: George's Creek. Part of tract occupied by GEORGE
CAMPBELL. Acknowledged by GEORGE CAMPBELL and wife, 21 May 1821.
To JONATHAN STINNETT, 21 May 1821.

517. 15 July 1820. JAMES LEE and wife, CATHERINE, Amherst County,
      to ELIAS WILLS, Amherst County...$1.00 105½ acres. Lines:
the river, JAMES WILLS. TINSLEY RUCKER and NELSON C. DAWSON, same
day, as to wife.

519. 8 April 1820. Order to Amherst County Justices of the Peace:
      JONATHAN TARDY and wife, COURTNEY, 1819, to WILLIS FRANKLIN...
65 acres. Done by THOMAS ALDRIDGE and EDMOND PENN, 7 June 1820.

520. 23 August 1820. ANDREW MONROE, Cumberland County, Kentucky,
      to JONATHAN P. WILSON, Campbell County...$220 138 3/4 acres
Rocky Run. Lines: PETER CASHWELL, JOSEPH HIGGINBOTHAM, LEWIS P.
SIMPSON, RICHARD C. HUCKSTEP. Bequeathed to me by uncle, ANDREW
MONROE, Amherst County. Witnesses: CHARLES WILSON, CHARLES L.
CHRISTIAN, J. S. DILLARD. To JONATHAN P. WILSON, 29 October 1820.

520. 22 August 1820. WILLIAM ARMISTEAD to GEORGE L. VAUGHAN...$1500
      house and lot in New Glasgow--3¼ acres; bought from SAMUEL
MEREDITH and wife, JANE, 20 April 1801. Lines: race path, DAVID S.
GARLAND, old field. To GEORGE L. VAUGHAN, 20 November 1820.

521. 8 May 1820. JAMES P. STEPHENS, Amherst County, to JOSEPH
      PENN...Deed of Trust; debt to PENDLETON and MOUNTCASTLE. $1.00;
long list, stove in Lovingston. Witnesses: HUDSON M. GARLAND,
JONATHAN DILLARD, DRURY D. CHRISTIAN.

522. 11 August 1820. EDMOND LIVELY, late of Amherst County, power
      of attorney to JAMES EVANS, Nelson County...all interest in
Amherst County and Nelson for my wife, JUDITH, from estate of JESSE
CAMPLER (PAMPLER?). Certified Franklin County: JONATHAN CALLAWAY
and EMOND TATE, same day.

523. 15 December 1819. WILLIAM P. MUSE, JR., to JONATHAN LONDON
      and JORDAN CREASY...Deed of Trust; debt to CHARLES PALMORE,
bondsman to JONATHAN WARWICK, administrator of JONATHAN CAMM--stock,
etc. Witnesses: EZEKIEL DAY, BARNETT EDWARDS. To JONATHAN LONDON,
15 January 1821. Acknowledged by WILLIAM P. MUSE, 11 August 1820.

523. No date. WILLIAM POLLARD, Amherst County, to JACOB PIERCE,
      Amherst County...Deed of Trust; debt to CHARLES H. CHRISTIAN,
$1.00 tobacco, crops, etc. Witnesses: C. PIERCE, THOMAS L. PIERCE.

524. 4 January 1820. CHARLES CLAY, Bedford, to son, PAUL A. CLAY,
      Bedford...'love and $1.00 82 acres north side Fluvanna; both
sides Otter Creek. Lines: ford path, river hill, RAWLEY's Island
(alias Big Island). Witnesses: ALEXANDER M. HEPBURN, HECTOR HARRIS,
JONATHAN ALEXANDER. Bedford Justices of the Peace: JOSEPH SLAUGHTER
and JONATHAN L. COBBS, 9 January 1820.

525. 12 October 1820. JONATHAN COLEMAN, Amherst County, to GEORGE L.
      COLEMAN...for deed conveyance agrees to board GEORGE L. COLEMAN
at my house; furnish bridle horse and $30 per year. Witnesses:
J. L. BLAIR, CORNELIUS POWELL, WILKINS WATSON.

526. 14 August 1820. WILKINS WATSON and wife, POLLY H., Amherst
      County, to CHARLES P. TALIAFERRO...$2600 2 3/4 acres Rutledge.
Lines: BEN STONE, MICAJAH CAMDEN--Montpelier Mills tract; late that
of SAMUEL SIMMONS. Witnesses: BENJAMIN HARRISON, THOMAS P. DILLARD.
To CHARLES P. TALIAFERRO, 18 December 1822.

526. 22 November 1817. JAMES CREWS and wife, ELIZABETH, Mercer
      County, Kentucky, to WILLIAM MITCHELL, Amherst County...$3000
154 acres. Part of estate of PETTIS THACKER and by court to ELIZABETH
and sister, SALLY BURFORD, two of PETTIS THACKER's children: lots
four and five; sur. of 9 November 1817, by REUBEN NORVELL. Witnesses:
WILLIAM PETTYJOHN, ROBERT RIDGWAY, EDWARD BUCKMAN. Mercer Justices
of the Peace: WILLIAM SHARP and PETER JORDAN, 23 January 1818, as
to wife. THOMAS ALLIN, Clerk; SAMUEL MC AFEE, Justice of the Peace.
Plat of 154 acres; page 528, PETTIS THACKER's tract: north side
Harris; lines of TEMPEY THACKER, WILLIAM PETTYJOHN.

528. 17 October 1820. JONATHAN WARE, JR., Amherst County, to
      ISAAC RUCKER...Deed of Trust; debt to ANDERSON WARE; $1.00,
furniture. Witness: HENRY P. RUCKER. To ISAAC RUCKER, 20 March
1822. 530 19 June 1820 GEORGE H. BURFORD and wife, MARY, Amherst
County, to LUNSFORD CARTER. Amherst County. $200 half acre lot in
Bethel--#8.

530. 5 September 1820. JOSEPH DILLARD, Amherst County, from PEACHY
      FRANKLIN, Amherst County...no amount; 350 acres north borders
Piney; both sides King's Creek. Patent to both, 1 December 1818.
Witnesses: HUDSON M. GARLAND, D. SHEPHARD, JONATHAN L. DILLARD,
RICHARD L. (J) WAUGH. To JOSEPH DILLARD, 11 December 1820.

531. 15 September 1820. JAMES PAMPLIN, Amherst County, to MICAJAH
      PENDLETON, Nelson County...Deed of Trust; debt to HORSLEY and
FARIS, Bent Creek. $1.00 50 acres; not to cultivate within four yards
of cemetery; where JAMES PAMPLIN lives. Lines: JONATHAN COLEMAN,
ROBERT L. JEFFERSON, ROWLAND VIA, LUFFBOROUGH, slave, stock, furniture.
Witnesses: JAMES D. WHITE, JOSEPH HORSLEY. To MICAJAH PENDLETON,
16 November 1820.

532. 8 August 1820. CHARLES P. TALIAFERRO to RICHARD HARRISON,
      Amherst County...$2000 380 acres south borders middle fork
Pedlar; bought from JAMES and WILLIAM FRAZER; patent to WALTER POWER,
1782. To RICHARD HARRISON, 27 April 1821.

533. 22 August 1820. JAMES BRIDGE, Amherst County, to JONATHAN
      BALLARD, Nelson County...$2000 debt; Deed of Trust; debt to
WILLIAM COFFEY, SR., Nelson; $1.00 stock, furniture, long list.
Witnesses: EDMOND T. COFFEY, GEORGE MONROE, PETER C. COFFEY. To
WILLIAM COFFEY, SR., July, 1823.

534. 27 May 1820. RICHARD MILLNER and wife, MARTHA, Pitsylvania,
      to WILLIAM MILLNER, JR., Bedford...$5361 750 acres both sides
Horsley. Lines: road, path, creek, NELSON CRAWFORD, WILLIAM
DEMPSEY. Pitsylvania Justices of the Peace: THOMAS GARRETT, WILLIAM
PRITCHETT, 16 June 1820.

536. 29 July 1819. JONATHAN EUBANK, JR. and wife, CATHERINE, Amherst
      County, to SAMUEL HANSBROUGH, Amherst County...210 acres $2600.
Lines: WILLIAM DEMPSEY, BENJAMIN SANDIDGE, Buffaloe Spring, road,
GODFREY TOLER, ARCHIBALD ROWSEY, JOSEPH HIGGINBOTHAM. Witnesses:
CHARLES L. BARRET, JAMES F. TALIAFERRO, LINZA BURKS.

537. Pitsylvania Justices of the Peace: BENJAMIN WATKINS and ROBERT
      HARRISON, 5 April 1820, as to RICHARD MILLNER and wife,
MARTHA, 16 November 1818, to JACK CARTER and LINDSEY SANDIDGE.

537. 22 August 1820. CHARLES TALIAFERRO and DAVID S. GARLAND as
      to JUDITH CHRISTIAN, wife of JONATHAN CHRISTIAN...grantee not
named.

538. 23 October 1819. GABRIEL SWANSON and wife, MATILDA, Franklin
      County, to ESABER PATE, same county...$300 for interest in
Amherst County and Nelson of estate of JONATHAN SWANSON, deceased,
Amherst County; GABRIEL is a son. Several tracts on JAMES; PATE may
sue for occupancy. Witnesses: WILLIAM CHILDRESS, DAVID P. TAYLOR,
DANIEL ARRINGTON.

539.　28 September 1820.　ZACH ISBELL and wife, SALLY, Amherst County,
　　　　to ALLISON MORRIS, Amherst County...$2000.　1.　879 acres.
Lines: grantor, road, COLONEL CHARLES TALIAFERRO, THOMAS WOODROOF,
deceased.　2.　120 3/4 acres adjacent to first.　Lines: CLEMENS,
WILLIAM WARE, deceased, THOMAS WOODROOF, deceased.　To ALLISON
MORRIS, January 4, 1821.

540.　28 August 1820.　WILLIAM WOODROOF, Amherst County, to wife,
　　　　ELIZABETH, for support and education of children...consideration:
property received from her deceased father and sisters.　CLAIBORNE W.
GOOCH, Richmond, is made trustee; eleven slaves named, alsy my interest
in my father's estate, furniture and stock.

541.　15 March 1820.　HENRY KIZER, Rockbridge, to COLEMAN and
　　　　BARRET, Amherst County...lease for eight years from 1 January
1820--saw mill on Pedlar and bought from JONATHAN MAYS.　Deed of
Trust to secure them.　Witnesses: JONATHAN RICHESON, ABRAM CARTER,
JONATHAN F. HALL, JONATHAN R. SHELTON, HUMPHREY GILBERT.

542.　11 August 1814.　Order to Bedford Justices of the Peace:
　　　　TINSLEY RUCKER and wife, NANCY, 11 March 1814, to RICHARD
HARRISON.　141½ acres.　Done, 9 February 1817: SAMUEL HANCOCK and
LAWRENCE MC GEORGE.

543.　30 August 1820.　MICAJAH CLARKE and wife, KEZIAH, Amherst
　　　　County, to SPENCER NORVELL and NELSON C. DAWSON, Amherst County...
Deed of Trust for debts.　$1.00 89 acres where MICAJAH CLARKE lives;
half acre lot in Madison; one military claim for 160 acres for which
MAJOR BUCKNER will furnish patent; one share in Nelson and Albemarle
Union Factory, horse, gun, tools, etc.　REUBEN NORVELL and TINSLEY
RUCKER as to wife, same day.

545.　15 August 1820.　THOMAS S. HOLLOWAY and CHARLES P. TALIAFERRO
　　　　as to CYNTHIA SIMMONS, wife of SAMUEL as to deed to --,
28 April 1820.

545.　7 September 1820.　WARNER GOODWIN to youngest son, JAMES W.
　　　　GOODWIN...love, cow and calk.

546.　18 September 1820.　STITH MEAD, Amherst County, to JONATHAN
　　　　ALCOCK and DANIEL HARWOOD, Amherst County and Henrico for them...
debt to MARY BLAKEY, Henrico.　She is guardian to her son and daughter,
REUBEN SMITH and ELIZA BLAKEY.　STITH is administrator of REUBEN
BLAKEY, deceased; debts to GEORGE BLAKEY and WILLIAM STREET, Henrico.
Two lots in Henrico on main road from Richmond to new bridges--legatee
lot 3--10 acres; lot 9--22 acres and divided by commissioners and
conveyed to PRUDENCE WATKINS MEAD, his wife, and recorded in Henrico.
Also my interest in MRS. MARY BLAKEY's dower of 140 acres which may
fall to me or heirs at her death; slaves from R. BLAKEY's estate;
balance left of property deeded to THOMAS MURRELL and THOMAS WIATT,
Amherst County, on trust; furniture.　Witnesses: THOMAS APPLING,
WILEY CAMPBELL, B. STONE.　To JONATHAN ALCOCK., 19 February 1821.

547.　21 September 1820.　WILLIAM HARRISON, Amherst County, to
　　　　JONATHAN T. HILL...Deed of Trust; various debts in North Carolina
and Virginia; $1.00, slaves; debts to RICHARD HARRISON on THOMAS
STAMPS' judgement, JONATHAN RUSSELL, JAMES SANDERS, PATRICK A.
FOUNTAIN, assignee of SAMUEL ALMONDS.　Witnesses: HUGH NORVELL,
AMBROSE RUCKER.

548.　11 September 1820.　PULLIAM SANDIDGE and wife, LUCY, Amherst
　　　　County, to RICHARD HARTLESS, Amherst County...$100 390 acres
north borders south fork Buffaloe.　Lines: LEONARD BALLOW, his own.
Witnesses: JACK CARTER, PULLIAM SANDIDGE, JR., PHILIP SMITH.　Order
delivered 20 December 1826.

549. 28 October 1820. HUGH TAGGART and wife, NANCY, Amherst County,
      to ROBERT TINSLEY, Amherst County...$1100 183 acres Buffaloe.
Lines: BENNETT HUDSON, GEORGE L. COLEMAN, ST. GEORGE TUCKER. Bought
from EDMOND HUDSON and HENRY CAMDEN. CHARLES TALIAFERRO and WILLIAM M.
WALLER, same day, as to wife.

551. 12 October 1820. GEORGE L. COLEMAN, Amherst County, to JONATHAN
      COLEMAN, Amherst County...consideration--benefits and rights
secured to GEORGE by JONATHAN, 12 October--all lands and interest in
mother's estate and that of grandfather, JONATHAN PENN, deceased;
slaves. Witnesses: CORNELIUS POWELL, J. S. BLAIN, WILKINS WATSON.

551. 21 July 1816. JAMES TURNER and wife, SPICEY, Amherst County,
      to GEORGE CAMPBELL, Amherst County...L190 220 acres Little
Piney. Lines: WILLIAM MOORE, WILLIAM EVANS' former tract. Witnesses:
STERLING CLAIBORNE, JONATHAN THOMPSON, JR., NELSON ANDERSON.

552. 30 October 1820. CLAUDIUS BUSTER and wife, NANCY, Kanawa
      County, to OLIVER TOWLES, JR., Lynchburg...$1.00. 1. 1062 acres
and 3/4. 2. 137½ acres--1200 acres. Plat annexed: surveyed by
CAPTAIN REUBEN NORVELL, Amherst County, surveyor. Witnesses:
JONATHAN M. SETTLE, HENRY DAVIS, M. S. LYNCH--first two as Lynchburg
Justices of the Peace. Plats show lines of CHARLES HOYLE, JONATHAN
MUNDY, STITH MEAD, MATTHEW RICKETTS, WILLIAM ROBINSON and names of
MARY and ANN BUSTER--1062 acres--from estate of COLONEL PHILIP
JOHNSON. Plat: 554 137½ acres CLAUDIUS and MARY BUSTER. Lines:
STITH MEAD, LINEAS BOLLING, mill dam, Terry--Falls Creek and late
property of COLONEL PHILIP JOHNSON.

544. 24 October 1817. JOSEPH KENNEDY et al. as heirs of JESSE
      KENNEDY...see page 379 for long list of heirs--to JOSEPH
DILLARD and JONATHAN LONDON--$2663.50. Lines: CHARLES L. CHRISTIAN,
THOMAS APPLING, JONATHAN ALCOCK, RICHARD ALCOCK, WILLIAM TILLER,
deceased, DAVID S. GARLAND--380½ acres, SUSANNAH's dower as widow of
JESSE KENNEDY--very poor scribe here. Witnesses: HUDSON M. GARLAND,
G. P. FARRAR, J. S. BLAIR. To JOSEPH DILLARD, 23 December 1820.
Acknowledged in Mason County, Kentucky by JANE D. KENNEDY, JONATHAN
FARRAR and wife, MARY H., 3 June 1819--1818 term, November. ADAM
BEATTY, Presiding Judge, 7 June 1819. MARSHALL KEY also named.

557. 23 September 1820. JOSEPH PRIOR and ALLEN PRIOR, Dearborn
      County, Indiana, POLLY and SALLY PRIOR, their wives and
daughters of MILLY PARKES, deceased, who was daughter of CHARLES
BURKS, deceased, Amherst County...power of attorney to WILLIAM PARKS,
Dearborn County, Indiana, as to estate of BURKS. Witnesses:
E. R. SPONE (?), JONATHAN LENOVER (?), JUDAH BAILEY. Justices of the
Peace: JAMES DILL, Clerk of Circuit Court, JONATHAN LIVINGSTON,
Associate Judge. JONATHAN, NANCY, WILLIAM and PEGGY PARKS, infants
of WILLIAM PARKS, between 14 and 21, chose father, WILLIAM, as
guardian. He also is guardian of WILLIAM and LOIUSA PARKS, his
children, under 14--WILLIAM has been named as above 14, too, 8 September
1820. SOLOMON MONWARING, Associate Judge.

560. 20 November 1820. JONATHAN LONDON and wife, TIRZA, Amherst
      County, to ELISHA BECKHAM, Amherst County...$650 80 acres
bought by JONATHAN LONDON from JAMES POWELL. Lines: north side
Lynch Road, A. B. DAVIES, north side Rutledge, THOMAS CREWS and
WILLIAM OLIVER--old lines, BENJAMIN BROWN.

561. 21 November 1820. JAMES NEVILL, Amherst County, to JOSEPH
      PENN, Amherst County...Deed of Trust; debt to JONATHAN PENN,
$1.00, stock, furniture, crops. To JONATHAN PENN, 18 November 1822.

562. 10 November 1820. JAMES TINSLEY and wife, SALLY, Amherst
      County, to EDWARD TINSLEY, Amherst County...$430.50 82 acres.
Lines: R. L. ELLIS, JONATHAN CAMM's heirs, GEORGE POWELL's heirs,
ANTHONY RUCKER, grantee. AMBROSE RUCKER and ROBERT TINSLEY as to
wife, same day.

564. 20 November 1820. JAMES PAMPLIN, Amherst County, to REES
     CUNNINGHAM...Deed of Trust; debt to WILLIAM L. WATTS, Nelson
County. 50 acres; graveyard excepted and not to cultivate within
four yards; where JAMES PAMPLIN lives. Liqes: JONATHAN COLEMAN,
ROBERT L. JEFFERSON, ROLAND VIA, LUFFBOROUGH, slave, stock, furniture,
boat timber. To WILLIAM L. WATTS, 2 April 1821.

566. 20 November 1820. THOMAS COLEMAN and wife, JUDITH, Amherst
     County, to REUBEN NORVELL, Amherst County...Deed of Trust;
debt to RICHARD BURKS, $1.00 170¼ acres Harris Creek. Lines:
SAMUEL COLEMAN. To RICHARD BURKS, 15 April 1822.

567. 20 November 1820. THOMAS COLEMAN and wife, JUDITH, Amherst
     County, to WILLIAM PENDLETON, JR., Amherst County...$34.75
6¼ acres south borders Harris. Lines: SAMUEL COLEMAN.

569. 20 November 1820. RICHARD BURKS and wife, MARY, Amherst
     County, to THOMAS COLEMAN, Amherst County...171¼ acres $1100.75
Harris Creek. Lines: SAMUEL COLEMAN, WILLIAM PENDLETON, JR., TINSLEY
RUCKER, WILLIAM PETERS, deceased. Part of tract bought by RICHARD
BURKS from THOMAS GRISSOM. To THOMAS COLEMAN, 24 April 1822.

570. 20 November 1820. RICHARD BURKS and wife, MARY, Amherst
     County, to WILLIAM WILLMER, Amherst County (WILLMORE)...$1000
110¼ acres south borders Harris. Lines: TINSLEY RUCKER, THOMAS
COLEMAN, BARBER. Tract bought from THOMAS GRISSOM. To W. WILLMORE,
8 October 1822. WILLMER is deed.

571. 1 June 1820. HARMON GENTRY and wife, SALLY, Amherst County,
     to RICHARD HARRISON, Amherst County...$850 52 3/4 acres Harris
Creek. Lines: ANTHONY RUCKER, grantee--formerly owned by said
HARRISON. Witnesses: JONATHAN T. HILL, GEORGE HOLLOWAY, THOMAS H.
BIAS. To RICHARD HARRISON, 17 October 1825.

571. 10 April 1820. MICAJAH CAMDEN and wife, POLLY, Amherst County,
     to THOMAS ALDRIDGE, Amherst County...$7000 37 acres. Lines:
Lynch road, grantor, LINDSEY COLEMAN--about 100 yards north of
Brick Tavern now occupied by SAMUEL SIMMONS, Migginson road, public
square on which is court house and jail, DR. JAMES POWELL, WILLIAM
LONG. Memo by THOMAS ALDRIDGE: I am to have enter (sic) alley on
east of lot sold by me to KINSEY and HILL from public lot MIGGINSON
read. To THOMAS ALDRIDGE, 2 August 1823.

572. 31 October 1820. OLIVER TOWLES, JR., Campbell County, to
     THOMAS WIATT, Amherst County...Deed of Trust; debt to CLAUDIUS
BUSTER, Kanawaha County, JOSHUA LONG, Spotsylvania...350 acres $1.00.
Lines: CHARLES HOYLE, WILLIAM ROBINSON, STITH MEAD, JULIMER's tract--
tract sold in Spotsylvania. Witnesses: JONATHAN M. SETTLE, HENRY
DAVIES, MICAJAH LYNCH. Acknowledged in Lynchburg before first two
Justices of the Peace. I have not seen any poorer writing in any
of books thus far. Same date: acknowledged.

574. 15 December 1820. PHEBE SALE, Amherst County, 1; RICHARD MAYS,
     Amherst County, 2; PHILIP THURMOND, Amherst County, 3...marriage
intended between PHEBE and MAYS and her estate is to be secured.
Bed, spinning wheel--1/6 as sale distributee, obligation to her from
WILLIAM DUNCAN, 25 December 1819. THURMOND is made her turstee.
Witnesses: WILLIAM MAYS, WILLIS MAYS, ANSELM MAYS.

576. 1 December 1820. GEORGE SHRADER, Amherst County, to GEORGE W.
     DILLARD, Amherst County...Deed of Trust; debt to CHARLES P.
TALIAFERRO and POWELL and TALIAFERRO, $1.00 40 acres Rocky Creek.
Lines: JACOB PIERCE, furniture, etc. To CHARLES P. TALIAFERRO,
1 September 1821.

577. 20 November 1820. WILLIAM DUNCAN, executor of JONATHAN CAMDEN,
to CHARLES TYLER, Amherst County...$133.34 53 acres. Part of
tract JONATHAN CAMDEN sold to BENJAMIN NOEL--270 acres; 117 acres of
it sold to WILLIAM WILLMORE--both sides Pedlar. Painter tract.
Lines: WILLIAM WILLMORE, JONATHAN ROBERSON, JONATHAN WARE. Witnesses:
JONATHAN B. DUNCAN, GEORGE W. VAUGHAN, JAMES POWELL.

578. 27 November 1820. JAMES CAMDEN and wife, POLLY, Amherst County,
to JONATHAN F. CAMDEN, Amherst County...$2455 122 3/4 acres
Piney. Lines: grantor, mouth of Little River, THOMAS S. HOLLOWAY,
JAMES POWELL--last two Justices of the Peace on same date as to wife.

579. 15 December 1820. RICHARD SMITH, SR. (JR?), to WIATT TURKLE...
no amount. Stonehouse Creek. Lines: EDMOND WILLIAMSON,
WILLIAM SALE, WILLIAM CASH, REV. WILLIAMSON, deceased, ENOCH CARPENTER.
RICHARD SMITH bought from JONATHAN BALL--34 acres excepted and sold
to GABRIEL PAGE. Witnesses: WIATT SMITH, SAMUEL MILLER, SHEROD --.

580. 27 November 1820. TINSLEY RUCKER and wife, NANCY, Amherst
County, to SAMUEL MILLER and JOSEPH ECHOLS, Lynchburg...Deed
of Trust; debt to JONATHAN MILLER. $1.00 202 acres Harris Creek and
southeast side of Tobacco Row in two tracts bought from ISAAC RUCKER
by TINSLEY RUCKER and GARLAND RUCKER--ISAAC RUCKER was administrator
of AMBROSE RUCKER, 22 September 1818. Lines: Top of Tobacco Row,
ROBERT JOHNSON, WILLIAM PENDLETON, HENRY MC DANILE. Other tract--
235 acres. Lines: DANIEL BURFORD, AMBROSE RUCKER, JR., AMBROSE
RUCKER, deceased, THOMAS GRISSOM. To JONATHAN MILLER, 2 November 1822.

584. 12 October 1819. ISAAC HARVEY and wife, AGATHA, formerly
TERRELL, Clinton County, Ohio, JEESE WILLIAMS and wife, SARAH,
formerly TERRELL, Warren County, Ohio...hrs. of MICAJAH TERRELL,
the elder, to JONATHAN LYNCH, Lynchburg. MICAJAH TERRELL, SR. sold
to MICAJAH TERRELL, JR., in life 340 acres both sides Bolling Creek;
no deed and JR. instituted friendly suit in Amherst County versus
heirs. JR. has sold to LYNCH. Lines: ROBERT MORRIS, BOLEN, near
Opossum Island Road, ROBINSON, WARWICK. Witnesses: M. T. WILLIAMS,
HANNAH J. WILLIAMS, JAMES HARRIS as to HARVEY, ISAAC THOMAS as to
WILLIAMS and HANNAH. Warren County: AMOS TULLIS and ROBERT HAYS,
Justices of the Peace as to WILLIAMS and wife, 16 October 1819.
MATTHEW CORWIN, JR., Clerk Common Pleas, 18 October 1819. Clinton
County, Ohio, JAMES HARRIS and JOSEPH CONGER, Justices of the Peace
as to HARVEY and wife, 12 October 1819. ISAIAH MORRIS, Clerk of
Common Pleas.

587. 1 January 1821. SAMUEL SCOTT and wife, JUDITH to JONATHAN
and JAMES J. DILLARD...Deed of Trust; debt to ALEXANDER JEWELL.
1. 110 acres where SAMUEL SCOTT lives. Lines: ROBERT GRANT, JAMES
DILLARD, DAVID S. GARLAND, JONATHAN LONDON (bought of JOSEPH HAWKINS).
2. Both sides Porrage 2 1/3 acres. Lines: THOMAS JEWELL, TURNER
PINN. Witnesses: PLEASANT STORY, REUBEN CARVER, WILLIAM CARVER.
To JAMES S. (D?) DILLARD, 18 April 1825.

589. 1 October 1820. THOMAS JEWELL, Amherst County, to SAMUEL
SCOTT, Amherst County...$500 2 1/3 acres both sides Porrage.
Lines: grantor. Witnesses: BEVERLY and NICHOLAS DAVIES, FREDERICK
FULTZ.

590. 23 May 1818. THOMAS ALDRIDGE and wife, CATHERINE, Amherst
County, to JAMES WILL, Amherst County, and GEORGE W. WITCOTT...
$500 two lots in New Glasgow--formerly those of WILLIAM MOSS,
deceased. Witnesses: WILLIAM KNIGHT, JONATHAN J. DILLARD, WILLIAM H.
ROSE, HILL CARTER, WILLIAM M. WALLER--last two as Justices of the
Peace as to wife, 15 November 1820.

591. 8 January 1821. JONATHAN WATTS, Amherst County, to JESSE
KENNEDY, Amherst County...Deed of Trust; debt to JONATHAN A.
SIMPSON; $1.00; tobacco, bee hives, corn, etc.

592. 15 August 1820. JONATHAN CAMDEN, Nelson County, to JESSE
     WRIGHT, Nelson County...$8.53 six acres on south side Piney.
Lines: JESSE MASSIE, JONATHAN CAMDEN, grantee. Witnesses: DABNEY
HILL, JONATHAN H. ROSE, CHARLES WINGFIELD, DAVID S. GARLAND.

592. 18 September 1820. JONATHAN HALL, SR. and wife, MARTHA, to
     heirs of NATHANIEL WILSON--not named...L2000 tobacco; patent
for 100 acres north side and joining Pedlar. Lines: WILLIAM GALT,
REUBEN TINSLEY, HUGH CAMPBELL, JAMES BALLINGER. Witnesses: WILLIAM
COLEMAN, JONATHAN R. SHELTON, WILLIAM PRICE, EZEKIEL GILBERT, WILLIAM
TENANT (?).

594. 15 January 1821. TINSLEY RUCKER to LUCAS P. THOMPSON...Deed
     of Trust; debt to JONATHAN N. ROSE and JONATHAN THOMPSON, JR.,
merchants; $1.00 stock bought from County, 19 December last, furniture,
slave. To LUCAS P. THOMPSON, 18 April 1821.

595. 26 December 1820. EZEKIEL GILBERT, Amherst County, to CHARLES L.
     BARRET...all interest in estate of grandmother, SUSANNAH CRENSHAW,
or my mother, JUDITH GILBERT--$50.00. Witnesses: THOMAS DAVIES,
K. H. YOUNG, REUBEN S. TYREE.

596. 29 November 1820. JESSE WADE, New Glasgow, to HENRY HAGER,
     same place...Deed of Trust; debt to JAMES S. PENDLETON; $1.00
long and interesting list of furniture. Witnesses: HEZEKIAH FULCHER,
JONATHAN L. DILLARD, D. L. SHEPHARD.

598. 9 November 1820. RICHARD HARRISON and wife, SOPHIA, Amherst
     County, to WILLIAM R. ROAN, Amherst County...$12,745 637¼ acres.
Lines: RUCKER's road, WILLIAM MC DANIEL, SPENCER NORVEL, SHELTON's
road, JAMES HILL, REUBEN NORVELL and AMBROSE RUCKER as to wife, same
day.

600. 30 October 1820. JOSEPH R. CARTER, executor of JONATHAN MAYS,
     with will, to JONATHAN RUSSELL, Amherst County...$526.50 169½
acres Pedlar. Lines: H. DIZER's saw mill, A. STATON, BIBB, COLEMAN
and BARRET on road. Margin blurred, but seem to be JONATHAN PRYOR.

601. 30 October 1820. JOSEPH R. CARTER, executor of JOSEPH MAYS,
     to CHARLES TULEY, Amherst County...$430.50 201 3/4 acres Pedlar.
Lines: COLEMAN and BARRET, A. CARTER, H. KIZER. To JONATHAN PRYOR,
per order of CHARLES TULEY, 2 May 1833. This seems to confirm previous
blurred margin.

602. 30 November 1819. MICAJAH PENDLETON and wife, MARY, Nelson
     County, to JONATHAN HORSLEY, JR...$4000 Elk Mills tract in
Amherst County and Nelson; three small surveys. 1. Two acres.
2. Two and a half acres and mill. One half conveyed by grantors to
JONATHAN HORSLEY, JR., 19 January 1813. 3. Five and a quarter acres
adjoining others. Lines: Mouth of Elk Island Creek at junction with
James; mill pond 9 3/4 acres. Witnesses: MARTHA M. PENDLETON,
WILLIAM S. LONDON, JAMES --, JONATHAN S. BECK (?), WILLIAM HORSLEY,
RICHARD PHILLIPS--last two Nelson Justices of the Peace as to wife,
10 January 1821. To JONATHAN HORSLEY, 18 February 1821.

604. 5 May 1820. JAMES DUNN and wife, NANCY, Amherst County, to
     THOMAS DUNN, Amherst County...$100 17½ acres north borders
Harris. Lines: MARTHA E. NORCUTT, REUBEN NORVELL, HUG's road (sic),
RACHEL NORCUTT--all to NANCY from estate of father, DANIEL NORCUTT.
REUBEN NORVELL and TINSLEY RUCKER as to wife, 15 May 1820.

606. 18 November 1820. TINSLEY RUCKER to JAMES S. DILLARD and
     CHARLES WINGFIELD, Amherst County...Deed of Trust; debts to
SAMUEL REED and Company, assignees of JOEL LEFTWICH, ARCHIBALD
ROBERTSON, surviving partner of BROWN and ROBERTSON, assignees of
ROBERT TINSLEY, executor of JONATHAN TINSLEY, CHARLES CRAWFORD as his
bondsman, slaves, furniture. To JAMES S. DILLARD, 21 May 1821.

607. 25 January 1820. JONATHAN CASHWELL, Lincoln County, Kentucky,
administrator of CHANDLER BOEN and grandson of BENJAMIN and
JONATHAN BOEN, infants of CHANDLER BOEN...power of attorney to friend,
PETER CASHWELL, Amherst County, to act in estate of JEREMIAH BOEN
who was brother of CHANDLER BOEN. WILLIAM BOEN is administrator of
JEREMIAH BOEN. THOMAS HELM, Clerk, 25 February 1820; JONATHAN WITHERS,
Presiding Justice of the Peace. Note: JEREMIAH BOURNE in our records
in office.

609. 14 September 1820. SPENCER NORVELL, Amherst County, to
JONATHAN D. MURREL, Lynchburg, and JONATHAN J. (?) FOX,
Richmond...Deed of Trust; bond assigned to PANNELL and NOWLINSON;
$1.00--slave; lately bought from SAMUEL NOWLIN. Witnesses: NATHANIEL B.
THURMOND, S. GARLAND, WILLIAM M. RIVERS.

610. 30 November 1819. JONATHAN HORSLEY and wife, MARY MILDRED, to
MICAJAH PENDLETON, both of Nelson County...$4565 209 acres James
River. Lines: MRS. ALLEN. Witnesses: WILLIAM S. LONDON, MARTHA M.
PENDLETON. To MICAJAH PENDLETON, 9 March 1827. WILLIAM HORSLEY and
RICHARD PHILIPS, Nelson Justices of the Peace as to wife, 10 January
1821.

611. 12 January 1821. D. and D. HIGGINBOTHAM and Company by agent,
CORNELIUS POWELL, to THOMAS DAY...Deed of Trust; $1.00--
released, furniture and stock.

612. 17 January 1819. Order to Amherst County Justices of the
Peace: HENRY WATTS and wife, ELIZA, 19 April 1813, to BENJAMIN
BROWN 430½ acres. Done, 1820, by JONATHAN COLEMAN and ROBERT TINSLEY.

613. 10 January 1821. Nelson Justices of the Peace as to MARY C.
PENDLETON, wife of MICAJAH PENDLETON, to JONATHAN HORSLEY,
19 June 1813...WILLIAM HORSLEY and RICHARD PHILLIPS, Justices of the
Peace.

613. 15 January 1821. AMBROSE RUCKER and DABNEY WARE as to SALLY
ISBELL, wife of ZACH ISBELL, to ALLISON MORRIS, 28 September
1820.

613. 2 February 1821. SALLY ISBELL to ALLISON MORRIS...$2000 paid
to her deceased husband, ZACHARIAH ISBELL, by MORRIS in lifetime.
Relinquished dower for $1.00 two tracts headwaters Harris on deed of
28 September 1820. Bought by ZACHARIAH ISBELL from RICHARD HARRISON
and JONATHAN CLEMENTS, 17 November 1817. Lines: grantor, JABEZ
CAMDEN, CHARLES TALIAFERRO, THOMAS WOODROOF, deceased, JONATHAN
CLEMENTS, JOICE CLEMENTS, WILLIAM WARE, RICHARD BURKS, BRANSFORD
HICKS. Also tract adjoining. Lines: HARRISON, CLEMENTS. WILLIAM
WARE, deceased. Witnesses: MARTIN M. DAWSON, WILLIAM PETER,
BLANFORD HICKS, LEONARD CARTER. 120 3/4 in second tract. To
ALLISON MORRIS, 24 December 1826.

615. 19 February 1821. THOMASH. BASS to THOMAS D. HILL...Deed of
Trust; debt to RICHARD HARRISON as bondsman when BASS was
appointed guardian of POLLY WOODROOF, infant of DAVID WOODROOF.
$1.00; interest of my wife in estate of DAVID WOODROOF. To S. GARLAND,
15 October 1821.

616. 17 February 1821. JONATHAN TAYLOE, Amherst County, to ROBERT Q.
SCOTT...Deed of Trust; GABRIEL SCOTT at request of JONATHAN
TAYLOE is bondsman to deliver to Sheriff horses and wagon; debt to
MORGAN and MC DANIEL, assignees of SAMUEL STEEL in suit. Horses and
wagon are used by JONATHAN TAYLOE to haul wood to Lynchburg.
Acknowledged Campbell County: JONATHAN MORRIS and W. C. MC ALLISTER,
Justices of the Peace, 17 September 1821.

617. 15 February 1821. HENRY BALLINGER and wife, POLLY, Amherst
     County, to JONATHAN RICHESON...Deed of Trust to secure THOMAS
RICHESON. HENRY BALLINGER owes JONATHAN and R. L. ELLIS on judgement
in Amherst County court versus HENRY BALLINGER and THOMAS RICHESON.
$1.00--all interest in estate of JONATHAN CLARKSON, Franklin County--
by marriage to my wife, POLLY, furniture, slave. To JONATHAN RICHESON,
15 October 1821.

618. 19 February 1821. CHARLES WINGFIELD to JACOB HAAS...Deed of
     Trust; $1.00 paid by CHISWELL DABNEY to secure HAAS; 147 acres.
Lines: BOWLINGG CLARK, deceased, JONATHAN H. GOODWIN tract bought
by CHARLES WINGFIELD from JONATHAN HEWITT--where CHARLES WINGFIELD
lives. To CK (CHARLES WINGFIELD?), 18 March 1822.

619. 19 June 1820. JONATHAN RICHESON and PHILIP THURMOND to JONATHAN
     HASS, Amherst County...$200 for tract where JONATHAN HASS lives
and sold under Deed of Trust by THURMOND and bought by RICHESON.
Lines: both sides Long Branch, road, WILLIAM DEMSEY, GORDAN's old
line, JONATHAN EUBANK. Tract was bought by JOSEPH MILSTRED from
JOSEPH HIGGINBOTHAM. Witnesses: CHARLES L. BARRET, JONATHAN W.
YOUNG, BENJAMIN HARRISON, GEORGE L. SHRADER.

620. 17 February 1821. NELSON PHILLIPS and wife, ROSAMOND, Campbell
     County, to PHILIP THURMOND, Amherst County...no amount; 128
acres Little Indian Creek. Witnesses: RICHARD H. BURKS, PAULUS A. E.
IRVINE, GEORGE --.

620. 19 September 1820. ELIZABETH FULCHER to HENRY FULCHER...$150
     all interest in estate of their deceased father, SAMUEL HUCKSTEP
(sic)--widow's dower and divided to ELIZABETH, WILLIAM CHRISTIAN,
RICHARD HUCKSTEP. Witnesses: SAMUEL CHRISTIAN, DABNEY HILL, WILLIAM
ANGUS.

621. 26 October 1820. MARIANT HARTLESS to RICHARD HARTLESS...interest
     in estate; not named; to pay him for trouble and expense. He
is to maintain her. Witnesses: JONATHAN BROWN, ANGUS MC CLOUD,
JOSEPH MILSTEAD, JONATHAN R. CLEMENT.

621. 6 September 1820. BENJAMIN SALE to RICHARD EUBANK...Deed of
     Trust; debt to RICHARD L. ELLIS; $1.00; tobacco crop. Witnesses:
THOMAS LAIN, AMBROSE RUCKER. D. T. PHILLIPS. To RICHARD EUBANK,
23 January 1835.

622. 23 November 1820. NANCY SHIELDS, on -- appointed JONATHAN PENN,
     STEPHEN WATTS and WILLIAM LEE, trustees...PENN and WATTS
renounce appointment. Witness: REUBEN NORVELL.

622. 10 February 1821. CAMMEL GOODE and wife, SUSANNAH, Adair
     County, Kentucky, to JONATHAN B. DUNCAN, Amherst County...$130--
all interest in estate of JONATHAN DUNCAN as death of widow, SARAH
DUNCAN--one thirteenth. Witnesses: LEONARD HENLEY, JAMES WOOD,
WILLIAM HENLEY.

623. 2 February 1821. JONATHAN R. SHELTON to THOMAS N. EUBANK...
     Deed of Trust; debt to JONATHAN and RICHARD L. ELLIS; $1.00
stock, furniture. Witnesses: JONATHAN F. TALIAFERRO, JONATHAN DAVIS,
PHILIP VEST. To RICHARD L. ELLIS, 18 February 1823.

623. 25 January 1821. ARMISTEAD RUCKER and wife, ELIZABETH,
     Pitsylvania, to RICHARD L. ELLIS, Amherst County...$700 100 acres
Pedlar--called Wincanton. Lines: grantee, JONATHAN ELLIS, DR. GILBERT,
GILLIAT GILBERT. ROBERT HARRISON and BENJAMIN WATKINS, Pitsylvania
Justices of the Peace, same date.

624. 19 February 1821. EDMOND PAGE to BENJAMIN HARRISON...Deed of
     Trust; debt to ALDRIDGE, MYERS and PENDLETON. $1.00 stock and
furniture.

626. 4 January 1821. LITTLEBERRY COLEMAN, Amherst County, to
JONATHAN WARE and WILLIAM JOPLING...Deed of Trust; debt to
MAGAN and MC DANIEL, Lynchburg, stock, furniture. Witnesses:
JONATHAN PRYOR, THOMAS EUBANK, GEORGE A. JOPLING.

626. 20 December 1820. WIATT SMITH, Amherst County, to LUCAS P.
THOMPSON...Deed of Trust; debt to DANIEL HIGGINBOTHAM on
judgement. SMITH is entitled by marriage to POLLY PHILLIPS in
estate of WILLIAM PHILLIPS who died intestate. MARY PHILLIPS,
Amherst County, widow, has dower; reversion to SMITH; FRANCIS
CHEATWOOD (formerly PHILLIPS); JACOB WOOD who married BARTHEMIA
PHILLIPS, GEORGE, DABNEY, and MOSES PHILLIPS--all children of WILLIAM
PHILLIPS. Sometime ago, WOOD conveyed his interest to WIATT SMITH--
SMITH conveys his one-sixth interest. Witnesses: JONATHAN SHEPHERD,
JONATHAN S. BLAIR, WIATT P. WATHER (?), CORNELIUS POWELL.

627. 22 March 1821. MATTHEW RICKETTS, Amherst County, to EDMOND N.
SALE, Lynchburg...$200 where I live--no acres. Lines:
BENJAMIN WATTS, EDMOND WATSON, WILLIAM I. ISBELL.

628. 8 April 1820. DANIEL and DAVID HOFFMAN (HOOFMAN in data) to
CHISWELL DABNEY...Deed of Trust; debt to WILLIAM STEEN; $5.00;
slaves. JONATHAN M. SETTLE and JACOB M. CARDOZA, Lynchburg Justices
of the Peace; same date.

629. 19 March 1821. GEORGE W. TRIBBLE, Amherst County, to JAMES
FULCHER, Amherst County...Deed of Trust; debt to DABNEY HILL;
$1.00; interest of GEORGE W. TRIBBLE's wife in estate of SAMUEL HILL.

629. 22 January 1821. STITH MEAD and wife, PRUDENCE WATKINS,
Amherst County, to WILLIAM BURD, Lynchburg...blank sum; three
acres. Lines: BENJAMIN SCHOOLFIELD, BURD, grantor, JAMES L. LAMKIN
and TINSLEY RUCKER as to wife, 31 January 1821. To WILLIAM BURD,
11 March 1822; 16 July 1832.

630. 9 October 1820. STITH MEAD and wife, as above, to HENRY WRIGHT,
Lynchburg...$70 two acre lot in Meadsville. Lines: grantor,
WIATT JOHNSON. Witnesses: JAMES WHEATLEY, JONATHAN WALKER, ARCHER
BROWN. Amherst County Justices of the Peace as above.

631. 22 December 1820. STITH MEAD and wife, as above, to WILLIAM
GRAVES, Amherst County...$5250 error: $52.50 1 3/4 acres
northeast side Main road from Lynchburg to ACH. Lines: WILLIAM
THURMOND, grantor, HENRY WRIGHT. Amherst County Justices of the
Peace as above. To WILLIAM GRAVES, 11 March 1822.

632. 1 November 1820. STITH MEAD and wife, as above, to DAVID
BRIGGS, Amherst County...$100 2½ acres No. 53 in Meadsville.
Lines: WILLIAM THURMOND, grantor. Same Justices of the Peace as
above.

633. 22 November 1820. STITH MEAD and wife, as above, to ANTHONY
PLEASANTS, Amherst County...$60 Lot 54 in Meadsville. Lines:
WIATT--formerly JOHNSON, Jay alley. Same Justices of the Peace.

634. 10 August 1820. THOMAS RICHESON, Amherst County, to WILLIAM
MILNER, Amherst County...$26 4 3/4 acres Horsley. Part of
tract bought by RICHARD L. ELLIS from JOSEPH MILLSTEAD and all around
grantee's tract bought from RICHARD MILLNER.

635. 21 March 1821. SAMUEL THURMOND, Amherst County, to JONATHAN
WARWICK, Sheriff...SAMUEL THURMOND in custody on exec. of
Amherst County court, 2 February 1821; JOHN PERKINS and Company for
benefit of J. D. URQUHART, trustee, for relief of insolvents--all
interest in house: Madison town on lot where he lives and bought
from BENJAMIN PERKINS.

635. 12 March 1821. JAMES M. (W.) WILSHIRE, Amherst County, to
JOSEPH WILSHIRE, Amherst County...$133 horse; beds, etc.
Witnesses: CHARLES A. CHRISTIAN, SAMUEL D. CHRISTIAN, WILLIAM POLLARD.

635. 17 March 1821. GARLAND MOORE, Amherst County, to EDWARD
      TINSLEY, Amherst County...Deed of Trust; debt to MERRIT W.
WHITE, $1.00, furniture.

636. 23 February 1821. WILLIAM WILLMIRE, Amherst County, to
      RICHARD H. BURKS and RUCKER NORVELL, Amherst County...Deed of
Trust; debt to RICHARD BURKS; $1.00 110 acres Harris Creek. Lines:
THOMAS COLEMAN, TINSLEY RUCKER, WILLIAM BARBER's survey--tract was
formerly part of GRISSOM estate; also slaves. Witnesses: DANIEL F.
CHRISTIAN, GEORGE MC DANIEL, SR., WILLIS BURKS.

637. 19 August 1820. JAMES DILLARD and wife, JANE, Amherst County,
      to JAMES S. and JONATHAN DILLARD and WILLIAM DILLARD, Amherst
County...$1.00 400 acres Mill and Porrage Creeks. Lines: JAMES
CHRISTIAN, ROBERT JOHNS, deceased. To WILLIAM DILLARD, 13 November
1843.

638. 4 April 1821. CHARLES L. CHRISTIAN and wife, SUSAN, WALTER L.
      CHRISTIAN, Amherst County, to REUBEN COLEMAN, Amherst County...
L20 98 acres Harris Creek. Lines: RICHARD HARDWICK, JABEZ CAMDEN,
WILLIAM PETERS, JAMES CHILDRESS, AMBROSE RUCKER.

639. 4 April 1821. WILLIAM WOODROOF and wife, ELIZABETH, Amherst
      County, to SAMUEL COLEMAN, Amherst County...L50 98 acres
Harris. Lines: RICHARD HARDWICK and others above, but former after
RUCKER's tract. To WILLIAM WOODROOF, 14 April 1821.

639. 4 April 1821. REUBEN COLEMAN and wife, FRANCES, Amherst
      County, to WILLIAM WOODROOF, Amherst County...L45 98 acres
Harris Creek. Lines: as above. To B. A. CRAWFORD, pre order of
WILLIAM WOODROOF, 5 May 1821.

640. 16 February 1821. HENRY H. WATTS and CHARLES MUNDY, Amherst
      County Justices of the Peace as to JANE DILLARD, wife of
JAMES, NARCISSA DILLARD, wife of JAMES S. DILLARD, NANCY F. DILLARD,
wife of JONATHAN DILLARD, 19 June 1820...deed to --.

640. 1 March 1821. BETSY BRYDIE, Richmond, to CHARLES MUNDY,
      Amherst County...$3255 651 acres; tract conveyed to CHARLES
MUNDY, 21 September 1818, by NANCY MC CREDIE (MC CURDIE): WILLIAM
DYER and wife, MARGARET, and WILLIAM BRYDIE. Lines: PARKS' Road,
JACOB PIERCE, Poor house tract, JACOB SCOTT, CHARLES HIGGINBOTHAM,
deceased, south border Rutledge, JAMES FRANKLIN, deceased. Richmond
Justices of the Peace: JAMES RAWLINGS and CHRISTOPHER TOMPKINS, same
day. To CHARLES MUNDY, 22 May 1821.

641. 16 April 1821. TINSLEY RUCKER, Amherst County, to DABNEY
      WARE, Amherst County...Deed of Trust; debt to AMBROSE RUCKER;
$1.00 slave, DANIEL. To DABNEY WARE, 1 May 1821.

642. 16 April 1821. GEORGE CAMPBELL and wife, LUCY, Amherst County,
      to WILLIAM CAMPBELL, Amherst County...$300 106 acres north side
south fork Piney. Lines: JONATHAN and BENJAMIN CAMDEN, JONATHAN
CAMPBELL, grantor. To WILLIAM CAMPBELL, 21 May 1821.

642. 16 April 1821. WILLIAM WILLMORE, Amherst County, to RICHARD
      BURKS and WILLIAM CRAWFORD...Deed of Trust; both on bond for
him; $1.00; slave, PRINCE.

643. 26 March 1821. MOSES MARTIN and JONATHAN J. MARTIN, Amherst
      County, to JONATHAN RICHESON, Amherst County and THOMAS
RICHESON, of Kentucky, but in Amherst County at present...Deed of
Trust; debt to THOMAS RICHESON. $1.00 500 acres--MOSES bought it
from JESSE RICHESON, furniture, etc.--long list; slave. Witnesses:
JEREMIAH SHOEMAKER, WILLIS GILLESPIE, JONATHAN TARDY, JONATHAN
TOMLINSON.

644. 10 January 1821. ABRAM CARTER, WILLIAM JOPLING, JOSEPH R.
      CARTER, executors of JONATHAN CRAWFORD, Amherst County, to
JONATHAN S. CARTER...$3391.50 399 acres Horsley. Lines: WILLIAM PRYOR.

645. 19 December 1820. THOMAS GOODRICH and wife, ELIZABETH,
      Amherst County, to JOSEPH R. CARTER, Amherst County...$2750
275 acres Pedlar. Lines: JONATHAN ELLIS (formerly SAMUEL GEST),
HAYNES, RICHARD EUBANK (formerly JONATHAN CRAWFORD), ABRAM CARTER,
JONATHAN ELLIS. CHARLES and BENJAMIN TALIAFERRO, Amherst County
Justices of the Peace, as to wife, 15 February 1821.

646. 20 March 1821. PEYTON ANDERSON, Amelia County, to STITH MEAD,
      Amherst County...$3200 80 acres. Lines: WILLIAM BURD,
B. SCHOOLFIELD, TAYLOR, grantee, WIATT, DABNEY. Acknowledged in
Richmond by PEYTON ANDERSON: JONATHAN H. ENSTACE and WILLIAM H.
FIZWHYLSOM, same date.

647. 10 October 1820. POLLY, THOMAS, and JONATHAN Y. JOHNSON, to
      ISHAM SCRUGGS...Amherst County Chancery decree: ISHAM SCRUGGS
versus POLLY JOHNSON, relict; MATILDA ARAMINTA, MARTHA ANN, MARY V.,
JONATHAN T. and CHARLES Y. JOHNSON, infant heirs of CHARLES Y.
JOHNSON, deceased--"guardian" (sic)--grantors for selves and infants--
two lots of half acre each: 56, 57--junction of third street and
fifth alley, fourth alley--in Madison--$1.00. Witnesses: THOMAS
MURRELL, THOMAS B. MEHONE, DAVID BLACK, JORDAN CREASY. Acknowledged
in Lynchburg, same date: ARCHIBALD ROBINSON and JONATHAN M. SETTLE,
Justices of the Peace.

647. 7 August 1820. CORNELIUS SALE, Amherst County, THOMAS SALE
      and wife, SALLY P., Bedford County, to THOMAS V. GOODRICH,
Amherst County...$700 100 acres Franklin Creek. Part of tract of
JONATHAN SALE, deceased, formerly. Surveyed by CHARLES L. CHRISTIAN,
22 July 1818. Lines: CORNELIUS SALE, JONATHAN SMITH, THOMAS
GOODRICH, JACOB PIERCE. Bedford Justices of the Peace: JACOB WHITE
and TAMERLAND W. W. DAVIES, as to SALLY P., 7 October 1820.

649. 24 March 1821. OLIVER TOWLES, JR., Lynchburg, from CLAUDIUS
      BUSTER and wife, ANN...about November, 1820, OLIVER TOWLES, JR.
bought from CLAUDIUS BUSTER two tracts of 1200 acres and deed sent to
JAMES LEWIS, Kanawaha, by mail for relinquishment of dower by ANN--
lost, so another deed with no description. Certified in Kanawaha by
ABRAM QUARRIER and JONATHAN WILSON, Justices of the Peace, 24 March
1821.

650. 24 April 1821. TINSLEY RUCKER to BENNET A. CRAWFORD and
      MERRIT M. WHITE, Amherst County...Deed of Trust; SAMUEL BURKS,
SR. (?) on bond of TINSLEY RUCKER and suit pending by PLEASANT
DAWSON to whom bond is made. $1.00 stock, crops on Tobacco Row
plantation where I live; wheat fan loaned to CHARLES WINGFIELD; about
seven is age of slave girl, another of about two years and one of
about two months and they are with their mother, HANNAH--also in
Deed of Trust. Also to secure my brother, GARLAND RUCKER, on debt
recorded in Bedford. To SAMUEL BURKS, 31 October 1822.

652. 23 April 1821. EDWARD CARTER, Amherst County, to HILL CARTER
      and STERLING CLAIBORNE, Amherst County...Deed of Trust for
$1.00 for benefit of SALLY and MARTHA ELDRIDGE FLOYD, children of
SAMUEL FLOYD--slave about seven. Witnesses: JONATHAN C. CARTER, JR.,
WHITTAKER CARTER.

653. 21 April 1821. T. S. HOLLOWAY and HENRY H. WATTS, Amherst
      County Justices of the Peace, as to SUSAN CHRISTIAN, wife of
CHARLES L. CHRISTIAN, 4 April 1821...deed to -- evidently to WILLIAM
WOODROOF for delivery to him, 9 May 1821.

653. 5 May 1821. RICHARD HARRISON and LINDSEY COLEMAN, Amherst
      County Justices of the Peace, as to ELIZABETH, wife of WILLIAM
WOODROOF, 4 April 1821, to --.

653. 7 May 1821. RICHARD HARRISON and CHARLES P. TALIAFERRO, Amherst
      County Justices of the Peace, as to FRANCES COLEMAN, wife of
REUBEN COLEMAN, 4 April 1821...to --.

653. 20 April 1821. TINSLEY RUCKER, Amherst County, to WIATT DUNCAN,
      Amherst County...Deed of Trust; debt to MARTIN BURKS. $1.00
slaves on Indian Creek plantation, stock, silver watch, gun. To
MARTIN BURKS, 31 October 1822.

654. 25 November 1820. EDITH BURFORD, Amherst County, to WILLIS
      WHITE, Amherst County...Deed of Trust; MERRIT M. WHITE is her
bondsman to administrators of SALLY GOODWIN, slave. To WILLIS WHITE,
2 April 1823. Witnesses: WILLIAM WHITE, JAMES MARTIN, GARLAND MOORE.

655. 29 January 1821. THOMAS HIGGINBOTHAM, JAMES BROWN, ROBERT
      RIVERS, late merchants of THOMAS HIGGINBOTHAM and Company, to
LINSEY BURKS, Amherst County...$1760 320 acres Maple and Cedar--
borders of Pedlar. Lines: BURFORD's Rolling road, his own, ROBERT
DAVIS, deceased, JOSIAH JOPLING, JONATHAN GOODRICH, JAMES NEWLEN.
Patent to JOSEPH CABELL, 20 August 1792. Witnesses: C. DABNEY,
ANTHONY, WILLIAM TURNER, JESSE BECK. Richmond Justices of the
Peace: JONATHAN H. EUSTARE and WILLIAM H. FITWHSOME, as to JAMES
BROWN, 17 February 1821. Acknowledged in Amherst County by ROBERT
RIVERS.

656. 7 February 1821. SALLY MITCHELL, wife of WILLIAM MITCHELL,
      12 July 1819, to -- ...TINSLEY RUCKER and JAMES L. LAMKIN,
Amherst County Justices of the Peace.

656. 24 May 1821. JONATHAN SWANSON, Amherst County, to BENNET A.
      CRAWFORD, Amherst County...Deed of Trust; debt to JAMES POWELL;
$1.00, furniture, etc. To JAMES POWELL, 29 April 1831, and 2 July
1831.

657. 15 January 1821. ROBERT ALLEN and wife, ELISABETH, Amherst
      County, to JONATHAN LACKEY, Bedford County...$73--all interest
in tract on headwaters of Thrasher and surveyed for both.

657. 12 May 1821. JONATHAN MOORE (so indexed, but appears to be
      WARE in spots. This is atrocious writing. MOORE is legal heir
of JAMES MOORE, deceased) to JONATHAN LONDON, Amherst County...$5000
paid to AMBROSE RUCKER and ALEXANDER MOORE, administrators of JAMES
MOORE (I have no JAMES WARE or MOORE fitting this case)--his interest
in tract on Porrage. Lines: JONATHAN HUTCHESON, THOMAS WILCOX's
heirs, ELIZABETH THURMON, RICHARD POWELL, JAMES PETIT, tract bought
from WILLIAM NIGHT. Tract which JAMES MOORE sold to JONATHAN LONDON
in life and where he lived: 336½ acres. JONATHAN, HEDDEN and LEWIS
WINGFIELD, Bedford Justices of the Peace as to grantor, same day.

658. 16 May 1821. JONATHAN M. GORDON and wife, AGNES W., Lynchburg,
      to JONATHAN ROBINSON, same place...$800 southwest end of town
of Madison; plat attached (not herein), lots: 66. 67, 73, 74.
Lines: junction first or Main and seventh alley; third street,
seventh alley--two acres. Agreeable to deed from JONATHAN LYNCH and
wife, MARY, to JONATHAN M. GORDON, 7 September 1817. Justices of the
Peace of Lynchburg, MICAJAH DAVIS, SR., and CHRISTOPHER WINFREE,
17 May 1821.

659. 1 December 1820. THOMAS RICHESON, at present of Amherst County,
      to JONATHAN RICHESON, Amherst County...$800--slave, WILL--good
blacksmith by trade. Witnesses: JAMES HARRIS, ALFRED RICHESON.
Memo: also tools with which will works.

660. 15 January 1821. JONATHAN LACKEY and wife, ANN, Bedford, to
      DUDLEY SANDIDGE, Amherst County...$146 146 acres Shasten's
Creek. Lines: JONATHAN HIGGINBOTHAM, deceased, ZACH TALIAFERRO.
To DUDLEY SANDIDGE, 17 March 1828. Bedford Justices of the Peace:
SAMUEL MITCHELL and LEWIS WINGFIELD, 31 March 1821, as to wife.

661. 19 May 1820. REUBEN NORVELL and wife, POLLY, Amherst County,
    to IRVIN LEE LONDON, Amherst County...$150 Porrage. Lines:
JAMES PINN, glade road, JAMES LONDON, SR., grantee. Part of 170 acres
sold by REUBEN NORVELL to JAMES PINN and conveyed to grantee by
mutual consent. JONATHAN THURMOND and JONATHAN M. SETTLE, Lynchburg
Justices of the Peace, as to REUBEN NORVELL; same day.

662. 12 May 1821. CHARLES HAYNES, Amherst County, to WILLIAM
    HAYNES, Amherst County...$100 all interest in estate of HARDEN
HAYNES, deceased, father, and in possession of mother, EDITH HAYNES.
Her dower: 150 acres where she lives. Lines: PHILIP THURMOND, SR.,
slave, JACOB, slaves: JOE, HANNAH and child, CAROLINE, slave, SALLY.
Also bonds from legatees of father. Witnesses: CHARLES L. BARRET,
R. L. ELLIS, JONATHAN W. YOUNG, MANSFIELD WARE, P. THURMOND,
JONATHAN ELLIS, R. N. EUBANK.

662. 21 December 1820. GEORGE CAMPBELL and wife, LUCY, Amherst
    County, to JESSE WRIGHT, Amherst County...$69 23 acres part of
tract; balance that of JONATHAN STINNET by deed to him. 23 acres
was taken from division of 179 acres. Lines: JESSE WRIGHT, WILLIAM
CAMPBELL, JONATHAN STINNETT. Witnesses: JAMES MILLER, GEORGE G.
WRIGHT, WILLIAM CAMPBELL.

663. 21 December 1820. WILLIAM CAMPBELL and wife, FRANCES, Amherst
    County, to JESSE WRIGHT, Amherst County...$238 54 acres part
of tract of GEORGE CAMPBELL--150 acres before division. Lines:
Little Piney. Witnesses: JAMES MILLER, GEORGE G. WRIGHT, GEORGE
CAMPBELL.

664. 20 February 1821. THOMAS ALDRIDGE and wife, CATHERINE, Amherst
    County, to EBENEZER HICKOK, Amherst County...$75 45 acres Piney.
Lines: Lynch road, JONATHAN N. ROSE, grantor, DAVID S. GARLAND and
EDMOND PENN as to wife, 19 March 1821. To EBENEZER HICKOK, 20 February
1827.

664. 3 May 1821. DANIEL M. BURFORD, Amherst County, to WILLIAM D.
    HILL, Amherst County...$150 all interest of wife, SUANNAH, as
legatee of JUDITH LYON, deceased, and power of attorney to HILL.
Witnesses: CATHERINE BURCH, ELIZA M. HILL.

665. 21 May 1821. GEORGE H. BURFORD, Amherst County, to POWHATAN
    CARTER, Amherst County...Deed of Trust; debt to MERRIT M.
WHITE; $1.00 stock, furniture, etc.

666. 5 June 1821. ELIZABETH and JONATHAN WATTS, Amherst County,
    husband and wife, to JONATHAN LONDON, Amherst County...$125 all
interest in tracts of THOMAS WILCOX, deceased--one eighth. CHARLES P.
TALIAFERRO and JAMES POWELL as to ELIZABETH, next day. To JONATHAN
LONDON, 17 September 1821.

667. 23 May 1821. WILLIAM PRYOR, Amherst County, to WILLIAM TERRY,
    Amherst County...$100 paid to LINDSEY SHUMAKER. 42 acres south
borders Horsley. Lines: DAVID CRAWFORD, deceased, DANIEL BURFORD,
deceased. Witnesses: JOHN PRYOR, ABRAM CARTER, RICHARD EUBANK.

667. 3 May 1821. TINSLEY RUCKER, 27 May 1819, made Deed of Trust
    to WILLIAM COOK and CHRISTOPHER ANTHONY...debt to SAMUEL
PHILLIPS. Advertised and sold to MARTIN P. BURKS--$1814 147 acres
Harris Creek and where TINSLEY RUCKER lives. Witnesses: DABNEY,
AMBROSE RUCKER, SAMUEL BURKS.

668. 3 March 1821. WILLIAM D. TAYLOR, Sellector for United States,
    to JONATHAN L. NEWBY under Congressional Act, 9 January 1815--
Amherst County in 19th District; tract in name of NICHOLAS JONES...
1815 tax. NEWBY bought 40 acres; only bidder; two years elapsed.
Twenty cents tax and twenty percent penalty. Certified in Richmond
by TAYLOR before C. TOMPKINS and RICHARD A. CARRINGTON, 26 March
1821.

670.   22 March 1821.   JONATHAN L. NEWBY, Richmond, to CHARLES WORTHAM
       and BENJAMIN TOMPKINS, Richmond...$10 40 acres Otter Creek.
Lines: WILLIAM MITCHELL, Certified in Richmond by JONATHAN L. NEWBY:
24 March 1821; WILLIAM H. FITZWHYLSOME and JONATHAN GODDIN.   To
ELLIOTT WORTHAM, 28 August 1840.

671.   10 July 1816.   WARNER GOODWIN, Amherst County, to JAMES L.
       PENDLETON...Deed of Trust; debt to THOMAS ALDRIDGE; $1.00, beds,
stock, etc.   Witnesses: JONATHAN THOMPSON, JR., JONATHAN S. BLAIR,
ROBERT HIGGINBOTHAM.

672.   26 September 1818.   HUMPHREY GILBERT, Amherst County, to
       JAMES BROWN, Amherst County...Deed of Trust; debt to COLEMAN
and BARRET; $1.00, stock, furniture.   Witnesses: JONATHAN RICHESON,
WIATT GATEWOOD, MOSES MARTIN.

673.   4 November 1817.   JAMES WOODROOF, Amherst County, to JAMES
       POWELL and NICHOLAS HARRISON, Amherst County...Deed of Trust;
$1.00, slave, MARY; for benefit of ELIZABETH, MARY T., FRANCIS C.,
RODA A., MALINDA L. and THOMAS P. WOODROOF.   ELIZABETH to have life
control.

674.   17 October 1818.   BENJAMIN RUCKER and wife, SALLY, Amherst
       County, to WILLIAM PETTYJOHN, Amherst County...$4264.12½ acres
274 acres both sides Lynch road.   Lines: PLEASANT DAWSON, BOLLING
CLARK, CHARLES WINGFIELD, JONATHAN BURFORD, TINSLEY road, ROBERT N. (H)
ROSE, WILLIAM MC DANIEL.   REUBEN NORVELL and NELSON C. DAWSON,
19 October 1818, as to wife.   Recorded 21 December 1821.

675.   7 December 1819.   CHARLES CHRISTIAN, Amherst County, to WILLIAM
       HORSLEY, HENRY H. WATTS, ROBERT L. JEFFERSON, Amherst County
and Nelson counties...$1.00; Deed of Trust; thirteen slaves named,
stock, furniture--to be hired and amounts to CHARLES CHRISTIAN each
year.   If he marries and has issue, trust ceases.   If he died without
issue, then one third to these: children of brother, JAMES CHRISTIAN,
ELIZABETH MURPHY, wife of JAMES MURPHY, and she is his sister--to
child or children; to SALLY HORSLEY, wife of WILLIAM HORSLEY--she,
too, is his sister--to child or children.   Witnesses: STEPHEN
WATTS, CHARLES L. COLLING (?), BENJAMIN WATTS.   To HENRY H. WATTS,
5 March 1830.

676.   2 October 1818.   THOMAS MOORE, REUBEN PENDLETON, JONATHAN ELLIS,
       NELSON CRAWFORD, LEWIS DAWSON, JAMES WARE, trustees of BETHEL,
to MOORMAN JOHNSON, Campbell County...$1.00 half acre lot: #17.

678.   17 February 1821.   WILLIAM MITCHELL and wife, SALLY, Amherst
       County, to MANSFIELD WARE, Amherst County...$1800 112 acres.
Lines: Horsley Creek, RICHARD L. ELLIS.   To MANSFIELD WARE,
17 September 1821.

679.   15 June 1821.   STITH MEAD and wife, PRUDENCE W., Amherst
       County, to WILLIAM THURMON, Lynchburg...$450 10 acres.   Lines:
JONATHAN TAYLOR, road, TINSLEY RUCKER and JAMES L. LAMKIN, Justices
of the Peace as to wife, same day.   To WILLIAM THURMON, 11 March 1822.

680.   16 June 1821.   TINSLEY RUCKER and wife, NANCY, Amherst County,
       to JONATHAN SMITH...Deed of Trust; AMBROSE RUCKER, DABNEY WARE,
SAMUEL BURKS are bondsmen for TINSLEY RUCKER to JONATHAN L. WINGFIELD
and assigned to JACOB HAAS. $1.00 156 acres Indian Creek and bought
by TINSLEY RUCKER from WILLIAM MARTIN.   Witnesses: THOMAS GRISSOM,
SAMUEL BURKS, ELIAS WILLS.

681.   17 May 1821.   JONATHAN COX and wife, FRANCES, MILLNER COX and
       wife, SALLY, WILLIAM PENDLETON and wife, PATSY, Amherst County,
to ELIAS WILLS, Amherst County...$1000 three lots; part of estate of
ARCHELAUS COX, deceased, and divided to his children: 30 acres to each.
Ninety acres #1, 2 and 6.   Same Justices of the Peace as page 679 as
to wives, 12 June 1821.

682. 30 May 1821. BENJAMIN OGDEN and wife, AGNES, Amherst County,
      to EDWARD TINSLEY, Amherst County...$180 18 acres next to
where EDWARD TINSLEY lives; part of where BENJAMIN OGDEN lives.
Witnesses: JAMES WARE, AMBROSE RUCKER, THOMAS LAINE, AMBROSE RUCKER
and JAMES WARE as to wife, same date.

683. 22 May 1821. GEORGE W. TAYLOR and wife, FANNY, Bedford County,
      to GUSTAVUS A. ROSE, Lynchburg...$749 107 acres both sides
Lynch road. Lines: WILLIAM MUSE. Witnesses: SAMUEL P. CHRISTIAN,
JONATHAN H. PATTERSON, WILLIAM SHELTON. Bedford Justices of the
Peace: JOAS. SLAUGHTER and JONATHAN L. COBBS, 5 May 1821 (sic) as
to wife.

684. 12 June 1821. GARLAND LUCAS, Amherst County, late private in
      CAPTAIN BENJAMIN HARDAWAY's Company, 35th Regiment, United
States Infantry, power of attorney to JONATHAN ALLEN, Amherst County...
to secure from proper place my bounty land. Witnesses: HUDSON M.
GARLAND, THOMAS ALDRIDGE, JACOB HEIGH. Copy of discharge: previously
treated.

685. 29 June 1821. ELIZABETH THURMOND, WILLIAM D. HILL and wife,
      NANCY, Amherst County, to heirs of RICHARD POWELL, deceased--
not named...$850 63 3/4 acres Porrage. Lines: JAMES PETTIT,
JONATHAN LONDON, ELIZABETH THURMOND, JAMES LIVELY, deceased,
RICHARD POWELL, deceased. Deed and plat executed in lifetime of
RICHARD POWELL, but not recorded. REUBEN NORVELL and JAMES L. LONDON
as to ELIZABETH THURMOND, 29 June 1821; also as to NANCY HILL.

686. 15 May 1821. BENJAMIN RUCKER, Amherst County, to RICHARD H.
      BURKS...Deed of Trust; $1.00; debt to RICHARD BURKS as bondsman
to ISAAC RUCKER, administrator of AMBROSE RUCKER, slaves named,
horse.

687. 10 March 1821. WILLIAM MITCHELL, Amherst County, to EDMOND
      WINSTON and WILLIAM LANGHORNE, Amherst County...$5.00 and L1500
bacon, in trust for support of his family; also to secure debts to
THOMAS MITCHELL, ROBERT HARVEY; two large bottles of spirits; one
dozen wine bottles with contents, oats, provender for horses, cattle,
carpenter and cooper tools, cogs in Farm Mills, 50 or 60 books,
profits from Farm Mills, profits from contract with Lynchburg and
Salem Turnpike Company and Freebridge Company. Witnesses: WILLIAM R.
MITCHELL, L. T. MITCHELL, HARVEY MITCHELL.

688. 2 July 1821. SAMUEL FLOYD, Amherst County, to STERLING
      CLAIBORNE...Deed of Trust; to support PEGGY FLOYD, wife of
SAMUEL, SALLY and MARTHA ELDRIDGE FLOYD, WILLIAM HENRY FLOYD, his
children--three feather beds, gun, etc.--to be divided at PEGGY's
death.

689. 4 July 1821. JAMES LONDON, Amherst County, to JAMES LONDON,
      JR...grantor is SR.--both of Amherst County; $180 19½ acres
both sides Jumping Branch. SR. bought from CAPTAIN CHARLES CHRISTIAN.
Lines: JONATHAN WARWICK, REUBEN NORVELL, JR. Witnesses: THOMAS
KNIGHT, RICHARD H. LONDON, SALLY LONDON, CHARLES MONDAY. To
JAMES L. WHITTINGTON. 1 January 1841 or 7 (?).

690. 21 July 1821. WILLIAM I. MAYS and ANSELM MAYS, Amherst County,
      to DABNEY SANDIDGE, Amherst County...Deed of Trust; debts to
JAMES W. SMITH; $1.00, black horse. Witnesses: R. HENLEY, PHILADELPHIA
SMITH, ROBERT TINSLEY and THOMAS SLDRIDGE, same day, as to all parties.

692.   4 June 1821.   GEORGE B. WOODSON, Marshall of Superior Court
      of Chancery, Lynchburg, to President and Board, Farmers' Bank
of Virginia (to CHARLES P. TALIAFERRO, a director, 24 August 1821)...
decree of Monday, 18 October 1819 between bank and defendants, ROBERT
MORRIS, WILLIAM MITCHELL, JAMES DUNNINGTON, ROBERT L. COLEMAN,
NICHOLAS HARRISON, JAMES PENN, JONATHAN M. SETTLE, SAMUEL GARLAND,
JONATHAN H. SMITH--Deed of Trust on Long Mountain tract of 930 acres,
executed by MORRIS to CHRISTOPHER ANTHONY and JONATHAN D. URQUHART,
181, due by 25 June 1819; tract in Campbell on Long Mountain; house
and lot in Lynchburg (GILPIN TUTTLE is a tenant). Sold, 17 February
1821 and agent for bank bought at $6411.50.   430 acres in Amherst
County and bought by MORRIS from GEORGE WINSTON and wife, DOROTHA;
also 620 acres adjoining and bought by ROBERT MORRIS from GEORGE MAY.
Witnesses: ALEXANDER TOMPKINS, JONATHAN M. GORDON, RICHARD THURMOND,
SR.   Certified as to WOODSON in Lynchburg, 27 July 1821, by JAMES
PENN and HENRY DAVIS.

696.   7 April 1821.   ERASMUS STRIBLING, Augusta County, to EDMOND
      EDRINGTON, same county...L5 176 acres conveyed by CARTER BEVERLY--
to JACOB KINNEY and STRIBLING and recorded in General Court, June,
1810, as trustees for benefit of WILLIAM MC MEEKIN and JAMES P.
HEATH.   KINNEY has died.   ALEXANDER ST. CLAIR and WILLIAM BOYD (BOYS),
Justices of the Peace of Augusta as to ERASMUS STRIBLING, same day.
To EDMOND EDRINGTON, 7 September 1821.

697.   23 August 1821.   THOMAS NEVILL and wife, ELIZABETH, Amherst
      County, to PETER BURROUGHS, Amherst County...$80 100 acres--
formerly that of JEREMIAH CONLETON, deceased, on Glade Creek.

699.   19 May 1820.   REUBEN NORVELL and wife, POLLY, Amherst County,
      to JAMES PENN, Amherst County...$1700 145 acres east side Glade
road. Lines: grantor, LARKIN LONDON, LEE LONDON. Part of tract
conveyed by JAMES LONDON to REUBEN NORVELL: 170 acres; balance at
request of PENN is to be conveyed to LEE LONDON.   Acknowledged in
Lynchburg by REUBEN NORVELL, same day, JONATHAN THURMON, Mayor, and
JONATHAN M. SETTLE, Alderman.   To LEE LONDON, present owner,
16 October 1848.

700.   2 March 1821.   WILLIAM D. TAYLOR, Collector of United States
      in Virginia, to JONATHAN L. NEWBY...delinquent tract of ROBERT
PRICE--34¢ for 1815 and not a resident: sold, 14 December 1818--
100 acres--part of tract. Lines: DAVID S. GARLAND; if a house is
thereon; 100 acres is part of 121 acres. C. TOMPKINS and RICHARD A.
CARRINGTON, Richmond Justices of the Peace, 27 March 1821, as to
TAYLOR.   To E. WILLS, 29 June 1822.

703.   21 August 1821.   RICHARD HARRISON and wife, SOPHIA, Amherst
      County, to JAMES L. PENDLETON and TIPTON B. HARRISON...Deed
of Trust; debt to ELIAS WILLS, JONATHAN M. SETTLE, STERLING CLAIBORNE;
$1.00; CLAIBORNE is bondsman for RICHARD HARRISON as guardian of
infants of SEATON M. PENN, deceased.   713 acres where RICHARD HARRISON
lives--balance of purchase from BENNETT RUCKER, JONATHAN MC BRIDE,
JAMES PETTIT, JOSHUA D. RUCKER, HARMON GENTRY, ISAAC RUCKER (agent
for JAMES TINSLEY), REUBEN RUCKER, named slaves, furniture, stock.
Also debts to NANCY SHIELDS, WILLIAM LEE, RICHARD BURKS, RICHARD H.
BURKS, BENJAMIN HARRISON as to bondsman to WILLIAM MORGAN and
partners.

705.   21 August 1821.   ELIAS WILLS released Deed of Trust, 8 April
      1820, from RICHARD HARRISON, to him; JONATHAN M. SETTLE,
RICHARD H. BURKS and JAMES L. PENDLETON.

505.   19 June 1821.   WALTER CHRISTIAN and wife, PATSY, Amherst
      County, to WILLIAM SIMMONS, Amherst County...$648 180 acres
Rocky Run. Lines: ABSALOM HOWL, PETER BURROUGHS, JACOB PIERCE,
CHARLES H. CHRISTIAN. Witnesses: REUBEN NORVELL, CHARLES L. CHRISTIAN,
CHARLES H. CHRISTIAN, RICHARD WILSON. To WILLIAM SIMMONS, 21 January
1823.

706. 20 August 1821. DAVID A. GILBERT, Amherst County, to MATTHEW
    BURKS, Nelson County...Deed of Trust; debt to RICHARD H. BURKS;
$1.00, furniture, interest in estate of parents--not named. Witnesses:
HARRY, WILLIS and JONATHAN F. BURKS. To MATTHEW BURKS, 21 July 1823.

707. 18 August 1821. WILLIAM WILLMORE and wife, SAUSANNA, Amherst
    County, to BENJAMIN NORVELL, Amherst County...$500 420 acres
Pedlar. Lines: CHARLES TYLER, JAMES ROWSEY--CHILDRESS' old place.
THOMAS CREWS and ISAAC RUCKER, same day, as to wife.

708. 21 August 1821. RICHARD HARRISON and wife, SOPHIA, Amherst
    County, to PHILIP LIVELY, Amherst County...$1350 180 acres--
part of two tracts bought by RICHARD HARRISON from STERLING CLAIBORNE;
also another tract of 50 acres.

709. 13 August 1821. JONATHAN WATTS, Amherst County, to CHARLES P.
    TALIAFERRO, Amherst County...Deed of Trust; $1.00 debt to
POWELL and TALIAFERRO--tobacco crop now growing. To CHARLES P.
TALIAFERRO, 9 January 1822.

710. 20 August 1821. WILLIAM L. WATTS and wife, MARY ANN, Nelson
    County, to JAMES D. WATTS, Nelson County...$1000 three tracts
on Buffaloe and both sides. Lines: MICAJAH PENDLETON--195 acres.
Tract on both sides Freeland Creek, north border Buffaloe. Lines:
JAMES FREELAND, deceased, JESSE CANADA, REUBEN THORNTON, SMITH TANDY,
JAMES ROWSEY--146 acres. Also tract on Buffaloe. Lines: ALLEN
BLAIR, STEPHEN WATTS--78 3/4 acres. To JAMES D. WATTS, 30 October
1860.

712. 14 December 1818. ELIZABETH FLINT, THOMAS FLINT, JAMES FLINT,
    NATHANIEL FLINT, CHRISTOPHER FLINT, JONATHAN FLINT and HANNAH
FLINT, Rockbridge, to ARCHY ROWSEY, Amherst County...$160 south
borders Pedlar; no acres set forth. Lines: HENRY HARTLESS, THOMAS
ALLEN, JOSEPH HIGGINBOTHAM. Rockbridge Justices of the Peace:
ALEXANDER SHIELDS and ROBERT WHITE, as to FLINTS, same day.

713. 25 June 1821. JAMES WARE and wife, ANN, Amherst County, to
    JONATHAN WILSON, Amherst County...$300 half acre lot in Bethel--
#11. JONATHAN ELLIS and RICHARD N. EUBANK, as to ANN, 23 August
1821. Delivered to -- June, 1824, in WILSON versus HENDERSON.

714. 4 August 1821. JONATHAN W. YOUNG, Amherst County, to JOSIAH
    ELLIS...Deed of Trust; debt to NANCY YOUNG as bondsman to
ELIJAH FLETCHER, JOSIAH ELLIS as bondsman to CHARLES L. BARRET and
Company; $1.00 paid by JAMES F. TALIAFERRO--interest in estate of
father, JONATHAN YOUNG, and in possession of NANCY. Witnesses:
GEORGE N. ROSE, BENJAMIN B. TALIAFERRO, ELI GARNETT. To JAMES F.
TALIAFERRO, 17 December 1821; returned 22 May 1822.

715. 1 September 1821. GEORGE A. BLAIR, Amherst County, to
    JONATHAN PRYOR, Amherst County...Deed of Trust; debt to
JONATHAN MYERS; $1.00, furniture.

716. 31 July 1821. THOMAS HIGGINBOTHAM and CHISWELL DABNEY, Amherst
    County, to JONATHAN WARD, SR., Pitsylvania...WILLIAM MITCHELL
and wife, SALLY, 31 July 1816, conveyed to THOMAS HIGGINBOTHAM and
CHISWELL DABNEY--798 3/4 acres on James nearly opposite Lynchburg;
one acre excepted at mouth of Harris given by JONATHAN WARD, SR. to
JONATHAN LYNCH, SR. and sold by EDMOND LYNCH to MITCHELL. Also
21½ acres excepted and conveyed by WILLIAM MITCHELL to GEORGE TUCKER.
Sold to WARD as highest bidder at $20,050. Lynchburg Justices of
the Peace: JONATHAN HANCOCK and ARCH. ROBERTSON as to THOMAS
HIGGINBOTHAM, 20 August 1821; Amherst County acknowledged by DABNEY
before clerk same day.

717. 4 August 1821. JONATHAN W. YOUNG, Amherst County, power of
    attorney to ELI GARNETT, Amherst County, to act for him...
Witnesses: CHARLES L. BARRET, JAMES F. TALIAFERRO, GEORGE N. ROSE.

717. 28 October 1820. BENJAMIN HIGGINBOTHAM, Amherst County, has
      received of brother, JOSEPH HIGGINBOTHAM, an old slave and
stock; to be returned upon demand. Witnesses: DAVID S. GARLAND,
JONATHAN EUBANK.

718. 7 February 1821. JAMES L. LAMKIN and TINSLEY RUCKER, Amherst
      County Justices of the Peace, as to SALLY MITCHELL, wife of
WILLIAM...31 July 1816, to -- .

718. 17 September 1821. EZEKIEL DAY and wife, ELISABETH S.,
      WILLIAM J AY and wife, SOPHIA W., Amherst County, to SOLOMON
DAY, Amherst County...Plank and Iron Brs. Lines: WILLIAM TURNER
(late), JAMES DAVIS, DANIEL DAY, JESSE BECK--170 acres. Also adjacent
tract. Lines: WILLIAM TURNER--31 acres $900. CHARLES MUNDY and
JAMES S. LAMKIN as to ELIZABETH S. and SOPHIA W., same day.

720. 15 September 1821. RICHARD WHITEHEAD and wife, PENCY,
      Pitsylvania, to BENJAMIN GOSNEY, same county...$2840 Harris
Creek. 1. North side Harris 106 acres and bought by RICHARD
WHITEHEAD of LEWIS DAWSON. 2. 105½ acres. Lines: JAMES WILLS,
bought by RICHARD WHITEHEAD from WILLIAM LEE. DAVID HUNT and NELSON
TUCKER as to wife in Pitsylvania, same day.

721. 28 August 1821. FREDERICK PAINTER, Amherst County, to THOMAS
      JORDAN and ANDERSON WARE, Amherst County...$1000 166 acres
south borders middle fork Pedlar. Witnesses: JONATHAN B. DUNCAN,
MAYO DAVIES, HENRY D. RUCKER.

722. 17 September 1821. HUGH TYGET, Amherst County, to DUDLEY
      SANDIDGE, Amherst County...HUGH TYGET has hired of EDMOND WATSON
a negro man, GEORGE, a blacksmith, for one year. JAMES W. SMITH is
his bondsman. Deed of Trust; said slave to be used by HUGH TYGET in
blacksmith shop. To SMITH, 5 August 1822, per WILLIAM DUNCAN.

723. 17 September 1821. JAMES PINN, Amherst County, to CHARLES
      MUNDY, Amherst County...Deed of Trust; to secure CATLETT
CAMPBELL who is bondsman to WILKINS WATSON and REUBEN NORVELL.
$1.00, cattle, stock, furniture, carpenter tools, crops. To
CATLETT CAMPBELL, 20 March 1820.

723. 3 September 1821. STERLING CLAIBORNE to DAVID S. GARLAND...
      Deed of Trust; debt to SAMUEL GARLAND, $1.00 600 acres. Lines:
Buffaloe Springs and bought from JOSEPH HIGGINBOTHAM. SAMUEL GARLAND
bondsman of STERLING CLAIBORNE to SAMUEL SPENCER, JONATHAN SCOTT.
Witnesses: SAMUEL HANNAH, FRANCIS L. MILLER, SEPTIMUS D. OWENS.

724. 18 September 1821. REUBEN COLEMAN and wife, FRANCES, Amherst
      County, to SAMUEL SIMMONS, Amherst County...$875 lot at ACH
on main road to Lynchburg--1 5/8 acres. To SAMUEL SIMMONS, 22 May
1822.

725. 8 September 1821. LINDSEY TINSLEY to JONATHAN WARWICK...this
      day LINDSEY TINSLEY taken by SAMUEL BRANSFORD, Sergeant of
Lynchburg Corporation, under execution of clerk of Amherst County in
favor of TIMOTHY FLETCHER, assignee of JONATHAN TAYLOR, for $500
debt; insolvent--to JONATHAN WARWICK for creditors. WARWICK as
Amherst County Sheriff--60 acres bought by LINDSEY TINSLEY from
GEORGE EUBANK, son of JONATHAN. Certified Lynchburg by LINDSEY
TINSLEY: ARCHIBALD ROBERTSON and JONATHAN HANCOCK, Justices of the
Peace.

726. 19 September 1821. JONATHAN LONDON and wife, TIRZA, Amherst
      County, to JAMES OGDEN, Amherst County...$1190 119 acres
Rutledge. Lines: RICHARD POWELL, deceased, path to mansion house,
JAMES LIVELY, MATTHEW LIVELY, JAMES HILL. RUBEN NORVELL and CHARLES
MUNDY, same day, as to wife.

727. 19 September 1821. JANE LIVELY, MATTHEW LIVELY and wife,
     LUCY, PHILIP LIVELY and wife, SUSAN, JAMES R. LIVELY, Amherst
County, to JAMES OGDEN, Amherst County...$1405 140½ acres Rutledge.
Lines: dower tract, JONATHAN MC DANIEL, DAVID WOODROOF, deceased,
JAMES HILL. Part of tract assigned to MATTHEW LIVELY out of lands
of deceased father, JAMES LIVELY.

728. 19 September 1821. REUBEN NORVEL and CHARLES MUNDY as to
     JANE, MATTHEW, PHILIP and JAMES R. LIVELY.

729. 21 May 1821. ROBERT L. COLEMAN and wife, MARY T., Bedford,
     to WILLIAM H. DIGGES, Nelson County...$4000 Amherst County
and Nelson tract on north side Buffaloe Ridge and part of tract
given to ROBERT L. COLEMAN by LINDSEY COLEMAN, deceased--676 acres.
Lines: a border. Bedford Justices of the Peace: BALDA MC DANIEL
and NATHANIEL J. MANSON, 18 June 1821, as to MARY T.

730. 24 September 1821. GEORGE SHRADER and wife, AGATHA, Amherst
     County, to JONATHAN PAMPLIN, Amherst County...L110 71½ acres
both sides north fork Elk Island Creek. Lines: WILLIAM LAINE,
GEORGE HILTON, deceased, WILLIAM VIA. Witnesses: REUBEN NORVEL,
THOMAS D. HILL, JONATHAN FRANKLIN.

731. 24 September 1821. EDMOND NOEL to WILLIAM DILLARD, Amherst
     County...Deed of Trust; $1.00 slave and five children named--
13, 9, 7, 3, 3 months. NOEL's wife mentioned, but not named. Debt
to RICHARDSON HENLEY.

732. 30 July 1821. JANE LIVELY, widow of JAMES LIVELY, PHILIP
     LIVELY, son of JAMES, and wife, SUSAN, to JONATHAN LONDON,
Amherst County...JAMES devised tract to JANE for her life by will,
and then equally to sons, MATTHEW, PHILIP and JAMES R. JANE agreed
with her sons, 2 April 1816, to make division and reserve one third
for herself: 280 acres; part of tract and including dower--$2,248.00
Rutledge and Porrage. Lines: JAMES HILL, RICHARD POWELL, deceased,
ELIZABETH THURMOND, JAMES R. LIVELY, MATTHEW LIVELY. Witnesses:
THOMAS D. HILL, GEORGE L. SHRADER, BENJAMIN NORVELL, REUBEN NORVELL
and CHARLES MUNDAY as to SUSAN and JANE, 19 September 1821. To
JANE LIVELY, 7 May 1822.

734. 21 March 1821. JONATHAN M. WALKER and wife, MARGARET,
     Buckingham County, to REUBEN NORVELL, Amherst County...$3,762
313½ acres James River. Lines: foot of JOHNSON's Mountain where
JAMES DILLARD's line crosses line, REUBEN CARVER, grantee, a lane.
Certified in Amherst County by grantor before HENRY H. WATTS and
CHARLES P. TALIAFERRO, next day. HENRY FLOOD and JONATHAN HARRIS,
Buckingham Justices of the Peace, as to his wife, 29 March 1821.
To REUBEN NORVELL, 18 March 1822.

735. 28 September 1821. WILLIAM ROACH, Amherst County, to JONATHAN
     THOMPSON, Campbell County...L140 800 acres in Ohio County,
Kentucky; middle fork ADAMS' fork Rough River. Lines: middle creek.
Bought from THOMPSON and wife, LYDIA, 14 February 18--, and recorded
in Campbell.

736. 10 June 1821. JONATHAN SCRUGGS to RHODA GRIFFITH...$250 lots
     56 and 57 in town of Madison--joins junction of third street,
fifth alley, fourth alley, JOHN MILLER--one acre. Witnesses:
THOMAS B. MAHONE, DANIEL MC CORMACK, SAMUEL SCRUGGS. Margin:
Recorded through mistake--not being ordered to record for want of
proof of another witness. Proved by MAHONE and MC CORMACK.

737. 27 September 1821. ARMISTEAD RUCKER, Pitsylvania, to WILLIAM
     SHELTON and ARTHUR B. DAVIES...Deed of Trust; debt to RICHARD
BURKS; $1.00 all interest in estate of my father, ANTHONY RUCKER,
deceased, slaves, furniture. Debt assigned to ARCHIBALD ROBERTSON
and Company and they have sued BURKS. To RICHARD BURKS, 25 July 1823.

738. 20 September 1821. GEORGE SHRADER, Amherst County, to PHENEAS
     PIERCE, Amherst County...seventy-five cents per day for use
of wagon and two horses, furniture, etc. Sold by GEORGE W. DILLARD,
trustee, in Deed of Trust; executed by GEORGE SHRADER--$200.
Witness: H. M. GARLAND.

738. 21 September 1821. WILLIS CARTER, Amherst County, to EDWARD A.
     CABELL...Deed of Trust; debt to DAVID JOHNSON, Rockbridge;
$1.00, furniture, stock. Witnesses: PEYTON JOHNSON, WILLIAM
SPEARS, JONATHAN W. (?) JOHNSON.

739. This is a long and involved document and it would be better
     understood, if we could find original papers in Richmond. I
have picked out all essential facts and names, but this seems to be
a suit that had dragged on for years. 28 November 1820. JAMES
CHRISTIAN and wife, CURDILLAH, JAMES MURPHY and wife, ELIZABETH,
WILLIAM HORSLEY and wife, SALLY, Nelson County, CHARLES CHRISTIAN.
Amherst County to REUBEN NORVELL, Amherst County...To REUBEN NORVELL,
18 March 1822--"long pending suit" between JAMES, ELIZABETH, SALLY
and CHARLES as children of GEORGE CHRISTIAN, deceased, and the
representatives of JONATHAN H. CHRISTIAN, deceased, to recover lands
and grantors agreed since to convey to REUBEN NORVELL interest in
any received from JONATHAN H. CHRISTIAN's representatives. Decree
of -- $2500 for their interest. Decree of Court of Appeals, Richmond,
18 March 1820--JOYCE CHRISTIAN, widow of JONATHAN CHRISTIAN, JONATHAN M.
WALKER and wife, SUSANNAH, heir--will annexed--versus JAMES,
ELIZABETH, CHARLES and SALLY CHRISTIAN, wife of GEORGE CHRISTIAN,
deceased, by REUBEN NORVELL, guardian, WILLIAM PRICE, Land Office
Registrar, JONATHAN BOOTH, DRURY BELL, JONATHAN STAPLES, WILLIAM
STAPLES, executors of THOMAS STAPLES--the said JONATHAN STAPLES,
HOBSON HOOD and wife, ELIZABETH, JAMES HARRIS and wife, ELLENOR,
JOSEPH DAVENPORT and wife, DOROTHY H., DAVID STAPLES, BEVERLY
STAPLES, JAMES HUGHES and wife, SARAH, CHRISTIAN NOEL and THOMAS
STAPLES, an infant, by guardian, JONATHAN STAPLES, and SAMUEL BELL--
upon appeals from Superior Court of Chancery, Richmond, last day of
May, 1808--between JOYCE CHRISTIAN et al. versus JAMES CHRISTIAN
et al.--JOYCE, widow of JONATHAN CHRISTIAN, JONATHAN M. WALKER and
wife, SUSANNAH, heirs, and JONATHAN M. WALKER, administrator with
will of JONATHAN CHRISTIAN. Decree is in error and reversed--will
of JAMES CHRISTIAN, SR., JONATHAN STAPLES holding under patent in
tract and also BOOTH--123 and 390 acres and where JONATHAN CHRISTIAN's
house stands--to convey to JOYCE in fee simple--one fourth of 400
acres to them on Stonewall granted to her testator. Patents to
JAMES CHRISTIAN, JR., and devised to their father, GEORGE CHRISTIAN.
Claims of DRURY BELL and SAMUEL BELL dismissed. Surveyed by JAMES
CHRISTIAN, SR., 27 February 1747, and transferred to JONATHAN and
GEORGE CHRISTIAN, 13 December 1771. H. DANCE, Circuit Clerk;
Certified in Nelson by NELSON ANDERSON and ALEXANDER BROWN as to
JAMES CHRISTIAN, JAMES MURPHY, WILLIAM HORSLEY and CHARLES CHRISTIAN,
28 November 1820, and their wives also named.

741. 20 September 1821. RICHARD MAYS to PHILIP THURMOND, Amherst
     County...Deed of Trust; debt to WILLIAM I. MAYS; $1.00; transfer
to WILLIAM I. MAYS by ANSEL MAYS; amount paid by WILLIAM to GEORGE W.
HUDSON for RICHARD MAYS, crops for this year and tools. Witnesses:
ROBERT W. CARTER, WILL M. WALLS, JAMES FULCHER.

742. 28 September 1821. CLAIBORNE W. GOOCH, Richmond, to DABNEY P.
     GOOCH, Amherst County...heirs of father, PHILIP GOOCH, deceased,
and late brother, WILLIAM B. GOOCH--CLAIBORNE W. GOOCH for self and
for WILLIAM F. GOOCH and ELIZABETH H. FERGUSON, formerly GOOCH--he
bought their interest and DABNEY P. in own right--a division: The
Folly, bought by PHILIP GOOCH from HARVIE and small tract joining on
side of Buffaloe Ridge bought from CHRISTIAN; also tracts on Elk Run
Creek--THOMPSON bought from JONATHAN THOMPSON; tract bought from
SAMUEL BELL; from executors of HENRY BELL; also revision interest of
PHILIP's widow or of WILLIAM B. GOOCH's widow. CLAIBORNE to DABNEY--
WRIGHT tract bought from ISAAC WRIGHT on Lime Kiln Creek; also interest
of WILLIAM B. GOOCH, save 300 acres on Tobacco Row Mt. and tracts in

205

Albemarle and Bedford of WILLIAM B. and PHILIP GOOCH which are to
be divided. CLAIBORNE W. GOOCH has sold some of these in Albemarle
and Bedford, and DABNEY agrees to ratify.

743. 16 October 1820. DRURY BELL and wife, CATHERINE, Nelson
     County, to REUBEN NORVELL of Amherst County...$750 148 acres (?)
on Lime Kiln. Lines: DRURY CHRISTIAN, deceased, COLEMAN's road--
tract in Court of Appeals decree between JAMES CHRISTIAN's representatives versus children of GEORGE CHRISTIAN. Witnesses: WILLIAM L. (?)
BELL, JONATHAN H. BELL, THOMAS COLEMAN, CHARLES P. TALIAFERRO,
P. THURMOND. To REUBEN NORVELL, 18 March 1822.

744. 15 October 1821. FLEMING CARTER, Amherst County, to JONATHAN S.
     BLAIR, Amherst County...Deed of Trust; debt to D. and D.
HIGGINBOTHAM and Company; $1.00, crops, furniture, stock.

745. 4 October 1821. ELLIS P. OMOHUNDRO and wife, POLLY D.,
     Amherst County, to JONATHAN A. SIMPSON, Amherst County...$950
122 3/4 acres Migginson Road on northwest side. Lines: PETER
CASHWELL, SAMUEL HUCKSTEP's estate, ANDREW MONROE, JOSEPH HIGGINBOTHAM's
old tract, CHARLES P. TALIAFERRO and CHARLES MUNDY as to POLLY D.,
15 October 1821.

746. 9 October 1821. CHARLES L. CHRISTIAN and wife, SUSANNAH,
     Amherst County, to WILLIAM EDMONDS, Kentucky...WILLIAM and
wife, POLLY, 15 June 1807, sold to grantors and WILLIAM L. CHRISTIAN,
146 acres Buffaloe. Lines: JONATHAN CHRISTIAN, JONATHAN COLEMAN,
WILLIAM S. CRAWFORD, REUBEN GATEWOOD, Watermillion (sic) Br. Decree
of Chancery, Lynchburg, 17 May 1821, made void aforesaid sale from
WILLIAM EDMONDS; $1.00 paid by WILLIAM EDMONDS. DAVID S. GARLAND
and THOMAS ALDRIDGE, 9 October 1821, as to CHARLES and ISAAC RUCKER
and CHARLES P. TALIAFERRO as to SUSANNAH, 18 October 1821.

747. 24 September 1821. CHARLES L. CHRISTIAN, Amherst County, to
     ELIJAH L. CHRISTIAN, Amherst County...in trust; $1.00; slaves
because of love for my wife, SUSANNAH, and children. To ELIJAH L.
CHRISTIAN, 20 July 1824.

748. 15 October 1821. WILLIAM DILLARD, Amherst County, to NELSON C.
     DAWSON...Deed of Trust; debt to GEORGE L. HOLLOWAY; $1.00
71½ acres. Lines: JONATHAN BOWLING on Lynch road; slaves.

749. 15 October 1821. JONATHAN A. SIMPSON, Amherst County, to
     BENNET A. CRAWFORD...Deed of Trust; debt to ELLIS P. OMOHUNDRO;
$1.00 122 1/3 acres. Lines: THOMAS HIGGINBOTHAM, PETER CASHWELL,
tract recently bought from ELLIS P. OMOHUNDRO. To BENNET A. CRAWFORD,
24 December 1822.

749. (two such pages) 16 May 1820. RICHARD MILLNER and wife,
     PATSY, Pitsylvania, to PHILIP THURMOND, Amherst County...$6000
645 acres tract bought from grantee by grantor. Lines: CHARLES
CARTER, THOMAS N. EUBANK, HARDEN HAYNES, deceased, Rocky Branch,
CHARLES ELLIS, RICHARD L. ELLIS, WILLIAM THURMOND. Pitsylvania
Justices of the Peace: BENJAMIN WATKINS and ROBERT HARRISON as to
wife, 29 May 1821.

750. 21 November 1816. JONATHAN POINDEXTER, SR., Loiusa County,
     to his son, THOMAS POINDEXTER, Louisa County...$100.00 400 acres
Buffaloe. Patent, 20 September 1758 (? blurred) and bought by
JONATHAN POINDEXTER from JONATHAN SERJEANT, Louisa, 22 July 1805.
Witnesses: JAMES (JAMES) BICKLEY, WILLIAM ANDERSON. Proved Louisa,
12 March 1821; WILLIAM ANDERSON, Deputy Clerk; JONATHAN HUNTER,
Clerk.

751. 15 October 1821. THOMAS HOLLOWAY and AMBROSE RUCKER as to
     ANNE RIVERS, wife of ROBERT RIVERS, as to deed of 14 January
1819, to --.

751. No date, but acknowledged in Warren County, Kentucky, 29 October
      1821--1820 (sic). WILLIAM L. CHRISTIAN and wife, NANCY,
Kentucky, to WILLIAM EDMUNDS, Kentucky...same facts as set forth in
deed on page 746--146 acres--resale for $1.00. Certified Warren
County, Kentucky by JONATHAN KEEL and W. C. PAYNE, 29 October 1821;
JONATHAN HOPSON, Clerk; JONATHAN PORTER, Presiding Justice.

753. 25 June 1819. BENNET RUCKER and wife, JOHANNA, Rutherford
      County, Tennessee to WILLIAM MC DANIEL, Amherst County...$100
301 acres. Lines: RICHARD HARRISON, JONATHAN BOLLING, ROBERT H.
ROSE. Rutherford County, Tennessee: second Monday, June, 1819, as
to wife--BLACKMAN COLEMAN, Clerk. Recorded: Amherst County,
19 November 1821.

754. 25 August 1821. WILLIAM I. MAYS, Amherst County, to WILLIAM
      CAMPBELL, Amherst County...$104 and L3000 tobacco 100 acres
both sides George's Creek, south border Piney. Lines: GEORGE
CAMPBELL. Witnesses: WILLIAM MAYS, CORNELIUS, SAMUEL and DANIEL
CAMPBELL.

755. 15 September 1821. WILLIAM D. HILL and wife, NANCY, Amherst
      County, to REUBEN NORVELL and PROSSER POWELL...Deed of Trust;
debt to SPENCER NORVELL and NELSON C. DAWSON; $1.00 89 acres Lynch
Road. Lines: CHARLES WINGFIELD, GUSTAVUS A. ROSE, WILLIAM MUSE,
TINSLEY RUCKER, BOLLING CLARK. Tract bought from SPENCER NORVELL
and NELSON C. DAWSON. Witnesses: WILLIAM TURNER, T. D. HILL,
AMBROSE RUCKER, WILLIAM I. BOWLING. JAMES L. LAMKIN and REUBEN
NORVELL as to wife, 24 October 1821.

756. 21 November 1821. RICHARD HARRISON and wife, SOPHIA, Amherst
      County, to ROBERT L. COLEMAN, Bedford, GEORGE L. HOLLOWAY
and JAMES L. PENDLETON, Amherst County...$1500 380 acres south
borders middle fork Pedlar--bought from CHARLES P. TALIAFERRO and
he bought from JAMES and WILLIAM FRAZER. Patent to WALTER POWER,
1782. Witness: SANDY C. BLAIR.

757. 19 November 1821. JONATHAN LONDON and wife, TIRZA, Amherst
      County, to SAMUEL WATTS, Amherst County...$180--all claims
to tracts of THOMAS WILCOCK, deceased--1/8th undivided part.
JONATHAN LONDON bought from JONATHAN WATTS and wife, ELIZABETH.
THOMAS L. HOLLOWAY and RICHARD HARRISON as to TIRZA, 19 November
1821.

      The script in this book is abominable in many places and it
has made the work difficult. I have done my best to give an
accurate picture depending upon the best interpretations possible
in many hard spots.

ABSTRACT OF DEED BOOK P OF AMHERST COUNTY, VIRGINIA

by

BAILEY FULTON DAVIS

1. 26 October 1821. POWHATAN BOLLING BELL, Amherst County, to
    JONATHAN M. WALKER, Buckingham...SAMUEL BELL, Amherst County,
by will--tract whereon he lived at death and where his widow, SARAH,
now lives; to be sold at her death or remarriage. POWHATAN is
entitled to one-fifth and sells his interest for $150.00. Witnesses:
R. KYLE, GREEN E. SMITH, R. H. WALTHALL. JAMES L. DILLARD and
HENRY H. WATTS, Amherst County Justices of the Peace.

1. 20 July 1821. BLAKE B. WOODSON, SAMUEL TAYLOR, administrator
    of THOMAS TAYLOR, JAMES LYLE, administrator of JAMES LYLE, to
TARLTON SAUNDERS...THOMAS TAYLOR, 14 January 1803, executor of Deed
of Trust to WOODSON--slaves; stock, etc. to secure LYLE and MC CREDIE
and recorded in Cumberland County. TAYLOR had died and SAMUEL TAYLOR
had qualified as administrator in Amherst County; GEORGE MC CREDIE
and JAMES LYLE of said firm have died and JAMES LYLE is adbn of
LYLE; property remotely situated for WOODSON to handle. SAUNDERS
paid $1.00 to sell in Lynchburg. 8 August 1821, certified in
Richmond by LYLE before RICHARD A. CARRINGTON and JONATHAN H.
ENSTARN (?) and 3 November 1821, in Lynchburg by TAYLOR before
JONATHAN VICTOR and A. ROBERTSON. On same date in Lynchburg,
SAUNDERS certified that he had sold NANCY for $430 and thus trust
is released.

4. 21 December 1821. JONATHAN COLEMAN and wife, SALLY W., Amherst
    County, to JAMES D. DILLARD, Orange County...to JAMES D. DILLARD,
21 December 1821--$6085.00 761 acres on Buffaloe Ridge and surveyed
by Amherst County surveyor, CHARLES L. CHRISTIAN. Lines: GOOCH,
MIXSON (sic) road, JONATHAN COLEMAN. THOMAS ALDRIDGE and ROBERT
TINSLEY, Amherst County Justices of the Peace.

5. 23 November 1821. NELSON C. DAWSON and AMBROSE RUCKER,
    Amherst County, patentees and trustees for heirs of BENJAMIN
and ANTHONY RUCKER...original inventors of the Batteaux or Tobacco
Boat now in use on James River and other waters of the United States
for transportation of produce and particularly adapted to swift and
shallow internal navigation of our rivers, and for right to use.
Patent issued to us by Secretary of United States, 3 April 1821, and
duly signed by President and Secretary of State and Attorney General
of United States. Power of attorney to JAMES WARE, Esq. to act in
North Carolina, Maryland, Virginia to collect from any users who
have no license from us. Note: my good friend, the late ALFRED
PERCY, JR., treats in detail this patent in his Piedmont Apoclapse
and I refer all interested persons to his work. He gives ANTHONY
RUCKER the credit, if I mistake not, but does not name BENJAMIN
RUCKER as a joint inventor. I feel sure that he had not seen this
deed or power of attorney. I found it a few months after his death.
If the book is not available, I suggest that his widow, MRS. ALFRED
PERCY, JR., Elon Road, Madison Heights, Virginia, be contacted.

6. 23 November 1821. Same men as above grant power of EDMOND
    RUCKER, Rutherford County, Tennessee to act in South Carolina,
Georgia, Kentucky, Tennessee and Alabama.

6. 23 November 1821. GEORGE H. BURFORD, Amherst County, to
    AMBROSE RUCKER, Amherst County...GEORGE H. BURFORD plans to
move to western country--$1.00 to secure creditors--interest in
estate of grandfather, GEORGE MC DANIEL, SR., deceased.

7. 29 October 1821. JOSEPH DILLARD and wife, JUDITH, Amherst
County, to JOSEPH KENNEDY, Amherst County...$1111.75 158 3/4
acres. Lines: WILLIAM TILLER, the road. Amherst County Justices
of the Peace DAVID S. GARLAND and THOMAS ALDRIDGE.

8. 28 October 1821. SALLY CREWS, Amherst County, to JAMES PENDLETON,
Amherst County...to JAMES PENDLETON, 13 November 1829--$2700.00
139 3/4 acres north fork Rutledge. Lines: LINDSEY MC DANIEL,
THOMAS CREWS. Witnesses: LINDSEY COLEMAN, JONATHAN B. FRANKLIN,
HENRY L. DAVIES.

8. 20 November 1821. HENRY MORRIS, Amherst County, 1; CHRISTOPHER
ANTHONY, Lynchburg, 2; HENRY HAGER, New Glasgow, 3; JAMES S. (L)
PENDLETON, Amherst County, 4; DAVID S. GARLAND, Amherst County, 5;
JAMES M. BROWN, Amherst County, 6...MORRIS owes PENDLETON and STERLING
CLAIBORNE--to JAMES S. PENDLETON, 22 May 1822--$1.00--long and
interesting list--maps, books, large academy bell, furniture--to
ANTHONY and HAGER as trustees.

10. 20 November 1821. NELSON C. DAWSON and wife, NANCY, Amherst
County, to SAMUEL GARLAND, Lynchburg; MARTIN PARKS, Amherst
County; AMBROSE RUCKER, Amherst County; JACOB HAAS, Bedford...
NELSON C. DAWSON owes HAAS as bondsman to SAMUEL G. DAWSON, 29 May
1819--$1-00--537 acres Harris Creek. Lines: LEWIS DAWSON, AMBROSE
BURFORD--slaves, names and ages. To ROBERT TINSLEY for HAAS,
19 January 1849.

11. 21 November 1821. WILLIAM C. WHITEHEAD, 1; LUCAS P. THOMPSON,
2; THOMAS ALDRIDGE, 3...$1.00; debt to THOMAS ALDRIDGE--all
interest in estate of father, BURCHER WHITEHEAD, deceased. To
LUCAS P. THOMPSON, 25 July 1822.

12. 20 November 1821. JONATHAN HANSARD, SR., Amherst County, to
children for $1.00...paid by PHILIP BURFORD, Madison County,
Alabama for HANSARD's daughter, MARY T. BURFORD, and children--slaves
and stock.

13. 1 November 1821. JONATHAN HANSARD, SR., Amherst County, to
GEORGE H. BURFORD, Amherst County...for my daughter, CAROLINE
MC BURFORD and any children--$1.00; slaves.

13. 13 September 1821. WILLIAM D. HILL, Amherst County, from
SPENCER NOWELL, SR. and NELSON C. DAWSON, SR., Amherst County...
trustees of MICAJAH and KEZIAH CLARK for life of MICAJAH CLARK.
Deed of Trust recorded in Amherst County; sold 27 July last for
$747.60--89 acres on Lynch road and where MICAJAH lived at death.
Lines: CHARLES WINGFIELD, JONATHAN MERRIT. BENJAMIN and CHARLES P.
TALIAFERRO, Amherst County Justices of the Peace.

14. 19 November 1821. JONATHAN LONDON and wife, TIRZA, Amherst
County, to JOSEPH DILLARD, Amherst County...$100.00 361 acres
north side Buffaloe and bought by LONDON and DILLARD of heirs of
JESSE KENNEDY, deceased. Amherst County Justices of the Peace:
THOMAS S. HOLLOWAY and RICHARD HARRISON.

14. 10 February 1807. JOSEPH DAWSON, Amherst County, to LEWIS
DAWSON, Amherst County...$1000.00 300 acres Harris Creek.
Lines: NELSON C. DAWSON, PLEASANT DAWSON, JAMES LEE, grantee.
Witnesses: BENJAMIN WILSON, JOHN LACY, JAMES LEE. Recorded
1 January 1822 and proved by JAMES LEE.

15. 17 November 1821. WILLIAM WILLMORE and wife, SUSANNAH, Amherst
County, to AMBROSE WILLMORE, Amherst County...hundred dollars
(sic) 119 acres. Lines: DR. GEORGE CABELL, EDMOND WINSTON, SAMUEL
WATTS. Bought from CHARLES COPPEDGE, deceased. BENJAMIN TALIAFERRO
and ISAAC RUCKER, Amherst County Justices of the Peace.

16. 16 November 1821. WILLIAM WATTS, Amherst County, to RICHARD N. EUBANK, Amherst County...Deed of Trust; debt to RICHARD L. ELLIS, agent for THOMAS MONTGOMERY. $1.00 cattle, etc. Witnesses: JONATHAN E. (C) TALIAFERRO, WILLIAM TOMLINSON. To RICHARD N. EUBANK, 18 February 1823.

17. 29 October 1821. JOSEPH DILLARD and wife, JUDITH, Amherst County, to WILLIAM WRIGHT, Nelson County...$1415.75 202½ acres. Lines: THOMAS APPLING, JONATHAN ALLCOCK, WILLIAM TILLER's heirs, CHARLES L. CHRISTIAN, DILLARD's road, DAVID S. GARLAND and THOMAS ALDRIDGE, Justices of the Peace. To WILLIAM WRIGHT, 24 May 1822.

18. 11 August 1821. THOMAS COPPEDGE, JR. as guardian, appointed by court, of JAMES W. and NANCY T. COPPEDGE, infants of CHARLES COPPEDGE, deceased, to WILLIAM WILLMORE, Amherst County... tract where CHARLES COPPEDGE lived and sold by him to WILLIAM WILLMORE in lifetime--119 acres.

18. 20 November 1821. ANDERSON H. MOSS, Amherst County, to WILLIS FRANKLIN, Amherst County...$5.00 75 acres--part of tract of WILLIAM MOSS, deceased, and lot of ANERSON as heir.

19. 21 November 1821. ARTHUR B. DAVIES, commissioner appointed by Amherst County Court, to JAMES LYLE, heir of JAMES LYLE, SR., deceased...300 acres sold by decretal order by WILLIAM WARE and CHARLES TALIAFERRO to GEORGE KIPPEN and Company--suit of said county versus JONATHAN BROWN et al. To JAMES LYLE, per T. SAUNDERS, 24 June 1822.

19. 29 October 1821. JEREMIAH COATES and wife, SALLY, to SALLY ELVIRA and CARY ANN HALL...$1.00 and $150.00 with interest from 29 October 1820 and $40 with interest--half acre and lot at ACH with house; JEREMIAH COATES and wife to occupy for six years and have chance to pay amounts. Note: suspended until deed from JEREMIAH COATES to HANNAH HALL is released. RICHARD HATTEN, guardian of grantees. To HATTEN, 20 August 1822.

20. 29 November 1821. JACOB TYREE, Amherst County, 1; MICAJAH CAMDEN, Amherst County, 2; EDMOND GOODRICH and ELIJAH STATON, Amherst County, 3...EDMOND GOODRICH and ELIJAH STATON on bond to THOMAS ALDRIDGE; $1.00 slaves named. To J. WOOD, 19 November 1827.

21. 3 March 1821. ROBERT MILLNER and wife, MARTHA, Bedford County, to WILLIAM MITCHELL, Amherst County...$42.00 42 acres Rocky Row (Roe)--bought by ROBERT MILLNER from "the ROACHES". Lynchburg Justices of the Peace: JONATHAN THURMON, ARCHIBALD ROBERTSON on same date.

22. 5 October 1821. JONATHAN BROWN, Amherst County, to MERIT M. WHITE, Amherst County...power of attorney to sell Amherst County tract. Lines: JONATHAN FLOOD, BENJAMIN SANDIDGE, LINDSEY BURKS. 202 acres and formerly that of HENRY HARTLESS. Witnesses: WILLIAM HANNAH, ANDERSON SANDIDGE, WILLIAM GATEWOOD, THOMAS L. HARRIS.

22. 19 November 1821. CHARLES L. CHRISTIAN and wife, SUSAN, Amherst County, to THOMAS APPLING, Amherst County...$100 100 acres Buffaloe. Lines: the road, DAVID S. GARLAND, JESSE KENNEDY, grantee, THOMAS L. HOLLOWAY and JAMES L. DILLARD, Justices of the Peace.

23. 25 October 1821. CHARLES L. CHRISTIAN and wife, SUSAN, and JAMES CHRISTIAN, Amherst County, to RICHARD PENDLETON, Amherst County...$100.00 100 acres Tobacco Row Mountain and Harris. Lines: grantee, THOMAS GRISSOM, deceased, AMBROSE RUCKER. Witnesses: D. P. GOOCH, ELIJAH L. CHRISTIAN, JONATHAN CHRISTIAN, B. T. L. HOLLOWAY and JAMES POWELL, Justices of the Peace.

24. 1 March 1820. EDWARD CARTER, SR., Amherst County, to RICHARD
     EUBANK, Amherst County...sum paid by THOMAS LAIN; 33 acres
Horsley. Lines: grantor, WILLIAM PRYOR, the creek, the "rode."
Witnesses: H. (?) R. EUBANK, ORMOND WARE, EDWARD CARTER, JR.
Final proof by "witnesses", 19 November 1821.

25. 27 September 1821. JAMES PINN, Amherst County, to JONATHAN
     COOPER, Amherst County...L100 150 acres Porrage and bought
from REUBEN NORVELL. Lines: grantor, ERVIN L. LONDON, glade road,
R. NORVELL, LARKIN LONDON.

25. 17 January 1822. MOSES RUCKER, Amherst County, to SAMUEL R.
     DAVIES, trustee, 2, and ELISHA RUCKER and FINNEY BRYANT, 2,
creditors...Deed of Trust; MOSES RUCKER is custody of law to
MEKIN A. SHELTON, SAMUEL SIMMONS, RICHARD HARRISON and thirds have
become bondsmen--otherwise prison for one year--$1.00--484 (?) acres.
Witnesses: WILL KIRKWOOD, WILLIAM MC CAUL, JONATHAN FRANKLIN. To
SAMUEL R. DAVIES, 24 January 1824.

26. 17 December 1821. Report of commissioners, HILL and EDWARD
     CARTER and WILLIAM MOORE, appointed to divide Indian Creek
tract...part of estate of WILLIAM S. CRAWFORD, between VANSTRUMP
CRAWFORD, WILLIAM L. CRAWFORD, ALEXANDER CRAWFORD, GABRIELLA CRAWFORD,
JULIANN CRAWFORD, children of WILLIAM S. CRAWFORD--August term, 1821.
Lots of 264 acres, 225 acres, 225 acres, 225 acres, 225 acres.
Plat and survey by REUBEN NORVELL, Amherst County surveyor, and part
of exhibit (not herein)--blank space for plat; difficult because of
situation of tract.

27. 28 December 1820. MOSES RUCKER, Amherst County, to ELISHA
     RUCKER...blank sum--all stock and crops to support family and
me. Witnesses: FINNEY BRYANT, LANDON TULEY.

28. 22 January 1822. STERLING CLAIBORNE, HILL CARTER, and MICAJAH
     CAMDEN, commissioners of Amherst County Court, divide slaves
named to JONATHAN, WILLIAM and ELIZABETH FULCHER, children of
JONATHAN FULCHER, deceased.

28. 7 January 1822. JESSE WOODROOF, Amherst County, to children
     for love...to MARTHA, HIRAM and TIPTON, all infants--$1.00 paid
by their grandfather, HARDEN WOODROOF--slaves named. I got them by
marriage to their mother. Witnesses: BENJAMIN BROWN, WILLIAM
BECKHAM, STEPHEN F. SUBLETT.

29. 3 December 1821. JONATHAN DAVIES and wife, ELIZABETH,
     Jefferson County, Kentucky, to CHARLES CRAWFORD, Shelby
County, Kentucky...$500 one-eleventh of Amherst County tract on
James River--whereon NICHOLAS DAVIES, father of JONATHAN lived and
died intestate. ROBERT BRECKENRIDGE and FORTUNATES COXLEY, Jefferson
County Justices of the Peace, WORDEN POPE, Clerk, JONATHAN BELL,
Presiding Justice of the Peace.

30. 28 November 1821. VANSTRUMP CRAWFORD, Amherst County, to
     WILLIAM M. WALLER, Amherst County...$3300 264 acres Mill
Creek--on division of Indian Creek tract by commissioners--late
that of WILLIAM CRAWFORD. Lines: JULIA CRAWFORD, PENN, BENJAMIN
RODGERS, grantee. Witnesses: G. S. HOLLOWAY, TIMOTHY FLETCHER,
ARTHUR B. DAVIES. To H. L. BROWN, 8 January 1845.

31. 26 December 1821. WILLIAM CAMPBELL and wife, FRANCES, Amherst
     County, to JONATHAN CAMPBELL, Amherst County...$200 106 acres
north side Little Piney. Lines: JONATHAN and BENJAMIN CAMDEN,
grantee, GEORGE CAMPBELL. Justices of the Peace: DAVID S. GARLAND
and THOMAS L. HOLLOWAY. To JONATHAN CAMPBELL, 26 December 1823.

33. 21 January 1822. JONATHAN TARDY, Amherst County, to PHILIP
     THURMOND and HENRY FRANKLIN, 2, Amherst County, and SAMUEL
TARDY, Lynchburg, 3...Deed of Trust; $1.00 paid by PHILIP THURMOND and
HENRY FRANKLIN, furniture in house of JONATHAN TARDY.

34. 29 December 1821. GEORGE, JONATHAN M. and DELILAH EUBANK, Amherst County, to ZA. DRUMMOND, Amherst County...to ZA. DRUMMOND 20 March 1822--$44.00 27½ acres on Taliaferro Mountain and bought from ANN M. KNOX. Lines: JAMES PENDLETON, grantee, BENJAMIN TALIAFERRO and WILLIAM JOPLING, Justices of the Peace.

36. 23 January 1822. ABSALOM RUCKER and wife, NANCY, Amherst County, 1; CHISWELL DABNEY, Amherst County, 2; GALT, BULLOCK and Company, Lynchburg, 3...Deed of Trust; $1.00 160 acres devised to RUCKER by father, ANTHONY RUCKER, deceased--by the mill of ANTHONY and to be taken off; part of old MH tract whereon ANTHONY lived and died. Witnesses: JAMES GARRETT. Certified in Lynchburg, JONATHAN VICTOR and JONATHAN HANCOCK, Justices of the Peace.

37. 29 January 1822. SAMUEL COLEMAN, Amherst County, to JAMES F. TALIAFERRO, Amherst County...$1.00; Deed of Trust; debt due POWELL and TALIAFERRO. To B. CRAWFORD, 2 January 1823. 110 acres on Harris and drawn by COLEMAN on division of father's (JONATHAN COLEMAN's) estate; also two slaves. Witnesses: JONATHAN W. YOUNG, JONATHAN S. COLEMAN, JAMES ORINBAUM (?).

38. 29 January 1822. NELSON CRAWFORD and CHARLES TALIAFERRO, Amherst County Justices of the Peace, as to SARAH BARRET, wife of CHARLES L. BARRET...as to dower in deed to --, 11 August 1817.

38. 1 February 1822. ARTHUR B. DAVIES and WILLIAM DILLARD to JAMES DILLARD, Amherst County...they have sold, as trustees, two tracts in Deed of Trust by TINSLEY RUCKER to secure JAMES DILLARD. 216 acres and 150 acres. Sold at ACH at $717.00. To WILLIAM DILLARD, 12 June 1822.

39. 9 February 1822. ELIAS WILLS and wife, MARY G., Amherst County, to WILLIAM GUTHERY, Amherst County...$2530.00 253 acres both sides Stovall Creek. Lines: grantee, J. BOWLING, RUCKER's road. To WILLIAM KENT, commissioner, to sell land of WILLIAM GUTHRIE, 11 July 1848. TINSLEY RUCKER and JAMESL. LAMKIN, Justices of the Peace as to grantors.

40. 23 January 1822. JONATHAN TAYLOE and wife, SALLY, Amherst County, to JONATHAN RICHESON, Amherst County...$6000.00 four acres plus near Lynchburg. Lines: James River, BENJAMIN SCHOOLFIELD, the branch. Part of conveyance by JONATHAN WARD, SR. to BENJAMIN PERKINS, 3 July 1816. JONATHAN HANCOCK and JONATHAN M. SETTLES, Lynchburg Justices of the Peace. To JONATHAN RICHESON, November 1822.

41. 23 January 1822. CHISWELL DABNEY, Amherst County, to BENJAMIN PERKINS, Amherst County...$1.00 relinquishment on above tract. Witnesses: T. A. HOLCOMB. Lynchburg Justices of the Peace: JOHN VICTOR and CHRISTOPHER WINFREE.

42. 23 January 1822. THOMAS A HOLCOMB to JONATHAN TAYLOE...$1.00 relinquished as above--Deed of Trust made to secure BENJAMIN PERKINS; here is mention of 74 acres and same Justices of the Peace as above.

42. 20 August 1821. LINDSEY BURKS, Amherst County, to WILLIAM HANNAH, Amherst County...$1000.00 on Maple and Cedar--branches of Pedlar. Lines: BURFORD's Rolling Road, ROBERT DAVIS, deceased, JOSIAH JOPLING, JONATHAN GOODRIDGE, JAMES NOWLAN.

43. 8 February 1822. JAMES COLEMAN, Amherst County, 1; SAMUEL GARLAND and GEORGE W. TURNER, 2; ARCHIBALD ROBERTSON, Lynchburg, 3...Deed of Trust; debt to ARCHIBALD ROBERTSON; $1.00; slaves named and ages. To ARCHIBALD ROBERTSON, 18 March 1823.

44. 15 February 1822. PHILIP THURMOND, Amherst County, to HENRY H. EVANS, Amherst County...$3003.00 named slaves.

44.   15 February 1822. PHILIP THURMOND, SR., Amherst County, to
      HENRY H. EVANS, Amherst County...$4271.00 645 acres where
PHILIP THURMOND, SR. lives. Lines: CHARLES CARTER, THOMAS EUBANK,
HARDEN HAYNES, deceased, Rocky Branch, CHARLES ELLIS, RICHARD L.
ELLIS, WILLIAM THURMOND, middle branch. To HENRY H. EVANS, 7 May
1822.

45.   15 February 1822. HENRY H. EVANS, Amherst County, to PETER P.
      THORNTON and THOMAS N. EUBANK, Amherst County, 2; PHILIP
THURMOND, 3...Deed of Trust to secure PHILIP THURMOND; $1.00 paid
by PETER P. THORNTON and THOMAS N. EUBANK. 645 acres on north side
Tobacco Row and twelve negroes. Lines as above. To L. P. THOMPSON
for P. THURMOND, 17 July 1822.

47.   2 January 1822. WILLIAM JOPLING and wife, SALLY, Amherst
      County, to GEORGE MORRIS, Amherst County...$670.50 223½ acres
Dancing and Cedar Creeks. Lines: FLEMING DUNCAN. JAMES WARE and
RICHARD N. EUBANK, Justices of the Peace.

48.   18 February 1822. RAWLEY FEAGANS, Amherst County, to children...
      $1.00 and love, to ELIZABETH MARSH, GEORGE, JANE and FRANCIS
FEAGANS--slaves, stock, furniture. Witnesses: BENNET A. CRAWFORD,
DANIEL F. CHRISTIAN, SPOTSWOOD PADGETT.

48.   22 January 1822. MOSES RUCKER, Amherst County, 1; SAMUEL R.
      DAVIES, Amherst County, 2; ELISHA RUCKER and FINNEY BRYANT,
Amherst County, 3...Deed of Trust; to secure ELISHA RUCKER and
FINNEY BRYANT as bondsmen to SAMUEL SIMMONS, MEKIN A. SHELTON,
RICHARD HARRISON; $1.00, corn, furniture, stock. Witnesses:
JONATHAN ALLEN, LINDSEY SANDIDGE, THOMAS T. HILL.

49.   7 March 1822. WILLIAM LEE and wife, ELIZABETH, Amherst
      County, 1; WILLIAM DILLARD, Amherst County, 2; GEORGE SEATON
HOLLOWAY, Amherst County, 3...Deed of Trust to secure GEORGE SEATON
HOLLOWAY. $1.00; two tracts. 1. 309 acres. Lines: DAVID WOODROOF,
WILLIAM MC DANIEL, the road, JONATHAN HANSFORD, ANTHONY RUCKER.
Conveyed by BENJAMIN RUCKER to LEE, 4 August 1814. 2. 127½ acres.
Lines: the road--Lynch's. Conveyed by WILLIAM WOODROOF to LEE,
25 June 1812; also interest in father's estate--not named.

50.   18 March 1822. ABRAM CARTER and wife, MARY, Amherst County,
      to ZA DRUMMOND, Amherst County...$35.00 15 acres headwaters
of Horsley. Lines: WILLIAM HARTLESS, EUBANK. To ZA DRUMMOND,
22 April 1822.

51.   16 March 1822. RICHARD BURKS and wife, POLLY, Amherst County,
      to ARCHIBALD ROBERTSON, Lynchburg...$5198.24 424 acres both
sides Harris Creek. Lines: JONATHAN AMBLER, JONATHAN SHELTON, DAVID
TINSLEY, ISAAC TINSLEY, and where BURKS lives; also 263 acres
bought from JAMES HARRISON and 161 acres bought from SAMUEL BURKS.
AMBROSE RUCKER and DABNEY WARE, Justices of the Peace.

52.   25 January 1822. JOSHUA D. RUCKER and wife, EMILY, Amherst
      County, to WILLIAM L. and JONATHAN D. BOWLING, Amherst County...
$1100 115½ acres west side Lynch road. Lines: JONATHAN BOWLING,
WILLIAM PETTYJOHN, a ridge. TINSLEY RUCKER and RICHARD HARRISON,
Justices of the Peace.

53.   22 October 1815. JONATHAN CREWS and wife, CHRISTINA, Amherst
      County, to THOMAS EDWARDS, Amherst County...$1.00 42 acres
north side Porridge. Lines: CHARLES MOORE, JONATHAN PADGETT, the
creek. Witnesses: JONATHAN WARWICK, CHARLES MUNDY, JAMES LONDON, JR.
Final proof by LONDON on 18 March 1822. To THOMAS EDWARDS, 29 May
1822.

53. 22 August 1821. ROBERT M. (N) EUBANK, Amherst County, to
JONATHAN EUBANK, Nelson County...$300.00 one thirteenth
interest in estate of JONATHAN EUBANK, deceased. Witnesses:
CHARLES P. TALIAFERRO, GEORGE W. DILLARD, THOMAS D. BLAIR.

54. 2 December 1815. JONATHAN WARWICK and CHARLES MUNDY, Amherst
County Justices of the Peace as to CHRISTIANIA CREWS, wife of
JONATHAN CREWS, to THOMAS EDWARDS...deed of 8 October 1815.

54. 2 March 1822. LEE H. BURKS, Amherst County 1; RICHARD H.
BURKS, 2; JONATHAN SHELTON, SR., Amherst County, 3...Deed of
Trust; debt to JONATHAN SHELTON, SR.; $1.00, slaves named, furniture;
to RICHARD H. BURKS, 18 October 1822.

55. 16 March 1822. RICHARD H. BURKS and MATTHEW BURKS, Nelson
County, 1; WILLIAM SHELTON and AMBROSE RUCKER, Amherst County, 2;
RICHARD BURKS, Amherst County, 3...Deed of Trust; debt to RICHARD
BURKS; $1.00; slaves. Witnesses: JONATHAN SHELTON, LINZA and
JONATHAN H. BURKS.

56. 15 March 1822. RICHARD BURKS, Amherst County, 1; WILLIAM
SHELTON and RICHARD H. BURKS, Nelson County. 2; ISAAC and
AMBROSE RUCKER, Amherst County, 2; RICHARD BURKS, Amherst County, 3...
Deed of Trust; debt to RICHARD BURKS--$1.00; slaves. Witnesses:
JONATHAN SHELTON, LINXA and JONATHAN H. BURKS.

56. 15 March 1822. RICHARD BURKS, Amherst County, 1; WILLIAM
SHELTON and RICHARD H. BURKS, Nelson County, 2; ISAAC and
AMBROSE RUCKER, WILLIAM WARE, ROBERT, ISAAC and ALEXANDER TINSLEY,
FLEMING COLEMAN...ISAAC and AMBROSE RUCKER are bondsmen for RICHARD
BURKS as executor of THOMAS GRISSOM, deceased, Amherst County--1819.
WILLIAM WARE is bondsman for BURKS as executor of GEORGE MC DANIEL,
deceased, Amherst County. ROBERT TINSLEY is bondsman to EDWARD
WATSON for RICHARD BURKS. ISAAC TINSLEY is bondsman to -- JOHNSON
and he and ALEXANDER TINSLEY are bondsmen to FOX. AMBROSE RUCKER
is bondsman to WILLIAM BATES. FLEMING COLEMAN is bondsman to
MILIER (?) RUCKER, Orange County. $1.00 paid by WILLIAM SHELTON and
RICHARD H. BURKS--slaves, stock, mountain tract of 196 acres. Lines:
ALEXANDER TINSLEY, WILLIAM JOPLING. Bought from JOSEPH MC RAY.

58. 2 January 1822. CHARLES JOHNSTON (?), Botetourt County, to
MATTHEW HARVEY, Botetourt County...$550.00 paid by SAMUEL
PANNEL and $1.00--three slaves and reference to Deed of Trust to
HARVEY, names and ages. 27 June 1820, SAMUEL PANNELL made gift of
Green Hill, Campbell County and acting trustee at sale of CAPTAIN
WILLIAM MITCHELL's Farm Mills--sold in Deed of Trust to secure
JAMES BRUCE--until CAPTAIN WILLIAM MITCHELL's youngest daughter by
present wife, SALLY, is 21 or married by mother's consent; SALLY's
youngest daughters or youngest son, youngest daughter is SARAH
LEWISCE. Witnesses: EDWARD JOHNSTON, HENRY L. LANGHORNE, WILLIAM
LOWRIE (?), JAMES T. WRIGHT. Certified in Lynchburg: JONATHAN
VICTOR and CHRISTOPHER WINFREE, Justices of the Peace. Note:
stencil seems damaged and name in first line is JOHNSTON.

59. 2 January 1822. CHARLES JOHNSTON, Botetourt, to MATTHEW
HARVEY, Botetourt...$250 paid by JAMES BRUCE, Halifax, and
$100 paid by HARVEY--slave, ELLEN, a woman, for benefit of MRS.
SALLY MITCHELL, Amherst County, and at death to MARTHA, second
daughter of MRS. MITCHELL. Witnesses and Justices of the Peace
as above.

60.   9 March 1822.   JONATHAN RICHESON, Amherst County, 1; JONATHAN D.
      URQUAHART, Lynchburg, 2; THOMAS A. HOLCOMB, 3...Deed of Trust;
to JONATHAN D. URQUAHART, 23 August 1822; debt to THOMAS A. HOLCOMB;
on purchase of tract opposite Lynchburg and where JONATHAN RICHESON
now lives--assigned to HOLCOMB by JONATHAN TAYLOE--bond of ROBERT
CAWTHON and THOMAS T. STONE--and assigned by HOLCOMBE to JONATHAN
WARD, SR.; bond of JONATHAN H. CLEMENTS, JONATHAN HAAS, THOMAS
GOODRICH, HENRY and WILLIAM FRANKLIN, WILLIAM STAPLES.   Tract conveyed
by CHISWELL DABNEY, trustee for JOHN WARD, SR. and THOMAS A.
HOLCOMBE, trustee, for BENJAMIN PERKINS; sold to RICHESON by
JONATHAN TAYLOE--also slaves, stock, furniture.   Certified by
Lynchburg Justices of the Peace JONATHAN VICTOR and CHRISTOPHER
WINFREE.

62.   11 March 1822.   WILLIAM WALLER SCOTT and wife, ELIZA, Amherst
      County, to WILLIAM PETTYJOHN, Amherst County...$20.00--tract
including spring.   REUBEN NORVELL and JAMES L. LAMKIN, Justices of
the Peace.

63.   15 October 1821.   WILLIAM CAMPBELL and wife, FRANCES, Amherst
      County, to DANIEL CAMPBELL, Amherst County...$300.00 100 acres
George's Creek.   Lines: GEORGE CAMPBELL.   Witnesses: JONATHAN
STINNETT, SAMUEL CAMPBELL, WILLIAM CAMPBELL.

64.   12 March 1822.   BENJAMIN HARRISON, Amherst County, HENRY H.
      WAATS, GEORGE S. HOLLOWAY, LUCAS P. THOMPSON, Amherst County, 2;
and sundry creditors, 3...slaves, furniture, etc. for $1.00.   Debts
due to THOMAS L. HOLLOWAY; debt due me from RICHARD HARRISON; interest
in my father's estate; debts due to WILLIAM B. JACOBS, THOMAS
ALDRIDGE, STERLING CLAIBORNE, JOSEPH EWERS; THOMAS S. CARTER,
LAVENDER LONDON, commissioners in estate of WILLIAM LAYNE, deceased;
D. and D. HIGGINBOTHAM and Company, JAMES S. PENDLETON and Company,
PEACHY FRANKLIN, DAVID HUNTER, JONATHAN SPENCER, JAMES NORVELL,
SAMUEL LAYNE, JAMES SAVAGE, JONATHAN JACOBS, JONATHAN PHILIPS,
WILLIAM TUCKER, ABSALOM HIGGINBOTHAM, JONATHAN PENN, JONATHAN EDMUNDS,
DAVID S. GARLAND, late sheriff, bank, JONATHAN MYERS.

66.   20 February 1822.   WILLIAM SALE and wife, LAVINIA, Amherst
      County, to HUGH TAGGART, Amherst County...$1290.00 193½ acres.
Lines: GOOLSBY heirs, BEVERLY WILLIAMSON's heirs, AMBROSE MC DANIEL,
JONATHAN SMITH, a road.   Witnesses: CORNELIUS POWELL, LUCAS P.
THOMPASON, ROBERT HIGGINBOTHAM.

66.   21 February 1822.   HUGH TAGGART and wife, NANCY, Amherst
      County, 1; CORNELIUS POWELL, Amherst County, 2; D. and
D. HIGGINBOTHAM and Company, merchants, 3...Deed of Trust; debt to
D. and D. HIGGINBOTHAM and Company as assignees of WILLIAM SALE.
$1.00 193 acres.   Lines: as above.   To CORNELIUS POWELL, 24 January
1823.

68.   15 November 1821.   RICHARD HARTLESS and wife, MARY, CHARLES L.
      BARRET, to RICHARD L. ELLIS, Amherst County...$200 42 acres.
Lines: JONATHAN FLOOD, W. H. CRUSALLE (?), WILLIAM COLEMAN, JOSEPH
TOWNSEND, THOMAS EUBANK, ISAAC RUCKER, RICHARD N. EUBANK--last two
as Justices of the Peace.   To RICHARD L. ELLIS, 2 January 1835.

69.   15 October 1821.   GEORGE CAMPBELL and wife, LUCY, Amherst
      County, to WILLIAM CAMPBELL, Amherst County...$200 150 acres
both sides Little Piney.   Lines: JOSEPH DILLARD, grantor.   Witnesses:
LAWSON and GEORGE CAMPBELL, NELSON MADDOX.

70.   17 September 1821.   LEWIS BROWN and wife, JUDITH, Lynchburg,
      to HENRY F. BEAUMONT, Lynchburg...To BEAUMONT, 24 April 1822;
$40 lot in town of Madison.   Lines: JORDAN CREASY, DAVID HOFFMAN--
105 foot front on Main road from Lynchburg to ACH--back 365 feet.
Bought from SAMUEL STEEL and LANDON C. RIEVES.   Lynchburg Justices
of the Peace: JONATHAN M. SETTLE and JONATHAN HANCOCK.

71. 18 March 1822. JAMES WARE and RICHARD N. EUBANK, Justices
     of the Peace, as to SALLY MITCHELL, wife of WILLIAM MITCHELL...
17 February 1821, deed to MANSFIELD WARE. To MANSFIELD WARE, 21 May
1822.

71. 28 February 1822. MOSES RUCKER, Amherst County, to SAMUEL R.
     DAVIES...Deed of Trust; debt to RICHARD L. ELLIS; $1.00 464 acres
where MOSES RUCKER lives. Lines: ARTHUR L. DAVIES, also crops,
stock, etc. To RICHARD L. ELLIS, March, 1823. Witnesses: EZEKIEL B.
GILBERT, ROSEMARY GUE, MARTIN N. DAWSON, P. THURMOND, GEORGE MORRIS,
JR., SHEROD M. GILLESPIE.

72. 16 March 1822. BEVERLEY T. BROWN, Amherst County, to THOMAS N.
     EUBANK, Amherst County...Deed of Trust; debt to RICHARD L.
ELLIS and EUBANK, Amherst County; $1.00; 120 acres where BEVERLY T.
BROWN lives. Lines: ROBERT CAWTHORN, HENRY FRANKLIN, slaves, stock,
my estate in hands of MARTIN HANCOCK, late guardian of Charlotte
County, and all coming to my wife. Witnesses: WILLIAM COLEMAN,
JONATHAN W. YOUNG, DAVID W. BURKS, CHARLES L. BARRET.

73. 1 January 1822. NELSON CRAWFORD, surviving executor of DAVID
     CRAWFORD, Amherst County, to ELIJAH FLETCHER, Lynchburg...DAVID
CRAWFORD in codicil directed sale of tract on south borders Buffaloe
and surveyed on entry by DAVID CRAWFORD, 19 April 1788; 216 acres;
$300.00. Lines: WILLIAM DIGGS, CHARLES L. CHRISTIAN, NATHAN
LOUGHBOROUGH. Plat on page 74; JAMES HIGGINBOTHAM, assistant
surveyor for REUBEN NORVELL. To ELIJAH FLETCHER, 23 April 1822.

74. 1 November 1822. DAVID GLASS, Amherst County, 1; THOMAS
     WRIGHT, Amherst County, 2; WILLIAM SHELTON, Amherst County, 3...
Deed of Trust; debt to WILLIAM SHELTON. Various items. To WILLIAM
SHELTON, 17 June 1823.

75. 20 March 1822. JONATHAN AMBLER and wife, CATHERINE, Richmond,
     to JONATHAN JACQUELINE AMBLER, Richmond, their son, for love
and $1.00...1467 acres--part of tract on Harris. To JONATHAN JACQUELINE
AMBLER, 11 November 1830. Lines: DANIEL CHRISTIAN, near ACH road,
GEORGE CABELL, EDMOND WINSTON, MC DANIEL, JONATHAN HANSARD, TINSLEY,
ISAAC TINSLEY, RICHARD BURKS, mountain road, lines between lower and
upper tract, road to Lynchburg. Certified in Richmond: JAMES RAWLINGS
and WILLIAM TAZWELL, Justices of the Peace, 20 March 1822.

77. 6 March 1822. JAMES HIX and wife, NANCY, Amherst County, to
     JONATHAN MOUNTCASTLE, New Glasgow, Amherst County...$990
123 3/4 acres north side Buffaloe. Surveyed by GEORGE W. HIGGINBOTHAM.
Lines: WILLIAM SANDIDGE, THRESHER's Creek, CHARLES and BENJAMIN
TALIAFERRO, Justices of the Peace.

78. 19 March 1822. THOMAS H. BASS, Amherst County, 1; BENNET A.
     CRAWFORD, Amherst County, 2; POWELL and TALIAFERRO, Amherst
County, 3...Deed of Trust; $1.00--all interest in estate of DAVID
WOODROOF, deceased, by marriage to his daughter, NANCY. To BENNET A.
CRAWFORD, 2 January 1823.

79. 8 January 1822. Commissioners: THOMAS N. EUBANK, JARRATT
     GILLIAM, JAMES WAUGH...in estate of JONATHAN GILLIAM, deceased.
Division of slaves to NANCY BURKS, formerly GILLIAM, heirs, SAMUEL
and ALFORD BURKS, heirs of JUDITH DAVIS: JONATHAN and MADISON DAVIS.
Note: I have commented on this DAVIS-GILLIAM angle before. A man
got furious when I sent him will of JONATHAN DAVIS wherein he named
these two sons. The man was "positive" that JONATHAN had only one
wife and that was second one by proof--which he did not believe.
See JONATHAN DAVIS in D will book. Slaves to JONATHAN P. GILLIAM,
POLLY and ELIZABETH GILLIAM--called "two daughers." Mansion house
tract to WILLIAM A. for widow's dower; JONATHAN P. GILLIAM--85 acres;
ELIZABETH GILLIAM--81½ acres.

79. 4 April 1822. NELSON CRAWFORD and CHARLES L. BARRET, Justices
     of the Peace, as to dower of CHARITY TOLER, wife of GODFREY
TOLER, 18 June 1810, to WILLIAM SHEPHERD.

79. 20 September 1821. GODFREY TOLER and wife, CHARITY, Amherst
     County, to WILLIAM B. SHEPHERD, Amherst County...$161.60
25¼ acres south side Banston (?) Mountain. Lines: RUCKER, grantee.
Same Justices of the Peace as above. To WILLIAM B. SHEPHERD, 15 April
1822.

80. 21 March 1822. JAMES R. LIVELY, Amherst County, 1; GEORGE S.
     HOLLOWAY, Amherst County, 2...$585.11 233 1/3 acres--one third
part devised by JAMES LIVELY to JAMES R. and his two brothers and in
possession of JONATHAN LONDON and JAMES OGDEN; also lines of two
brothers, THOMAS EDWARDS, JONATHAN MC DANIEL, Widow BOURNE.
Witnesses: LUCAS P. THOMPSON. To GEORGE S. HOLLOWAY, 7 May 1822.

81. 10 March 1821. JONATHAN COLEMAN and wife, SARAH W., Amherst
     County, to JONATHAN MOUNTCASTLE, New Glasgow...$1932.00
322 acres south side Turkey Mountain. Lines: grantor, DAVID S.
GARLAND, MANTIPLY, NELSON MANTIPLY. Surveyed by GEORGE W. HIGGINBOTHAM.
Witnesses: D. SHEPHERD, H. HAGER, WILLIAM L. FULCHER, JONATHAN
DILLARD. To STAPLES per order, 31 January 1824, of JONATHAN
MOUNTCASTLE.

82. 19 March 1822. BENAMMIN STONE, Amherst County, to ROBERT
     GARLAND, Nelson County...May 5, 1815, deed of trust to ROBERT
WALKER, Amherst County; slaves--love of BENAMMI STONE for GARLAND
who married STONE's daughter, NANCY, and $10.00. Release of WALKER
as trustee and sale of slaves to GARLAND. Witnesses: BEVERLY
DAVIES, WILLIAM ARMISTEAD. Release signed by WALKER, 15 April 1822.

82. 21 March 1822. RICHARD HARRISON and wife, SOPHIA, Amherst
     County, to LAWSON G. WKLTSHIRE, Amherst County...$360 160 acres
Pedlar. Lines: PRICE, CRAWFORD, WILLIAM HIGGINBOTHAM, JOSEPH
HIGGINBOTHAM, BENJAMIN SANDIDGE, TUNKETT (?), JAMES FRAZIER,
deceased.

83. 15 March 1822. ANGUS MC CLOUD and wife, KEZIAH, Amherst
     County, to JONATHAN H. CLEMENTS, Amherst County...$1000 three
tracts of 307 acres east side Long Mountain and both sides south
fork of Buffaloe. 1. 48 acres. Lines: AARON HIGGINBOTHAM, NEIL
CAMPBELL. 2. 161 acres. Lines: BENJAMIN SANDIDGE. 3. 98 acres.
Lines: BENJAMIN SANDIDGE, NEIL CAMPBELL, JAMES HIGGINBOTHAM.
ISAAC RUCKER and RICHARD N. EUBANK, Justices of the Peace.

84. 21 January 1822. ELIAS WILLS and wife, MARY G., Amherst
     County, to DAVIDSON BRADFUTE, Lynchburg, 2; President and
Directors of Farmers' Bank of Virginia, 3...Deed of Trust. JONATHAN M.
SETTLE on note; $1.00 652 acres where ELIAS WILLS lives. Lines:
WILLIAM GUTHREY. Witnesses: J. M. GORDON, Lynchburg; TINSLEY RUCKER
and JAMES L. LAMKIN, Justices of the Peace.

86. 20 March 1822. CHISWELL DABNEY, Amherst County, to CHARLES
     WINGFIELD, Amherst County...$1.00 all interest in 147 acres
by Deed of Trust from JACOB HAAS, 19 February 1821.

86. 22 April 1822. WILLIAM H. CAMDEN and wife, MARY J., Amherst
     County, to ZA DRUMMOND, Amherst County...$50 19 3/4 acres north
borders Buffaloe. Lines: BOURN, HUBNER (?). Bought from WALTER D.
CHRISTIAN. To ZA DRUMMOND, 15 October 1825.

87. 22 April 1822. JONATHAN PRYOR, Amherst County, to THOMAS N.
     EUBANK, Amherst County...Deed of Trust; $1.00 debt due RICHARD L.
ELLIS and ELLIS and EUBANK, Amherst County; 1500 acres in Rockbridge.
Lines: HENRY BANKS, ZED SHOEMAKER. 2. 123 acres. Lines: MOSES
MARTIN. 3. 60. Lines: JONATHAN and ORMOND WARE. Two and three in
Amherst County. Stock, furniture, etc. Witnesses: JOSIAH ELLIS,
CHARLES C. CARTER, JONATHAN E. TALIAFERRO.

217

88. 22 April 1822. JONATHAN PRYOR, Amherst County, to RICHARD N.
     EUBANK, Amherst County...$1.00; Deed of Trust; debt to JAMES
WARE. To JAMES WARE, 22 May 1822; tobacco, crop in Rockbridge and
Amherst County; about L8000. Witnesses: JOSHUA L. ELLIS, NATHANIEL
DAVIS, JONATHAN E. TALIAFERRO.

89. 10 November 1821. JONATHAN RICHESON and wife, NANCY, Amherst
     County, to JACK CARTER and RICHARD HARTLESS, Amherst County...
$284.00 81 acres south fork Buffaloe. Lines: JACK CARTER's house.
Witnesses: THOMAS J. STONE, JONATHAN H. CLEMENT, GEORGE W. RAY,
ANGUS MC CLOUD, BEVERLY T. BROWN. BENJAMIN TALIAFERRO and ISAAC
RUCKER, Justices of the Peace.

89. 20 March 1822. STERLING CLAIBORNE, Amherst County 1; THOMAS
     ALDRIDGE, Amherst County, 2; and JONATHAN P. COBBS, 2;
JONATHAN M. SETTLE and WILLIAM L. BELL and Company, 3...Deed of
Trust; debt to JONATHAN M. SETTLE and WILLIAM L. BELL and Company;
$1.00 261 acres Piney River. Lines: THOMAS ALDRIDGE, JONATHAN N.
ROSE. Lately bought from WILLIS FRANKLIN. To ALLEM MC DANIEL,
17 June 1822.

91. 10 November 1821. JONATHAN RICHESON and wife, NANCY, Amherst
     County, to ROBERT CORTHAN and THOMAS STONE, Amherst County...
$1104.00 301 acres south fork Buffaloe. Lines: AARON HIGGINBOTHAM,
HARTLESS. Witnesses: ANGUS MC CLOUD, BEVERLY T. BROWN, JACK CARTER,
JONATHAN H. CLEMENTS, A. SANDIDGE. ISAAC RUCKER and BENJAMIN
TALIAFERRO, Justices of the Peace.

91. 8 April 1822. CATLETT CAMPBELL, 1; JONATHAN WARWICK, 2;
     D. and D. HIGGINBOTHAM...Deed of Trust; $5.00, slaves named
and ages, furniture, stock.

92. 8 March 1822. EDMOND PAGE, 1; BENNET A. CRAWFORD, 2; THOMAS
     WRIGHT, Amherst County, 3...Deed of Trust; $1.00; black mare,
may sell at SAMUEL SIMMONS' tavern. To T. KNIGHT, 4 November 1822.

93. 14 March 1822. RICHARD BURKS and wife, POLLY, Amherst County,
     to MATTHEW BURKS, Nelson County...$425.00 122½ acres south
borders Harris Creek. Lines: JONATHAN AMBLER, RICHARD PENDLETON,
THOMAS COLEMAN. To MATTHEW BURKS, 12 November 1822.

94. 10 April 1822. ARCHELAUS P. MITCHELL, 1; PETER RUCKER, 2;
     ELISHA RUCKER, 3...Deed of Trust; debt to ELISHA RUCKER and
LANDON TULERY as bondsmen on good behavior bond for twelve months.
221 acres Fluvanna River. Lines: WILLIAM HANNAH and whereon
ARCHELAUS P. MITCHELL lives; stock, furniture. Witnesses:
PETER C. MOORE, LANDON TULEY, TANDY TULERY (EY), JONATHAN R. SHELTON.

94. 13 February 1822. NATHANIEL HILDRETH, Amherst County, 1;
     HENRY HAGER, New Glasgow, 2; JAMES L. PENDLETON and Company, 3...
$1.00, stock, tobacco. Witnesses: JOSEPH STAPLES.

95. 30 October 1821. JONATHAN RICHESON and wife, NANCY, Amherst
     County, to JONATHAN H. CLEMENTS, Amherst County...$112 28 acres
both sides south fork Buffaloe. Part of 400 acres. Lines: grantee.
Witnesses: THOMAS J. STONE, JACK CARTER, ANGUS MC CLOUD, BEVERLY T.
BROWN, GEORGE W. RAY. To JONATHAN H. CLEMENTS, 15 May 1826.

96. 8 April 1822. SOLOMON RICHIE, Amherst County, 1; SAMUEL R.
     DAVIES, Amherst County, 2; JONATHAN BURKS, Amherst County, 3...
JR. $1.00 100 acres Pedlar. Witnesses: JESE KENNEDY, WILLIAM H.
CAMDEN, WILL KIRKWOOD, SANDY C. BLAIR.

97. 16 February 1805. WALTER CHRISTIAN, JR., Amherst County, to
     JONATHAN COLEMAN, Amherst County...$331.75 331 3/4 acres both
sides Buffaloe Ridge and both sides MIGGINSON's road--ferry road--
near the Ridge Spring. Lines: PHILIP GOOCH, grantee, W. S. CRAWFORD,
JAMES WEBSTER, HIGGINBOTHAM, ROBERT MEANES (?). Witnesses: EDMOND T.
COLEMAN, ROBERT WALKER, THOMAS ALDRIDGE. Final proof by WALKER,
15 April 1822.

98. 11 April 1822. RICHARD HARRISON and wife, SOPHIA, Amherst
     County, to ROBERT L. COLEMAN, Amherst County...$1386 198 acres
both sides Pedlar. Part of tract bought from STERLING CLAIBORNE and
conveyed to PHILIP LIVELY.

98. 5 January 1820. WILLIAM WOODROOF, Amherst County, 1; JONATHAN
     SHELTON and EDMOND WINSTON, Amherst County, 2...bonds due
MAJOR PRICE, Pitsylvania and RICHARD BURKS, bondsmen. $1.00, slaves
named. Witnesses: LEE H. BURKS, ALEXANDER MOOR, R. H. BURKS.

100. 30 October 1821. JONATHAN RICHESON and wife, NANCY, Amherst
      County, to HENRY FRANKLIN, Amherst County...$350 ___ (illegible)
two tracts south side Cold Mountain and both sides Mitchell Creek.
500 acres. 1. 200 acres top of Fork Mountain to NEIL CAMPBELL's
patent, Michel Cove Creek. 2. 300 acres. Lines: first tract.
Witnesses: PEACHY FRANKLIN, GEORGE MYERS, ROBERT A. PENN, ST. GEORGE
TUCKER, ANDERSON MOSS, THOMAS L. CARTER. BENJAMIN TALIAFERRO and
ISAAC RUCKER, Justices of the Peace.

101. 15 October 1821. HILL CARTER and WILLIAM M. WALLER, Justices
      of the Peace, as to JANE CHRISTIAN, wife of SAMUEL D. CHRISTIAN...
13 March 1819, to DABNEY HILL. To SAMUEL D. CHRISTIAN, 6 November
1822.

101. 23 March 1822. JONATHAN BROWN, Amherst County, to THOMAS N.
      EUBANK, Amherst County...Deed of Trust; debt to RICHARD L.
ELLIS; ELLIS and EUBANK; $1.00 201 acres. Lines: JONATHAN FLOID,
LINDSEY BURKS, BENJAMIN SANDIDGE, JESSE RICHESON. Bought from
HENRY HARTLESS, SR. Witnesses: BEVERLY T. BROWN, P. THURMOND, JR.,
LINZA BURKS, WILLIAM BOYD. To RICHARD N. EUBANK, 18 February 1823.

102. 23 April 1822. STERLING CLAIBORNE and wife, JANE, Nelson
      County, to ZA DRUMMOND, Amherst County...$800.00; no acres;
Buffaloe. Bought of JOSEPH HIGGINBOTHAM--northeast side Buffaloe.
Lines: grantee's tract bought of PULLIAM SANDIDGE, JAMES GOVAN,
BENJAMIN SANDIDGE. To ZA DRUMMOND, 19 August 1822.

102. 25 April 1822. RICHARD HATTEN and wife, HANNAH, Amherst
      County, to COLEMAN and BARRET, Amherst County...$50 22 acres.
Lines: THOMAS MORRIS. Tract allotted to HANNAH as one third dower
of MOSES HALL, deceased. AMBROSE RUCKER and CHARLES P. TALIAFERRO,
Justices of the Peace.

103. 24 April 1822. RICHARD HARVIE, Amherst County, 1; SAMUEL R.
      DAVIES, Amherst County, 2; NANCY SHIELDS, Amherst County, 3...
$1.00 reference to Deed of Trust of 21 August 1821, to secure
JONATHAN M. SETTLE and NANCY has endorsed in SETTLE's place--all
property in first Deed of Trust. Witnesses: BENJAMIN RUCKER,
JAMES PETTIT.

104. 25 April 1822. JAMES GILBERT, Amherst County, to ABSALOM
      RUCKER, Amherst County...power of attorney. Witnesses:
S. R. DAVIES, JONATHAN FRANKLIN, WILLIAM I. IEBELL, THOMAS TERRY.

104. 21 February 1821. Recorded 22 April 1822. DAVID S. GARLAND
      and BENJAMIN BROWN...Deed of Trust of 21 April 1816--WILLIAM M.
WALLER, 1; WILLIAM GALT, Richmond, 2; DAVID S. GARLAND and BENJAMIN
BROWN, 3. 900 acres paid in full and released. Richmond Justices
of the Peace: C. TOMPKINS and WILLIAM FITZWHYLSON.

105. 17 April 1822. CHARLES WINGFIELD, Amherst County, to TINSLEY
RUCKER, Amherst County, 2; JONATHAN L. WINGFIELD, Amherst
County, 3...Deed of Trust; debt to JONATHAN L. WINGFIELD; $1.00,
wagon, horse, stock.

106. 1 April 1822. DAVID BRIGGS, Amherst County, to STITH MEAD,
Amherst County...$100.00 2½ acre lot No. 53 in Meadsville.
Lines: WILLIAM THURMAN, the branch, MEAD. Witnesses: JONATHAN R.
SIMMONS, BENJAMIN SIMMONS, WILLIAM REYNOLDS.

106. 1 April 1822. ANTHONY PLEASANTS, Lynchburg, to STITH MEAD,
Amherst County...$60.00 Lot 54 in Meadsville. Lines: MEAD
(formerly WIATT), JOHNSON, an alley. Witnesses: BENJAMIN A. PHILLIPS,
ROBERT COBBS, JO. HARDWICK, TINSLEY RUCKER and JAMES L. LAMKIN,
Justices of the Peace of Amherst County.

107. 11 April 1822. WILLIAM THURMOND and wife, ELIZA L., Lynchburg,
to STITH MEAD, Amherst County...$55.00; tract joining JONATHAN
TAYLOE, field by the road. SAMUEL NOWLIN and JONATHAN THURMAN,
Lynchburg Justices of the Peace.

108. 1 April 1822. WILLIAM GRAVES and wife, LETHA, Amherst County,
to STITH MEAD, Amherst County...$52.50 71 3/4 acres northwest
side of main road from Lynchburg to ACH. Lines: WILLIAM THURMAN,
MEAD, HENRY WRIGHT. Witnesses: THOMAS MURRILL, JORDAN CREASY,
NATHAN WILLIAMSON. TINSLEY RUCKER and JAMES L. LAMKIN, Justices of
the Peace.

109. 9 May 1822. REUBEN PENDLETON, Amherst County, 1; GEORGE W.
TURNER and SAMUEL GARLAND, 2; ARCHIBALD ROBERTSON, 3; also
debts to BENJAMIN BROWN, ALISON OGDEN, MERIT M. WHITE, PROSSER POWELL's
administrator, MANSFIELD WARE, RICHARD SHELTON, SR.'s executor,
SOPHIA POWELL to WILLIAM SHELTON, executor Deed of Trust...$1.00 named
slaves and ages, stock. JONATHAN THURMON and SAMUEL NOWLING, Lynchburg
Justices of the Peace as to PENDLETON and TURNER.

111. 20 May 1822. LEE H. BURKS, Amherst County, 1; RICHARD H. BURKS
and GEORGE W. TURNER, Amherst County, 2; ARCHIBALD ROBERTSON,
3...Deed of Trust; debt to ARCHIBALD ROBERTSON on assignment from
RICHARD SHELTON, JR., executor of RICHARD SHELTON, SR.; $1.00; slaves
and ages.

112. 1 April 1822. ELIJAH BECKHAM, Amherst County, to CORNELIUS
POWELL, Amherst County, of firm of D. and D. HIGGINBOTHAM and
Company...Deed of Trust; $1.00; stock and furniture. Witnesses:
JONATHAN S. BLAIR, CHARLES W. CHRISTIAN, JONATHAN SHEPHERD.

113. 7 May 1822. WILLIAM LEE, Amherst County, to GEORGE S. HOLLOWAY,
Amherst County...$1375.07 436½ acres Lynch road. Lines:
JESSE WOODROOF. Witnesses: STERLING CLAIBORNE, JONATHAN THOMPSON, JR.,
BENJAMIN HARRISON.

113. 21 May 1822. JACOB TYREE, Amherst County, to CORNELIUS POWELL
and TANDY TUTHERFORD, Amherst County, 2; DANIEL HIGGINBOTHAM
and Company, Amherst County, 3...Deed of Trust; $1.00; slaves. Sent
to CORNELIUS POWELL by LEE C. CHRISTIAN, 16 January 1824.

114. 29 April 1822. STITH MEAD and wife, PRUDENCE, Amherst County,
to JONATHAN RICHESON, Amherst County...$1500 98½ acres main
road from Lynchburg to ACH. Lines: grantor, WIATT, CHISWELL DABNEY,
BURD, B. SCHOOLFIELD, JONATHAN TAYLOE. Justices of the Peace:
JAMES L. LAMKIN and TINSLEY RUCKER.

115. 6 June 1822. JONATHAN HUDSON, Amherst County, to LUCAS P.
THOMPSON, Amherst County, 2; PEACHY FRANKLIN and BENNET HUDSON,
Amherst County, 3...Deed of Trust; debts to BENJAMIN WARNER, THOMAS
ALDRIDGE; suit in Amherst County court--furniture, etc.

116. 3 May 1822. JONATHAN RICHESON and wife, NANCY, Amherst County,
     to CHRISTOPHER ISBELL, Amherst County...$1380 98¼ acres Main
road from Lynchburg to ACH. Lines: WIATT, MEAD, CHISWELL DABNEY,
BURD, B. SCHOOLFIELD, JONATHAN TAYLOE. Justices of the Peace:
JAMES L. LAMKIN and TINSLEY RUCKER.

118. 19 January 1822. ANDREW M. STATON and wife, ANNY (AMY?),
     CHARLES STINNET and wife, ELIZABETH, Amherst County, to
JONATHAN ELLIS, Amherst County...$480.00 120 acres Pedlar. Lines:
JONATHAN RUSSELL, MARTIN BIBB, JONATHAN TERRY, JONATHAN ELLIS.
Justices of the Peace: BENJAMIN TALIAFERRO and CHARLES L. BARRET.

119. 6 May 1822. WILLIAM LEE confirms sale by his agent, STERLING
     CLAIBORNE, to GEORGE S. HOLLOWAY...slaves at $1262.25.
Witnesses: WILL DILLARD, J. C. LEE.

120. 30 May 1822. WILLIAM LEE to GEORGE S. HOLLOWAY...$180.00
     slave, LINDY. Witnesses: as above.

120. 3 June 1822. WILLIS HIGGINBOTHAM, FELICINIA PARISH, Louisiana,
     power of attorney to JONATHAN ROSSER, Amherst County, for self
and LINDSEY JACKSON HIGGINBOTHAM, JONATHAN KERR and wife, FRANCES,
BAILEY HIGGINBOTHAM, JOSEPH R. CAMPBELL...to act as to estate of
MOSES HIGGINBOTHAM, Amherst County--I am duly appointed; also
estate of FRANCES, widow of MOSES HIGGINBOTHAM. To JONATHAN ROSSER,
6 January 1825.

121. 8 June 1822. JONATHAN WATTS, 1; SAMUEL R. DAVIES, 2; CHARLES
     NEIGHBORS, 3...all of Amherst County; $1.00 to secure CHARLES
NEIGHBORS on bond in WATTS versus LONDON; stock and furniture.

122. 17 June 1822. RICHARD EUBANK, Amherst County, to JOSEPH R.
     CARTER, Amherst County...to secure him on bonds to COLONEL
WILLIAM JOPLING, Amherst County; THOMAS LAIN, Amherst County;
JONATHAN ROBERTSON, Rockbridge--46 acres adjoining WILLIAM PRYOR
and bought by EUBANK from THOMAS LAIN, 1 March 1820; also 33 acres
bought from EDWARD CARTER. 1 March 1820; also slaves.

123. 27 May 1822. RICHARD HARTLESS and wife, MARY, Amherst County,
     to ANNIS HARTLESS, Amherst County...$360.00 40 acres bought
from JONATHAN RICHESON; 20 acres bought from PULLIAM SANDIDGE.
Lines: ROBERT CAUTHORNE, tobacco house. Witnesses: BEVERLY T.
BROWN, JACK CARTER, JONATHAN PAINTER. Justices of the Peace:
BENJAMIN TALIAFERRO and JONATHAN COLEMAN.

124. 28 May 1822. WILLIAM DILLARD, Amherst County, to JAMES
     BOWLING, Amherst County...Deed of Trust by NELSON C. DAWSON
to secure--GEORGE S. HOLLOWAY; defaulted and sold to BOWLING for
$325.50. 71½ acres. To JAMES BOWLING, SR., 15 July 1822.

125. 17 June 1822. JAMES HIX, Amherst County, to JONATHAN WARWICK,
     Amherst County...on execution of D. and D. HIGGINBOTHAM--150
acres.

125. 22 February 1822. HARRISON HUGHES, Stokes County, North
     Carolina, to WILLIAM PATTEN or PANURE?, Amherst County...
$100.00; estate now in hands of mother and willed by father to me--
one half. Witnesses: WILLIAM D. HILL, WILLIAM C. MUSE, REUBEN D.
HILL.

126. 15 January 1821. JAMES MOORE, 1; STERLING CLAIBORNE, Amherst
     County, 2; ALDRIDGE, MYERS, PENDLETON, Amherst County, 3...Deed
of Trust; $1.00; beds, etc.

127. 20 May 1822. JONATHAN COLEMAN and CHARLES P. TALIAFERRO,
Amherst County Justices of the Peace, as to PATSY CHRISTIAN,
wife of WALTER CHRISTIAN, 19 June 1821, to W. SIMMONS...To W.
SIMMONS, 21 January 1823. Note: grantee's name is not in document,
but note on margin shows delivery to him.

127. 27 June 1822. RICHARD EUBANK, Amherst County, to WILLIAM
ARMISTEAD, Amherst County...$1.00; debt to CALEB RALLS, PULLIAM
SANDIDGE, ELIJAH FLETCHER for lands. 1. 33 acres from EDWARD CARTER
and where RICHARD EUBANK lives. 2. 46 acres joining fnd from THOMAS
LAIN and wife, ELIZABETH. Also slaves, crops. Witnesses: ABRAM and
CREED C. CARTER, SARAH ROBERTS, JAMES EUBANK, ROBERT M. and B. EUBANK.
To THOMAS N. EUBANK, 14 February 1840. Note: a whole page in book
is blank, but numbers are in sequence.

129. 9 January 1822. OLIVER TOWLES and wife, CYNTHIA, Lynchburg,
to CHARLES HOYLE, Lynchburg...$1.00; 350 acres PALMORE's
tract. Lines: JONATHAN MUNDY, HOYLE, MEAD, O Possum Island road.
Witnesses: JONATHAN B. DABNEY. Lynchburg Justices of the Peace:
THOMAS A. HOLCOMEE and MICAJAH DAVIS, JR. To G. A. HOYLE per order
of CHARLES HOYLE, 28 June 1823.

130. 12 July 1822. POLLY CHILDRESS, Amherst County, widow and
administratrix of JAMES CHILDRESS, late of Henrico, who died
intestate...to daughter, JANE CRUTCHER--one of childre of late husband
and wife of ABSALOM P. CRUTCHER, Amherst County, and her children.
$1.00--slaves. Witnesses: WILL DILLARD, ALEXANDER MUNDY, EDMOND
PADGET.

131. 12 July 1822. REUBEN PENDLETON, Amherst County, 1; ARCHIBALD
ROBERTSON, SAMUEL REED, BOYD MILLER, late of ARCHIBALD ROBERTSON
and Company, Lynchburg, 2; and SAMUEL GARLAND, Lynchburg, 3...Deed of
Trust to SAMUEL GARLAND; $1.00 440 acres whereon REUBEN PENDLETON
lives; part of 500 acres surveyed for REUBEN PENDLETON, 23 March
1796, by JAMES HIGGINBOTHAM. Lines: CAMM, deceased, GEORGE TINSLEY,
DABNEY T. PHILIPS. Justices of the Peace of Lynchburg: SAMUEL NOWLIN
and ALBON MC DANIEL, aldermen.

132. 19 June 1822. STITH MEAD and wife, PRUDENCE, Amherst County,
to WILLIAM WARWICK, Amherst County...$1200 233 acres Boling
Creek. Four surveys. 1. Lines: PHIL JOHNSON--now C. HOYLE, LUCY
ROBINSON, MRS. ROBINSON, old road, H. TENNISON--now MEAD, path,
grantee, THOMAS JOHNSON, WILLIAMS, now MEAD, 128 5/8 acres and from
WILLIAMS to MEAD. 2. Lines: WILLIAMS, PHIL JOHNSON, road opposite
old schoolhouse, Lynchburg road and bought from DOW--14 3/4 acres.
3. Lines: COLONEL PHIL JOHNSON, Lynchburg road near O Possum Island
road, small road, TERRY's Path, WILLIAM ROBINSON. Bought from LUCY
ROBINSON. 41 3/4 acres. 4. Lines: WILLIAMS, now MEAD, LUCY
ROBINSON, grantee, THOMAS WIATT and bought from TENNISON--50 acres.
Lynchburg Justices of the Peace: JONATHAN THURMAN and CHRISTOPHER
WINFREE. Amherst County Justices of the Peace: JAMES L. LAMKIN and
REUBEN NORVELL. To WILLIAM WARWICK, 20 May 1823.

133. 4 July 1822. SAMUEL DAWSON, Amherst County, to CHARLES
PALMER, Amherst County, 2; JONATHAN Y. JOHNSON, 3...$57.05
paid by CHARLES PALMER; beds, etc. JONATHAN Y. JOHNSON is administrator
of THOMAS JOHNSON. To secure JONATHAN MERRIT, bondsman. To CHARLES
PALMER, 21 October 1822.

134. 14 June 1822. WILLIAM ROBINSON and CHISWELL DABNEY, Amherst
County, trustees in Deed of Trust from STITH MEAD, 14 July
1819...MEAD releases JAMES GILLIAM who signs. Witnesses: W. NORVELL--
233 acres.

135. 19 June 1822. WILLIAM ROBINSON and CHISWELL DABNEY to STITH
MEAD, Amherst County...$1.00 and order above--233 acres;
reference to Deed of Trust above. Lynchburg Justices of the Peace:
CHRISTOPHER WINFREE and MICAJAH DAIES, JR.

135. 9 January 1822. Deed of Trust: OLIVER TOWLES to THOMAS WIATT
      and CLAUDIUS BUSTER, 31 October 1820...Lines: CHARLES HOYLE,
WILLIAM ROBINSON, STITH MEAD--350 acres PALMER's tract. Paid and
OLIVER TOWLES has sold to CHARLES HOYLE. Witnesses: JONATHAN B.
DABNEY. Lynchburg Justices of the Peace: THOMAS HOLCOMB and MICAJAH
DAVIES.

136. 23 March 1821. SAMUEL MEREDITH and wife, ELIZABETH, Fayette
      County, Kentucky, by JAMES BRECKINRIDGE, attorney, to DAVID S.
GARLAND, Amherst County...$2262.00--all interest in tract on both
sides Buffaloe and adjoins New Glasgow, DAVID S. GARLAND, JONATHAN
COLEMAN, JONATHAN PENN, JAMES L. PENDLETON, EDMOND PENN--1257 acres.
Devised by SAMUEL MEREDITH, deceased, to WILLIAM MEREDITH, MARY MAY,
SAMUEL MEREDITH, JANE H. GARLAND and (wife of DAVID S. GARLAND) and
WILLIAM B. HARE for support of SARAH ARMISTEAD--one fifth. Witnesses:
JOSEPH PENN, J. P. COBB, ROBERT TINSLEY, H. HAGER.

137. 2 July 1822. JONATHAN M. EUBANK, Amherst County, to THOMAS N.
      EUBANK, Amherst County...Deed of Trust; debt to WILLIAM
DILLARD, ELLIS and EUBANK, RICHARD L. ELLIS, THOMAS and DANIEL
HIGGINBOTHAM, MORGAN and MC DANIEL, GEORGE T. WILLIAMS and Company.
$1.00 200 acres part of JORDAN tract and interest in 228 acres bought
of WILLIAM LONG. Witnesses: JONATHAN PRYOR, A. B. EUBANK, WILLIAM
GRANBERRY.

138. 27 March 1822. RICHARD HARTLESS and wife, MARY, Amherst County,
      to CHARLES L. BARRET, Amherst County...to CHARLES L. BARRET,
11 October 1824--$2000.00 three tracts. 1. Bought of JONATHAN
SMITH--170 or 180 acres. 2. Tract bought of EDWARD VICKERS--170
or 180 acres. 3. Adjoining 1 and 2--VICKER's old tract in Amherst
County and Rockbridge. Witnesses: JONATHAN W. YOUNG, DAVID W. BURKS,
ELI GARNETT, BENJAMIN TALIAFERRO and JONATHAN COLEMAN, Amherst
County Justices of the Peace.

139. 15 July 1822. WILLIAM DILLARD, Amherst County, to JAMES
      BOWLING, Amherst County...Deed of Trust to secure NELSON C.
DAWSON, JR. $1.00 71½ acres sold 28 May 1822 to BOWLING for $325.50.
to JAMES BOWLING, 27 July 1822. This seems to be Deed of Trust by
DAWSON to DILLARD and not paid and sold by DILLARD to BOWLING.

140. 8 July 1822. RICHARD HARRISON and wife, SOPHIA, Amherst
      County, to SAMUEL BURKS, Bedford, and WILLIAM L. BURKS, Campbell
County...L405 both sides Christian Mill Creek--405 acres. Lines:
CHRISTIAN, SAMUEL SIMMONS, JOSEPH SWANSON, BELL (?), CHARLES CHRISTIAN.
TINSLEY RUCKER and JAMES L. LAMKIN, Justices of the Peace.

141. 11 April 1822. JONATHAN PENN, JR., acting executor of JONATHAN
      PENN, SR., Amherst County, to JONATHAN SMITH, Amherst County...
by Amherst County will to sell and divide to grandchildren--at late
mansion house on same date--289½ acres Indian Creek tract sold for
$1745.68. Lines: ISAAC SCOTT, JONATHAN HUDSON, JONATHAN TUCKER,
PENDLETON, JESSE CASH. To JONATHAN SMITH, 19 August 1822.

142. 9 July 1822. LINDSEY BURKS, Amherst County, to THOMAS N.
      EUBANK, Amherst County...Deed of Trust; debts to RICHARD L.
ELLIS, ELLIS and EUBANK, $1.00, four named slaves, stock, etc.
Witnesses: JONATHAN E. TALIAFERRO, JOSIAH ELLIS, GEORGE EUBANK,
M. PENDLETON, ELLIOTT WORTHAM, JONATHAN G. SMITH. To R. N. EUBANK,
18 February 1823.

144. 12 July 1822. JONATHAN PRYOR to THOMAS N. EUBANK, Amherst
      County...Deed of Trust; debt to JOSHUA L. ELLIS, bondsman for
PRYOR on bond to JONATHAN ELLIS and THOMAS N. EUBANK, curators of
SUSANNAH BECKLEY, deceased, and in court; $1.00--crops. To JOSHUA L.
ELLIS, 17 March 1823. Witnesses: R. N. EUBANK, M. PENDLETON,
JONATHAN E. TALIAFERRO.

144. 12 July 1822. JONATHAN PRYOR to THOMAS N. EUBANK...Deed of
        Trust; debt to THOAMS LAIN as bondsman to BRADFORD HANNAH and
Company; $1.00; 1500 acres in Rockbridge on BENNETT's run and lot
in town of Springfield; two tracts in Amherst County--Brown Mountain
Creek--123 acres and 60 acres next to ORMOND WARE and JONATHAN WARE;
stock, furniture, books, maps, etc. Witnesses: WIATT DUNCAN,
JONATHAN E. TALIAFERRO, JOSHUA L. ELLIS.

145. 25 June 1822. JONATHAN COLEMAN and wife, SALLY, Amherst
        County, to DAFID S. GARLAND, Amherst County...$415.72 30 acres
north border Buffaloe, part of tract and surveyed, 7 November 1821.
Lines: SAMUEL MEREDITH, deceased, grantor, grantee.

146. 19 June 1822. JONATHAN WILSON and wife, AALLY, town of
        Bethel, Amherst County, to MERIT M. and WILLIAM WHITE, Bethel...
$300--lot 11 1½ acres. Witnesses: WILLIAM ARMISTEAD, THOMAS D.
HILL, ABSALOM RUCKER.

147. 27 May 1822. RICHARD HARTLESS and wife, MARY, Amherst County,
        to CHARLES L. BARRET, Amherst County...$75.00 50 acres.
Lines: JAMES FRAZIER, deceased. Witnesses: BEVERLY T. BROWN,
JACK CARTER, JONATHAN PAINTER. Justices of the Peace: BENJAMIN
TALIAFERRO and JONATHAN COLEMAN.

148. 27 May 1822. RICHARD HARTLESS and wife, MARY, Amherst County,
        to CHARLES L. BARRET, Amherst County...$75.00 50 acres. Lines:
JAMES FRAZIER, deceased, James River, THOMAS ALLEN. Justices of the
Peace as above.

149. 15 July 1822. REUBEN NORVELL, Amherst County, to WILLIAM
        JINKINS, Amherst County...$50.00 5¾ acres. Lines: Farm Mills
road, WILLIAM MUSE, ELIAS WILLS.

150. 15 July 1822. STERLING CLAIBORNE and GEORGE S. HOLLOWAY...
        agreement--900 acres--debt to JABEZ CAMDEN--pending in Lynchburg
chancery--cancelled a debt from CLAIBORNE, included BRADFORD and
HANNAH and Company, RIEVES debt, JAMES S. PENDLETON's debt. CLAIBORNE
owes HOLLOWAY $25,000 and to be paid in various amounts. CLAIBORNE
executed Deed of Trust on 900 acres and Buffaloe tract next to
Buffaloe Springs, brick house tract near ACH, Rocky Creek Mills
tract and house and lot in Lynchburg. To L. P. THOMPSON, attorney
for GEORGE S. HOLLOWAY, 27 July 1822. Returned and filed.

150. 15 July 1822. GEORGE S. HOLLOWAY to STERLING CLAIBORNE...
        margin as above--$5,000 900 acres formerly that of HENRY
HOLLOWAY and abought from VERNON METCALFE.

151. 15 July 1822. STERLING CLAIBORNE, Amherst County, to GEORGE S.
        HOLLOWAY, Amherst County...margin as above--$1.00 900 acres
and other tracts as set forth in deed above--535 acres Buffaloe
Springs--minus parcels sold to HAAS and DRUMMOND, Brick House tract--
450 acres and bought from JONATHAN H. SMITH near ACH, Ricky Creek
Mills and tract--130 acres and house and lot in Lynchburg and bought
from NICHOLAS HARRISON.

152. 21 June 1822. LINDSEY TINSLEY and wife, LUCY, Amherst County,
        to LINDSEY BURKS, Amherst County...$2544.00 150 acres Swamping
Camp Creek, Buffaloe. Lines: fence, BENJAMIN SANDIDGE, JOO. BROWN,
JESEE RICHESON. BENJAMIN TALIAFERRO and ISAAC RUCKER, Justices of
the Peace.

153.   20 July 1822.   STITH MEAD, Amherst County, to ROBERT MIMS
       and STEPHEN S. DUIGUID, Lynchburg...Deed of Trust; $1.00;
all interest in land sold JONATHAN RICHESON (RICHARDSON), Amherst
County; 11½ acres sold to CHRISTOPHER and WILLIAM I. ISBELL with
blacksmith shop; also 90¾ acres bought from SAMUEL STEEL; two lots
on half acre each in Madison Town; LUCY ROBINSON's land; three
acres bought from LEWIS ROBINSON; 32 acres in Henrico near Richmond;
six slaves; blacksmith tools, library, watch, furniture, etc.   To
protect JAMES GILLIAM on bond to JAMES TALIAFERRO.   REUBEN NORVELL
and JAMES L. LAMKIN, Justices of the Peace.   Page 154ff inventory of
MEAD's property--long and interesting--to protect WILLIAM THURMAN;
many names: W. STEEL, M. BLAKEY, CHRISTOPHER G. MOORING, JONATHAN
CLARKSON for moving him to Bedford.

157.   17 June 1822.   JONATHAN WARWICK, Amherst County Sheriff, to
       TIMOTHY FLETCHER...LINDSEY TINSLEY took insolvent oath on behalf
of FLETCHER and JONATHAN TAYLOE versus TINSELY; surrendered 60 acres
bought from GEORGE EUBANK, son of JONATHAN.   Conveyed to Sheriff and
he advertised and sold at $250.00.

157.   15 August 1822.   ABSALOM RUCKER, Amherst County, 1; JAMES L. (S)
       LAMKIN, Amherst County, 2; G. A. ROSE and ROSE and PATTERSON,
3...Deed of Trust; notes due G. A. ROSE and ROSE and PATTERSON;
$1.00 named slaves.   To G. A. ROSE, 14 March 1823.

158.   1 July 1822.   JAMES WARE, Amherst County, to WILLIAM G.
       PENDLETON, Richmond...$5000.00 50 acres Horsley Creek.   Lines:
RICHARD L. ELLIS, road from Pedlar River to CRAWFORD's Gap, WIATT
DUNCAN's Spring branch, MANSFIELD WARE, mills thereon--Pedlar Mills,
distillery, store, dwelling house, half acre reserved and conveyed
to POLLY EUBANK and in possession of RICHARD EUBANK, half acre in
hands of JONATHAN DAVIS--for 100 years, one shilling--rent; Deed of
Trust; debt of $5000 due Bank of Virginia.   Amherst County Justices
of the Peace: WILLIAM JOPLING and RICHARD N. EUBANK.   Richmond
Justices of the Peace: SAMUEL MC CRAW and JONATHAN H. EUSTACE.   To
WILLIAM G. PENDLETON, 1822.

161.   2 January 1822.   WILLIS FRANKLIN and wife, POLLY, Amherst
       County, to STERLING CLAIBORNE, Amherst County...$2610.00 260
acres--mansion and residence of WILLIAM MOSS, deceased--lot of
grantors in 260 acres.   Lots to POLLY FRANKLIN, JONATHAN TARDY's
wife, ARTHUR HOPKINS' wife, ANDERSON MOSS, JR., children of WILLIAM
MOSS, deceased, on division.   Witnesses: SARAH A. ROSE, MILDRED
ROSE, SALLY ROSE.

162.   13 September 1822.   WILLIAM H. GIBSON and wife, ELVIRA,
       Amherst County, to RICHARD A. BUCKNER, Green County, Kentucky...
$1000 200 acres in Green and patent from Commonwealth of Kentucky,
28 June 1798, to JONATHAN HUDGINS, JR.   Lines: RODGER THOMPSON,
GLOVER's old fort, small branch, entering Green, top of the cliff.
Certified in Amherst County by grantor. NELSON CRAWFORD and WILLIAM
JOPLINS, Justices of the Peace.

163.   19 August 1822.   ABSALOM RUCKER, Amherst County, 1; SAMUEL
       GARLAND, GEORGE W. TURNER, 2; ARCHIBALD ROBERTSON, 3...Deed
of Trust; debt to ARCHIBALD ROBERTSON--to GEORGE W. TURNER, 17 February
1823--and THOMAS LAINE and RICHARD SHELTON, JR. and assigned by them
to ROBERTSON--$1.00 named slaves and children.

164.   20 August 1822.   JANE M. CLAIBORNE, wife of STERLING CLAIBORNE,
       relinquished dower of ZA DRUMMOND...JAMES POWELL and JONATHAN
COLEMAN, Justices of the Peace.

164. 21 May 1822. I note that script is different and very bad--
      EDWARD and ANSELM LYNCH, executors of JONATHAN LYNCH, Campbell
County, to HENRY S. LANGHORNE, Amherst County...JONATHAN LYNCH died
31 October 1820, testate--will in Lynchburg Hustings Court--MAREY
(sic) LYNCH, executrix, EDWARD, WILLIAM B., MICAJAH and ANSELM LYNCH,
executors--only EDWARD and ANSELM qualified; to sell land to raise
money for debts--79 acres north side James in Amherst County; $632.00.
Lines: grantee, the field, little below old Madison WH. Lynchburg
Justices of the Peace: MICAJAH DAVIS and S. NOWLING. To HENRY S.
LANGHORNE, per CHARLES IRVINE, 1 October 1822.

166. 9 August 1821. President, Directors of Farmer's Bank to
      HENRY S. LANGHORNE, Campbell County...$6090.75 492 acres.
Lines: WILLIAM WARWICK, JONATHAN LYNCH, GEORGE WHITLOCKE, -- PATTON,
James River. Tract conveyed to bank by ROBERT MORRIS and wife by
Deed of Trust, 29 June 1818, and bought by bank at sale by Marshall
of Superior Court of Lynchburg Chancery. ROBERT POLLARD, President;
JONATHAN RUTHERFORD and JONATHAN H. ENSTACE, Lynchburg Justices of
the Peace.

167. 20 August 1822. Memo of agreement by RICHARD H. BURKS, attorney-
      in-fact for RICHARD and AMBROSE BURKS...to AMBROSE RUCKER--
crops at plantation of RICHARD BURKS in Amherst County; lately sold,
but not delivered to ARCHIBALD ROBERTSON; RUCKER to sell and pay
debts due from BURKS--about $114 and RICHARD H. BURKS as bondsman
in various Amherst County suits.

168. 17 September 1822. SAMUEL COLEMAN, 1; GEORGE S. HOLLOWAY and
      STERLING CLAIBORNE, 2; WILLIAM DILLARD, 3...Deed of Trust; debt
to WILLIAM DILLARD; $1.00 105 acres. Lines: THOMAS COLEMAN, DANIEL F.
CHRISTIAN, FLEMING COLEMAN--where STERLING CLAIBORNE lives; also
120 acres bought of WILLIAM WILLMORE. Lines: THOMAS COLEMAN, GRALAND
RUCKER; also named slaves. To WILLIAM DILLARD, 14 June 1824.

170. 26 April 1822. JONATHAN AMBLER, Richmond, to son, JONATHAN
      JACQUELINE AMBLER, Richmond...love and $1.00; named slaves
on the Lower Place in Amherst County and tract conveyed to son,
20 March 1822. WILLIAM, usually known as the Head Man and about 50
or 55; PETER, about 50 or 55; old MARTIN, about 50; ABRAHAM, about
25; MANSFIELD, about 21; ADAM, about 40--long list and interesting--
CHRISTOPHER, a blacksmith aged 23; CENTIA, a baby a few weeks old;
SALLY, the weaver; old NELLY; horses, one in Louisa, one bought from
MAJOR EDMOND PENDLETON, Louisa, several bought at sale of late HENRY
KEITH. JAMES PWALING and WILLIAM TAZEWELL, Richmond Justices of the
Peace.

172. 15 July 1822. (very dim) SARAH F. CARTER, widow of JOB CARTER;
      JACOB CREAT and wife, MILDRED V. (late CARTER); ISAAC N. CARTER
and MARY F. CARTER, heirs of JOB CARTER, by CUTHBERT S. ANDERSON, to
CHARLES CRAWFORD, Shelby County, Kentucky...to JAMES BULLOCK, 19 March
1823--decree of Circuit Court at Frankfort, Kentucky, 13 March 1822--
CHARLES CARTER versus SARAH F. CARTER et al.--ordered to convey
Horsley tract in Amherst County on Gun Mountain. Lines: CHARLES
CRAWFORD, WILLIAM JOBLIN, JONATHAN CRAWFORD, CALEB RALLS, 30 acres,
ISAAC WRIGHT, ROBERT JOHNSON, deceased. Certified by C. S. ANDERSON,
FRANCIS P. BLAIR, Circuit Clerk, HENRY DAVIDGE, Circuit Judge,
Franklin County, Kentucky. JONATHAN ADAIR, GOVERNOR CABELL BRECKENRIDGE,
Section, 16 September 1822, Amherst County.

174. 3 June 1822. JONATHAN PENN, JR., acting executor of JONATHAN
      PENN, SR., late of Amherst County, to NANCY SHIELDS, Amherst
County...SR. by will directed land sale and money to grandchildren--
Indian Creek tract at $6 96/100 per acre: $2132.10--all of title.
Lines: WILLIAM WALLER, JOANNA HIGGINBOTHAM, Little Creek, PENDLETON,
north bank of Creek--309 acres. Witnesses: S. CLAIBORNE, SAMUEL
SIMMONS, WILLIAM MC DANIEL.

175. 18 September 1822. NANCY SHIELDS, Amherst County, to JAMES W.
SMITH, Amherst County...$2000.00 309 acres--semmingly tract
above. Lines: opposite a school house, Thorofare Road, WOODS'
survey. Witnesses: CHARLES TUCKER, TINSLEY RUCKER and RICHARD
HARRISON, Justices of the Peace. To JAMES W. SMITH, 1824.

176. 20 June 1822. ELIZABETH TINSLEY, widow of WILLIAM TINSLEY,
ISAAC TINSLEY and wife, NANCY, Amherst County, to GEORGE M.
and ALEXANDER TINSLEY, Amherst County...$418.00 52½ acres Harris
Creek. Lines: Bethel and WARE's road junction, JOSHUA TINSLEY,
deceased. EDMOND WINSTON and REUBEN NORVELL, Justices of the Peace.
To ISAAC TINSLEY, 20 November 1826.

178. 20 June 1822. ELIZABETH TINSLEY as above, ISAAC TINSLEY and
wife, NANCY, Amherst County, to ALEXANDER TINSLEY, Amherst
County...$1.00 thirty square poles on Bethel road. Justices of the
Peace as above.

179. 1 September 1822. STERLING CLAIBORNE, Amherst County, to
SARAH ANN and MILDRED J. (I) ROSE, Amherst County...$2600
261 acres--former residence of WILLIAM MOSS, deceased, and conveyed
to STERLING CLAIBORNE by WILLIS FRANKLIN and wife. Sent to grantees,
14 December 1824.

180. 24 July 1822. JONATHAN WARWICK, Sheriff of Amherst County...
JAMES PENN took insolvent oath--JAMES LONDON versus JAMES PENN--
PENN made deed on 4 June 1822.

180. 4 June 1822. JAMES PENN, Amherst County, to JONATHAN WARWICK,
Amherst County Sheriff...about to take insolvent oath; decree
of JAMES LONDON versus PENN. Witnesses: LINDSEY COLEMAN, T. S.
HOLLOWAY, W. WATSON.

180. 19 August 1822. Agreement by JAMES C. BURFORD, REUBEN and
WILLIAM BURFORD, to JOSEPH MC CARY and AMBROSE BURFORD...$200
claim of ROBERTSON and Company versus MARY (later NANCY) BURFORD--
negroes in possession of NANCY, her life interest. Witnesses:
AMBROSE RUCKER.

181. 20 August 1822. ABSALOM RUCKER, Amherst County, to SAMUEL
GARLAND, 2; ARCHIBALD ROBERTSON, Lynchburg, 3...Deed of Trust;
debt to ARCHIBALD ROBERTSON; $1.00 slaves named, stock, furniture,
interest in estate of father, ANTHONY RUCKER.

182. -- June 1822. JONATHAN PENN, JR., acting executor of JONATHAN
PENN, SR., Amherst County, to JONATHAN DILLARD, Amherst County...
under will; sale at late MH. Indian Creek tract $3.09 per acre;
$906.96 293½ acres. Lines: LAWHORNE, SCOTE, WILLIAM DILLARD, RICHARD
MAYS, CAMPBELL's old line, CASH.

184. 24 September 1822. JOSEPH B. MAYS, Amherst County, 1; WILLIAM M.
WALLER, Amherst County, 2; JAMES W. SMITH, Amherst County, 3...
15 June 1818, SMITH became bondsman on guardian bond for JOSEPH B.
MAYS--wards: NANCY W., BEVERLY W., TALIAFERRO W. and ROBERT B. MAYS,
orphans of ELIZABETH MAYS, deceased. $5.00 230 acres where JOSEPH B.
MAYS lives. Lines: JESSE MAYS, THOMAS WILLIAMSON, BEVERLY WILLIAMSON,
deceased. Tract belonged to ROBERT MAYS, father of JOSEPH B. MAYS.

185. 24 September 1822. SAMUEL COLEMAN, 1; DAVID S. GARLAND, 2;
RICHARD H. BURKS, 3...Deed of Trust; $1.00 122 acres on
Tobacco Row. Lines: JONATHAN AMBLER, RICHARD PENDLETON, GARLAND
RUCKER, WILLIAM WILLMORE, THOMAS COLEMAN. To DAVID S. GARLAND,
15 August 1825.

186. 28 August 1822. CHARLES MOORE and wife, POLLY, to JONATHAN
      LONDON, Amherst County...$1490 262 3/4 acres headwaters Rocky
Run. Lines: JONATHAN CASHWELL, JAMES GRISSOM's old line, a road,
ANDREW MONROE, deceased. THOMAS CREWS and RICHARD HARRISON, Justices
of the Peace. To JONATHAN LONDON, 18 November 1822.

187. 4 July 1822. CHRISTOPHER ISBELL, Amherst County, to WILLIAM I.
      ISBELL, Amherst County...power of attorney--JAMES L. LAMKIN,
Justice of the Peace.

187. 8 June 1822. WILLIAM PARKS, Dearborn County, Indiana, attorney
      for JOSEPH and ALLEN PRYOR, guardian of JONATHAN, NANCY, PEGGY,
WILLIAM, JR. and LAVINIA PARKS...Power of attorney to MARTIN PARKS,
Amherst County to act in estate of CHARLES BURKS, deceased, Amherst
County, for heirs of MILLY PARKS, deceased, as heir of RICHARD BURKS.
Witnesses: J. L. WINGFIELD, WILLIAM H. and SAMUEL G. PARKS. Recorded
Amherst County, 16 September 1822, and proved by witnesses.

188. 26 August 1822. CHRISTOPHER ISBELL, 1; CHRISTOPHER ANTHONY, 2;
      REUBEN NORVELL, 3...REUBEN NORVELL is bondsman for CHRISTOPHER
ISBELL to THOMAS F. BOULDIN, assignee of JONATHAN A. and MARSHALL J.
COUCH--Bedford Court; Deed of Trust; $5.00; long list of named
slaves. TINSLEY RUCKER and JAMES L. LAMKIN, Justices of the Peace.
To REUBEN NORVELL, 8 April 1823.

189. 5 February 1819. CHRISTOPHER ISBELL and wife, ELIZABETH,
      WILLIAM I. ISBELL and wife, LUCY, Amherst County, to STITH
MEAD, Amherst County...$10,000 three lots on Lynch road. Lines:
road, shop corner of MEAD, LYNCH old line, NATHAN L. WILLIAMSON,
CREASY--7 3/4 acres second lot conveyed to WILLIAM I. ISBELL by
JONATHAN LYNCH, 4 April 1817; third lot deed of 2 March 1818--by
SAMUEL STEEL to WILLIAM ISBELL. JAMES NEWHALL and JONATHAN M.
SETTLE, Lynchburg Justices of the Peace. Recorded Amherst County,
8 October 1822.

190. 16 September 1822. ARCHY ROWSEY, Amherst County, to THOMAS
      FLINT, Rockbridge...$160 83 acres Pedlar. Lines: THOMAS
ALLEN, JOSEPH HIGGINBOTHAM, HENRY HARTLESS. Tract conveyed to
ARCHY ROWSEY by ELIZABETY FLINT and CHILDREN as heirs of JONATHAN
FLINT, deceased. JONATHAN SEYBORN and ROBERT WHITE, Rockbridge
Justices of the Peace.

191. 17 February 1822. JACOB TYREE and wife, MARTHA, Amherst
      County, to TANDY RUTHERFORD, Amherst County...$900 246 acres
south borders Buffaloe and bought from WIATT and JONATHAN DUNCAN.
Lines: CHARLES DUNCAN, JAMES GARLAND, deceased, JAMES WOOD, PATSY
DUNCAN, MICAJAH CAMDEN. Witnesses: LEROY CAMDEN, JAMES WOOD, JAMES W.
SMITH. To TANDY RUTHERFORD, 14 January 1841. Note: see will of
TANDY RUTHERFORD in R will section of my works.

192. 17 September 1822. ACHILLES P. MITCHELL to LUCAS P. THOMPSON
      and STERLING CLAIBORNE, Amherst County...$1000 225 acres on
James River. Lines: WILLIAM HANNAH and where ACHILLES P. MITCHELL
lives. Witnesses: ISAAC RUCKER, POWHATAN D. FRANKLIN, ELIJAH L.
CHRISTIAN. To STERLING CLAIBORNE, 8 December 1824.

192. 20 August 1822. GEORGE S. HOLLOWAY to STERLING CLAIBORNE...
      agreement of 15 July 1822--voied for $1.00 paid to HOLLOWAY.

193. 20 August 1822. Memo of agreement between same parties as
      above...Deed of Trust voided; Deed of Trust as to JABEZ CAMDEN's
debt.

194. 20 August 1822. Same parties...reference to Deed of Trust for
      $15,000 and CLAIBORNE reconveys to HOLLOWAY for $1.00; 900 acres
formerly that of HENRY HOLLOWAY and bought by him from VERNON METCALFE.

228

194. 30 September 1822. RICHARD HARTLESS, Amherst County, to
     JONATHAN WARWICK, Sheriff of Amherst County...RICHARD HARTLESS
has been taken on writ by HENRY A. CHRISTIAN, assignee of ROBERT R.
NEIGHBOURS, assignee of CALEB RALLS; assignee of PULLIAM SANDIDGE;
also writ by D. and D. HIGGINBOTHAM, SAMUEL R. DAVIES--HARTLESS
takes insolvent oath and conveys to Sheriff. 300 acres nedt to
HENRY FRANKLIN. Witnesses: ROBERT CAMM, JESSE MUNDY, MICHALE
MC MAHON. To WILLIAM DILLARD, Deputy Sheriff. November 1822.

195. 30 September 1822. RICHARD HARTLESS, Amherst County, to
     JONATHAN WARWICK, Amherst County Sheriff...margin as above;
HENRY A. CHRISTIAN as above; HARTLESS took insolvent oath when sued
by CHRISTIAN--35 acres to Sheriff--recently appropriated by a warrant
and patent to be made. Witnesses: as above.

196. 19 August 1822. SAMUEL R. DAVIES to GEORGE BURKS...ARTHUR B.
     DAVIES, guardian of SAMUEL R. on -- to said BURKS for $2000.00.
SAMUEL was not of age, but now ratifies.

196. 19 August 1822. STERLING CLAIBORNE to DABNEY T. PHILLIPS...
     rent of plantation bought by STERLING CLAIBORNE from GEROGE S.
HOLLOWAY--five years from 1 January next. DABNEY T. PHILLIPS to pay
one fourth of crops per year and to take good care of tract.
Witnesses: B. DAVIES.

197. 24 September 1822. RICHARD BURKS by attorney, RICHARD H.
     BURKS, to SAMUEL COLEMAN...$1220 122 acres on Tobacco Row.
Lines: JONATHAN AMBLER, RICHARD PENDLETON, GARLAND RUCKER, WILLIAM
WILLMORE, THOMAS COLEMAN.

197. 19 August 1822. DABNEY T. PHILLIPS, 1; RICHARD BURKS, 2;
     DABNEY P. GOOCH, WILLIAM SHELTON, 3...Deed of Trust to secure
DABNEY P. GOOCH and WILLIAM SHELTON; suit in Lynchburg District by
NANCY PHILIPS--SHELTON as next friend--versus CATLETT WILLS et al.;
$1.00, slaves, stock, books, etc.; interest in estate of late father,
WILLIAM PHILIPS, and held by mother, MARY PHILIPS.

198. 14 September 1822. DR. JAMES M. BROWN and wife, RHODY, Amherst
     County, to NELSON MANTIPLY, Amherst County...$206.67 62 acres
north side Turkey Mountain and Buffaloe. Lines: CAPTAIN JONATHAN
COLEMAN, grantee, WILLIAM MANTIPLY, RUSH HUDSON, SR. Witnesses:
JOSEPH STAPLES, STEPHEN TURNER, JONATHAN D. WARE. To NELSON MANTIPLY,
18 November 1822.

199. 6 August 1822. ELIZABETH THURMAN, Amherst County, to only
     son, WILLIAM D. HILL, Amherst County...$1.00 named slaves
and ages, stock, furniture--life interest to her; stock to be
delivered to POLLY RICKETTS. Witnesses: JONATHAN LONDON, SALLY
RICKETTS, REUBEN D. HILL.

200. 6 August 1822. NANCY YOUNG, widow of JONATHAN YOUNG, Amherst
     County, 1; JAMES W. SMITH, 2; PHILIP LIVELY, WILLIAM and
JONATHAN B. DUNCAN, 3...$1.00 to secure ELIJAH FLETCHER on debt of
late husband. PHILIP LIVELY, WILLIAM and JONATHAN B. DUNCAN have
made bond to FLETCHER and she conveys to JAMES W. SMITH--slaves,
stock. Witnesses: CHARLES MASSIE, BENJAMIN B. TALIAFERRO, JONATHAN
PENDLETON, GEORGE CORNELIUS.

201. 23 August 1822. LEWIS P. THOMPSON, Amherst County, to JONATHAN
     WHITEHEAD, Nelson County...WILLIAM C. WHITEHEAD, 21 November
1821, conveyed all interest in estate of BURCHER WHITEHEAD, his
father, in Deed of Trust; defaulted, to secure THOMAS ALDRIDGE,
advertisement in Lynchburg paper and sold at ACH, 29 August 1822
(sic) and ALDRIDGE bought at $51.00 as agent of JONATHAN WHITEHEAD.

201. 19 March 1822. (Recorded) Plat of 21 acres on both sides
      RUCKER's old road--subject of dispute between ELIAS WILLS and
JAMES DAVIS who objected to processing; County Court order to survey
and jury to judge; done 21 July 1821. Jury found for DAVIS. Lines:
JONATHAN LONDON, ELIAS WILLS, RUCKER's road.

202. 15 August 1822. LINDSEY BURKS, Amherst County, to THOMAS N.
      EUBANK, Amherst County...Deed of Trust; debts to RICHARD L.
ELLIS, ELLIS and EUBANK; $1.00 156 acres where LINDSEY BURKS lives
or interest in it; named slaves, claim on WILLIAM HANNAH and JONATHAN
HAYNES; whiskey--328 gallons. To RICHARD N. EUBANK, 18 February
1823.

203. 3 May 1822. JOSEPH KENNEDY and wife, ELIZABETH, Amherst
      County, to THOMAS SPPLING, Amherst County...$224.75 31 acres
north borders Buffaloe and part of where JOSEPH KENNEDY lives.
Lines: DILLARD's road. THOMAS S. HOLLOWAY and ROBERT TINSLEY, Justices
of the Peace.

204. 1 January 1823. PULLIAM SANDIDGE, Amherst County, to ZA DRUMMOND,
      Amherst County...$4000.00 300 acres both sides Buffaloe and
where PULLIAM SANDIDGE lives. Lot of ELIJAH FLETCHER and plat made
for WILLIAM S. CRAWFORD, not herein. Witnesses: CHARLES L. BARRET,
JOSHUA SANDIDGE, JAMES W. SMITH, MANSFIELD WARE. To ZA DRUMMOND,
17 February 1823.

204. 12 July 1822. REUBEN PENDLETON, Amherst County, 1; ROBERT
      TINSLEY, Amherst County, 2; DAVID S. GARLAND, WILLIAM W. SCOTT,
      JAMES WARE, JAMES L. and WILL G. PENDLETON, 3...six shillings
paid by ROBERT TINSLEY; debt to ARCHIBALD ROBERTSON; interest in
ten slaves received from estate of JAMES GARLAND, deceased, and right
of self and children. CAMPBELL suit: REUBEN PENDLETON versus
GABRIEL SCOTT; also stock, furniture. To DAVID S. GARLAND, 5 May
1823.

206. 10 March 1821. JONATHAN HAAS and wife, SUSAN, Amherst County,
      to WILLIAM MITCHELL, Amherst County...$1400 3½ acres Horsley;
part of tract bought by EDMOND GOODRICH. Lines: JOSIAH ELLIS,
JAMES WARE, a spring. Witnesses: R. HENLEY, MIRANDA PRICE HAAS.
WILLIAM JOPLING and BENJAMIN TALIAFERRO, Justices of the Peace.

207. 19 August 1822. THOMAS COLEMAN, Amherst County, 1; AMBROSE
      RUCKER, Amherst County, 2; JONATHAN COLEMAN, Amherst County, 3...
Deed of Trust; $1.00 120 acres Harris Creek. Part of tract of
grantor and bought from heirs of DANIEL COLEMAN. Lines: FANNY
SCOTT's hollow, WILLIAM WILLMORE (formerly THOMAS GRISSOM), DANIEL L.
CHRISTIAN, JONATHAN AMBLER, THOMAS GRISSOM's old place. To AMBROSE
RUCKER, 6 October 1827.

207. 22 October 1822. JAMES WARE, Amherst County, 1; RICHARD L.
      ELLIS, Amherst County, 2; WILLIAM G. PENDLETON, Richmond, 3...
Deed of Trust; debt to WILLIAM G. PENDLETON. Sent to WILLIAM G.
PENDLETON, 26 October 1822, per H. HAGER--$1.00 Pedlar Mills on
Horsley. Lines: road from Pedlar River to CRAWFORD's Gap, RICHARD N.
EUBANK, DUNCAN's Spring Branch, MANSFIELD WARE, RICHARD L. ELLIS,
JONATHAN DAVIS. Justices of the Peace: JONATHAN ELLIS and RICHARD N.
EUBANK.

209. 20 August 1822. ANTHONY RUCKER, Amherst County, 1; SPENCER
      NORVELL, Amherst County, 2; ROSE and PATTESON, Lynchburg, 3...
Deed of Trust; $1.00; names slaves. Witnesses: SPENCER D. NORVELL.
SPENCER NORVELL is called SR.

210. 11 April 1822. DANIEL and DAVID HOFFMAN, merchants; WILLIAM
       STEEN, 2; to CHISWELL DABNEY, 3...Deed of Trust to secure
WILLIAM STEEN; $1.00 slaves named: LITTLE BEN, a tanner, etc.
ALEXANDER SHIELDS and ROBERT WHITE, Rockbridge Justices of the Peace
as to DANIEL HOFFMAN. ALBON MC DANIEL and JONATHAN THURMOND,
Lynchburg Justices of the Peace as to DAVID HOFFMAN.

211. 22 August 1822. THOMAS J. STONE, Amherst County, to THOMAS N.
       EUBANK, Amherst County...Deed of Trust; debt to ELLIS and
EUBANK; $1.00, slave, stock. Witnesses: JONATHAN C. TALIAFERRO,
JONATHAN DAVIS, WILLIAM F. GRANBERRY.

212. 16 September 1822. JACOB SMITH, Amherst County, to CHARLES
       TUCKER, Amherst County...$1885 400 acres Franklin Creek.
Lines: JAMES SMITH. Bought from JONATHAN SMITH, 13 March 1813.
Gross and not by acre, if less. To CHARLES TUCKER, 22 August 1823.

212. 26 April 1822. MILBURN HOGG and wife, MARTHA, Washington
       County, Kentucky, to RICHARD L. ELLIS, Amherst County...$600.
1. 89 acres on Maple Creek, branch of James--to me from deceased
father, JONATHAN HOGG--55 acres on division. Lines: WILLIAM NOEL.
2. 34 acres from deceased brother, JONATHAN HOGG, the younger, and
we bought from his heirs. JOHN HUGHES, JR., Washington County Clerk,
Springfield, Kentucky. Note: I have a good nit of Washington County
data for I had privilege of being pastor of Springfield Baptist
Church for over eight years. I am interested in MILBURN name and
GLASSCOCK, too, and note that his man bears first name of MILBURN.

213. 16 September 1822. SAMUEL COLEMAN, Amherst County, to THOMAS N.
       EUBANK, Amherst County...Deed of Trust; $1.00 to secure ELLIS
and EUBANK, slaves. To RICHARD N. EUBANK, 17 July 1823.

214. 16 September 1822. JONATHAN WARE and wife, PEGGY, Amherst
       County, to ZA DRUMMOND, Amherst County...$15.00 six acres
headwaters of Puppie Creek. Lines: grantee, Red Hill top. To
ZA DRUMMOND, 17 February 1823.

214. 23 January 1822. GEORGE MARKHAM, Powhatan, 1; LINEAS BOLLING,
       Buckingham, 2; JAMES L. DILLARD and WILLIAM M. RIVES, 3...Deed
of Trust; debt to LINEAS BOLLING; decree of Chancery in Richmond
District. BRETT RANDOLPH et al. versus BERNARD MARKHAM's executors;
slaves. CHRISTOPHER TOMPKINS and WILLIAM H. FITZWHYLOM, Richmond
Justices of the Peace.

215. 15 September 1822. AMBROSE B. EUBANK, Amherst County, to
       THOMAS N. EUBANK, Amherst County...Deed of Trust; debt to
ELLIS and EUBANK, THOMAS WHITTENTON, ARMISTEAD OTEY, WILLIAM DILLARD.
$1.00 slaves, furnitre. To R. N. EUBANK, 18 July 1823.

216. 16 September 1822. PRESTON H. GARLAND, Amherst County, to
       JACOB PEARCE, Amherst County...$1800 254 acres south borders
Buffaloe and east side Braxton Ridge. Lines: grantee, a branch,
top of ridge, road. To JONAS PIERCE, 22 August 1835, as executor
of JACOB PEARCE.

217. 3 August 1822. JONATHAN COOPER and JENSEY PINN, wife of
       JAMES PINN, Amherst County, to JAMES LONDON, JR., Amherst
County...$250.00 45 acres Porridge Creek. Part of tract JAMES PINN
bought from REUBEN NORVELL. Lines: LARKIN LONDON, top of the hill,
the branch, the stanle, REUBEN NORVELL, ANDREW STEWART. Witnesses:
WIATT LONDON, JOSHUA CASWY, RICHARD L. LONDON.

218. 25 September 1822. LEE H. BURKS to RICHARD SHELTON...$1.00;
       crop on mountain plantation where he lives. RICHARD SHELTON
to sell and pay debt to GEORGE MC DANIEL's executors--R. BURKS is
bondsman. Balance to WILLIAM TINSLEY's executors. To RICHARD
SHELTON, 12 November 1822.

218. 28 August 1822. JONATHAN WARWICK, Sheriff, to CORNELIUS
POWELL...JAMES HIX, 17 June 1822, conveyed to Sheriff--150
acres. Advertised and bought by CORNELIUS POWELL.

218. 5 January 1822. JAMES WEBB, GEORGE G. WESCOT and wife,
NANCY, now of Rockbridge, to JONATHAN JAMES DILLARD, Amherst
County...$2000.00 house and lot in New Glasgow--that of WILLIAM MOSS,
deceased, and sold to THOMAS ALDRIDGE and by THOMAS ALDRIDGE to
grantors on --. Rockbridge Justices of the Peace: JONATHAN
MC CLELLAND and ROBERT WHITE.

219. 1 June 1822. JOSEPH JARVIS and wife, NANCY, Rockbridge, to
ANDERSON WARE, Amherst County...$50.00 66 acres south borders
Pedlar. Lines: JAMES FRAZIER, deceased, JONATHAN MC CLAIN. JOSEPH
HIGGINBOTHAM, JOSEPH KING, THOMAS ALLEN. BENJAMIN TALIAFERRO and
ISAAC RUCKER, Justices of the Peace.

220. 1 October 1822. GEORGE CAMPBELL and wife, LUCY, Amherst
County, to JONATHAN CAMPBELL, Amherst County...$160 48 acres
north side Little Piney; part of tract. Lines: JONATHAN and
BENJAMIN CAMDEN, grantee, DAVID S. GARLAND and JAMES M. BROWN,
Justices of the Peace. To JONATHAN CAMPBELL, 26 December 1823.

221. 22 October 1822. PHILIP LIVELY and wife, SUSAN, Amherst
County, to GEORGE S. HOLOWAY, Amherst County...$900 180 acres--
two tracts bought from RICHARD HARRISON. 50 acres. Witnesses:
ROBERT CAMM, WILL DILLARD, B. DAVIES. To GEORGE S. HOLOWAY,
21 November 1822.

222. 22 October 1822. JAMES R. LIVELY to PHILIP LIVELY...$2097.00
233 acres--one-third of tract devised by JAMES LIVELY, deceased,
to JAMES R. and his two brothers and adjoins their parts; in possession
of JONATHAN LONDON and JAMES OGDON. Lines: JONATHAN MC DANIEL,
THOMAS WDWARDS, widow BROWN. To PHILIP LIVELY, 1824.

223. 22 October 1822. GEORGE S. HOLLOWAY, Amherst County, releases
JAMES R. LIVELY, Amherst County...233 acres--reference to deed
of 21 March 1822.

223. 4 November 1822. SAMUEL GOWING, Amherst County, and ELIZABETH
BRYANT, Amherst County, 1; WILL STAPLES, Amherst County, 2;
JAMES L. PENDLETON and Company, 3...$1.00; Deed of Trust; debt to
JAMES L. PENDLETON and Company--about L3000 tobacco; one cow bought
of HENRY FRANKLIN, stock, furnitre--to enjoy until 1 March 1823.
Witnesses: WILLIS FRANKLIN, ANDREW H. MOSS, JAMES L. WATTS.

224. 23 October 1822. MARTIN B. BURKS and wife, LOUISA C., Bedford
County, to GUSTAVUS A. ROSE, Campbell County...$2250 147 acres
north borders Harris. Lines: RODERICK TALIAFERRO, deceased, CHARLES
WINGFIELD. Conveyed to MARTIN B. BURKS by CHRISTOPHER ANTHONY,
WILLIAM COCK, 3 May 1821. Lines: intersection of Dawson and Lynch
roads, RODNEY TALIAFERRO, deceased, GEORGE CARRINGTON, MOSES
HIGGINBOTHAM, ELIAS WILLS. Bedford Justices of the Peace: THOMAS
SALE and JACOB WHITE.

225. 23 October 1822. JAMES L. LAMKIN and REUBEN NORVELL as to
NANCY RUCKER, wife of TINSLEY RUCKER...deed to CHRISTOPHER
ANTHONY, 2 November 1822 (sic).

225. 4 November 1822. SAMUEL BURKS, SR., Amherst County, 1; GARLAND
RUCKER, Bedford, 2; NANCY RUCKER, wife of TINSLEY RUCKER,
Amherst County, 3...SAMUEL BURKS for love of daughter, NANCY, and
infants; $1.00; long list of items. To GARLAND RUCKER per T. RUCKER,
13 November 1822. REUBEN NORVELL and JAMES L. LAMKIN, Justices of
the Peace.

226.   4 November 1822.   JAMES LEE, WILLIAM L. BELL, MARTHA H. BELL,
       EDMOND WOODROOF, NELSON DAWSON, JR. and wife, FANNY, all of
Virginia, power of attorney to DANIEL DAY, Amherst County to act in
North Carolina estate of WILLIAM B. DAMERON, as heirs...DAMERON late
of Virginia. Also JONATHAN H. BELL, BENJAMIN DAWSON and wife,
SUSANNA, BENJAMIN WATTS and wife, FANNY D.

227.   21 November 1822.   Dower to widow of THOMAS WILCOX, deceased;
       all heirs of age...MH and 52 acres adjoining; plat not herein;
161 acres to be sold and ELI BURCH bought at $1205.30. JAMES DAVIS,
WILLIAM and DANIEL DAY, commissioner. Part of 213 acres on north
side Porrige. REUBEN NORVELL, surveyor. Note error: date is
August 15, 1821.

227.   21 November 1822.   POLLY CHILDRESS, relict of JAMES CHILDRESS,
       deceased, late of Henrico, ROBERT and ABSALOM P. CRUTCHER,
Amherst County, power of attorney to THOMAS WRIGHT, Amherst County...
to rent Henrico tract--property of JAMES CHILDRESS and interest of
all legatees. Acknowledged by all in Amherst County.

229.   18 November 1822.   RICHARD PENDLETON, Amherst County, to
       JONATHAN P. BURKS, Madison County, Alabama...to provide support
of RICHARD PENDLETON's daughter, POLLY, wife of WILLIAM H. HAYNES,
Amherst County, and her children and future ones--$10.00; slaves
and furniture; when children are 21.

230.   6 November 1822.   TINSLEY RUCKER, Amherst County, to SPENCER
       NORVELL, Amherst County...power of attorney to act in estate
of WILLIAM WARE, as to daughter, NANCY W. RUCKER, deceased, and to
pay executors of HUGH NORVELL, deceased, and BENJAMIN NORVELL.
Witnesses: ROBERT and WILLIAM RIDGWAY.

230.   1 June 1822.   JONATHAN PENN, JR., acting executor of JONATHAN
       PENN, SR., late of Amherst County, to JONATHAN J. DILLARD and
HENRY H. WATTS, Amherst County...under will to sell and divide sums
to grandchildren--156 acres at $8.01 per acre--$1249.56. Indian
Creek tract and joins JONATHAN HUDSON.

231.   5 October 1822.   Madison trustees to JORDAN CREASY, Amherst
       County...$1.00 old lot 38 and now 9; First Street or Main and
fifth alley--half acre. PLEASANT DAWSON, REUBEN PENDLETON, NELSON C.
DAWSON, WILLIAM TURNER, ELIAS WILLS, JONATHAN WIATT, trustees.
Witnesses: TIM FLETCHER, D. R. EDLEY, EZEKIEL DAY, WILLIAM RIVES,
C. DABNEY.

232.   11 November 1822.   ROBERT P. CRUTCHER, Amherst County, to
       PEACHY FRANKLIN, Amherst County...Deed of Trust; debt to
JONATHAN MARQUIS--to redeem slave, HENRY, in hands of Amherst County
Sheriff; $1.00 for HENRY. Witnesses: LUCAS P. THOMPSON, J. YAGER,
GEORGE G. WESTCOTE. To JONATHAN MARQUIS, 26 January 1824.

232.   18 November 1822.   SEBELL CAMDEN, Amherst County, to WILLIAM
       DUNCAN for support of my son, LEROY CAMDEN...slave; at LEROY's
death to my three daughters: NANCY WHITEHEAD, ESTHER GOODWIN,
SUSANNAH DUNCAN. To WILLIAM DUNCAN, 20 June 1825. Witnesses:
WIATT DUNCAN, JAMES WOOD, SAMUEL BYERS.

233.   18 November 1822.   JONATHAN L. WINGFIELD, Amherst County, to
       brother, CHARLES WINGFIELD, Amherst County...love and for
support of him and family. Furniture, etc. Witnesses: J. HAAS,
RICHARD SHELTON.

233.   18 November 1822.   WILLIAM CARTER and wife, MILLY, Buckingham
       County, to LEWIS LAYNE, Amherst County...$900 106½ acres south
waters of Buffaloe and Green Spring branch--part of tract. Lines:
grantee, CHARLES L. CHRISTIAN, WILLIAM S. CRAWFORD, deceased.

234. 9 November 1822. ROBERT RIVERS and wife, NANCY, Amherst County,
     to JORDAN CREASY, Amherst County...$400 old 38 and now 9 in
Madison--half lot. Lynchburg Justices of the Peace: MICAJAH DAVIS
and JONATHAN THURMOND. To JORDAN CREASY, 8 April 1826.

235. 18 November 1822. WILLIS RUCKER, Amherst County, 1; JAMES
     GARLAND and DABNEY P. GOOCH, 2; DABNEY T. PHILLIPS, 3...
DABNEY T. PHILLIPS and ANDREW MORELAND on bond to DAVID S. GARLAND
and WILLIAM SHELTON, executors of RICHARD SHELTON. $1.00 slaves.
To GOOCH, 5 May 1823.

235. 18 June 1822. JONATHAN PENN, JR., acting executor of JONATHAN
     PENN, SR. to ABRAHAM MARTIN, JR. and JONATHAN TUCKER. Sold at
late MH, April, 188 acres Indian Creek at $451--later amount is
$847.88. Lines: JONATHAN TUCKER, HUDSON, WILLIAM MOORE, creek ford.

235. 20 November 1822. DANIEL F. CHRISTIAN, 1; PETER F. CHRISTIAN, 2;
     JONATHAN CHRISTIAN, B., 3...debt to JONATHAN CHRISTIAN, B.
$1.00 550 acres and where JONATHAN CHRISTIAN, B. lives. Lines:
south side Buffaloe, THOMAS APPLING, JOSEPH KENNEDY, Rocky Creek,
GEORGE SHRADER, Mill Pond, STERLING CLAIBORNE, PHILLIP GOOCH estate,
JONATHAN DILLARD, Migginson road, JONATHAN COLEMAN, WILLIAM EDMUNDS,
also slaves and stock.

238. 20 November 1822. JONATHAN CHRISTIAN, B., Amherst County, to
     DANIEL F. CHRISTIAN, Amherst County...$5500 at $10 per acre--
550 acres where JONATHAN CHRISTIAN, B lives. Lines: south side
Buffaloe, crossing to THOMAS APLING, JOSEPH KENNEDY, mouth of
Rocky Creek, GEORGE SHRADER, JOSEPH DILLARD of Culpeper--life estate
reserved for wife and self. To DANIEL F. CHRISTIAN, 8 May 1823.
Note: I have pointed out elsewhere that the B by JONATHAN's name
stands for JONATHAN of Buffaloe.

239. 18 November 1822. EDMOND GOODRICH, Amherst County, to friend,
     JAMES WOOD, Amherst County...power of attorney to collect bond
of 6 January 1818, assigned to me by RICHARDSON HENLEY, Amherst
County, assignee of THOMAS GOODRICH versus JOSEPH R. and ABRAM
CARTER, Amherst County, and all unsettled Amherst County business.
Witnesses: LEROY CAMDEN, JAC TYREE, WILLIS DUNCAN.

239. 18 November 1822. ELIJAH STATON, Amherst County, to JAMES
     WOOD, Amherst County...power of attorney to conduct Amherst
County business. Witnesses: JAC TYREE, WILLIS and CHARLES DUNCAN.

239. 5 October 1822. HENRY, GEORGE and JAMES CLARK, Amherst
     County, to DAVID S. GARLAND, Amherst County...$608 for land
on headwaters of Pedlar and Blue Ridge. 72 acres on top of Blue
Ridge and joins WALTER POWERS. 46 acres on top of Blue Ridge.
JAMES M. BROWN and EDMOND PENN, Justices of the Peace.

240. 21 December 1821. LINDSEY SANDIDGE and wife, CLARA G., Amherst
     County, to WILLIAM HANNAH...$1800 Franklin Creek, no acres.
Witnesses: JONATHAN and ELIHU TARDY, WILLIAM COLEMAN, CHARLES L.
BARRET and ISAAC RUCKER, Justices of the Peace.

241. 23 October 1822. HENRY, GEORGE and JAMES CLARK, Amherst County,
     to DAVID S. GARLAND, Amherst County...$247.50 99 acres Pedlar.
Granted to JONATHAN JARVIS. BENJAMIN TALIAFERRO and ROBERT TINSLEY,
Justices of the Peace.

242. 7 October 1822. WILLIAM WILLMORE and wife, SUSANNAH, Amherst
     County, to DAVID S. GARLAND, Amherst County...$750 167 acres
Pedlar. Lines: WILLIAM GRISSOM, HENRY CAMDEN, GARLAND, HALL,
WILLIAM GALT. JAMES M. BROWN and EDMOND PENN, Justices of the Peace.

242. 11 August 1821. THOMAS HICKS, Amherst County, to LUCAS P.
     THOMPSON, Amherst County...Deed of Trust; debts to JONATHAN
THOMPSON, JR.; $1.00; Nelson County tract of 158 acres. Lines:
DR. HUBARD, WILLIAM S. CABELL, JONATHAN P. COBBS, THOMAS HAWKINS,
ELIZABETH POWELL, widow of LUCAS POWELL. Bought from THOMPSON on
even date, stock, furniture.

243. 16 November 1822. THOMAS ALDRIDGE, Amherst County, Justice
     of the Peace, DAVID S. GARLAND, Justice of the Peace, as to
POLLY C. FRANKLIN, wife of WILLIS FRANKLIN, to STERLING CLAIBORNE.

243. 6 April 1822. JAMES MURRAY BROWN and wife, RHODY, Amherst
     County, to DAVID S. GARLAND, Amherst County...$50 part of tract
near New Glasgow and surveyed 12 November 1821--one acre plus.
Lines: both, Lexington road.

244. 22 November 1822. JAMES HATTON, Amherst County, 1; BENNET A.
     CRAWFORD, Amherst County, 2; JONATHAN HATTON, Amherst County, 3...
debt to JONATHAN HATTON; $1.00; black walnut tables and cupboard, etc.

245. 5 October 1822. JONATHAN MOOHN, Amherst County, to BRANFORD
     HICKS and FLEMING COLEMAN, Amherst County, 2; SAMUEL GARLAND,
Lynchburg, 3...JONATHAN and son, BENNETT, owe SAMUEL GARLAND on
judgement--$1.00; tobacco crop, furniture, etc. Witnesses: SAMUEL
COLEMAN, THOMAS COLEMAN, CHARLES P. TALIAFERRO.

246. 26 November 1822. WILLIAM G. PENDLETON and wife, MARY,
     Richmond; JAMES L. PENDLETON and wife, CATHERINE, Amherst
County, to PHILIP NORBORNE NICHOLAS and WILLIAM MC KESVIS (NEHERVIS),
Richmond, 2; President and Directors of Farmers' Bank of Virginia, 3...
8 January 1822 to CAMPBELL per MANSFIELD WARE; 9 April 1830, sent to
JONATHAN GORDON, Campbell County tract on Whipping Creek by WILLIAM G.--
Locust Thicket tract of 1736 acres. Lines: late that of DUDLEY
TERRILL, Lynchburg road, PHILIP PAYNE, Buckhorn branch, DR. JONATHAN
SLAUGHTER. Part of 1800 acres from ROBERT ALEXANDER to WILLIAM G.
PENDLETON and wife, MARY G., 24 December 1813. JAMES conveys 753 acres
on Buffaloe and both sides of road from New Glasgow to Lynchburg.
Lines: DAVID S. GARLAND, bought by THOMAS ALDRIDGE from JONATHAN
CAMM and conveyed by THOMAS ALDRIDGE and wife, CATHERINE, to JAMES L.
PENDLETON, 29 April 1818. Richmond Justices of the Peace: WILLIAM H.
FITZWHYLSOM and JONATHAN H. EUSTACE.

250. 13 November 1822. JONATHAN PETER, Bedford County, to RICHARD
     DAVIS, Bedford, 2; JONATHAN SLEDD, Bedford, 3...$1.00; interest
in estate of father, WILLIAM PETER, deceased, Amherst County. THOMAS
SALE and JACOB WHITE, Bedford Justices of the Peace.

251. 26 October 1822. WILLIAM H. CABELL and wife, AGNES G. G.,
     Buckingham County, to JOSEPH C. CABELL, Nelson County...tract
bought from NELSON CRAWFORD on both sides Pedlar--4350 acres. Patent
to CRAWFORD and NICHOLAS CABELL--except 600 acres sold by them to
SAMUEL DEANE--under will of NICHOLAS CABELL, father of WILLIAM H.--
HILL CARTER and EDMOND WINSTON, Amherst County, to be committee and
$1.00 paid to seal. Witnesses: MAYO CABELL, EDWARD A. CABELL,
J. M. BROWN, LITTLEBERRY N. LIGON.

252. 18 November 1822. CHARITY MOSS, H. initial, to THOMAS ALDRIDGE,
     Amherst County...$700 50 acres--share in estate of father,
WILLIAM MOSS, Amherst County, deceased--reference to division by
commissioner. DAVID S. GARLAND and JAMES L. DILLARD, Justices of
the Peace.

252. 18 November 1822. WILLIAM LONG to BENNET A. CRAWFORD and
     THOMAS WRIGHT, Amherst County...$1.00; debt to JOSEPH ECHOLS,
Lynchburg; tobacco on plantation called Lanewille. To THOMAS WRIGHT,
17 May 1823.

253. 21 December 1822. HENRY FULCHER and wife, DELILAH, Amherst
County, to THOMAS MILES, Amherst County...$250 52 acres;
JONATHAN COLEMAN and EDMOND PENN, Justices of the Peace. To THOMAS
MILES, 6 June 1840.

253. 21 December 1822. JAMES FULCHER and wife, SALLY, to THOMAS
MILES, Amherst County...$700 140 acres conveyed by ELIZABETH
FULCHER to STERLING CLAIBORNE as trustee for JAMES FULCHER. Justices
of the Peace as above.

254. 10 August 1821. WILLIAM ATKINSON, BENAJA CLEVELAND and wife,
PATSY, legal heirs of ISAIAH ATKINSON, deceased, Amherst County,
to PETER BURROUGHS, Amherst County...$2000.00 334 acres Rocky Run.
Lines: JACOB PIERCE, WALTER CHRISTIAN, ABSALOM HOWL, CATLETT CAMPBELL,
WILEY CAMPBELL. Lynchburg Justices of the Peace as to wife of
CLEVELAND: SAMUEL NOWLIN and JONATHAN THURMAN.

255. 27 November 1822. JONATHAN PUGH, SR., 1; SAMUEL P. LAIN, 2;
WILLIAM MC DANIEL, 3...debt to WILLIAM MC DANIEL; $1.00, stock,
furniture, wheelwright tools, loom.

256. 1 January 1823. REUBEN PENDLETON, Amherst County, to JAMES
LLE, Amherst County...to CORNELIUS CROW, 9 August 1823--$1.00;
slave bought at sale of MILLNER COX; debt due REUBEN NORVELL,
commissioner, bondsmen: ARCHELAUS REYNOLDS and CORNELIUS CREW.
Lynchburg Justices of the Peace: SAMUEL NOWLIN and JONATHAN THURMAN.

257. 15 January 1823. MARTIN LONDON, Smith County, Tennessee, to
brother, JONATHAN LONDON, Amherst County, as to Amherst County
business...To JONATHAN LONDON, 18 March 1824.

258. 7 January 1823. WILLIAM H. GAYLE, Amherst County, to SAMUEL McD.
MOORE, Rockbridge County...$1.00; debt to bondsman: SAMUEL McD.
REID in debt suits by WILLIAM LUSK, Rockbridge; bond by JONATHAN
THOMPSON, JR. and GAYLE to Sheriff of Kanawaha County--THOMPSON as
guardian of legatees of JONATHAN GAYLE, deceased, for benefit of
SPENCER FALCONER versus ROWLAND SANDIDGE, JONATHAN RICHESON, RICHARD
HARTLESS--bond of 31 December 1822; slave about thirteen. JONATHAN
LEYBURN and ALEXANDER SHIELDS, Rockbridge Justices of the Peace.

259. 22 January 1823. WILLIAM SIMMONS and wife, ESTHER, Amherst
County, to ABSALOM HOWL, Amherst County...L204 108 acres Rocky
Run. Lines: grantee, JACOB PIERCE, CHARLES W. CHRISTIAN.

259. 23 January 1823. HENRY H. EVANS and PHILIP THURMOND, SR. to
THOMAS N. EUBANK, Amherst County, 2; RICHARD L. ELLIS, Amherst
County, 3; ELLIS and EUBANK, Amherst County, 4...to secure debts to
RICHARD L. ELLIS and ELLIS and EUBANK; $1.00; slaves, stock, copper
still, crops, furniture. JONATHAN ELLIS and DABNEY WARE, Justices
of the Peace.

260. 21 January 1823. THOMAS EDWARDS, Amherst County, and wife,
ELIZABETH...THOMAS for her support and protection of dower--life
estate--tract bought of WILLIAM MOORE. Lines: THOMAS WILCOX,
deceased; road from my MH to Migginson road and WILLIAM D. HILL and
whereon I have lately built--50 acres and slaves.

261. 29 November 1822. JONATHAN WARWICK, late Sheriff, to WILLIAM
DILLARD, Amherst County...RICHARD HARTLESS, 30 September 1822,
took insolvent oath--300 acres. Lines: HENRY FRANKLIN; also 35 acres
and reference to deed; advertised and sold, 29 November 1822, at home
of HARTLESS and bought by DILLARD--300 acres at $111.00 and 35 acres
at $9.00--plus $1.00. To WILLIAM DILLARD, 24 October 1823.

262. 4 January 1823. WILLIAM BURTON to HUDSON M. GARLAND...all
interest to certain proceeding in Superior Court of Amherst
County versus Justices of the Peace of Amherst County for not providing
and keeping a sufficient jail for county. Witness: S. R. DAVIES.

262. 3 February 1823. SAMUEL and JAMES COLEMAN, Amherst County, 1; ALLEN TALBOT, 2; ELIJAH FLETCHER, Amherst County, 3...$1.00 145 acres. Lines: WILLIAM PETERS, deceased, HARDWICK heirs, JABEZ COLEMAN, JAMES WILLMORE. To ELIJAH FLETCHER, 23 February 1824.

263. 27 December 1822. CHALRES WILLS and wife, MARY G., Amherst County, 1; DAVIDSON BRADFUTE, Lynchburg, 2; President and Directors of Bank of Virginia, 3...$1.00 652 acres where CHARLES WILLS lives. Lines: WILLIAM GUTREY. JAMES L. LAMKIN and RICHARD HARRISON, Justices of the Peace.

264. 15 November 1822. WILL LONG to THOMAS CREWS, WILLIAM and BETSY BRYDIE, heirs of ALEXANDER BRYDIE...all interest in amount from sale of WHITEHALL by decree: NEILL MC CALL in Richmond Chancery; also sale of The Grove in case of CHARLES CLARK, Lynchburg Chancery. To THOMAS CREWS, 13 October 1823. Note: I have made comment that we are unable to tract Sweet Briar title, but it is stated that Sweet Briar House--president's home--was once that of THOMAS CREWS. Some CREWS descendants have an old picture wherein the place is called Locust Ridge. In Q is another title as to this same group, but no definite description.

265. 24 September 1821. MATTHEW BURKS, Nelson County, to SAMUEL COLEMAN, Amherst County...$1220 122½ acres south borders Harris. Lines: JONATHAN CMBLER, RICHARD PENDLETON, THOMAS COLEMAN.

265. 7 February 1823. WILLIS RUCKER, Amherst County, 1; SAMUEL GARLAND and GEORGE W. TURNER, Lynchburg, 2; ARCHELAUS ROBERTSON, Lynchburg, 3...SAMUEL GARLAND and GEORGE W. TURNER, bondsmen for WILLIS RUCKER as guardian of brothers, JONATHAN L. D. and RICHARD F. RUCKER; debt to ARCHELAUS ROBERTSON; THOMAS WRIGHT on bond to RICHARD SHELTON, JR. and assigned to ARCHELAUS ROBERTSON; $1.00; slaves, furniture, interest in estate of JONATHAN RUCKER and in possession of widow, NANCY. Lynchburg Justices of the Peace: JONATHAN HANCOCK and ALBON MC DANIEL. To GEORGE W. TURNER, 17 February 1823.

266. 2 December 1822. JONATHAN BROWN, Amherst County, to WILLIAM ARMISTEAD, Amherst County...$1.00 to secure MERIT M. and WILLIAM WHITE 201 acres headwaters of south fork Buffaloe. Lines: JESSE RICHESON, LINDSEY BURKS, JONATHAN FLOOD, BENJAMIN SANDIDGE and where JONATHAN BROWN lately lived.

267. 17 February 1823. STERLING CLAIBORNE and wife, JANE M., to JONATHAN HAAS...$1120 112 acres near Buffaloe Springs. Lines: side of the road. Memo: one acre deducted for DAVID CLARKSON and 112 acres left. To JONATHAN HAAS, 18 March 1824.

168. 4 February 1823. WILLIAM HARTLESS and wife, NANCY, Amherst County, to JESSE RICHESON, Amherst County...$1314.00 438 acres Brown Mountain Creek, branch of Pedlar. NELSON CRAWFORD and WILLIAM JOPLING, Justices of the Peace. To JESSE RICHESON, 19 March 1824.

269. 6 December 1822. WALTER WILLIAMS and wife, MOURNING, PETER P. THORNTON to RICHARD L. ELLIS...$300 54½ acres headwaters Maple Creek. Lines: ANDERSON WARE, ALLISON MORRIS, a branch, bought from WILLIAM NOEL and by WILLIAMS to PETER P. THORNTON and by THORNTON to ELLIS. Witnesses: WILLIAM SHELTON, JONATHAN MEHONE, AMBROSE MORELAND, JORDAN CREASY. To RICHARD L. ELLIS, by JONATHAN W. YOUNG, 25 August 1823.

270. 17 February 1823. GEORGE S. HOLLOWAY, Amherst County, to JACOB HAAS, Amherst County...$600 two tracts bought by PHILIP LIVELY from RICHARD HARRISON and sold by LIVELY to HOLLOWAY, 22 October 1822. 1. 180 acres. 2. 50 acres. Lynchburg Justices of the Peace: JONATHAN THURMAN and SAMUEL NOWLIN.

270. 11 January 1822. WIATT SMITH, Amherst County, to HENRY HAGER,
      Amherst County, 2; JAMES L. PENDLETON, 3, and Company...$1.00;
beds, etc. Witnesses: JOSEPH STAPLES, SAMUEL W. CHRISTIAN.

272. 19 February 1823. MERIT M. WHITE and wife, JUDITH P., 1;
      WILLIAM ARMISTEAD, 2; ROBERT and ALEXANDER TINSLEY, 3...
ALEXANDER TINSLEY on bond to WILLIAM MORGAN, GEORGE S. HOLLOWAY,
Bank of Virginia, GARLAND, WALTON, and PENN; $1.00 paid by WILLIAM
ARMISTEAD; slaves and children; furniture, stock, crops, six lots
in Bethel: 17, 18, 21, 22, 23, 24--9/10 interest in them; goods at
WHITE's store in Bethel; four batteaux; interest in estate of
JOSHUA TINSLEY, deceased. Witnesses: JONATHAN WILLS, JONATHAN HANCOK
and ALBON MC DANIEL, Lynchburg Justices of the Peace. To ALEXANDER
TINSLEY, 20 October 1823.

274. 26 January 1822. MOSES MARTIN, SR., Amherst County, to BENNET A.
      CRAWFORD, Amherst County...$500 100 acres Brown Creek. Road
over PRYOR's Gap passes through it. Part of tract bought from JESSE
RICHESON. Lines: REUBEN L. TYREE, ford of creek. Subject to Deed
of Trust for benefit of THOMAS RICHESON which MARTIN claims was
obtained by fraud--has sued in Lynchburg Chancery to amend. ELIZABETH,
wife of MARTIN, signs. Witnesses: CHARLES L. BARRET, J. W. YOUNG,
JOSEPH TOWNSEND, EDWARD LANKFORD. CHARLES L. BARRET and NELSON
CRAWFORD, Justices of the Peace.

275. 25 February 1823. CHARLES DAIRY, debtor, to SAMUEL R. DAVIES, 2;
      JESSE KENNEDY, 3...Deed of Trust to secure JESSE KENNEDY;
bond to WIATT DUNCAN, JONATHAN L. BLAIR; $1.00 180 acres--tract bought
from ROBERT RIVERS. Lines: CORNELIUS SALE, a tract by entry--25 or
30 acres next to 180; tract in Harrisburg, County, Pennsylvania.
500 acres; interest in Superior Court suit, Amherst County, between
self and ROBERT RIVERS; slander--suit between self and THOMAS
ALDRIDGE in same court; all claims versus Amherst County for work on
public bridge on Buffaloe between New Glasgow and ACH; levy made to
DAVID S. GARLAND; all interest in estate of REUBEN COLEMAN, deceased--
mason's work; claim versus THOMAS WILLIAMSON. To SAMUEL R. DAVIES,
13 June 1823.

276. 27 August 1822. BARKSDALE SLEDD and wife, LUCY, Bedford
      County, to TINSLEY RUCKER, Amherst County, 2; WILLIAM I.
IEBELL, Amherst County, 3...judgements due WILLIAM I. IEBELL; $1.00
for benefit of ALEXANDER GARVEN--slaves, stock, claim versus estate
of WILLIAM PETERS, deceased, in pending suit; claim versus WIATT
SMITH, JONATHAN DUNCAN, JAMES TANKERSLEY, JACK MITCHELL, PHILIP
THURMOND. Bedford Justices of the Peace: THOMAS SALE and JACOB
WHITE.

277. 1 March 1823. WILLIAM P. MUSE, Amherst County, to MILLNER
      COX, Amherst County...all interest in estate bought from
HARRISON HUGHES; part of estate of WILLIAM HUGHES, SR., Amherst
County; $100--also power of attorney to COX. Witnesses: WILLIAM D.
HILL, AMOS THACKER, JONATHAN F. (H) GOODWIN, SR. To MILLNER COX,
8 March 1823.

278. 13 March 1823. WILLIAM R. ROANE, Amherst County, to MATTHEW,
      JONATHAN F., LUCINDA, WILLIAM P., NINNY EALENOR BURKS, SARAH
ANN, MARY JANE, HENRIETTA MILDRED, and EMELINE ELIZABETH BURKS...$1.00
carriage and harness; children of RICHARD BURKS, Amherst County.
Witnesses: WILLIAM SHELTON, ISAAC TINSLEY, DABNEY WARE and EDMOND
WINSTON, Justices of the Peace.

279. 8 March 1823. WILLIAM P. MUSE, 1; SAMUEL R. DAVIES and JONATHAN
      TOLBERT, 2; WILLIAM SMITHSON, 3...WILLIAM SMITHSON bondsman in
suit: JEREMIAH H. HYLTON versus MUSE--Amherst County Court; suit of
JONATHAN WARWICK, administrator versus MUSE. $1.00; 21½ acres 17½
acres and adjoins WILLIAM P. MUSE and REUBEN NORVELL. 7½ acres bought
from WILLIAM JENKINS. 40 acres--Deed of Trust on it to MILLNER COX.
Three acres "in the Lynchburg 4 from Town" (sic).

238

280.	13 March 1823. RAWLEY FEAGANS, Amherst County, to GEORGE
	FEAGANS, Amherst County...to secure debt to GEORGE; $1.00;
slaves, stock, furnitre. Witness: ROBERT CAMM.

280.	6 March 1823. RICHARD H. BURKS and wife, POLLY, WILLIAM SHELTON,
	trustee of RICHARD BURKS, Amherst County, to WILLIAM R. ROANE,
Amherst County...$700 184 acres east side Tobacco Row. Bought from
ROBERT MC CALPHIN by RICHARD BURKS. Lines: road to CRAWFORD's Gap,
near AMBROSE LUCAS' house. Reference to Deed of Trust, 15 March
1822. Witnesses: THOMAS D. HILL, WILLIAM KNIGHT, ISAAC TINSLEY,
JONATHAN F. BURKS. DABNEY WARE and EDMOND WINSTON, Justices of the
Peace.

280.	21 April 1823. JAMES L. PENDLETON and RICHARD H. BURKS, 1;
	ELIAS WILLS and wife, MARY G., 2; RICHARD HARRISON and JONATHAN M.
SETTLE, 3...wills and wife on 8 April 1820, executed Deed of Trust
to JAMES L. PENDLETON and RICHARD H. BURKS on 105½ acres and bought
from BENJAMIN GOSNEY.

281.	1 March 1823. THOMAS WIATT, executor of JONATHAN MILLER, to
	CHISWELL DABNEY...$400 24 3/4 acres near Lynchburg. Lines:
LYNCH, grantee, Lynch road. Lynchburg Justices of the Peace:
CHRISTOPHER WINFREE and T. A. HOLCOMBE.

282.	6 March 1823. RICHARD H. BURKS and wife, POLLY, Amherst County,
	to WILLIAM R. ROANE, Amherst County...$50 50 acres Harris Creek
and Tobacco Row. Lines: former tract of R. BURKS and sold to
WILLIAM R. ROANE, ISBELL, old patent line. Witnesses: TERRY.
Surveyed by CHARLES L. CHRISTIAN. Other witnesses: WILLIAM SHELTON,
ISAAC TINSLEY, RICHARD H. BURKS, WILLIAM KNIGHT, THOMAS D. HILL,
JONATHAN F. BURKS. Justices of the Peace: EDMOND WINSTON and
DABNEY WARE. TERRY seems to be W. TERRY and adjoining owner.

283.	18 January 1823. WILLIAM STAPLES, Campbell County, to DANIEL
	STAPLES, Amherst County...$5000 33 acres German Mills in Amherst
County. Lines: the river, below mouth of Porrage, DILLARD.

284.	18 January 1823. GEORGE STAPLES, Amherst County, to JAMES
	STAPLES, Campbell County...$900 10½ acres Island in James
River--one mile above mouth of Porrage and opposite WILLIAM GALT--
Chase Island.

285.	17 March 1823. WILLIAM LAVENDER, Amherst County, 1; CORNELIUS
	POWELL, Amherst County, 2; D. and D. HIGGINBOTHAM and Company,
3...$1.00; furniture, interest in slave in mother's possession in
North Carolina; debt from JONATHAN PENN, farm tools. To JAMES D.
HIGGINBOTHAM, agent for county, 7 June 1824.

286.	15 March 1823. WILLIAM CLARKSON, Amherst County, 1; to
	JONATHAN MOSS and RICHARS SMITH, JR., 2; HENRY FRANKLIN, 3...
$1.00, stock, furniture, tools.

287.	And Page 288 are blanks in book, but no mention of any missing
	data. This involves 289 as well--blank.

290.	15 March 1832. MERIT M. and WILLIAM WHITE, Bethel, to WILLIAM
	ARMISTEAD, Amherst County...$1.00--WILLIAM ARMISTEAD is bondsman
to executor of RICHARD SHELTON, BOYD MILLER and Company, ARCHELAUS
ROBERTSON and Company--suit pending in Amherst County Superior
Court, ROBERT TINSLEY, bedford, ALEXANDER TINSLEY, Amherst County--
bondsman to WILLIAM MORGAN, GEORGE S. HOLLOWAY, JONATHAN TALBOT,
deputy to JAMES M. BROWN, Amherst County Sheriff--stock in Bethel
store, slave, furniture. Witnesses: JONATHAN ROBINSON, THOMAS
LAINE, EDWARD CARTER.

291. 11 March 1823. CLIFTON HARRIS, Albemarle County, to WESLEY
CHRISTIAN...consideration: 160 acres southwest quarter of
Township 54, south in Range 17, west--in military tract--Act of
6 May 1812, in Missouri, and patent 4 March 1819. Amherst County
tract on south side Blue Ridge. Lines: HENRY HARTLESS--100 acres.
Witnesses: BENJAMIN TALIAFERRO, JONATHAN F. TALIAFERRO, DABNEY
SANDIDGE.

292. 20 February 1823. CHARLES WINGFIELD and wife, ELIZABETH,
Amherst County, to JACOB HASS, Bedford...$450 134 acres. Lines:
ELIJAH MAYS, BOLLING, JONATHAN BOND, deceased. Justices of the Peace:
NELSON DAWSON and JAMES L. LAMKIN. To JACOB HASS, 19 March 1828.

294. 18 January 1823. WILLIAM STAPLES, Campbell County, to son,
GEORGE STAPLES, Amherst County...love and to support son--256
acres on James River. Lines: SAMUEL TURNER, CAPTAIN JAMES DILLARD,
DAVID STAPLES.

294. 17 March 1823. WALTER CHRISTIAN, Amherst County, to THOMAS N.
EUBANK, Amherst County...$1.00; debts to RICHARD L. ELLIS and
ELLIS and EUBANK, slaves. Witnesses: JONATHAN W. YOUNG, JESSE
RICHESON, SAMUEL W. DICKEN. To RICHARD L. ELLIS, 20 May 1823.

296. 25 February 1823. ISAAC SCOTT and wife, MARTHA, Amherst County,
to JONAH PIERCE, Amherst County...$300 245 acres Rocky Run.
Lines: JACOB PIERCE, JONATHAN TYLER, DANIEL CHEATWOOD. One-seventh
interest of MARTHA as daughter of WILLIAM DILLARD, deceased.
Witnesses: WILLIAM M. WALLER, HOWARD CASH, EDWARD WOOTEN. Justices
of the Peace: HENRY H. WATTS and WILLIAM M. WALLER.

297. 6 November 1822. JAMES POWELL and LINDSEY COLEMAN as to JANE
CHRISTIAN, wife of SAMUEL D. CHRISTIAN, 15 March 1819...deed
to DABNEY HILL. To DABNEY HILL, 19 May 1824.

297. 17 March 1823. CORNELIUS SALE, Commissioner, to ABRAM MARTIN,
Amherst County...decree of court between heirs of JONATHAN
MARTIN, SR., Amherst County, intestate. SALE and JONATHAN SMITH and
--, Commissioners, sold Franklin Creek tract of 150 acres and
including 21 acres sold by JONATHAN MARTIN to ABRAM MARTIN in lifetime;
reference to orders and to deed to JONATHAN MARTIN from JACOB SMITH,
deceased, Amherst County--blank sum, bondsman not named. Witnesses:
MATTHEW KNIGHT, JAMES H. MARTIN, PLEASANT LAWHORN.

299. 14 February 1823. SARAH H. ARMISTEAD, Amherst County, to
JONATHAN P. COBBS and wife, JANE M., Nelson County...for love
of SARAH for niece, JANE M. and $1.00; in trust to COBBS for wife.
Lines: Lynch road, DAVID S. GARLAND, the Glebe, held in trust by
JAMES L. PENDLETON for SARAH under will of father, COLONEL SAMUEL
MEREDITH, deceased. SARAH to enjoh for life and at death, COBBS to
enter--reference to JANE's children, but not named. Justices of the
Peace: EDMOND PENN and ROBERT TINSLEY.

301. 20 March 1823. JONATHAN COLEMAN, Amherst County, 1; GEORGE M.
TURNER, Lynchburg and JONATHAN TALBORT, Amherst County, 2;
SAMUEL GARLAND, Lynchburg, 3...$1.00--tract from ELIZABETH COLEMAN
to JAMES COLEMAN as legatee, slaves.

302. 21 April 1823. JONATHAN MYERS, Amherst County, 1; LINDSEY
MC DANILE, Amherst County, 2; WILLIAM MC DANIEL and JAMES
PENDLETON, Amherst County, 3...$1.00; WILLIAM MC DANIEL and JAMES
PENDLETON as bondsmen to SHEPHERD and WEBB in suit pending Amherst
County Superior Court, Bank of Virginia; one negro woman of dark
complexion and children; other slaves, furniture, stock. To LINDSEY
MC DANIEL, 4 October 1824.

303. 7 December 1822. WALTER CHRISTIAN to THOMAS C. CHRISTIAN...$50
slave, ADAM. Witnesses: ROBERT and COURTNEY CHRISTIAN. To
THOMAS C. CHRISTIAN, 11 January 1834.

304. 29 March 1823. WILLIAM MUSE, SR., 1; WILLIAM D. HILL, 2;
     JONATHAN H. GOODWIN, 3...$1.00, beds, tools. Witnesses:
CATHERINE BURCH, EDMOND J. HILL.

305. 8 April 1823. PLEASANT LAWHORNE, Amherst County, 1; DABNEY
     SANDIDGE, Amherst County, 2; WILLIAM MARTIN, Amherst County, 3...
$1.00, stock, tools.

307. 31 December 1822. THOMAS H. BASS and wife, NANCY, Amherst
     County, to JONATHAN MC DANIEL, Amherst County...$800 interest
in estate of DAVID WOODROOF, JR., Amherst County, deceased. Witnesses:
THOMAS CREWS, PHILIP LIVELY, LINDSEY MC DANIEL, THOMAS G. HOLLOWAY
and LINDSEY COLEMAN, Justices of the Peace. To JONATHAN MC DANIEL,
23 June 1829.

307. 19 April 1823. SHEROD M. GILLASPIE, Amherst County, 1; RICHARD N.
     EUBANK, Amherst County, 2; WILLIAM JOPLING, Amherst County, 3,
agent for HOLEMAN JOPLING, Nelson County...$1.00; horse, furniture,
tools. Witnesses: J. W. YOUNG, J. E. TALIAFERRO. Note: This is
CAPTAIN SHERAD MOORE GILLESPIE, son of GEORGE GILLESPIE, and brother
of my wife's ancestor, WILLIAM GILLESPIE, who married ANN HUDSON and
went to Madison County, Kentucky.

308. 15 April 1823. DAVID STAPLES, Amherst County, 1; CHARLES
     MUNDY and JONATHAN DILLARD, Amherst County, 2; DANIEL DAY,
Amherst County, 3...$1.00; 33 acres. Lines: mouth of Porrage,
DILLARD. To DANIEL DAY, 21 March 1831.

310. 21 April 1823. ROBERT LAWHORN, Amherst County, 1; SAMUEL R.
     DAVIES, Amherst County, 2; THOMAS LAWHORN, Amherst County, 3...
$1.00, furniture, stock.

311. 21 April 1823. CHRISTOPHER ISBELL, Amherst County, 1; CHRISTOPHER
     ANTHONY, Amherst County, 2; REUBEN NORVELL, Amherst County, 3...
REUBEN NORVELL bondsman to THOMAS T. BALDWIN, assignee of JONATHAN
and MARSHALL J. COUCH, siere facias in Bedford Superior Court. $5.00;
long list of slaves.

312. 28 August 1822. JONATHAN RUCKER, Amherst County, to AMBROSE
     RUCKER, Amherst County...to secure him for slave hire and
bondsman to N. C. DAWSON; $1.00, stock, crops. Witnesses: DABNEY
WARE, JOSEPH MC CARY, WILLIAM WARE. To AMBROSE RUCKER, 1823.

313. 14 April 1823. NELSON CRAWFORD, Amherst County, to BENJAMIN B.
     TALIAFERRO, Amherst County...deed of gift--BENJAMIN TALIAFERRO
married JUDITH, daughter of NELSON CRAWFORD--180 acres. Part of tract.
Lines: WILLIAM SHEPHERD, THOMAS MORRIS.

314. 22 April 1823. RICHARD HATTEN, Amherst County, 1; LUCAS P.
     THOMPSON, Amherst County, 2; J. S. PENDLETON, Amherst County, 3...
$1.00, stock, furniture, tools, crops. Justices of the Peace:
REUBEN NORVELL and JONATHAN COLEMAN.

315. 24 April 1823. JAMES WILMORE, Amherst County, to CORNELIUS
     POWELL, Amherst County...$1.00; debt to DAVID and DANIEL
HIGGINBOTHAM and THOMAS HIGGINBOTHAM, merchants, Amherst County,
LINDSEY COLEMAN, JAMES POWELL. 140 acres. Lines: JAMES POWELL,
HARDWICK heirs, JAMES COLEMAN. Bought from JONATHAN MC DANIEL--
stock, furniture. To CORNELIUS POWELL, 2 June 1823.

316. 24 January 1823. HENRY ROACH, Amherst County, to HENRY LANDON
     ROACH, Amherst County...$1.00 and love for his son, HENRY
LANDON ROACH--125 acres. Lines: GEORGE ROACH, HENRY ROACH, grantee's
house, WILLIAM MITCHELL, ARCHIBALD GILLIAM, WILLIAM ROACH, Wilderness
Creek. THOMAS N. EUBANK and JONATHAN ELLIS, Justices of the Peace.

317. 9 April 1823. JONATHAN N. ROSE and wife, MARY, Nelson County,
        to JONATHAN P. COBBS and JAMES S. PENN, 2; SPOTSWOOD GARLAND,
3...$1.00 GARLAND is bondsman to JOSEPH E. ROYAL and THOMAS A.
HOLCOMB, executors of WILLIAM ROYAL, GUSTAVUS A. ROSE, SAMUEL P.
CHRISTIAN. Late Amherst County residence on left on main road from
ROSE and THOMPSON's Mill to New Glasgow--300 acres. Part of tract
given to JONATHAN N. by father, PATRICK ROSE, by deed. At that time
it contained 530 acres. Lines: THOMAS ALDRIDGE, WILLIAM MOSS'
heirs, ROSE, THOMPSON, named slaves, stock, crops, furniture. Also
owes WILLIAM M. WALLER, Amherst County, DAVID S. GARLAND, ELIZABETH N.
PRICE, Nelson County, ROBERT S. ROSE, New York, MORGAN and MC DANIEL,
BRADFORD and HANNAH Company, JAMES S. PENDLETON and Company, D. and
D. HIGGINBOTHAM, ALDRIDGE and MYERS, JOSEPH MARX, Richmond. Memo:
part released to ROSE to dispose of. Lines: main road, about
100 yards above house occupied by WILLIAM STAPLES, the Mill, ROSE
and THOMPSON--five to seven acres. To SPOTSWOOD GARLAND, 1823.

321. 7 March 1823. RICHARD HATTEN, Amherst County, 1; DABNEY SANDIDGE,
        Amherst County, 2; WILLIAM MARTIN, SR., Amherst County, 3...
$1.00 rent bond to WILLIAM HANNAH and JAMES M. SMITH, constable;
stock, tools, furniture. Memo: for benefit of HANNAH. Witnesses:
A. ROBERTSON. To DABNEY SANDIDGE, 19 June 1823.

323. 17 March 1823. JONATHAN COLEMAN and wife, SARAH, Amherst
        County, to JONATHAN DILLARD, Amherst County...$30 1½ acres.
Lines: JONATHAN CHRISTIAN, GOOCH, a road, JAMES D. DILLARD.

323. 12 October 1822. JONATHAN J. MARTIN, CHARLES BARRET, 2, to
        WILLIAM COLEMAN, Amherst County, 3...$1.00; to secure CHARLES
BARRET; stock, furniture, etc. Witnesses: GEORGE W. YOUNG, WILLIAM
COLEMAN, workman, MOSES TAYLOR, WILLIAM ROGERS.

324. 19 May 1823. ROBERT P. CRUTCHER, Amherst County, 1; PEACHY
        FRANKLIN, Amherst County, 2; JONATHAN MOUNTCASTLE, Amherst
County, 3...$1.00; named slaves, furniture, tools.

325. 19 May 1823. WILLIAM WOOD, Amherst County, to SAMUEL P.
        CHRISTIAN, Buckingham County...$..00; judgements in Amherst
County Court: HORSLEY and FARRIS, JONATHAN HORSLEY, JR., agent for
ARCHIBALD HYLTON, administrator of JONATHAN HYLTON--stock, furniture,
property lent me by WILLIS CARTER.

326. 9 May 1823. ELIAS WILLS and wife, MARY G., Amherst County, to
        WILLIAM PENDLETON, Amherst County...$700 105½ acres on James
River and where RICHARD WHITEHEAD lived and sold by him to BENJAMIN
GOING, Pittsylvania, and by BENJAMIN GOING to ELIAS WILLS. Lines:
JAMES WILLS. Justices of the Peace: NELSON C. DAWSON and JAMES L.
LAMKIN. To WILLIAM PENDLETON, 28 April 1824.

328. 14 May 1823. HUGH TAGGART, Amherst County, 1; DAVID S. GARLAND,
        Amherst County, 2; to JOSEPH PENN, Amherst County, 3...$1.00
to protect DAVID S. GARLAND; stock, furniture, horse cart at LINDSEY
SANDIDGE's. Witnesses: J. HAIGH, RICHARD J. WAUGH, JONATHAN S.
BLAIR, SAMUEL W. CHRISTIAN.

328. 10 May 1823. SAMUEL COLEMAN, Amherst County, 1; GEORGE W.
        TURNER and BLANFORD HIX, 2; ARCHELAUS ROBERTSON, Lynchburg, 3...
and debts to WILLIAM BLACK, JONATHAN and BENNET MOOHN. $1.00; tract
on Harris. Lines: THOMAS COLEMAN, 110 acres and conveyed by SAMUEL
COLEMAN to JAMES F. TALIAFERRO on Deed of Trust to secure POWELL and
TALIAFERRO and assigned to ROBERTSON; 105 and 120 acres conveyed to
HOLLOWAY and CLAIBORNE for benefit of WILLIAM DILLARD on HARRIS.
Lines: THOMAS COLEMAN, DANIEL F. CHRISTIAN. Also tract adjoining
CABELL's tract on Bear Mountain--42½ acres; slaves, stock, furniture,
tools. Memo: no claims--versus above by JONATHAN S. COLEMAN and
WINSTON L. COLEMAN.

330.   9 November 1822.   WILLIAM JENKINS and wife, MARGARET, Amherst
       County, to WILLIAM P. MUSE, Amherst County...$50 5½ acres
east side and joining MITCHELL's road.   Lines: grantee, ELIAS
WILLS, MILLNER COX.   Bought from REUBEN NORVELL.   REUBEN NORVELL and
JAMES L. LAMKIN, Justices of the Peace.

331.   19 May 1823.   ELIAS WILLS, 1; to DAVID S. GARLAND and sundry
       creditors: STERLING CLAIBORNE, WILLIAM TURNER, JONATHAN WILLS,
THOMAS HIGGINBOTHAM, SAMUEL GARLAND in own right and agent for
BOYD MILLER, Farmers Bank of Virginia at Lynchburg, ARCHELAUS ROBERTSON,
JAMES L. PENDLETON, WILLIAM B. JACOB, DANIEL MORGAN...$1.00 300 acres
next to where ELIAS WILLS lives and that not previously conveyed;
four slaves in Fluvanna named; stock, tools, furniture in Amherst
County and Fluvanna.   STERLING CLAIBORNE on bond in Superior Court
of Amherst County--suit of JONATHAN TIMBERLAKE, appealed.

333.   21 March 1823.   RICHARD L. ELLIS, 1; ELLIS and EUBANK, 2; to
       LINDSEY BURKS, Amherst County, 3...covenant with BURKS to live
with them as overseer for 1823 and 1824--where BURKS lives on Long
Mountain and bought from him by them in two Deeds of Trust; slaves,
tools, stock, furniture--long and interesting list--$150.00 per year;
bacon for family, to be directed by RICHARD L. ELLIS and ELLIS and
EUBANK.   Witnesses: JONATHAN W. YOUNG, THOMAS S. STONE, ROWLAND
SANDIDGE.

334.   29 April 1823.   SAMUEL COLEMAN, Amherst County, 1; SAMUEL GARLAND
       and GEORGE W. TURNER, 2; ARCHELAUS ROBERTSON, 3...$1.00; slaves
and ages.   Lynchburg Justices of the Peace: SAMUEL NOWLING and
DANIEL BROWN.

335.   20 May 1823.   ISAAC TINSLEY, Amherst County, 1; EDMOND WINSTON, 2;
       ALEXANDER TINSLEY, Amherst County, 3...ALEXANDER TINSLEY on
bond on execution in Superior Court of Amherst County for ARCHELAUS
ROBERTSON, SAMUEL READ, BOYD MILLER, late merchants of ROBERTSON and
Company who sued for MILLER.   Slaves at $1.00.   Witnesses: RICHARD
BURKS, D. T. PHILLIPS, WILLIAM WHITE.   CAPTAIN ISAAC TINSLEY is at
liberty to sell--signed: ALEXANDER TINSLEY.

336.   20 May 1823.   BENJAMIN HIGGINBOTHAM, Amherst County, to DAVID S.
       GARLAND, Amherst County...$450 for support of SUSANNAH SMITH,
wife of JAMES SMITH, estate delivered of JOSEPH HIGGINBOTHAM,
deceased--31 slaves "of all sizes" devised by JOSEPH to BENJAMIN
HIGGINBOTHAM.   To --, agent for DAVID S. GARLAND, 10 November 1823.

336.   1 January 1823.   WILLIAM SHELTON to WILLIAM ARMISTEAD for
       benefit of SHELTON's daughter, ELIZA JANE, wife of RICHARD H.
BURKS, and her children--apart from him...$1.00; slaves, furniture.
To WILLIAM ARMISTEAD, 15 August 1823.

337.   25 May 1823.   WILLIAM S. APPLEBERRY, 1; GUSTAVUS A. ROSE, 2;
       SPENCER NORVELL, 3, DELAWARE HILL, JOSEPH MC CARY, Amherst
County, 3...$1.00; NORVELL is bondsman for WILLIAM S. APPLEBERRY to
WILLIAM LEE for benefit of GEORGE S. HOLLOWAY and others: SPENCER
NORVELL, DELAWARE HILL and JOSEPH MC CARY; slaves, stock, etc.
Signed THOMAS D. HILL.   To SPENCER NORVELL per WILLIAM S. APPLEBERRY,
12 April 1824.

337.   14 May 1823.   SOLOMON RITCHIE, Amherst County, 1; ISAAC RUCKER,
       Amherst County, 2; ANDERSON WARE, Amherst County, 3...$1.00
100 acres where SOLOMON RITCHIE lives; middle fork Pedlar; stock.

339.   21 May 1823.   OBADIAH HENDERSON, Amherst County, 1; ARTHUR B.
       DAVIES, Amherst County and WILLIAM DILLARD, Amherst County, 2;
JAMES S. DILLARD, Amherst County, 3...$1.00; slaves, stock, etc.
To JAMES S. DILLARD, 28 July 1823.

340. 29 May 1823. JESSE WOODROOF, Amherst County, 1; LINDSEY
      MC DANIEL, Amherst County, 2; ELIZABETH WOODROOF, and wife of
JESSE WOODROOF, 3...She relinquished dower in 306 acres; $1.00;
slaves came to him when he married her. Witnesses: S. R. DAVIES,
STEPHEN SUBLETT, JONATHAN ALLEN.

341. 28 May 1823. JESSE WOODROOF and wife, BETSY, Amherst County,
      to LINDSEY MC DANIEL, Amherst County, 2; JONATHAN MYERS, GALT,
BULLOCK and Company, WILLIAM MC DANIEL, THOMAS CREWS, JONATHAN
MC DANIEL, ROBERT WALKER, executors of DAVID WOODROOF, 3...$1.00
300 acres. Lines: WILLIAM MC DANIEL, THOMAS CREWS. Witnesses:
JONATHAN M. TOWNLEY, THOMAS D. HILL, WIAT LONDON, JONATHAN ALLEN,
WILLIAM P. CASHWELL. EDMOND WINSTON and CHARLES P. TALIAFERRO,
Justices of the Peace.

343. 31 May 1823. JESSE WOODROOF and wife, BETSY, to same parties
      as above--plus SAMUEL and STEPHEN HEISKELL, Amherst County...
SAMUEL R. DAVIES for fees--$5.00 each for riding to house of JESSE
WOODROOF, and BENNET A. CRAWFORD for attorney fees--$20; DR. GUSTAVUS A.
ROSE, medical fees; STEPHEN SUBLETT, overseer; HUDSON M. GARLAND,
attorney fees; $1.00; 300 acres where JESSE WOODROOF lives; crops.
Justices of the Peace as above.

344. 4 June 1823. AMBROSE WILLMORE, 1; SAMUEL R. DAVIES, 2;
      LINDSEY COLEMAN, 3...$1.00; debts to LINDSEY COLEMAN; ROBERT
WALKER, bondsman in suit of TIMOTHY FLETCHER, assignee of RICHARD
HARRISON, trustee for NANCY SHIELDS, JONATHAN MYERS--chancery suit.
119 acres where AMBROSE WILLMORE lives. Lines: EDMOND WINSTON,
SAMUEL WATTS. To LINDSEY COLEMAN, 9 May 1826.

346. 5 June 1823. FIELDING BROWN, Amherst County, to CORNELIUS
      POWELL, Amherst County, 2; creditors, 3...D. and D. HIGGINBOTHAM
and Company, H. L. DAVIES, JACOB SMITH, DRURY TUCKER, JONATHAN B.
DUNCAN, WILLIAM M. WALLER, THOMAS ALDRIDGE. $1.00; slaves, stock,
etc. To S. W. CHRISTIAN, agent for D. and D. HIGGINBOTHAM and Company.

347. 5 June 1823. JAMES S. PENDLETON, Amherst County, 1; SAMUEL
      GARLAND, Lynchburg, 2; JONATHAN D. MURRELL, Lynchburg, 3...$1.00
slaves. Lynchburg Justices of the Peace: JONATHAN HANCOCK and
SAMUEL NOWLING. To JONATHAN D. MURRELL, 21 June 1824.

349. 27 May 1823. RICHARD BURKS, Amherst County, to MATTHEW BURKS,
      Tennessee...for benefit of ELIZA JANE BURKS, wife of RICHARD H.
BURKS, and children (also future ones) by my son, RICHARD H. BURKS;
$10.00; slave, REUBEN--until children are of age or married. Sent
to MATTHEW BURKS, 19 August 1823.

350. 8 June 1823. JONATHAN L. WINGFIELD, Amherst County, 1; WILLIAM
      ARMISTEAD, Amherst County, 2; WILLIAM BURFORD, Amherst County,
3...$1.00; 165 acres west side Tobacco Row and where JONATHAN L.
WINGFIELD lives and bought from JACOB HAAS. Lines: RODNEY MC CULLOCH,
CALBE WATTS. To WILLIAM ARMISTEAD, 22 August 1826.

351. 23 May 1823. THOMAS WIATT and RICHARD TYREE to WILLIAM ROBINSON
      and JESSE BECK,..SAMUEL J. HARRISON, 8 July 1819, executor
Deed of Trust--180½ acres. Lines: LINEAS BOLLING, CHRISTOPHER ISBELL,
PHILIP JOHNSON, deceased. Bought by HARRISON from REUBEN POWELL.
Advertised and sold 18 April 1823; brought $8.00 per acre--$1444.
SAMUEL NOWLING and SMITHSON H. DAVIS, Lynchburg Justices of the
Peace. To JONATHAN M. WILLIAMS, administrator of WILLIAM ROBINSON,
12 April 1825.

353. 13 June 1823. WILLIAM WALLER SCOTT and wife, ELIZA A., Amherst
      County, to WIATT PETTYJOHN, Amherst County...$800 33½ acres and
crops--James River Island a few miles above Lynchburg; right to take
wagons over lands of SCOTT. JAMES L. LAMKIN and NELSON C. DAWSON,
Justices of the Peace. To WIATT PETTYJOHN, 19 April 1824.

354. 1 May 1823. THOMAS EDWARDS, 1; CHARLES MUNDY and JONATHAN
    DILLARD, 2; DANIEL DAY, 3...$1.00; two slaves. Witnesses:
THOMAS KNIGHT, WILLIAM DAY, WILLIAM D. HILL. To DANIEL DAY, 3 December
1823.

355. 9 November 1822. THOMAS GOODRICH and wife, ELIZABETH, JONATHAN
    DAMRON and wife, PHEBE, JONATHAN B. GOODRICH and wife, REBECCA,
WIATT DUNCAN and wife, MARY, EDMOND GOODRICH and wife, ELIZABETH,
GIDEON C. GOODRICH and wife, ELIZABETH, JONATHAN HAAS and wife,
SUSAN, BENNETT G. BATES and wife, CATHERINE, WILLIAM SLEDD and wife,
ABIGAIL to WILLIAM MITCHELL, Amherst County...$757.75 180 3/4 acres
west side Tobacco Row. Lines: WIATT DUNCAN, the road. Margin:
R:182 for relinquishment of dower of wife of JONATHAN HAAS. JONATHAN
ELLIS and WILLIAM JOPLING as to wives of THOMAS GOODRICH, WIATT
DUNCAN, EDMOND GOODRICH, GIDEON C. GOODRICH, BENNETT G. BATES. To
GIDEON G. (C) GOODRICH (signed GIDEON C. GOODRICH, 20 October 1825),
per order of WILLIAM MITCHELL.

356. 16 June 1823. ELIJAH L. CHRISTIAN, Amherst County, 1; HENRY H.
    WATTS, Amherst County, 2; DABNEY P. GOOCH, Amherst County, 3...
$1.00; slave boy.

358. 8 April 1823. RICHARD HARRISON, Amherst County, 1; NANCY
    SHIELDS, Amherst County, 2; THOMAS D. HILL, Amherst County, 3...
NANCY SHIELDS has made bond to WILLIAM L. and S. BURKS and one to
JONATHAN WARD--$1.00 crops where RICHARD HARRISON lives, tools;
RICHARD HARRISON to have support for family and to control hands.
To NANCY SHIELDS, 21 July 1823.

359. 14 June 1823. EATON CARPENTER to DRURY TUCKER...$968 121 acres
    Long Branch. Lines: BARNETT CASH, WIATT TUCKER. To DRURY
TUCKER, by HUGH PAGE, 24 June 1843.

360. 9 November 1822. Same grantors--GOODRICH et al. as on page 355
    to WIATT DUNCAN, Amherst County...$1254 209 acres west side
Tobacco Row Mountain. Lines: WILLIAM MITCHELL, RODERICK MC CULLOCH,
CHARLES ELLIS, THURMOND, HARDIN HAYNES, deceased, JONATHAN EUBANK,
deceased, JAMES WARE. Same citation as to wives. To WIATT DUNCAN,
29 October 1825.

361. 12 June 1823. JONATHAN HUDSON, Amherst County, 1; JAMES
    FULCHER, Amherst County, 2; JAMES W. SMITH, Amherst County, 3,
and WILLIAM M. WALLER and Company, Amherst County, 3...margin
scratched--to JAMES FULCHER by CHARLES BARRETT, 9 January 1824--$1.00
93 acres Little Piney. Lines: WILLIAM MOORE, JONATHAN TUCKER,
stock, furniture. Acknowledged by JAMES FULCHER, 2 February 1824.
Witnesses: JONATHAN SMITH, WILLIAM NEVILL, WILLIAM MAYS.

363. 4 June 1823. JAMES S. PENDLETON, Amherst County, to WILLIAM G.
    PENDLETON, Richmond...were partners of JONATHAN G. MOUNTCASTLE
in mercantile business for two years--to 31 July 1820; PENDLETONS
bought out MOUNTCASTLE and operated until 1 January 1822 and dissolved.
Books in hands of JAMES S. PENDLETON; many unpaid accounts--agreement
to place books in hands of JOSEPH PENN, Amherst County. Witness:
DAVID S. GARLAND.

364. 28 May 1823. JONATHAN PAMPLIN, Nelson County, 1; JAMES
    PAMPLIN, JR. and SAMUEL LOVING, 2; WILLIAM L. WATTS, 3...$1.00
72½ acres both sides north fork Elk Island Creek in Nelson, stock.
Lines: WILLIAM LAINE. Sent to Nelson County Court per WILLIAM L.
WATTS, 19 September 1823. Witnesses: J. GARLAND, BEVERLY HARGROVE,
DANIEL NASH.

365. 7 April 1823. DAVID S. GARLAND and wife, JANE M., to WILLIAM
    KNIGHT, Amherst County...$253.75 lot in New Glasgow on west
side Main Street and next to lot 20 occupied by MRS. HUDSON. Also
tract next to town in rear and to east of 4, 5, 6, 7 and occupied
by WILLIAM KNIGHT--5 1/8 acres.

366. 20 February 1823. CHARLES L. BARRET and wife, SALLY, Amherst
      County, to ROBERT TINSLEY, Amherst County...$175.00 50 acres
both sides middle fork Pedlar. Lines: THOMAS JORDAN, ANERSON WARE;
also 50 acres on both sides Pedlar. Lines: THOMAS JORDAN, ANDERSON
WARE, THOMAS ALLEN. NELSON CRAWFORD and BENJAMIN TALIAFERRO, Justices
of the Peace.

367. 31 January 1822. WILLIAM KNIGHT and wife, MARGARET, Amherst
      County, to LUCAS P. THOMPSON, Amherst County...$50 lot 22 in
New Glasgow--joining #--of JAMES S. PENDLETON and by him lately
bought of WESCOT and WEBB--north side Main and bought from DAVID S.
GARLAND, 25 September 1814--book M, page 569 is reference given.
Signed PEGGY KNIGHT. THOMAS ALDRIDGE and EDMOND PENN, Justices of
the Peace.

368. 7 May 1823. JAMES S. PENDLETON, Amherst County, DAVID S.
      GARLAND, Amherst County...on 12 July 1822 REUBEN PENDLETON
executed Deed of Trust to SAMUEL GARLAND, Lynchburg, for benefit of
ARCHELAUS ROBERTSON and Company--recorded 15 July. SAMUEL GARLAND
now sells to PENDLETON and GARLAND--tract sold 22 February 1823, upon
premises and bought by JONATHAN N. ANDERSON, agent for ROBERTSON and
Company at $2120; sold to SAMUEL GARLAND for $3055.35--440 acres and
part of 500 acres conveyed to REUBEN PENDLETON, 23 March 1796, by
JAMES HIGGINBOTHAM. Lines: JONATHAN CAMM, deceased, GEORGE TINSLEY,
DABNEY T. PHILIPS, near TRENT's ferry and where REUBEN lived for many
years past. To DAVID S. GARLAND, 1 September 1824.

369. 24 January 1823. LIENDAMAN NOWELL and wife, MATILDA, Jessamine
      County, Kentucky, to JAMES ERVING, Jessamine County, Kentucky...
$1229.00 150 acres Harris Creek--lately recieved by LIENDAMAN NOWELL
and wife of STUART and TALIAFERRO. Lines: DANIEL NORCUTT, PLEASANT
DAWSON, WILLIAM BURFORD. SAMUEL H. CRAIG and JONATHAN DOWNING,
Justices of the Peace; JEFF PRICE, Deputy Clerk for DANIEL B. PRICE,
JONATHAN PERRY, Presiding Justice of the Peace--all of Jessamine
County, Kentucky.

371. 25 December 1822. JAMES MARTIN and wife, NANCY, Amherst County,
      to JAMES M. MARTIN, Amherst County...love and $1.00; 80 acres
Irish Creek. Lines: WILLIAM SLEDD, deceased, JONATHAN ROBERTSON,
ARCHIBALD GILLIAM, JAMES MARTIN. Witnesses: JESSE, VARLAND and
AMELIA RICHESON. NELSON CRAWFORD and CHARLES L. BARRET, Justices
of the Peace.

372. 31 February 1823. THOMAS DAVIS, Amherst County, to friend,
      SAMUEL R. DAVIES, Amherst County...power of attorney to bid
for slaves in hands Buckingham Sheriff--three children--on schedule
made for me by WILLIAM BURTON in Amherst County Court and for my
benefit--not over $300.00. Witness: BEVERLY DAVIES.

372. 17 April 1823. MERIT M. WHITE and wife, JUDITH P., WILLIAM
      WHITE and wife, POLLY, Bethel in Amherst County, to WILLIAM
ARMISTEAD and RICHARD L. ELLIS, Amherst County, 2; CHARLES ELLIS
and JONATHAN ALLEN, Richmond, 3, merchants: ELLIS and ALLEN...$1.00
lot 18 in Bethel whereon is storehouse and lumber house; four lots
whereon MERIT M. WHITE lives--21, 22, 23, 24; one improved lot bought
of JONATHAN WILSON and where JONATHAN WILSON lives; three other lots--
numbers not recollected--JAMES HUNTLEY lives on one and others not
improved; also stock in Bethel store, cattle, etc.; slaves (two
watermen); two batteaux; all interest of MERIT and wife in estate of
JOSHUA TINSLEY, late of Amherst County--mansion house where TINSLEY
lived at death about -- acres. Reference to Deed of Trust to WILLIAM
ARMISTEAD to secure ROBERT and ALEXANDER TINSLEY. Witnesses:
EDWARD CARTER, JR., JONATHAN WILSON, JAMES HUNTLEY. To CHARLES
ELLIS, 17 September 1823.

375. 21 June 1821. THOMAS ALDRIDGE and wife, CATHERINE, Amherst
      County, and New Glasgow, to WILLIAM MORGAN, Lynchburg...$236800
Amherst County and Nelson tract of 2368 acres. Lines: THOMAS
LANDRUM, JAMES FRANKLIN's estate, NATHANIEL MANTIPLY's estate, HILL
CARTER, JONATHAN N. ROSE, EBENEZER HICKOK, STERLING CLAIBORNE to Tye
River, to estate of WILLIAM S. CRAWFORD, NORVEL SPENCER's estate,
Geddes road, Lynch Road. All of tract bought by THOMAS ALDRIDGE
from COLONEL PATRICK ROSE, deceased, except 45 acres sold to EBENEZER
HICKOK, heirs of WILLIAM MOSS, deceased, STERLING CLAIBORNE, JONATHAN
THOMPSON. Some seem to refer to tracts bought by ALDRIDGE from these
parties. EDMOND PENN and THOMAS CREWS, Justices of the Peace.

376. 23 December 1822. CHARLES P. TALIAFERRO and wife, LOUISA,
      Amherst County, to JAMES POWELL, Amherst County...$1500 one
half of tract on Rutledge. Lines: BENAMMI STONE, ARTHUR B. DAVIES,
2 3/4 acres on which stands Mont Pelier Mills, late property of
JAMES FRANKLIN, deceased. Dower relinquished in S:390 margin.

377. 4 May 1822. NELSON C. DAWSON on -- bought of PATRICK P. BURTON
      his interest in named slaves...assigned in dower to wife of
DAWSON in right of her interest in estate of former husband, PHILIP
BURTON--and cancelled this day as to curtail; PATRICK P. BURTON has
paid NELSON C. DAWSON who says that he holds slaves only for right
of wife and such estate that she has of PHILIP BURTON's by Act of
Assembly in case. BURTON has same right to female slaves. Witnesses:
C. DABNEY, C. ANTHONY, WILLIAM M. RIVES. Memo: DAWSON sold one
whilst he had title and not required to deliver, but at death of wife
is to pay for slave. If slave dies before his wife, then to pay is
due. Same witnesses.

378. 23 June 1823. WILLIAM MORGAN and wife, ELIZABETH, Lynchburg,
      to WILLIAM HUDNATH MORGAN, Lynchburg...$23,680 2380 acres in
Amherst County and Nelson and bought from THOMAS ALDRIDGE and wife,
CATHERINE, 21 June 1823. ALBON MC DANIEL and JONATHAN HANCOCK,
Lynchburg Justices of the Peace. To WILLIAM HUDNATH MORGAN, July,
1823.

379. 4 July 1823. JEREMIAH COATS and wife, SALLY, Amherst County,
      to BEVERLY DAVIES, Amherst County, 2; SAMUEL R. DAVIES, 3...
$1.00 half acre lot where JEREMIAH COATS lives. EDMOND PENN and
LINDSEY COLEMAN, Justices of the Peace.

380. 19 March 1823. ALEXANDER CUTLOR and SAMUEL PATTERSON, Rockbridge
      Justices of the Peace, as to SALLY HILL, wife of WASHINGTON
HILL...17 May 1819, to THOMAS GOODRICH.

381. 19 March 1823. WILLIAM M. WALLER and EDMOND PENN as to RHODA
      BROWN, wife of JAMES M. BROWN, 14 September 1822, to N. MANTIPLY,
17 July 1823...Order recorded page 198 (margin).

381. 14 February 1823. AMBROSE RUCKER and DABNEY WARE, as to POLLY
      BURKS, wife of RICHARD BURKS...16 March 1822, to MATTHEW BURKS.

382. REUBEN NORVELL and JAMES L. LAMKIN, 9 November 1822, as to
      NANCY RUCKER, wife of TINSLEY RUCKER, to JOSEPH ECHOLS...
27 November 1820.

382. 14 March 1823. JOSEPH SHELTON and LEE W. HARRIS, Nelson
      Justices of the Peace, as to BETSY FORTUNE, wife of ZACHARIAH
FORTUNE...13 February 1804, to JONATHAN FORTUNE.

382. 9 July 1823. JONATHAN COLEMAN and ROBERT TINSLEY as to
      POLLY H. WATSON, wife of WILKINS WATSON...22 July 1816,
GEORGE TUCKER. To GEORGE TUCKER, 18 July 1823.

383. 21 July 1823. THOMAS ALDRIDGE, GEORGE, JONATHAN and MARY
     MYERS, Amherst County, to RICHARD H. JONES, Baltimore, Maryland...
power of attorney--to act in estate of BARBARA MYERS, late of Baltimore,
as legatees under will. Witnesses: JOSEPH DILLARD, LUCAS P. THOMPSON.
Note: I showed this to my good friend, HENRY MYERS, Sheriff of
Amherst County, and suggested that he write to Baltimore to find out
about this will.

383. 21 June 1823. ELIAS WILLS and wife, MARY G., Amherst County,
     to JAMES L. LAMKIN, 2; GUSTAVUS A. ROSE and WILLIAM TURNER,
Amherst County, 3...WILLIAM TURNER is bondsman on suit in Campbell
Superior Court by ARCHELAUS ROBERTSON and Company: $5.00; Mill tract
on Harris of 117 acres and made up of 103 acres bought from BANISTER
TINSLEY and 14 acres bought from LEE and REYNOLDS; 90 acres on Harris.
Lines: JAMES LEE, ARCHELAUS REYNOLDS and bought from JONATHAN MAHONE
and conveyed to ELIAS WILLS by heirs of ARCHELAUS COX, deceased. A
small tract on Lynch road bought of DANIEL NORCUTT--WILLS' blacksmith
shop on it--13 acres. NELSON C. DAWSON and RICHARD HARRISON,
Justices of the Peace. To GUSTAVUS A. ROSE, 18 December 1823.

387. 26 June 1821. JONATHAN N. ROSE and JONATHAN THOMPSON, JR.,
     merchants of firm of ROSE and THOMPSON, Amherst County, to
LUCAS P. THOMPSON, Amherst County...JONATHAN THOMPSON, SR., Nelson
County, and COLONEL PATRICK ROSE, Amherst County, are bondsmen to
JAMES WILLS, SR., NATHAN WILLS, A. C. KENEAR, -- MOOR, SAMUEL C.
BRENT, J. DMITH, SR. and JR. $1.00; 41 acres Piney--merchant mill
and pond--ROSE MILLS and bought from THOMAS ALDRIDGE on --; and by
JONATHAN N. ROSE and wife to ROSE and THOMPSON as social property.
Witnesses: EDWARD LANKFORD, JONATHAN WHITE, THOMAS HICKS.

391. 18 April 1823. JONATHAN N. ROSE and wife, MARY, Nelson County,
     to JONATHAN THOMPSON, JR., Amherst County...$1.00 where
JONATHAN N. ROSE lately lived in Amherst County--right hand side of
main road from ROSE's Mill to New Glasgow and some on left of road--
100 yards above WILLIAM STAPLES' house; hill above mill; part of tract
deeded to JONATHAN N. ROSE by his father, PATRICK ROSE, deceased.
Lines: ROSE and THOMPSON, HILL CARTER, THOMAS ALDRIDGE, JONATHAN P.
COBBS, JAMES PENN; to secure debts to JAMES D. BRENT. Witnesses:
EDWARD LANKFORD, JONATHAN HARVEY, GEORGE GEAGANS. Memo: $1.00 for
crops.

393. 21 January 1822. JONATHAN RICHESON and wife, NANCY, Amherst
     County, to JAMES B. HARRIS, Amherst County...$50 74 acres and
near Lynchburg. Lines: James River, BENJAMIN SCHOOLFIELD, mouth of
branch. Bought from JONATHAN TAYLOE and wife, SALLY, 23 January
1822 (sic). Witnesses: WILLIAM I. ISBELL, H. WILLIAMSON, THOMAS
MURRELL.

394. 1 July 1823. PEYTON KEITH, Amherst County, to JAMES L. WATTS,
     Amherst County...WATTS is son-in-law of KEITH by marriage to
LUCY M. KEITH--for support by loan; $1.00 slave and four children.
Witnesses: JOSEPH BROWN, MARSHALL M. KEITH, JAMES W. KEITH.

394. 3 May 1823. ARTHUR B. DAVIES and wife, SUSAN M., Amherst
     County, to SAMUEL R. DAVIES, Amherst County...$500 600 acres--
lot of ELIZABETH DAVIES, deceased, widow of NICHOLAS C. DAVIES,
deceased--as dower and now to her children--eleven and ARTHUR B.
DAVIES is one and conveys 1/11th.

395. 19 July 1823. JOSEPH SWANSON, Amherst County, to sister-in-
     law, POLLY SWANSON, wife of brother, JONATHAN SWANSON...love
and $1.00; horse, cart and gear for POLLY and children.

396. 30 June 1823. JESSE WOODROOF and wife, ELIZABETH, Amherst
County, to HUDSON M. GARLAND, Amherst County, 2; JONATHAN
MC DANIEL, THOMAS CREWS, JAMES POWELL, Amherst County 3...JONATHAN
MC DANIEL, THOMAS CREWS, JAMES POWELL bondsmen in Superior Court of
Nelson to WILLIAM B. JACOBS--$1.00; 306 acres. Lines: JONATHAN
MC DANIEL and where JESSE WOODROOF lives; slaves, stock, tools,
interest in estate of JESSE's mother, debt due from THOMAS MOORE,
CORNELIUS PIERCE, WILLIAM BECKHAM. Witnesses: JAMES R. LIVELY,
STEPHEN SUBLETT, WILLIAM CASHWELL.

397. 14 August 1799. ROWLAND JONES and wife, ANN, Campbell County,
to POWHATAN BOLLING, Buckingham County...$200 260 acres Stovall
and Juniper Creeks and surveyed for WILLIAM EVANS, 5 April 1788, and
patent to WILLIAM EVANS, 1 November 1791. Sold by WILLIAM EVANS to
SACKVILLE KING and Company and by them to JONES. Lines: TURNER
CHRISTIAN, grantee, IVY HILL, STEPHEN HAM, JOSEPH CREWS, BENJAMIN
COFLAND. To POWHATAN BOLLING's executor, 18 August 1823. Witnesses:
REUBEN CRAWFORD, JONATHAN MC DANIEL, HENRY TURNER, SAMUEL ROSE.
Proved by REUBEN CRAWFORD and HENRY TURNER, 21 April 1800, in Amherst
County; July 21, 1823 by JONATHAN MC DANIEL and "other witness."

399. 20 July 1823. JAMES LAINE, Amherst County, 1; BEVERLY DAVIES,
Amherst County, 2; HENRY L. DAVIES, Amherst County, 3...$1.00;
stock, etc. To HENRY L. DAVIES, 10 June 1828.

400. 22 July 1823. JACOB PIERCE, Amherst County, to ISAAC POWELL,
Madison County, Alabama...27 December 1827, sent to ISAAC POWELL
per WILEY CAMPBELL, to Alabama--JACOB agreed with COLONEL SEMER
(SEYMOUR?) POWELL, Powhatan County, to free ISAAC when 31 years of
age. He now frees him.

400. 17 July 1823. JACOB PIERCE and wife, LIZZA, Amherst County,
to JOSEPH KENNEDY, Amherst County...L20 20 acres. Lines:
Spring branch to DAVID S. GARLAND, Buffaloe, JESSE KENEDY, deceased.
Signed: ELIZABETH PIERCE.

401. 26 July 1823. BENJAMIN FORTUNE, 1; HILL CARTER, 2, to MANSFIELD
WARE, Amherst County, 3...debt to HILL CARTER; $1.00--HILL CARTER
bondsman to CORNELIUS POWELL, administrator of JESSE JONES; Sheriff
of Amherst County in suit of D. and D. HIGGINBOTHAM and Company,
THOMAS LATEN, JAMES S. PENDLETON and Company. Furniture, stock,
tools, crops, accounts in smith's shop, HILL CARTER is partner.
Witnesses: LUCAS P. THOMPSON, L. and JAMES L. FULCHER.

403. 25 July 1823. JONATHAN MAHONE, Amherst County, 1; JONATHAN W.
MAHONE and DAVID R. RDLEY, Amherst County, 2, to WINSTON H.
LUCAS, 3...debt to JONATHAN W. MAHONE and DAVID R. RDLEY; $1.00;
stock, furniture, gun. DANIEL BROWN and ALBON MC DANIEL, Lynchburg
Justices of the Peace. To DAVID R. RDLEY, 18 August 1823.

405. 31 July 1823. MICAJAH CAMDEN and wife, POLLY, Amherst County,
to JACOB PIERCE, Amherst County...$1900 ten acres near ACH and
includes tavern house occupied by REUBEN COLEMAN. Lines: three
feet south of front of tavern, corner to prison, middle of Lynch
road, SAMUEL HEISKELL, a fence, a drain, ARTHUR B. DAVIES, MEGGINSON's
road. RICHARD HARRISON and ROBERT TINSLEY, Justices of the Peace.

407. 31 July 1823. MICHAJAH CAMDEN and wife, POLLY, Amherst County,
to ARTHUR B. DAVIES, Amherst County...$1100 55 acres. Lines:
Rutledge Creek at mouth of a branch, a road, LINDSEY COLEMAN, JACOB
PIERCE, grantee, a branch. Justices of the Peace as above.

408. 31 July 1823. MICAJAH CAMDEN and wife, POLLY, Amherst County,
to SAMUEL HEISKELL, Amherst County...$380 three or four acres
at ACH. Lines: grantee, ARTHUR B. DAVIES, main road, land sold
JACOB PIERCE this day. Justices of the Peace as above.

409. 31 July 1823. RICHARD HARRISON and ROBERT TINSLEY as to POLLY above to A. B. DAVIES.

409. 14 June 1823. ARTHUR L. DAVIES and wife, --, SAMUEL B. DAVIES and wife, ELIZABETH, JANE, HOWELL DAVIES and wife, ABBY, JONATHAN J. CABELL and wife, HARRY ANN, CATHERINE E. MERIWETHER, EDITHA CLAY, FRANCIS R. DAVIES and wife, --, ARTHUR B. DAVIES and wife, SUSAN, ROBERT L. COLEMAN and wife, MARY T., NATHANIEL J. MANSON and wife, SARAH, ADDISON TALIAFERRO and wife, HARRY ANN, MAYO DAVIES, JONATHAN DAVIES, BEVERLEY DAVIES, SAMUEL R. DAVIES, NICHOLAS DAVIES, WHITING DAVIES, and EDITHA DAVIES, infants and heirs of NICHOLAS DAVIES, who was one of the sons and heirs of HENRY L. DAVIE, deceased, WILLIAM L., PHILIP HENRY, ELIZABETH, CATHERINE, GEORGE, HARRY ANN, MARTHA and VIRGINIA DAVIES, infants of TAMERLAND W. W. DAVIES, deceased, who was also a son and heir of HENRY L. DAVIES, and also HENRY L. DAVIES, son of NICHOLAS DAVIES, deceased, who was one of sons and heirs of HENRY L. DAVIES, deceased, and who is absent from the Commonwealth, by JAMES BENAGH, commissioner of Superior Court of Chancery in Lynchburg and appointed by decrees to convey--to JAMES WAUGH, ISABELLA WAUGH, widow of EDWARD WAUGH, deceased--Chancery decree in Lynchburg, 21 October 1818: LUCY W. DAVIES, administratrix of HENRY L. DAVIES, and TAMERLANE W. W. DAVIES, administrator of HENRY L. DAVIES versus EDWARD and JAMES WAUGH, ARTHUR L. DAVIES, SAMUEL B. DAVIES, HOWELL DAVIES, CATHERINE E. MERIWETHER, CHARLES CLAY and wife, EDITHA, JONATHAN J. CABELL and wife, HENRY ANN, ELIZABETH DAVIES, widow, FRANCIS R. DAVIES, ARTHUR B. DAVIES. HENRY L. DAVIES, MAYO DAVIES, JONATHAN DAVIES, BEVERLEY DAVIES, SAMUEL R. DAVIES, NICHOLAS DAVIES, WHITING DAVIES, HARRY ANN DAVIES, and EDITHA DAVIES, children of NICHOLAS DAVIES--last seven are infants--Marshall of Court assigned ELIZABETH DAVIES and ROBERT L. COLEMAN, guardians "and MARY" (sic)-- "this wife," these devisees of ADDISON DAVIES, deceased. Decree: defendant, HENRY L. DAVIES, is out of commonwealth, but others duly notified in December, 1817, and no answers filed by CHARLES CLAY and wife, EDITHA, JONATHAN J. CABELL and wife, HARRY ANN, ARTHUR L. and MAYO DAVIES (margin: to GEORGE D. MERIWETHER, 23 September 1823), heirs of HENRY L. DAVIES, to execute fee simple deed to JAMES and EDWARD WAUGH--agreement during lifetime of HENRY L., February, 1808, and WAUGHS to pay plaintiffs L116-16-4, with interest from 1 May 1810. If they refuse, then deed to be filed with County Clerk for them and to pay plaintiffs within six months. Infant defendants may show cause at any time. HENRY L. DAVIES is allowed seven years. Lynchburg Chancery Court, 24 May 1823. ELIZABETH, widow of ADDISON, EDWARD WAUGH has died, HARRY ANN had married ADDISON TALIAFERRO, and NATHANIEL J. MANSON by death of ELIZABETH DAVIE has interest as devisee of ADDISON DAVIES, deceased. Order to proceed in name of GEORGE D. MERIWETHER, administrator of HENRY L. DAVIES, JANE DAVIES, widow, WILLIAM S., PHILIP HENRY, ELIZABETH CATHERINE, GEORGE, HARRY ANN, MARTHA and VIRGINIA DAVIES--children of TAMERLANE W. W. DAVIES, infants, by SAMUEL B. DAVIES, next friend as plaintiffs and in name of ADDISON TALIAFERRO and wife, HENRY ANN (late DAVIES), NATHANIAL J. MANSON, devisee of ADDISON DAVIES. Tract from HENRY L. DAVIES to heirs for $1.00--to JAMES and ISABELLA WAUGH, widow of EDWARD WAUGH, and PEMBROKE WAUGH, son and heir of EDWARD WAUGH--244 acres. Lines: JAMES WAUGH, reference to final agreement in suit of Superior Court of Lynchburg, 9 February 1808. JONATHAN HANCOCK and DANIEL BROWN, Lynchburg Justices of the Peace. BALDA MC DANIEL and JOSEPH SLAUGHTER, Bedford Justices of the Peace, as to JONATHAN J. CABELL: ROBERT L. COLEMAN et al. Note: this is really an involved document. I recall working in Bedford some years ago on DAVIES data and there is much of it in that county.

416. 18 August 1823. RICHARD PENDLETON, Amherst County, to JAMES BRIGHT, -- Tennessee and ROBERT TINSLEY, Amherst County...for benefit of TINSLEY's daughter, PAMELIA ZEVELEY, widow of JONATHAN H. ZEVELEY, and her children. Slave. To ROBERT TINSLEY, 19 December 1823.

417. 18 August 1823. WILLIAM TURNER, JONATHAN PENN, JONATHAN
      MYERS, SPENCER NORVELL, JAMES L. (S) PENDLETON, Amherst County,
power of attorney to HENRY H. WATTS...sumd from GEORGE S. HOLLOWAY,
late of Amherst County, as bondsman to JONATHAN WARWICK, Sheriff, and
GEORGE, as deputy. To HENRY H. WATTS, 19 August 1823.

418. 28 July 1823. HENRY FARNKLIN and wife, JANE, Amherst County,
      to JOSEPH STAPLES, Amherst County...$1.00 500 acres. Lines:
AMBROSE TOMLINSON, AARON HIGGINBOTHAM; bought from JONATHAN RICHESON;
slaves, stock, tools--to secure WILLIAM STAPLES, bondsman to THOMAS A.
HOLCOMB, Lynchburg--WILLIAM STAPLES and JONATHAN MOUNTCASTLE, some
years ago--shortly after death of JEREMIAH FRANKLIN, father of HENRY,
were bondsmen as he qualified as administrator of JEREMIAH FRANKLIN.
Witnesses: JONATHAN THOMPSON, GEORGE FEAGANS, EDWARD FEAGANS, JONATHAN
STAPLES. To JOSEPH STAPLES, 16 February 1824.

422. 1 July 1823. OLIVER TOWLES, SR. and wife, AGATHA, Amherst
      Counth, to JONATHAN M. WILLIAMS and WILLIAM ROBINSON, Amherst
County...$1.00 137¾ acres Falls' Creek. Lines: WILLIAM ROBINSON,
JESSE BECK, WILLIAM WARWICK, THOMAS TERRY, LINEAS BOLLING, DANIEL
BROWN, ALBON MC DANIEL, Lynchburg Justices of the Peace, as to grantor
by JONATHAN B. DABNEY, attorney-in-fact. ROBERT RIVES and ALEXANDER
BROWN, Nelson County Justices of the Peace as to AGATHA. To JONATHAN M.
WILLIAMS, 20 September 1831.

424. 2 August 1823. RICHARD H. BURKS, 1; MATTHEW BURKS and WILLIAM
      ARMISTEAD, Amherst County, 2; WILLIAM SHELTON, Amherst County,
3...$1.00; debts to JONATHAN BURKS, Rockbridge, and suit; BROCKENBROUGH
and HARVIE, Richmond; ELLIS and ALLEN, Richmond; slaves, mare.

425. 13 August 1823. ANDERSON SANDIDGE, Amherst County; AARON
      HIGGINBOTHAM, 2; WILLIS WHITE, Amherst County, 3...$1.00;
WILLIS WHITE bondsman to WILLIAM KNIGHT and transferred to ROBERT
TINSLEY Amherst County suit; stock, crops. To WILLIS WHITE, 16 February
1824.

427. 15 August 1823. ANTHONY RUCKER, JR., Amherst County, 1;
      SAMUEL R. DAVIES, Amherst County, 2; NANCY SHIELDS, Amherst
County, 3...ANTHONY RUCKER, JR. as sold NANCY SHIELDS slaves derived
by him--by wife--from WILLIAM EADES, brother of wife--presumed that
WILLIAM EADES is dead--has been gone from Amherst County for six
years and no intelligence from him. $1.00 paid by SAMUEL R. DAVIES--
interest in estate of ANTHONY RUCKER to children of BATTLETT EADES--
RUCKER's wife is one. Witnesses: JONATHAN SCOTT, J. R. LIVELY,
JONATHAN FRANKLIN.

428. 19 May 1823. EDWARD DAVIDSON, Amherst County, to WILLIAM P. H. R.
      DAVIDSON, Amherst County...$1.00 debt to STEPHEN DAVIDSON, JR.,
Amherst County; slaves, tools. Witnesses: D. FULTZ, MICAJAH
DAVIDSON, JONATHAN STRATTON. To trustee, 22 September 1823.

429. 18 August 1823. THOMAS GOODRICH and wife, ELIZABETH, 1;
      to MATTIN TASK and WILLIAM M. RIVES, 2; JACOB HAAS, 3, and
JOSEPH R. CARTER, 3...$1.00; 260 acres. Lines: PULLIAM SANDIDGE,
THOMAS V. GOODRICH, slaves, furniture. To JOSEPH R. CARTER, 17 May
1824.

431. 18 August 1823. JONATHAN DILLARD and wife, NANCY, Amherst
      County, to WILLIAM S. TURNER, Amherst County...$300 1¼ acres
south side Megginson road. Lines: JONATHAN CHRISTIAN, GOOCH, the
road. To WILLIAM S. TURNER, 17 October 1831.

431. 9 August 1823. PEACHY CASH, Amherst County, 1; JAMES S.
      PENDLETON, Amherst County, 2; to JOSEPH PENN, 3...$1.00; furniture,
etc.; claim versus JONATHAN CAMDEN, JR. and BENJAMIN CAMDEN for service
as overseer. Witnesses: BARTHOLOMEW WHITEHEAD, WILLIAM E. SMITH,
SAMUEL S. PENDLETON.

433. 26 July 1823. THOMAS COPPEDGE, SR., Amherst County, to
      CORNELIUS POWELL, Amherst County...$1.00; debt to DAVID, DANIEL
and THOMAS HIGGINBOTHAM, merchants, Amherst County; furniture, crops.
Witnesses: JAMES COLEMAN, JONATHAN S. BLAIR, SAMUEL W. CHRISTIAN.
To JAMES D. HIGGINBOTHAM, -- June 1824.

435. 11 August 1823. THOMAS ALDRIDGE and wife, CATHERINE, Amherst
      County, to PAUL C. CABELL, Halifax County...$2500 tenement;
dwelling house, store at New Glasgow--4 1/8 acres. Lines: ROBERT
HIGGINBOTHAM's grocery, Main Street, alley, the garden, WILLIAM
CLARKE, DAVID S. GARLAND, church lot. DAVID S. GARLAND and ROBERT
TINSLEY, Justices of the Peace.

436. 9 July 1823. JAMES S. PENDLETON and RICHARD H. BURKS, Amherst
      County, 1; to ELIAS WILLS and wife, MARY G., 2; RICHARD HARRISON
and JONATHAN M. SETTLE, 3...8 April 1820, ELIAS WILLS executor
Deed of Trust to RICHARD HARRISON and JONATHAN M. SETTLE on 131 acres--
part of it bought from BENJAMIN GOSNEY--103 acres bought from BANISTER
TINSLEY on Harris Creek; slaves--seven of them--paid and for $1.00
a release. DABNEY WARE and REUBEN NORFELL, Justices of the Peace as
to RICHARD H. BURKS.

438. 18 August 1823. RHODA GRIFFITH, Lynchburg, to WILLIAM I.
      ISBELL, Amherst County or Madison (town of), 2; THOMAS B.
MEHONE, 3...$1.00 two lots in Madison--56 and 57; junction of Third
Street and Fifth alley, fourth alley, JONATHAN MILLER--one acre.
Furniture, etc. Witnesses: JONATHAN TAYLOE, THOMAS MURRELL,
NATHAN P. BREEDLOVE.

440. 1 May 1823. JESSE KENNEDY, 1; WILLIAM KELLY, 2; JOSEPH KENNEDY,
      3...JOSEPH KENNEDY bondsman to JONATHAN POINDEXTER, JONATHAN
ROBINSON, Rockbridge; $1.00; house and lot near ACH--west side Lynch
road. Lines: JAMES POWELL, SAMUEL SIMMONS, now occupied by WILLIAM
KELLY--3/4 acres, stock, furniture, one fiddle, estate due at death
of mother, SUSANNAH ALFRED, from estate of JESSE KENNEDY, the elder;
claim versus CORNELIUS POWELL--suit in Lynchburg Chancery. To
WILLIAM KELLY, 16 April 1827.

442. 19 August 1823. THOMAS ALDRIDGE and wife, CATHERINE, Amherst
      County, to WASHINGTON HILL...$4000 36 acres at ACH; except lot
sold to KENNEDY and HILL; reference to Lynchburg Chancery suit; also
half acre sold: RODNEY DAVIES, buyer; includes The Brick Tavern and
bought from MICAJAH CAMDEN. DAVID S. GARLAND and EDMOND PENN,
Justices of the Peace. To WASHINGTON HILL's attorney, 1827.

443. 7 August 1823. JEREMIAH COATS and wife, SALLY, to MARY ANN
      COATS, Amherst County...$180 half acre lot at Courthouse of
Amherst County; reference to Deed of Trust to SARAH ANN ELVIRA and
CARY ANN HALL, JEREMIAH to receive rents until SARAH ANN HALL is
of age.

444. 13 August 1823. RICHARD PENDLETON, Amherst County, to JAMES
      BRIGHT, Tennessee, and ROBERT TINSLEY, Amherst County, for
benefit of PENDLETON's daughter, PAMELIA ZEVELEY, widow of JONATHAN H.
ZEVELEY, deceased...children and heirs of any deceased children--
$1.00; slave.

445. 19 August 1823. WASHINGTON HILL to HILL CARTER, 2; THOMAS
      ALDRIDGE, 3...$1.00; Brick Tavern at ACH and bought from
THOMAS ALDRIDGE and wife, 19 August 1823. To HILL's attorney, 1827.

446. 19 August 1823. JAMES PAGE, Amherst County, to SAMUEL GARLAND
      and JONATHAN TALBOT, Amherst County, 2; ALLEN TALBOT, 3...$1.00
paid by SAMUEL GARLAND and JONATHAN TALBOT; slave, furniture, tools,
crop.

447. 18 November 1818. RACHEL NORCUTT, sister and heir of CHARLES
      HIGGINBOTHAM, deceased, Amherst County, to DAVID S. GARLAND...
$300 for all interest in tract at CHARLES HIGGINBOTHAM where CHARLES
lived at death; south side Buffaloe and both sides Rutledge--one
sixth. Witnesses: REUBEN NORVELL, WILLIAM S. MUSE, JAMES, JOSEPH
and WILLIAM NORCUTT.

448. 20 August 1823. HUMPHREY GILBERT, Amherst County, 1; BEVERLEY
      DAVIES, Amherst County, 2; JAMES and HUDSON M. GARLAND, 3...
$1.00; interest in estate of deceased mother, JUDITH GILBERT--conveyed
to JAMES FRANKLIN in trust during life and at death to her children--
"by her mother, SUSANNAH CRENSHAW." To CHARLES A. BARRET per order
of JAMES and HUDSON M. GARLAND, 27 January 1825.

450. 9 August 1823. JONATHAN FRANKLIN, 1; JAMES FULCHER, 2; THOMAS
      ALDRIDGE, 3...$1.00 "waggon" and four horses, two horses bought
from THOMAS ALDRIDGE. Witnesses: EDMOND PENN, LUCAS P. THOMPSON,
GEORGE MYERS.

451. 15 August 1823. ANTHONY RUCKER, Amherst County, to NANCY
      SHIELDS, Amherst County...$200 slave and four children--in
right of wife in estate of WILLIAM EADES who is supposed to be dead.
Witnesses: J. R. LIVELY, JONATHAN SCOTT, JONATHAN FRANKLIN. To
RICHARD HARRISON, 2 March 1824.

452. 27 August 1823. JONATHAN HUDSON, 16 June 1823, executor Deed
      of Trust to JAMES FULCHER...93 acres Little Piney. Lines:
WILLIAM MOORE, JONATHAN TUCKER. Has been sued by DAVID, DANIEL and
THOMAS HIGGINBOTHAM, merchants, in Amherst County Court; has taken
insolvent oath and transferred to JAMES M. BROWN, Sheriff.

452. 29 August 1823. JONATHAN SHELTON, Amherst County, to WILLIAM
      ARMISTEAD, Amherst County, SAMUEL BURKS, SR., Amherst County,
WALTER OTEY, Madison County, Alabama...for benefit of daughter,
ELIZABETH K., who is wife of LEE H. BURKS--apart from him--and at
death to any children--$1.00; slave girl about fifteen. AMBROSE
RUCKER and DABNEY WARE, Justices of the Peace as to SHELTON and
BURKS.

454. 29 August 1823. WILLIAM SHELTON, Amherst County, to same
      parties as above...$1.00--for benefit of daughter, ELIZA JANE,
wife of RICHARD H. BURKS, at death to any children; girl slave about
sixteen. Same Justices of the Peace as above.

455. 6 August 1823. THOMAS MOORE, Bedford, to BENJAMIN A. DONALD...
      $1.00; slave in hands of PETER WALKER, Amherst County, for
benefit of daughter, ELIZA H. WALKER and children. Witnesses:
JONATHAN N. ANDERSON, HOWSON L. WHITE, JONATHAN MOORE. To PETER
WALKER, 25 August 1824. JOSEPH SLAUGHTER and JONATHAN L. COBBS,
Bedford Justices of the Peace.

456. 1 June 1823. CHARLES L. MITCHELL and SAMUEL MITCHELL, by JAMES
      BENAGH, Commissioner of Superior Court of Chancery, Lynchburg,
to GEORGE CABELL, Campbell County--Court of 24 October 1822, Lynchburg,
by GEORGE CABELL versus MITCHELLS above--and JONATHAN N. SPOTSWOOD
JONES, executors of said L. JONES...Defendants out of county and in
legal form, but did not appear. Motion made that MITCHELLS relinquish
to CABELL all right in tract sold by their father, SAMUEL MITCHELL,
to L. JONES. MITCHELLS are non-residents and JAMES BENAGH appointed
to convey; they may contest; $1.00; Campbell and Amherst County tracts
and references to two deeds of 16 March 1803, to L. JONES and one of
1 June 1805, between L. JONES and GEORGE CABELL. THOMAS HOLCOMB and
JONATHAN VICTOR, Justices of the Peace of Lynchburg.

458. 8 September 1823. GEORGE CAMPBELL, 1; JONATHAN STINNETT, 2;
      WILLIAM CAMPBELL, 3; BARTLETT CAMPBELL, 4; CARY F. CAMPBELL, 5...
$1.00; debts to CHARLES TUCKER and Amherst County suit; furniture,
tools, crops. Witnesses: JAMES MILLER, JAMES CAMBELL, GEORGE CAMPBELL,
JR. To JONATHAN STINNETT, 19 April 1824.

460. 1 August 1823. RICHARD H. BURKS and wife, ELIZA JANE, Amherst
County, to WILLIAM SHELTON, Amherst County...$1000 634 acres
Pedlar. Lines: DAVID S. GARLAND, near WHITE's Gap and on Blue
Ridge. Conveyed to ARTHUR B. DAVIES, JAMES POWELL, STERLING CLAIBORNE.
CLAIBORNE in Deed of Trust by HENRY CAMDEN, two connected surveys.
JAMES S. DILLARD and RICHARD HARRISON, Justices of the Peace, as to
RICHARD H. BURKS. AMBROSE RUCKER and DABNEY WARE, Justices of the
Peace, as to wife of RICHARD H. BURKS.

461. 15 October 1823. ARCHEY ROWSEY, Amherst County, 1; JAMES
ROWSEY, 2; to JESSE RICHESON, Amherst County, 3...$1.00;
stock, furniture, tools, four acres.

462. 15 September 1823. ELISHA RUCKER, Amherst County, 1; WILLIAM
ARMISTEAD, Amherst County, 2; ANDREW MORELAND, Amherst County,
3...$1.00; to secure ANDREW MORELAND on appeal of judgement in Amherst
County Court; bondsman to P. P. THORNTON, trustee, for PHILIP THURMOND
for property sold ELISHA RUCKER at THURMOND's sale. Slaves.

463. 20 August 1823. STERLING CLAIBORNE, Amherst County, to
WILLIAM S. and CHARLES BULLER CLAIBORNE, Amherst County...$6000
101 acres on Rocky Creek and next to Rocky Creek Mills. Tract sold
by JONATHAN CHRISTIAN, B, to RICHARD HARRISON and by him sold to
STERLING CLAIBORNE. Also 2/3 of the mill and 2/3 of 29 acres adjoining
it.

464. 1 September 1823. STERLING CLAIBORNE to SARAH ANN and MILDRED
ROSE...$5000 tract near ACH on road from Greenway--430 acres.
Lines: BENAMMI STONE, CHARLES MUNDY, CHARLES HUNT CHRISTIAN. Brick
dwelling thereon and occupied by JAMES GARLAND. Bought by CLAIBORNE
from JONATHAN H. SMITH. Witnesses: RICHARD W. FOX, CHARLES B.
WILLIAMS, WILLIAM H. GOODWIN. To grantees, 14 December 1824.

465. 23 September 1823. STERLING CLAIBORNE, 1; to WILLIAM H. ROSE, 2;
WILLIAM B. ROANE, 3...$1.00; bonds due THOMAS A. HOLCOMBE and
ROBERT L. COLEMAN, trustees for NICHOLAS HARRISON and SAMUEL GARLAND,
agent for BOYD MILLER and JAMES M. BROWN. 400 acres. Tract adjoins
Buffaloe Springs on Buffaloe.

465. 22 September 1822. MICAJAH CAMDEN, Amherst County, 1; ROBERT
TINSLEY, Amherst County, 2; DAVID S. GARLAND and THOMAS ALDRIDGE
and JONATHAN PENN, Amherst County, 3...$1.00; debts to JONATHAN
MYERS, assigned of GIDEON RUCKER, assigned of REUBEN COLEMAN--slaves
named and ages.

467. 22 September 1823. MICAJAH CAMDEN, 1; ROBERT TINSLEY, 2; LUCY
HUDSON, 3...WILLIAM M. WALLER, acting executor of JONATHAN
SMITH, WILLIAM SALE, Amherst County, 3...$1.00, stock--30 hogs and
eighteen pigs; thirty horned cattle, crops, tools, furniture, etc.

469. 22 September 1823. JAMES S. PENDLETON, Amherst County, to
DAVID S. GARLAND and WILL G. PENDLETON, Richmond, 2, and various
creditors: BENJAMIN BLAKE as administrator of ISRAEL and FRANCES
GLASSCOCK, JANE ALDRIDGE as legatee of RICHARD COGHILL in right of
wife as legatee of ROBERT ALDRIDGE, DAVID S. GARLAND, Virginia Bank,
SAMUEL TURNER's widow, JAMES FRANKLIN, PEACHY FRANKLIN...$1.00; 758
acres on Buffaloe and 128 acres on Indian Creek bought from PHILIP
THURMOND, JR., slaves; slaves allotted by executors of JAMES GARLAND
to REUBEN and FRANCES PENDLETON. Witnesses: JOHN A. SIMPSON and
NICHOLAS DAVIES. This is a long list as to those owed and others are:
PETER BURROUGHS, WILLIAM M. WALLER, JOSEPH PENN, WILLIAM ARMISTEAD,
NICHOLAS HARRISON, RODNEY TALIAFERRO, JONATHAN TALBOT, PENDLETON and
MOUNTCASTLE, HENRY M. DIDLAKE, GEORGE T. WILLIAMS, D and D. HIGGIN-
BOTHAM, WILLIAM S. CABELL, JONATHAN D. MURRELL. I think that this
GLASSCOCK data probably is to be found in Fauquier. I have so many
loose ends to pursue that I have never got to dote on my own family
research. In my family is statement that great-grandfather, JONATHAN
MATHIS BYRD, that his wife, LUCY ANN WILLIAMS, was daughter of
BRYANT WILLIAMS and wife, NANCY (nee MILBURN). There is a deed in

Graves County, Kentucky, -- records burned--brought in after the
fire--showing BRYANT WILLIAMS and wife, NANCY, selling land on
Mayfield Creek. JONATHAN BYRD also stated that NANCY MILBURN was
daughter of a MILBURN who married a GLASSCOCK. In Washington County,
Kentucky, is a WILLIAM MILBURN who married CUZZY (KESIAH?) GLASSCOCK.
They disappear and I wonder if they are my ancestors who went to
Purchase in Kentucky. In old circuit data is suit showing a GLASSCOCK
with wife, NANCY, and he is shown to be heir of a GLASSCOCK in
Fauquier. These names seem to ring a Fauquier bell to me, but I
will not be dogmatic. I am still chasing BRYANT WILLIAMS and the
MILBURN and GLASSCOCK lines.

473. 25 September 1823. JONATHAN WISE, Amherst County, 1; FIELDING
      BROWN, Amherst County, 2; JOSEPH BROWN, Amherst County, 3...
JOSEPH BROWN on bond to JESSE KENNEDY; $1.00; furniture, tobacco,
tools, claims versus JAMES S. PENDLETON, JONATHAN PORTER, JONATHAN
SMITH, WILLIAM JACOBS of Culpeper. To FIELDING BROWN, 7 June 1824.

474. 24 September 1823. SPENCER NORVELL, Amherst County, 1;
      CHISWELL DABNEY, Amherst County, 2; EDMOND WINSTON, Amherst
County, 3...EDMOND WINSTON on bond to Bank of Virginia; $5.00; slaves
named. Witnesses: BENJAMIN NORVELL, G. A. ROSE, CHARLES TUCKER.

476. 27 February 1823. ANDERSON TINSLEY and wife, CYNTHIA, Giles
      County, Tennessee to BANISTER TINSLEY, Bedford County...$600
lot seven--part of estate of JOSHUA TINSLEY, deceased--59 acres.
Lines: ALEXANDER TINSLEY, mill road, SHELTON's road, GEORGE M.
TINSLEY, Harris Creek, grantee. Witnesses: MATTHEW P. STURDIVANT,
AMBROSE RUCKER and DABNEY WARE, Justices of the Peace, as to ANDERSON
TINSLEY.

477. 20 September 1823. AMBROSE RUCKER and wife, BETSY, Amherst
      County, to SAMUEL BURKS, SR., Amherst County...$191.25 90 acres
Salt Creek on southeast side of Mountain. Lines: SAMUEL BURKS on
mountain, JONATHAN CAMM, deceased, Pedlar road. To DR. DAVID
PATTERSON and returned, 1 June 1838.

478. 22 September 1823. AMBROSE RUCKER, Amherst County, to JACOB
      HAAS, Bedford...$3.00 14 acres Clark Creek. Lines: RODNEY
MC CULLOCH, JONATHAN L. WINGFIELD, NICHOLAS C. DAVIES, deceased,
CALEB WATTS. Bought from CALEB WATTS in 1809.

479. 27 September 1823. JONATHAN THOMPSON, JR., trustee, JONATHAN N.
      ROSE and wife, MARY, to WILLIAM M. WALLER, Amherst County...
$3094.00 221 acres Piney. Lines: HILL CARTER, Mill lot, JONATHAN N.
ROSE, THOMAS ALDRIDGE, main road between Rose Mills and New Glasgow
and above house occupied by WILLIAM STAPLES, WILLIAM MORGAN (formerly
THOMAS ALDRIDGE), mill tract of ROSE and THOMPSON. THOMAS ALDRIDGE
and ROBERT TINSLEY, Justices of the Peace.

481. 6 September1823. PULLIAM SANDIDGE and wife, LUCY, Amherst
      County, to ZA DRUMMOND, Amherst County...$2500 320 acres both
sides Buffaloe; DAVID S. GARLAND and ISAAC RUCKER, Justices of the
Peace. To ZA DRUMMOND, 20 October 1823.

482. 25 September 1823. SALLY ISBELL, administratrix of ZACHARIAL
      ISBELL, deceased, to WILLIAM I. ISBELL, Amherst County...
considerations: two judgements of $3671.64 in Amherst County Court
versus ZACHARIAH ISBELL by WILLIAM I. ISBELL; slaves named. Witnesses:
REUBEN NORVELL and WILLIAM PENDLETON, JR. To WILLIAM I. ISBELL,
20 November 1823.

482. 25 September 1823. WILLIAM I. ISBELL to SALLY ISBELL...$500
      slaves named above. Witnesses: as above. To SALLY ISBELL,
8 September 1831.

483.	19 November 1818. Order to JAMES WARE and RICHARD N. EUBANK,
	to quiz JANE EUBANK, wife of THOMAS N. EUBANK as to deed of
24 November 1817 to LARKIN BYAS...600 acres. Done, 13 September 1823.

484.	20 May 1823. ALEXANDER TINSLEY stated that CAPTAIN ISAAC
	TINSLEY may take or sell property in Deed of Trust...September 22,
1823 EDMOND WINSTON for $1.00 paid by ISAAC TINSLEY releases rights
to negro man.

485.	24 July 1823. BENJAMIN TALIAFERRO and ISAAC RUCKER as to
	SUSANNAH WILLMIRE, wife of WILLIAM WILLMORE...7 October 1822,
deed to DAVID S. GARLAND.

485.	12 September 1823. SUSANNAH, WILLIAM and THOMAS TUCKER,
	Amherst County, to REUBEN T. MARTIN and wife, JUDITH, formerly
TUCKER, Kentucky, under will of THOMAS TUCKER, Amherst County...
slaves in possession of SUSANNAH and divided into four lots by JESSE
RICHESON, ABRAM CARTER, CHARLES L. BARRET. Final distribution of
THOMAS TUCKER's estate. SUSANNAH for life and then to heirs: WILLIAM
and THOMAS TUCKER and JUDITH MARTIN; lands excepted. Witnesses:
PHILIP THURMOND, JR., PHILIP THURMOND, MARTIN PARKS.

486.	14 April 1823. OLIVER TOWLES, at present in Cape Girardeau
	County, Missouri--the clerk here had a hard time with this one
and spelled it as "Gurardo"...power of attorney to JONATHAN B.
DABNEY, attorney of Campbell County, Virginia--to sell various
Virginia tracts. Missouri Justices of the Peace: GEORGE HENDERSON
and JONATHAN ABERNATHIE. To BLAIR DABNEY, 20 October 1823.

487.	7 August 1823. ROBERT C. SCOTT and GABRIEL J. SCOTT, Campbell
	County, to WILLIAM M. RIVES, Lynchburg, and JONATHAN HANCOCK, 2;
THOMAS and DANIEL HIGGINBOTHAM, merchants, and JAMES BULLOCK, 3...
to T. and D. HIGGINBOTHAM by JESSE HIGGINBOTHAM, 25 October 1823--
$1.00; suit in Campbell County Superior Court: HENRY M. DIDLAKE
et al.; JAMES BULLOCK 100 acres in Bedford. Lines: James River,
Indian (?) Creek, ANNA SCOTT, widow of WILLIAM SCOTT--life estate by
will; MAYO DAVIES, Island in James--seven acres and devised to
GABRIEL J. SCOTT by will of father, WILLIAM SCOTT; also slaves.
DANIEL BROWN and ALBON MC DANIEL, Lynchburg Justices of the Peace.

490.	20 October 1823. JAMES W. SMITH and wife, ELIZABETH, Amherst
	County, to JACOB SMITH, Amherst County...$175--interest in
tract lately devised by JONATHAN SMITH to JAMES W. SMITH and in
possession of SALLY SMITH, widow of JONATHAN SMITH--1/10th. To
JACOB SMITH, 30 June 1829.

491.	20 October 1823. JAMES W. SMITH and wife, ELIZABETH, to
	JACOB SMITH, Amherst County...$900 234½ acres where JAMES
lives on CARTER's mill creek. Lines: BARTLETT CASH, LYNE S.
TALIAFERRO, JAMES CASH, JAMES FRANKLIN.

492.	19 October 1823. SALLY ISBELL, administratrix of ZACHARIAH
	ISBELL, Amherst County, to CHRISTOPHER ISBELL, Amherst County...
$225 horses, furniture. Amount reported by Lynchburg M.C as due
him--CHRISTOPHER ISBELL.

493.	1 October 1823. DAVID TINSLEY, Amherst County, to ROBERT
	TINSLEY, Amherst County...power of attorney. Witnesses:
ANSON TINSLEY. To ROBERT TINSLEY, 19 April 1829.

493.	19 October 1823. WILLIAM TURNER, Amherst County, to daughter,
	ELIZABETH TURNER...love--slaves.

494.	20 October 1823. JAMES DILLARD, Amherst County, 1; SAMUEL R.
	DAVIES, Amherst County, 2; JONAS PIERCE, Amherst County, 3...
$1.00 one seventh of 245 acres Rocky Run. Lines: JACOB PIERCE,
JONATHAN TYLER, DANIEL CHEATWOOD, deceased--inherited from father,
WILLIAM DILLARD. Witnesses: DAVID FULTZ, STEPHEN DAVIDSON, JONATHAN G.
WINGFIELD.

495. 6 March 1823. EDWARD and ANSELM LYNCH, executors of JONATHAN
      LYNCH, Campbell County, to JONATHAN PERCIVAL, Campbell County...
JONATHAN LYNCH died testate, 3 October 1820--Lynchburg Court. MARY
LYNCH appointed executrix and EDWARD, WILLIAM B., MICAJAH and ANSELM
LYNCH, executors. EDMOND (EDWARD) and ANSELM qualified. JONATHAN
directed sale of lands to pay debts. $1000 12 acres nearly opposite
Lynchburg, James River island. ALBON MC DANIEL and SMITHSON H. DAVIS,
Lynchburg Justices of the Peace. To JONATHAN PERCIVAL, 27 August 1832.

497. 16 October 1823. JAMES COLEMAN, Amherst County, 1; SAMUEL
      GARLAND and GEORGE W. TURNER, 2; ARCHELAUS ROBERTSON, 3...
various debts of JAMES COLEMAN--to ROBERTSON, DANIEL F. CHRISTIAN.
$1.00; tobacco crop. ALBON MC DANIEL and JONATHAN VICTOR, Lynchburg
Justices of the Peace. To ARCHELAUS ROBERTSON, 25 May 1824.

498. 16 October 1823. SAMUEL GOWING and ELIZABETH BRYANT, 1;
      JOSEPH PENN, 2; JAMES S. PENDLETON and WILLIAM G. PENDLETON, 3...
$1.00; crops, furniture. Witnesses: JONATHAN THOMPSON, JR., LUCAS
POWELL, JONATHAN N. ROSE. To JAMES S. PENDLETON, 4 November 1823.

500. 2 October 1823. ABSALOM PARKER CRUTCHER, Amherst County, for
      love and $1.00 to NANCY PUGH, daughter of JONATHAN PUGH...cow
and calf.

500. 23 September 1823. ARTHUR L. DAVIES and wife, LUCY C.,
      Gloucester County, to RICHARD L. ELLIS, Amherst County...$1890
270 acres. Lines: JONATHAN CAMM's heris, a lane. JONATHAN WICTOR
and JAMES ROSE, Lynchburg Justices of the Peace as to grantors.

501. 27 October 1823. MAYO CABELL, acting executor of COLONEL
      WILLIAM CABELL, to EDWARD A. CABELL...$6740 no acres. Lines:
KEITH, grantee.

502. 20 October 1823. ELIJAH ROSON, Amherst County, to MATTHEW
      WEBBER, 2; JONATHAN WINEBARGER, 3...$1.00; furniture, debt due
from ROBERT RIVES, LANDON RIVES, JONATHAN THOMPSON, THOMAS MASSIE, JR.,
ELISHA PETERS.

503. 12 November 1823. AMBROSE WILMORE and wife, LUCINDA, to
      LINDSEY COLEMAN--to CAPTAIN COLEMAN, 17 August 1827; 18 December
1826...$200 119 acres. Lines: DR. GEORGE CABELL, EDMOND WINSTON,
SAMUEL WATTS. Sold to WILLIAM WILLMORE by CHARLES COPPEDGE, deceased,
and by him conveyed to AMBROSE WILLMORE.

504. 1 October 1823. WILLIAM RIPPETOE, Amherst County, to daughter,
      SUSAN RIPPETOE, Amherst County...love and $1.00; beds, stock,
crops. Witnesses: HENRY and WILLIAM H. CAMDEN, WILLIAM DAVIDSON,
JESSE RICHESON, WILLIAM GATEWOOD.

504. 17 November 1823. ISAAC TINSLEY, Amherst County, to RODERICK
      DAVIES, 2; ALEXANDER TINSLEY, 3...ALEXANDER agrees to be
bondsman to WILLIAM MORGAN versus property of MERIT M. WHITE, ALEXANDER
TINSLEY, ISAAC TINSLEY, RICHARD BURKS, $1.00; slave and child.
Signed by ISAAC TINSLEY and ALEXANDER TINSLEY. Witnesses: PHILIP
LIVELY and ARCHIBALD REYNOLDS.

505. 17 November 1823. PULLIAM SANDIDGE and wife, LUCY, Amherst
      County, to JAMES F. TALIAFERRO, 2; JAMES POWELL and DABNEY
SANDIDGE, 3...JAMES POWELL and DABNEY SANDIDGE on bond by PULLIAM
SANDIDGE versus ELIJAH FLETCHER--$1.00; 350 acres on Long Mountain.
Lines: CALEB RALLS and where PULLIAM SANDIDGE lives; also tract
adjoining on Swamping Camp Creek--158 acres and where ROWLAND SANDIDGE
lives, wagon, stock, furniture.

507.   6 September 1823.   PHILIP THURMOND, Amherst County, deceased,
      died intestate, ELISAH THURMOND, son, Linvingston County,
Kentucky...power of attorney to wife, POLLY M., same county.
ROBERT C. BINGHAM, County Clerk, JAMES FORD, Presiding Justice.
Recorded Amherst County 19 November 1823.   To WILLIAM TUCKER, per
order of POLLY M. THURMOND, 1823.

509.   22 November 1823.   JABEZ CAMDEN and wife, NANCY, Amherst
      County, to CHARLES B. PENN, Botetourt County, Virginia...$1.00;
106 acres.   Lines: grantor.   Tract was conveyed to JABEZ CAMDEN by
grantee.   T. S. HOLLOWAY and LINDSEY COLEMAN, Justices of the Peace.

510.   9 October 1823.   TALBERT NOEL and wife, NANCY, Amherst County;
      SAMUEL HOGG and wife, DELSEY, Amherst County, to THOMAS MORRIS,
Amherst County...$475 81½ acres both sides Maple Creek.   THOMAS N.
EUBANK and JAMES WARE, Justices of the Peace.

511.   17 November 1823.   PULLIAM SANDIDGE and wife, LUCY, to JAMES
      POWELL and DABNEY SANDIDGE as bondsmen versus ELIJAH FLETCHER...
Superior Court, Lynchburg--judgement versus PULLIAM and JAMES
SANDIDGE, PULLIAM SANDIDGE, JR., JACK CARTER in Superior Court of
Amherst County; slaves.   Witnesses: G. A. ROSE, HENRY T. HARRIS.

512.   8 October 1823.   STEPHEN HAM, late of Amherst County, by will
      of 1 September 1810, bequeathed to me, LUCY TURNER, Sumner
County, Tennessee and equal part with his other children--at death
of my mother, MILDRED HAM--JESSE BECK and CHARLES MUNDY, executors...
power of attorney to STEPHEN H. TURNER, Sumner County, Tennessee to
receive from executors.   WILLIAM WOODALL and REUBEN SEARCY, Acting
Justices of the Peace.   ALFRED H. DOUGLAS, Clerk of Pleas and Quarter
Sessions.   JAMES DOUGLAS, Presiding Justice of the Peace.

514.   6 January 1823.   NANCY SHIELDS, Amherst County, to GEORGE L.
      HOLLOWAY...GEORGE L. HOLLOWAY has sold her tract--formerly that
of WILLIAM LEE and where she lives--366 acres, south of road from
JONATHAN HANSARD to ACH at $10. (ten) per acre.   Schedule of payments
in slaves, etc.   May pay bonds on various persons in Amherst County,
Campbell, Bedford, Botetourt, Rockbridge of Nelson; tract subject
to dower of ELIZABETH WOODROOF and ELIZABETH LEE.   Commissioners:
WILLIAM MC DANIEL, EDMOND WINSTON, DAVID S. GARLAND.   Witnesses:
WILLIAM MC DANIEL, WILLIAM GILBERT, RICHARD HARRISON.   Plat on 514.
Lines: WILLIAM MC DANIEL, DAVID WOODROOF's heirs, JAMES HILL, RUCKER
heirs, JOSHUA TINSLEY's heirs, Davis road, Lynch road, GEORGE S.
HOLLOWAY.   To NANCY SHIELDS, 6 September 1824.

514.   13 November 1823.   DABNEY T. PHILLIPS, Amherst County, WILLIAM
      ARMISTEAD, 2; ANDREW MORELAND, WILLIAM SHELTON, MARY PHILLIPS,
RICHARD L. ELLIS, GEORGE D. PHILLIPS and JAMES GARLAND, 3...bond to
RICHARD SHELTON's executors, GEORGE MC DANIEL's executors. $1.00;
slaves, crops, furniture.   Plat in estate of WILLIAM PHILLIPS which
is held by MARY PHILLIPS, widow.

516.   18 November 1823.   BANISTER TINSLEY and wife, MILLY, Bedford
      County, to ALEXANDER TINSLEY, Amherst County...$50 all interest
in TINSLEY Mill.   BANISTER TINSLEY is legatee of JOSHUA TINSLEY--
twenty acres, stock, 1/24 part.   AMBROSE RUCKER and DABNEY WARE,
Justices of the Peace, as to BANISTER TINSLEY and wife.

517.   14 November 1823.   THOMAS S. HOLLOWAY, 1; LINDSEY COLEMAN, 2;
      ARTHUR L. DAVIES, 3...debts to WILLIAM WATSON, JONATHAN MERRIT,
JAMES TURK, NICHOLAS C. KINNEY, JAMES DILLARD, JONATHAN P. COBBS;
reference to Amherst County suits; $1.00; slaves.   Witnesses:
JAMES S. PENDLETON, BEVERLY DAVIES, NICHOLAS DAVIES.

519. 12 May 1823. ELIZABETH LEE, late of Amherst County, and now
      of Barren County, Kentucky, power of attorney to brother,
CHARLES B. PENN, Botetourt...to recover dower in tracts of late
husband, WILLIAM LEE, Amherst County; suit to recover for daughter;
tract sold to GEORGE S. HOLLOWAY in 1822, but not paid. Witnesses:
WILLIAM EDMUNDS, TERRANCE COONEY, WILLIAM LONGAN, clerk, LEONIDAS H.
MAURY, Presiding Justice of the Peace.

520. 22 November 1823. JABEZ CAMDEN and wife, NANCY, Amherst
      County, to JAMES POWELL, Amherst County, 2; JAMES POWELL,
Amherst County, 3, to secure CHARLES B. PENN, 3...$1.00 700 acres.
Lines: WILLIAM STINNETT, WILLIAM CAMDEN's heirs, ZACH ISBELL,
WILLIAM PETERS, deceased, ELIZABETH COLEMAN's heirs. THOMAS S.
HOLLOWAY and LINDSEY COLEMAN, Justices of the Peace. To CHARLES B.
PENN, 22 November 1824.

521. 3 April 1823. ROBERT TINSLEY, trustee, OLIVER TINSLEY and
      wife, SOPHIA, Bedford, to GUSTAGUS A. ROSE, Amherst County...
$1100 121½ acres Lynch road. Sold by OLIVER TINSLEY to TINSLEY
RUCKER and Deed of Trust by RUCKER and wife, NANCY, to ROBERT
TINSLEY. Sold at public auction, 15 March 1822. Bedford Justices
of the Peace BALDA MC DANIEL and NATHANIEL J. MANSON.

522. 1 December 1823. HENRY L. CRUTCHER, Williamson County,
      Tennessee, power of attorney to HUDSON M. GARLAND, Amherst
County...to execute a bond to judge of Superior Court of Chancery,
Lynchburg District versus DAVID and D. HIGGINBOTHAM and Company,
administrators of GRANVILLE HENDERSON and ROBERT P. CRUTCHER,
defendants.

523. 4 December 1823. PHILIP M. DORNIN, Lewis County, Kentucky,
      power of attorney to JOSEPH KENNEDY, Amherst County...to act
in right of my wife, JANE D., late KENNEDY.

523. 5 December 1823. ABSALOM RUCKER, Amherst County, 1; SAMUEL
      GARLAND and GEORGE W. TURNER, 2; ARCHELAUS ROBERTSON, 3...$1.00
To ABSALOM RUCKER, 25 May 1824; slave, stock, tools, interest in
father's estate. SAMUEL NOWLIN and DANIEL BROWN, Lynchburg Justices
of the Peace.

524. 3 December 1823. ROBERT C. SCOTT, Campbell County, Marshall
      of Superior Court, Chancery, Lynchburg; 5 November 1823 two
suits between ROBERT C. SCOTT versus DUDLEY JONES, MILTON BENNETT,
THOMAS D. BENNETT, LEWIS BENNETT, DORCAS and THOMAS J. MOORMAN,
GEORGE MARTIN and wife, ELIZABETH, JONATHAN FOWLER and wife, VARILLA,
WILLIAM SHAW and wife, PATSY, HOWARD MARTIN and wife, LUCY, JONATHAN
WEBB, GEORGE F. MERIWETHER for THOMAS JONES, ANSELM CLARKSON and wife,
MILDRED, JAMES MARTIN, JONATHAN BURTON, GEORGE EWE (EVE), CHARLES
MUNDY, THOMAS B. TRENT (WEST?), MARTHA GOODE, GRIEF BARKSDALE, MOSES
PRESTON, JONATHAN SAMMIER (?) versus OLIVER MC REYNOLDS, Sheriff of
Campbell County, GABRIEL J. and WILLIAM WALTER SCOTT and WILLIAM
SCOTT. Chancellor's decree, 24 May 1822--non-performance: CHARLES
MUNDY versus ROBERT C. SCOTT and SCOTT to convey to heirs of THOMAS
JONES, deceased, where he lives, 202 acres and derived from them.
CHARLES MUNDY, assignee of JAMES DUNNINGTON versus SCOTT. JONATHAN
HANCOCK and SAMUEL NOWLING, Lynchburg Justices of the Peace. Page 527
is a schedule of slaves of SCOTT and other property. REUBEN PRICE,
father of my wife, died intestate; mother, ANN SCOTT.

528. 18 November 1823. ROBERT RIVERS and wife, ANNE, Madison
      County, Alabama, to WILLIAM M. RIVES, Lynchburg...$2000 404 acres
Buffaloe. Lines: WIDOW SHIELDS, LONG, JONATHAN PENN. Conveyed by
THOMPSON NOEL to ROBERT RIVERS. Witnesses: JAMES ST. CLAIR, WILLIAM
VOLTAIRE LOVING, FRED JONES, HENRY RIGNEY, Justices of the Peace
in Alabama. THOMAS RANDOM, Clerk.

529. 22 February 1823. WIATT BAILEY, W. initial, and wife, DOLLY,
      Smith County, Tennessee, to GEORGE MC TINSLEY, Amherst County...
$650. 1. Lines: WILLIAM R. ROANE, ANTHONY RUCKER, deceased,
MERIT M. WHITE, ALEXANDER TINSLEY--55 acres Harris Creek--share of
DOLLY from deceased father, JOSHUA TINSLEY--MH tract. 2. DOLLY's
undivided interest in Mountain tract on Pedlar. LITTLE B. HUGHES
and WILLIAM MOORES, Justices of the Peace in Tennessee County.

531. 15 December 1823. POLLY M. THURMOND, attorney for husband,
      ELISHA THURMOND, as heir of PHILIP THURMOND, to WILLIAM and
THOMAS TUCKER, Amherst County...$325--ELISHA is of Livingston
County, Kentucky, and heir--all of interest. 21 January 1824, to
WILLIAM TUCKER--erased in part.

531. 1 December 1823. JACOB HAAS, Bedford, to niece, MARINDA P.
      HAAS, Amherst County...slave and bought by me from JONATHAN
HAAS, Amherst County.

532. 15 December 1823. THOMAS N. EUBANKS and HILL CARTER to
      President and Directors of Literay Fund--bond--THOMAS EUBANKS
appointed treasurer by School Commissioners...I have not tried to
trace thehistory of education in Amherst County, but modern history
alone is enough to keep one busy. I attended the meeting of the
supervisors yesterday, April 3, 1966, and it was a rough one. I
have commented on fact that the southern section of the county is
rapidly growing. My wife, MILDRED MILLER DAVIS, teaches in Amelon
School which is fairly new, but it is so crowded that another teacher
had to be secured after school began for another first grade.
Elon is a little village which is in the throes of an expanding
population growth. It is situated at the foot of Tobacco Row Mountain
and the people have been asking for a new school. Some supervisors
want to consolidate Elon with Amelon and Pleasant View until they
see the way to build a new school at a cost of somewhere between
$250,000 and $300,000. This is not at all pleasing to the Elon folk
and they came--over 100 strong--to the meeting yesterday. The air
was rather hot at times and words were hurled from the supervisors
to the group. One of the former even stated that it looked as if the
group wanted "to cram a new school down our throats." One Elon person
stated that if they went to Amelon and Pleasant View, they would
NEVER get a new school. Another one jumped up and said that he
wanted to make a motion that they just stay in the courtroom until
something was done in the way of a new school. My good friend,
EUGENE CAMPBELL, is pastor of Elon Baptist Church and he finally got
the floor and poured oil on the troubled waters and got them to decide
to go home. I feel that the supervisors are really interested in
getting a new school for Elon, but they are trying to work out the
money angles since so much building has been done in the county in the
recent past. The county has borrowed a vast amount to finance the
new work at various schools and the supervisors do not want to over-
extend themselves. The Elon people are to be pitied for they are
sending children to an antiquated edifice. It is to be hoped that a
satisfactory solution will soon be reached.

532. 22 November 1823. THOMAS LAINE, Amherst County, to MICAJAH
      PENDLETON...debt to HORSLEY and FARRIS, Bent Creek...$1.00;
stock, furniture, property loaned to JACOB ANDREWS. Witnesses:
JAMES PAMPLIN. To JONATHAN HORSLEY, 1 November 1827.

533. 2 January 1824. JOSEPH B. MAYS, Amherst County, to SAMUEL
      MILLER...$262 one-fifth interest in estate of ROBERT MAYS,
deceased, in hands of widow, SUSANNAH. To SAMUEL MILLER, 1 January
1836.

534. 3 January 1824. JABEZ CAMDEN, Amherst County, to GEORGE B.
WOODSON, Campbell County...Chancery decree, Lynchburg; debt
to STERLING CLAIBORNE, Nelson County, for benefit of JACOB SWOPE,
Augusta County; 14 May 128, to GEORGE B. WOODSON by CHARLES B.
PENN--700 acres. Lines: WILLIAM STINNETT, WILLIAM CAMDEN's heirs,
ZACH ISBELL, WILLIAM PETERS, deceased, ELIZABETH CAMM, deceased.
JABEZ CAMDEN has executed Deed of Trust to JAMES POWELL to secure
CHARLES B. PENN.

535. 9 January 1824. WILLIS DUNCAN, Amherst County, to JAMES WOOD,
Amherst County...$200 197 acres south borders Buffaloe.
Lines: JONATHAN DUNCAN, JACOB SMITH, deceased, JONATHAN YOUNG.

536. 23 December 1823. NELSON C. DAWSON, Amherst County, to JACOB
HAAS, Bedford County...no amount. Slaves named in right of
wife, NANCY. Witness: DAVID AUSTIN.

537. 2 December 1825. NELSON C. DAWSON and wife, NANCY T., to
JACOB HAAS, Bedford...$6000 530 acres where DAWSON has lived
for many years past. Lines: south bank Harris Creek, PLEASANT
DAWSON, JONATHAN BURFORD, deceased, DANIEL BURFORD, RICHARD SHELTON,
VAL COX, JONATHAN CAMM, LEWIS DAWSON. AMBROSE RUCKER and DABNEY
WARE, Justices of the Peace. To JACOB HAAS, 17 December 1832.

538. 19 January 1824. Recorded; December --, 1823 JACOB HAAS,
Bedford, to AMBROSE RUCKER, SAMUEL GARLAND and MARTIN PARKS...
$5.00 for all right in above tract.

539. 25 December 1823. JACOB HAAS, Bedford, to NELSON C. DAWSON,
Amherst County...rents stipulated; lease on 530 acres conveyed
this day--three years from 1 January 1824--$1.00 for first year and
$100 per year for rest of lease. To take good care of timber and
land. Witness: DAVID AUSTIN.

539. 15 January 1824. BENJAMIN TALIAFERRO and wife, MILDRED, Amherst
County, to JAMES F. TALIAFERRO, Amherst County...$220.00 318½
acres both sides Puppie Creek; part of where BENJAMIN TALIAFERRO
lives. Lines: WILLIAM SMITH, deceased, JONATHAN YOUNG's heirs,
CHARLES P. TALIAFERRO north side of road below TALIAFERRO's old
store, JAMES PENDLETON. To JAMES F. TALIAFERRO, 29 January 1824.

540. 20 December 1823. ARCHELAUS GILLIAM, Amherst County, to
THOMAS A. and GEORGE W. MORRIS, Amherst County...$700 396 acres.
Lines: south side Pedlar, JAMES ROWSEY, JONATHAN ROBERSON, BENJAMIN
TALIAFERRO, JAMES MARTIN, PETER MARTIN, RICHARD L. ELLIS. THOMAS N.
and RICHARD N. EUBANK, Justices of the Peace.

542. 15 January 1824. THOMAS ALDRIDGE and wife, CATHERINE, Amherst
County, to CHARLES L. BARRET, Amherst County...$3000 three
acres. Lines: PAUL CABELL's lot in New Glasgow and is where tanyard
stands, CABELL's garden, notch in fence, DAVID S. GARLAND, a branch.
EDMOND PENN and ROBERT TINSLEY, Justices of the Peace.

543. 30 December 1823. JAMES HIX and wife, NANCY, CORNELIUS POWELL
and wife, ELIZABETH, to DANIEL HIGGINBOTHAM, Amherst County...
$1278.26 about 150 acres Buffaloe. Lines: AMBROSE MC DANIEL,
EDMOND COLEMAN, deceased, WILLIAM DUNCAN, JONATHAN MOUNTCASTLE--
except 45 acres held by HIX in own right. Part of share of NANCY
HIX in division of estate of AARON HIGGINBOTHAM and surrendered when
HIX took oath of an insolvent. Sold by JONATHAN WARWICK, Sheriff
to CORNELIUS POWELL who warrants only what Sheriff conveyed to him.
JONATHAN COLEMAN and CHARLES L. BARRET as to HIX and wife. THOMAS
ALDRIDGE and BENJAMIN TALIAFERRO as to POWELL and wife. To JONATHAN J.
LONDON, agent, 23 December 1831.

545. 23 September 1823. THOMAS WIAT and PLEASANT M. MILLER,
    executors of JONATHAN MILLER, Lynchburg, to CHISWELL DABNEY,
Amherst County...$2620--two tracts adjoining. 1. 37 acres. Lines:
north side Main road from Lynchburg to ACH--short distance below
house occupied by THOMAS WIAT, BURD, JONATHAN MILLER, deceased.
2. 24 3/4 acres. Lines: Main road, first tract. Knox County,
Tennessee: DAVID NELSON and JAMES DAVIDS (?), Justices of the Peace,
as to MILLER. CHARLES MC CLUNG, Clerk of Court, WILLIAM SWAN,
deputy, ROBERT HOUSTON, Presiding Justice of the Peace. SMITHSON H.
DAVIS and JAMES ROSE, Lynchburg Justices of the Peace as to WIAT.

547. 29 October 1823. EDWIN and JONATHAN F. WIAT, Knoxville,
    Tennessee, to CHISWELL DABNEY, Amherst County...$5.00 all
interest in tracts above. Same Knox officials.

548. 25 December 1823. DAVID and MARS S. HOFFMAN, Amherst County,
    to CHISWELL DABNEY, Amherst County...$5.00 all interest in
same tracts as above. SMITHSON H. DAVIS and JAMES ROSE, Lynchburg
Justices of the Peace.

550. 25 December 1823. JACOB HAAS, Bedford, to NELSON C. DAWSON...
    Friendship and esteem for him and wife, NANCY--life loan of
slaves; survivor clause; then to my legal representatives. Witness:
DAVID AUSTIN.

550. 19 December 1823. DAVID TOMLINSON, JR., Amherst County, to
    CHARLES L. BARRET, Amherst County...debts to WILLIAM and
JONATHAN TOMLINSON, executors of AMBROSE TOMLINSON; $1.00; slave.
Witnesses: BARTLETT CLEMENTS, AMBROSE TOMLINSON, ELIJAH BARNES,
SAMUEL HANSBROUGH, DAVID TOMLINSON, SR.

551. 30 December 1823. DANIEL HIGGINBOTHAM, Amherst County, to
    DABNEY SANDIDGE, 2; NANCY HIX, 3, wife of JAMES HIX, Amherst
County...18 October 1847, to DABNEY SANDIDGE and returned; 2 November
1847, to WILLIAM HIX to send to Kentucky--NANCY at marriage owned
130 acres on Buffaloe. Lines: AMBROSE MC DANIEL, EDMOND COLEMAN,
WILLIAM DUNCAN, WASH HILL--now JONATHAN MOUNTCASTLE. Descended to
her from father, AARON HIGGINBOTHAM; JAMES HIX became life tenant
and took insolvent oath. Part of tract and 40 acres of his own--
about 150 acres. Sold by JONATHAN WARWICK, Sheriff, to CORNELIUS
POWELL. DANIEL HIGGINBOTHAM bought from POWELL on equal date.
NANCY has agreed to relinquish dower and DANIEL HIGGINBOTHAM will
settle $300 in money and property on her and children; $1.00; young
slaves--five and three years of age for her benefit and her children.
JONATHAN COLEMAN and CHARLES L. BARRET, Justices of the Peace.

553. 25 September 1823. JONATHAN PATTEN and wife, SARAH, Lynchburg,
    to WILLIAM OWENS, Lynchburg...$313 11 acres bought from ROBERT
MORRIS. Lines: HENRY LANGHORN, PHILIP JOHNSON, deceased, BENJAMIN
PERKINS, a road. SMITHSON H. DAVIS and JONATHAN VICTOR, Lynchburg
Justices of the Peace; also RICHARD J. TILDEN.

554. 30 December 1823. JAMES HIX, Amherst County, to DABNEY SANDIDGE,
    Amherst County...NANCY, wife of JAMES, at marriage owned tract--
lines as in deed on page 551; she had relinquished dower to about
123 1/3 acres; 102 acres was that of JAMES in his own right. In
favor of JONATHAN MOUNTCASTLE and in 46 acres which JAMES bought from
JOANNAH and GEORGE W. HIGGINBOTHAM in favor of DANIEL HIGGINBOTHAM.
JAMES estate relinquishes $1200 to comply; $1.00--relinquished
interest in estate of AARON HIGGINBOTHAM and held by his wife, NANCY,
now deceased; slave; JONATHAN COLEMAN and CHARLES L. BARRET, Justices
of the Peace. Mailed to ALBERT HIXKS in Kentucky 25 February 1845.

555. 27 January 1824. CHARLES L. CHRISTIAN and ELIJAH L. CHRISTIAN,
    Amherst County, to SAMUEL R. DAVIES, Amherst County, 2;
WILLIAM KELLY, Amherst County, 3...$1.00; slave for benefit of wife
and children of CHARLES L. CHRISTIAN. ELIJAH is trustee.

556.   29 January 1824.   ISAAC TINSLEY, 1; DABNEY SANDIDGE, Amherst
       County, 2; NANCY TINSLEY, Amherst County, 3...NANCY relinquished
dower to JONATHAN HANSFORD on even date and $1.00; slaves, horses,
furniture. Witnesses: SAMUEL R. DAVIES and JONATHAN HANSARD, SR.
To DABNEY SANDIDGE, 20 November 1826.

557.   10 January 1824.   JONATHAN HUTCHESON and wife, LUCINDA, Amherst
       County, to LORENZO DOW, Amherst County...$100 369 acres undivided;
interest in tract of JOSHUA TINSLEY, deceased, Pedlar. Lines:
JONATHAN CRAWFORD--one-eighth part. AMBROSE RUCKER and DABNEY WARE,
Justices of the Peace. To LORENZO DOW, 29 December 1825.

558.   3 February 1824.   ISAAC TINSLEY and wife, NANCY, 1; SAMUEL R.
       DAVIES, and ISAAC HANSARD, 2; JONATHAN HANSARD, 3...JONATHAN
HANSARD on bond as administrator of WILLIAM TINSLEY, deceased, for
ISAAC TINSLEY. $1.00; 280 acres Harris Creek. THOMAS CREWS and
CHARLES P. TALIAFERRO, Justices of the Peace.

559.   27 January 1824.   STELLA W. BELL, Amherst County, to CORNELIUS
       POWELL, Amherst County...$1.00; debts to DAVID, DANIEL and
THOMAS HIGGINBOTHAM--all interest in tract from her father, SAMUEL
BELL, to his children and where her mother, SALLY T. BELL, lives--
1/5th part. Lines: HENRY H. WATTS. Witnesses: STEPHEN WATTS,
JAMES CHRISTIAN, WILLIAM HORSLEY, WILLIAM WRIGHT, HENRY H. WATTS.
Memo: trustee may sell and balance to be paid DR. MACE C. SPENCER,
AMBROSE R. PLUNKET and Campbell County man, CAPTAIN MOON. Witnesses:
as above.

560.   6 January 1824.   THOMAS ALDRIDGE, Amherst County, to HILL CARTER,
       Amherst County...power of attorney to act--also to STERLING
CLAIBORNE and JONATHAN C. CARTER, JR. Witnesses: JACOB HAIGH,
THOMAS S. CARTER, JONATHAN TALBOT.

561.   23 September 1823.   THOMAS WIAT and PLEASANT M. MILLER,
       executors of JONATHAN MILLER, Lynchburg, to JONATHAN M.
WILLIAMS, Amherst County...$3200 two adjoining tracts. 1. 109
acres. Lines: HOYLE's road, WILLIAM ROBINSON, old road, east side
main road from Lynchburg to ACH, DABNEY, ISBELL, ROBERT MORRIS,
THOMAS JOHNSON. 2. 20½ acres. Lines: tract above, JONATHAN MUNDY,
JONATHAN HANSARD, road, C. DABNEY, WILLIAM ROBINSON. Knox County,
Tennessee. DAVID NELSON and JAMES DAVIDS, Justices of the Peace
as to MILLER, CHARLES MC CLUNG, clerk of Court of Pleas, WILL SWAN,
deputy. ROBERT HOUSTON, Presiding Magistrate. Lynchburg Justices
of the Peace, SMITHSON H. DAVIS and JAMES ROSE as to WIAT.

564.   18 March 1824.   JONATHAN C. CARTER, JR., Amherst County, to
       STERLING CLAIBORNE, Amherst County...$1.00, 2; HILL CARTER and
THOMAS ALDRIDGE, 3...bonds due MURRELL, PENDLETON and Company--appeal
in Nelson Superior Court; named slaves; tobacco on THOMAS PENN's
plantation in Nelson; gig and horse. Certified to Nelson clerk,
19 March 1824. ARTHUR B. DAVIES, clerk of Amherst. To HILL CARTER,
23 March 1824.

ABSTRACT OF DEED BOOK Q OF AMHERST COUNTY, VIRGINIA

by

BAILEY FULTON DAVIS

1. 25 December 1823. DAVID HOFFMAN and wife, MARY S., CHISWELL
    DABNEY and wife, ANN, Amherst County, to JONATHAN M. WILLIAMS,
Amherst County...$5.00--release of all claims versus WILLIAMS on two
tracts. 1. 109¼ acres. 2. 20½ acres. Bought by WILLIAMS from
THOMAS WIATT and PLEASANT M. MILLER, executors of JONATHAN MILLER,
Lynchburg. SMITHSON H. DAVIS and JAMES ROSS, Lynchburg Justices of
the Peace.

2. -- 1823. EDWIN and JONATHAN F. WIATT, Knoxville, Tennessee, to
    JONATHAN M. WILLIAMS, Amherst County...$5.00 to release as above.
October 29, 1823, DAVID NELSON and JAMES DARDIS, Knox County Justices
of the Peace; CHARLES MC CLUNG, Clerk of Court of Pleas and Quarterly
Session by WILL SWAN; ROBERT HOUSTON, Chairman of Magistrates. Note:
This JONATHAN M. WILLIAMS has long intrigued me. Descendants in
Texas say that the M. stood for MORGAN. To date, I am unable to esta-
blish his parentage.

3. 10 January 1824. ALEXANDER TINSLEY and wife, PERMELIA, Amherst
    County, to GEORGE M. TINSLEY, Amherst County...$100.00 one-
eighth of tract of estate of JOSHUA TINSLEY--Pedlar. Lines: JONATHAN
CRAWFORD. About 369 acres. Witnesses: AMBROSE RUCKER, DABNEY WARE,
JOSHUA T. CLEMENTS and first two as Justices of the Peace, too.

5. 10 January 1824. GEORGE M. TINSLEY to ALEXANDER TINSLEY...one-
    fourth of TINSLEY's Mill on Harris Creek--20 acres; stock.
Witnesses: as above. Note: I have never tried to trace this site,
but believe that it is the same one as Cash's Mill. My son, THURMAN
BLANTON DAVIS, lives just a short piece from this mill on Harris. I
am told that there is an old TINSLEY cemetery in the vicinity, but
have not checked on this as yet.

5. 20 February 1824. ANDERSON L. CREWS, 1; JAMES S. PENDLETON, 2;
    SAMUEL TURNER, 3...$1.00; stock; slave boy. These deeds of trust
are generally made to second parties to secure third parties.

7. 11 December 1823. GEORGE S. HOLLOWAY, late of Amherst County,
    to HENRY H. WATTS and NICHOLAS C. KINNEY...to HENRY H. WATTS,
15 October 1824--$50.00. 1. One moiety in 916 acres held as tenants
in common by GEORGE and his sister, ELIZABETH KINNEY, derived from
uncle, HENRY HOLLOWAY. 2. Tract adjacent WILLIAM MC DANIEL and
JESSE WOODROOF--50 acres--bought from WILLIAM LEE. 3. -- acres
adjoining STERLING CLAIBORNE and JACOB PIERCE and old mill thereon--
bought under Deed of Trust from SHRADER and DILLARD. Witnesses:
WILLIAM ANDERSON, FRANCES M. TILES (?), EDMOND T. BAINBRIDGE. Memo--
to pay STEPHEN WATTS, HENRY H. WATTS, WILLIAM TU NER, JAMES S. DILLARD,
SPENCER NORVELL, THOMAS L. HOLLOWAY, JONATHAN PENN, JAMES POWELL and
JONATHAN MYERS. Acknowledged in New Orleans, Louisiana by GEORGE S.
HOLLOWAY, 12 December 1823: MARTIN GORDON, Clerk; JOSHUA LEWIS,
Presiding Justice of the Peace of First District.

8. 2 March 1824. ANTHONY and REBECCA RUCKER, Amherst County, to
    NANCY SHIELDS, Amherst County...To NANCY SHIELDS, 14 January
1824--$600--interest in estates of ANTHONY RUCKER and WILLIAM EADES.
Witnesses: JONATHAN SCOTT, RICHARD HARRISON. NANCY will pay part
out of amount for which ANTHONY RUCKER is in custody and due JONATHAN M.
SETTLE or WILLIAM MORGAN--surviving partner of JONATHAN M. SETTLE and
Company.

9. 15 March 1824. ELIJAH L. CHRISTIAN, 1; SAMUEL R. DAVIES, 2;
    WILLIAM KELLY, Amherst County, 3...$1.00; slave woman about
thirty and to bsued(?) by WILLIAM KELLY.

10.   1 March 1824.   REBECCA RUCKER, wife of ANTHONY RUCKER, releases
      all claims versus estate of WILLIAM EADES...conveyed to NANCY
SHIELDS (MRS.).   Witnesses: R. HARRISON.   To NANCY SHIELDS, 4 June
1824.

10.   7 January 1824.   WILLIAM M. RIVES, 1; ROBERT, NANCY and NATHANIEL
      RIVES, JR. (?), 2; PATRICK P. BURTON, 3...PATRICK P. BURTON on
note to Bank of Virginia, Lynchburg and also endorsed by RICHARD
WALKER. $5.00 404 acres south side Buffaloe.   Lines: ROBERT WALKER,
JONATHAN PENN, MRS. SHIELDS.   Bought from ROBERT RIVES and wife.
SAMUEL NOWLIN and JONATHAN HANCOCK, Lynchburg Justices of the Peace.

11.   19 March 1824.   ELIAS WILLS and wife, MARY G., Amherst County,
      to DR. G. A. ROSE, JONATHAN D. WILLS and BENJAMIN NORVELL, 2;
PATSY WILLS, wife of MATTHEW WILLS, Fluvanna, 3...PATSY has relin-
quished dower in two tracts in Fluvanna sold by MATTHEW to ELIAS
WILLS. 1. 155 acres on north side Rivanna. 2. 181 acres on
Cary Creek and south side of Rivanna--$5.00 131 acres in Amherst
County on north side Harris.   Lines: REUBEN PENDLETON, G. TINSLEY,
the road.

12.   1 November 1823.   WILEY DICKERSON and wife, MARY, Amherst
      County, to SIMS BROCKMAN, Amherst County...no amount.   To
T. B. BROCKMAN, 17 May 1875--both sides of road from WAUGH's Ferry
to Amherst County old Court House.   Part of tract sold by ROBERT
RIVERS to DICKERSON--419½ acres.   Lines: EDWARD CARTER, JAMES FRANKLIN,
old road, WILLIAM MANTIPLY, Mill Creek, EDMOND COLEMAN, main road.
Certified by Albemarle Justices of the Peace as to grantors: RICHARD
DUKE and ACHILLES BROADHEAD.

14.   1 November 1823.   WILLEY DICKERSON and wife, MARY, to ARCHIBALD B.
      DUKE, Albemarle...no amount.   428½ acres both sides Carter
Mill Creek.   Lines: road from WAUGH's Ferry to old ACH, JONATHAN
SMITH, EDMOND COLEMAN's heirs, JAMES FRANKLIN's heirs.   Part of tract
bought from ROBERT RIVERS, Albemarle Justices of the Peace as above.

15.   7 October 1823.   REUBEN T. MARTIN and wife, JUDITH, Breckenridge
      County, Kentucky, to WILLIAM TUCKER and THOMAS TUCKER, Amherst
County...$265 for interest in estate of THOMAS TUCKER--430 acres.
NELSON CRAWFORD and CHARLES L. BARRET, Amherst County Justices of
the Peace as to grantors, 3 December 1823.

16.   5 March 1824.   ROBERT C. HENDRICKS, Amherst County, to DANIEL F.
      CHRISTIAN, Amherst County...to DANIEL F. CHRISTIAN, 23 May 1836--
$40.00 11 acres Harris Creek.   Lines: fork of roads to CRAWFORDS and
WARES Gaps, BLUFORD HICKS.   Witnesses: DRURY CHRISTIAN, BARNETT MOHN,
MARBLE STINNETT, JUDITH F. CHRISTIAN.

Just here is blank page and error in copying by some clerk. Page 15
is crossed out and is continuation of Albemarle Justices of the Peace
DUKE and BROADHEAD. There is a repeat of REUBEN T. MARTIN's deed
and page 16 is also crossed out and is deed above of ROBERT C.
HENDRICKS.

17.   16 March 1824.   THOMAS WILLS, Amherst County, 1; WILLIAM
      SHELTON, Amherst County, 2; JONATHAN WARWICK, administrator
of JONATHAN CAMM, 3...$1.00 slave hire due JONATHAN WARWICK; stock;
furniture; tools.

18.   16 May 1823.   JONATHAN SWANSON and wife POLLY, Amherst County,
      to JOSEPH SWANSON, Amherst County...$300. 1.   250 acres on
Buffaloe Ridge. 2. 90 acres.   Tract sold by JOSEPH SWANSON to
WILLIAM JORDON.   Both hold by death of father, JONATHAN SWANSON.
JAMES and JAMES S. DILLARD, Justices of the Peace.

19. 14 November 1823. Madison trustees to THOMAS B. MAHONE, Amherst
County...$1.00 lot 55 at junction of third street and fifth
alley to domicile of DAVID HOFFMAN--half acre; lot 31 junction of
second street and sixth alley--half acre. Trustees: DAVID TINSLEY,
ELIAS WILLS, NELSON C. DAWSON, JONATHAN WIAT, WILLIAM TURNER. Witnesses:
DAVID R. EDLEY, TIMOTHY FLETCHER, REUBEN NORVELL, JAMES S. PENDLETON.

20. 24 February 1824. WILLIAM ROBINSON, Amherst County, to
JONATHAN M. WILLIAMS, Amherst County...to JONATHAN M. WILLIAMS,
2 September 1831--$640.50. 91 acres--WILLIAM ROBINSON's interest in
137¾ acres bought by both from MAJOR OLIVER TOWLES, late of Lynchburg
and Campbell-Falls Creek. Lines: WILLIAM ROBINSON's dwelling,
MAJOR WM. WARWICK, THOMAS TERRY, SR., LINEAS BOWLING. Rented by them
to SAMUEL TAYLOR. NELSON C. DAWSON and JAMES L. TOMKINS, Justices
of the Peace.

21. 19 March 1824. WILLIAM COLEMAN, Amherst County, to WILKINS
WATSON, Amherst County...$600--interest in estate of father,
GEORGE COLEMAN, and to widow, JUDITH, as dower; slaves of estate.
To WILKINS WATSON, 13 December 1831.

22. 17 March 1824. HENRY FRANKLIN, Amherst County, 1; JONATHAN
THOMPSON, JR., 2; WILLIAM STAPLES, Amherst County, 3...to
JONATHAN THOMPSON, JR., 23 June 1824--$1.00 two negresses--to settle
title a suit is in Superior Court of Lynchburg Chancery: WILLIAM
STAPLES versus PHOEBY FRANKLIN, mother of HENRY FRANKLIN; crops; debt
due from ABNER FRANKLIN, North Carolina; note in hands of BENJAMIN
FRANKLIN, North Carolina; debt due from SAMUEL HAYCOCK and in hands
of CAPTAIN JAMES GARLAND, United States Army; debt from WILLIS
FRANKLIN, Alabama; THOMAS A. HOLCOMB, executor of ROYALL. Witnesses:
STEPHEN BOWLES, JONATHAN STAPLES, WILLIAM STAPLES, JR.

24. 17 March 1824. CHARLES WINGFIELD and wife, ELIZABETH, Amherst
County, to GUSTAVUS A. ROSE, Amherst County...to C. DABNEY,
agent for MRS. HUGHES, 19 December 1853--$1080.00. Lines: DANIEL
NORCUTT at Lynch road, MICAJAH CLARK (now WILLIAM D. HILL), BOWLING
CLARK, Spring Branch, TINSLEY's Road. JAMES L. LAMKIN and WILLIAM M.
WALLER, Justices of the Peace.

25. 24 July 1823. WILLIAM WILMORE and wife, SUSANNAH, Amherst
County, to WILLIAM BATES, Amherst County...to WILLIAM BATES,
20 November 1832--$500. 1. 125 acres on both sides Pedlar. Lines:
DAVID S. GARLAND, HENRY CAMDEN, JAMES MARTIN, CRAWFORD, Galt at the
branch. 2. 117 acres Pedlar--formerly that of JONATHAN CAMDEN, SR.--
Painter Falls. Lines: HENRY CAMDEN, JONATHAN ROBERTSON. BENJAMIN
TALIAFERRO, ISAAC RUCKER, Justices of the Peace.

26. 6 March 1824. CHRISTOPHER ISBELL, Amherst County, 1; NORBORNE M.
TALIAFERRO, Lynchburg, 2; WILLIAM I. ISBELL, Amherst County, 3...
to NORBORNE M. TALIAFERRO, 24 June 1824--$5.00--slaves and 200 acres
bought from REUBEN CARVER. Witnesses: JONATHAN M. WILLIAMS,
JONATHAN TAYLOE, HENRY WILLIAMSON. Memo: CHRISTOPHER ISBELL
executed Deed of Trust to secure REUBEN NORVELL to CHRISTOPHER ANTHONY.
Released. WILLIAM I. ISBELL transfers to PAUL JONES.

28. 23 February 1824. ROBERT GARLAND, Amherst County, to JAMES P.
GARLAND, Nelson County...$1.00 and release of dower by NANCY,
wife of ROBERT in tract lately sold to JAMES S. PENN in Nelson--
next to town of Lovingston--"Garlanza." slave for benefit of NANCY
for life. Witnesses: SAMUEL LOVING, WILLIAM H. LOVING, JAMES BOID.

29. 17 March 1824. THOMAS GOODRICH, 1; GIDEON GOODRICH, 2;
JONATHAN HAAS, 3...$1.00 debts--JONATHAN HAAS cases to estate
of JOSEPH HIGGINBOTHAM; to WASH HILL--tobacco crop "where I occupy";
other crops, carpenter tools.

29. 22 March 1824. BLUFORD CAMDEN, Amherst County, to LINDSEY
COLEMAN, Amherst County, 2; JAMES POWELL, Amherst County, 3...
to JAMES POWELL, per CHARLES P. TALIAFERRO, 23 November 1824--stock,
etc.

30.   3 April 1824.   BARTLETT CLEMENTS, Amherst County, to WILLIAM
      DUNCAN, 2; ISAAC and HENRY RUCKER, Amherst County, 3...ISAAC
and HENRY RUCKER on bond to executor of AMBROSE TOMLINSON and ISAAC
is bondsman for BARTLETT CLEMENTS as guardian of his three daughters:
POLLY, JOICY and NANCY CLEMENTS to receive their share in estate of
AMBROSE TOMLINSON estate shares. $1.00--five slaves; two "horse
beasts", furniture. Witnesses: ANDERSON WARE, BENNET G. BATES,
JONATHAN CLEMENTS, WILLIAM HAISLEP.

31.   24 March 1824.   ABRAM CARTER and wife, MARY, Amherst County,
      to PETER RUCKER, Amherst County...$400 100 acres Horsley Creek.
Lines: WILLIAM SHEPHERD, GODFREY TOLER, WILLIAM DEMPSEY--formerly
WILLIAM SCHOOLFIELD, NELSON CRAWFORD and WILLIAM JOPLING, Justices
of the Peace.

32.   13 April 1824.   LINDSEY SANDIDGE, Amherst County, 1; RICHARD
      CRAWFORD, Amherst County, 2; JAMES W. SMITH, Amherst County, 3...
to RICHARD CRAWFORD, 25 July 1825--$1.00, interest in Amherst County
court decree by DUNCAN and SMITH, 141 acres where LINDSEY SANDIDGE
lives and has been there for sometime--Buffaloe. Lines: BENJAMIN
SANDIDGE, JOSEPH DODD estate, also slaves, stock, etc. Witnesses:
JONATHAN SCOTT, GEORGE W. BAILEY, SAMUEL HEISKELL.

33.   12 April 1824.   WILLIAM TOMLINSON, Amherst County, to RICHARD
      CRAWFORD, 2; JAMES W. SMITH, 3 and ALLEN TALBOT, Amherst
County, 3...to JAMES W. SMITH, October 1824--$1.00---suit in Amherst County,
WILLIAM TOMLINSON and LINDSEY SANDIDGE versus PAUL JONES, assignee of
PULLIAM SANDIDGE, BENNETT CRAWFORD--380 acres on Buffaloe where
WILLIAM TOMLINSON lives--north fork. Lines: AMBROSE TOMLINSON,
deceased; slaves, stock, furniture and interest in estate of deceased
father, AMBROSE TOMLINSON. Witnesses: as above.

35.   12 April 1824.   LINDSEY SANDIDGE, Amherst County, 1; RICHARD
      CRAWFORD, Amherst County, 2; JAMES W. SMITH and ALLEN TALBOT,
Amherst County, 3...$1.00; suit as above--tract where LINDSEY SANDIDGE
lives on Buffaloe. Lines: BENJAMIN SANDIDGE: JOSEPH DODD's estate--
141 acres. Witnesses: as above.

36.   12 April 1824.   JONATHAN STINNETT, Amherst County, 1; JACOB
      HAIGH, Amherst County, 2; THOMAS ALDRIDGE, Amherst County, 3...
$1.00 crops, stock, furniture. Witnesses: RICHARD J. WAUGH, THOMAS S.
CARTER, WILLIAM H. KNIGHT.

38.   2 November 1823.   ARCHIBALD DUKE, Albemarle, to ELISHA H.
      THURMOND, GEORGE CARR and GIDEON C. TREVILLIAN, Albemarle...to
P. WELBURN (?) DEEKS, administrator of THURMOND, 22 August 1855--
$1.00 120 acres in Amherst County. Lines: south side main road to
LINDSEY COLEMAN, JONATHAN SMITH, CARTER's old mill, JAMES FRANKLIN,
EDWARD CARTER. Albemarle Justices of the Peace: JEFFERSON RANDOLPH
and JAMES CLARKE.

40.   3 November 1823.   SIMS BROCKMAN, Orange County, to ELISHA H.
      THURMOND, GEORGE CARR and GIDEON C. TREVILLIAN, Albemarle...
$1.00 87 acres--part of 849 acres in Amherst County. Lines: same
as above. Albemarle Justices of the Peace as above as to BROCKMAN.

42.   30 March 1824.   THOMAS NORVELL, 1; WILLIAM R. ROANE, 2; THOMAS D.
      HILL, Amherst County, 3...$1.00, furniture and tools.

43.   22 November 1823.   This is different and beautiful script.
      THOMAS MORRIS and wife, NANCY, Amherst County, to MURRY
HENDERSON (HENDSON--I suspect that it is really HENSON for such a
man was here), Amherst County, $400 100 acres Bankson's Mountain,
not far from Pedlar River. Lines: JONATHAN SANDIDGE, JERRY DEAN.
THOMAS N. and RICHARD N. EUBANK, Justices of the Peace.

45. 11 March 1824. MATTHEW BURKS, now of Amherst County, to
     WILLIAM SHELTON, Amherst County, 2; DAVID A. GILBERT, executor
Deed of Trust, 20 August 1821, to secure RICHARD H. BURKS interest in
estate of parents--to MATTHEW BURKS...Also slaves and furniture. Sold
at Bethel on August -- last and estate of HENRY GILBERT, deceased,
also sold--$25.00. Witnesses: WILLIAM ARMISTEAD, J. L. WINGFIELD,
THOMAS WRIGHT, JAMES MC DANIEL.

48. 1 May 1824. JONATHAN PRYOR, Amherst County, to RICHARD HENLY,
     2; WILLIAM DILLARD, 3...$1.00 stock, furniture, etc.

49. 13 (?) March 1824. THOMAS EDWARDS and present spouse, ELIZABETH,
     to her--slaves; mare--life estate and then back to heirs in
general...To ELIZABETH EDWARDS, 13 July 1837. Witnesses: JOSEL LYON
and WILLIAM D. HILL. Memo of 21 April 1824. Witnesses: NICHOLAS
DAVIES, JESSE MUNDY.

50. 5 March 1824. LEWIS NICHOLS and wife, LEVICY, Campbell County,
     to WILLIAM BURD, Lynchburg...$50 18 acres north side James.
Lines: HENRY TRENT, WILLIAM LEE, deceased, THOMAS COCK and ADAM
CLEMENT, Campbell County Justices of the Peace.

52. 5 February 1824. DANIEL F. CHRISTIAN and wife, POLLY, to
     JOSEPH R. CARTER, Amherst County, 2; ABRAM CARTER, Amherst
County, 3...ABRAM CARTER on bond of POLLY CHRISTIAN--then COLEMAN
and since married to DANIEL CHRISTIAN. To ABRAM CARTER, 4 February
1828--about 1819 autumn--$1.00 between 3 and 400 acres. Lines:
JONATHAN AMBLER, GEORGE CABELL, deceased, WILLIAM PETERS, deceased--
where THOMAS COLEMAN formerly lived and now ROBERT GRANT lives there
as tenant. Witnesses: JONATHAN PRYOR, ROBERT H. CARTER, SAMUEL
COLEMAN. Mention of suit in Lynchburg: CHRISTIAN and wife versus
THOMAS COLEMAN, administrator of ELIZABETH COLEMAN. Margin: dower
relinquished U:256.

54. 2 April 1824. THOMAS FLINT, Rockbridge, to JONATHAN M. BROWN,
     Amherst County Sheriff...FLINT is in Rockbridge jail in debt
suit by ABRAM CARTER for Superior Court there; FLINT is about to take
oath of insolvent -$1.00--four shares of undivided tract in Amherst
County on Pedlar branches. Lines: ANDERSON WARE; 83 acres.
ALEXANDER SHIELDS and JONATHAN MC CLELLAND, Rockbridge Justices of
the Peace.

55. 28 April 1824. TANDY S. TYLER, Amherst County, 1, to SAMUEL R.
     DAVIES, Amherst County, 2; LAWSON G. TYLER, Amherst County,
3...$1.00 furniture.

56. 12 April 1824. ALLEN TALBOTT to ELIJAH FLETCHER...to ELIJAH
     FLETCHER, 19 October 1824--SAMUEL and JAMES COLEMAN, 3 February
1823, executor Deed of Trust to ALLEN TALBOTT on 140 acres. Lines:
WILLIAM PETERS, deceased, HARDWICK heirs, JABEZ CAMDEN, JAMES WILMORE.
Sold at $230 on 12 April 1824.

57. 29 April 1824. JONATHAN STINNETT, Amherst County, to CORNELIUS
     POWELL and JAMES D. HIGGINBOTHAM...debt to D. and D. HIGGINBOTHAM
and Company--to J. D. HIGGINBOTHAM, agent for Company, 7 June 1824--
$1.00 150 acres Little Piney. Lines: JESSE WRIGHT, WILLIAM DILLARD,
WILLIAM CAMPBELL, JOSEPH DILLARD. Where JONATHAN STINNETT lives;
also crops; stock, tools. Witnesses: ALEXANDER BROWN, R. J. WAUGH,
SAMUEL W. CHRISTIAN.

58. 27 May 1823. JONATHAN FRY, administrator of WILLIAM HALL,
     to WILLIAM H. KNIGHT, Amherst County...$1.00 95 acres Pedlar.
Lines: FREDERICK PRICE, JONATHAN D. CRAWFORD. Witnesses: THOMAS
ALDRIDGE, GEORGE G. WESTCOTT, J. YAGER.

59.   13 January 1824.   SAMUEL SPENCER and wife, NANCY, and STERLING
      CLAIBORNE, Amherst County, under Deed of Trust in Nelson to
DANIEL HIGGINBOTHAM...to JONATHAN J. LONDON, agent, 23 December 1831--
$4500 paid by HIGGINBOTHAM and $100 paid by CLAIBORNE--Nelson and
Amherst County tract and all to SAMUEL SPENCER on division of father,
WILLIAM SPENCER and where SAMUEL SPENCER lives--p892 acres. Lines:
TERISHA TURNER, SAMUEL TURNER, the road. County lines cut tract.
RICHARD PHILLIPS and JONATHAN P. COBBS, Nelson Justices of the Peace.

60.   20 April 1824.   NANCY SHIELDS, Amherst County, to ROBERT L.
      COLEMAN...to R. HARRISON, present trustee, 19 February 1832--
for benefit of SOPHIA HARRISON, wife of RICHARD HARRISON, and str. of
NANCY SHIELDS--free from his control and at death to such children
as she may leave and heirs of any who are dead--$1.00; named slaves.

61.   12 May 1824.   THOMAS COLEMAN, Amherst County, 1; JONATHAN D.
      MURRELL and GEORGE W. TURNER, Campbell County, 2; BOYD MILLER,
City of London, England, 3; ARCHIBALD ROBERTSON, Lynchburg, 4;
SAMUEL GARLAND, Lynchburg, 5...THOMAS COLEMAN owes BOYD MILLER as
surviving partner of WILLIAM BROWN and Company; and debt due ARCHIBALD
ROBERTSON: bond of JAMES COLEMAN and SAMUEL COLEMAN, TINSLEY RUCKER,
DANIEL F. CHRISTIAN, RICHARD BURKS, REUBEN NORVELL--all creditors.
Tract where he lives and his lot from estate of his mother; also
adjacent tract with mill--about 250 acres. Lines: WILLIAM PETERS,
JONATHAN AMBLER on Harris, also all that bought from RICHARD
BURKS and in trust to REUBEN NORVELL, 20 December 1820; slaves.
SAMUEL NOWLING and ALBON MC DANIEL, Lynchburg Justices of the Peace.

63.   8 May 1824.   JONATHAN N. ROSE and JONATHAN THOMPSON, JR.,
      Amherst County, 1; FREDERICK CABELL, Nelson, 2; JONATHAN
HORSLEY, JR., Amherst County, 3...to JONATHAN HORSLEY, JR., 10 December
1824; to JAMES ROSE, 14 April 1826--$2000 paid by HORSLEY--40 acres
Piney River tract--merchant mill and tools, tubs, saw mill, pond
race--Rose Mills--all save 3½ acres bought by ROSE and THOMPSON
from THOMAS ALDRIDGE. Witnesses: HEZEKIAH S. FULCHER, JAMES SMILEY (?),
WILLIAM H. KNIGHT, VAL. FULCHER.

65.   8 March 1824.   MOSES WRIGHT and wife, ELIZABETH, Amherst County,
      to JONATHAN CAMPBELL, Amherst County...$600 100 acres Piney.
Lines: grantee, DAVID S. GARLAND. HILL CARTER and WILLIAM M. WALLER,
Justices of the Peace.

66.   10 May 1824.   WILLIAM TOMLINSON, Amherst County, 1; DABNEY
      SANDIDGE, Amherst County, 2; JAMES W. SMITH, Amherst County, 3...
PAUL JONES, assignee of PULLIAM SANDIDGE, 22 March 1824, sued in
Amherst County versus WILLIAM TOMLINSON and LINSEY SANDIDGE--JAMES W.
SMITH is deputy for JAMES M. BROWN, Sheriff, SMITH and ALLEN TALBOT
became bondsman, 1 April 1824, for them to Sheriff and they broke
bond. SMITH is bondsman for WILLIAM TOMLINSON in RICHARD S. ELLIS
versus WILLIAM TOMLINSON and BARTLETT CLEMENTS. $1.00 334 acres on
north fork Buffaloe. Lines: ABRAM MARTIN, AMBROSE TOMLINSON, deceased,
where WILLIAM TOMLINSON lives; stock, crops, furniture, interest in
estate of deceased father, AMBROSE TOMLINSON. Witnesses: JONATHAN
SMITH, GARLAND MAYS, WILLIAM MAYS.

68.   19 May 1824.   STERLING CLAIBORNE and wife, JANE, Nelson County,
      to THOMAS GOODWIN, Nelson County...$2816.00 352 acres Buffaloe
and next to Buffaloe Springs. Lines: JAMES GOVAN, JONATHAN EUBANK,
JONATHAN HAAS, BENJAMIN SANDIDGE, ZA. DRUMMOND. Bought from JOSEPH
HIGGINBOTHAM--save for 71 acres sold by STERLING CLAIBORNE to ZA.
DRUMMOND and 112 acres sold to JONATHAN HAAS. Certified in Lynchburg
by STERLING CLAIBORNE before JONATHAN VICTOR and ALBON MC DANIEL. To
THOMAS GOODWIN, 1824 and 26 February 1829.

69. 20 September 1820. JONATHAN P. COBBS and wife, JANE, Nelson
     County, to DAVID S. GARLAND, Amherst County...to DAVID S. GARLAND,
6 April 1828--$4000 five acres plus north end of town of New Glasgow.
Lines: east side Lynch road, JAMES M. BROWN, grantor. Also two
lots of half acre each in New Glasgow--numbers 12 and 13. Twelve
formerly sold to HENRY CAMDEN and by him sold to MICAJAH CAMDEN and
by MICAJAH CAMDEN sold to JAMES P. GARLAND. EDMOND PENN and WILLIAM M.
WALLER, Amherst County Justices of the Peace.

70. 24 December 1818. RICHARD MILLNER and wife, MARTHA, to JESSE
     RICHESON, Amherst County, and LEXINGTON PARISH...$250 125 acres.
Lines: THOMAS TUCKER, Pedlar River, crossing river, Enchanted Creek.
Witnesses: JAMES WARE, WILLIAM JOPLING, CHARLES L. BARRET, THOMAS
WILLS.

71. 20 January 1824. DAVID CLARKSON, Amherst County, 1; JOEL F.
     SMITH, Amherst County, 2; ZACHARIAH DRUMMOND, Amherst County, 3...
to ZACHARIAH DRUMMOND, 19 July 1824--$1.00 one acre near Buffaloe and
bought from JOSEPH HIGGINBOTHAM, deceased; one shot gun. Witnesses:
HENRY F. and JAMES W. SMITH, WILLIAM W. DAVIES, WILLIAM COLEMAN.

72. 15 December 1823. WILLIAM MAYS, Amherst County, 1; DUDLEY
     SANDIDGE, Amherst County, 2; JAMES W. SMITH, Amherst County, 3...
$1.00 furniture; stock. To JAMES W. SMITH, 17 November 1824.
Witnesses: JONATHAN SMITH, EDWARD WARTON (?), GARLAND MAYS.

73. 28 May 1824. CHARLES H. CHRISTIAN, Amherst County, 1; BEVERLEY
     DAVIDS, Amherst County, 2; SAMUEL D. CHRISTIAN, SAMUEL R.
DAVIES and RICHARD LANDRUM, Amherst County, 3...SAMUEL D. CHRISTIAN,
SAMUEL R. DAVIES and RICHARD LANDRUM on bonds--guardian and to executor
of WILLIAM TILLER--$1.00--slaves bought from TILLER estate; furniture.
To BEVERLEY DAVIDS, 1 December 1828.

74. 29 May 1823. CHARLES H. CHRISTIAN, Amherst County, to son,
     CHARLES HARRIS CHRISTIAN, Amherst County...$1.00 slaves.

75. 11 June 1824. AMBROSE RUCKER, Amherst County, 1; JONATHAN
     MILLER, Lynchburg, 2; ABRAM R. NORTH and ALBON MC DANIEL,
Lynchburg, 3...to ALBON MC DANIEL and ABRAM R. NORTH on debt to
JONATHAN MILLER; slaves named and ages. If defaulted, to sell at
door of Franklin Hotel, Lynchburg.

76. 12 June 1824. AMBROSE RUCKER and wife, BETSY, Amherst County, 1;
     JONATHAN MILLER and DAVID R. EDLEY, Lynchburg, 2; sundry credi-
tors, 3...JAMES GILLIAM, ABRAM MARTIN, ABRAM R. NORTH, WILLIAM THURMOND,
JONATHAN HOLLING, LORENZO D. HENDERSON, THOMAS GRISSOM, Virginia
Bank at Lynchburg, WILLIAM MORGAN, DAVID TINSLEY...To AMBROSE RUCKER,
14 October 1824; returned and to JONATHAN WYTEE (?), 18 January 1847--
and D. E. MURELL (?)--$1.00 287 acres and 1/4 on Miller's Creek in
Amherst County--bought from RICHARD HARRISON in 1805; 328 acres
adjacent and bought from ISAAC TINSLEY in 1812; 60 acres adjacent
last and bought from RICHARD ELLIS in 1813; 27½ acres joining 1 and 2
and bought from GEORGE MC DANIEL in 1813--could be 2772 acres--script
has changed and; also 1350 acres adjacent last tracts and bought
from GEORGE MC DANIEL in 1817; 839 acres bought from ARTHUR L. DAVIES,
Gloucester County; 391 acres below--Pedlar road on Salt Creek--part
of tract from ARTHUR L. DAVIES--one eighth of estate of JOSHUA TINSLEY,
deceased, on Cole (sic) Mountain and bought from ANDERSON TINSLEY,
son of JOSHUA; one third of Tinsley Mill stock on Harris and bought from
RICHARD HARRISON in 1815; also 2/24 part of mill bought from JOSHUA
TINSLEY's heirs; named slaves; stock; crops; blacksmith tools; farm
tools--very long list--one fifth deducted for overseerer, ABRAM MARTIN;
also one sixth of crop at house place and share due NATHAN RUCKER.
Other creditors: THOMAS MORRIS, SR., ZACH ISBELL, ABRAM R. NORTH,
ALBON MC DANIEL, -- MONTGOMERY, JAMES TINSLEY, KYLE and Company,
WILLIAM RUCKER, DABNEY PHILLIPS, ELIZABETH CAMM, -- MARSHALL, estate
of GEORGE MC DANIEL, GEORGE MC DANIEL, SR., WILLIAM DORRIS or DOWNS(?),
LINDSEY DAVIS, estate of JOSEPH ECHOLS, WILLIAM EADSON, estate of
ANTHONY RUCKER, RICHARD ELLIS. Proved by ROBERT, ANSON and DAVID
TINSLEY, 21 March 1825.

80. 14 June 1824. ANTHONY RUCKER, 1; WILLIAM MC DANIEL, WILLIAM
TUCKER, ARCHIBALD ROBERTSON, ROBERT H. GRAY, 2; to LINDSEY
MC DANIEL, 3...$1.00 horse, gun, furniture, debt due from NANCY
SHIELDS. Witnesses: STERLING CLAIBORNE, WILLIAM DILLARD, RICHARD
HARRISON.

81. 11 June 1824. ALEXANDER TINSLEY and wife, PAMELIA, Amherst
County, and SAMUEL R. DAVIES, trustee, 2; GALT and BULLOCK,
DIACLESIN REYNOLDS, MILLNER COX, ANDERSON TINSLEY, WESTLEY DUNCAN,
GEORGE and BANISTER TINSLEY, 3...to SAMUEL R. DAVIES, 3 May 1825--
REUNEN COX, WIATT BAILEY. ALEXANDER TINSLEY is administrator of
JOSHUA TINSLEY and TINSLEY names are bondsman. $1.00, slaves.
Relinquishment of dower in R:159.

82. 25 June 1824. PULLIAM SANDIDGE, SR. to PULLIAM SANDIDGE, JR...
SR. has sold tract to CALEB RALLS on Long Mountain. 400 acres
and Buffaloe tract of 300 acres and Cold Mountain tract of 90 acres.
LUCY, wife of SR., will not sign unless provided for so SR. makes
JR. her trustee--wagon, horse, sheep, crops (overseer part excepted),
one anvil--$1.00--LUCY has life estate.

83. 25 June 1824. GEORGE W. DILLARD, trustee--GEORGE SHRADER,
executor Deed of Trust, 1 December 1820, to HENRY H. WATTS
(to HENRY H. WATTS, 15 October 1824)...Lines: JACOB PIERCE--40 acres
and mill--creditors of SHRADER: CHARLES P. TALIAFERRO and JAMES
POWELL. Advertised and bought by GEORGE S. HOLLOWAY who asked that
deed be made to HENRY H. WATTS--$1.00.

84. 24 June 1824. WILLIAM E. SMITH, Amherst County, 1; JAMES S.
PENDLETON, Amherst County, 2; PETER BURRUS, Amherst County, 3...
$1.00 mare, cattle, hogs, furniture.

86. 28 June 1824. GEORGE HOLLOWAY, Orange County, to sisters,
CATHERINE, ELIZABETH and SARAH HOLLOWAY...carriage, harness,
mare, horse, furniture and interest in my father's estate. To
WILLIAM HENLEY, 11 February 1831, as husband of ELIZABETH HOLLOWAY.

86. 25 June 1824. FLEMING SCOTT, 1; JONATHAN FRANKLIN, Amherst
County, 2; JACOB SCOTT, Amherst County, 3...$1.00; JACOB
SCOTT is bondsman to COLONEL ELLIS P. OMOHUNDRO, JONATHAN SIMPSON,
BENAMMI STONE, JAMES P. GARLAND, JONATHAN L. HARRIS, MATTHEW BURKS,
JAMES POWELL--crops on tract of CHARLES HIGGINBOTHAM, deceased.

88. 10 June 1824. PULLIAM SANDIDGE, SR. and wife, LUCY, to
JONATHAN BROWN, Amherst County...$1000 201 acres Buffaloe and
Long Mountain. Lines: AMBROSE TOMLINSON, HENRY HARTLESS, deceased.
To JONATHAN BROWN, 15 May 1826. BENJAMIN TALIAFERRO and ISAAC
RUCKER, Justices of the Peace.

89. 17 June 1824. CHARLES TINSLEY and wife, FRANCES, Amherst County,
to JONATHAN DAVIS, Amherst County...$245 2 May 1833 to JONATHAN
DAVIS--east side Pedlar and whereon are Sulphur Spring Mills--66½ acres.
Lines: ABRAM CARTER. JAMES WARE and RICHARD N. EUBANK, Justices of
the Peace.

90. 15 December 1823. BENNETT G. BATES, Amherst County, 1; ISAAC
RUCKER, Amherst County, 2; WILLIAM BATES and THOMAS DRYDON, 3...
also debt to CARUTHERS and SHIELDS, Lexington merchants; ELLIS and
EUBANK. $1.00, slaves, stock. Witnesses: DANIEL BATES, W. S.
THORNTON, AMBROSE E. JONES. To WILLIAM BATES, 29 September 1825.

92. 24 May 1824. ZA DRUMMOND and wife, ISABELLA M., Amherst County,
to CHARLES P. TALIAFERRO, Amherst County...$600 45 2/5 acres
Puppie Creek--ZA DRUMMOND's part of former tract of JONATHAN TALIAFERRO
and held as dower by late ELIZABETH TALIAFERRO. BENJAMIN TALIAFERRO
and ISAAC RUCKER, Justices of the Peace.

93. 24 May 1824. ZA DRUMMOND and wife, ISABELL M., Amherst County,
to JAMES GOVAN, Hanover County...$152 19 acres Buffaloe. Lines:
grantee, ridge road. Justices of the Peace as above.

271

94. 24 May 1824. PULLIAM SANDIDGE and wife, LUCY, Amherst County,
     to ELIJAH FLETCHER, Campbell County...to ELIJAH FLETCHER,
19 October 1824--$180 118 acres Buffaloe. Lines: ZA DRUMMOND,
JAMES GOVEN. Justices of the Peace as above.

95. 3 June 1824. PULLIAM SANDIDGE, SR. to PULLIAM SANDIDGE, JR...
     To JR., 11 January 1825. SR. has sold 201 acres to HENRY
HARTLESS; also six other tracts of 300; 149 acres; 200 acres; 250;
200 acres; 180 acres. To satisfy LUCY, his wife, slaves, furniture,
149 acres on Long Mountain. $1.00 life interest.

96. 24 May 1824. PULLIAM SANDIDGE and wife, LUCY, to ELIJAH
     FLETCHER, Campbell County...$550 390 acres on Davis Mountain.
To ELIJAH FLETCHER, 19 October 1824. Same Justices of the Peace.

98. 14 November 1823. Madison Trustees to BENJAMIN A. PHILLIPS,
     Lynchburg...$1.00 lot 46 second street and third alley--half
acre. Lot 47--second street and third alley; lot 26--second street
and third alley. Trustees: DAVID TINSLEY, NELSON C. DAWSON,
JONATHAN WITT, ELIAS WILLS, WILLIAM TURNER. Witnesses: D. R. EDLEY,
TIMOTHY FLETCHER, REUBEN NORVELL, JAMES S. PENDLETON.

99. 25 June 1824. Agreed by PULLIAM SANDIDGE and ELIJAH FLETCHER...
     Long Mountain tract of 300 acres where PULLIAM SANDIDGE lives--
PULLIAM SANDIDGE to convey. Lines: WILLIAM HAISLEY, CALEB RALLS
(bought by DUDLEY SANDIDGE and J. CARTER), to deliver on or before
1 January next and may sow small grain.

99. 29 March 1824. NELSON CRAWFORD, acting executor of CALEB RALLS,
     Amherst County, to DUDLEY SANDIDGE, Amherst County...RALLS by
will directed sale and to divide to children and sold at Mansion house
25 February year aforesaid--400 acres on Long Mountain at --. Lines:
top of Long Mountain, LINDSEY BURKS, the road, JONATHAN RICHESON,
JONATHAN CLEMENTS, CHRISTIAN, HORSLEY. To DUDLEY SANDIDGE, 17 March
1828.

101. 21 June 1824. JOSEPH STAPLES, Amherst County, 1; HENRY FRANKLIN,
      Amherst County, 2; WILLIAM STAPLES, Amherst County, 3...to
WILLIAM STAPLES, 15 March 1833--$2225 500 acres--Deed of Trust by
HENRY FRANKLIN and wife, JANE, 28 July 1823 and JOSEPH STAPLES sold
by consent of HENRY FRANKLIN. HENRY FRANKLIN bought from JONATHAN
RICHESON. Lines: AMBROSE TOMLIN, AARON HIGGINBOTHAM. WILLIAM
STAPLES bought at $1805 and slaves in Deed of Trust at $120 and $300.

102. 23 June 1824. HENRY FRANKLIN, Amherst County, 1; JONATHAN
      THOMPSON, JR., Amherst County, 2; WILLIAM STAPLES, Amherst
County, 3...$1.00 crops near the Cold Mountain--STAPLES on bond to
THOMAS A. HOLCOMBE; and on AB of HENRY FRANKLIN as administrator of
father, JEREMIAH FRANKLIN; bond to JOSEPH STAPLES.

103. 23 June 1824. JESSE WOOD, 1; ROBERT TINSLEY, 2; ABRAM EWERS,
      3...CALEB WOOD on bond $1.00 furniture, stock.

105. 24 June 1824. THOMAS WILLIAMSON, 1; HEZEKIAH FULCHER, 2; JAMES
      FULCHER, 3...$1.00 slaves names and ages; furniture. To JAMES
FULCHER, 23 March 1829.

105. 24 June 1824. HENRY FRANKLIN and wife, JANE C., Amherst County,
      1; BENJAMIN FRANKLIN, North Carolina, 2; HENRY FRANKLIN, Amherst
County, 3...HENRY married JANE C. MOSS, daughter of WILLIAM MOSS--
intestate--WILLIAM owned considerable land on Piney and JANE entitled
to one-eighth. Husband wants to sell and she agrees, if $400 bestowed
on her and children. On -- she executed deed to him. 500 acres which
HENRY bought of JONATHAN RICHESON near Cold Mountain. HENRY wished to
sell this and she agreed, if $300 bestowed on her, and release of dower
to JOSEPH STAPLES. To bestow amounts, HENRY transfers to BENJAMIN
FRANKLIN a debt of about $700 due by bond. BENJAMIN is to buy North
Carolina tract for amount and deed is to be made to JANE C. and
children with BENJAMIN as trustee.

117.   24 June 1824.   MICAJAH CAMDEN and wife, MARY, Amherst County,
       to JONATHAN ROBINSON, Rockbridge...to JACOB M. RUFF, 26 October
1839; $3000 535 3/4 acres south borders Huff. Lines: grantor,
DAVID S. GARLAND, ROBERT WALKER, JABEZ CAMDEN, GEORGE S. HOLLOWAY,
JAMES POWELL, BENJAMIN TALIAFERRO and CHARLES L. BARRET, Justices
of the Peace.

109.   13 July 1824.   WALTER L. CHRISTIAN, Amherst County, to CHARLES L.
       CHRISTIAN, Amherst County...$150 71 acre tract bought from
BENJAMIN WARNER. Lines: WILLIAM DILLARD, deceased, DANIEL CHEATWOOD.
To CHARLES L. CHRISTIAN, 21 February 1825.

110.   14 November 1823.   EDWARD LYNCH and ANSELM LYNCH, executors
       of JONATHAN LYNCH, Campbell County, to WILLIAM I. ISBELL,
Amherst County...JONATHAN LYNCH died 31 October 1820, testate--
Lynchburg Hustings Court--appointed MARY LYNCH, EDWARD, WILLIAM B.,
MICAJAH and ANSELM LYNCH as executors and they are only ones who
qualified. To sell as much as needed to pay debts--half acre near
top of the hill around the road from toll bridge--$16.75. Lines:
southeast corner of lot 1 in Madison; BENJAMIN PERKINS. SMITHSON H.
DAVIS and ALBON MC DANIEL, Lynchburg Justices of the Peace.

111.   10 July 1824.   JAMES WILLMORE, Amherst County, 1; JAMES D.
       HIGGINBOTHAM, Amherst County, 2; D. and D. HIGGINBOTHAM and
DANIEL HIGGINBOTHAM and Company, Amherst County, 3...to SAMUEL W.
CHRISTIAN, agent, 17 May 1826. $1.00 140 acres. Lines: JAMES
POWELL, HARDWICK heirs, JONATHAN COLEMAN. Bought from JONATHAN
MC DANIEL, stock, tools, crop, etc., amount due from CHARLES DAVIES.
Witnesses: RICHARD J. WAUGH, WILLIAM C. JORDAN, SAMUEL W. CHRISTIAN,
MANSFIELD WARE.

113.   15 July 1824.   JONATHAN TINSLEY, Amherst County, to RICHARD N.
       EUBANK, Amherst County...debts to RICHARD L. ELLIS and JONATHAN
and R. L. ELLIS, Amherst County. $1.00 58 acres. Lines: WALTER
WILLIAMS, LINDSEY TINSLEY on Peavine Mountain; furniture, tools,
crops.

114.   19 July 1824.   RICHARD WOOD, 1; JOSEPH PENN, 2; ROBERT TINSLEY,
       3...$1.00 slaves named: FRANCES and child, WASHINGTON.

115.   19 July 1824.   MARTIN PARKS to RANDOLPH CASH...18 August 1823,
       THOMAS GOODRICH executor Deed of Trust to MARTIN PARKS and
WILLIAM M. RIVERSS. Cash bought for $126 260 acres.

115.   1 March 1824.   JAMES FULCHER, Amherst County, to WILLIAM MOORE...
       to WILLIAM MOORE, 9 January 1825. JONATHAN HUDSON executor
Deed of Trust and WILLIAM MOORE bought for $151.00 93 acres. Witnesses:
DILLARD H. PAGE, JONATHAN STINNETT.

116.   10 March 1824.   JOSEPH KENNEDY and wife, ELIZABETH, Amherst
       County, to WILLIAM O'BRYANT, Amherst County...$21 three acres
northeast side of DILLARD's road, RICHARD ALLCOCK, WILLIAM WRIGHT,
grantee lives on it. Witnesses: JESSE KENNEDY.

117.   19 July 1824.   ALLEN TALBOT, 1; STERLING CLAIBORNE, 2; JONATHAN
       TALBOT, WILLIAM MC DANIEL, JAMES W. SMITH, 3...$1.00 slaves
named, stock, etc.

117.   17 July 1824.   WILLIS CARTER to WILLIAM J. FREELAND...$60
       160 acres in Territory of Arkansas--northeast quarter of Section 1
of Township 3, north, Range 11 West. Obtained by WILLIS CARTER for
service in last war.

118.   19 July 1824.   ANDERSON C. KIDD, 1; JONATHAN THOMPSON, JR., 2;
       STERLING CLAIBORNE, 3...$1.00 crops, stock, carpenter's tools,
etc.

119. 25 June 1824. PULLIAM SANDIDGE, SR. and wife, LUCY, to
      PULLIAM SANDIDGE, JR...$500 118 acres Buffaloe. Lines:
ZA DRUMMOND, FLUCKER (sic), GIVINS. BENJAMIN TALIAFERRO and ISAAC
RUCKER, Justices of the Peace.

120. 25 June 1824. PULLIAM SANDIDGE and wife, LUCY, to ELIJAH
      FLUCKER (sic)...$550 300 acres Buffaloe and Pedlar. Lines:
JACOB CARTER, CHARLES BARRET "layed off" for me over the Cold Mountain,
WILLIAM HASLEP, CAPTAIN RUCKER's muster field, RIGHT's Scoul (sic)
hous (sic), old Stilhous (sic) br. DUDLEY SANDIDGE's Spring Branch.
Justices of the Peace as above.

121. 14 November 1823. Madison trustees to WILLIAM I. ISBELL...
      $1.00 lot 40--third street andClark Street--half acre; lot 41--
third and Clark, half acre; lot 63--third street and first alley,
3/4 acres. Four lots--1, 2, 22, 23--First or Main and Clark--two
acres. Lot 3--First or Main and Clark--running north half acre.
Signed by DAVID TINSLEY, NELSON C. DAWSON, JONATHAN WIATT, ELIAS
WILLS, WILLIAM TURNER. Witnesses: D. R. EDLEY, TIMOTHY FLETCHER,
REUBEN NORVELL, J. S. PENDLETON.

122. 26 July 1824. WILLIAM VIA, 1; PETER CHRISTIAN, 2; REBECCA
      LAYNE, 3...$1.00 stock, furniture. Witnesses: BEVERLY DAVIES.
To J. F. CHRISTIAN, 26 November 1824.

123. 20 July 1824. JAMES R. LIVELY, 1; LINDSEY COELMAN, 2; JAMES
      POWELL, 3...JAMES POWELL on bond for JAMES R. LIVELY as constable;
$1.00--interest in estate of JAMES LIVELY, deceased, and widow's
dower--about eight slaves, furniture, tools. Witnesses: SAMUEL R.
DAVIES, NICHOLAS DAVIES, WILLIAM BOURNE.

124. 26 July 1824. HOLLAND GOODRICH to THOMAS COPPEDGE, JR...$43.87
      stock priced by head. Witnesses: JONATHAN LONOGAN, WILLIAM
WILCHER, JAMES W. COPPEDGE.

124. 31 July 1824. ROBERT GARLAND, Amherst County, 1; DANIEL
      PERROW and WILLIAM H. LOVING, 2; JAMES P., SPOTSWOOD and
BURR GARLAND, 3...ROBERT owes JAMES P. GARLAND in Nelson Circuit
Court on judgement; JAMES P. is surviving partner of JAMES P. GARLAND
and JAMES HENDERSON--JAMES P. GARLAND and Company; for hire of negro
boy, too and JAMES P. GRALAND is on bonds in Albemarle, Nelson,
Amherst County, and Superior Court of Chancery in Lynchburg. SPOTSWOOD
GRALAND on bond to JAMES LOVING's administrator and SUSANNAH FRANKLIN
for benefit of BURR GARLAND on appeal to Amherst County Superior
Court. $1.00; named slaves; stock; furniture; etc. HILL CARTER and
WILLIAM M. WALLER, Justices of the Peace. To JAMES P. GARLAND,
5 October 1824.

128. 25 March 1824. LANDON C. RIVES and wife, ANNE MARIA, Nelson,
      to ELIJAH MAYS, Nelson County...$1692.50 199 acres Juniper
Creek and bought from MAYS and wife, ELIZABETH, 9 January 1818.
Lines: JOSEPH MAYS, DAWWON. To ELIJAH MAYS, 17 April 1826.
ROBERT J. KINCAID and SAMUEL LOVING, Nelson Justices of the Peace.

129. 25 November 1823. BENJAMIN NOEL and wife, JUDITH, Amherst
      County, to JONATHAN WARE, Amherst County...$25 1 3/4 acres south
side Pedlar. Lines: grantee. ISAAC RUCKER and WILLIAM JOPLING,
Justices of the Peace.

131. 9 August 1824. WILLIAM S. APPLEBERRY, 1; WILLIAM R. ROANE, 2;
      THOMAS D. HILL, 3...WILLIAM S. APPLEBERRY owes MOSS, MORRIS and
JOPLING Company on Amherst County judgement and THOMAS D. HILL on
bond. $1.00 interest in estate of HUGH NORVELL, deceased.

132.   7 August 1824. DANIEL F. CHRISTIAN and wife, POLLY, Amherst
       County, to PETER F. CHRISTIAN, Amherst County...$2860 400 acres
Harris and both sides of creek--where ROBERT GRANT lives. Lines:
Bare Mountaon. Also 126 acres where DANIEL F. CHRISTIAN lives on both
sides of Harris. Lines: WILLIAM PENDLETON, the road, BLANFORD
HICKS, ZACH ISBELL, JACOB PHILLIPS, SAMUEL COLEMAN. Also tract
where FRANCIS FEAGANS lives of 45 acres. Lines: the branch, the
road, BROWN, WILLIAM PENDLETON, BURFORD. HILL CARTER and LINDSEY
COLEMAN, Justices of the Peace.

134.   12 August 1824. PETER F. CHRISTIAN, 1; SAMUEL R. DAVIES, 2;
       DANIEL F. CHRISTIAN, 3...$1.00 128 on Harris; 45 acres on
Harris; 400 acres on Harris and sold by DANIEL F. and wife, POLLY,
to PETER F. in 1824.

136.   11 August 1824. WILLIAM CASHWELL, Amherst County, to THOMAS
       STRANGE, Amherst County, 2; PETER CASHWELL, Amherst County, 3...
$1.00 ten slaves named and ages; crops. To THOMAS STRANGE, 28 February
1826.

138.   8 July 1824. DRURY BELL, Amherst County, to SAMUEL HANNAH and
       MARTIN M. DAVENPORT, Lynchburg, 2; BELL and ROSE, Lynchburg, 3...
$1.00 named slaves, stock, tools. Witnesses: W. M. TALIAFERRO,
S. H. DAVIS and T. A. HOLCOMB, Lynchburg Justices of the Peace. To
trustee per order of WILLIAM MORGAN, 1824,

140.   14 August 1824. JONATHAN RUCKER, Amherst County, 1; PETER P.
       THORNTON, 2; ELISHA RUCKER, Rockbridge, 3...to P. THURMOND,
agent, 20 March 1828; returned 24 June and to P. THURMOND again.
ELISHA RUCKER is bondsman to RICHARD L. ELLIS, $1.00 stock, furniture,
crops with ANDREW MORELAND this year. P. THURMOND signed as agent.

142.   16 August 1824. CORNELIUS PEARCE, 1; SAMUEL R. DAVIES, 2;
       JACOB and JONAS PIERCE, Amherst County, 3...JACOB and JONAS
PIERCE on bond--constable; $1.00; shot gun; horse. DAVIES is called
CRAWFORD, trustee, and evidently clerical error for it is signed
DAVIES.

143.   13 August 1824. RICHARD HARRISON, 1; NANCY SHIELDS, 2; THOMAS D.
       HILL, 3...to protect NANCY SHIELDS as bondsman to JONATHAN WARD,
WILLIAM L. and SAMUEL BURKS, AMBROSE WILLMORE--$1.00 crops, furniture,
two lottery tickets, boats.

144.   10 August 1824. JONATHAN PADGETT and wife, PEGGY, Amherst
       County, to NANCY PADGETT, Amherst County...48 acres at $5.00
per acre; on road from Galt's mill to CH. Bought by JONATHAN PADGETT
from MOSES PENN. Lines: Rocky Run, Porrage, road, EPHRAIM PADGETT,
JONATHAN WARWICK, JAMES LONDON, THOMAS HUTCHESON, THOMAS EDWARDS,
grantee, grantor. LINDSEY COLEMAN and EDMOND WINSTON, Justices of
the Peace.

146.   2 July 1824. JOSHAU SANDIDGE, Amherst County, to ZA DRUMMOND,
       2; CHARLES L. BARRET, 3; COLEMAN and BARRET, 4; CHARLES L.
BARRET and Company, 5...$1.00 stock, crops, etc. Witnesses: WILLIAM
COLEMAN, GEORGE TAYLOR, PULLIAM SANDIDGE, ALLEN TALBOTT, WILLIW WHITE.

148.   25 November 1823. BENJAMIN NOEL and wife, JUDITH, Amherst
       County, 1; JAMES ROWSEY, Amherst County, 2...$30 14 acres south
side Pedlar. Lines: WILLIAM HORSLEY, JONATHAN WARE, grantee. Sent
to TALBOT NOEL, per order to JAMES ROWSEY, 20 February 1832. ISAAC
RCUER and WILLIAM JOPLING, Justices of the Peace. RUCKER above--error.

150.   31 July 1824. BENJAMIN NOEL and wife, JUDITH, to NATHAN G.
       MORRIS, Amherst County...$520 348 acres Pedlar. Lines:
CHARLES TYLER, a branch, JONATHAN ROBINSON, JAMES ROWSEY, JONATHAN
WARE. Justices of the Peace as above.

152.   16 August 1824. THOMAS GOODRICH, 1; MARTIN PARKES, 2; JACOB
       HAAS, 3...$1.00 slave, stock, etc. Carpenter's tools. To
JACOB HAAS, 1 October 1824.

153. 25 December 1823. DAVID HOFFMAN and wife, MARY S., CHISWELL
      DABNEY and wife, ANN, Amherst County, to THOMAS WIATT and
PLEASANT M. MILLER, executors of JONATHAN MILLER, Lynchburg, and
bondsmen: JONATHAN WIATT and EDWARD LYNCH...$5.00 release of all
claims versus estate. SMITHOSON H. DAVIS and JAMES ROSE, Lynchburg
Justices of the Peace. To CHISWELL DABNEY, 17 January 1825.

156. 2 June 1824. JACK CARTER to FRANCES CARTER, Amherst County...
      100 acres on Buffaloe. Lines: JONATHAN CLEMENTS, Long Mountain,
ANNIS HARTLESS, WILLIAM DILLARD, ELIZABETH FULCHER, DUDLEY SANDIDGE--
consideration: one negro wench and child--SALLIE and FRANK.
Witnesses: HENRY FRANKLIN, WILLIAM CLEMENTS, PULLIAM SANDIDGE.

157. 16 August 1824. ROBERT C. SCOTT to CHARLES MUNDY, Sheriff of
      Amherst County...SCOTT has taken insolvent oath--to CHARLES
MUNDY, 18 November 1824, by JOSEPH PETTYJOHN, deputy. Sheriff--suit
of GARLAND, WALTON and PENN--judgement in Campbell County lease that
he and brother, THOMAS N. SCOTT, have made with AMBROSE RUCKER and
crops.

158. 14 August 1824. ROBERT TINSLEY, Amherst County, to DAVID S.
      GARLAND, Amherst County...$175 50 acres both sides Pedlar.
Lines: THOMAS JORDAN, Blar's Creek (sic), THOMAS ALLEN. Fifty acres
both sides middle fork of Pedlar. Lines: THOMWS JORDAN, mill rave
area to be reserved and cut. Granted WILLIAM MACKEY, if he built
mill on his river land.

160. 12 August 1824. ANDREW MORELAND, Amherst County, to WILLIAM
      ARMISTEAD, Amherst County, 2; THOMAS LAIN, Amherst County, 3...
To WILLIAM ARMISTEAD, 8 December 1824. $1.00 debts due WILLIAM SHELTON
and THOMAS LAIN--slaves, crops on tract rented from HUGH PAXTON,
Rockbridge, and Amherst County crops, stock. Rockbridge tract near
mouth of North River, debt due GEORGE T. WILLIAMS and Company, assignee
of NELSON C. DAWSON, THOMAS WILLS who sues for ARCHIBALD ROBERTSON,
WILLIAM MORGAN, assignee of BELL and ROSE, MARY PHILLIPS, assignee of
DABNEY T. PHILLIPS, ALBON MC DANIEL, estate of JOSEPH ECHOLS,
assignee of WILEY COPER, NANCY SHIELDS, estate of ANTHONY RUCKER,
WILLIAM JORDAN, ELIZABETH CAMM, EDMOND WINSTON. Slaves in hand of
Amherst County sheriff or deputies. Witnesses: CHALRES TUCKER,
NAHUM OSGOOD, EDMOND WINSTON.

164. 12 August 1824. HENRY LAYNE, Amherst County, to DAVID S.
      GARLAND, Amherst County...$200 90 acres south borders Pedlar.
Lines: grantee, WILLIAM HALL. Witnesses: ROBERT TINSLEY, JO PENN,
H. M. GARLAND. To DAVID S. GARLAND, 27 September 1832.

166. 1823. EDWIN and JONATHAN F. WIATT, Knoxville, Tennessee, to
      JONATHAN M. WILLIAMS, Amherst County...$5.00 release as above,
page 2 of this book to THOMAS WIATT and PLEASANT M. MILLER, administrators of JONATHAN MILLER, Lynchburg. To C. DABNEY, 17 January 1825.

168. 17 August 1824. WIATT DUNCAN and wife, MARY, Amherst County,
      to JAMES D. HIGGINBOTHAM and WILLIAM DUNCAN, Amherst County...
to L. P. THOMPSON, attorney for D. and D. HIGGINBOTHAM and Company,
17 January 1826--$1.00 to secure company. 209 acres Horsley Creek.
Lines: THOMAS N. EUBANK, WILLIAM MITCHELL; where WIATT DUNCAN lives.

170. 17 August 1824. JAMES WAUGH, commissioner of Amherst County
      court to LUKE RAY...to LUKE RAY, 23 November 1825--$400 200 acres.
Lines: grantee, ALLISSON MORRIS, SAMUEL NICELY, JAMES WAUGH.
JONATHAN SLEDD's tract at death.

171. 15 April 1823. RICHARD HARRISON and wife, SOPHIA, Amherst
      County, to SAMUEL SIMMONS, Amherst County...Deed of Trust by
HENRY CAMDEN to JAMES POWELL, ARTHUR B. DAVIES and STERLING CLAIBORNE--
two tracts of 327 and 307 acres. POWELL and DAVIES sold to RICHARD
HARRISON and RICHARD H. BURKS--$1000.00.

173.   30 July 1824. GEORGE B. WOODSON, Marshall of Superior Court
       of Chancery, Lynchburg, to THOMAS CREWS, Amherst County...
3 November 1823, THOMAS CREWS, WILLIAM BRYDIE, NANCY MC CREDIE,
BETSY BRYDIE versus WILLIAM LONG and wife, BETSY, JONATHAN and
RICHARD ELLIS, THOMAS ALDRIDGE, GEORGE MYERS, JAMES L. PENDLETON,
WILLIAM MASSIE (or MANN?), JONATHAN MYERS and Company--to sell and
pay any surplus to LONG and wife. Sold, 11 June 1823--to THOMAS
CREWS at $1.00--81½ acres. ALBON MC DANIEL and CHARLES L. DIBRELL,
Lynchburg Justices of the Peace.

175.   19 August 1824. THOMAS ALDRIDGE and wife, CATHERINE, Amherst
       County, to JONATHAN ROBERTSON, Rockbridge...$1110 98 acres north
fork Piney. Fifty acres south fork Piney. Lines: JONATHAN MAMMON.
EDMOND PENN and CHALRES L. BARRET, Justices of the Peace.

177.   17 August 1824. DAVID FULTZ, 1; ROBERT WINGFIELD, Amherst
       County, 2; ISAAC RUCKER, Amherst County, 3, and executor of
AMBROSE RUCKER...$1.00 slave and children.

178.   17 August 1824. GABRIEL J. SCOTT, Campbell County, to HENRY B.
       ELY, Campbell County and WILLIAM W. SCOTT, Amherst County, 2;
THOMAS W. SCOTT, Campbell County, SALLY N. SCOTT, wife of ROBERT C.
SCOTT, Amherst County, 3...to N. M. TALIAFERRO, 1824--THOMAS SCOTT
is bondsman for GABRIEL for keeping the limits of the Campbell County
jail. Last April or May GABRIEL left limits of jail and in June, last,
made Deed of Trust to HENRY and WILLIAM for THOMAS, SAMUEL M. SCOTT,
BARNETT FINCH, JR. (other bondsman) in Bedford. Suit of REUBEN PENDLETON
versus GABRIEL for recovery of two negroes: GILBERT and NICHOLAS.
GABRIEL intends to apply for injunction in Lynchburg District Court
on judgement last August term or to judge of Superior Court of
Campbell. Wishes to continue to support wife and children of ROBERT C.
SCOTT--SALLY R. SCOTT. ROBERT has taken insolvent oath--$1.00--all
claims versus brother, ROBERT C.--Lynchburg Chancer suit. ROBERT C.
is plaintiff versus OLIVER MC REYNOLDS, late sheriff of Campbell;
GABRIEL J. SCOTT, WILLIAM W. SCOTT, WILLIAM PENDLETON. Another
suit: ROBERT C. versus DUDLEY JONES et al--two negroes named above.
AMBROSE RUCKER and DABNEY WARE, Justices of the Peace.

182.   27 August 1824. PHILIP LIVELY, 1; JONATHAN B. DUNCAN, 2;
       WILLIAM DUNCAN, 3...To WILLIAM DUNCAN, 1825--$1.00 all interest
in dower of NANCY YOUNG, widow of JONATHAN YOUNG--where she lives--
420 acres. Lines: BENJAMIN TALIAFERRO, CHARLES TALIAFERRO, deceased;
slaves, stock. Also 2/7 interest in dower of -- LIVELY, widow of
JAMES LIVELY--includes mine and that of CORNELIUS CAMPBELL by sale,
slaves, stock.

186.   10 Spetember 1824. WILLIS RUCKER, Amherst County, to WILLIAM
       ARMISTEAD, Amherst County, 2; WILLIAM SHELTON and JANE E.
RUCKER, 3...WILLIAM SHELTON on bond for WILLIS RUCKER as guardian of
RICHARD T. and JONATHAN D. L. RUCKER--account of JANE E. $1.00;
various items; cooper tools; interest in estate of FRANCIS C. COLE,
deceased.

188.   10 September 1824. PHILIP LIVELY and wife, SUSAN, Amherst
       County, to WILLIAM MC DANIEL, Amherst County, 2; NANCY SHIELDS,
Amherst County, 3...$100--to RICHARD HARRISON, agent, 20 June 1825--
233 acres. Lines: JONATHAN MC DANIEL, MRS. BROWN, JONATHAN LONDON,
deceased. Devised by JAMES LIVELY, SR. to son, JAMES R., and by him
sold to PHILIP and his interest in father's estate--in hands of JANE
LIVELY; stock. EDMOND WINSTON and RICHARD HARRISON, Justices of
the Peace.

189.   14 November 1823. Madison Trustees to WILLIAM P. CORRELL,
       Lynchburg...$1.00 lot 60 at junction of third street and third
alley--half acre. DAVID TINSLEY, NELSON C. DAWSON, JONATHAN WIATT,
ELIAS WILLS, WILLIAM TURNER. Witnesses: D. R. EDLEY, TIMOTHY
FLETCHER, REUBEN NORVELL, J. L. PENDLETON. Assigned to JONATHAN R.
SIMMONS by CORRELL, 24 December 1823. Witnesses: JONATHAN HARDWICK,
EDWIN D. MEREDITH.

191. -- November 1809. HUGH CAMPBELL and wife, ELIZABETH, CHARLES L.
     BARRET, JAMES and ANN BARRET, Amherst County, to JOSHUA TINSLEY,
Amherst County...to GEORGE M. TINSLEY, 15 November 1824--$1211 two
tracts of 380¼ in all--north fork Pedlar and on side of Long Mountain.
1. 225¾ acres. 2. 150 acres. Lines: NEIL CAMPBELL, deceased.
No explanation as to late recording of deed.

193. 30 June 1823. OLIVER TOWLES, SR., and wife, AGATHA, to ODEN
      CLAY...to CHISWELL DABNEY, 1825--$1.00 520 acres--one undivided
interest of estate of PHILIP JOHNSON, deceased, and bought by
OLIVER TOWLES, SR. from CLAUDIUS BUSTER. Lines: CHALRES HOYLE,
GOODWIN--part most distant from Lynchburg--Poison Field. Witnesses:
GEORGE HOYLE, H. L. LANGHORNE, JOSEPH TURNER.

194. 2 June 1824. JONATHAN B. DABNEY and wife, ELIZABETH L.,
      Campbell County, to MEREDITH LAMBETH, Campbell County...$1.00
tract where OLIVER TOWLES, JR. lived--now deceased--and interest
of ELIZABETH L. as heir. Lines: ODEN G. CLAY, CHARLES HOYLE--residue
of 1002 3/4 acres formerly that of CLAUDIUS BUSTER and wife, NANCY,
and by them conveyed to OLIVER TOWLES, JR. 350 acres of it sold to
CHARLES HOYLE, Lynchburg in life of OLIVER TOWLES. 520 acres fartherst
from Lynchburg to ODEN G. CLAY. THOMAS FOX and JONATHAN ORGAN,
Campbell County Justices of the Peace and also ALEXANDER AUSTIN and
THOMAS COCKE, Justices of the Peace.

196. 7 September 1824. OLIVER M. TOWLES, Attacapas, Louisiana,
      "Co.", to MEREDITH LAMBETH, Campbell County...$1.00 one-eighth
of tract of OLIVER TOWLES, JR., deceased. Lines: as above. By
attorney, JONATHAN B. DABNEY. Last two Justices of the Peace above
of Campbell County as to DABNEY.

197. 28 June 1824. LANDON E. RIVES and wife, ANNA MARIA, Nelson
      County, to MEREDITH LAMBETH, Campbell County...$1.00 one-eighth
of tract above as heirs. ROBERT J. KINCAID and SAMUEL LOVING,
Nelson Justices of the Peace.

199. 19 August 1824. CHARLES DUNCAN, 1; JAMES D. HIGGINBOTHAM, 2;
      D. and D. HIGGINBOTHAM and Company, 3...To JAMES D. HIGGINBOTHAM,
19 October 1824--$1.00 judgement in Amherst County court. 155 3/4
acres. Lines: HENRY CAMDEN, PRESTON GARLAND, TANDY RUTHERFORD,
MICAJAH CAMDEN. Bought from GEORGE DUNCAN, stock, tools, etc.
Witnesses: LUCAS P. THOMPSON, SAMUEL W. CHRISTIAN, RICHARD T. WAUGH.
Memo: JAMES WOOD bondsman for DUNCAN to JAMES S. PENDLETON and
Company or PENDLETON and MOUNTCASTLE--judgement versus DUNCAN and
WOOD in Amherst County court--to protect WOOD, JAMES HIGGINBOTHAM
will sell, if required. Witnesses: as above.

202. 25 September 1824. ISAAC SCOTT, Amherst County, to JAMES D.
      HIGGINBOTHAM, 2; D. and D. HIGGINBOTHAM and Company, 3...$1.00
tobacco on my plantation, corn, stock, furniture. To JAMES D.
HIGGINBOTHAM, 19 October 1824.

204. 23 September 1824. JACK CARTER and wife, KEZIAH, Amherst
      County, to BENJAMIN SANDIDGE, Amherst County...$1400 142 acres
between main branches of Buffaloe, Mill tract. Lines: AMBROSE
TOMLINSON, deceased, JONATHAN TOMLINSON, grantee, Mill Mountain.
BENJAMIN TALIAFERRO and ISAAC RUCKER, Justices of the Peace.

206. 11 October 1824. JONATHAN N. ROSE to LUCAS P. THOMPSON...ROSE
      and JONATHAN THOMPSON, JR. owe THOMAS LANDRUM, WILLIAM STAPLES,
MARY ROSE, STERLING CLAIBORNE (tobacco land rent), JONATHAN CREWS,
BENJAMIN GAYLE's guardian, SIMON CRISP, SARAH FRANKLIN, THOMAS WOOD.
$1.00 one half of ROSE Mills and tract, saw mill and shops, out
houses, crops in Amherst County and Nelson on land rented from
STERLING CLAIBORNE. ROSE Mill is on Piney.

208.	23 September 1824.	JACK CARTER and wife, KEZIAH, Amherst County,
	to LINDSEY SANDIDGE, Amherst County...to LINDSEY SANDIDGE,
17 November 1824--$1000 365 acres both sides Buffaloe. Bought from
RICHARD MILLNER and wife, MARTHA, by LINDSEY SANDIDGE and JACK CARTER,
26 November 1818. BENJAMIN TALIAFERRO and ISAAC RUCKER, Justices of
the Peace.

210.	31 July 1824.	JONATHAN WARE, SR., executor of WILLIAM WARE,
	deceased, to WILLIAM JOPLING and NELSON CRAWFORD, Amherst
County...$1030 57½ acres. To WILLIAM JOPLING, 21 April 1828--west
side Horsley. Lines: JONATHAN S. CARTER, RICHARD EUBANK, LAIN's
Spring Branch, road from old CH to WAUGH's ferry, mill site and
known as the Mill Tract. JAMES WARE and RICHARD N. EUBANK, Justices
of the Peace.

211.	28 September 1824.	THOMAS LANGHORNE, Amherst County, 1; JOSEPH
	STAPLES, Amherst County, 2; WILLIAM M. WALLER, Amherst County,
3...$1.00 stock, furniture, tobacco.

213.	18 September 1824.	RICHARD WOOD to ELIZABETH and SALLY WOOD...
	$500 stock, furniture--long and interesting list. Witnesses:
JONATHAN STRATTON, MOORE F. CARTER, EDWARD H. CARTER.

214.	-- July 1824.	GEORGE B. WOODSON, Marshall of Superior Court
	Chancery, Lynchburg District, to WILLIAM BRIDIE NAPIER...decree
of 3 November 1823: THOMAS CREWS, WILLIAM BRIDIE, NANCY MC BRIDE(IE)
and BETSY BRIDIE--not use of MC with one name--versus WILLIAM LONG;
wife, BETSY; JONATHAN and RICHARD ELLIS; THOMAS ALDRIDGE; GEORGE
MYERS, JAMES S. PENDLETON, WILLIAM MARR and JONATHAN MYERS--to sell
Lainville tract. Sold, 9 January. Lines: JAMES POWELL, -- RIVERS,
NANCY SHIELDS, LINDSEY COLEMAN. 650 acres. $1.00. JONATHAN VICTOR
and S. H. DAVIS, Lynchburg Justices of the Peace. Recorded:
14 August 1824.

215.	29 September 1824.	SPENCER NORVELL, Amherst County, to CHISWELL
	DABNEY and JAMES L. LAMKIN, Amherst County...THOMAS D. HILL and
ELIAS WILLS are bondsmen to NANCY SHIELDS, Amherst County. $1.00--
assigned to ELIJAH FLETCHER--slave. To ELIJAH FLETCHER, 3 January
1825.

216.	29 September 1824.	WILLIAM SHELTON, Amherst County, to RICHARD L.
	ELLIS, Amherst County, and THOMAS N. EUBANK, Amherst County...
$1.00--to RICHARD L. ELLIS, 19 April 1825--852 acres devised from
father and where WILLIAM SHELTON lives; interest in estate of ABRAM
DANIEL, deceased; helf by his widow; interest by will in estate of
JOSHAU SHELTON, deceased--one moiety of 634 acres and conveyed by
RICHARD H. BURKS by deed, cattle, furniture, tools, books, Bethel lot
and interest in estate of HENRY GILBERT, deceased. Two slaves in
Alabama conveyed to M. BURKS, trustee, for his benefit; other slaves.

218.	1 October 1824.	DABNEY T. PHILLIPS, Amherst County, to DAVID S.
	GARLAND, Amherst County...$200 21 acres--his lot from estate
of WILLIAM PHILLIPS, deceased, on south side Buffaloe.

218.	15 January 1824.	CHARLES L. BARRET and wife, SARAH, Amherst
	County, and THOMAS ALDRIDGE, Amherst County, to SAMUEL W.
CHRISTIAN for DANIEL HIGGINBOTHAM...16 July 1829--to DANIEL HIGGINBOTHAM,
Lynchburg. $1.00. Lines: PAUL CABELL in New Glasgow, DAVID S.
GARLAND--tanyard thereon and recently bought from THOMAS ALDRIDGE,
PAUL CABELL's garden. EDMOND BENN and ROBERT TINSLEY, Justices of
the Peace.

220. 25 September 1824. HUGH TAGGART and wife, NANCY; CORNELIUS
    POWELL, trustee, to DANIEL HIGGINBOTHAM...to JONATHAN J.
LONDON, agent, 23 December 1831--Deed of Trust on 21 February 1822,
to CORNELIUS POWELL and defaulted. 18 September 1824, sold to
DANIEL HIGGINBOTHAM for $700. $1.00 193½ acres. Lines: GOOLSBY
heirs, BEVERLY WILLIAMSON's heirs, AMBROSE MC DANIEL, a road,
JONATHAN SMITH. Bought from WILLIAM SALE. HILL CARTER and THOMAS
ALDRIDGE, Justices of the Peace.

222. 8 October 1824. THOMAS ALDRIDGE and wife, CATHERINE, Amherst
    County, to SAMUEL R. DAVIES, Amherst County...$50 half acre.
Lines: WASH HILL--north of ACH, a road, Clerk's office, Lynchburg
road. CHARLES L. BARRET and WILLIAM M. WALLER, Justices of the Peace.

223. 9 October 1824. FLEMING CASHWELL, Amherst County, 1; BENNET A.
    CRAWFORD, Amherst County, 2; JAMES POWELL, Amherst County, 3...
$1.00 furniture, crops as overseer of BENAMMI STONE.

224. 11 September 1824. SAMUEL SIMMONS and wife, CYNTHIA, Amherst
    County, to ARTHUR B. DAVIES, Amherst County...$110 3½ acres.
Lines: grantee, JAMES POWELL's mill.

225. 4 October 1824. LUCAS POWELL, Amherst County, to CHARLOTTE
    and COURTNEY POWELL...$300 slave. Witnesses: JONATHAN
THOMPSON, JR.

225. 8 October 1824. LUCAS POWELL to MARY POWELL...$200 slave.

226. 29 July 1824. LUCY ROBERTSON (this is spelling employed, but
    it is also ROBINSON in other data in Amherst County) to WILLIAM
ROBERTSON--to JONATHAN M. WILLIAMS, administrator of WILLIAM ROBERTSON,
11 April 1825--wishes to make equal distribution to her children and
WILLIAM has bought interest of following children: HENRY, LEWIS,
THOMAS, JOSEPH BEVERLY, PHOEBE TENNERSON, DOLLY MC DANIEL, deceased--
love for son, WILLIAM, 132 acres north border Bolling Creek--part of
my MH tract. Lines: MEAD, the road, Opossum Island road, HOYLE,
WIATT--life reservation set forth. REUBEN NORVELL and JAMES L.
LAMKIN, Justices of the Peace.

227. 11 October 1824. WILLIAM JOPLING, Amherst County, 1; BENNET A.
    CRAWFORD, Amherst County, 2; CHARLES CRAWFORD, Kentucky;
LEONARD HENLEY, ABRAM CARTER, NELSON CRAWFORD, Amherst County, 3...
3 on bond to JONATHAN WARE, executor of WILLIAM WARE, Amherst County.
To BENNET A. CRAWFORD, 20 November 1830--$1.00 400 acres where
WILLIS JOPLING lives. Lines: WILLIAM PRYOR, JONATHAN S. CARTER,
CHARLES C. CARTER--includes MH, slaves, stock, furniture, crops.

229. 9 October 1824. LUCAS POWELL, Amherst County, to JONATHAN
    THOMPSON, JR., debts to BROWN and RIVES Company, MORRIS and
JAMES, RICHMOND (BENJAMIN POWELL, Nelson County is bondsman), N. LOFTUS
and Company (MARY POWELL is bondsman)...$1.00, stock, mare in hand of
EDWARD JONES, Lynchburg, crops on ROSE land and THOMPSON near ROSE
Mills; two houses in Amherst County and two in Nelson County.

231. 11 October 1824. JONATHAN THOMPSON, JR. and JONATHAN N. ROSE, 1;
    JAMES ROSE, 2; MARY ROSE, wife of JONATHAN N. ROSE, 3...April,
1823, JONATHAN N. ROSE and JONATHAN THOMPSON, JR., sold to WILLIAM M.
WALLER 221 acres--part conveyed to him and dower relinquished
27 September 1823--11 3/4 acres left and for dower, JONATHAN N.
conveys to MARY with JAMES ROSE, trustee; $1.00. Lines: next to
tract sold to WALLER, JONATHAN N. ROSE, trustee in tract sold to
JONATHAN L. PENN, JONATHAN P. COBBS, mill tract.

232. 8 October 1824. JOSEPH DILLARD, Amherst County, to ROBERT
    TINSLEY, Amherst County, 2; DAVID S. GARLAND and JONATHAN
DILLARD, 3...JOSEPH DILLARD owes Virginia bank at Lynchburg; $1.00;
debt to SAMUEL GARLAND; ten slaves named and ages, furniture, stock.
To ROBERT TINSLEY, 24 September 1827.

235. 13 October 1824. BENAMMI STONE, Amherst County, to JAMES P.
     GARLAND, Nelson County, 2; ROBERT GARLAND and wife, NANCY,
Amherst County, 3...to JAMES P. GARLAND, 16 August 1826-November,
1813, ROBERT GARLAND married NANCY, daughter of STONE and BENAMMI
STONE made Deed of Trust to ROBERT WALKER, now deceased, for NANCY's
benefit and husband--two slaves. It was acknowledged in clerk's
office, but, for some reason, was never recorded--lost. Love for
son-in-law and my daughter and also for my daughter, KITURAH, and
children. KITURAH is wife of JAMES P. GARLAND.

236. 15 October 1824. NELSON C. DAWSON and DABNEY WARE as to BETSY
     RUCKER, wife of AMBROSE RUCKER, 2 June 1824, to JONATHAN MILLER
and DAVID R. EDLEY.

237. 5 October 1824. AMBROSE RUCKER and wife, BETSY, Amherst
     County, 1; wife is 2; EDWIN L. RUCKER and WILLIAM B. RUCKER,
Amherst County, 3...reference to Deed of Trust to DAVID R. EDLEY and
JONATHAN MILLER and to protect wife who relinquished dower--$1.00--
all profits from land in Deed of Trust; proceeds of suit versus
THOMAS LAIN in Amherst County; bond versus LEONARD CARTER in Amherst
County court; suit in Lynchburg Chancery versus SAMUEL BURKS, JR.
NELSON C. DAWSON and DABNEY WARE, Justices of the Peace.

238. 20 September 1824. CHARLES MUNDY and JESSE BECK, executors
     of STEPHEN HAM, to ARCHILLUS REYNOLDS, Amherst County...to
WILLIAM KENT, 27 March 1846 or 66-hard to read--$2452.50 490½ acres
Stovall Creek. Lines: LINEASS BOLLING, WILLIAM BURFORD, SR.,
JESSE BECK, WILLIAM TURNER, a branch, SAMUEL ANDERSON, WILLIAM GALT--
where HAM lived.

240. 18 October 1824. THOMAS WILLIAMSON, Amherst County, to JAMES
     FULCHER, Amherst County...$1.00 power of attorney as to business
in Amherst County and Nelson counties. Witnesses: LUCAS P. THOMPSON,
JAMES D. HIGGINBOTHAM. To JAMES FULCHER, 1829.

241. 10 October 1824. WILLIAM STINNETT, Amherst County, 1; DANIEL
     HIGGINBOTHAM, 2; D. and D. HIGGINBOTHAM and Company, 3...$1.00--
to SAMUEL W. CHRISTIAN, 30 November 1829--170 or 180 acres both sides
Huff. Lines: PETER G. CAMDEN, JABEZ CAMDEN--where WILLIAM STINNETT
lives. Witnesses: WILLIS DUNCAN, JONATHAN PRYOR, MICAJAH and PETER G.
CAMDEN.

242. 27 September 1824. BENJAMIN NORVELL, 1; JAMES L. LAMKIN, 2;
     REUBEN NORVELL, 3...$5.00--To REUBEN NORVELL, 16 May 1825--
REUBEN NORVELL is bondsman with SPENCER D. and HUGH NORVELL, deceased,
JAMES BENAGH. Slaves, stock, furniture, interest in claim of
TINSLEY RUCKER versus WILLIAM WARE's executor and transferred by
TINSLEY RUCKER to BENJAMIN NORVELL; to heirs of HUGH NORVELL and
interest in estate by will.

244. 16 October 1824. WILLIAM S. LONDON, 1; EDWARD A. CABELL, 2;
     LAVENDER LONDON, AUSTIN WRIGHT, JONATHAN DILLARD, WILLIAM M.
WALLER and Company, D. and D. HIGGINBOTHAM and Company, JAMES S.
PENDLETON and Company, JACOB HAIGH and Company--suits pending in
Amherst County...$1.00--all medical accounts, horses, silver, watch.
Also debts to HORSLEY and FARIS, DABNEY P. BRYANT.

245. 25 September 1824. ISAAC RUCKER, Overseer of Poor, to BENNET G.
     BATES...bound out to BATES, JONATHAN FLINT, age of 13 until 21
to learn carpenter's trade. WILL JOPLING also signed.

246. 8 October 1824. DAVID TINSLEY, SR. and wife, ANN, Amherst
     County, to ARCHIBALD ROBERTSON, Lynchburg...to ARCHIBALD ROBERTSON,
18 November 1824--$60 six acres. Lines: both, ISAAC TINSLEY, deceased,
JONATHAN HUTCHINSON, road from old chappel (sic) across creek--on
Harris Creek. AMBROSE RUCKER and DABNEY WARE, Justices of the Peace.

247.   9 October 1824. RICHARD EUBANK and wife, PEGGY, Amherst County,
        to THOMAS N. EUBANK, Amherst County...$1000 199½ acres Horsley
Creek. Lines: HAYNES, NELSON CRAWFORD's mill, LANE, mouth of branch.
JAMES WARE and RICHARD N. EUBANK, Justices of the Peace.

248.   21 October 1824. ABRAM MARTIN, JR., Amherst County, 1; THOMAS
        COPPEDGE, JR., Amherst County, 2; JONATHAN TUCKER, Amherst
County, 3...$1.00, JONATHAN TUCKER on bond to JONATHAN PENN, JR.,
executor of JONATHAN PENN, SR. 188 acres Indian Creek. Lines:
JONATHAN TUCKER, also slave, crops coming from AMBROSE RUCKER,
furniture. Witnesses: BEVERLY DAVIES, RICHARD CRAWFORD, NICHOLAS
DAVIES.

249.   25 October 1824. JONATHAN B. TALIAFERRO, Amherst County;
        PETER G. CAMDEN, 2; to SAMUEL R. DAVIES, 3...$1.00 crops,
stock, furniture. Witnesses: A. MUNDY, HOWELL L. BROWN, JONATHAN
SCOTT.

250.   23 July 1824. SARAH ANN and MILDRED J. ROSE to THOMAS ALDRIDGE...
        by father's will have interest in tract called Bellevitte.
STERLING CLAIBORNE has sold part of it to THOMAS ALDRIDGE who hath
sold to WILLIAM MORGAN--between seven and 800 acres. STERLING CLAIBORNE
has paid them $500 to release title--$1.00 paid by THOMAS ALDRIDGE
and title released.

251.   27 September 1823. HENRY MORRIS, Lynchburg, to D. and D.
        HIGGINBOTHAM and Company...$1.00--legacy of wife, ANN JENEFER
MORRIS, daughter of MRS. ELIZABETH NIXON, deceased, by late DR. (?)
DANIEL JENEFER, Chas. County, Maryland. Witnesses: JAMES D.
HIGGINBOTHAM, ACHILLES D. JOHNSON. To JONATHAN J. LONDON, agent for
D. and D. HIGGINBOTHAM and Company, 1 June 1833.

252.   23 October 1824. JAMES HIGGINBOTHAM, Amherst County, 1;
        JAMES D. HIGGINBOTHAM, Amherst County, 2; D. and D. HIGGINBOTHAM
and Company, Amherst County, 3...to trustees, 14 May 1825--$1.00
165½ acres. Lines: JONATHAN HIGGINBOTHAM, deceased, EDWARD A. CABELL,
JOSEPH DILLARD, slaves--where JAMES D. HIGGINBOTHAM lives.

253.   1 November 1824. SIMEON A. BURCH, Amherst County, to JOSEPH R.
        CARTER, 2; ROBERT H. CARTER, 3...to ROBERT H. CARTER, 23 November
1824; $1.00; furniture, etc. Rent bond on blacksmith slave.

254.   5 August 1824. WILLIAM J. FREELAND, 1; MERIWETHER LEWIS, 2;
        DONGALD FERGUSON, JR., 3...to W. P. WOODROOF for MERIWETHER LEWIS,
3 November 1824--SARAH ABBIT has recovered juggment in Buck. versus
WILLIAM J. FREELAND for debt due from late firm of GARLAND and
FREELAND; bound with NELSON FREELAND and appealed; $1.00; all interest
in books of firm of DUVAL and Company; half third interest in blacksmith
shop--PHILIP DUVAL and Company; interest in dower of widow of DAVID
WOODROOF, Amherst County, in right of his wife and share bought from
WILLIAM HARRISON who married a sister of his wife; interest in dower
of late widow of -- WOODROOF of Buck--she has since married CAPTAIN
JONATHAN HOOD, Buck. Part of wife is that of WILLIAM HARRISON,
daughter of JONATHAN WOODROOF. Crops in Amherst County and Nelson
in partnership with GEORGE SPILLER. Witnesses: RICHARD CLARKE,
SILAS B. VAWTER, CHARLES L. CHRISTIAN, WIATT P. WOODROOF.

256.   9 October 1824. MICAJAH CAMDEN and wife, MARY, Amherst County,
        to DANIEL HIGGINBOTHAM, Amherst County...$2300 460 acres both
sides Beaver Creek; branch of Buffaloe, and both sides main road
from WILLIAM SANDIDGE to ACH. Lines: grantor, HENRY CAMDEN, CHARLES
DUNCAN, TANDY RUTHERFORD, GEORGE H. BRALEY, SPICEY DUNCAN, LEONARD
HENLEY, ST. GEE TUCKER. To JONATHAN J. LONDON, 23 December 1831,
top of Mobley's Mountain. Witnesses: PETER G. CAMDEN, WILLIS DUNCAN,
CHARLES L. BARRET and EDMOND PENN, Justices of the Peace.

257. 18 October 1824. JAMES POWELL and wife, MILDRED, Amherst
      County, to THOMAS CREWS, Amherst County...$3000 two acres or
thereabouts with manufacturing mills--Montpelier and late property
of JAMES FRANKLIN, deceased. To THOMAS CREWS, 24 September 1828.

258. 4 November 1824. PLEASANT WINSTON, Richmond, to BOWLING CLARK,
      Campbell County...PLEASANT WINSTON intends to make Deed of
Trust for creditors--to C. DABNEY, 10 May 1830--lot with two brick
houses on D or Carey Street, Richmond--back towards the river and
occupied by G. and J. COSLEY, tenants. ELIZABETH C. is wife of
PLEASANT WINSTON and has consented to relinquish dower, if protected--
$1.00 two tracts in Campbell County. 1. About 450 acres. 2. About
120 acres. Also tract in Amherst County of about 96 acres--maiden
tracts of ELIZABETH C. from father—one-seventh; bank stock; at death
of her mother; debt due from HENRY CLARK; slaves in Campbell County--
ages and names. A. PLEASANTS and J. H. EUSTACE, Richmond Justices
of the Peace.

260. 30 October 1824. WILLIAM PAMPLIN, JAMES PAMPLIN, LEORY PAMPLIN,
      ROBERT ROGERS who married MARY PAMPLIN, ISHAM JOHNSON who
married SALLY PAMPLIN, JAMES PAMPLIN, JR., administrator of JONATHAN
PAMPLIN--now residents on James River in Amherst County, Nelson,
and Buckingham--all devisees of ROBERT PAMPLIN, late of Louisiana--
power of attorney to SAMUEL GARLAND, Lynchburg, to receive amount
from estate devised us and late NICHOLAS PAMPLIN, deceased--he died
1818 intestate and no issue--heirs under will of ROBERT PAMPLIN. To
SAMUEL GARLAND, 12 November 1824 by A. ROBERTSON, Buck. County:
JAMES PAMPLIN, JR., WILLIAM, JAMES, LEROY PAMPLIN, ROBERT ROGERS,
ISHAM JOHNSON. Justices of the Peace: WILLIAM WALTON and JONATHAN
HARRIS, JR.

262. 15 October 1824. THOMAS ALDRIDGE, Amherst County, to HILL
      CARTER...power of attorney. Witnesses: LUCAS P. THOMPSON,
JAMES S. PENDLETON, STERLING CLAIBORNE.

263. 15 November 1824. JACOB HAAS, Bedford, to brother-in-law,
      THOMAS GOODRICH and wife, ELIZABETH, Amherst County...love--
long list of items--during my eill and pleasure.

263. 13 November 1824. JESSE CAMPBELL, Amherst County, 1; JONATHAN
      MASSIE, 2; JONATHAN CAMPBELL, 3...$1.00 furniture, stock,
crops.

265. 15 November 1824. THOMAS G. GOODRICH, Amherst County; JACOB
      HAAS, Bedford, 2; BOYD MILLER and DAVID S. GARLAND, 3...to
S. GARLAND, 30 June 1825--THOMAS GOODRICH with JONATHAN HAAS, bondsmen,
made bonds to JOSEPH HIGGINBOTHAM and assigned to BOYD MILLER and
DAVID S. GARLAND; suit in Amherst County; HIGGINBOTHAM's executors;
$1.00 tobacco where he lives; tobacco made by RICHARD SMITH--1/3;
books, tools--unsold by trustee, MARTIN PARKS.

266. 15 November 1824. JAMES C. BURFORD, Amherst County, 1; JOSEPH
      MC CRAY, Amherst County, 2; DABNEY WARE, Amherst County, 3...
$1.00 debts to MOORE and Company; JESSE RICHESON, administrator of
ANTHONY RUCKER; suit in Amherst County; JAMES WARE; slaves named.

267. 10 February 1820. JONATHAN HUTCHINSON and wife, LUCINDA,
      Amherst County, to THOMAS HUTCHINSON, Amherst County...$1050
70 acres Porrage. Lines: CHARLES MUNDY, grantee, THOMAS EDWARDS,
grantor--bought of HIGGINBOTHAM; lane dividing tract JONATHAN HUTCHINSON
bought of JAMES LONDON, JR.--Sugar Hill; WIATT. Witnesses: JONATHAN
LONDON, CHARLES PALMORE, HARRISON GENTRY. Acknowledged November 15,
1824 by JONATHAN HUTCHINSON.

268. 13 March 1824. CORNELIUS POWELL, tract of WILLIAM H. CAMDEN,
and D. and D. HIGGINBOTHAM and Company, 1 October 1821 to
DANIEL HIGGINBOTHAM...To SAMUEL W. CHRISTIAN, 6 February 1828--$150
paid at public auction at home of WILLIAM H. CAMDEN 260 acres and
where HENRY CAMDEN lives. One of tracts conveyed by HENRY to
WILLIAM H. on --. POWELL, 13 March 1824, sold for $50 to DANIEL
HIGGINBOTHAM--Pedlar tract--Rowsey tract 160 acres and bought by
WILLIAM H. CAMDEN et al. from HENRY CAMDEN.

269. 17 November 1824. ALLEN TALBOT, Amherst County, 1; HEZ J.
FULCHER, Amherst County, 2; JAMES FULCHER, Amherst County, 3...
debts to NELSON CRAWFORD, executor of CALEB RALLS, HENRY L. DAVIES,
JAMES M. BROWN, late Amherst County sheriff--appointed by BROWN--to
protect JAMES FULCHER as bondsman. $1.00, crops, silver watch.

272. 17 November 1824. JONATHAN WARWICK, late sheriff of Amherst
County, to JOSEPH PENN, Amherst County...SAMUEL THURMOND took
insolvent oath at suit of JONATHAN PERKINS for benefit of J. D. URQUHART
in Amherst County--house and lot in Madison; duly advertised by
deputy sheriff, GEORGE S. HOLLOWAY. JOSEPH PENN bought at $25.00.

272. 29 October 1824. JAMES PLEASANTS and wife, SUSANNAH, to THOMAS
ALDRIDGE...$430 270 acres--230 acres of it to SUSANNA from
father, COLONEL HUGH ROSE--40 acres bought from GUSTAVUS A. ROSE and
joins. Richmond Justices of the Peace: JONATHAN H. EUSTACE and
A. PLEASANTS.

273. 8 September 1823. NATHAN WILLIAMSON, Amherst County, to
HENRY WILLIAMSON, Amherst County...$300 1¼ acres Lynch road
from Lynchburg to ACH and where NATHAN WILLIAMSON lives. Witnesses:
JORDAN CREASY, THOMAS MURRELL, JAMES TERRY.

274. 15 November 1824. SAMUEL P. LAYNE, Amherst County, 1; BEVERLY
SEAY, Nelson, 2; JAMES SEAY, Nelson, 3...JAMES SEAY on bond to
BRNJ GARLAND--termination of suit between SAMUEL GARLAND and THOMAS
CREWS; $1.00; slave; furniture; stock.

275. 23 July 1824. D. P. GOOCH to ELIJAH L. CHRISTIAN...$142.42 to
release Deed of Trust by CHRISTIAN to HENRY H. WATTS, for
benefit of GOOCH.

275. 20 November 1824. JAMES WILMORE, Amherst County, to JONATHAN
FRANKLIN, Amherst County...Deed of Trust on 140 acres. Lines:
JAMES POWELL, HARDWICK heirs, JAMES COLEMAN and bought from JONATHAN
MC DANIEL. Deed of Trust, 24 April 1823, to JAMES D. HIGGINBOTHAM
and one of --. $20.27 paid by JONATHAN FRANKLIN until 1 May 1826 as
tenant. Witnesses: ROBERT TINSLEY, POWHATAN D. FRANKLIN, GUS. ROSE.

276. 24 July 1824. HILL CARTER and EDMOND PENN as to JANE MARIA
CLAIBORNE, wife of STERLING CLAIBORNE, 17 February 1823, to
JONATHAN HAAS.

276. 15 December 1824. BLUFORD CAMDEN, Amherst County, 1; BEVERLY
DAVIES, Amherst County, 2; CHARLES P. TALIAFERRO, Amherst
County, 3...$1.00; CHARLES P. TALIAFERRO on bond to HUGES in Amherst
County court; hogs.

277. -- 1824. JONATHAN PATTEN, 1; ELIJAH FLETCHER and WILLIAM S.
CRAWFORD, 2; SARAH, CORINER, JONATHAN PATTEN, JR., SOPHIA
PATTEN, WILLIAM A. PATTEN, 3...JONATHAN married present wife, SARAH,
formerly CRAWFORD, and heir of WILLIAM S. CRAWFORD, Amherst County--
division by Amherst County decree--as merchant has disposed of much
of estate--his share--$1.00 paid by ELIJAH FLETCHER and WILLIAM S.
CRAWFORD--all interest in dower estate--two tracts--one known as
Tusculum, by name of Tye River; tract in Harrison County; slaves,
personal property--any future children of wife. Lynchburg Justices of
the Peace: ALBON MC DANIEL and DANIEL BROWN as to PATTEN and
FLETCHER. Note: Tusculum still stands.

279. 7 October 1818. Order to Bedford Justices of the Peace: JAMES
EWING and JONAH DAVIS--POLLY WILLIAMSON, wife of JONATHAN,
28 November 1815, to ALEXANDER SALE--interest in estate of BEVERLY
WILLIAMSON. Done, 29 November 1820; recorded Amherst County,
20 December 1824.

280. 20 December 1824. STEPHEN EWERS, 1; WILLIAM S. CRAWFORD, 2;
JONATHAN and ABRAHAM EWERS, 3...$1.00 stock, furniture. To
WILLIAM S. CRAWFORD, 11 January 1825.

280. 5 October 1824. CHRISTOPHER and WILLIAM I. ISBELL, Amherst
County, 1; DAVID HOFFMAN, LEWIS GREGORY, NATHAN B. THURMAN,
THOMAS O. ACREE, 2; SAMUEL SCHOOLFIELD, all of Lynchburg...debts to
SAMUEL SCHOOLFIELD; $1.00; 19 acres. Lines: near fish dam above
Lynchburg, Harris, grantors. Also house and lot--half acre occupied
by WILLIAM I. ISBELL on road from toll bridge to CH. SAMUEL SCHOOLFIELD
named slaves. SAMUEL NOWLING and ALBON MC DANIEL, Lynchburg, Justices
of the Peace. To N. M. TALIAFERRO, 23 March 1825.

282. 1 December 1824. HILL CARTER and wife, MARY, Amherst County,
to BARTHOLOMEW WHITEHEAD, Amherst County...$200 30 acres Piney.
Lines: grantee, CATHERINE CAMPBELL. Bought from GEORGE CAMPBELL.
Witnesses: ROBERT GARLAND, J. G. READ, JAMES W. SMITH. To BARTHOLOMEW
WHITEHEAD, 21 February 1825.

283. 10 December 1824. BENJAMIN TALIAFERRO, Amherst County, to
RICHESON HENLEY, Amherst County...love of BENJAMIN TALIAFERRO
for daughter, POLLY, who married RICHESON HENLEY; $1.00 80 acres on
Blue Ridge and borders of Shady Mountain Creek.

283. 4 May 1824. BARTLETT CLEMENTS, Amherst County, to ISAAC
RUCKER, SR...power of attorney for use of my three children:
POLLY, JOSCY, and NANCY CLEMENTS--to recover from estate of AMBROSE
TOMLINSON--amount due me as guardian of my three children, when of
age. Witnesses: LINDSEY SANDIDGE, DAVID TOMLINSON, AMBROSE RUCKER.

284. 28 November 1822. JESSE BECK and wife, ANN, DANIEL and SOLOMON
DAY and wife, RACHEL, Amherst County, to GEORGE MARKAHM,
THOMAS MURRELL, WILLIAM ROBINSON, WILLIAM DAY, EZEKIEL DAY, JAMES LEE,
CHARLES MAYSE, JAMES BOWLING and WILEY CAMPBELL, trustees, Amherst
County...$1.00 two acres--free use of spring and adjoins Beck at or
near the meeting house on said tract. Methodist Church of U.S.A.;
minister to call meeting to fill vacancies on board. Witnesses:
WILLIAM TURNER, CHARLES MUNDY, HENRY TURNER.

285. 5 August 1824. Augusta Justices of the Peace, JAMES A. MC CUE
and BENJAMIN BRYAN, as to ELIZABETH E. HENDREN, wife of REV.
JONATHAN HENDREN, 21 April 1817, to CHARLES H. and WALTER D. CHRISTIAN.
Note: did not look up deed, but 17 could be 11.

285. 25 November 1824. JONATHAN BRADY, Nelson County, to JAMES ROSE...
$52.60 furniture. Witnesses: JOSEPH STAPLES, BARNETT CASH.

286. 30 December 1824. WALTER L. CHRISTIAN to CHARLES MUNDY, Amherst
County Sheriff...WALTER L. CHRISTIAN in custody as daughter of
EDWARD WATSON et al. Takes insolvent oath--two tracts. 1. 71 acres.
Lines: WILLIAM (?), deceased, DANIEL CHEATWOOD. 2. 500 acres also
interest under will of late father, JONATHAN CHRISTIAN, B. To JOSEPH
PETTYJOHN, 17 January 1825. Witnesses: SAMUEL R. DAVIES, WILKINS
WATSON, JAMES G. CHRISTIAN.

286. 5 October 1824. WILLIAM I. ISBELL and wife, LUCY, 1; JONATHAN
MILLER and DAVID R. EDLEY, 2; to SAMUEL MILLER and EDWIN S.
RUCKER, 3...debts to JONATHAN MILLER and DAVID R. EDLEY as trustees
of AMBROSE RUCKER--to trustees, 21 March 1827--$1.00 391 acres Salt
Creek. Bought from AMBROSE RUCKER and wife, ELIZABETH, 5 October
1824q Lynchburg Justices of the Peace: SAMUEL BROWN and JONATHAN
VICTOR.

288. 4 January 1825. CATLETT CAMPBELL and wife, NANCY, Amherst
        County, to CHARLES WILSON, Amherst County...to R. WILSON,
27 August 1835--$50 73 acres. Lines: grantee, JONATHAN LONDON on
road--his estate, JONATHAN WARWICK, ABSALOM HOWL. JAMES POWELL and
LINDSEY COLEMAN, N.P.'s.

290. 20 December 1824. FREDERICK CABELL, Nelson County, to ROBERT S.
        ROSE, Seneca County, New York...all interest in Deed of Trust,
8 May 1824, between JONATHAN N. ROSE and JONATHAN THOMPSON, JR.,
FREDERICK CABELL, 2; JONATHAN HORSLEY, 3, Amherst County, and recorded
17 May 1824.

290. 21 June 1824. ROBERT TINSLEY, Amherst County, to JAMES and
        SALLY TINSLEY, Amherst County...$492 146 acres. Lines:
JONATHAN COLEMAN, BENNETT HUDSON, WILLIAM MANTIPLY--where grantees
live--life estate of JAMES and then to SALLY for life. Witnesses:
H. M. GARLAND.

291. 27 November 1824. ARCHELAUS P. MITCHELL to CHARLES MUNDY,
        Amherst County Sheriff...ARCHELAUS P. MITCHELL is in custody on
suit of ELLIS and EUBANK and TIMOTHY FLETCHER takes insolvent oath--
225 acres on James and conveyed by Deed of Trust to PETER RUCKER,
another Deed of Trust to LUCAS P. THOMPSON and STERLING CLAIBORNE.
Witnesses: LINDSEY COLEMAN, ROBERT TINSLEY, CHARLES P. TALIAFERRO.
To A. MUNDY, Deputy Sheriff, 18 January 1825. Note: TIMOTHY FLETCHER
was a brother of ELIJAH FLETCHER and there is much of him in the
splendid book on ELIJAH FLETVHER's letters by my good friend,
MISS MARTHA VON BRIESEN, Sweet Briar College.

292. 31 December 1824. P. P. BURTON and wife, EMILY, Bedford County,
        to JAMES POWELL, Amherst County...$1800 404 acres south side
Buffaloe. Lines: PENN, WALKER, SHIELDS--by lines and not by acres.
Lynchburg Justices of the Peace: BALDA MC DANIEL and N. J. MANSON--
note error--they are Bedford Justices of the Peace.

293. 1 January 1825. JAMES POWELL, Amherst County, 1; ROBERT J.
        YANCEY, Bedford, and WILLIAM ARMISTEAD, Amherst County, 2;
PATRICK P. BURTON, Bedford, 3...$1.00 to secure the purchase of
Amherst County tract joining JONATHAN PENN, NANCY SHIELDS--404 acres
on Buffaloe. To ROBERT TINSLEY, trustee, 15 July 1827.

294. 21 December 1824. ROBERT J. YANCEY, NATHANIEL RIVES, JR.,
        trustees, to P. P. BURTON...$1800 404 acres south side Buffaloe
near ACH. Lines: WALKER, PENN, SHEILDS. ALBON MC DANIEL and DANIEL
BROWN, Lynchburg Justices of the Peace.

295. 17 January 1825. WILLIAM DAVENPORT, Amherst County, to
        JONATHAN L. DAVENPORT and THOMAS WINGFIELD, Amherst County...
$1.00--to secure wife, SARAH, and children; WILLIAM DAVENPORT is
lately possessed of personal estate of $750. Slave.

297. 16 December 1824. DABNEY HILL, Amherst County, 1; HEZEKIAH S.
        FULCHER, Amherst County, 2; WILLIAM ANGUS, 3...WILLIAM ANGUS
on bond to ALEXANDER MUNDY, Deputy Sheriff of Amherst County for
CHARLES MUNDY, Sheriff, on execution of DAVID, DANIEL and THOMAS
HIGGINBOTHAM, merchants; $1.00 slaves; stock; furniture. Witnesses:
ALEXANDER MUNDY, JONATHAN W. CAMPBELL, WIATT TUCKER.

298. 15 January 1825. JAMES WARE, Amherst County, 1; RICHARD N.
        EUBANK, Amherst County, 2; RICHARD L. ELLIS, Amherst County, 3...
to RICHARD E., January 1826 pre JONATHAN W. YOUNG--ELLIS has paid
Bank of Virginia at Lynchburg an amount, 6 October 1824, for note of
JONATHAN WARE, SR. $1.00 slaves; furniture; stock. Witnesses:
MANSFIELD WARE, WILLIAM ROACH, J. W. YOUNG, J. L. WINGFIELD.

299. -- January 1825. JONATHAN BONDS, Amherst County, 1; JONATHAN
        ALCOCK, Amherst County, 2; LEWIS LAYNE, Amherst County, 3...
LEWIS LAYNE on bond to JONATHAN PHILLIPS' administrator. $1.00--
NANCY FRANKLIN, guardian (six)--stock.

300. 15 October 1824. SAMUEL BURKS and wife, MARY, WILLIAM L.
BURKS and wife, ELIZABETH, Campbell County, to JAMES P. BULLOCK,
Campbell County...$1300 405 acres. Lines: CHRISTIAN, SAMUEL
SWANSON, JOSEPH SWANSON, the branch, BELL and CHRISTIAN, crossing
creek, CHARLES CHRISTIAN. JONATHAN E. WOODSON and JO MC ALLISTER,
Campbell County Justices of the Peace as to SAMUEL BURKS and wife,
BENJAMIN HADEN and HENRY T. EALY, Campbell Justices of the Peace as
to WILLIAM L. BURKS and wife.

301. 31 January 1825. JAMES POWELL, Amherst County, 1; ROBERT
TINSLEY, Amherst County, 2; JONATHAN PENN, Amherst County, 3...
J. P. owes Bank of Virginia and PENN on note; also owes P. P. BURTON;
$1.00 340 acres Huff Creek. Lines: JAMES WILMORE, SAMUEL WATTS,
named slaves.

304. 8 November 1824. AMBROSE RUCKER, Amherst County, to CHARLES
MUNDY, Amherst County Sheriff...on execution of DAVID and
WILLIAM KYLE, merchants--KYLE and Company--applied to Justices of
the Peace, DABNEY WARE and THOMAS CREWS, and took insolvent oath.
Declares following tracts: 322 or 323 acres bought from ISAAC TINSLEY;
287¾ acres bought from RICHARD HARRISON; 27½ acres bought from
GEORGE MC DANIEL, JR.; 60 acres bought from RICHARD N. ELLIS; 839
acres bought from ARTHUR L. DAVIES; 1350 acres bought from GEORGE
MC DANIEL, SR. 4 acres bought of ANDERSON TINSLEY, heir of JOSHUA
TINSLEY--Cold Mountain; interest in 2/3 of TINSLEY's Mill on Harris.

305. 4 February 1825. ELIZABETH MARSH, Amherst County, to FRANCIS
FEAGANS, JAMES and SALLY MARSH, Amherst County...$1.00 and
love for her brother, son, and daughter; stock, etc. Witnesses:
DRURY CHRISTIAN, WILLIAM NORTH, PUTNAM NORTH.

305. 12 November 1824. WILLIAM TURNER, SR., Amherst County and wife,
SALLY, to WILLIAM BURFORD, SR., Amherst County...to CHARLES
MAYS, 19 August 1833--$108 18 acres south side Plank Branch. Lines:
JESSE BECK, ARCHELAUS REYNOLDS, WILLIAM TURNER. Dower relinquished
U:266.

306. 39 December 1824. NELSON C. DAWSON and wife, ANN T., Amherst
County, to LEWIS DAWSON, Amherst County...$700--no acres--
south side Harris. Lines: AMBROSE BURFORD, WILLIAM PETTYJOHN,
grantee. AMBROSE RUCKER and DABNEY WARE, Justices of the Peace.

307. 27 January 1824. ROBERT L. WILKINS and wife, ELIZABETH (formerly
HARDWICK), Lynchburg, to ANSON TINSLEY, Amherst County...$150
36 acres Huff. Lot no. -- lately surveyed by REUBEN NORVELL in division
of estate of JONATHAN and ELIZABETH COLEMAN and by commissioners--
TINSLEY was one--to heirs. ELIZABETH was heir. Lines: WILMORE;
lot 3; JAMES POWELL; the branch. ALBON MC DANIEL and AUGUSTINE
LEFTWICH, Lynchburg Justices of the Peace. ROBERT is called ROBERT C.
in summary.

309. 6 July 1824. JONATHAN PERCIVAL and wife, MARGARET, 1; CHISWELL
DABNEY, 2; JONATHAN LYNCH, 3...JONATHAN LYNCH on bond at
Farmer's Bank of Virginia. $1.00 15 acres all that part of James
River island immediately below Lynchburg--formerly that of JONATHAN
LYNCH, SR., deceased, and conveyed to JONATHAN PERCIVAL by EDWARD
and ANSELM LYNCH, executors. JONATHAN VICTOR and SAMUEL NOWLIN,
Lynchburg Justices of the Peace. DANIEL BROWN and JONATHAN VICTOR
as to wife.

311. 21 February 1825. PLEASANT MALLORY, Amherst County, to
HENRY J. ROSE, New Glasgow, 2; WILLIAM H. ROSE, New Glasgow, 3...
$1.00 horse, furniture--fee paid A. B. DAVIES, 21 February 1825--
70 cents; shoemaker's tools; long list.

312. 19 January 1825. WILLIAM TURNER, JESSE BECK, JAMES L. LAMKIN,
THOMAS MURRELL, commissioners of Court to sell estate of THOMAS
JOHNSON, deceased, to WILLIAM WARWICK, Amherst County...to JONATHAN M.
OTEY, administrator, 3 October 1833--WILLIAM JOHNSON and SUSAN JOHNSON
versus JONATHAN JOHNSON et al.--$1899 316½ acres near Lynchburg--
where THOMAS JOHNSON lived at death. Lines: north bank Bolling
Creek; grantee, MRS. ADAMS, grantee (formerly MEAD), CHARLES HOYLE,
PHILIP JOHNSON, deceased--half acre for cemetery--heirs of THOMAS
JOHNSON. JONATHAN VICTOR and DANIEL BROWN, Lynchburg Justices of the
Peace as to grantors.

314. 3 June 1823. PHILIP BURFORD and wife, CAROLINE M., Madison
County, Alabama, to ANSON TINSLEY, Amherst County...To J. T.,
JR., 6 April 1839--BURFORD's share in estate of PHILIP BURFORD, SR.--
his father, Amherst County. Lines: DAVID TINSLEY, JAMES BARNETT,
SPENCER NORVELL--$500 about 35 acres and where SR. lived at death.
THOMAS BRANDON, Clerk of Court in Alabama; SAMUEL CHAPMAN, Judge of
County Court.

316. 9 August 1824. HECTOR ATKINSON, Lynchburg, 1; JOEL ATKINSON,
2; SUSANNAH FRANKLIN, 3...to MRS. FRANKLIN, 6 October 1835--
$1.00 HECTOR ATKINSON's interest in estate of JOEL FRANKLIN, deceased,
and in hands of widow, SUSANNAH. In right of his wife, SALLY W. B.,
daughter of JOEL and SUSANNAH. Witnesses: HEZEKIEL S. FULCHER,
WILLIAM CAMPBELL, ROBERT W. CARTER.

318. 16 November 1824. GEORGE SHRADER and wife, AGNES, Amherst
County, 1; DABNEY P. GOOCH, Amherst County, 2; HENRY H. WATTS,
Amherst County, 3...to HENRY H. WATTS, 16 February 1829--$5.00 40 acres
Rocky Run. Lines: JACOB PEARCE--water grist mill thereon and where
GEORGE SHRADER lives. CHARLES P. TALIAFERRO and REUBEN NORVELL,
Justices of the Peace.

320. 25 January 1825. WILLIAM TOMLINSON, 1; THOMAS N. EUBANK, 2;
RICHARD L. ELLIS, 3...to RICHARD L. ELLIS, 19 May 1834--
BARTLETT CLEMENTS on bond to ELLIS--$1.00 334 acres where WILLIAM
TOMLINSON lives; stock; interest in father's estate. Witnesses:
JONATHAN W. YOUNG, SIMEON A. BRUCH, JONATHAN DAVIS, H. CRUSOLLES.

321. 21 February 1825. THOMAS ALFRED and wife, SUSSANAH, Amherst
County, to THOMAS WRIGHT, Amherst County...SUSANNAH is widow of
JESSE KENNEDY, Amherst County...THOMAS ALFRED made Deed of Trust to
her, son, JOSEPH KENNEDY-- (illegible) by will left slave to his
mother and dower tract. In trust to THOMAS WRIGHT. Witnesses:
JESSE KENNEDY.

323. 23 February 1825. PHINEAS L. PIERCE, Amherst County, to JACOB
PIERCE, Amherst County...$5.00 200 acres part of tract bought
from REUBEN COLEMAN--two adjacent tracts, 6 August 1811--also 200
acres conveyed by JACOB to PHINEAS, 20 July 1818--to include dwelling
house. Witnesses: JONATHAN CHRISTIAN, ROBERT PATRICK, PETER F.
CHRISTIAN, CHARLES L. CHRISTIAN.

324. 10 January 1825. MARY HUDSON, wife of JONATHAN HUDSON, to
WILLIAM MOORE, Amherst County...$30 93 acres Little Piney.
Lines: grantee, JONATHAN TRECK (?). Conveyed to her husband by
Deed of Trust from JAMES FULCHER. WILLIAM M. WALLER and CHARLES L.
BARRET, Justices of the Peace.

325. 17 February 1825. PULLIAM SANDIDGE, JR., Amherst County, 1;
SAMUEL B. DAVIES and RICHARD CRAWFORD, Amherst County, 2;
ELIJAH FLETCHER, 3...$1.00 about 118 acres. Lines: ZA DRUMMOND,
JAMES GOVAN, ELIJAH FLETCHER and where JOANNA SANDIDGE lives.
ELIJAH FLETCHER on bond to LUCY SANDIDGE--Lynchburg Chancery versus
LINDSWY and PULLIAM SANDIDGE. ALBON MC DANIEL and DANIEL BROWN,
Lynchburg Justices of the Peace.

327. 19 June 1824. CHARLES P. TALIAFERRO and wife, LOUISA, Amherst
     County, to THOMAS HIGGINBOTHAM, Amherst County...To SAMUEL W.
CHRISTIAN, agent, 24 July 1830--$1808 226 acres both sides Rutledge.
Lines: BENJAMIN BROWN, WILLIAM BROWN, PETER CASHWELL, grantee.
CHARLES and BENJAMIN TALIAFERRO, Justices of the Peace.

328. 20 September 1824. JESSE WOODROOF, Amherst County, to ARCHIBALD
     ROBERTSON, Lynchburg...all interest in dower estate of my mother,
widow of DAVID WOODROOF, JR., slaves, furniture--one seventh. Witnesses:
ALLEN TALBOT, WILLIAM H. CAMDEN. To ARCHIBALD ROBERTSON, 23 March
1825.

329. 25 February 1824. WILLIAM BRIDIE NAPIER, Richmond, 1; WILLIAM S.
     CRAWFORD, Amherst County, 2; WILLIAM H. DYER, Richmond, 3...
9 January last NAPIER bought at public sale under decree of Lynchburg
Chancery Court--life estate of BETSY LONG to 650 acres called Lainsville;
$1.00 paid by WILLIAM S. CRAWFORD and WILLIAM H. DYER in consideration
of BETSY's relinquished dower--254 acres and 1/4--part of said tract.
Sells 395½ acres. Lines: Tribulation, south border Buffaloe,
northwest side Lynch road and four miles from New Glasgow and 17
from Lynchburg. Lines: WASH HILL, LINDSEY COLEMAN, NANCY SHIELDS,
ROBERT RIVERS--residue of Lainsville tract after deducting 254½ acres.
W. CAWLING and WILLIAM H. FIZWHYLSOM, Richmond Justices of the Peace.

330. 26 January 1825. ROBERT SHARPE, Richmond to WILLIAM H. DYER,
     Richmond and WILLIAM S. CRAWFORD, Amherst County...$1.00 slave
and furniture--to WILLIAM LANE per order of WILLIAM S. CRAWFORD,
8 December 1825--for benefit of MRS. BETSY LONG, wife of WILLIAM
LONG, Amherst County--life estate. W. CAWLING and JAMES RAWLINGS,
Richmond Justices of the Peace.

332. 24 November 1824. JONATHAN TALBOT, Amherst County, to JOSEPH
     PENN, Amherst County, 2; JONATHAN PENN, Amherst County, 3...
$1.00 JONATHAN PENN on note to Bank of Virginia; slaves. Witnesses:
N. M. TALIAFERRO, J. POWELL, JACOB PEARCE.

334. 12 March 1824. SAMUEL R. DAVIES, trustee, to WILLIAM JORDAN,
     Amherst County...CHARLES DAIRY, 25 February 1823, executor
Deed of Trust to SAMUEL R. DAVIES--Sold 25 June 1823 180 acres.
Lines: Sale and 25 or 30 acres adjacent at $31.75.

335. 21 February 1824. WILLIAM LONG and wife, BETSY, Amherst County,
     to WILLIAM BRYDIE NAPIER, Richmond...$1.00 254½ acres. Lines:
LAMONT's Spring, JONATHAN PENN, R. RIVERS, near creek, WASH HILL,
JAMES POWELL, ROBERT WALKER. Witnesses: VAN TRUMP CRAWFORD.
LINDSEY COLENA and THOMAS CREWS, Justices of the Peace.

336. 22 January 1825. THOMAS WIATT and PLEASANT M. MILLER, executors
     of JONATHAN MILLER, to JONATHAN M. WILLIAMS, Amherst County...to
JONATHAN M. WILLIAMS, 12 April 1825--$230 11½ acres near Lynchburg.
Lines: West by Lynch road, northeast and south by lands heretofore
conveyed to grantee on -- 1823. WIATT attorney-in-fact for MILLER.
THOMAS A. HOLCOMBE, SMITHSON H. DAVIS, Lynchburg Justices of the
Peace. I may have commented on PLEASANT M. MILLER, son of JONATHAN--
I have seen JOHN MILLER's will in Lynchburg. My wife is daughter of
PLEASANT GREEN MILLER, son of JONATHAN, who was son of JONATHAN from
Wythe County to Estill County, Kentucky. JONATHAN of Wythe married
MALINDA REPASS in Wythe. Data shows that PLEASANT M. MILLER went to
Tazewell, Tennessee. It is probably just coincidental that the name
of PLEASANT shows in two MILLER families.

338. 31 January 1825. WILLIAM WARWICK and wife, FRANCES, Amherst
     County, to JONATHAN M. WILLIAMS, Amherst County...to JONATHAN M.
WILLIAMS, 12 April 1825--$360 60 acres both sides Bowling Creek.
Lines: grantee, a spring, grantor, CHARLES HOYLE. THOMAS A. HOLCOMB
and CHARLES L. DIBRELL, Lynchburg Justices of the Peace.

340. 21 March 1825. JAMES ROSE, Amherst County, 1; LUCAS P. THOMPSON,
Amherst County, 2; JONATHAN J. DILLARD, Amherst County, 3...
To LUCAS P. THOMPSON, 23 October 1835--$1.00 debt to for sums to buy
house and lot in New Glasgow. Lien on house and lot.

342. 21 March 1825. JONATHAN J. DILLARD, Amherst County, to JAMES
ROSE, Amherst County...consideration: slave, ADAM, and $1800--
house and lot in New Glasgow bought from WESTCOTT and WEBB. Lines:
front side near street which separates it from the Tavern house
occupied and belonging to COLONEL JAMES DILLARD, alley between lot
of JAMES S. PENDLETON, JONATHAN MOUNTCASTLE's store house and
TAYLOR's shop, DAVID S. GARLAND.

343. 31 December 1824. JAMES WARE and wife, NANCY, Amherst County,
to RICHARD L. ELLIS, Amherst County, 2; JOSEPH ALLEN, 3...to
R. N. EUBANK, 30 April 1825; returned and sent to ELLIS, 1826--WARE
on 26th of same month and year owed WILLIAM G. PENDLETON and made
Deed of Trust to R. L. ELLIS--Pedlar Mills on Horsley--PENDLETON
has assigned to ALLEN, MICAJAH PENDLETON, and THOMAS LAIN, bondsman.
$1.00 said tract. Also tract bought by WARE from EDMOND GOODRICH--
15 acres N S Harris between creek and road and adjacent tract bought
by WARE from CHARLES ELLIS and GOODRICH. THOMAS N. and RICHARD N.
EUBANK, Justices of the Peace.

347. 21 March 1825. CHARLES MUNDY, Amherst County Sheriff, to
DUDLEY SANDIDGE, Amherst County...to DUDLEY SANDIDGE, 17 March
1828--WALTER L. CHRISTIAN took oath of insolvent in suit of EDWARD
WATSON in Superior Court of Amherst County and suit of POWELL and
TALIAFERRO versus him. Real estate conveyed 13 December 1824, to
Sheriff JOSEPH PETTYJOHN, Deputy Sheriff, advertised tract held jointly
as tenant with WILLIAM HORSLEY--500 acres. Sold on court day,
21 February 1825, and SANDIDGE bought at $75.00.

349. 21 March 1825. WILLIAM WARE, Amherst County, 1; ORMUND WARE
and EDWIN L. RUCKER, Amherst County, 2; DABNEY WARE, Amherst
County, 3...DABNEY WARE on bonds to NELSON C. DAWSON, 1817; ARCH
ROBERTSON and Company for benefit of BOYD MILLER and negro hire--
$1.00 paid by ORMUND WARE and EDWIN L. RUCKER's slave about 40,
CHARLES; stock. Witnesses: AMBROSE RUCKER, ANDERSON WARE.

351. 23 March 1825. THOMAS WILLS, Amherst County, 1; JONATHAN D.
DAVIS, Amherst County, 2; JAMES DAVIS and THOMAS N. EUBANK,
Amherst County, 3...to J. D. D., 20 November 1829--$1.00 JAMES DAVIS
and THOMAS N. EUBANK on bond for THOMAS WILLS to BENJAMIN DONALD,
guardian of ELIZABETH CAMM; interest is saw mill on tract of JAMES
DAVIS and grist mill being built next to mill; stock; furniture.

353. 22 March 1825. JONATHAN H. BELL, Amherst County, 1; NELSON C.
DAWSON and JAMES LEE, Amherst County, 2; WILLIAM L. BELL, 3...
$1.00 slave; furniture; long and interesting list; also interest in
20 or 30 acres--part of tract of WILLIAM DAMRON, deceased.

355. 22 March 1825. JOEL F. SMITH, Amherst County, 1; DABNEY
SANDIDGE, Amherst County, 2; JAMES GOVAN, 3...to trustee,
21 December 1825--and release--14 September 1827, to BENJAMIN
TALIAFERRO. $1.00 slave, furniture.

356. 1 November 1824. CALEB RALLS died testate and divided estate
to children. ROBERT LEBREE, Lincoln County, Kentucky, married
NANCY RALLS, one of CALEB's children. Power of attorney to JONATHAN
MURRELL, Kentucky, and THOMAS EUBANK, Virginia, to receive legacy
or sums due; may sue in chancery. THOMAS HELM, County Clerk;
BENJAMIN HAILL, Presiding Justice of the Peace.

358. 18 March 1825. JONATHAN WARWICK and wife, POLLY, Amherst
County, to CHARLES WILSON, Amherst County...$150.00 7½ acres.
Lines: CAMPBELL, grantee.

359. 22 March 1825. THOMAS N. EUBANK, Commissioner of Amherst
     County Court to COLEMAN and BARRET, Amherst County...MOSES
HALL, deceased, tract--decree to sell. Lines: south by JONATHAN F.
HALL; east by NELSON CRAWFORD; north by THOMAS MORRIS and GEORGE
KIPPEN and Company--formerly JONATHAN BROWN; west by Pedlar River.
No amount.

360. 23 March 1825. JONATHAN MERIT, Amherst County, 1; SAMUEL J. C.
     DAWSON, 2; PETER DAY, Botetourt County, 3...$5.00 paid by
SAMUEL J. C. DAWSON; slaves; stock; furniture; copper still.

361. 30 November 1824. SPENCER NORVELL, SR., Amherst County, to
     daughter, FRANCES APPLEBERRY...love and $1.00--to B. NORVELL,
21 December 1826--furniture. Witnesses: GEORGE NORVELL, JR.,
ELIJAH HAM, WASHINGTON M. NORVELL, BENJAMIN NORVELL, JAMES M. DANIEL.

362. 23 March 1825. CATLET CAMPBELL and wife, NANCY, Amherst County,
     to JONATHAN WARWICK, Amherst County...exchange of 7¾ acres.
Lines: grantee, CHARLES WILSON, forks of road, JONATHAN JONDON,
deceased. Nothing as to sum or other tract.

363. 3 March 1825. THOMAS WRIGHT, Amherst County, 1; WILLIAM
     ARMISTEAD, Amherst County, 2; WILLIAM SHELTON, JAMES M.
DANIEL, SR. and JR. (probably MC DANIEL), JONATHAN H. WRIGHT--
guardian of CATHERINE M. WRIGHT...WILLIAM SHELTON, bondsman, to
HENRY L. DAVIES, guardian for slave hire; debt to JONTAHAN MILLER
and -- trustees for AMBROSE RUCKER; $1.00 two guns, stock, interest
in estate of MARY WRIGHT, relict of JONATHAN WRIGHT, late of Bedford.
AMBROSE RUCKER and RICHARD HARRISON, Justices of the Peace.

366. 24 March 1825. JONATHAN TYLER, Amherst County, 1; SAMUEL P.
     CHRISTIAN, Buckingham, 2; LAWSON G. TYLER, -- County, 3...
about 47½ acres. Lines: WILEY CAMPBEL, JACOB PIERCE, estate of
WILLIAM DILLARD, estate of DANIEL CHEATWOOD and where JONATHAN TYLER
lives--slaves; stock; furniture; crops--and interest in estate of
WILLIAM DILLARD, deceased.

368. 23 February 1825. JACOB PIERCE and wife, ELIZABETH, Amherst
     County, to PHINEAS PIERCE, Amherst County...$5.00 ten acres
near CH and includes tavern occupied by REUBEN COLEMAN. Lines: in
front of tavern, prison, middle of Lynch road, SAMUEL HEISKELL,
fence corner, west bank of a drain, ARTHUR B. DAVIES, MIGGINSON's
road. Witnesses: JONATHAN, PETER F., CHARLES L. CHRISTIAN, ROBERT
PATRICK.

370. 7 April 1825. THOMAS CREWS, Amherst County, to WILLIAM S.
     CRAWFORD, Amherst County...to WILLIAM LONG per order, 8 December
1825--agreement between THOMAS CREWS and WILLIAM and BETSY LONG
wherein they surrend title from estate of GABRIEL PENN; also propor-
tion of sum that may be recovered from securities of JAMES PENN,
executor of GABRIEL PENN--Chancery suit in Lynchburg; and that part
of Lainville tract west of Camden (south road--50 acres; also in
consideration of BETSY LONG's dower in 81½ acres next to LINDSEY
COLEMAN and NANCY SHIELDS. $1.00 paid by CRAWFORD--long and
interesting list of furniture; stock; slaves.

371. 22 January 1825. WILLIAM JOPLING, Amherst County, to son,
     GEORGE A. JOPLING, Amherst County...$1.00 and love--interest
in estates of BETSY and WILLIAM WARE, Amherst County. Witnesses:
M. PENDLETON, DAVID W. BURKS.

372. 8 April 1825. WILLIAM JOPLING and wife, SALLY, Amherst County,
     1; WILLIAM ARMISTEAD, Amherst County, 2; RICHARD L. ELLIS,
Amherst County, 3; JONATHAN and RICHARD L. ELLIS, Amherst County, 4;
ELLIS and EUBANK, Amherst County, 5 to ROBERT N. EUBANK, 30 April 1825...
debts to above and MORGAN and MC DANIEL, Lynchburg. $1.00 slaves and
ages; stock; furniture; crops--40 acres where WILLIAM JOPLING lives.
Lines: WILLIAM PRYOR, SR., CHARLES C. CARTER. Witnesses: JONATHAN W.
YOUNG, ALEXANDER N. JONES, G. A. JOPLING.

375. 8 April 1825. WILLIAM JOPLING, 1; ALEXANDER MUNDY, 2;
HOLMAN JOPLING, Nelson County, 3...to ALEXANDER MUNDY,
29 December 1829--$1.00 interest in 57 acres on west side Horsley.
Lines: JONATHAN S. CARTER, RICHARD EUBANK. In possession of
WILLIAM JOPLING and NELSON CRAWFORD.

376. 13 April 1825. JONATHAN TOMLINSON, Amherst County, 1;
JAMES D. HIGGINBOTHAM, Amherst County, 2; D. and D. HIGGINBOTHAM
and Company, Amherst County, 3...$1.00 slaves--ages and names.
Witnesses: JESSE and JOSEPH HIGGINBOTHAM.

378. 17 December 1824. GEORGE B. WOODSON, Lynchburg Marshall of
Chancery, to ELIJAH FLETCHER, Lynchburg...decree of 21 May
1824: CAMDEN versus CLAIBORNE--to sell and pay plaintiffs--500 acres.
Lines: MICAJAH CAMDEN, WILLIAM STINNETT. S. H. DAVIS and CHARLES L.
DIBRELL, Lynchburg Justices of the Peace.

380. 7 April 1825. PETER CASHWELL, Amherst County, 1; SAMUEL R.
DAVIES and W. S. CRAWFORD, Amherst County, 2; ELIJAH FLETCHER,
3...$1.00 to ELIJAH FLETCHER, 21 March 1826--between 5 and 600 acres.
Lines: THOMAS HIGGINBOTHAM, WILLIAM BOURNE, ABNER PADGETT, THOMAS
EDWARDS, EPHRAIM PADGETT, JONATHAN WARWICK, JONATHAN SIMPSON--slaves
named. DANIEL BROWN and ALBON MC DANIEL, Lynchburg Justices of the
Peace.

382. 18 April 1825. WILLIS GILLASPIE, Amherst County, 1; WILLIAM J.
THURMOND, Amherst County, 2; STERLING J. THURMOND, 3...$1.00
stock. Witnesses: JONATHAN J. FULCHER, ALEXANDER N. JONES,
GEORGE MC DANIEL, JR. (?).

383. 13 April 1825. DAVID TOMLINSON, JR., Amherst County, to
RICHARD L. ELLIS, Amherst County...debt to estate of AMBROSE
TOMLINSON, deceased. $1.00 all interest in deceased father's
estate and in hands of my mother. Witnesses: WILLIAM CARTER,
DABNEY WARE, JAMES WARE.

384. 5 January 1825. CALEB WATTS and wife, SUSANNAH, Amherst
County, to MARTIN PARKS, Amherst County...$60.00 27 acres
Clark Creek, border of Pedlar. Lines: both; PARKS' road from his
house to Bethel Road; THOMAS WATTS', deceased, spring branch.
Witnesses: WILLIAM H. PARKS, MITCHELL WATTS, SAMUEL G. PARKS, J. J.
WINGFIELD, GEORGE BURKS.

387. 12 August 1824. HENRY HEGER, Amherst County, 1; JONATHAN
RUSSELL, Amherst County, 2; JOSEPH R. CARTER and WILLIAM
COLEMAN, Amherst County, 3...JOSEPH R. CARTER and WILLIAM COLEMAN
on bond to NELSON CRAWFORD, executor of CALEB RALLS--about January 15
last; $1.00 furniture; stock. Witnesses: DANIEL HALL, RICHARD
CRAWFORD, CHARLES MOFFITT, THOMAS M. PRYOR. Note: CRAWFORD's name
in wrong place and erased.

388. 1 February 1825. ELLIOTT WORTHAM, Amherst County, to JAMES
DAVIS, Amherst County...$105.00 mare; cows; tools.

389. 8 March 1825. ISAAC RUCKER, SR., and wife, MARY, Amherst
County, to WILLIAM HOLLIDAY, Westmoreland County...to WILLIAM
HOLLIDAY, 20 August 1831--to get dower release--$2500 511 acres in
three surveys on both sides north fork Pedlar and bought from
FIELDING HOLIDAY 438 acres of T for release. Witnesses: JAMES F.
TALIAFERRO.

390. 10 March 1825. PULLIAM SANDIDGE, SR. to JACK CARTER...PULLIAM
    SANDIDGE has sold WILLIAM WILSON one "sartain" tract of 300
acres in the county "of this in the State of Canctuckey" on Reef (?)
Creek--to complete title by release of wife, LUCY, who refuses until
Amherst County tract is conveyed to her does so by trustee--40 acres
Pedlar. Lines: DUDLEY SANDIDGE, ELIJAH FLUCHER (sic), CHARLES
CRESTON. Witnesses: PULLIAM SANDIDGE, JR., LINZA BURKS, WILLIAM B.
SHEPPARD. Memo: LUCY has dower "rites" in Mill tract to JAMES
SANDIDGE, Buffaloe tract to JOSEPH HIGGINBOTHAM, Luck Mt. tract to
ADKERSON, Luch Mountain tract to WILLIAM WILLMORE, Flashy Creek to
WILLIAM CARTER, Fork Mountain to JACOB PHILLIPS, Long Mountain to
"diferent" persons--949 acres, Buffaloe tract to same--926 acres;
Cold Mountain tract to RICHARD HARTLESS 390 acres; Long Mountain to
HENRY HARTLESS 201 acres; Cantucky tract to WILLIAM NELSON 300 acres.
Each is spelled "Eacors." "Ther" is six tracts of the above land
that I don't "now" the number of "Eacors" "til" I see the deeds in
the office.

392. 13 April 1825. DAVID TOMLINSON, JR., to ISAAC RUCKER, Amherst
    County...to J. W. YOUNG, 15 May 1826--debts to R. L. ELLIS
and ELLIS and EUBANK; $1.00 all interest in estate of JOSEPH DODD,
deceased; tobacco crop made and in hands of "his mother"--one fifth;
furniture; crop now making with MRS. DODD. Witnesses: WILLIAM
CARTER, DABNEY WARE, JAMES WARE.

394. 26 March 1820. MURRY HENSON and wife, ELIZABETH, Amherst
    County, to PETER RUCKER, Amherst County...$250 100 acres both
sides Aculking Branch; part of former tract of JONATHAN ROBERTS,
deceased. Lines: COLEMAN and BARRET, CHARLES MOFFITT, WILLIAM
MITCHELL. Witnesses: ROBERT H. CARTER, PETER P. THORNTON, THOMAS N.
EUBANK. THOMAS N. and RICHARD N. EUBANK, Justices of the Peace.
Very poor script here.

396. 25 April 1825. JONATHAN TOMLINSON, 1; THOMAS N. EUBANK, 2;
    RICHARD L. ELLIS, 3; ELLIS and EUBANK, 4...suits pending in
Amherst County; $1.00 100 3/4 acres where JONATHAN TOMLINSON lives.
Lines: AMBROSE TOMLINSON, deceased, BENJAMIN SANDIDGE--slaves--
ages and names; furniture; stock; tools. Witnesses: JONATHAN D.
DAVIS, CHARLES C. CARTER, MANSFIELD WARE, J. W. YOUNG.

398. 23 April 1825. SAMUEL P. LAYNE to NICHOLAS DAVIES...debt to
    NICHOLAS DAVIES. $1.00 mare.

398. 28 April 1825. WILLIAM JOPLING, Amherst County, 1; WILLIAM
    ARMISTEAD, Amherst County, 2; SAMUEL GARLAND, Lynchburg, 3...
to A. ROBERTSON, 8 May 1825--owes ARCH. ROBERTSON and ROBERT MOORE
and Company. Rather than take insolvent oath--400 acres. Lines:
WILLIAM PRYOR, JONATHAN S. CARTER, CHARLES C. CARTER and where
WILLIAM JOPLING lives--interest in tract on Horsley. Lines:
JONATHAN S. CARTER, RICHARD EUBANK, slave, stock, furniture, interest
in estate of WILLIAM and BETSY WARE, deceased, crops.

401. 19 April 1825. THOMAS R. TERRY and wife, CATHERINE; WILLIAM
    HOLLINSWORTH and wife, LUCY, Amherst County, to JONATHAN M.
WILLIAMS, Amherst County...$260 interest in estate by will of WILLIAM
ROBINSON (you will note that earlier LUCY ROBERTSON made a deed to
son, WILLIAM, and I cited that it was also ROBINSON)--this is same
family--WILLIAM was father of LUCY and CATHERINE--2/3 of 180½ acres.
Lines: LINEAS BOLLING, CHRISTOPHER ISBELL, CHARLES HOYLE, grantee.
Bought by WILLIAM ROBINSON and JESSE BECK from THOMAS WIATT and
RICHARD TYREE, 23 May 1823. REUBEN NORVELL, NELSON C. DAWSON,
EDMOND PENN, CHARLES L. BARNET, Justices of the Peace.

403. 31 May 1823. LITTLEBERRY COLEMAN, Amherst County, 1; JONATHAN
    WARE, Amherst County, 2; ORMUND WARE, Amherst County, 3...ORMUND
WARE on bond to WILLIAM ARMISTEAD. $1.00; cattle; furniture; tools;
crops. Witnesses: ALLEN TALBOT, WILLIAM L. FULCHER, WILLIAM
ARMISTEAD.

404. 27 April 1825. WILLIAM SHELTON, Amherst County, 1; RICHARD L.
      ELLIS, THOMAS N. EUBANK, SAMUEL GARLAND, 2; ARCH. ROBERTSON,
Lynchburg, 3...to ARCH. ROBERTSON, by GEORGE W. TURNER, agent,
27 October 1825; debts also to ROBERT MOORE and Company for benefit
of ROBERTSON; suit pending in Amherst County Superior Court; all
interest in property of Deed of Trust to ELLIS and EUBANK.

406. 14 January 1825. JAMES HILL, SR., Amherst County, 1; JAMES
      OGDON, Amherst County, 2; JAMES HILL, JR., Monroe County, 3...
to JAMES OGDON, 12 November 1825; $1.00 debt to JAMES HILL, JR. from
13 February 1821, and then date of 15 March 1818; slaves. Witnesses:
PHILIP LIVELY, STAGE DAVIS, WILLIAM KNIGHT.

408. 30 April 1825. WILLIAM CARTER, Amherst County, 1; JAMES D.
      HIGGINBOTHAM, Amherst County, 2; D. and D. HIGGINBOTHAM and
Company, Amherst County, 3...to JAMES D. HIGGINBOTHAM, 8 August 1825--
Amherst County suits; $1.00 interest in estate of late COLONEL WILLIAM
WARE, Amherst County, in right of wife, PAULINE CARTER, except part
conveyed to ORMUND WARE--that part assigned to PATSY WARE, as dower;
stock; furniture; crops.

411. 3 May 1825. THOMAS CREWS and EDMOND PENN as to POLLY H. WATSON,
      wife of WILKINS WATSON, 14 August 1820, to CHARLES P. TALIAFERRO.

412. 15 May 1825. WILLIAM SMITH and wife, NANCY, Amherst County,
      to GEORGE MYERS, Amherst County...to GEORGE MYERS, 20 June
1825--$100 459 acres Carter's Mill Creek. WILLIAM SMITH acquired
as heir of father, JONATHAN SMITH, deceased, and undivided--subject
to life estate of widow, SARAH SMITH--if any brothers and sisters
are without issue, and not selling.

414. 16 May 1825. ALEXANDER TINSLEY, Amherst County, 1; SAMUEL R.
      DAVIES, Amherst County, 2; ARCHELAUS REYNOLDS and PAMELIA
TINSLEY, wife of ALEXANDER, 3...REYNOLDS agrees to unite with
ALEXANDER on bond from Superior Court, Amherst County--JAMES TINSLEY's
name then appears; PAMELIA agrees to relinquish dower on tract sold
SAMUEL R. DAVIES by ALEXANDER and transferred to WILLIAM ARMISTEAD
in Deed of Trust for MERIT M. WHITE. ALEXANDER owes DAVIES; $1.00;
property in Deed of Trust, 11 June 1824, to DAVIES.

416. 20 May 1825. WILLIAM I. ISBELL, Amherst County, 1; N. M.
      TALIAFERRO, Lynchburg, 2; PAUL JONES, Lynchburg, 3...scratched:
to N. M. TALIAFERRO, 22 March 1826--$1.00 slaves bought by WILLIAM I.
ISBELL from PAUL JONES who had sold them to CHRISTOPHER ISBELL--;
tract bought by WILLIAM I. ISBELL from AMBROSE RUCKER. Lines:
THOMAS LAYNE, Bethel tract of between 350 and 400 acres. JONATHAN
VICTOR and CHRISTOPHER WINFREE, Lynchburg Justices of the Peace.

418. 1 August 1823. JONATHAN T. HILL, Lynchburg; SAMUEL GARLAND,
      Lynchburg, 2; NATHAN LOFTUS and Company, Nelson County, 3...
$1.00 interest in dower estate of CLARA WOODROOF--half of 1/7 two
females; suit in -- County versus WILLIAM KNIGHT, trustee; conveyed
by HILL to JOSEPH PENN in Lynchburg Corporation Court; slave in
hands of his mother, MRS. HARRISON--life estate; furniture in Bell
Tavern, Lynchburg. Certified from Lynchburg to Amherst County,
5 July 1824; JAMES BENAGH, Deputy Clerk.

420. 13 April 1825. JONATHAN HAAS and wife, SUSAN, Amherst County,
      to THOMAS GOODWIN, Nelson County...$1.00 112 acres bought
from STERLING CLAIBORNE. Long Branch near Buffaloe Springs and both
sides. To THOMAS GOODWIN, 3 April 1826. Lines: road; grantee;
GEORGE and JONATHAN M. EUBANK, Swapping Camp road. Witnesses:
JAMES M. YANCEY, WILLIAM HAMLET, SAMUEL BALLARD. HAWES N. COLEMAN
and JONATHAN J. COLEMAN, Nelson Justices of the Peace and BENJAMIN
TALIAFERRO and WILLIAM JOPLING, Amherst County Justices of the
Peace.

422. 13 April 1825. JONATHAN HAAS and wife, SUSAN, Amherst County,
        to THOMAS GOODWIN, Nelson County...$1.00--margin as above--
13 acres Long Branch; border of Buffaloe. Bought from JONATHAN
RICHARDSON and formerly that of JOSPEH MILSTRED. Lines: GEORGE
EUBANK, JONATHAN M. EUBANK, tract bought by JONATHAN HAAS from
STERLING CLAIBORNE, STITH HAMNER road (?), WILLIAM DEMSEY. Justices
of the Peace as above.

424. 11 April 1825. BEVERLY DAVIES, Amherst County, to CHARLES L.
        BARRET, Amherst County...HUMPHREY GILBERT, 20 August 1823,
executor Deed of Trust to BEVERLY DAVIES--all interest in estate of
deceased mother, JUDITH GILBERT--Deed of Trust to JAMES FRANKLIN
for her benefit and JAMES and HUDSON M. GARLAND. HUMPHREY GILBERT
did not pay and CHARLES L. BARRET bought at $30.00.

426. 23 May 1823. JONATHAN HAAS, Amherst County, to SAMUEL GARLAND,
        Lynchburg...$1.00 debts to DAVID S. GARLAND; slave bought which
was that of JOSEPH HIGGINBOTHAM, BOYD MILLER nad Company, WILLIAM M.
WALLER and Company, THOMAS HOLCOMBE, GALT and BULLOCK--150 acres on
south borders of Potomac in Hamsher (sic) County--tract near
Winchester, Frederick County--formerly that of HENRY BANKER; remaining
interest in estate of EDMOND GOODRICH, deceased--interesting list
of items; books; etc.; account versus STERLING CLAIBORNE; note versus
GEORGE EUBANK; GEORGE W. RAY; LINDSEY BURKS; WILLIAM OVERTON; PHILIP
VEST; GARLAND MOORE; LINDSEY TINSLEY; MOSES TAYLOR; RODNEY THORNTON.

427. 12 March 1825. JONATHAN COOPER, Amherst County, to son,
        RICHARD COOPER, Augusta County...to RICHARD COOPER, 8 June
1825--150 acres south side middle fork Pedlar and bought from
JOSEPH HIGGINBOTHAM, 17-, 1809. JONATHAN WAYT and JONATHAN C. SOWER,
Augusta Justices of the Peace.

429. 30 May 1825. JOSEPH DILLARD, Amherst County, 1; PEACHY FRANKLIN
        and WILLIAM S. CRAWFORD, Amherst County, 2; ELIJAH FLETCHER, 3...
to ELIJAH FLETCHER, 19 December 1825--$1.00 300 acres where JOSEPH
DILLARD lives. Lines: JAMES HIGGINBOTHAM, JONATHAN HIGGINBOTHAM,
deceased, PAUL CABELL, WILLIAM S. CRAWFORD, deceased, WILLIAM
HIGGINBOTHAM. DAVID S. GARLAND and EDMOND PENN, Justices of the
Peace.

431. 10 May 1825. JAMES WARE, Amherst County, to MANSFIELD WARE,
        Amherst County; GEORGE A. JOPLING; JONATHAN WARE, SR.; WILLIAM
JOPLING; MICAJAH PENDLETON; WILLIAM WARE, Amherst County to secure
them on note to Bank of Virginia--all books; accounts; interest in
batteaux on James River. THOMAS N. and RICHARD N. EUBANK, Justices
of the Peace.

432. 20 June 1824. WILLIAM G. NIMMO, Lynchburg, to JAMES GARLAND,
        Pitsylvania County, 2; SAMUEL GARLAND, Lynchburg, 3; PATSY
NIMMO, wife of ROBERT T. NIMMO, now of Pitsylvania, 4...$1.00 for
benefit of his mother, PATSY, wife of ROBERT T. NIMMO--slave; stock,
in possession of his father and mother. JONATHAN VICTOR and DANIEL
BROWN, Lynchburg Justices of the Peace. Acknowledged in Pitsylvania
by WILLIAM G. NIMMO; WILL TUNSTEAD, Clerk.

434. 10 June 1825. ABRAHAM EWERS and wife, ANNA, Amherst County,
        to JOHN ALCOCK, THOMAS APLING, and WILLIAM L. WATTS, trustees
for Methodist Church, Amherst County...this is difficult: advisable
to MT. GEOZIN (?), Amherst County, to more convenient site adjoining
old site and now on ABRAHAM EWERS' land--trustees agree to convey
old site for $1.00. Lines: JONATHAN ALCOCK, ALLEN BLAIR--2 or 3
acres.

435. 18 June 1825. SAMUEL SMITHSON...to SMITHSON, JR. (sic),
        Amherst County. Witnesses: JONATHAN VEST, WILLIAM M. SMITHSON.

436. 21 June 1825. JANE ALDRIDGE, now of Amherst County, 1;
     JOSEPH PENN, Amherst County, 2; CATHERINE PENDLETON, wife of
JAMES S. PENDLETON, Amherst County, 3...$1.00 slaves for benefit
of CATHERINE and children.

437. 1 June 1825. CATHERINE PADGET, Amherst County, 1; DAVID
     STAPLES, Amherst County, 2; WILLIAM TURNER, Amherst County, 3...
$1.00 WILLIAM TURNER on bond to ARCH. ROBERTSON, executor of JAMES M.
BROWN--furniture, etc.

437. 4 June 1825. EDMOND PAGE, 1; JAMES D. HIGGINBOTHAM, 2;
     D. and D. HIGGINBOTHAM and Company, Amherst County, 3...to
JAMES D. HIGGINBOTHAM, 14 July 1825; suit in Amherst County; $1.00;
furniture; tools; stock; crops.

439. 30 May 1825. LUCY ROBINSON, at present of Bedford, to
     WILLIAM WARWICK, Amherst County...to WILLIAM WARWICK by CHISWELL
DABNEY, 19 August 1829--deed in Amherst County to my son, WILLIAM
ROBINSON, late of Amherst County--132 acres. (This is the ROBERTSON
item cited)--Bolling Creek--life reservation; now sold to WILLIAM
WARWICK. Lines: WILLIAM ROBINSON, AGATHA ROBINSON, STITH MEAD,
BECK's mill road, Opossum Island road, LINEAS BOWLING, THOMAS WIATT.
RICHARD HOBSON and BALDA MC DANIEL, Bedford Justices of the Peace.

440. 11 June 1825. NANCY YOUNG, Amherst County, to HIRAM YOUNG,
     Amherst County...$335 45 acres where NANCY YOUNG lives--420
acres from deceased husband, JONATHAN YOUNG, for life; slaves;
furniture; tools. Witnesses: JAMES F. TALIAFERRO, JAMES PENDLETON,
CHARLES MASSIE.

441. 12 November 1824. JAMES P. BULLOCK, Campbell County, to
     RICHARD H. (A) LONDON, Amherst County...to RICHARD A. LONDON,
17 October 1825--$350 100 acres Christian Mill Creek. Part of tract.
Lines: BELL, SWANSON. Signed also by ELIZABETH F., wife of BULLOCK.
BALDA MC DANIEL and SAMUEL NOWLIN, Lynchburg Justices of the Peace.

442. 7 June 1825. WILLIAM DOWNS, 1; JAMES D. HIGGINBOTHAM, 2;
     D. and D. HIGGINBOTHAM and Company, 3...to JAMES D. HIGGINBOTHAM,
14 July ----; $1.00 horse; furniture; tools; interest in estate of
deceased father, HENRY DOWNS.

444. 4 November 1824. PLEASANT WINSTON, Richmond, to BOWLING CLARK,
     Campbell County...to C. DABNEY, 16 May 1830--intends to execute
Deed of Trust on two brick houses on Cary Street, Richmond and occupied by S. and J. COSBY, tenants. ELIZABETH, wife of PLEASANT
WINSTON, consents and to secure her--$1.00 two tracts in Campbell
-1. 450 acres.. 2. 120 acres; 3 Amherst County tract of 96 acres--
maiden tracts of ELIZABETH from father by will--at death of his
mother-in-law; debt from HENRY CLARK; slaves in Campbell County--if
any children "at her death." A. PLEASANTS and J. H. EUSTACE, Richmond
Justices of the Peace. Recorded in Campbell County: JONATHAN
ALEXANDER, Clerk.

446. 30 May 1825. WILLIAM HOLLANDSWORTH and wife, LUCY, JONATHAN M.
     WILLIAMS and wife, ELIZABETH A., THOMAS R. TERRY and wife,
CATHERINE, Amherst County, to WILLIAM WARWICK, Amherst County...
$1056.00--to WILLIAM WARWICK, by C. DABNEY, 19 August 1829--132 acres
Bolling Creek. Tract conveyed to WILLIAM ROBINSON, father of
females, by his mother, LUCY. Lines: AGATHA ROBINSON, HOLLANDSWORTH,
WILLIAMS, TERRY, MEAD, Opossum Island road, BECK's mill road, LINEAS
BOWLING, THOMAS WIATT. Devised to WILLIAM to his three daughters
by Amherst County will. LINDSEY COLEMAN, JAMES POWELL, NELSON C.
DAWSON, and JAMES L. LAMKIN, Amherst County Justices of the Peace.

448.   15 June 1825.   JACOB SCOTT, Amherst County, to JONATHAN
       FRANKLIN, Amherst County...to JAMES P. GARLAND, 31 July 1838--
$5.00 133 1/3 acres where JACOB SCOTT lives; stock; furniture.   Debts
to JONATHAN SCOTT, CHARLES P. TALIAFERRO, M. JOHNSON, HENRY CRUTCHER,
JAMES P. GARLAND, WILLIAM WATSON, ROBERT WALKER, JONATHAN MOUNTCASTLE,
HENRY L. DAVIES, DAVID S. GARLAND, DANIEL NASH, ALEXANDER MUNDY,
JAMES PAMPLIN, D. and D. HIGGINBOTHAM, GIDEON GOOCH, JONATHAN ALCOCK,
WILEY CAMPBELL, JAMES PAGE.

449.   10 March 1825.   ISAAC RUCKER and CHARLES L. BARRET as to
       MILDRED TALIAFERRO, wife of BENJAMIN TALIAFERRO, 15 January 1824,
to JAMES F. TALIAFERRO.

450.   4 September 1824.   EDWARD LYNCH and wife, MARY, Lynchburg,
       to JONATHAN LYNCH, Lynchburg...to JONATHAN LYNCH, 24 June
1835--JONATHAN LYNCH, SR., died 31 October 1820, testate, Lynchburg--
to six children: MATILDA ROBERTS, ZALINDA DAVIS, EDWARD LYNCH,
POLLY LEGGET, WILLIAM B. LYNCH, MICAJAH LINCY. $150 one sixth part
Amherst County on James.   Lines: RICHARDSON, JONATHAN TAYLOE,
JONATHAN ROBINSON, beginning at RICHARDSON's line above toll bridge
to branch below Horse ford.   SAMUEL NOWLING and DANIEL BROWN,
Lynchburg Justices of the Peace.

451.   7 March 1825.   WILLIAM BEVERLEY TOWLES, Campbell County, to
       MEREDITH LAMBERT, Campbell County...$1.00 tract OLIVER TOWLES,
JR., owned and WILLIAM BEVERLEY TOWLES is an heir.   Lines: ODEN G.
CLAY, CHARLES HOYLE.   Residue of 1062 acres and formerly that of
CLAUDIUS BUSTER and wife, NANCY, and conveyed to OLIVER TOWLES, JR.--
350 acres part nearest Lynchburg; conveyed to OLIVER TOWLES, JR. to
CHARLES HOYLE; 520 acres fartherest from Lynchburg to ODEN G. CLAY
by OLIVER TOWLES, JR.   CHARLES L. DIBRELL and S. H. DAVIS, Lynchburg
Justices of the Peace.

452.   24 June 1825.   NELSON C. DAWSON, JR. to THOMAS STRANGE, 2;
       BENJAMIN R. DAWSON, 3...$1.00, slave, stock, furniture, tools,
crops.

by

BAILEY FULTON DAVIS

1. 23 April 1825. SAMUEL CAMPBELL, Amherst County, 1; WILLIAM M.
    WALLER, Amherst County, 2; PATRICK ROSE's executor, JAMES ROSE,
3...$1.00 stock; furniture; stock. Witnesses: JONATHAN SCOTT.

2. 30 June 1825. ALLEN TALBOT, 1; STERLING CLAIBORNE, 2; MELVILLE
    TALBOT and NANCY J. THORNTON, 3...$1.00 paid by STERLING
CLAIBORNE; cattle; furniture; slaves.

3. 23 March 1825. AJAX J. WALKER, 1; JONATHAN E. LEWIS, 2;
    A. B. DAVIES, PAUL C. CABELL, H. L. DAVIES, 3...A. B. DAVIES,
PAUL C. CABELL and H. L. DAVIES on bond to CHARLES P. TALIAFERRO,
ISAAC RUCKER, NELSON C. DAWSON, JAMES L. LAMKIN, Amherst County
Justices of the Peace. $1.00--tract in Caswell County, North
Carolina--acres. Lines: DAN RIVER, E. M. WILLIAMS, WALKER's planta-
tion in Pitsylvania, E. HUNT. Slaves named; long list; cattle.
Witnesses: THOMAS J. WALKER. Memo: reserves right to sell personal
property and land to pay bank in Newburn County, North Carolina.

5. 2 July 1825. CORNELIUS POWELL, 1; LINDSEY COLEMAN, 2; JAMES
    POWELL, 3...to JAMES POWELL, 1 May 1830--JAMES POWELL on bond
to JONATHAN PENN's executors, DAVID S. GARLAND, Lynchburg District
Court suit, JAMES M. BROWN's estate. $1.00 slaves, cattle, furniture,
tools, crops, interest in estate of STEPHEN PERROW at widow's death.

6. 25 June 1825. WILLIAM CAMPBELL, Amherst County, 1; JAMES D.
    HIGGINBOTHAM, 2; D. and D. HIGGINBOTHAM and Company, 3...to
JAMES D. HIGGINBOTHAM, 14 July 1825--$1.00 Amherst County suit by
D. and D. HIGGINBOTHAM and Company; interest in estate of father,
GEORGE CAMPBELL, deceased, and held by my mother, ELIZABETH; bond
due by COLONEL CHARLES CARTER to my father in suit in Amherst County
Superior Court--two shares, cattle, furniture, stock.

8. 12 July 1825. DAVID RIPPETOE, 1; JONATHAN PENN, 2; JAMES
    POWELL, 3...debt to JAMES POWELL; medical account; mill
account for support of family of DAVID RIPPETOE; $1.00 stock, etc.

9. 18 July 1825. WILLIAM J. ROBERTS and wife, MARTHA, EDMOND
    PENN and wife, JANE, ELIZABETH H. SMITH, THOMAS LUNSFORD LOMAX...
power of attorney to ROBERT STANARD and JONATHAN METCALFE to sell
tract in town of Fredericksburg on WILLIAM (?) St.; parts of 129 and
130 lots; also tract in Spotsylvania; DRUMMOND's mill bought by
WILLIAM DRUMMOND from FONTAINE MAURY--1½ acres; also tract adjacent
mill and bought by WILLIAM DRUMMOND from SETH BARTON--eight acres
plus; at WILLIAM DRUMMOND's death descended to ANN FOX DRUMMOND who
died intestate and decreed to her heirs: JANE JOHNSTON, now deceased,
MARTHA LOMAX, now wife of WILLIAM J. ROBERTS, JANE PENN, wife of
EDMOND PENN, and ELIZABETH H. SMITH. JANE JOHNSTON devised her
interest to THOMAS LUNSFORD LOMAX. Witnesses: WILLIAM M. WALLER,
JOSEPH STAPLES, WILLIAM H. KNIGHT, JONATHAN G. MOUNTCASTLE.

10. 18 July 1825. JAMES S. PENDLETON, Amherst County, 1; JOSEPH
     PENN, Amherst County, 2; CATHERINE PENDLETON, wife of JAMES S.
PENDLETON, 3...CATHERINE has relinquished dower in house and lot in
New Glasgow sold by WILLIAM G. and JAMES S. PENDLETON to JONATHAN
MOUNTCASTLE and ROBERT TINSLEY; also tract sold by JAMES S. to same
parties; tract on HARRIS sold by husband to DAVID S. GARLAND; tract
sold to first parties above on west side of road from New Glasgow to
ACH; $1.00--interest in detinue judgement in Campbell County in favor
of REUBEN PENDLETON versus GABLE SCOTT for two slaves; enjoined in
Superior Court at Lynchburg District Court--at her death to her
children. To trustee, 19 June 1827.

11. 11 June 1825. NANCY and JUDAH MARTIN, Amherst County, to
     JESSE RICHESON, Amherst County...$14.00 two acres Pedlar.
Lines: JESSE RICHESON's mill race, dam across Pedlar--to JESSE
RICHESON, 21 July 1828. Witnesses: WILLIAM HANNAH, LINDSEY SHOEMAKER,
JONATHAN G. SMITH, W. A. RICHESON, AMBROSE TOMLINSON.

12. 16 July 1825. JONATHAN MOUNTCASTLE and wife, TAMSEY, and
     ROBERT TINSLEY, Amherst County, to RICHARD L. ELLIS and
CHISWELL DABNEY, Amherst County, 2; LEWIS WEBB, 3...to RICHARD L.
ELLIS, 30 January 1825. WILLIAM G. and JAMES S. PENDLETON and grantors
owe LEWIS WEBB on Amherst County suit; $1.00 house andlot occupied by
JAMES S. PENDLETON in New Galsgow and lately conveyed by him and
WILLIAM G. PENDLETON to grantors. Two lots in New Glasgow--1 is
store occupied by JAMES ROSE and the other by MOUNTCASTLE; tract
within mile of New Glasgow--330 acres. Lines: DAVID S. GARLAND,
JONATHAN COLEMAN; also 7½ acres adjacent lot mentioned and bought
from DAVID S. GARLAND; tract on Buffaloe of 122 acres. Lines:
BARNETT CASH, WILLIAM DUNCAN, WILLIAM SANDIDGE, tract of 200 acres
adjacent last tract; slaves. DAVID S. GARLAND and CHARLES L. BARRET,
Justices of the Peace.

16. Blank page.

17. 18 July 1825. RICHARD HARRISON, 1; JAMES R. LIVELY, 2;
     WILLIAM TUCKER, 3...to trustee, 9 January 1826. $4.00 batteaux;
tools; five lottery tickets.

18. 24 June 1825. GEORGE W. HIGGINBOTHAM and wife, JOANNA C.,
     Amherst County, to EATON CARPENTER, Amherst County...to E. P.
TUCKER, executor of EATON CARPENTER, 3 October 1848--$320 64 acres
both sides Thrasher Creek. Lines: grantee, WILLIAM HANNAH, GILLAT's
heirs, ABRAM MARTIN. Former tract of AARON HIGGINBOTHAM, deceased.
BENJAMIN TALIAFERRO and JAMES POWELL, Justices of the Peace.

19. 18 April 1825. WILLIAM G. PENDLETON and wife, MARY G., Richmond;
     JAMES S. PENDLETON and wife, CATHERINE, Amherst County, to
JONATHAN G. MOUNTCASTLE and ROBERT TINSLEY, Amherst County...$2000
tract and buildings in New Glasgow. Lines: JAMES ROSE on south,
LUCAS P. THOMPSON on north, and fronts on Main Street. Bought by
PENDLETONS as late merchants of JAMES S. PENDLETON and Company of
WEBB and WESTCOTT. PRESTON SMITH and MARTIN DRURY, Richmond Justices
of the Peace and EDMOND PENN and WILL M. WALLER, Amherst County
Justices of the Peace.

21. 16 July 1825. WILLIAM SHELTON, Amherst County, 1; WILLIAM
     ARMISTEAD and EDMOND WINSTON, Amherst County, 2; JAMES MC DANIEL,
SR., Amherst County, 3...$1.00 slaves named; furniture; tools; 852
acres decised to WILLIAM SHELTON by deceased father, RICHARD SHELTON,
and where WILLIAM SHELTON lives; also 634 acres bought by SW from
RICHARD H. BURKS and wife, ELIZA JANE; interest in estate of ABRAM
DANIEL, deceased, Cumberland, and held by widow; interest in estate
of JOSHUA SHELTON, deceased; interest in estate of HENRY GILBERT,
deceased, Amherst County; four shot guns; half acre lot in Bethel
"with AMBROSE RUCKER"; two slave boys in Tennessee conveyed to --,
trustee by RICHARD H. BURKS.

23. 15 July 1825. JONATHAN and JAMES S. DILLARD, Amherst County,
     to ALEXANDER JEWELL, Amherst County...to ALEXANDER JEWELL,
12 April 1832--SAMUEL SCOTT owes ALEXANDER JEWELL from 1820 and made
Deed of Trust to grantors and defaulted, 1 January 1821; $675.92
110 acres. Lines: ROBERT GRANT, JAMES DILLARD, DAVID S. GARLAND,
JONATHAN LONDON's tract bought of JOSEPH HAWKINS. Two tracts on
both sides Porrage 2 1/3 acres with saw mill. Lines: THOMAS
JEWELL, TURNER PINN, JAMES DILLARD and HENRY H. WATTS, Justices of
the Peace.

24. 18 July 1825. JAMES S. PENDLETON and wife, CATHERINE, Amherst
    County, to JONATHAN G. MOUNTCASTLE, Amherst County, and
ROBERT TINSLEY, Amherst County...$6.00 per acres 128 acres Indian
Creek. Lines: ISAAC SCOTT, JAMES W. SMITH. Bought from PHILIP
THURMOND, JR. EDMOND PENN and WILLIAM M. WALLER, Justices of the
Peace.

26. 23 June 1825. ALFRED GUTHRIE, Amherst County, to WILLIAM
    BOWLING, Amherst County...$450 interest in estate of deceased
father, WILLIAM GUTHRIE; dower of mother, ELIZABETH GUTHRIE, excepted.

28. (27 not numbered, but goes on opposite page from 26 to 28)
    10 June 1822. GEORGE W. VAUGHAN, Halifax County, North
Carolina, but at present of Richmond, Virginia to MICAJAH CLARK,
Richmond...Deed of Trust to secure MICAJAH CLARK $1.00 tract near
New Glasgow 3 1/4 acres and bought from WILLIAM ARMISTEAD, 22 August
1820. JONATHAN H. EUSTACE and WILLIAM H. FIZWHYLSOM, Richmond
Justices of the Peace.

29. 3 August 1825. JACOB SMITH, Amherst County, to GEORGE MYERS,
    Amherst County...$636 234½ acres where JACOB SMITH lives on
Carter's Mill Creek. Lines: BARTLETT CASH, deceased, JAMES FRANKLIN,
LYNE S. TALIAFERRO, JAMES CASH.

30. 2 August 1825. LINDSEY SANDIDGE and wife, CLARA G., Amherst
    County, 1; ALEXANDER MUNDY and JAMES W. SMITH, Amherst County. 2;
BENJAMIN SANDIDGE, Amherst County, 3...$1.00 224 acres bought by
LINDSEY SANDIDGE and JACK CARTER from RICHARD MILLNER, 16 November
1818; slaves; stock; furniture; tools. To BENJAMIN SANDIDGE,
22 August 1825. JONATHAN COLEMAN and WILLIAM M. WALLER, Justices
of the Peace.

32. 2 August 1825. LINDSEY SANDIDGE and wife, CLARA G., Amherst
    County, to BENJAMIN SANDIDGE, Amherst County...$319 141 acres--
to BENJAMIN SANDIDGE, 22 August 1825; Buffaloe. Lines: grantee,
JOSEPH DODD, deceased; where LINDSEY SANDIDGE lives. Justices of
the Peace as above.

33. 3 August 1825. CHARLES C. CARTER and wife, JANE S., Amherst
    County, to HILL CARTER, Amherst County and GEORGE M. PAYNE,
Buckingham, trustees...on same date Deed of Trust executed--460 acres
where CHARLES C. CARTER lives and undivided interest in Walnut
Grove; $1.00 for benefit of JANE and children--slaves.

34. 15 August 1825. SAMUEL R. DAVIES, trustee, to GEORGE M.
    TINSLEY...Deed of Trust by ALEXANDER TINSLEY and wife, PAMELIA,
11 June 1824; ALEXANDER and GEORGE M. were joint tenants in 50 acres
which they bought from ISAAC TINSLEY; GEORGE M., at the request of
ALEXANDER, bought at $157. To GEORGE M. TINSLEY, 17 October 1825.

35. 15 August 1825. ROBERT A. PENN, Amherst County, to JONATHAN
    PENN, Amherst County...power of attorney.

36. 13 August 1825. WILLIAM W. SCOTT, Amherst County, to NORBORNE
    TALIAFERRO, Lynchburg; THOMAS H. SCOTT, Campbell County and
HUGH R. SCOTT...to HUGH R. SCOTT, 15 August 1827--HUGH R. SCOTT has
this day sold WILLIAM W. SCOTT tract devised by father, WILLIAM
SCOTT, to said HUGH R. SCOTT; half now occupied by ANN SCOTT; old
tract of 950 acres in Campbell and Bedford; $9000 due by bond from
WILLIAM W. SCOTT; $1.00 slaves; 260 acres in Amherst County in right
of wife, ELIZA, late PENDLETON. Witnesses: WILLIAM SHELTON, JAMES M.
DANIEL, JR., ROBERT C. SCOTT.

38. 8 August 1825. JAMES PENN, Lynchburg, to N. M. TALIAFERRO,
    Lynchburg and ELIJAH FLETVHER, Lynchburg, 2; J. POWES (seems
to be POWES), ELIJAH FLETVHER...$1.00 all interest in estate of
father, -- PENN and reference to deed by "said PENN to JAMES PENN
and KYLE on --. Witnesses: JONATHAN T. HILL.

39.   8 April 1823.   JONATHAN CLARK and wife, MARY, Miami County,
      Ohio, to REUBEN PETERS, Amherst County...$60 141 acres head-
waters Pedlar and south side Blue Ridge. Lines: Gervan's survey,
CLARK, EDMINSTON. Formerly that of JAMES HARTLESS and CLARK and
wife are his heirs--their part sold to PETERS. RICHARD W. HARTLESS,
heir, devised his part to GEORGE CLARK, minor son of JONATHAN and
MARY CLARK. Witnesses: THOMAS MACY, JOSEPH BELAM. DAVID JENKINS,
Justice of the Peace in Ohio. JONATHAN W. TUFORD, Clerk.

41.   29 July 1823.   DANIEL L. BURFORD and wife, RUTH, Amherst
      County, to REUBEN COX, Amherst County...to REUBEN COX, 3 September
1835--$90 18 acres south side Harris. Lines: grantee, a branch,
REUBEN NORVELL and AMBROSE RUCKER, Justices of the Peace.

43.   5 January 1825.   JAMES POWELL and wife, MILDRED, Amherst
      County, to WILLIAM C. CHRISTIAN, Amherst County...$1500 404 acres
south side Buffaloe; not sold by acres, but by boundaries. Lines:
PENN, WALKER, SHIELDS. Witnesses: JONATHAN FRANKLIN, JONATHAN
SCOTT, POWHATAN D. FRANKLIN. THOMAS CREWS and LINDSEY COLEMAN,
Justices of the Peace.

44.   15 December 1823.   AARON HIGGINBOTHAM's legatees: ABSALOM
      HIGGINBOTHAM and wife, POLLY, Amherst County; WASHINGTON HILL
and wife, SALLY, Rockbridge; JAMES HIX and wife, NANCY, Amherst
County; AARON HIGGINBOTHAM and wife, ELIZABETH, Amherst County;
GEORGE W. HIGGINBOTHAM and wife, JOANNA, Amherst County; JAMES
SHIELDS and wife, ELIZABETH, Nelson County to LINDSEY SANDIDGE and
wife, CLARA G., Amherst County...$1.00 390 acres Thrasher's Creek
and Franklin Creek. Lines: ABRAHAM MARTIN, AARON HIGGINBOTHAM,
deceased. Witnesses: CORNELIUS SALE, WILLIAM TUCKER, FIELDING
BROWN. BENJAMIN TALIAFERRO and JAMES POWELL, Amherst County Justices
of the Peace as to NANCY HIX; JOANNAH C. HIGGINBOTHAM, POLLY HIGGIN-
BOTHAM, wife of ABSALOM HIGGINBOTHAM. JONATHAN J. COLEMAN and JAMES
WOOD, JR., Nelson County, Justices of the Peace as to ELIZABETH
SHIELDS.

46.   18 December 1823.   Same HIGGINBOTHAM legatees as above, but
      LINDSEY SANDIDGE and wife, GLARY G., join to convey to GEORGE W.
HIGGINBOTHAM and wife, JOANNA C...$1.00 four tracts. 1.   270 acres
south side Piney Mr. land. Lines: THOMAS WILLIAMSON, BENJAMIN
CARPENTER. 2.   55 acres both sides Thrasher Creek. Lines: EATON
CARPENTER. 3.   33 acres Indian Creek. Lines: JAMES S. PENDLETON.
4.   46 acres north side Buffaloe. Lines: WILLIAM DUNCAN. Land of
AARON HIGGINBOTHAM, deceased. Witnesses: as above and same Justices
of the Peace.

49.   18 December 1823.   Legatees as above to JAMES HIX and wife,
      NANCY, Amherst County...$1.00 125 acres north side Buffaloe.
Lines: COLEMAN, AARON HIGGINBOTHAM, deceased, tract. Witnesses
and Justices of the Peace as above.

52.   18 December 1823.   Same legatees to WASHINGTON HILL and wife,
      SALLY, Rockbridge...$1.00 100 acres north side Buffaloe. Lines:
WILLIAM SANDIDGE. Witnesses and Justices of the Peace as above.

55.   18 December 1823.   Same legatees to AARON HIGGINBOTHAM and wife
      ELIZABETH S., Amherst County...$1.00 126 acres south side
Buffaloe. Lines: WILLIAM DUNCAN. Same witnesses and Justices
of the Peace as above.

57.   18 December 1823.   Same legatees to JAMES SHIELDS and wife,
      ELIZABETH, Nelson County...$1.00 144 acres both sides Stone
House Creek. Lines: JAMES HIX, WILLIAM TUCKER. Same witnesses
and Justices of the Peace as above.

60. 18 December 1823. Same legatees to ABSALOM HIGGINBOTHAM, Amherst County...$1.00 416 acres Thrasher Creek. Lines: EATON CARPENTER. 2. 34 acres south side Buffaloe. Lines: SANDIDGE. Witnesses and Justices of the Peace as above.

63. 16 August 1825. SAMUEL R. DAVIES, Amherst County, to ARCHIBALD ROBERTSON, Lynchburg...3 February 1824, ISAAC TINSLEY and wife, NANCY, executor Deed of Trust to SAMUEL R. DAVIES and ISAAC HANSARD to secure JONATHAN HANSARD as bondsman for ISAAC TINSLEY as administrator of father, WILLIAM TINSLEY. ARCHIBALD ROBERTSON, administrator of ISAAC TINSLEY, asked for sale and DABNEY SANDIDGE, trustee of MRS. NANCY TINSLEY, consents--8 May last JONATHAN HANSARD had possession, but ROBERTSON insisted upon sale and ROBERTSON bought at $5.01 per acre. Other trustee declined to act, but DAVIES conveys--232½ acres. Lines: Harris Creek, Ambler's road, Bethel road, HANSARD's field, AMBLER.

65. 23 July 1825. ALLEN TALBOT, Amherst County, to HEZEKIAH S. FULCHER, Amherst County...debt to NELSON CRAWFORD, executor of CALEB RALLS, HENRY L. DAVIES, guardian of --; JAMES FULCHER on bond; debts to late JAMES M. BROWN, late Amherst County Sheriff, as deputy-- ALLEN TALBOT by appointment. Deed of Trust, 17 November 1824, but since JAMES FULCHER became bondsman DAVID S. GARLAND assignee of P. P. THORNTON--Superior Court Amherst County; $1.00 crops; stock in hands of Marshall of Lynchburg Superior Court; slaves devised by -- JONES to MARY THORNTON for life; remainder to children by then husband, STERLING THORNTON; later conveyed by RICHARD JONES to STERLING THORNTON and wife for lives.

67. 15 August 1825. ROBERT A. PENN, Amherst County, to FIELDING BROWN, Amherst County...$150 interest of my wife, LUCY C. (formerly LUCY C. COLEMAN) in personal estate of GEORGE COLEMAN, deceased, and held by MRS. JUDITH tucker, formerly COLEMAN, as dower in estate of GEORGE COLEMAN. To FIELDING BROWN, 15 October 1825.

68. 16 August 1825. -3 February 1824. ISAAC TINSLEY and wife, NANCY..Deed of Trust to SAMUEL R. DAVIES and ISAAC HANSARD-- bought by ARCHIBALD ROBERTSON, and paid $112.30--part. ROBERTSON is administrator of ISAAC TINSLEY and insists upon retaining rest of amount. ROBERTSON executes lien until paid to SAMUEL R. DAVIES.

68. 1 February 1825. GEORGE HOWARD, Amherst County, to COURTNEY CHRISTIAN, wife of ROBERT CHRISTIAN...love and affection--mare etc. free from control of husband. Witnesses: W. S. THORNTON, THOMAS A. MORRIS. Sent to COURTNEY CHRISTIAN, 20 February 1827. WILLIAM M. WALLER and JONATHAN COLEMAN, Justices of the Peace.

69. 1 July 1825. GEORGE CAMPBELL and wife, LUCY, Amherst County, to WILLIAM ANGUS, Amherst County...to HILL CARTER, agent, 19 June 1827--dower relinquished in -?L2. $650 240 acres where WILLIAM ANGUS lives--Little Piney. Lines: WILLIAM MOORE, JONATHAN STINNETT, JONATHAN CAMPBELL. HILL CARTER and WILLIAM M. WALLER, Justices of the Peace.

70. 17 August 1823. ANDREW MORELAND, Amherst County, 1; WILLIAM ARMISTEAD, Amherst County, 2; THOMAS LAIN, Bethel, 3...$1.00 crops, furniture, tools.

71. 17 August 1825. AMBROSE WILLMORE and wife, LUCINDA, Amherst County, to JAMES POWELL, Amherst County...$1120 140 acres headwaters Huff. Dower relinquished. S:440.

72. 20 September 1824. LEMUEL TOLER, Buckingham, 1; GRANDERSON
     MOSELEY, 2; MORRIS and JOPLING, MARY HUGHES, THOMAS DANIEL,
ALEXANDER TREDWELL, or FRETWELL--surviving partner of JONATHAN
FRETWELL and Company, AUSTIN M. APPLING, WOODSON and STAPLES, LEMUEL
TOLER, JR., REBECCA HUGHES, PETER F. JEFFERSON...debt to all $1.00.
30 acres. Lines: JONATHAN ALCOCK, slaves, furniture. ROLFE ELDRIDGE,
Deputy Clerk of Buckingham. Memo: GRANDERSON MOSELEY suggested that
it be recorded in Amherst County; property removed to Amherst County.

75. 19 August 1825. ROBERT A. PENN, Amherst County, to ROBERT
     TINSLEY,...$1.00 slaves to secure JONATHAN COLEMAN.

77. 29 August 1825. PETER BURRUS--signed BURROUGHS--and wife,
     ELIZABETH, Amherst County, to CHARLES WILSON, Amherst County...
$54 13½ acres. Lines: ABSALOM OWL, grantee, CATLETT CAMPBELL;
the field. THOMAS CREWS and LINDSEY COLEMAN, Justices of the Peace.

78. 3 September 1825. LUCAS POWELL, Amherst County, to JONATHAN
     THOMPSON, JR...$1.00 interest in crops adjacent Rose Mills;
portion of crop in Nelson; rented from JONATHAN N. ROSE and JONATHAN
THOMPSON, JR. One fourth belongs to MARY; CHARLOTTE and COURTNEY
POWELL who furnished a fellow and plough; debt to PEACHY FRANKLIN,
assignee of MOORE F. CARTER; to guardian of BENJAMIN H. GAYLE,
HENRY ROSE, JONATHAN THOMPSON, SR.; Sheriff of Nelson; blacksmith
accounts.

79. 14 September 1825. CHARLES and RICHARD STINNETT, Amherst
     County, to JESSE HIGGINBOTHAM, Amherst County, 2; DAVID and
DANIEL HIGGINBOTHAM and Company, 3...$1.00 stock and furniture.
To L. S. CHRISTIAN, 28 June 1826.

81. 14 September 1825. JONATHAN M. EDWARDS, Lincoln County,
     Kentucky, to WILLIS RUCKER, Amherst County...power of attorney
to act: interest in estate of GEORGE MC DANIEL. Witnesses:
JONATHAN R. IRVINE, WILLIAM J. BOWCOCK, ABNER SISSON. To WILLIS
RUCKER, 23 March 1854. 14 September 1825 DABNEY WARE as to JONATHAN M.
EDWARDS who was then in Amherst County.

82. 10 September 1825. JONATHAN ALLCOCK and wife, ELIZABETH,
     Amherst County, to JONATHAN HORSLEY, Amherst County...debt
to MICAJAH PENDLETON--$1.00 between 90 and 100 acres north side
Buffaloe. Lines: THOMAS APPLING, grantor, JAMES D. WATTS. Bought
from MICAJAH PENDLETON on first day of this month. WILLIAM HORSLEY
and RICHARD PHILLIPS, Nelson Justices of the Peace as to JONATHAN
ALLCOCK.

84. 10 September 1825. JAMES D. WATTS and wife, JANE, to JONATHAN
     HORSLEY, JR...to JONATHAN HORSLEY, 20 December 1830; debt to
MICAJAH PENDLETON; $1.00 95 acres south side Buffaloe. Lines:
grantor, LEWIS LAYNE; recently bought from MICAJAH PENDLETON.
Witnesses: D. P. GOOCH, RICHARD PHILLIPS. Same Nelson Justices
of the Peace as above.

86. 1 September 1825. MICAJAH PENDLETON and wife, MARY C.,
     Nelson County, to JONATHAN ALLCOCK...$1300 between 95 and
100 acres north side Buffaloe. Lines: THOMAS APPLING, grantee,
JAMES D. WATTS. Share of MICAJAH PENDLETON on division of larger
tract between him and MACE FREELAND. Patent to JAMES FREELAND.
Same Justices of the Peace as above.

87. 1 August 1825. MICAJAH PENDLETON and wife as above to LEWIS
     LAYNE...$1.00 300 3/4 acres south side Buffaloe. Lines:
grantee. Part of tract of JAMES FREELAND. Same Justices of the
Peace as above.

89.   4 June 1824.   JABEZ CAMDEN and wife, NANCY, Amherst County,
          to BLUFORD CAMDEN, Amherst County...$600 664 acres--to BLUFORD
CAMDEN, by ROBERT GRANT, 4 February 1850.   Lines: mouth of a lane,
JAMES COLEMAN, WILLIAM STINNETT, WILLIAM PETRES, grantor, ZACH ISBELL,
deceased, ALLISON MORRIS, CHARLES TALIAFERRO's estate on top of
Tobacco Row Mountain, M. W. CAMDEN.   Witnesses: PETER G. CAMDEN,
FIELDING BROWN, JONATHAN WISE.

90.   24 August 1825.   THOMAS CREWS, Amherst County, to EDWARD
          LLOYD, Lynchburg...$3125 800 acres where THOMAS CREWS lives.
Lines: BENJAMIN BROWN, JONATHAN MC DANIEL, LINDSEY MC DANIEL,
JAMES PENDLETON.   Deed of Trust.   Witnesses: ELIJAH and TIMOTHY
FLETCHER.   To EDWARD LLOYD, 17 October 1825.

92.   19 September 1825.   DAVID S. GARLAND and wife, JANE H., Amherst
          County, to JONATHAN ROBINSON, Rockbridge...to JACOB M. RIFF,
26 October 1839--$1713 285½ acres both sides Huff; south border
Buffaloe.   Lines: MICAJAH CAMDEN, JONATHAN ROBINSON, AJAX WALKER,
CHARLES B. PENN, BURCHER WHITEHEAD, deceased.   Patent to JAMES
HIGGINBOTHAM.   CHARLES L. BARRET and WILLIAM M. WALLER, Justices
of the Peace.   In summary, grantee is called JONATHAN RICHESON.

94.   1 September 1825.   JEMIMA JENKINS to WILLIAM JINKINS...$10
          one acre headwaters Buck Branch and where "said JINKINS lives."
Witnesses: GEORGE W. PETTYJOHN, REUBEN NORVELL and JAMES L. LAMKIN,
Justices of the Peace.

95.   29 September 1824.   NANCY SHIELDS, Amherst County, WILLIAM
          TURNER and HENRY L. DAVIES, 2...to HENRY L. DAVIES, 19 June
1826; returned--to WILLIAM TURNER, 2 October 1829, returned; to
trustees by JONATHAN PENN, 24 October--slaves (many); one bought
from GEORGE S. HOLLOWAY; tract on Buffaloe and one mile from ACH
and bought from MATTHEW WATSON; interest in estate of ANTHONY
RUCKER; furniture; tools; debts due CHAPMAN JOHNSON, STERLING CLAIBORNE,
JONATHAN L. HARRIS, THOMAS ALDRIDGE, GUSTAVUS A. ROSE, GEORGE S.
HOLLOWAY, MARTIN LONDON (one of legatees of BARTLETT EADES), WILLIAM
MORGAN, surviving partner of JONATHAN M. SETTLE and Company; bondsmen:
JAMES PETTIT, WILLIAM MC DANIEL, WILLIAM TURNER.   To deliver slaves
to AMANDA LEE at death of N. SHIELDS or children, if any; also
slaves to SEATON M. PENN, PAULUS HARRISON, FRANCIS ANN PENN, SOPHIA
HARRISON and children by RICHARD HARRISON.   Witnesses: CHARLES
WILSON, P. S. PEARCE.

98.   23 September 1825.   JONATHAN MERRITT and wife, RHODA, Amherst
          County, to JONATHAN L. MERRITT...$266.25 53½ acres Stervant
Creek.   Lines: CHARLES WINGFIELD, MILLNER COX, BOLER CLARK, deceased.

99.   26 September 1825.   GABRIEL PAGE, commissioner of Amherst
          County Court to JONAS PIERCE, Amherst County...March term,
1823 decree between FRANCIS PAGE et al. versus SUSAN CHRISTIAN et al.--
to sell tracts of BARTLETT OWENS, deceased, and distribute to
interested parties.   Advertised sale at ACH, 19 September 1825;
court day.   PIERCE bought at $2.75 per acre; $1.00 125 acres south
side Buffaloe.   Lines: DAVID S. GARLAND, JACOB SCOTT, JONAH PIERCE.
Witnesses: L. P. THOMPSON.   It is noted that survey is appended,
but it is not herein.

100.   26 September 1825.   WILLIAM WARE to DABNEY WARE...all crops
          but rent is reserved to landlord.   DABNEY WARE to sell and
apply on bond due from WILLIAM WARE.   Witnesses: WILLIAM TUCKER,
DABNEY T. PHILLIPS.

100.   -- September 1825.   JONATHAN ALLEN, Amherst County, 1; JAMES N.
          EDMUNDS, Amherst County, 2; LEWIS TINDALL, Amherst County, 3...
to LEWIS TINDALL, 21 February 1827--$1.00 one fifth of property in
hands of JACOB TYREE and decised to me by SAMUEL ALLEN, deceased;
also LEROY CAMDEN's fifth bought by me; GARLAND LUCAS' claim to
county land and recorded in Amherst County.

102. 10 -- 1825. SARAH WOODSON, administratrix of JONATHAN WOODSON,
     to CHRISTOPHER ISBELL, Amherst County...to WILLIAM I. ISBELL,
agent, 12 April 1826--$154.04 and $5.12 on judgement recovered by
CHRISTOPHER ISBELL versus her in Lynchburg Corporation Court and
$500 due him for boarding her and children and educating children.
Interest in slave, GEORGE--JONATHAN WOODSON instituted suit versus
JOSEPH PENN and pending in Amherst County Superior Court. Witnesses:
WILLIAM I. ISBELL, THOMAS MURRELL. Recorded 26 September 1825.
(Note: word should be "instituted" above.)

103. -- September 1825. ALEXANDER MUNDY, Deputy, for CHARLES MUNDY,
     Sheriff, Amherst County, to TIMOTHY FLETCHER, Lynchburg...
ROWLAND SANDIDGE arrested and took insolvent oath, 19 September 1825,
and Sheriff sold 226 acres and SANDIDGE's interest in estate of
JONATHAN WILLIAMSON in right of wife--after death of widow, SARAH
WILLIAMSON. FLETCHER bought at $21.00. Recorded 17 October 1825.

104. 18 October 1825. JOSEPH MC CRAY and wife, SOPHIA, to LYDIA
     CARY...$100 seven acres on Harris; bought from DANIEL L.
BURFORD. AMBROSE RUCKER and DABNEY WARE, Justices of the Peace.

106. 19 July 1825. GEORGE B. WOODSON, Lynchburg District Chancery
     Court Marshall, to HENRY L. LANGHORNE, Campbell County...decree
of 20 May 1824: JONATHAN N. ROSE, THOMAS MOORE, JR., trustees,
versus JONATHAN PATTON, SOPHIA CRAWFORD, ARTHUR B. DAVIES, RICHARD
PERKINS and JONATHAN MOORE--sold, 12 July 1824--contingent to town
of Lynchburg; tract bought by BENJAMIN PERKINS from ROBERT MORRIS
39 acres and bought by LANGHORNE for $1.00. DANIEL BROWN and ALBON
MC DANIEL, Lynchburg Justices of the Peace.

108. 17 October 1825. SAMUEL CAMPBELL, 1; HEZEKIEH S. (L.) FULCHER, 2;
     JAMES FULCHER, 3...to trustee, 23 May 1826--14 acres. Lines:
HILL CARTER, interest in dower tract of ELIZABETH CAMPBELL, wife of
GEORGE CAMPBELL, SR., deceased.

109. 14 May 1825. THOMAS CLEMENTS and wife, ROSANNA, Amherst
     County, to EDWIN S. RUCKER, Amherst County...$50 interest in
Tinsley Mill tract--one-twenty-fourth part--20 acres; interest as
heir of JOSHUA TINSLEY, deceased. NELSON C. DAWSON and AMBROSE
RUCKER, Justices of the Peace.

110. 1 October 1825. JESSE CASH, 1; DUDLEY SANDIDGE, Amherst
     County, 2; JONATHAN SMITH, Amherst County, 3...to JONATHAN
SMITH, 20 March 1826; $1.00 cattle; furniture; interest as overseer
for this year for COLONEL JONATHAN DILLARD; one-fourth on Indian
Creek.

112. 18 October 1825. REUBEN HENDERSON, Bedford, 1; ARTHUR B.
     DAVIES, Amherst County, 2; SAMUEL R. DAVIES, Amherst County, 3...
$1.00 bay horse about nine years old. Witness: C. POWELL.

113. 5 October 1825. RODERICK MC CULLOCH, Amherst County, to
     WILLIAM H. MC CULLOCH, Amherst County...to WILLIAM H. MC CULLOCH,
23 November 1826--love and $1.00 200 acres on James River; life
reservation to RODERICK MC CULLOCH. Lines: James on south;
EDWARD WAUGH; ARHTUR L. DAVIES; also all land I own on east side of
Ferry road. Lines: A. L. DAVIES, WILLIAM ROACH, LUKE RAY. If
WILLIAM H. claims any other estate, to be divided to residue of my
children as heirs of their mother, ELIZABETH, and then he forfeits.
Witnesses: PETER P. THORNTON, SAMUEL B. DAVIES, JOSEPH GLASGOW,
ROBERT H. MC CULLOCH, BENJAMIN T. SHACKELFORD, NELSON DAVIS.

114. 5 October 1825. RODERICK MC CULLOCH, Amherst County, to
     ROBERT H. MC CULLOCH, Amherst County...love and $1.00 tract
on Ferry road on east, ARTHUR L. DAVIES, JAMES WAUGH. Witnesses:
as above--minus ROBERT MC CULLOCH and plus WILLIAM H. MC CULLOCH.

114. 8 November 1825. JANE LIVELY, Amherst County, to HIRAM
      YOUNG, Amherst County...love for daughter-in-law, SUSAN LIVELY,
wife of PHILIP LIVELY; $1.00; slave for benefit of SUSAN and children.

115. 8 November 1825. HIRAM YOUNG, Amherst County, to JANE LIVELY...
      valuable consideration all interest in estate of JAMES LIVELY;
interest of ANNE CAMPBELL, daughter of JAMES LIVELY and by Deed of
Trust by PHILIP LIVELY--conveyed to YOUNG.

116. 8 November 1825. JANE LIVELY to daughter, ANNE CAMPBELL,
      Kentucky and children...her interest in estate of JAMES LIVELY
by will; if ANNE marries, then not under husband's control.

117. 14 November 1825. JACOB HAAS, Bedford, to AMBROSE RUCKER,
      son of ISAAC, Amherst County, 2; ISAAC COLLETT, Ohio, and
County of --...for benefit of ELIZABETH GOODRICH, wife of THOMAS
GOODRICH--they are poor and destitute; not under control of THOMAS.
$5.00--horse, furniture, etc. to assist THOMAS and wife to remove
to Ohio; at death of ELIZABETH, COLLETT is to sell and divide to
children of JONATHAN HAAS: THOMAS, JACOB and FREDERICK HAAS, when
of age.

118. 14 November 1825. JACOB HAAS, Bedford, to AMBROSE RUCKER,
      son of ISAAC, and ISAAC COLLETT, Ohio...$5.00 for benefit of
SUSANNA HAAS, wife of his brother, JONATHAN HAAS, and her three
children--poor and destitute--wagon, stock, furniture, etc. to assist
in their removal to Ohio to buy land and to be trustees. At SUSANNA's
death to children when of age.

120. 7 November 1825. WILL JOPLING and ISAAC RUCKER as to JONATHAN
      HAAS and wife, SUSANNA, 9 November 1822, to -- two such items
on 120f.

122. 18 November 1825. JOEL BOWLES, 1; NATHANIEL BOWLES, 2;
      MILDRED DAWSON, 3, all of Amherst County...$1.00 crops, stock,
furniture.

123. 1 August 1825. THOMAS SALE and wife, SALLY P., Bedford, to
      CORNELIUS SALE, Amherst County...to JONATHAN THOMPSON, JR.
for CORNELIUS SALE, 3 September 1839--$2500 500 acres Thrasher
Creek; border of Buffaloe. Lines: A. HIGGINBOTHAM. Tract bought
by both from heirs of JONATHAN SALE--600 acres here. JACOB WHITE
and EDWARD GWATHIM, Bedford Justices of the Peace.

125. 31 October 1825. FRANCES SHACKELFORD, Madison County, Kentucky,
      to SAMUEL B. DAVIES, Bedford...$1184 76½ acres Horsley and south
side of Buffaloe Ridge--spur of Tobacco Row Mountain about one fourth
of a mile above Pedlar Mills. Lines: WIATT DUNCAN, CHARLES ELLIS,
WILLIAM MITCHELL, RICHARD L. ELLIS. Part of estate of late ELIZABETH
MC CULLOCH and divided to children--FRANCES is one of them.
JAMES WARE and RICHARD N. EUBANK, Amherst County Justices of the Peace.

127. 29 October 1825. EDITH EUBANK, Amherst County, to WILLIAM
      HAYNES, Amherst County...for life of EDITH--plantation and
slaves. Consideration: HAYNES to furnish EDITH and ELIZABETH P.
HAYNES, his sister, ample support. EDITH is his mother. WILLIAM
has bought at sale of JONATHAN EUBANK, deceased, and husband of
EDITH, by paying bond to GALT BULLOCK and Company, Lynchburg.
Witnesses: RICHARD N. EUBANK, JONATHAN PRYOR, ROBERT H. CARTER.
To HENRY E. HAYNES, administrator of WILLIAM HAYNES, 17 May 1836.

128. 3 November 1825. JAMES C. TERRY, 1; SAMUEL TAYLOR and WILLIAM I.
      ISBELL, 2; THOMAS TERRY and CHRISTOPHER ISBELL, 3...$5.00
slaves. THOMAS TERRY and CHRISTOPHER ISBELL on bond to WILLIAM
TURNER, Commissioner of Amherst County, to sell and divide estate
of THOMAS JOHNSON, deceased--$250. December 29, 1824.

131. 26 October 1825. ROBERT L. COLEMAN and wife, MARY T.,
      Bedford, to JOSEPH T. REISE (RUSE?), Bedford...$1800 430 acres.
Lines: HAAS, BURKS, MC CLURE, county line, DAVID S. GARLAND,
CHRISTIAN. 202 acres. Lines: COOPER, JARVIS, HARCLES, B. TALIAFERRO,
HAAS, CHRISTIAN. NATHANIEL J. MANSON and BALDA MC DANIEL, Bedford
Justices of the Peace. To JOSEPH T. REISE, 20 March 1826.

133. 29 October 1825. JONATHAN J. DILLARD, Amherst County, to
      HENRY H. WATTS, Amherst County...power of attorney. Witnesses:
LUCAS P. THOMPSON, R. L. WAUGH, STERLING CLAIBORNE.

134. 21 November 1825. HUMPHREY GILBERT, 16 May 1820, executor
      Deed of Trust to TINSLEY RUCKER who has removed from Virginia...
GILBERT appoints ORMUND WARE in his stead as trustee.

135. 22 November 1825. CHARLES C. CARTER, 1; HILL CARTER, 2;
      THOMAS N. EUBANK, 3; RICHARD L. ELLIS, 4...$1.00 stock,
slaves (9), furniture, crops. To JONATHAN W. YOUNG, 17 April 1826.

137. 7 November 1825. MANSFIELD WARE and wife, SUSAN PETTIS,
      Amherst County, to RICHARD N. EUBANK, Amherst County...to
RICHARD N. EUBANK, 29 September 1829--$1000 112 acres. Lines:
south side Horsley, R. L. ELLIS. Witnesses: JAMES WARE, R. L. ELLIS,
JAMES D. WARE, PETER P. THORNTON. JAMES POWELL and EDMOND PENN,
Justices of the Peace.

138. 26 October 1825. ROLAND BIAS and wife, NANCY, Amherst County,
      to LARKIN BIAS, Amherst County...to WILLIAM ARMISTEAD,
18 March 1834--$150 150 acres Pea Vine Mountain. Lines: DAVID
BURKS, SR., ROLAND GILLESPIE, WALTER WILLIAMS--where ROLAND BIAS
lives. Witnesses: WILLIAM ARMISTEAD, ROBERT N. EUBANK, NELSON DAVIS,
JONATHAN D. DAVIS, JAMES WARE. JAMES WARE and RICHARD N. EUBANK,
Justices of the Peace.

140. 19 November 1825. JAMES WARE, Amherst County, to JONATHAN
      DAVIS, Amherst County...$55 17 acres where JONATHAN DAVIS
formerly lived. Lines: RICHARD ELLIS on west.

141. 27 July 1825. JAMES DAVIS and wife, SALLY, Amherst County,
      to JONATHAN ELLIS, Amherst County...$1.00 10 acres Maple
Creek. Lines: Island in creek, grantor, R. L. ELLIS. Witnesses:
R. L. ELLIS, JONATHAN DUDLEY DAVIS, ELLIOTT WORTHAM, M. PENDLETON.

142. 27 October 1825. JESSE MAYS and wife, NANCY, Amherst County,
      to WILLIAM M. WALLER, Amherst County...$1.00 and $580.50
210 acres Stone House Creek. One moiety interest of JESSE from
father, ROBERT MAYS--106 acres. Lines: CHARLES TUCKER, deceased,
PETER CASH, AARON HIGGINBOTHAM, deceased. Also tract of 104 acres
bought by JESSE from PIERCE W. MAYS. Lines: JESSE MAYS, PETER
CASH, BEVERLY WILLIAMSON, deceased. DAVID S. GARLAND and EDMOND
PENN, Justices of the Peace.

145. 1 September 1825. MICAJAH PENDLETON and wife, MARY, to
      JAMES D. WATTS...$700 95 acres south side Buffaloe. Lines:
grantee, small tract conveyed by MICAJAH PENDLETON to LEWIS LAYNE,
WILLIAM H. DIGGES. Part of tract divided between MICAJAH PENDLETON
and MACE FREELAND and patent to JAMES FREELAND. Nelson County
Justices of the Peace, WILLIAM HORSLEY and RICHARD PHILLIPS as to
grantors.

148. 20 December 1825. WILLIAM C. WHITEHEAD, Amherst County, 1;
      SAMUEL W. CHRISTIAN, Amherst County, 2; D. and D. HIGGINBOTHAM
and Company, Amherst County, 3...$1.00 furniture, stock, tools.

307

150.   1 August 1825. REUBEN NORVELL, Amherst County, to CHRISTOPHER
       ANTHONY and GEORGE N. NORVELL, Lynchburg...to secure various
creditors; $5.00 600 acres adjacent JAMES CHRISTIAN's Quarter of
253 acres; tract adjacent of 250 acres; tract adjacent of 400 acres
second tract on Otter--240 acres. Tract where REUBEN NORVELL lives
of 330 acres; slaves; stock; furniture; tools; two stills. ALBON
MC DANIEL and JONATHAN W. BAGWELL, Lynchburg Justices of the Peace.

152.   19 December 1825. LORENZO D. LYONS, Amherst County, to JAMES D.
       JOHNS, Amherst County...to JAMES D. JOHNS, 5 March 1826--$35
one-eighth interest in tract of JOSHUA TINSLEY on Pedlar. Lines:
JONATHAN CRAWFORD--369 acres. Reference to deed by JONATHAN
HUTCHINSON and wife, LUCINDA, to LORENZO D. LYONS, 10 January 1824.

153.   10 November 1825. Division between heirs of WILLIAM PETTYJOHN's
       three sons, JOSEPH PETTYJOHN and wife, NANCY, WIATT PETTYJOHN
and wife, JANE, GEORGE WASHINGTON PETTYJOHN and wife, NANCY T...to
JOSEPH PETTYJOHN, 19 January 1829, and plat also delivered. Note:
plat is not herein, but is probably the one on the last page of this
book. GEORGE WASHINGTON PETTYJOHN is the ancestor of my daughter-in-
law, MARY GAYLE PETTYJOHN, who married my third son, THURMAN BLANTON
DAVIS--all are entitled under father's will to tract on Harris and
James 735 acres. Agree to divide and reference to plat and survey
of 29 November 1822, by REUBEN NORVELL and annexed. JOSEPH gets
208½ acres on north side Harris; WIATT gets 230½ acres south side
Harris; GEORGE W. gets 286 acres including mansion house adjacent
the river and 10 acres of woodland adjacent SCOTT and PENDLETON.
Subject to rights of WILLIAM PETTYJOHN's widow under will. Each
pays $1.00 and at death of their mother each will pay balance and
satisfy by will of WILLIAM PETTYJOHN. Testator's grandson, SETH
WOODROOF, has privilege of working part of the land. NELSON C.
DAWSON and REUBEN NORVELL, Justices of the Peace. Recorded,
17 November 1828.

157.   25 December 1825. BENJAMIN SALE to RICHARD L. ELLIS to secure
       debt due RICHARD L. ELLIS of $40.00; tobacco crop to be taken
as soon as season will admit of getting it in order. Witnesses:
J. E. TALIAFERRO and J. W. YOUNG. Note: I was reared at Shelbyville,
Kentucky, which is the third largest burley market in the world,
but have lived in western Kentucky where dark fired was the main
tobacco crop. It has been interesting to note the differences in
terms used to denote readiness of crop to strip and get ready for
market. In some sections they use the phrase "in case" and in other
areas they use the term, "in order." In olden days they had to
depend upon rain to moisten it to the proper condition, but in modern
days they use coke burners to help condition it. It must not be
allowed to get "too high" for this prevents proper handling.

158.   2 January 1826. JONATHAN B. DUNCAN, trustee in Deed of Trust,
       27 August 1824, from PHILIP LIVELY, to HIRAM YOUNG, Amherst
County...all interest in dower tract of NANCY YOUNG, widow of
JONATHAN YOUNG 420 acres. Lines: BENJAMIN TALIAFERRO, CHARLES
TALIAFERRO, deceased. $72.00. Witnesses: POWELL, ST. GEORGE
TUCKER, JONATHAN COLEMAN. To HIRAM YOUNG, 17 June 1833.

159.   10 January 1826. AMBROSE RUCKER and RICHARD HARRISON as to
       PAMELIA TINSLEY, wife of ALEXANDER TINSLEY, 11 June 1824...
to SAMUEL R. DAVIES, trustee, 24 January 1826.

160.   1 February 1826. SAMUEL R. DAVIES, trustee, to PAMELIA
       TINSLEY, wife of ALEXANDER TINSLEY...Deed of Trust and sale
made 50 acres whereon ALEXANDER TINSLEY lives. One third of
TINSLEY MILL, slave and child, furniture. Apart from husband.
Reference to deed of 11 June 1824.

161. 17 February 1826. SAMUEL COLEMAN, Amherst County, 1; GEORGE W.
      TURNER, 2; SAMUEL GALT, GRALAND, WALTON and PENN, DANIEL L.
BURFORD, BOYD MILLER, assignee of RICHARD HARRISON, SAMUEL GARLAND
for benefit of BOYD MILLER, 3...to SAMUEL G., 6 March 1825--judgements
in Amherst County court versus SAMUEL COLEMAN and JAMES COLEMAN;
$1.00; remaining interest in slave conveyed by SAMUEL COLEMAN to
GEORGE W. TURNER and BLANSFORD HICKS, 10 May 1823, in Deed of Trust;
also Deed of Trust to S. GARLAND and TURNER, 29 April 1823; another
to JAMES F. TALIAFERRO; interest that may be recovered of WILLIAM
DILLARD in Lynchburg Chancery; tract conveyed to STERLING CLAIBORNE.
Witnesses: THOMAS D. HILL, POWHATAN D. FRANKLIN, WILLIAM TUCKER.

163. 17 February 1826. SAMUEL COLEMAN, Amherst County, to BARNETT
      MOOHN, Amherst County...four or five years past SAMUEL COLEMAN
sold BARNETT MOOHN 120 acres on Harris for $400; som paid to
assignees of SAMUEL COLEMAN; balance due WILLIAM BLACK and SAMUEL
GARLAND; SAMUEL COLEMAN has delivered tract. Lines: WILLIAM
PETERS, deceased; JABEZ CAMDEN, ZACH ISBELL, deceased. Witnesses:
as above.

164. 12 November 1825. JAMES P. BULLOCK and wife, ELIZA F., Campbell
      County, to JONATHAN CREWS, Halifax County...to JONATHAN CREWS,
3 November 1831--$1186 355 acres Christian Mill Creek. Lines:
SIMMONS, SWANSON, CHRISTIAN, BELL, CHARLES L. CHRISTIAN. AUGUSTINE
LEFTWICH and SAMUEL NOWLIN, Lynchburg Justices of the Peace.

166. 18 February 1826. ROBERT TINSLEY, Bedford, 1; JONATHAN J.
      TINSLEY, 2; LUCY TINSLEY, wife of LINDSEY TINSLEY, Amherst
County, 3; and SALLY and POLLY TINSLEY, infants of said LINDSEY
TINSLEY by a former wife and those by present wife: PULLUM...Lines:
ELIZA, OLIVER and MARTHA and future ones--love of ROBERT for the
children of his brother's wife and children--reduced to penury by
indiscretions of LINDSEY--$1.00 slaves with ages and names--to educate
and support until youngest is 21. May, if trustee consents, be
removed to any western states or territories. Lynchburg Justices
of the Peace as above.

169. 25 February 1826. WILLIAM BURFORD, SR., Amherst County, to
      CHARLES MAYS, JR., Amherst County...$1.00 and services 409½
acres. Lines: north by JESSE BECK, east by WILLIAM TURNER and
ARCHIBALD REYNOLDS, south by LINEAS BOWLING, west by JAMES B.
COFFLIN and BENJAMIN WATTS. One grist mill and saw mill; three
acres on Harris. Lines: AMBROSE BURFORD, REUBEN COX, named slaves,
furniture, blacksmith tools, crops, all Deed of Trusts. Witnesses:
WILLIAM KENT, SAMUEL MAYS, WILLIS REYNOLDS. No date at beginning;
this is recorded date at end of document.

170. -- December 1825. ROBERT CONNE, Culpeper, to BENJAMIN
      WIGGINTHON, Bedford...to BENJAMIN WIGGINTHON, 1829--$650
1300 acres. Patent to WILLIAM WIDDEBURN, 17 April 1796, and by
WILLIAM WIDDEBURN by deed, 16 October 1806--proved District Court,
Fredericksburg--to CHARLES GRYMES who with wife and JONATHAN MINOR--
to them by Deed of Trust, 1 May 1805. WILLIAM WARD and JER. STROTHER,
Justices of the Peace of Culpeper. This is confusing, but reads thus.

172. 19 February 1826. JAMES HILL, JR. and wife, ELIZABETH, Munroe
      County, to JAMES HILL, SR...$350 41½ acres. Lines: Lunch
road, Church road. WILLIAM GRAHAM and JONATHAN HENCHMAN, Munroe
Justices of the Peace.

173. -- October 1804. CHARLES GRYMES and wife, JANE, Spotsylvania
      County, to JONATHAN MINOR, same county...for benefit of ROBERT
CONNE, Culpeper, 15 October 1804. Lines: Piney, south fork Shoe
Creek 1320 acres. CHARLES GRYMES bought from WILLIAM WIDDERBURN; to
sell and balance to pay WILLIAM WIDDERBURN. Witnesses: DABNEY HERNDON,
HUGH MERCER, J. CANNONS. Memo: sold 6 December 1804 to ROBERT
CONNE, Culpeper for L140. THOMAS TAYLOR and Company, auctioneers,
Richmond. JO CHEW, Deputy Clerk of Frederick County.

175. 1 May 1804. CHARLES GRYMES and wife, JANE, Spotsylvania, to
ROBERT CONNE...CHARLES GRYMES bought from WILLIAM WIDDERBURN
and wife, ANN, King George County, 16 October 1804; CHARLES GRYMES
conveyed to JONATHAN MINOR, Fredericksburg, 1804, in trust; JONATHAN
MINOR sold in Richmond to ROBERT CONNE, Culpeper and MINOR joins
GRYMES and wife in conveying 1320 acres Little Piney. Witnesses:
WILLIAM BROOK, DAVID C. KER, GEORGE HITCH (?), JO CHEW, Deputy Clerk.
Recorded Amherst County, 26 March 1826.

177. 28 August 1824. ROBERT TINSLEY, Bedford, to JONATHAN J.
TINSLEY, Bedford--son of ROBERT--to JONATHAN J. ROBERTSON,
15 November 1833...gift--Irish Creek and in Amherst County and
Rockbridge atop Blue Ridge. Lines: WILLIAM SILES, WILLIAM CLARK,
deceased, grantor. 445 acres bought from HENRY HARTLESS. Witnesses:
WILLIAM C. PORTER, JONATHAN HOWARD, JONATHAN P. SWINNEY.

178. 5 September 1825. THOMAS A. MORRIS, Amherst County, to JAMES H.
MARTIN, Amherst County...$300 seven acres east side of his (?)
lands. Lines: ALIN WOOD, RICHARD L. ELLIS. Witnesses: CHARLES
and LINDSEY MARTIN, JAMES WARE, RICHARD N. EUBANK.

179. 16 March 1826. JOSHUA SANDIDGE and wife, JANE, Amherst
County, to THOMAS ALLEN, Amherst County...$100 two tracts on
Pedlar of 196 acres. Lines: JONATHAN D. CRAWFORD, DAVID S. GARLAND.
As heirs of NATHANIEL WILSON, deceased. BENJAMIN TALIAFERRO and
CHARLES L. BARRET, Justices of the Peace.

180. -- 1826. BENJAMIN R. DAWSON and wife, SUSAN, Amherst County,
to JESSE WOODROOF, Amherst County...$1000 ($1.00) 76 acres.
Lines: THOMAS CREWS, WILLIAM MC DANIEL, grantee. Sold by WILLIAM
WOODROOF to BENJAMIN R. DAWSON. Recorded: 20 March 1826.

181. 3 September 1825. WILLIAM TURNER and wife, SARAH, Amherst
County, to ELLIS P. OMOHUNDRO, Amherst County...to WILLIAM
TURNER, 27 April 1827--$584 292 acres Stovall Creek. Lines: Galt
road, SAMUEL ANDERSON, deceased, WILLIAM GALT, deceased, DAVID
STAPLES, THOMAS JEWELL, A. JEWELL, HENRY TURNER, STAPLES' road.
Witnesses: N. P. BREEDLOVE, GEORGE STAPLES, STEPHEN B. TURNER.

182. 14 March 1826. BENJAMIN WATTS and wife, FANNY D., Amherst
County, to LEWIS MAYS, Amherst County...$120.39 26 3/4 acres
Stovall Creek. Lines: road, old field. NELSON C. DAWSON and JAMES L.
LAMKIN, Justices of the Peace.

184. 1 July 1825. FRANCIS PETERS, Amherst County, 1; ALEXANDER
MUNDY, Amherst County, 2; BLANFORD HIX, Amherst County, 3...
$1.00; debt to ARCHIBALD ROBERTSON, Superior Court Amherst County
judgement; THOMAS COPPEDGE, administrator of CHARLES COPPEDGE and
BLANFORD HIX is on bond; slaves; furniture. Witnesses: STERLING
CLAIBORNE, WILL DILLARD, THOMAS COLEMAN.

186. 11 March 1826. JAMES F. TALIAFERRO, Amherst County, to
SAMUEL GARLAND, Lynchburg...to SAMUEL GARLAND, 29 December
1828--Deed of Trust by SAMUEL COLEMAN, Amherst County, 29 January
1822, to JAMES F. TALIAFERRO. For benefit of POWELL and TALIAFERRO
and assigned to ARCHIBALD ROBERTSON--slaves; tract both sides of
Harris Creek. Lines: THOMAS COLEMAN, DANIEL F. CHRISTIAN, FLEMING
COLEMAN--110 acres and inherited from father's estate.

187. 29 September 1825. DAVID BURKS, JUNIOR, to PETER RUCKER...
$100 203 acres north side Banks' Mountain and joining Pedlar.
Lines: THOMAS MORRIS, JER. DEAN, JONATHAN SANDIDGE, WILLIAM CARTER,
deceased, BENJAMIN HIGGINBOTHAM, PETER CARTER, JONATHAN BROWN,
Fallen Branch. Witnesses: PETER P. THORNTON, WIATT DUNCAN, GIDEON C.
GOODRICH, JOSEPH R. CARTER.

189.   17 February 1825.   REUBEN NORVELL, Amherst County, to ROBERT
       STANARD, Richmond...$5.00 75 acres--to THOMAS DAMON or DAWSON?,
present owner, 23 September 1844--Farm Mill road, Wills' Mill road,
Dawson Mill road, ELIAS WILLS, GUSTAVUS A. ROSE, DANIEL NORCUTT.

190.   7 October 1825.   PETER CARTER and wife, ELIZABETH, Amherst
       County, to PETER RUCKER, Amherst County...$50 16 acres west
side Bankston Mountain; branch of Pedlar; taken off of larger
tract of PETER CARTER's--1796 acres. Lines: grantee tract bought
from DAVID BURKS, JR., JONATHAN BROWN, deceased, NELSON CRAWFORD
and WILLIAM JOPLING, Justices of the Peace.

191.   26 October 1825.   REUBEN NORVELL, trustee for WILLIAM P. MUSE
       and MILLNER COX, Amherst County, to WILLIAM D. HILL, Amherst
County...$50 three acres Lynch road. Lines: GUSTAVUS A. ROSE.
Sold under Deed of Trust and bought by MILLNER COX and at his request
to HILL.

192.   22 March 1826.   JONATHAN COLEMAN and wife, SARAH W., Amherst
       County, to PENELOPY PHILLIPS, widow of JONATHAN PHILLIPS, and
SOPHIA PHILLIPS, granddaughter of JONATHAN PHILLIPS...JONATHAN COLEMAN
owed JONATHAN PHILLIPS and HENRY H. WATTS, his administrator under
will, is willing to take land to satisfy. $97.70 40 acres. Part of
tract and joining same; NATHANIEL LOUGSBOUROUGH. To widow for life
and then to SOPHIA. Plat--head of Elk Island Creek. PENELOPY is
called ELOPHY and date is 10 January 1826, in summary.

194.   18 February 1826.   ROBERT S. WILKINS and wife, ELIZABETH G.,
       Lynchburg, to BLANSFORD HICKS, Amherst County...$35 four acres:
to ROBERT S. WILKINS, 1826--Drawn by grantors in division of estate
of JONATHAN and ELIZABETH COLEMAN, deceased--grandparents of
ELIZABETH G.--both sides Harris. Lines: LINDSEY HARDWICK (legatee),
DANIEL F. CHRISTIAN. Plat in office--not herein--THOMAS A. HOLCOMBE
and ALBON MC DANIEL, Lynchburg Justices of the Peace.

195.   16 January 1826.   CATLETT CAMPBELL and wife, NANCY, Amherst
       County, to CHARLES WILSON, Amherst County...to CHARLES WILSON,
10 October 1832--Dower in U:394, and delivered to B. WILSON, 27 August
1833--$60 70 acres. Lines: grantee, JOEL CAMPBELL, SR., PETER
BURROUGHS. Residue of tract bought by CATLETT CAMPBELL from JAMES
POWELL and all that CATLETT CAMPBELL owns in Amherst County.
Witnesses: ALLISON OGDEN, JAMES D. HIGGINBOTHAM, GUSTAVUS A.
EDWARDS.

197.   15 August 1825.   LEWIS DAWSON, Amherst County, to THOMAS
       CLEMENTS, Amherst County...$40 eight acres Harris Creek.
Lines: GEORGE M. TINSLEY, THOMAS CLEMENTS. NELSON C. DAWSON and
JAMES L. LAMIKIN, Justices of the Peace--LAMKIN.

198.   25 March 1826.   JOSEPH DODD, Amherst County, SAMUEL R. DAVIES,
       Amherst County, 2; EDWARD WATSON, Amherst County, 3...to
SAMUEL R. DAVIES, 12 June 1829--$1.00 EDWARD WATSON on bond to JOEL F.
SMITH; 226 acres formerly that of JOSEPH DODD, deceased. Lines:
BENJAMIN SANDIDGE, stock, furniture, tools, crops.

199.   27 March 1826.   MICAJAH CAMDEN, JR., Amherst County, 1;
       WILLIAM S. CRAWFORD, Amherst County, 2; ELIJAH FLETCHER,
Lynchburg, 3...to ELIJAH FLETCHER, 20 September 1830; $1.00 373 acres.
Lines: MICAJAH CAMDEN, SR. JR. lately bought it from ELIJAH FLETCHER.
DANIEL BROWN and ALBON MC DANIEL, Lynchburg Justices of the Peace.

201.   18 February 1826.   CHARLES C. CARTER and wife, JANE S.,
       Amherst County, to THOMAS E. and GEORGE T. PLEASANTS, Amherst
County...$3600 460 acres. Lines: JONATHAN MC DANIEL, WILLIAM
JOPLING and is home tract of CHARLES C. CARTER. THOMAS N. EUBANK
and HILL CARTER, Justices of the Peace.

203. 25 March 1826. THOMAS ALLEN and wife, MARY, Amherst County,
     to ALFRED RICHESON, Amherst County...$60 no acres; interest
as heirs of NATHANIEL WILSON and to THOMAS ALLEN by JOSHUA SANDIDGE
and wife. Witnesses: ISAAC RUCKER, SR., BARTLETT CLEMENTS.
BENJAMIN and CHARLES P. TALIAFERRO, Justices of the Peace.

205. 27 March 1826. ELIJAH FLETCHER, Lynchburg, to MICAJAH CAMDEN,
     JR...$800; no acres. Lines: MICAJAH CAMDEN, SR., WILLIAM
STINNETT--formerly that of JABEZ CAMDEN and called Whitehead
tract. To ELIJAH FLETCHER from Marshall of Lynchburg Superior
Court of Chancery. DANIEL BROWN and ALBON MC DANIEL, Lynchburg
Justices of the Peace.

206. 13 December 1825. RICHARD HARRISON and JAMES L. LAMKIN as
     to MARY G. WILLS, wife of ELIAS WILLS, 19 March 1824...to --
relinquishment of dower, Q:11; to G. A. ROSE, JONATHAN D. WILLS,
BENJAMIN NORVELL.

206. 5 November 1824. JONATHAN CAMDEN, JR. and wife, SALLY, and
     BENJAMIN CAMDEN, to JONATHAN CAMPBELL, Amherst County...to
JONATHAN CAMDEN, JR., 17 June 1829--$285 81 acres north side of
south fork Piney. Lines: GILBERT HAYS, GEORGE MONROE. Tract
conveyed by GEORGE GILLESPIE and wife, MARY, to JAMES ROBERTS, then
of Goochland, 5 October 1792. DAVID S. GARLAND and EDMOND PENN,
Justices of the Peace.

208. -- November 1825. WILLIAM H. MC CULLOCH and wife, MARY C.,
     Amherst County, to MARY THORNTON, ISABELLA WAUGH and ROBERT H.
MC CULLOCH, Amherst County; ELIZABETH DAVIES, Bedford; NANCY E.
GLASGOW, Rockbridge; and FRANCES SHACKELFORD, Madison County,
Kentucky...$1000 one-seventh part on west side Tobacco Row Mountain.
Lines: RICHARD L. ELLIS, MARTIN PARKS, JONATHAN WINGFIELD, CALEB
WATTS--588 3/4 acres.

209. 14 October 1825. DABNEY WARE and wife, ELIZABETH, Amherst
     County, to JONATHAN R. IRVINE, Bedford...to JONATHAN R.
IRVINE, 16 August 1830--$1800 282 acres Grayham Creek. Lines:
AMBROSE RUCKER, SAMUEL BURKS, deceased, WILLIAM and JONATHAN SHELTON,
NELSON C. DAWSON.

211. 5 April 1826. WILLIAM WEAVER, Fluvanna, to MARY CAWTHORN,
     widow of ROBERT CAWTHORN, Amherst County, 2; ISAAC RUCKER, SR.,
and WILLIAM DUNCAN, Amherst County, 3...marriage shortly intended
between WILLIAM WEAVER and MARY. MARY has estate in Fluvanna and in
hands of her mother, MRS. WILLIAMSON; at death to be disposed of by
MARY. She will not claim estate of WILLIAM WEAVER; $1.00; if WILLIAM
WEAVER survives, then to him. Witnesses: JOSEPH C. DODD, HENRY
FRANKLIN, JONATHAN FLOOD, PULLIAM SANDIDGE, RICHARD SMITH, JR.

214. 2 January 1826. REUBEN NORVELL, trustee for WILLIAM P. MUSE,
     Amherst County, to MILLNER COX, Amherst County...$140 40 acres
both sides Mitchell's road. Lines: grantor, GEORGE W. TAYLOR,
grantee. To REUBEN NORVELL in Deed of Trust by MUSE; debt due COX.

215. 3 March 1826. JAMES W. SMITH and wife, ELIZABETH L., Amherst
     County, to SAMUEL D. CHRISTIAN, Amherst County...$2000 309
acres Indian Creek. Lines: WILLIAM M. WALLER, a branch, west side
thorofar (sic) Woods' survey, JOANNA HIGGINBOTHAM, Little Creek,
PENDLETON, B branch of Indian Creek. Witnesses: H. S. FULCHER,
JONATHAN TUCKER, CLAIBORNE TUCKER. BENJAMIN and CHARLES P. TALIAFERRO,
Justices of the Peace.

217. 17 April 1826. JONATHAN WARE, Amherst County, to WILLIAM G.
     CAMPBELL, Amherst County...$280 50 acres south borders of
north fork Piney. Patent to MATTHEW MOORE, 1769.

218. 17 April 1826. ROBERT LAWHORN, Amherst County, 1; WILLIAM
     MARTIN, SR., Amherst County, 2; JONATHAN LAWHORN, JR., Amherst
County, 3...$1.00 stock and furniture.

220.   22 April 1826.   TANDY TOOLEY and wife, SALLY, Amherst County,
       to WESTLEY E. CHRISTIAN, Amherst County...$100 50 acres
Johnson Branch. WILLIAM JOPLING and ISAAC RUCKER, Justices of the
Peace.

221.   22 April 1826.   ZED. SHOEMAKER, Amherst County, to WILLIAM
       PRYOR, JR., Amherst County...to WILLIAM PRYOR, JR. by JONATHAN
PRYOR, 21 January 1857--$200 105 acres south borders Lovelady Creek.
Lines: JAMES TAYLOR, CHARLES P. TALIAFERRO, WILLIAM H. CABELL,
grantor, JAMES GATEWOOD's Spring. JAMES WARE and ISAAC RUCKER,
Justices of the Peace.

223.   8 October 1820.   PETER CARTER and wife, ELIZABETH, Amherst
       County, to JOB CARTER, Amherst County...$200 201 acres, both
sides Pedlar; residue of 217 acres patent to PETER CARTER, 1796.
Lines: BENJAMIN HIGGINBOTHAM--now CHARLES P. TALIAFERRO, WILLIAM H.
CABELL. Former tract of JONATHAN BROWN, deceased. Sixteen acres
taken off and sold to PETER RUCKER; RUCKER's tract bought of DAVID
BURKS, JR. NELSON CRAWFORD and WILLIAM JOPLING, Justices of the
Peace. Recorded 8 October 1825 and Justices of the Peace term this
as date of deed.

224.   25 January 1826.   WILLIAM BATES and wife, SALLY, Amherst
       County, to WILLIAM NOEL, Amherst County...$200 117 acres Pedlar.
Lines: CHARLES TYLER, JONATHAN ROBINSON, grantor. Witnesses:
ISAAC RUCKER, SR., FREDERICK PAINTER. BENJAMIN TALIAFERRO and ISAAC
RUCKER, Justices of the Peace.

226.   4 May 1826.   HENRY CAMDEN and wife, LUCY, Amherst County, to
       HIRAM YOUNG, Amherst County...$60 23 acres. Lines: his own,
JONATHAN YOUNG, deceased. Witnesses: WILLIAM C. DUNCAN, JONATHAN O.
DUNCAN, GEORGE H. DUNCAN.

227.   1 May 1823.   ELIZABETH PUGH, Amherst County, to her son,
       GEORGE EDMUND PUGH, Amherst County...love and $1.00 furniture.
Signed: ELIZABETH BECKHAM. Witnesses: CHARLES PALMORE, WILLIAM
BOWMAN. Summary calls her BECKHAM.

227.   5 May 1826.   LEWELLIN J. REYNOLDS, 1; NICHOLAS DAVIES,
       HOWELL L. BROWN, 2; SAMUEL R. DAVIES, 3 and trustees...debts
due SAMUEL R. DAVIES; $1.00 tract bought from SAMUEL R. DAVIES this
day.

228.   5 May 1826.   SAMUEL R. DAVIES, trustee, to LEWILLIN J. REYNOLDS...
       11 June 1824, Deed of Trust to SAMUEL R. DAVIES by ALEXANDER
TINSLEY and wife. Sold at ACH, 4 May 1826--part of property on
Harris. Lines: WILLIAM R. ROANE. LEWILLIN J. REYNOLDS bought at
$400.

229.   10 January 1826.   JONATHAN FRANKLIN, WILLIAM R. ROANE, 2;
       ROBERT TINSLEY, Amherst County, 3...$175 paid by ROBERT
TINSLEY; horses; wagon; furniture; Debt to WILLIAM R. ROANE.
Witnesses: RICHARD CRAWFORD, JONATHAN SCOTT, P. D. FRANKLIN.

231.   7 March 1826.   JOEL CAMPBELL, JR. and wife, ELIZABETH, Amherst
       County, to DABNEY HILL, CA...to DABNEY HILL, 4 June 1827--$150.
Lines: the river, JONATHAN F. CAMDEN, CRAWFORD. Part of tract of
estate of JONATHAN FULCHER, deceased. 36 acres. JAMES POWELL and
LINDSEY COLEMAN, Justices of the Peace.

232.   13 December 1823.   JONATHAN HUTCHESON and wife, LUCINDA,
       Amherst County, to ARCHIBALD ROBERTSON, Lynchburg...to
ARCHIBALD ROBERTSON, 16 March 1830. $461.50 tract on main branch of
Harris; part of mansion house tract of JOSHUA TINSLEY, deceased, and
lot two by commissioners of Amherst County. Lines: creek, Bethel
road, ISAAC TINSLEY, deceased, 71½ acres Survey of 27 January 1823,
by REUBEN NORVELL. JAMES POWELL and THOMAS CREWS, Justices of the
Peace.

234.   23 March 1826.   SIMEON ROBINSON, Amherst County, to CHARLES
       MUNDY, Sheriff of Amherst County...alias capias by SARAH
JEFFERSON, executrix of JONATHAN JEFFERSON versus JONATHAN F.
ROBERTSON and SIMEON ROBINSON; takes insolvent oath; all interest
in estate of deceased father, JONATHAN ROBINSON, Amherst County;
mother, LUCY ROBINSON.   Note: I think that his father was WILLIAM
and this is evidently clerical error.

235.   20 April 1826.   THOMAS EDWARDS and wife, ELIZABETH, Amherst
       County, to JONATHAN HUTCHESON, Amherst County...to J. F.
HUTCHINSON, 19 January 1826; $1.00 71½ acres south side Porrage.
JAMES POWELL and THOMAS CREWS, Justices of the Peace.

236.   2 June 1826.   CHRISTOPHER ISBELL, Amherst County, 1; JONATHAN H.
       GOODWIN and CHISWELL DABNEY, Amherst County, 2; JONATHAN H.
GOODWIN, SR., Amherst County, 3...$1.00; named slave.   ALBON MC DANIEL
and ABRAM R. NORTH, Lynchburg Justices of the Peace.

238.   14 June 1826.   ANDREW M. STATON, JR. and THOMAS STATON,
       Amherst County, to JONATHAN W. YOUNG, Amherst County...to
R. L. ELLIS, 23 January 1835; debt due ELLIS; $1.00 furniture;
stock; crops.

240.   12 June 1826.   RICHARD L. ELLIS hired to ANDREW M. STATON, SR...
       for two and a half years for $1.00; furniture; stock.   Bought
at my house this day by ELLIS and EUBANK on execution.   Witnesses:
THOMAS STATON, J. W. YOUNG, ANDREW M. STATON, GEORGE W. YOUNG.

241.   21 April 1826.   JONATHAN LYNCH and wife, ANNA, Campbell
       County, to WILLIAM WARWICK, Amherst County...to JONATHAN M.
OTEY, administrator per note, 30 October 1833--$2000 340 acres
both sides Bolling Creek.   Lines: HENRY LANGHORNE, BOLLING, near
Opossum Island road, WIATT, grantee, fork of Bolling Creek, up south
fork.   JESSE BURTON and THOMAS FOX, Campbell County Justices of the
Peace.

242.   24 March 1826.   CHRISTIAN COLEMAN, Amherst County, 1; BLANSFORD
       HICKS and FLEMING COLEMAN, Amherst County, 2; SAMUEL GARLAND,
Lynchburg, 2...$1.00; slaves sold this day by GARLAND to COLEMAN.
One woman conveyed by POLLY CHRISTIAN--formerly COLEMAN to CHRISTIAN
COLEMAN.   Witnesses: SAMUEL COLEMAN 02 such names; JAMES and THOMAS
COLEMAN.

244.   20 June 1826.   RICHARD N. EUBANK and wife, MARY C., Amherst
       County, to MANSFIELD WARE, Amherst County...$1000 3/4 acres
brick house and lot at Pedlar Mills whereon RICHARD N. EUBANK now
lives.   THOMAS EUBANK and JAMES WARE, Justices of the Peace.

245.   13 November 1826.   MANSFIELD WARE, 1; DAVID S. GARLAND, 2;
       RICHARD L. ELLIS, 3...to JONATHAN W. YOUNG, agent for RICHARD L.
ELLIS, 23 April 1829; $1.00 lot near and joining Pedlar Mills and
bought from RICHARD N. EUBANK--in forks of Pedlar and Horsley.
Witnesses: RICHARD N. EUBANK, PETER P. THORNTON, JONATHAN D. WARE.

246.   6 July 1826.   SAMUEL J. WIATT, Lynchburg, to CHARLES L. BROWN,
       Lynchburg, 2; SARAH E. BROWN, Lynchburg, 3...to ROBERT M.
BROWN, for CHARLES L. BROWN, 17 September 1850--$1.00 slaves for
benefit of SARAH E. BROWN.

247.   17 July 1826.   WILLIAM D. HILL, 1; CHISWELL DABNEY, 2;
       JONATHAN M. WILLIAMS, 3...JONATHAN M. WILLIAMS on bond to
CHARLES MUNDY, Sheriff of Amherst County; suit of ALEXANDER GARVIN,
assignee of WILLIAM I. ISBELL, WILLIAM D. HILL versus ZACH ISBELL's
estate in hands of SALLY and CHRISTOPHER ISBELL, administratrix and
administrator--$5.00 slaves; two tracts about five minutes from
Lynchburg or is it miles: probably latter and occupied by HILL.
1.   89 acres. Lines: Lynch road, GUSTAVUS A. ROSE, CHARLES WINGFIELD
and bought from trustees of MICAJAH CAMDEN, deceased.   2.   3 acres.
Lines: Lynch road, G. A. ROSE, bought from MILLNER COX and formerly
that of WILLIAM P. MUSE; two slaves; all interest in estate of mother,
furniture, tools, stock.

249. 12 May 1826. WILLIAM D. HILL, Amherst County, to ALEXANDER
      GARVIN, Amherst County...$246.40 46½ acres Porrage Creek.
Lines: THOMAS WILCOX, JAMES LIVELY, JONATHAN LONDON, RICHARD
POWELL, deceased.

250. 3 March 1826. SAMUEL D. CHRISTIAN, Amherst County, to JAMES W.
      SMITH, Amherst County...$1100 309 acres Indian Creek. Lately
bought from SMITH, 3 March 1826. Witnesses: WILLIAM DUNCAN, JONATHAN
and RICHARD SMITH.

251. 1 July 1826. CHARLES MARTIN and wife, JOYCE, Amherst County,
      to DAVID TOMLINSON, Amherst County...$40--to DAVID TOMLINSON,
23 April 1827. Big Plow River in Amherst County--this is a new one
on me, as I recall--31 acres patent to AMBROSE TOMLINSON, asce (sic)
of JAMES CLEMENTS and since allotted to CHARLES MARTIN and wife by
commissioners in division of AMBROSE TOMLINSON, deceased. Lines:
AMBROSE TOMLINSON. Also undivided tract of widow, MARY TOMLINSON.
ISAAC RUCKER and JAMES POWELL, Justices of the Peace.

252. 24 July 1826. WILLIAM TURNER, Amherst County, 1; HUDSON M.
      GARLAND, Amherst County, 2; AMBROSE RUCKER and ALEXANDER MARR,
administrators of JAMES MARR, Amherst County...to ALEXANDER MARR,
7 May 1827--$1.00 slaves. WILLIAM TURNER is surviving obliger of
JONATHAN LONDON--judgement in Amherst County Superior Court.

255. 2 August 1826. CHALRES BIBB, Amherst County, to JONATHAN W.
      YOUNG, Amherst County...to R. S. ELLIS, 23 January 1835; debts
due ELLIS; interest in father's estate; furniture--$1.00. Witnesses:
ROBERT C. BIBB, J. E. TALIAFERRO, BENNETT TINSLEY, RICHARD STINNETT,
GEORGE W. YOUNG.

256. 22 June 1826. JONATHAN GUTHRIE, Augusta, to ELIZABETH GUTHRIE,
      Amherst County...$270 54 acres--JOHN's part of father's estate.

256. 21 August 1826. REUBEN NORVELL to WILLIAM D. HILL...all
      interest in "within conveyed tract." Margin: O:755(?) 1821.

257. 20 November 1825. WILLIAM MC DANIEL, trustee of PHILIP LIVELY
      in Deed of Trust to secure NANCY SHIELDS, 10 September 1824...
233 acres. Lines: JONATHAN MC DANIEL, MRS. BOURNE, JONATHAN LONDON,
deceased. Tract devised to JAMES R. LIVELY by father, JAMES, SR.
and by him sold to PHILIP. NANCY SHIELDS bought at $815.50.

257. 11 January 1826. REUBEN NORVELL, attorney-in-fact for JOEL
      THACKER and SALLY BURFORD, Kentucky; JEMIMA JENKINS, AMOS
THACKER and wife, SUSANNAH, ROBERT RIDGWAY and wife, POLLY, Amherst
County, to WIATT PETTYJOHN, Amherst County...$630--to WIATT PETTYJOHN,
18 September 1826--70 acres Harris Creek; allotted to TEMPY THACKER
out of estate of father, PETTIS THACKER. REUBEN NORVELL and JAMES L.
LAMKIN, Justices of the Peace.

259. 28 September 1824. THOMAS MITCHELL, Caswell County, North
      Carolina to JAMES P. GARLAND, Nelson County, 2; NANCY GARLAND,
wife of ROBERT GARLAND, Amherst County, 3...23 February 1824,
ROBERT GRALAND executed Deed of Trust to JAMES P. GARLAND; slave.
Three slaves of ROBERT's were sold yesterday at Nelson Court House
and bought by MITCHELL at $332. Three slaves were in Deed of Trust
by ROBERT GARLAND to DANIEL PERROW and WILLIAM H. LOVING. NANCY
wishes to exchange slaves--better adapted to her use; $1.00.
Witnesses: LINDSEY COLEMAN, JR. and S. GARLAND.

260. 21 August 1826. WILLIAM COLEMAN, Amherst County, 1; SAMUEL W.
      DICKEY, Amherst County, 2; CHARLES L. BARRET, Amherst County,
3...$1.00 mare, carpenter's tools. To WILLIAM COLEMAN, 6 January
1830.

261. 18 July 1826. PETER CASH, Amherst County, to son, REUBEN CASH...
furniture, stock, tools for use of son at father's pleasure--
for REUBEN, wife, and children. Witnesses: JAMES and WASHINGTON
CASH. To REUBEN CASH, 11 November 1831.

261. 19 December 1825. Slave division to legatees of JAMES GARLAND,
deceased....Five slaves at $2700. To WILLIAM G. PENDLETON,
JAMES WARE and wife, NANCY, formerly PENDLETON, SOPHIA PADGETT,
formerly PENDLETON, JAMES S. and MICAJAH PENDLETON, ELIAS WILLS and
wife, POLLY, formerly PENDLETON, W. W. SCOTT and wife, ELIZA,
formerly PENDLETON, CORNELIUS CROW and wife, JANE, formerly PENDLETON,
FRANCIS, SAMUEL, MARTHA and HARRIET PENDLETON. JAMES S. PENDLETON
represents WILLIAM G. PENDLETON, JAMES WARE, MICAJAH PENDLETON,
SOPHIA PADGETT, ROBERT and SAMUEL PENDLETON--seven parts. RICHARD
EUBANK represents FRANCIS PENDLETON, ELIAS WILLS represents MARTHA
and HARRIET, CROW and SCOTT for selves and wives, ELIAS WILLS,
guardian of MARTHA and HARRIET, JAMES WARE, guardian of SAMUEL and
ROBERT PENDLETON, $1.00 mutually paid. Long list as to adjustment
of payments.

263. 22 August 1826. JONATHAN S. CARTER and wife, ELIZABETH, 1;
ROBERT TINSLEY, 2; THOMAS N. EUBANK, 3 and DABNEY SANDIDGE, 3...
all of Amherst County. JONATHAN S. CARTER has obtained injunction
from Lynchburg Chancery versus ABRAM CARTER, WILLIAM JOPLING and
JOSEPH R. CARTER as to further judgements versus him in Amherst
County Superior Court and THOMAS N. EUBANK and DABNEY SANDIDGE are
bondsmen. $1.00 399 acres formerly that of JONATHAN CRAWFORD,
deceased. Lines: WILLIAM JOPLING, WILLIAM PRYOR, slaves.

265. 21 August 1826. JONATHAN ALLCOCK, THOMAS APLING and LEWIS
LAYNE, Commissioners to act upon estate of WILLIAM TILLER,
deceased, Amherst County...$171 paid by RICHARD LANDRUM, Nelson
County. 80 acres west side of road adjacent to mansion house of
WILLIAM TILLER. Lines: JOSEPH KENNEDY. Witnesses: WIATT LONDON
and JOSEPH SWANSON.

266. 19 December 1825. ELIAS WILLS in own right and as guardian
of MARTHA G. and HARRIET R. PENDLETON, CORNELIUS CROW, JAMES S.
PENDLETON in own right and as guardian of SAMUEL PENDLETON, ROBERT
and FRANCIS PENDLETON, WILLIAM W. SCOTT, 1 to JAMES S. PENDLETON, 2;
REUBEN PENDLETON, 3...love for REUBEN and $5.00 to ROBERT TINSLEY,
6 December 1827--paid by JAMES PENDLETON, SR.; two slaves for
benefit of REUBEN and to secure ROBERT TINSLEY on Deed of Trust.
Witnesses: C. DABNEY, L. P. THOMPSON, HILL CARTER.

267. 25 August 1826. JONATHAN N. ROSE and JONATHAN THOMPSON, JR.,
partners in ROSE and THOMPSON, Amherst County, to SAMUEL SIMMONS,
Amherst County ROSE MILLS...to JONATHAN THOMPSON, JR., 27 September
1826--on Piney; 41 acres; reserving flat near spring of MARY ROSE
and WILLIAM M. WALLER on south side Mill pond; to secure SAMUEL
SIMMONS a path to spring; also 98 acres bought by JONATHAN THOMPSON,
JR. from ANDERSON H. MOSS, guardian of WILLIAM MOSS, infant heir of
WILLIAM MOSS, deceased, Amherst County; ANDERSON MOSS did not complete
title and could not until WILLIAM was 21. JONATHAN THOMPSON, JR.
paid only $238 and made bond for $212 at maturity of WILLIAM ANDERSON
MOSS made bond to protect JONATHAN THOMPSON, JR. SAMUEL SIMMONS takes
deed with no recourse; assessed by DAVID S. GARLAND; HILL CARTER
and JONATHAN P. COBBS. SAMUEL SIMMONS sells to ROSE and THOMPSON
541 acres on Buffaloe Ridge and bought by him from RICHARD HARRISON
and about a two acre lot on Buffaloe Ridge and bought by him from
RICHARD HARRISON and about a two acre lot at ACH on which stands
tavern house for $3000. ROSE MILL price deducted at $1000. Several
liens on mill. Witnesses: JONATHAN W. DEAN, JESSE FORTUNE,
ELIZABETH T. LAWLER. DAVID S. GARLAND and HILL CARTER, Justices of
the Peace.

316

270.   26 August 1826.   JAMES WOLFE to brother, SAMUEL WOLFE...$1.00
       paid by HUDSON M. GARLAND; for benefit of MARIA A. WOLFE,
wife of SAMUEL; furniture; bought this day of SAMUEL WOLFE--initial
of M used here for $350; have assigned him my claim upon my father's
estate. Will go to children of MARIA at her death. Witnesses:
STERLING CLAIBORNE, H. J. ROSE, WILLIAM G. CLAIBORNE.

271.   21 August 1826.   JACOB SCOTT, 1; RICHARD CRAWFORD, 2; ROBERT
       TINSLEY, 3...to secure debt due from JONATHAN H. PARISH and
self to JAMES S. PENDLETON and Company, assignees of WILLIAM C.
CHRISTIAN for benefit of ROBERT TINSLEY on Amherst County court
judgement. $1.00 133 1/3 acres where JACOB SCOTT lives; crops on
land rented from HIGGINBOTHAM estate; stock.

272.   12 September 1826. (very poor script here) WILLIAM H. WINGFIELD
       to MEREWETHER LEWIS...debt to estate of WILLIAM PATTERSON, late
merchant at Bent Creek; MILLER and ROBERTS, Lynchburg; DR. REUBEN D.
PALMER; GEORGE BOOKER; FREELAND and FERGUSON and Company; J. and
J. KYLE, Richmond; J. MC KELOR, Richmond; S. PARKELL, trustee and
Company (sic); WEAVER and SPEAR, Richmond; LEWIS WEBB and Company;
PARKER and WRIGHT. $1.00; interest in estate of deceased father and
in hands of mother in Amherst County--by will and at her death--one
ninth; interest of wife under Deed of Trust from his grandfather,
MACE FREELAND; to WILLIAM J. FREELAND et al. and recorded in
Buckingham. On page 273 is long list of open accounts of HAIL J.
FREELAND, etc.

274.   13 September 1826.   BARNETT EDWARDS, Greenbrier County, to
       GUSTAVUS A. EDWARDS, Amherst County...power of attorney to
recover from W___ (illegible) ROBINSON, administrator of ROBERT
ROBINSON from 23 August 1819; amount due legatees of ROBERT
ROBINSON. Witnesses: N. DAVIES, E. WATSON.

274.   15 May 1826.   HENRY L. DAVIES (spelled DAVIS), 1; to RICHARD
       CRAWFORD, 2; BEVERLY and SAMUEL R. DAVIES, 3...$1.00--to
BEVERLY DAVIES, administrator: A. B. DAVIES, 15 June 1838--slaves.
Witnesses: A. B. DAVIES, N. DAVIES, ROBERT L. COLEMAN.

275.   8 July 1826.   ABRAHAM MARTIN and wife, FRANCES, Amherst County,
       to EATON CARPENTER, Amherst County...to E. P. TUCKER, executor
of EATON CARPENTER, 3 October 1848--$150 115 acres north Thrasher
Creek. Lines: grantee, ZACH TALIAFERRO. BENJAMIN TALIAFERRO and
CHARLES P. TALIAFERRO, Justices of the Peace.

277.   25 January 1826.   ROWLAND SANDIDGE, Amherst County, to CAROLINE
       SANDIDGE, Amherst County...$200 53 acres both sides Swamping
Camp Creek. Patent to ROWLAND SANDIDGE, 6 January 1808. Lines:
JONATHAN WARE, HORSLEY, CHRISTIAN.

277.   17 April 1819.   STITH MEAD and wife, PRUDENCE, Amherst County, 1;
       WILLIAM I. ISBELL, Amherst County, 2; THOMAS WIATT and CHISWELL
DABNEY, Amherst County, 3...to CHISWELL DABNEY, 22 March 1827--$1.00
three tracts on Lynch road. Lines: shop corner to MEAD and bought
from SAMUEL STEEL and LANDON C. RIVES; CREASY--7 3/4 acres. 3 3/4 acres
bought by WILLIAM I. ISBELL from JONATHAN LYNCH, 4 April 1817. Half
acre to WILLIAM I. ISBELL from SAMUEL STEEL, 2 March 1818. All
conveyed to STITH MEAD by CHRISTOPHER ISBELL and wife, ELIZABETH,
and WILLIAM I. ISBELL and wife, LUCY, 5 February 1819. Witnesses:
WILLIAM H. CLARK, J. LYNCH, THOMAS WIATT.

279.   2 May 1824.   VAN TROMP CRAWFORD to ELIJAH FLETVHER...$700
       interest in life estate of mother, SOPHIA CRAWFORD--Tye River
tract; also tract where she lives--dower in estate of WILLIAM S.
CRAWFORD. 800 acres and 379 acres. Witnesses: DAVID R. EDLEY,
TIM FLETCHER, SAMUEL R. DAVIES.

280. 16 September 1826. JONATHAN H. COLEMAN and wife, TABITHA,
Amherst County, to DAVID S. GARLAND, Amherst County...to DAVID
S. GARLAND, September, 1833--$1500 335 acres both sides south fork
Buffaloe; made up of five smaller tracts. Lines: BENJAMIN SANDIDGE,
HUGH CAMPBELL, JACK CARTER, ROBERT CAWTHORNE, branch, JAMES HIGGIN-
BOTHAM. BENJAMIN and CHARLES P. TALIAFERRO, Justices of the Peace.

282. 25 September 1826. ALEXANDER MUNDY and JAMES W. SMITH to
BENJAMIN SANDIDGE...LINDSEY SANDIDGE and wife, CLARA, executor
Deed of Trust, 2 August 1825. Advertised at Buffaloe Springs and
Lynchburg; sold 7 March 1826, at $1803.50. 224 acres. Bought by
LINDSEY SANDIDGE and JACK CARTER from RICHARD MILLNER on 16 November
1818; slaves; furniture; tools; stock.

284. 22 September 1826. JAMES SEAY, Nelson County, to PEYTON
KEITH, Amherst County...to PEYTON KEITH, 15 October 1826--
$300 137 in Nelson and Amherst County. Lines: JOSEPH SEAY,
HIGGINBOTHAM, mouth of the creek. WATTS. Witnesses: JOSEPH,
CALVIN and NELSON SEAY and JAMES L. WATTS.

285. 25 September 1826. BENJAMIN SANDIDGE, Amherst County, to
GEORGE W. HIGGINBOTHAM, Amherst County...love of BENJAMIN for
son, LINDSEY SANDIDGE and wife, CLARA, and children. $1.00; slaves;
tools; furniture.

286. 23 September 1826. JONATHAN FULCHER and wife, ELIZABETH,
Amherst County, to DABNEY HILL, Amherst County...to DABNEY
HILL, 4 June 1827--$200 tract allotted JONATHAN FULCHER from estate
of father, JONATHAN FULCHER--lot 5 36 acres. Little Piney. Lines:
grantee, CRAWFORD.

287. 25 September 1826. MOSES HIGGINBOTHAM, Tazewell County, to
son, AARON HIGGINBOTHAM, same County...power of attorney.
THOMAS and WILLIAM GILLESPIE, Justices of the Peace. Note: I have
corresponded with GILLESPIES in this area and have seen published
data. They stemmed from Pennsylvania and seem to have no connection
with the Amherst family.

288. 3 October 1826. MOSES HIGGINBOTHAM, by attorney, AARON
HIGGINBOTHAM, Tazewell County, to JOSEPH HIGGINBOTHAM, Amherst
County...$150 tract of CHARLES HIGGINBOTHAM, deceased--his interest
of one-sixth; Buffaloe. Lines: DAVID S. GARLAND, JACOB SCOTT.
About 200 acres.

289. 8 September 1826. JAMES LEE, Amherst County, to JOSEPH
PETTYJOHN, Amherst County...to JOSEPH PETTYJOHN, 23 November
1826--$1297.50 121½. Lines: WIATT PETTYJOHN, grantor, ARCHELAUS
REYNOLDS, Harris Creek, grantee. Witnesses: ROBERT TINSLEY.

290. 29 August 1826. THOMAS P. JORDAN and ANDERSON WARE, to
FREDERICK PAINTER, SR...$1000 166 acres both sides south border
of middle fork of Pedlar. From grantee to grantors by deed. Signed
by wives: LEVISA JORDAN and CYNTHIA A. H. WARE. Witnesses:
J. L. WINGFIELD, JONATHAN CLARKSON, GEORGE HULEF (?), ISAAC RUCKER,
SR. BENJAMIN and CHARLES P. TALIAFERRO, Justices of the Peace.

291. 16 October 1826. DAVID S. GARLAND to MURRAY LATHAND and
Company, Liverpool, England to demand of JAMES and Sons,
Liverpool...later JAMES BROWN and Sons--tobacco consigned to them.

291. 16 October 1826. SAMUEL CAMPBELL, Amherst County, to SAMUEL W.
CHRISTIAN, Amherst County...to trustee, 19 October 1826--to
secure D. and D. HIGGINBOTHAM and Company. Amherst County suit
decree 30 April 1823; $1.00 14 acres. Lines: HILL CARTER, GEORGE
CAMPBELL, deceased, one third of 64 acres of GEORGE CAMPBELL's heirs;
Piney. Witnesses: HILL CARTER and occupied by ELIZABETH CAMPBELL;
also all interest as heir of GEORGE CAMPBELL--one-ninth. Stock;
furniture.

292. 6 October 1826. ISAAC SCOTT, 1; SAMUEL W. CHRISTIAN, 2; D. and
      D. HIGGINBOTHAM and Company, 3...$1.00 165 acres Indian Creek.
Lines: JONATHAN SMITH, DAVID S. GARLAND, JONATHAN MOUNTCASTLE,
ROBERT TINSLEY, stock, crops, etc. Witnesses: ROBERT TINSLEY,
A. MUNDY, B. DAVIES.

294. 1 April 1826. PETER BURROUGHS and wife, ELIZABETH P., Amherst
      County, to WILEY CAMPBELL, Amherst County...$1044.87 321½ acres
Rocky Run. Lines: JACOB PEARCE, ABSALOM HOWL, CHARLES WILSON,
CATLETT CAMPBELL, grantee, JAMES DILLARD and HENRY H. WATTS,
Justices of the Peace.

295. 8 September 1826. WILLIAM TOMLINSON, Amherst County, to
      R. L. ELLIS, Amherst County...$1.00; to R. L. ELLIS, 23 January
1835--to secure ELLIS; all present crops.

296. 31 October 1826. JAMES CRAWFORD, Amherst County, 1; ISAAC
      RUCKER, Amherst County, 2; JONATHAN MC COWN, Rockbridge, 3...
$1.00; stock. Witnesses: S. R. DAVIES, E. WATSON, BENJAMIN BROWN,
JR.

297. 14 November 1826. BENJAMIN SALE, Amherst County, to RICHARD L.
      ELLIS, Amherst County...$10; to RICHARD L. ELLIS, 23 January
1835; to secure RICHARD L. ELLIS; crops. Witnesses: J. W. YOUNG,
JAMES GILLIAM.

298. 11 September 1826. WILLIAM HASLEP and wife, SUSANNAH, Amherst
      County, to ISAAC RUCKER, 2; JONATHAN H. CLEMENTS, Amherst
County, 3...to JONATHAN H. CLEMENTS, 26 September 1827--$1.00 two
tracts on headwaters Brown Mountain Creek. 99 acres where WILLIAM
HASLEP lives and 46 acres adjacent; cattle; furniture; crops.
Witnesses: AMBROSE RUCKER, SAMUEL LOWMAN, BARTLETT CLEMENTS,
JONATHAN CLARKSON.

300. 1 November 1826. JOSEPH B. MAYS, Amherst County, to WILLIAM M.
      WALLER, 2...to WILLIAM M. WALLER, 23 March 1832--$20 two acres;
Stonehouse Creek and extreme southwest corner of tract. Lines:
BEVERLY WILLIAMSON, deceased. Witnesses: GARLAND MAYS, GEORGE W.
HIGGINBOTHAM.

301. 14 November 1826. WILLIAM J. THURMOND, Amherst County, 1;
      JONATHAN W. YOUNG, Amherst County, 2; GEORGE BURKS, Amherst
County, 3...10 June last GEORGE BURKS became bondsman for WILLIAM J.
THURMOND to JONATHAN P. BURKS--to JONATHAN W. YOUNG, 19 February
1827--$1.00 slave, FANNY. Witnesses: CHARLES L. BARRET, MOORE F.
CARTER, WIATT DUNCAN.

302. 31 October 1826. JONATHAN BURKS, Amherst County, 1; ISAAC
      RUCKER, SR., Amherst County, 2; THOMAS P. JOURDAN, Amherst
County, 3...THOMAS P. JOURDAN on bond to RICHARD L. ELLIS for
delivery of property to CHARLES MUNDY or lawful deputies at ACH,
20 November next; $1.00; slaves; stock, etc.

304. 6 October 1826. ROBERT H. MC CULLOCH, Amherst County, to
      MARTIN PARKS, Amherst County...$1055 138 3/4 acres Pedlar.
Lines: MARY MONTGOMERY, DAVID BURKS. Tract assigned by commissioners
to ROBERT H. MC CULLOCH in division of date of mother, ELIZABETH
MC CULLOCH, to children. Witnesses: WILLIAM H. MC CULLOCH.

305. 21 November 1826. ELIAS WILLS and wife, MARY G., Amherst
      County, 1; CHISWELL DABNEY, Amherst County, 2; ARCHLAUS
REYNOLDS, Amherst County, 3...ARCHLAUS REYNOLDS on bond for ELIAS
WILLS on injunction bond to JONATHAN TIMBERLAKE, JR.; Superior
Court, Lynchburg Chancery, 15 November 1826; $5.00 also Amherst County
court: WILLS versus TIMBERLAKE; 652 acres where ELIAS WILLS lives
and in trust to DAVID BRADFUTE to secure Farmer's Bank of Virginia
on debts, 27 December 1822.

307.　17 April 1826.　JESSE BECK and wife, ANNA, Amherst County, to
　　　JONATHAN M. WILLIAMS, Amherst County...to JONATHAN M. WILLIAMS,
2 September 1831; $360 one third of 180½ acres.　Lines: LINEAS
BOWLING, CHRISTOPHER ISBELL, PHILLIP JOHNSON, deceased.　Bought by
WILLIAM ROBINSON and JESSE BECK from THOMAS WIAAT and RICHARD TYREE,
23 May 1823.　SMITHSON DAVIS and DANIEL BROWN, Lynchburg Justices of
the Peace as to JESSE BECK and AMBROSE RUCKER and DABENY WARE as to
his wife.

309.　18 November 1826.　CORNELIUS POWELL to DANIEL HIGGINBOTHAM...
　　　JAMES WILMORE on 24 April 1823, made Deed of Trust to CORNELIUS
POWELL for benefit of D. and D. HIGGINBOTHAM and Company; JAMES
POWELL; LINDSEY COLEMAN.　Sold, 3 November 1826, on premises and
D. HIGGINBOTHAM by agent, SAMUEL W. CHRISTIAN, bought for $171.00;
$1.00 140 acres.　Lines: JAMES POWELL, HARDWICK heirs, JAMES COLEMA.
Witnesses: JAMES S. PENDLETON, LUCAS P. THOMPSON, JONATHAN PENN.

311.　4 November 1826.　JOSEPH B. MAYS and wife, SALLY, Amherst
　　　County, to JAMES FULCHER, Amherst County...$700 235½ acres
both sides south fork Stonehouse Creek.　Lines: THOMAS WILLIAMSON,
GEORGE W. HIGGINBOTHAM, WILLIAM M. WALLER, BEVERLY WILLIAMSON,
deceased.　WILLIAM M. WALLER and HILL CARTER, Justices of the Peace.

313.　3 November 1826.　BENJAMIN A. PHILLIPS, Lynchburg, 1; SAMUEL
　　　and MORRIS H. GARLAND, 2; ALEXANDER TOMPKINS and Company, 3...
to secure A. BRIDGLAND and JONATHAN IRVINE, bondsman--to trustees,
4 May 1827; $1.00 four lots in Madison of half acre each; I improved
and others vacent bought from trustees of town.　AUGUSTINE LEFTWICH
and JONATHAN HANCOCK, Lynchburg Justices of the Peace.

315.　25 November 1826.　WILLIS HIGGINBOTHAM, BARTLETT K. (?)
　　　HIGGINBOTHAM, LINDSEY HIGGINBOTHAM, JACKSON HIGGINBOTHAM,
JONATHAN CARR and wife, FRANCES, JOSEPH CAMPBELL and wife, PERMELIA,
by WILLIS HIGGINBOTHAM, attorney-in-fact, to JOSEPH HIGGINBOTHAM...
$150 one-sixth of tract on both sides Rutledge--200 acres.

316.　27 November 1826.　JONATHAN N. ROSE and wife, MARY, JONATHAN
　　　THOMPSON, JR. and wife, CAROLINE E., Amherst County, to
SAMUEL SIMMONS, Amherst County...to SAMUEL SIMMONS, 16 January 1839;
$1.00 use of spring near the mill lately owned by grantors; also
path to spring; to begin at house occupied by ROSE; within forty
yards above same.　HILL CARTER and WILLIAM M. WALLER, Justices of
the Peace.

317.　27 November 1826.　SAMUEL SIMMONS and wife, SYNTHIA, Amherst
　　　County, to JONATHAN N. ROSE and JONATHAN THOMPSON, JR.,
Amherst County...to secure them on debt--to JONATHAN THOMPSON, JR.
25 July 1827--$1.00 and reference to deed of equal date from them
to SAMUEL SIMMONS; also tract adjacent 74 acres and contract between
them, 25 August 1826.　HILL CARTER and JONATHAN COLEMAN, Justices
of the Peace.

320.　Same date as above:　ROSE and THOMPSON and wifes as above to
　　　SAMUEL SIMMONS, Amherst County...to SAMUEL SIMMONS by mail,
4 May 1829--$11330 about 41 acres Rose Mills on Piney; plat annexed
(not herein); subject to reservations of 25 August 1826; and reference
to Deed of 3 December 1817--three acres conveyed to grantors by
THOMAS ALDRIDGE.　HILL CARTER and WILLIAM M. WALLER, Justices of
the Peace.

322.　27 November 1826.　SAMUEL SIMMONS and wife, CYNTHIA, Amherst
　　　County, to ROSE and THOMPSON as above...to JONATHAN THOMPSON,
JR., 20 August 1828; $3000 531 acres on Buffaloe plat annexed--not
herein--also lot at ACH of about two acres; reference to agreement
of 25 August 1826.　HILL CARTER and JONATHAN COLEMAN, Justices of
the Peace.

323.   11 December 1826. JOSEPH MC CRAY and wife, SOPHIA, Amherst
       County, to AMBROSE RUCKER and MATTHEW DAVIDSON, M.D. of
Rockbridge...to secure creditors--to AMBROSE RUCKER, 21 May 1827--
DAVID TINSLEY, JESSE RICHESON, administrator of ANTHONY RUCKER,
WILLIAM MORGAN and Company; assignees of ELIAS WILLS, SAMUEL GARLAND,
assignee of AMBROSE R. BURFORD, ELIZABETH DAVIDSON--during life;
JANE MC CRAY (now MC GUFFEN), ROSE and PATTERSON, JONATHAN THOMPSON,
LINDSEY COELAN, JONATHAN MILLER and DAVID R. EDLEY, trustees of
AMBROSE RUCKER, JONATHAN MYERS, NELSON C. DAWSON, SR., JAMES MILLER,
Rockbridge, WILLIAM BAILEY, Lynchburg, WILLIAM MC DANIEL, administrator
of BENJAMIN MILES, JAMES MC DANIEL, -- BOWEN, Lynchburg, LORENZO D.
HENDERSON--$5.00; interest in tract held by MARY BURFORD, widow of
JAMES BURFORD, as dower--160 or 170 acres--one-tenth. Thomas or
Miller Creek. Lines: JAMES BENNETT, also one-seventh of MARY's
dower; slaves; cattle; tools.

326.   12 December 1826. BENJAMIN HIGGINBOTHAM to CHARLES MUNDY,
       Sheriff of Amherst County...BENJAMIN HIGGINBOTHAM in prison in
suit of HUDSON M. GARLAND for JONATHAN L. DAVENPORT; takes insolvent
oath; interest in estate of late brother, JOSEPH HIGGINBOTHAM
except that sold to DAVID S. GARLAND and JAMES POWELL.

327.   29 March 1824. NELSON CRAWFORD, acting executor of CALEB
       RALLS, Amherst County, to TANDY TULEY, Amherst County...under
will to sell--to J. B. ROBERTSON, JR., for T. BERRY, 14 September
1893--sold 25 February in year aforesaid at late mansion house--300
acres Lovelady tract at 36 cents per acre. Lines: CHARLES P.
TALIAFERRO. Witnesses: WILKINS WATSON, RICHARD CRAWFORD, HUGH NELSON
CRAWFORD, BENNET A. CRAWFORD. Recorded 18 December 1826.

328.   25 September 1826. JAMES BENAGH to WILLIAM L. BURKS...
       SAMUEL BURKS and wife, MARY, 28 May 1826, executor Deed of
Trust to JAMES BENAGH; all interest of SAMUEL BURKS in estate of
father, SAMUEL BURKS, deceased, at mother's death. Sold this day
at ACH for $495--one-ninth of estate--to take at mother's death.
ALBON MC DANIEL and AUGUSTINE LEFTWICH, Lynchburg Justices of the
Peace.

330.   20 December 1826. JOYCE CLEMENTS, Washington County, Kentucky,
       to ALLISON MORRIS, Amherst County...$100 100 acres headwaters
of Harris Creek. Lines: grantee, NELSON CRAWFORD and WILLIAM
JOPLING, Justices of the Peace. JOYCE appeared in Amherst County.
This is interesting to me since I lived in Washington County for
eight years. The CLEMENTS family there is largely Roman Catholic
and stems from the Maryland migration before 1800. Some of them are
now in Union county and other parts of Kentucky. EARL CLEMENTS,
one time U.S. Senator and Governor of Kentucky, is from Union and
descends from the Washington County clan, but is not a member of the
Roman Catholic faith.

331.   1 November 1826. ANDERSON TINSLEY, Giles County, Tennessee,
       to WILLIAM STEEL, Giles County, Tennessee...power of attorney
to recover from ALEXANDER TINSLEY, Amherst County, $250 due.
Witnesses: CHARLES G. WILCOX. E WARD D. JONES and JONATHAN BRAMLETT,
Justices of the Peace in Tennessee. GERMAN LESTER, Clerk of Pleas
and Quarterly Sessions.

333.   20 February 1824. JONATHAN M. WILLS, 1; GARRET M. QUARLES, 2;
       PATSY WILLS, wife of MATTHEW WILLS and her children: JONATHAN D.,
WILLS, PATSY NORVELL, SUSAN and MARY WILLS...$1000 slaves; furniture;
cattle; tools; apart from her husband. JONATHAN TIMBERLAKE,
Fluvanna Clerk.

335.   6 January 1827. WILLIAM B. NAPIER, Richmond, to AJAX WALKER,
       Amherst County...$900 254½ acres bought by WILLIAM B. NAPIER
from WILLIAM LONG and wife, BETSY, 21 February 1824.

336. 6 January 1827. Delivered to MRS. NANCY GARLAND on lean--
   furniture, stock...to JAMES P. GARLAND, 26 April 1833; to be
returned undamaged. Signed by JAMES P. GARLAND. Memo: bought of
ROBERT GARLAND under Deed of Trust to W. H. LOVING and D. PERROW.

337. 16 January 1827. CHALRES MUNDY and wife, MARY, Amherst County,
   to their son, JESSE MUNDY, Amherst County...power of attorney
to recover Kentucky lands and to sell or rent. To JESSE MUNDY,
15 January 1827.

338. 13 November 1826. ISAAC RUCKER, JR., Amherst County, to
   JONATHAN SHEPHERD, Amherst County...to trustee, 27 October
1827--debt to DAVID S. GARLAND for dealings in his store; $1.00
stock; furniture; tobacco. Interest in estates of ROBERT COLHERN (?),
and WILLIAM BROWN. Witnesses: S. M. GARLAND, WILLIAM MC CAUL,
CHARLES L. BARRET and EDMOND PENN, Justices of the Peace.

339. 5 January 1827. WILLIAM J. THURMOND, Amherst County, to
   JONATHAN W. YOUNG, Amherst County, 2; WILLIAM HAYNES, Amherst
County, 3...to JONATHAN W. YOUNG, 19 February 1827--WILLIAM HAYNES
on bond to JONATHAN FULCHER and Bank of Virginia, Lynchburg; $1.00
slaves. Witnesses: CHARLES L. BARRET, WILLIAM MITCHELL, MOORE F.
CARTER.

341. 3 June 1824. MAYO DAVIES and wife, LUCINDA; HENRY L. DAVIES
   and wife, ANN; ADDISON TALIAFERRO and wife, HENRY ANN; and
SAMUEL R. DAVIES, Amherst County, to BEVERLY DAVIES, Amherst County...
grantors as heirs of NICHOLAS DAVIES, Amherst County--together with
FRANCIS K., ARTHUR B., JONATHAN, BEVERLY, NICHOLAS, EDITHA, and
WHITING DAVIES--ELIZABETH DAVIES, widow, had dower of 600+ acres.
Pedlar River. Lines: CALEB WATTS. ELIZABETH has died and descended
to heirs. BEVERLY DAVIES has bought five shares; one-eleventh of each
share at $2500. WILLIAM JOPLING and BENJAMIN TALIAFERRO, Justices
of the Peace.

345. 15 January 1827. GEORGE W. HIGGINBOTHAM and wife, JOANNA C.,
   Amherst County, to CHARLES TUCKER, Amherst County...to CHARLES
TUCKER, 26 January 1827--sic--dower relinquished S:8--$541.93 196 3/4
acres Coteral Creek and south side Piney Mountain. Lines: grantee,
THOMAS WOODROOF, deceased, grantor, JAMES TUCKER, WILLIAM M. WALLER.
Part of tract of AARON HIGGINBOTHAM's heirs.

347. 5 January 1827. RUSSEL DAWSON and wife, --, Bedford County, 1;
   SAMUEL and M. H. GARLAND, Lynchburg, 2; ARCHIBALD ROBERTSON
and Company, Lynchburg, 3...judgement in Bedford; $1.00; interest in
estate of SAMUEL BURKS, deceased, Amherst County, stock, furniture.
JONATHAN HANCOCK and AUGUSTINE LEFTWICH, Lynchburg Justices of the
Peace as to RUSSEL DAWSON; wife is not named.

349. 15 January 1826. SAMUEL R. DAVIES to ELIJAH FLETCHER...to
   ELIJAH FLETCHER, 4 April 1834--Deed of Trust; August, 1824, to
secure PETER F. CHRISTIAN--to DANIEL F. CHRISTIAN and S. R. DAVIES;
sold 2 October 1826; blank sum; 120 acres and 45 acres. Harris
Creek. This is not clear as to exact person making Deed of Trust,
but should be PETER F. making it, I believe; have not checked.

350. 23 November 1826. JAMES DILLARD and HENRY H. WATTS as to
   RACHEL TURNER, wife of HENRY TURNER...21 November 1814, to --.

350. 20 October 1825. GEORGE CAMPBELL and wife, LUCY, Amherst
   County, to JONATHAN CAMPBELL, Amherst County...$50.00 150 acres
north side Little Piney. Lines: CAMPBELL, JONATHAN CAMPBELL.
Witnesses: WILLIAM CASH, DABNEY HILL, BENJAMIN W. CAMPBELL.

352. 1 June 1826. JONATHAN HUTCHERSON and wife, LUCINDA, Amherst
County, to CHARLES W. TINSLEY, Amherst County...to ST. GEORGE
AMBLER, present owner, 7 June 1845--$50.00; interest in TINSLEY's
Mill as legatees of JOSHUA TINSLEY--20 acres; stock.

353. 19 January 1827. WALTER WILLIAMS, Lynchburg, 1; RICHARD L.
ELLIS and WILLIAM GATEWOOD, Amherst County, 2; THOMAS N. EUBANK,
Amherst County, 3...debts to THOMAS N. EUBANK and SAMUEL B. MITCHELL
on decree of Superior Court, Lynchburg; $1.00; tract bought by
WALTER WILLIAMS from WILLIAM GATEWOOD and BENJAMIN NOEL--150 acres;
all of his Amherst County lands. Lines: LARKIN BYAS, ROWLAND
GILLESPIE. DANIEL BROWN and ALBON MC DANIEL, Lynchburg, Justices
of the Peace.

355. 20 December 1826. JESSE L. PERRY, Campbell County, to
THOMAS P. DILLARD, Amherst County...to GEORGE W. DILLARD,
20 April 1827--$1.00 for benefit of niece, SOPHIA F. DILLARD, wife
of THOMAS P. DILLARD--niece--late PERRY; slave; to her children at
her death. Same Justices of the Peace as above.

357. 13 January 1827. DABNEY T. PHILLIPS, trustee for NANCY PHILLIPS
and children, Amherst County, 1; SAMUEL and MAURICE H. GARLAND,
Lynchburg, 2; WILLIAM PENDLETON, JAMES LEE, WIATT PETTYJOHN, WILLIAM W.
SCOTT, commissioners of Amherst County to sell lands of GEORGE
POWELL, deceased, Amherst County; decree of PADGETT versus POWELL
heirs--PADGETT's wife was party, but not named--Amherst County suit.
DABNEY T. PHILLIPS owes WILLIAM PENDLETON, JAMES LEE, WIATT PETTYJOHN,
and WILLIAM SCOTT in partial payment of tract and is required to
secure balance; $1.00; 150 acres. Lines: grantor, Trent's ferry
tract, PROSSER POWELL, BENJAMIN OGDEN, R. G. HADEN (formerly CAMM),
DAVID S. GARLAND (formerly REUBEN PENDLETON), AUGUSTINE LEFTWICH
and ALBON MC DANIEL, Lynchburg Justices of the Peace. To PROSSER
POWELL for G. POWELL's children, 22 January 1829.

359. 29 February 1827. JOSHUA BARBER, Amherst County, 1; S. R.
DAVIES, Amherst County, 2; WILINS WATSON, Amherst County, 3...
$1.00 cow, furniture, crops.

359. 31 January 1827. ELISHA RIDER, Amherst County, to WALTER B.
BOSWELL, Amherst County, 2; WILLIAM C. JOHNSON, Warren County,
Kentucky, 3...to WALTER B. BOSWELL, 6 April 1829; debt to WILLIAM C.
JOHNSON for money received of the executor of his father, WILLIAM
JOHNSON, deceased; $1.00; cattle, furniture.

361. 17 January 1827. ELISHA RIDER, Amherst County, 1; WALTER B.
BOWSWLL, 2; HENRY L. DAVIES, 3 and EZEKIEL A. EAST, 3...debt
to HENRY L. DAVIES and EZEKIEL A. EAST; $1.00; packaging machine;
wool carding machine.

362. 29 January 1827. WILLIAM WAUGH, 1; STERLING CLAIBORNE, 3;
creditors, 3...$1.00; stock of goods in my store at New Glasgow;
debt to mother, PAMELIA WAUGH, MC KEE, ROBINSON and Company, Lynchburg, Amherst County and Nelson creditors: JONATHAN PATTEN, Lynchburg; WILLIAM ELLIOTT, Alabama; JAMES PEARSON, Alabama; CHARLES L.
BARRET; CLAIBORNE is trustee for mother. Witnesses: HENRY J. ROSE,
GEORGE W. DILLARD, J. S. PENDLETON.

364. 20 September 1826. CHARLES L. CHRISTIAN and wife, SUSANNA,
Amherst County, to C. W. GOOCH, Richmond...$100 71 acres and
where CHARLES L. CHRISTIAN lives and bought by WALTER L. CHRISTIAN
from BENJAMIN WAREEN; conveyed by WALTER L. CHRISTIAN to CHARLES L.
CHRISTIAN, 31 July 1809 and 13 July 1824. Lines: DANIEL CHEATWOOD,
deceased; WILLIAM DILLARD, deceased; C. W. GOOCH; REUBEN PADGETT,
deceased; includes nine acres from WILLIAM DILLARD to BENJAMIN
WARREN, 20 January 1806. JAMES DILLARD and HENRY H. WATTS, Justices
of the Peace.

365.　28 October 1825.　THOMAS HASKINS, Prince Edward County, to
　　　WILLIAM S. CRAWFORD, Amherst County...to WILLIAM S. CRAWFORD,
30 April 1828--$1.00 for benefit of ANN F. D., SARAH, JANE, CATHERINE
PENN, infants of EDMOND and JANE PENN--my interest in estate of
GABRIEL PENN by will--at widow's death.　THOMAS HASKINS states that
he married GABRIEL PENN's daughter, PAMILLIA.　Witnesses:　EDMOND
PENN, THOMAS CREWS, A. O. NASH.

366.　15 September 1826.　WILLIAM L. SAUNDERS and wife, MARY, to
　　　RICHARD G. HADEN, all of Campbell County...$1634 226 acres
John's Creek; allotted to MARY, formerly CAMM, from estate of deceased
husband, JONATHAN CAMM, Amherst County.　Lines:　SMITHSON H. DAVIS
and ALBON MC DANIEL, Lynchburg Justices of the Peace.

367.　23 January 1824.　THOMAS ALDRIDGE and THOMAS CREWS, Amherst
　　　County, to JONATHAN METCALFE, Fredericksburg and WILLIAM S.
CRAWFORD, Amherst County...to WILLIAM S. CRAWFORD, 30 April 1828;
and EDMOND PENN and wife, Amherst County, 3.　17 January 1815, Deed
of Trust EDMOND PENN to DAVID S. GARLAND and THOMAS CREWS--all of
PENN's interest by marriage to JANE, formerly JOHNSOTON--house and
lot in Fredericksburg; tracts in Greenbrier of WILLIAM DRUMMOND,
deceased; furniture; interest in estate of father, GABRIEL PENN,
at death of SARAH PENN, widow.　Sold, 15 November 1823, at tavern
door of PEACHY FRANKLIN, New Glasgow, and bought by ALDRIDGE for
$100; $10 for furniture; small amounts for other items.　Deed made
for separate use of JANE for Fredericksburg tract; THOMAS ALDRIDGE
is entitled to debts due his Company; JONATHAN and GEORGE MYERS;
JONATHAN PENN; JONATHAN ROBERTSON; JONATHAN P. COBBS.　$1.00 and
JANE relinquished dower in 1100 acres in Greenbrier (more above);
house and lot in Fredericksburg.　Deed of Trust for benefit of JANE.
CHARLES L. BARRET and JONATHAN COLEMAN, Justices of the Peace.

371.　16 September 1826.　STERLING CLAIBORNE and wife, JANE M.;
　　　WILLIAM S. and CHARLES B. CLAIBORNE to THOMAS LANDRUM...$260
13 acres Naked Creek.　Lines:　grantee, JAMES FRANKLIN, deceased;
Lynchburg road.　EDMOND PENN and CHARLES L. BARRET, Justices of
the Peace.

372.　20 January 1827.　SAMUEL H. RAY, Amherst County, 1; JONATHAN W.
　　　YOUNG, Amherst County, 2; BENNETT TINSLEY, Amherst County, 3...
BENNETT TINSLEY on bond to RICHARD L. ELLIS and ELLIS and EUBANK--to
trustee, 23 April 1827--$1.00 interest in estate of deceased father.
Witnesses:　JONATHAN D. WARE, REUBEN S. WARE, HIRAM YOUNG.

373.　27 January 1827.　AMBROSE R. HANSARD, Amherst County, 1;
　　　SAMUEL and MAURICE H. GARLAND, Lynchburg, 2; ROBERT H. GRAY,
MOURNING CHRISTIAN, WILLIAM M. RIVES, 3...to ROBERT H. GRAY,
24 September 1827--$1.00; interest in estate of father, JONATHAN
HANSARD, deceased.　Amherst County--one-ninth; will is in controversy.

374.　13 January 1827.　WILLIAM PENDLETON, JAMES LEE, WIATT PETTYJOHN,
　　　WILLIAM W. SCOTT, Commissioners:　LINDSEY B. PADGETT and wife
and widow and infants of late GEORGE PWOELL; DABNEY T. PHILLIPS,
trustee of NANCY PHILLIPS, widow, and children...DABNEY T. PHILLIPS
bid $3.35 per care or $469 for 140 acres for GEORGE POWELL tract.
Lines:　D. T. PHILLIPS, PROSSER POWELL, BENJAMIN OGDEN, R. F. HADEN
(formerly JONATHAN CAMM), DAVID S. GARLAND (formerly REUBEN PENDLETON)--
where GEORGE POWELL lived and died and bought from JAMES WARE.
AUGUSTINE LEFTWICH and ALBON MC DANIEL, Justices of the Peace in
Lynchburg.

375.　13 February 1827.　LEWIS DAWSON, Amherst County, to WILLIAM
　　　PETTYJOHN, Amherst County...$100--to WILLIAM PETTYJOHN, and
returned, 21 January 1833--16 3/4 acres Fawn Creek.　Lines:　road,
both, AMBROSE BURFORD.　NELSON C. DAWSON and JAMES L. LAMKIN,
Justices of the Peace.

376.   24 February 1827. JAMES H. MARTIN and wife, ROBINA L., 1;
       HUDSON M. GARLAND, 2; WILLIAM MARTIN, Amherst County, 3...
ROBINA L. at marriage became entitled to share of her father's
estate, by will--EDWARD WINGFIELD, Albemarle, was her father and
to ROBINA at death of mother, NANCY WINGFIELD; $1.00 all interest
in said estate. Witnesses: EDMOND W. HILL, MOSES H. MARTIN,
JONATHAN LAWHORN. BENJAMIN and CHARLES P. TALIAFERRO, Justices
of the Peace.

377.   15 March 1827. ALEXANDER P. CRAWFORD to ELIJAH FLETCHER...
       to ELIJAH FLETCHER, 15 March 1827--$500 all interest as heir
of WILLIAM S. CRAWFORD, Amherst County; widow, SOPHIA's interest.

378.   17 March 1827. ALEXANDER P. CRAWFORD and wife, ANN, to
       BENJAMIN CAMDEN...to W. S. CRAWFORD, 29 March 1827--$5250
225 acres Indian Creek; allotted to Amherst County on division of
father's estate. Lines: WILLIAM MOON, WILLIAM S. CRAWFORD, WILLIAM M.
WALLER. CHARLES P. TALIAFERRO and RICHARD N. EUBANK, Justices of
the Peace.

379.   21 February 1827. ANDERSON WARE and wife, CYNTHIA, Amherst
       County, to SAMUEL HOGG, Amherst County...$290 115 acres.
Lines: RICHARD L. ELLIS, SAMUEL NIECLY. Witnesses: WILLIAM STATON,
CHARLES CREASY THOMAS, SAMUEL GARLAND.

380.   30 November 1826. WILLIAM J. THURMOND, 1; WILLIAM TURNER,
       THOMAS TUCKER, JONATHAN J. FULCHER, 2; WILLIAM TUCKER and
JONATHAN PRYOR, 3...to WILLIAM TUCKER and JONATHAN PRYOR. $1.00
one-seventh interest in father's estate; slaves; debt to Farmer's
Bank. To JONATHAN PRYOR, 16 August 1830.

381.   19 February 1827. PETER CASHWELL, Amherst County, 1; SAMUEL R.
       DAVIES and TIMOTHY FLETCHER, 2; ELIJAH FLETCHER, 3...to
SAMUEL R. DAVIES, 19 November 1828--$1.00 between four and 500 acres.
Lines: THOMAS HIGGINBOTHAM, WILLIAM BOUREN, ABNER PADGETT, JONATHAN
WARWICK, JONATHAN SIMPSON, slaves. AUGUSTINE LEFTWICH and JONATHAN
HANCOCK, Lynchburg Justices of the Peace.

382.   22 June 1814. PETTIS THACKER and wife, MOLLY, Amherst County,
       to WILLIAM MITCHELL, Lynchburg...9 May 1829, to present owner,
JAMES BRUCE--$397.50 39 3/4 acres Harris Creek. Lines: Mitchell
Mill tract. Part of where PETTIS THACKER lives. Lines: grantor,
JONATHAN WARD, grantee. Witnesses: REUBEN NORVELL, WILLIAM PETTYJOHN,
JONATHAN COX. Final proof, 20 March 1827, by COX.

383.   8 March 1827. HENRY L. LANGHORNE and wife, FRANCES, Campbell
       County, to THOMAS R. TERRY, Amherst County...$6000 551 3/4
acres. Lines: WILLIAM S. MILLER, OWENS, ADAMS, WARWICK, BOWLING,
James River, mouth of branch a little below Lynchburg. Three tracts.
One bought from President and Directors, 9 August 1821; one bought
from EDWARD LYNCH and ANDELM LYNCH, executors of JONATHAN LYNCH,
1 May 1822; one bought from GEORGE B. WOODSON, late Marshall of
Chancery, Lynchburg on -- tt. of GEORGE WHITLOCK. ALBON MC DANIEL
and DANIEL BROWN, Lynchburg Justices of the Peace.

385.   15 February 1827. JONATHAN MOUNTCASTLE and wife, TAMSEY,
       Amherst County, to TITUS W. VIGUS...to TITUS W. VIGUS,
1 September 1828, by SAMUEL W. CHRISTIAN--$900 lot in New Glasgow.
Lines: DAVID S. GARLAND. Bought from JAMES BRADFUTE. (field?)

386.   19 March 1827. JONATHAN J. FULCHER, 1; WILLIAM J. THURMOND, 2;
       SAMUEL D. CHRISTIAN, 3...to HEZEKIAH S. FULCHER, 28 April
1828--furniture, tools, stock; $1.00. Witnesses: PHILIP THURMOND,
ANDREW HANNAH, ROBERT SEBREE.

387. 5 March 1827. WILLIAM J. THURMOND, 1; THOMAS TUCKER and
     WILLIAM TURNER, 2; WILLIAM TUCKER and JONATHAN PRYOR, Amherst
County, 3...to WILLIAM TUCKER and JONATHAN PRYOR; all interest in
200 acres Rockcastle and Duck Creeks in Rockcastle County, Kentucky;
half of undivided moiety; $1.00; Chancery suit in Kentucky: THURMOND
versus BENNETT C. SHACKELFORD heirs.

388. 19 March 1827. JONATHAN SAVAGE, Amherst County, to WILLIAM H.
     GARLAND, Amherst County...$50 stock; furniture.

389. 21 March 1827. WESLEY E. CHRISTIAN and wife, LUCY, Amherst
     County, to ALFRED RICHESON, Amherst County...consideration:
tract adjacent JONATHAN TULEY; 50 acres; tract of HENRY HARTLESS--
100 acres. Lines: HENRY HARTLESS; bought from CLIFTON HARRIS,
11 March 1823.

390. 22 March 1827. PLEASANT LAWHORNE, Amherst County, 1; WILLIAM
     MARTIN, SR., Amherst County, 2; JONATHAN LAWHORN, Amherst
County, 3...$1.00 stock; crops.

391. 20 March 1827. CHARLES C. CARTER to HILL CARTER and RICHARD N.
     EUBANK...to secure JAMES S. PENDLETON and Company and WILLIAM M.
WALLER and Company and other creditors--suit in Superior Court,
Amherst County; JAMES EUBANK, GARLAND, WALTON and PENN, D. and D.
HIGGINBOTHAM and Company, HOLMES and BREWSTER, DR. E. B. GILBERT;
$1.00 title to Walnut Grove estate and in hands of mother, ALPHIA
CARTER; estate of unfortunate brother, OTHER W. CARTER. Certified
in Nelson County, 28 March 1827; SPOTSWOOD GARLAND, Clerk.

393. 19 March 1827. WILLIAM CAMPBELL, son of GEORGE, Amherst
     County, 1; SAMUEL M. CHRISTIAN, Amherst County, 2; D. and D.
HIGGINBOTHAM and Company, Amherst County, 3...$1.00 mare; interest
in estate of deceased father and held by my mother, ELIZABETH;
bond due from COLONEL CHARLES CARTER to my father--Superior Court
of Amherst County; I hold two shares, stock, furniture, tools.

394. 14 February 1827. JOSHUA MAYS and wife, SALLY, Rockbridge,
     to JONATHAN TERRY, Amherst County...$1800 157½ acres. Lines:
JONATHAN ELLIS, deceased, PETER P. THORNTON, survey and plat--not
herein--by JONATHAN PRYOR. Lines: Lovelady Creek. WILLIAM JOPLING
and CHARLES L. BARRET, Justices of the Peace.

396. 23 March 1827. JAMES S. PENDLETON, Amherst County, 1; RICHARD
     EUBANK, Amherst County, 2; MICAJAH PENDLETON, 3...to L. P.
THOMPSON, 26 June 1829--MICAJAH PENDLETON on bond (guardian) for
ROBERT PENDLETON to EDMOND MASSIE; $1.00; furniture; half interest
in tanyard; half debts due MICAJAH PENDLETON.

397. 8 March 1827. THOMAS R. TERRY, Amherst County, 1; CHISWELL
     DABNEY and GEORGE W. NELSON, 2; HENRY S. LANGHORNE, Campbell
County, 3...HENRY S. LANGHORNE on note to Farmer's Bank of Virginia,
Lynchburg--to HENRY S. LANGHORNE, 1 March 1828--$5.00 451 3/8 acres.
Lines: WILLIAMS, MILLER, OWENS, ADAMS, WARWICK, BOWLING, James
River up to first branch above Bollin's tt. Bought this day from
said LANGHORNE and wife; slaves, wagon, tools. ALBON MC DANIEL and
DANIEL BROWN, Lynchburg Justices of the Peace.

400. 28 March 1827. ELIAS WILLS and wife, MARY G., Amherst County,
     to SETH WOODROOF, Amherst County...to SETH WOODROOF, 19 November
1827--$200 13½ acres west side Lynch road. Lines: DR. G. A. ROSE,
WILLIAM D. HILL. Bought some years ago from DANIEL NORCUTT. REUBEN
NORVELL and NELSON C. DAWSON, Justices of the Peace.

402. 14 April 1827. WILLIAM W. BOWLING, Amherst County, to ELIZABETH
     GUTHRIE, Amherst County...$265 53 acres Stovall Creek. ALFRED
GUTHRIE's portion of WILLIAM GUTHRIE's estate and his mother's
dower--conveyed to BOWLING. Witness: WILLIAM KENT.

403. 10 March 1827. BENJAMIN CAMDEN, 1; WILLIAM S. CRAWFORD, 2;
ALEXANDER P. CRAWFORD, 3...to WILLIAM S. CRAWFORD, 21 July 1828--
$1.00 tract on Indian Creek; no acres. Lines: WILLIAM M. WALLER,
WILLIAM L. CRAWFORD, WILLIAM MOORE. CHARLES P. TALIAFERRO and
RICHARD N. EUBANK, Justices of the Peace.

405. 9 March 1827. GEORGE W. RAY, Amherst County, 1; SAMUEL W.
CHRISTIAN, Amherst County, 2; D. and D. HIGGINBOTHAM and
Company, Amherst County, 3...to SAMUEL W. CHRISTIAN, 18 September
1827--$1.00 one-seventh of property of my deceased father, LUKE RAY--
about 500 acres; 1/7th of slaves named; stock, furniture. Witnesses:
REUBEN D. WARE, JONATHAN D. WARE, B. C. RAY.

406. 13 October 1826. SAMUEL D. CHRISTIAN and wife, JANE, Amherst
County, to THOMAS IVERS, Amherst County...to SAMUEL D.
CHRISTIAN for dower, 26 February 1830--$1.00 125 acres both sides
Megginson road. Lines: ABSALOM HOWL, STERLING CLAIBORNE, grantor,
ALEXANDER MUNDY.

407. 1 February 1827. THOMAS IVERS, Amherst County, 1; WILLIAM
BOURNE, Amherst County, 2; LEWIS P. SIMPSON, Amherst County,
3...to WILLIAM BOURNE, 17 September 1827--$1.00 125 acres above.

408. 7 April 1827. HUDSON M. GARLAND, Amherst County, 1; ROBERT
TINSLEY, Amherst County, 2; JAMES GARLAND, JAMES BOYD and
EDWARD A. CABELL, Nelson County, 3, and SAMUEL GARLAND, Lynchburg, 3...
JAMES GARLAND on bond to JONATHAN D. MURRELL on judgement in Amherst
County Superior Court; JONATHAN F. PATTEN, Lynchburg, Nelson County
judgement. One acre adjacent New Glasgow and bought from JAMES
FRANKLIN, deceased; slaves; books.

410. 16 April 1827. WILLIS GILLASPIE, Amherst County, to CHARLES
DARY, Amherst County...$800 200 acres. Lines: CORNELIUS
SALE.

410. 5 January 1827. DAVID TINSLEY, SR., to daughter, RUTH BURFORD,
and her children...$1.00 and love; amount paid by ROBERT
TINSLEY, trustee; slaves; free from husband's control. Witnesses:
AMBROSE RUCKER, R. P. BURK, EDWARD TINSLEY.

411. 16 April 1826. ROBERT CAMM, Amherst County, to BENJAMIN A.
DONALD, Bedford County...$800 210 acres John's Creek; branch
of James. To STEPHEN ADAMS per letter, 1 August 1847 (67?).

411. 1 March 1827. LINDSEY HARDWICH, Lynchburg, to BLANFORD HICKS,
Amherst County...$40 Harris Creek; lot -- in division of
ELIZABETH COLEMAN, deceased--six or seven acres. Survey by NORVELL
for division; ALBON MC DANIEL and JONATHAN HANVETT (?), Lynchburg
Justices of the Peace.

412. 14 November 1823. Madison trustees to ARCHER LEWIS, Lynchburg...
$1.00 lots 53 and 54--half acre each; also No. 52 and 51--half
acre each. DAVID TINSLEY, NELSON C. DAWSON, JONATHAN WIATT, ELIAS
WILLS, WILLIAM TURNER. Witnesses: D. R. EDLEY, TIMOTHY FLETCHER,
REUBEN NORVELL, J. S. PENDLETON. SMITHSON H. DAVIS and CHRISTOPHER
WINFREE, Lynchburg Justices of the Peace.

414. 16 April 1827. JONATHAN MASSIE, Amherst County, to SAMUEL M.
GARLAND, Amherst County...contract of 11 November 1826, between
JONATHAN MASSIE and DAVID S. GARLAND and JONATHAN MASSIE bought
three slaves--to deliver tobacco by 1 June 1828; Deed of Trust to
secure DAVID S. GARLAND; $1.00 three slaves; stock; furniture; crops.
EDMOND PENN and WILLIAM M. WALLER, Justices of the Peace.

415. 27 September 1826. JONATHAN MERRIT, Amherst County, 1; JAMES L.
LAMKIN, Amherst County, 2; HENRY CLARKE, executor of BEVERLY
CLARKE, 3...to PETER DAY, 28 October 1847, by order of JAMES L. LAMKIN--
debt from 8 January 1825; $1.00; furniture; cattle, etc. AUGUSTINE
LEFTWICH and SMITHSON H. DAVIS, Lynchburg Justice of the Peace.

417. -- July 1826. JONATHAN COLEMAN, Amherst County, 1; JOSEPH
      PENN, Amherst County, 2; JONATHAN PENN, Amherst County, 3...
to JOSEPH PENN, 29 October 1828--JONATHAN PENN on bond to D. and
D. HIGGINBOTHAM and Company; Superior Court Amherst County judgement;
$1.00; named slaves. Witnesses: ROBERT TINSLEY, WILL DILLARD,
POWHATAN D. FRANKLIN. Recorded: 23 April 1827.

419. 3 April 1827. ELIAS WILLS, Amherst County, 1; DAVID S. GARLAND,
      Amherst County, 2; EDWARD A. CABELL, Amherst County, 3...to
DAVID S. GARLAND, 27 September 1827--DAVID GARLAND on Deed of Trust,
19 May 1823--various items and amounts; EDWARD A. CABELL bought at
sale; two narrow axes, etc. at $1.00; interesting list and long as to
prices; slaves and ages. ELIAS WILLS wishes to rebuy many items and
long list at $1612.10; Deed of Trust on many slaves and items to
protect GARLAND. Witnesses: SAMUEL M. GARLAND, H. M. GARLAND,
JONATHAN SHEPHERD, PATRICK H. GARLAND.

424. 25 April 1827. JONATHAN WARE, SR., to EDMOND D. WINSTON,
      RICHARD L. ELLIS, WILLIAM ARMISTEAD, Amherst County...to
protect Farmer's Bank of Virginia in Superior Court of Amherst
County--versus WILLIAM JOPLING and JONATHAN WARE; also versus JONATHAN
WARE and MICAJAH PENDLETON; suit of RICHARD HADEN; $1.00; 380 acres.
Lines: DAVID S. GARLAND. Bought from JONATHAN LUSK, slaves.

426. 19 April 1827. LINDSEY SANDIDGE, Amherst County, 1; SAMUEL W.
      CHRISTIAN, Amherst County, 2; D. and D. HIGGINBOTHAM and
Company, Amherst County, 3...$1.00 south border Buffaloe. Lines:
BENJAMIN SANDIDGE, AARON HIGGINBOTHAM. Bought about 1814 or 15
from JAMES HIGGINBOTHAM.

428. 23 March 1827. JONATHAN FRANKLIN, Amherst County, 1; STERLING
      CLAIBORNE, 2; various creditors, 3...$1.00; all furniture and
thirteen feather beds in use at tavern in use at house occupied by
JONATHAN FRANKLIN; cattle; eleven tables at tavern; kitchen furniture
in use at tavern; tools; at Amherst CH; blacksmith tools. Debts to
MRS. LUCY SPENCER, WILLIAM TURNER, JAMES HILL, EDWARD WATSON,
trustee of MRS. ARMISTEAD, LINDSEY COLEMAN, AJAX WALKER, POWHATAN D.
FRANKLIN, administrator of REUBEN COLEMAN, WILLIAM L. WATTS, GEORGE
HILTON's estate, FRANCES COLEMAN, JONATHAN COLEMAN, JAMES W. SMITH.

430. 26 April 1827. SAMUEL M. WOLFE, Amherst County, SAMUEL M.
      and HUDSON M. GARLAND, JR., 2; JAMES GARLAND, 3...$1.00;
furniture.

431. 31 March 1827. CHARLES MARTIN and wife, JOISEY, Amherst County,
      to DAVID TOMLINSON, SR., Amherst County...to --, 21 April 1828;
$104.87 interest in estate of AMBROSE TOMLINSON, SR.; devised to
his wife, NANCY; reference to Amherst County will. ISAAC RUCKER and
CHARLES L. BARRET, Justices of the Peace.

433. 4 May 1827. JESSE RICHESON and wife, CATHERINE, Amherst
      County, to AMBROSE TOMLINSON, Amherst County...$250 125 acres.
Lines: THOMAS TUCKER, Pedlar and Enchanted Creek. CHARLES L.
BARRET and ISAAC RUCKER, Justices of the Peace.

434. 4 May 1827. AMBROSE TOMLINSON and wife, MARY, Amherst County,
      to VARLAND and WILLIAM RICHESON, Amherst County, 2; JESSE
RICHESON, Amherst County, 3...$1.00; 125 acres above; also interest
in estate of AMBROSE TOMLINSON, SENIOR; dev. to wife, MARY, for life;
stock; furniture; interest of AMBROSE TOMLINSON and wife in estate of
JAMES MARTIN, SR. Justices of the Peace as above.

437. 8 May 1827. FIELDING BROWN, Amherst County, 1; GEORGE W.
      DILLARD, Amherst County, 2; various creditors, 3...JAMES ROSE,
DAVID S. GARLAND for accounts at store in New Glasgow, JONATHAN PENN,
STERLING CLAIBOREN, ROBERT HIGGINBOTHAM, HIRAM YOUNG, SAMUEL GARLAND,
JONATHAN DUNCAN. $1.00; slaves and furniture.

438. 3 May 1827. Chatham County, Georgia, Eastern District,
        ANTHONY PORTER, Justice of the Peace as to seal of WILLIAM
MOREL, Deputy Clerk; BENJAMIN SHIFTALL and ISAAC RUCKER, Justices
of the Peace as to MRS. ANN CRAWFORD, 15 March 1827, to --.

440. 23 February 1827. JESSE MAYS, Giles County, Tennessee, to
        friend, JAMES W. SMITH, Amherst County...power of attorney to
collect my legacy from estate of my father, ROBERT MAYS, who died
in Amherst County. Witnesses: SAMUEL KERCHIVAL, A. G. UNDERWOOD,
T. W. TANEY, GERMAN LISTER, Clerk. E. D. JONES, Presiding Justice
of the Peace.

441. -- March 1827. JONATHAN DAVIES and wife, ELIZABETH, Jefferson
        County, Kentucky, CHARLES CRAWFORD, Shelby County, Kentucky,
to BEVERLY DAVIES, Amherst County...all interest in tract which
descended to JONATHAN DAVIES and wife at death of ELIZABETH DAVIES,
widow of NICHOLAS C. DAVIES; reference to deed by JONATHAN DAVIES
to CRAWFORD, but wife had not released dower. MATTHEW LOVE and
ROBERT N. MILLER, Jefferson Justices of the Peace; WORDEN POPE,
Clerk; JONATHAN BELL, Presiding Justice of the Peace. Shelby
County: MARK HARDIN and GEORGE MILLER, Justices of the Peace;
JAMES S. WHITEKER, Clerk. JAMES YOUNG, Presiding Justice of the
Peace.

443. 21 February 1827. JAMES ANGUS and wife, MARY, formerly TUCKER,
        Giles County, Tennessee to friend, JAMES W. SMITH, Amherst
County...power of attorney to execute deed to CHARLES TUCKER, Amherst
County, as to any land descending to CHARLES TUCKER and MARY ANGUS.
Witnesses: T. W. YANCEY, WILLIS S. MC LENRIC (?), E. D. JONES--last
two are Justices of the Peace. GERMAN LISTER, Clerk.

445. 6 June 1827. JONATHAN P. GILLIAM, Botetourt, 1; JONATHAN W.
        YOUNG and MOORE F. CARTER, Amherst County, 2; EZEKIEL B.
GILBERT, Amherst County, 3...EZEKIEL B. GILBERT on bond to administra-
tor of JONATHAN GILLIAM; $1.00; all interest in estate of RICHARD
JONES and of his father, JONATHAN GILLIAM--life estate to MARY,
widow. THOMAS N. EUBANK and CHARLES L. BARRET, Justices of the
Peace.

446. 18 June 1827. THOMAS D. HILL, Amherst County, 1; ARTHUR B.
        DAVIES, Amherst County, 2; JAMES HILL, Amherst County, 3...
JAMES HILL, SR. owes 1; $1.00. This is confusing: JAMES HILL to
ARTHUR B. DAVIES; 268 acres where I live on Lynchburg road. Lines:
JAMES OGDEN, WILLIAM R. ROANNE. Witnesses: JAMES HILL, SR. (sic),
THOMAS WHITTON, JONATHAN H. WILLS. Assigned to THOMAS D. HILL and
S. R. D. same date. Witnesses: JONATHAN HORSLEY, SR.

447. 18 June 1827. EDMUND DAVIS and wife, MILDRED, Amherst County,
        to HIRAM YOUNG, Amherst County...$75 100 acres tract given
to EDMUND DAVIS by United States government; lot 17; 4th quarter
of eighth township in third range; military services; 5 June 1826.
JAMES WARE and CHARLES L. BARRET, Justices of the Peace. To HIRAM
YOUNG, 17 November 1828. No state is set forth herein.

448. 17 March 1827. PETER CASH, Amherst County, to WASHINGTON
        CASH, Amherst County...$450 150 acres Stone House Creek.
Lines: CHARLES TUCKER, WILLIAM M. WALLER, GARLAND PAGE, JAMES CASH.
BENJAMIN and CHARLES P. TALIAFERRO, Justices of the Peace.

448. 5 March 1827. PULLIAM SANDIDGE, JR., Lincoln County, Kentucky,
        to AUSTIN DAVIS, Amherst County...ROWLAND SANDIDGE made contract
to DAVIS, and $800; tract conveyed to PULLIAM SANDIDGE by PULLIAM
SANDIDGE and wife; Buffaloe. Lines: ZA DRUMMOND, RANDLE CASH,
ELIJAH FLETCHER--118 acres. To AUSTIN DAVIS, -- January 1829.
Witnesses: T. HELM, THOMAS HELM, Clerk, JONATHAN MC ROBERTS, Presiding
Justice of the Peace. Recorded Amherst County, 18 June 1827.

449. 20 March 1827. WILLIAM TURNER, Amherst County, to ELIZABETH
BECKHAM, Amherst County...to MAJOR J. B. COFFLIN, 24 February
188, and returned--$10; one acre. Lines: SOLOMON and DANIEL DAY,
WILLIAM TURNER. Witnesses: CHARLES PALMORE, N. P. BREEDLOVE.

450. 19 June 1827. CHARLES DUNCAN, Amherst County, 1; SAMUEL W.
CHRISTIAN, Amherst County, 2; D. and D. HIGGINBOTHAM and
Company, Amherst County, 3...on judgements in Amherst County Court;
JAMES D. HIGGINBOTHAM, trustee, 19 August 1824, has died; $1.00;
155 3/4 acres. Lines: HENRY CAMDEN, PRESTON GARLAND, TANDY RUTHERFORD,
MICAJAH CAMDEN. Bought from GEORGE DUNCAN et al.--cattle, tools,
furniture, crops.

451. 18 June 1827. DAVID TOMLINSON, LL (sic), 1; SAMUEL W.
CHRISTIAN, Amherst County, 2; D. and D. HIGGINBOTHAM and
Company, Amherst County, 3...$1.00; to SAMUEL W. CHRISTIAN, 30 June
1827--107 acres. Lines: ABRAM CARTER, JAMES TOMLINSON, JO.
RICHESON (formerly); came to me by marriage to MARY TOMLINSON,
daughter of AMBROSE TOMLINSON.

452. 4 May 1827. EDWARD TINSLEY and GEORGE TINSLEY, Amherst
County, 1; JONATHAN MILLER and DAVID R. EDLEY, 2; SAMUEL
MILLER and EDWIN S. RUCKER, 3...$1.00 10/24 of a mill on Harris-
Tinsley's Mill. SMITHSON H. DAVIS and AMMON HANCOCK, Lynchburg
Justices of the Peace.

453. 23 March 1825. ROBERT HAMBLETON, 1; WILSON PETERS and
WILLIAM H. LOVING, 2; JAMES S. PENN, all of Nelson County...
$1.00 JAMES S. PENN as assigned of JONATHAN WHITEHEAD; WILLIAM M.
WALLER and JAMES S. PENN, trustees of THOMAS PENN--JAMES FULCHER,
bondsman. 1 January 1823. Nelson County suit; slaves. Recorded
Amherst County, 18 June 1827.

454. -- June 1827. EDWARD LANKFORD, Amherst County, 1; SAMUEL M.
GARLAND, Amherst County, 2; WILLIAM M. WALLER, Amherst County,
3...WILLIAM M. WALLER, on bond to JAMES S. PENDLETON and Company for
benefit of LUKE and LUCY--er (sic); $1.00; stock; furniture; tools;
bond on ELIJAH PUGH and JONATHAN CHEWNING to JONATHAN SHEPHERD and
WILLIAM MURRILL and assigned to me; bond of WILLIAM CAMPBELL; crops.

456. 20 June 1827. JOEL F. SMITH, Amherst County, 1; HENRY FRANKLIN,
Amherst County, 2; RICHARD SMITH, JR., and DABNEY SANDIDGE,
STERLING CLAIBORNE, 3...$1.00; slaves. Reference to Deed of Trust
to DABNEY SANDIDGE.

456. 2 June 1827. CHARLES STINNETT, Amherst County, 1; SAMUEL W.
CHRISTIAN, Amherst County, 2; D. and D. HIGGINBOTHAM and
Company, Amherst County, 3...$1.00; judgement in Amherst County
court; cattle; crops. To SAMUEL W. CHRISTIAN, 7 July 1827.

457. 20 June 1827. CHARLES M. CHRISTIAN, Amherst County, 1; DAVID J.
WHITE and CHARLES F. BURKS, 2; CLARKE FERGUSON and Company;
JONATHAN P. PHELPS and Company, HENRY H. WATTS, LUCY CHRISTIAN,
MOURNING CHRISTIAN, STEVEN DAVIDSON, son of GILES, 3...to CLARK
FERGUSON and Company by CHARLES L. CHRISTIAN, agent, no date--$1.00
70 3/4 acres. Lines: DRURY CHRISTIAN, deceased, CAPTAIN JONATHAN
CHRISTIAN, deceased; also 142 acres. Lines: JONATHAN M. WALKER,
slaves, 1/5 interest in estate of HENRY CHRISTIAN, and allotted to
MOURNING CHRISTIAN as dower; interest as heir of DRURY CHRISTIAN.
Witnesses: JOSEPH KYLE.

459. 27 June 1827. JAMES POWELL, Amherst County, 1; THOMAS R.
BROWN, Lynchburg, 2; ARCHIBALD ROBERTSON, JONATHAN PENN,
ROBERT L. and JONATHAN COLEMAN, 3...bonds due P. P. BURTON; $1.00;
354 acres adjacent CH and where JAMES POWELL lives; 240 acres
adjacent JONATHAN ROBERTSON, deceased, and bought from ANDREW
MUNROE; slaves.

461.   11 July 1827.   BENNET A. CRAWFORD, Amherst County, to WILLIAM I.
      and CHRISTOPHER ISBELL, Amherst County...$3500 10 year lease;
tract adjacent Bethel and known as Bethel Tract--370 or 403 acres;
lately owned by NICHOLAS C. DAVIES and NELSON CRAWFORD. Lines:
RICHARD L. ELLIS, road from Pedlar Mills to Bethel; also clover lot
below Bethel Warehouse; Bethel spring. AMMON HANCOCK and S. H. DAVIS,
Lynchburg Justices of the Peace.

462.   9 June 1827.   THOMAS SMITH, Amherst County, to SAMUEL W.
      CHRISTIAN to secure D. and D. HIGGINBOTHAM and Company on
execution from Amherst County Clerk...to SAMUEL W. CHRISTIAN,
8 August 1827--$1.00; interest in estate of PEARCE MAYS by marriage
to MARIAH MAYS, daughter of MAYS, furniture, etc. Witnesses:
JAMES L., JESSE and EUGENE HIGGINBOTHAM.

463.   27 June 1827.   JONATHAN WARE, Amherst County, to THOMAS RICE,
      Bedford...$910 200 acres north side and joining north fork
Pedlar; on side of Cold Mountain. Patent to JAMES SMITH, 10 August
1766, and by him conveyed to PATRICK LOVING and by LOVING to JAMES
BAILEY. Lines: JOSEPH HIGGINBOTHAM, AUGUSTINE LEFTWICH and JONATHAN
HANCOCK, Lynchburg Justices of the Peace.

464.   16 July 1827.   ROWLETT GILL, 1; SAMUEL W. CHRISTIAN, 2;
      CHARLES MASSIE, 3...CHARLES MASSIE on bond on execution from
Clerk's office in name of D. and D. HIGGINBOTHAM and Company versus
ROWLETT GILL; $1.00; furniture; interest in crops as overseer of
MRS. JOANNA ELLIS--one fifth.

465.   17 July 1827.   PETER P. THORNTON, 1; ARTHUR B. DAVIES, 2;
      WILLIAM HANNAH and WILLIAM H. MC CULLOCH, 3...WILLIAM HANNAH
and WILLIAM H. MC CULLOCH on bond to RICHARD L. ELLIS from Superior
Court of Amherst County in RICHARD L. ELLIS's name as surviving
partner of JONATHAN and RICHARD ELLIS; $1.00 292 acres where
PETER P. THORNTON lives; slaves named; cattle, etc.

466.   16 July 1827.   PETER P. THORNTON, trustee of ROLAND GILLESPIE,
      Amherst County, to ABRAM CARTER, Amherst County...$212 100 acres
Horsley. Lines: GODFREY TOLER, WILLIAM DEMPSEY, WILLIAM SHEPHERD.

466.   20 July 1827.   ANDERSON SANDIDGE, Amherst County, 1; SAMUEL W.
      CHRISTIAN, Amherst County, 2; D. and D. HIGGINBOTHAM and
Company, Amherst County, 3...to SAMUEL W. CHRISTIAN, 30 July 1827--
$1.00 all interest in estate of WILLIAM WARE and PATSY WARE (wife
of WILLIAM WARE) by marriage to BELINDA WARE, their daughter; slaves
named; lands and personal estate of both WARES. Witnesses: R. N.
EUBANK, WILLIAM DEMPSEY, LINDSEY SANDIDGE, WILLIAM WAUGH.

468.   16 July 1827.   MARY SMITH, 1; RICHARD SMITH, 2; -- JR., JAMES W.
      SMITH, 3...to JAMES W. SMITH, 17 September 1827. JAMES W. has
this day loaned MARY $100; $1.00 named slaves. Witnesses: DUDLEY
SANDIDGE, JONATHAN and EDWARD SMITH.

469.   5 December 1823.   JSO. THOMPOSN, Nelson County, 1; SPOTSWOOD
      GARLAND and JONATHAN WHITEHEAD, 2; JAMES S. PENN, WILLIAM M.
WALLER, JAMES S. PENN, trustees of THOMAS PENN, 3...$1.00; horse;
cattle; sheep; furniture; crops. Recorded Amherst County, 18 June
1827.

BROWN (cont.)
Andrew 45
Andrew A. 43
Anna 128
Anne 94
Archer 194
B. 77, 92, 150, 156
B., Jr. 67
Benjamin 67, 73, 74,
  87, 89, 92, 95,
  105, 116, 128, 134,
  139, 150, 155, 168,
  171, 181, 188, 192,
  211, 219, 220, 289,
  304, 319
Beverly T. 216, 218,
  219, 221, 224
Charles 19
Charles L. 314
Daniel 112, 175, 177,
  243, 249, 250, 251,
  256, 259, 284, 286,
  287, 288, 292, 295,
  297, 305, 311, 312,
  320, 323, 325, 326
Fielding 244, 255, 301,
  302, 304, 328
George M. 95
H. L. 211
Henry 4, 12, 27, 35,
  56, 67, 76, 78, 87,
  128
Howell L. 282, 313
J. M. 85, 101, 235
Jacob 23, 25, 44, 175
James 101, 106, 162,
  166, 178, 197, 199,
  318
James M. 20, 21, 23,
  26, 27, 32, 58,
  92, 126, 128, 135,
  164, 171, 209, 229,
  232, 234, 239, 247,
  253, 254, 269, 270,
  284, 296, 298, 302
James Murray 235
James, Sr. 166
Jesse 62
Jonathan 3, 25, 43, 45,
  87, 94, 95, 101,
  117, 124, 128, 131,
  193, 210, 219, 237,
  271, 291, 310, 311,
  313
Jonathan H. 126
Jonathan M. 268
Jonathan P. 34
Joo. 224
Joseph 118, 248, 255
Judith 215
Lewis 161, 215
Lucy C. 302
Mary 131
Matthew 122, 139
Murphy 2, 4, 7, 10, 94
Rachel 45
Reid 174
Rhoda 247
Rhodoy 229, 235
Robert M. 314
Sally 95
Samuel 285
Sarah E. 314
Stephen 167
Thomas R. 330
Wiatt W. 61
Willia 64
William 1, 12, 16, 20,
  57, 58, 87, 105,
  115, 116, 269, 289,
  322
Willis 12, 65, 90
BRUCE, James 84, 132, 163,

BRUCE (cont.)
James (cont.) 184,
  214
BRYAN, Benjamin 285
BRYANT, Benjamin 26
Berry 44, 58, 78
Dabney P. 281
Eliabeth 232, 257
Finney 78, 211, 213
Jonathan 10, 88, 107
Joseph 182
Lewis 34, 58
Littleberkry 9, 33
Richard 9
Sylvanus 9
Vicey 92
William 54, 92
BRYDIE, -- 10
Alexander 28, 54, 55,
  58, 119, 157, 167,
  237
Betsy 157, 167, 195,
  237, 277
Charles 107
Nancy 157
William 157, 167, 195,
  237, 277
BUCKMAN, Edward 186
BUCKNER, Major 187
Richard A. 225
BUCKS, -- 177
BUGG, Allen 7, 29, 65, 66
Ann 42
Nancy 29
Sharod 42
Sherad 99
Sherod 54
BULLOCK, -- 150, 244,
  271, 295
Eliza F. 309
Elizabeth F. 296
Galt 306
James 127, 148, 160,
  171, 183, 225, 256
James P. 287, 296, 309
Jonathan 38, 52, 69,
  74, 80, 85, 95,
  111, 165, 169
BURCH, Catherine 198, 241
Elizabeth 98
Eli 233
Jonathan 98, 109
Simeon A. 282, 288
BURD, -- 220, 221, 262
William 130, 138, 139,
  141, 156, 175, 194,
  196
BURFORD, -- 33, 197, 268,
  275
Ambrose 12, 50, 52, 57,
  123, 138, 142, 145,
  209, 227, 287, 309,
  324
Ambrose R. 321
Archibald 60
Caroline M. 288
Cynthia 74
Daniel 3, 12, 17, 30,
  31, 32, 41, 50, 61,
  66, 68, 73, 76, 79,
  84, 108, 120, 124,
  128, 150, 151, 173,
  179, 190, 198, 261
Daniel, Jr. 12, 50,
  51, 54, 70, 73, 79,
  105, 123
Daniel L. 84, 301, 305,
  309
Daniel M. 105, 198
Daniel S. 98
Daniel, Sr. 50, 51,
  105, 115
Edith 197

BURFORD (cont.)
George H. 64, 123,
  145, 161, 186, 198,
  208, 209
James 283, 321
James C. 227
John, Jr. 50
Jonathan 3, 12, 17,
  105, 115, 148, 157,
  199, 261
Jonathan D. 77
Jonathan, Jr. 50, 51,
  52, 70
Jonathan L. 101, 102,
  111
Jonathan, Sr. 51
Lewis 138
Mary 74, 84, 186,
  227, 321
Mary T. 209
Nancy 227
P. 123
Phil 31
Philip 11, 41, 74,
  209, 288
Philip, Jr. 74
Philip, Sr. 288
Reuben 108, 227
Ruth 84, 150, 301,
  327
Sally 50, 186, 287,
  315
Sarah 50, 68, 70, 73,
  76
Sary 17
Susanna 79
Susannah 74, 102, 198
William 22, 39, 50,
  51, 60, 68, 70, 73,
  74, 76, 84, 86,
  102, 151, 155, 227,
  244, 246
William J. 73
William, Sr. 281, 287,
  309
BURGE, Drury 179
Green M. 179
BURK, R. P. 327
Samuel 22
BURKS, -- 124, 173, 307
Alford 216
Ambrose 226
Charles 22, 56, 70,
  88, 133, 137, 188
Charles F. 330
Charles M. 172
Charles, Sr. 22, 50,
  113
David 35, 65, 66, 68,
  70, 72, 92, 98,
  104, 111, 133, 134,
  137, 307
David J. 31
David, Jr. 74, 98,
  311, 313
David Junior 310
David, Sr. 72, 82,
  113
David W. 216, 223,
  291
Eliza Jane 243, 244,
  253, 254, 299
Elizabeth 113, 137,
  159, 287
Elizabeth K. 253
Emeline Elizabeth 238
George 50, 113, 122,
  137, 229, 292, 319
Harry 202
Henrietta Mildred 238
Henry 95
Jonathan 19, 43, 94,
  113, 117, 124, 128,

www.ingramcontent.com/pod-product-compliance
Lightning Source LLC
Chambersburg PA
CBHW021846020426
42334CB00013B/206